A Companion to the Civil War and Reconstruction

BLACKWELL COMPANIONS TO AMERICAN HISTORY

This series provides essential and authoritative overviews of the scholarship that has shaped our present understanding of the American past. Edited by eminent historians, each volume tackles one of the major periods or themes of American history, with individual topics authored by key scholars who have spent considerable time in research on the questions and controversies that have sparked debate in their field of interest. The volumes are accessible for the non-specialist, while also engaging scholars seeking a reference to the historiography or future concerns.

Published

A Companion to the American Revolution
Edited by Jack P. Greene and J. R. Pole

A Companion to 19th-Century America
Edited by William L. Barney

A Companion to the American South
Edited by John B. Boles

A Companion to American Indian History
Edited by Philip J. Deloria and Neal Salisbury

A Companion to American Women's History
Edited by Nancy Hewitt

A Companion to Post-1945 America
Edited by Jean-Christophe Agnew and Roy Rosenzweig

A Companion to the Vietnam War
Edited by Marilyn Young and Robert Buzzanco

A Companion to Colonial America
Edited by Daniel Vickers

A Companion to 20th-Century America
Edited by Stephen J. Whitfield

A Companion to the American West
Edited by William Deverell

A Companion to American Foreign Relations
Edited by Robert Schulzinger

A Companion to the Civil War and Reconstruction
Edited by Lacy K. Ford

A Companion to American Technology
Edited by Carroll Pursell

A Companion to African-American History
Edited by Alton Hornsby

BLACKWELL COMPANIONS TO HISTORY

Published

A Companion to Western Historical Thought
Edited by Lloyd Kramer and Sarah Maza

A Companion to Gender History
Edited by Teresa A. Meade and Merry E. Wiesner-Hanks

BLACKWELL COMPANIONS TO BRITISH HISTORY

Published

A Companion to Roman Britain
Edited by Malcolm Todd

A Companion to Britain in the Later Middle Ages
Edited by S. H. Rigby

A Companion to Stuart Britain
Edited by Barry Coward

A Companion to Eighteenth-Century Britain
Edited by H. T. Dickinson

A Companion to Early Twentieth-Century Britain
Edited by Chris Wrigley

In preparation

A Companion to Tudor Britain
Edited by Robert Tittler and Norman Jones

A Companion to Britain in the Early Middle Ages
Edited by Pauline Stafford

A Companion to Nineteenth-Century Britain
Edited by Chris Williams

A Companion to Contemporary Britain
Edited by Paul Addison and Harriet Jones

BLACKWELL COMPANIONS TO EUROPEAN HISTORY

Published

A Companion to the Worlds of the Renaissance
Edited by Guido Ruggiero

A Companion to the Reformation World
Edited by R. Po-chia Hsia

In preparation

A Companion to Europe Since 1945
Edited by Klaus Larres

A Companion to Europe 1900–1945
Edited by Gordon Martel

BLACKWELL COMPANIONS TO WORLD HISTORY

In preparation

A Companion to the History of the Middle East
Edited by Youssef M. Choueiri

A COMPANION TO THE CIVIL WAR AND RECONSTRUCTION

Edited by

Lacy K. Ford

Blackwell
Publishing

© 2005 by Blackwell Publishing Ltd
except for editorial material and organization © 2005 by Lacy K. Ford

BLACKWELL PUBLISHING
350 Main Street, Malden, MA 02148–5020, USA
108 Cowley Road, Oxford OX4 1JF, UK
550 Swanston Street, Carlton, Victoria 3053, Australia

The right of Lacy K. Ford to be identified as the Author of the Editorial Material in this Work has
been asserted in accordance with the UK Copyright, Designs, and Patents Act 1988.

First published 2005 by Blackwell Publishing Ltd

Library of Congress Cataloging-in-Publication Data

A companion to the Civil War and Reconstruction / edited by Lacy Ford.
p. cm. — (Blackwell companions to American history ; 12)
Includes bibliographical references and index.
ISBN 0–631–21551–4 (alk. paperback)
1. United States—History—Civil War, 1861–1865—Historiography. 2. United States—
History—Civil War, 1861–1865. 3. United States—History—Civil War, 1861–1865—
Social aspects. 4. Reconstruction (U.S. history, 1865–1877)—Historiography.
5. Reconstruction (U.S. history, 1865–1877) 6. United States—Social conditions—
1865–1918. I. Ford, Lacy K. II. Series.

E468.5.C64 2005
973.7—dc22

2004011684

A catalogue record for this title is available from the British Library.

Set in 10/12pt Galliard
by Graphicraft Ltd., Hong Kong
Printed and bound in the United Kingdom
by TJ International, Padstow, Cornwall

The publisher's policy is to use permanent paper from mills that operate a sustainable forestry policy,
and which has been manufactured from pulp processed using acid-free and elementary chlorine-free
practices. Furthermore, the publisher ensures that the text paper and cover board used have met
acceptable environmental accreditation standards.

For further information on
Blackwell Publishing, visit our website:
www.blackwellpublishing.com

Contents

Notes on the Contributors

John Ashworth is Professor of American History at the University of Nottingham, United Kingdom. He is the author of *"Agrarians" and "Aristocrats": Party Political Ideology in the United States, 1837–1846* (1983) and *Slavery, Capitalism and Politics in the Antebellum Republic: Volume I, Commerce and Compromise, 1820–1850* (1996). He is currently completing *Slavery, Capitalism and Politics in the Antebellum Republic: Volume II, Towards a Bourgeois Revolution, 1850–1861*.

Charles C. Bolton is Professor and Chair of History at the University of Southern Mississippi. He is the author of *Poor Whites of the Antebellum South: Tenants and Laborers in Central North Carolina and Northeast Mississippi* (1994) and co-editor of *The Confessions of Edward Isham: A Poor White Life of the Old South* (1998). He recently completed a book manuscript entitled "The Hardest Deal of All: The Battle over School Integration in Mississippi, 1870–1980."

O. Vernon Burton is University Distinguished Teacher/Scholar at the University of Illinois at Urbana-Champaign. Past president of the Agricultural History Society, he is the author of more than 100 essays and author or editor of eight books, including *In My Father's House Are Many Mansions: Family and Community in Edgefield, South Carolina* (1985).

Matthew Cheney is a graduate student in Library and Information Sciences at the University of Illinois at Urbana-Champaign. His research interests include the American South, automatic metadata creation and document linkage, and the ethics of moral obligation.

Peter A. Coclanis is Albert R. Newsome Professor of History and Associate Provost for International Affairs at the University of North Carolina-Chapel Hill. He is the author of, among other works, *The Shadow of a Dream: Economic Life and Death in the South Carolina Low Country, 1670–1920* (1989), which won the Allan Nevins Prize of the Society of American Historians. He is currently working on a history of the international rice trade in the period between 1650 and 1940.

Daniel Crofts is Professor of History and Chair of the History Department at the College of New Jersey. His books include *Reluctant Confederates: Upper South Unionists in the Secession Crisis* (1989), *Old Southampton: Politics and Society in a Virginia County, 1834–1869* (1992), and *Cobb's Ordeal: The Diaries of a Virginia Farmer, 1842–1872* (1997).

Mary DeCredico is Professor of History and Department Chair at the US Naval Academy, Maryland. Her *Patriotism for Profit: Georgia's Urban Entrepreneurs and the Confederate War Effort* (1990) won the Museum of the

Confederacy's Jefferson Davis Award for outstanding scholarship on the Confederate era. She is also the author of *Mary Boykin Chesnut: A Confederate Woman's Life* (2002) and is currently working on a book manuscript entitled "War Comes to Richmond, 1860–1865."

Douglas R. Egerton is Professor of History at Le Moyne College, Syracuse, NY. He is the author of *He Shall Go Out Free: The Lives of Denmark Vesey* (1999), *Charles Fenton Mercer and the Trial of National Conservatism* (1989), and *Gabriel's Rebellion: The Virginia Slave Conspiracies of 1800 and 1802* (1993), which was awarded the annual book prize by the Society for Historians of the Early Republic.

Lacy K. Ford is Professor of History at the University of South Carolina. He is the author of *Origins of Southern Radicalism: The South Carolina Upcountry, 1800–1860* (1988), winner of the 1989 Francis B. Simkins Prize, and a number of essays and articles on nineteenth- and twentieth-century southern history. He is currently completing a book, "Constructing the Old South: White Attitudes Toward Race, Slavery and Power, 1787–1835."

Gaines M. Foster is Professor of History at Louisiana State University and author of *Ghosts of the Confederacy: Defeat, the Lost Cause, and the Emergence of the New South, 1865–1913* (1988) and *Moral Reconstruction: Christian Lobbyists and the Federal Legislation of Morality, 1865–1920* (2002).

Kevin Gannon received his PhD from the University of South Carolina in 2002 and is Assistant Professor of History at Grand View College in Des Moines, Iowa. He is the author of "Escaping 'Mr. Jefferson's Plan of Destruction': The Idea of a New England Confederacy, 1803–1804," *Journal of the Early Republic* (2003). He is currently completing a book manuscript entitled "Nationalism's Opposite: States' Rights, Nullification, and Secession in the North, 1789–1860."

Michele Gillespie is Kahle Family Professor at Wake Forest University, North Carolina.

She is the author of *Free Labor in an Unfree World: White Artisans in Slaveholding Georgia* (2002), and has co-edited several books, including *Neither Lady Nor Slave: Working Women in the Old South* (2002) and *The Devil's Lane: Sex and Race in the Early South* (1997).

David Herr is an Assistant Professor of American History at St Andrews Presbyterian College, North Carolina. His research interests include slavery and multimedia integration in history. He is currently working on an examination of the relationship among non-elite whites and slaves.

Larry Hudson is Associate Professor of History at the University of Rochester, New York. He is author of *"To Have and to Hold": Slave Work and Family Life in Antebellum South Carolina* (1997). He is completing "'Crossing Jordan': Plantation Slavery in the United States," and editing a collection of essays on the "Private and Public Worlds of Frederick Douglass."

John Larson is Professor of History at Purdue University, Indiana, and past co-editor of the *Journal of the Early Republic*. He is author of *Bonds of Enterprise: John Murray Forbes and Western Development in America's Railway Age*, 2nd edn. (2001) and *Internal Improvement: National Public Works and the Promise of Popular Government in the Early United States* (2001). His current project deals with environmental history and the capitalist culture of exploitation and is tentatively entitled "Profligate Mother: Nature, History, and the Rise of a Capitalist Ethos in America 1700–1900."

R. Tracy McKenzie is Associate Professor of History at the University of Washington, Seattle. A specialist in southern social and economic history, he is the author of *One South or Many? Plantation-Belt and Upcountry in Civil War-Era Tennessee* (1994). He is currently completing a book on a bitterly divided Appalachian town during the Civil War.

Scott Marler is currently completing his dissertation on nineteenth-century southern merchants, "Rural Merchants in a New South: Louisiana, 1840–1900," at Rice University, Texas, where he has also served on the editorial staff of the *Journal of Southern History* since 2000. He has published articles in *Louisiana History*, the *Journal of the Historical Society*, and the third edition of the *Dictionary of American History*.

Michael Morrison is Associate Professor of History at Purdue University, Indiana. He is the author of *Slavery and the American West: The Eclipse of Manifest Destiny and the Coming of the Civil War* (1997), co-editor with James Brewer Stewart of *Race and the Early Republic: Racial Consciousness and Nation-Building in the Early Republic* (2002), and co-editor with Melinda S. Zook of *Revolutionary Currents: Nation Building in the Transatlantic World* (2004). In 1998 the Carnegie Foundation for the Advancement of Teaching named him Indiana Professor of the Year.

Teresa Murphy is Associate Professor of American Studies at George Washington University, Washington, DC. She is the author of *Ten Hours Labor: Religion, Reform, and Gender in Early New England* (1992). Her current projects include the manuscript "Angels of History: Women and Historical Imagination in the Early Republic" as well as a textbook on US Women's History.

Michael Perman is Research Professor in the Humanities at the University of Illinois at Chicago. He is the author of *Reunion without Compromise: The South and Reconstruction, 1865–1868* (1973), *The Road to Redemption: Southern Politics, 1869–1879* (1984), *Emancipation and Reconstruction*, 2nd edn. (2003), and *Struggle for Mastery: Disfranchisement in the South, 1888–1908* (2001). He also edited *Major Problems in the Civil War and Reconstruction*, 2nd edn. (1998).

Carol Reardon is Associate Professor of History at Penn State University, University Park, Pa. Her *Pickett's Charge in History and Memory* (1997) won the 1998 Forrest C. Pogue Prize from the Eisenhower Center for American Studies and the Philip S. Klein Prize

from the Pennsylvania Historical Association. She has served as visiting faculty at the US Army War College, US Military Academy, and Marine Corps Command and Staff College. She is currently completing a book about naval aviation in the Vietnam War that focuses on an A-6 Intruder squadron's experiences in 1972.

Joseph P. Reidy is Professor of History and Associate Provost at Howard University, Washington, DC. He is the author of *From Slavery to Agrarian Capitalism in the Cotton Plantation South: Central Georgia, 1800–1880* (1992) and is a co-editor of the four volumes of *Freedom: A Documentary History of Emancipation, 1861–1867* (1982–93) and the Lincoln Prize-winning *Free at Last: A Documentary History of Slavery, Freedom, and the Civil War* (1992). He currently is working on a study of black sailors in the US Navy during the Civil War.

Heather Richardson is the author of *The Greatest Nation of the Earth: Republican Economic Policies during the Civil War* (1997) and *The Death of Reconstruction: Race, Labor, and Politics in the Post-Civil War North, 1865–1901* (2001). She is currently completing a book on Reconstruction for Yale University Press.

Nina Silber is Associate Professor of History at Boston University, Massachusetts. She is the author of *The Romance of Reunion: Northerners and the South, 1865–1900* (1993) and co-editor of *Divided Houses: Gender and the Civil War* (1992). Her new book on northern women and the Civil War home front will be published in spring 2005 by Harvard University Press.

James B. Stewart is James Wallace Professor of History at Macalester College, Minnesota. He is the author of biographies of abolitionists Joshua R. Giddings, Wendell Phillips, and Willam Lloyd Garrison, and (with George R. Price) of Hosea Easton, as well as of *Holy Warriors: The Abolitionists and American Slavery* (1997), a general history of the abolitionist movement. His most recent publications address the evolution of racial politics in the free states from 1776 to 1861.

Jeannie Whayne is Professor of History and chair of the Department of History at the University of Arkansas. She received her doctorate degree in 1989 from the University of California, San Diego. She has authored, co-authored, edited, and co-edited several books. Her *New Plantation South: Land, Labor and Federal Favor in Twentieth Century Arkansas* won the Arkansiana Award in 1996. Her edited books include *Arkansas Delta: A Land of Paradox* (1993) and *Shad-* *ows Over Sunnyside: An Arkansas Plantation in Transition, 1830–1945* (1993).

Steven Woodworth is Associate Professor of History at Texas Christian University. His *Jefferson Davis and his Generals* (1990) and *Davis and Lee at War* (1995) each won the Fletcher Pratt Award of the New York Civil War Round Table. He is currently completing "Nothing But Victory: The Army of the Tennessee, 1861–1865."

Introduction: A Civil War in the Age of Capital

LACY K. FORD

Even at a distance of seven score years, the Civil War era remains the most riveting epoch in all of American history for scholars and the general public alike. In his sweeping synthesis of the capitalist world during the third quarter of the nineteenth century, *The Age of Capital, 1848–1875*, the gifted Marxist historian Eric Hobsbawm noted with characteristic British understatement that the scholarly investigation of the "nature and origins of the American Civil War" had generated seemingly "endless dispute among historians" (Hobsbawm 1975: 154). Though the relative proportions have varied over time, the causes of the war, the contingencies of the war itself, and the long-term impact of the war on American society have all received abundant attention from scholars through the decades, turning the "battle of the books" over the Civil War era into the Hundred Years War of American intellectual life, a contest whose principal casualties have been pulp forests and red-eyed graduate students. Contributors to this volume accepted the daunting task of surveying this voluminous literature, or at least the most recent waves, and making sense of it for informed readers of the early twenty-first century. The volume is organized around the traditional tripartite themes of causation, war, and consequences, but its topics reflect the introduction of important new categories of analysis since the early 1960s.

Writing in the mid-1970s from his outsider perspective, Hobsbawm readily concluded that it could "scarcely be denied that slavery . . . was the major cause of the friction and rupture between the Northern and Southern states," but he also pointed out that "the real question is why it [slavery] should have led to secession and civil war rather than to some sort of formula for coexistence." After all, Hobsbawm suggested, "militant abolitionism alone was never strong enough to determine the Union's policy" and "Northern capitalism" could easily have found it "convenient to come to terms with and exploit a slave South," along the same lines as international businesses worked advantageously with a twentieth-century South Africa characterized by apartheid. Moreover, Hobsbawm noted, the Union victory that emerged from the conflict represented "the triumph of American capitalism and the modern United States," but, while slavery was abolished, it hardly reflected the triumph "of the Negro, slave or free." With the ultimate "failure" of Reconstruction, which Hobsbawm characterized as a program of forced democratization across racial lines, conservative white southerners regained control of the region and maintained a racist home rule for decades over occasional and usually feckless federal complaints and in spite of increasing resistance from the region's African American population. Ironically, in a chapter entitled "Winners," Hobsbawm concluded that the post-war South remained "poor, backward and resentful, the whites resenting the not-forgotten defeat, and the blacks the disfranchisement and ruthless subordination imposed by the whites" (Hobsbawm 1975: 153–7).

In many respects this volume in Blackwell's *Companion* series might be better titled "The United States in the Age of Capital," as the chapters focus largely on the years between the emergence of sectional crisis over the Wilmot Proviso in 1846 and the end of political Reconstruction in 1877. In broad brush, the contributions cover the historiography, much of it written since Hobsbawm's magisterial 1975 account of capital's triumph in the western world, offering 23 chapters covering three central themes of the era: how, why, and when slavery produced an American Civil War, the direction of the war itself and its immediate consequences for American society, and the process of Reconstruction, with its mixed and disappointing results.

Setting the stage for the rest of the volume, Douglas R. Egerton's chapter, "Slavery and the Union, 1789–1833," explores the literature on slavery in the world of the founders. Egerton contends that critical regional differences defined the young nation's approach to slavery and slavery-related issues from the time the founders drafted the constitution onward. In New England and most of the northern states, where the proportion of slaves as a part of the total population was small and where local economies depended only marginally on slave labor, post-revolutionary ideal-ism quickly put slavery on the road to a gradual end. But, as Joanne Pope Melish (1998) has pointed out, as the gradual emancipation process unfolded, these states also began to purge the long-time presence of slavery from their civic memory. Moreover, even as gradual emancipation removed slaves from the social landscape in these free-labor states, public policy continued to reflect high, and perhaps even intensified, levels of white supremacist thought and severely circumscribed social, political, and economic opportunity for free blacks in the region, recasting both former slaves and blacks free from birth as second-class citizens. In the Chesapeake region, with its long history of slave-based tobacco production, slavery remained entrenched even as the region's aging tobacco economy experienced cyclical decline. The rhetoric of leading Chesapeake state politicians endorsed gradual emancipation; but the actions of these same upper South politicians failed to match their rhetoric and did little to hasten emancipation. Ultimately, in both the upper South and the lower North, a fragile and awkward consensus emerged around colonization as the best method of gradually ending slavery while preventing the creation of a large free black population. To complicate matters further, black agency in the Caribbean, primarily in the form of the Haitian Revolution, played a key role in forging white attitudes, both in frightening southern slaveholders into concern for their future safety and in prompting President Jefferson to acquire Louisiana to facilitate the "diffusion" of slaves out of the Chesapeake and South Atlantic regions, where concentrations of slaves on a Haitian scale existed in a few locales. Jefferson and other upper South defenders of the approach praised diffusion as a beneficent means of weakening slavery and preparing the way for eventual emancipation. In the booming cotton regions of the lower South, however, little sympathy for colonization emerged other than as a means for removing potentially troublesome free blacks from an expanding slave society. In the South Carolina lowcountry, where spectacular rice fortunes emerged from the work of the region's preponderant slave population, Charleston authorities investigating the aborted Denmark Vesey insurrection scare advocated a tighter regimen of slave management that would reduce the limited autonomy slave resistance had carved out for slaves and their families while also launching a full-throated rhetorical attack on slavery's critics in the early 1820s.

But as white southerners grappled with how to wind slavery down or expand it westward, depending on their preferred policy, the world the founders knew gradually disappeared into the vortex of the market revolution. During the years following the war of 1812, a series of transportation improvements and related technological innovations prompted a dramatic expansion and quickening of the young republic's market economy. Market relations penetrated regions previously isolated from their reach and thickened in areas where they already flourished. To be sure, the market revolution emerged at different times and proceeded at different paces in different parts of the country, but it was everywhere an evolution of the capitalist economy. In many parts of the North, and in scattered enclaves elsewhere, the market revolution brought with it industrialization, understood as a process of capital-intensive factory production, and the rise of a class of largely propertyless wage laborers. In other areas, the market revolution meant simply the expansion and intensification of commercial agriculture and trade, and in the lower South, the market revolution represented the westward expansion of plantation agriculture and the extension of staple agriculture into upland regions previously dominated by subsistence production.

Moreover, as the chapters herein by John Larson and Michael Morrison explain, the American public often interpreted the market revolution through the lens of political ideology. As Larson notes, "by the time of the election of Andrew Jackson in 1828, the market revolution had become both an engine of social change and a self-conscious topic of public debate." Defenders of the market revolution saw it as a rising tide that lifted all boats. From this standpoint, one eventually championed by the Whig party, the growth and development of the American economy allowed more and more Americans to move from subsistence to competence, from competence to comfort, and even from comfort to prosperity. Over time, Henry Clay's Whig party, which both inherited and enhanced the Federalist vision of a robust national government active in promoting economic stability and progress, wanted federal policies which would foster the market revolution by providing a stable and abundant currency, financing internal improvements, enacting tariffs to protect emerging American industry from potentially ruinous British competition, and slowing the pace of westward expansion to encourage intensive development in established areas. On the other hand, many Jacksonian Democrats tended to view the market revolution as a threat to the independence of petty producers, the yeoman farmers and artisans (whom Jefferson had praised as the yeomanry of the cities), and threatened to plunge these unsuspecting avatars of personal independence into the dangerous if exciting vortex of the market. Other Democrats had less quarrel with the market revolution than with the notion of using the government to endow already powerful interests with special favors to the disadvantage of rising entrepreneurs. But both groups of Democrats saw the function of government in the age of market revolution as one of protecting individual producers from powerful corporations and an

expanding government, while Whigs wanted to use the power of government posit-
ively to foster entrepreneurship, economic development, and social progress.

Moreover, as Thomas Haskell (1985) has argued, the market revolution also
helped generate a new way of conceptualizing American efforts to address social
problems. According to James Brewer Stewart's essay on reform in the antebellum
North, the market revolution proved central to the emergence of the broad sense of
humanitarianism which guided northern reform efforts through the age of Jackson
and beyond. The exact nature of this relationship between an expansion of market
activity and the rise of humanitarianism as a reform impulse remains the subject of
considerable historiographical controversy, but the role of the market revolution in
constructing an "ideological modernity" during the 1830s appears critical to the
emergence of the reform impulse in antebellum America. According to Stewart, the
teachings of humanitarian reform undoubtedly owed much to the expansion of
market economics and market values. He even suggests that the colonization movement represented the Whig attempt to apply the market doctrine of progress to the
stubborn problems of slavery and race. Rather than a "chimerical project" involving
the mass transport of over 2 million slaves and the possible compensation of many
slaveholders for surrendering their property, moderate Whigs like Henry Clay saw
colonization as a viable alternative to an enduring status quo, as a benevolent form
of government activism that both accelerated the end of American slavery and
strengthened the white republic.

Yet while acknowledging the importance of the market revolution to antebellum
reform, Stewart nonetheless locates the principal origins of abolitionist sentiment
in the social message of a radical wing of the evangelical awakening of the early
nineteenth century. A spiritual cousin of the market revolution, the Second Great
Awakening also shaped the antebellum reform movements. Indeed, the "sensibilities
of empathy" which abolitionists used "when imagining the silent sufferings of the
powerless and exploited slaves" – the "plight of the suffering stranger" – owed as
much to the evangelical awakening as to the market revolution, Stewart suggests.
Ideological modernity, however, also brought with it a stern and more forbidding
face. Abolition gained respect in the North only when its opponents overstepped
republican bounds in their attempts to quiet slavery's opponents. Violent reprisals
against abolitionists, along with open southern disdain and defiance, actually strengthened the antislavery movement over the long term.

Teresa Murphy's survey of the literature on women and gender in the antebellum
North maintains that the market revolution "transformed the lives . . . of women in
the North" even though historians have disagreed sharply over the exact nature of
those changes. As the Second Great Awakening transformed the role of women
from that of reproducing republican virtue to that of inculcating Christian piety in
the next generation, the notion of a "cult of true womanhood" emerged and the
role of women as the peculiar guardians of domestic virtue led to the development
of a notion of gender-specific "separate spheres" in which women were responsible
for the household and childrearing while men trafficked in the competitive secular
worlds of business and politics. Women maintained their households as havens of
virtue and comfort and provided a refuge from the heartless world of the marketplace and stump. But from their assigned positions as guardians of domestic virtue,
middle-class women quickly recognized that households could be protected only by

the promotion of community virtue as well as individual piety. Excessive drinking, gambling, prostitution, and even poverty threatened family life and demanded collective social action, action frequently best coordinated by reform-minded middle-class women and their Protestant minister allies. With virtue in their hearts and time on their hands, ministers and reform-minded women soon ventured out of the home and into the streets, subtly blurring the distinction of separate spheres, and slipping quietly into the first crusades of the Benevolent Empire. Most middle-class women reformers sought mere amelioration of conditions for the poor and vigilance against public vice. They wanted to smooth out the rough edges of society rather than radically alter the antebellum northern social structure being created by the market revolution. A smaller number of perfectionist reformers sought the eradication of evil through personal perfection, but these perfectionists either rejected collective action outright or remained profoundly suspicious of the efficiency of collective social action compared to personal moral transformation. Over time, forays into causes like opposition to Indian removal, temperance, and property law reform gradually drew reform-minded women out of the household and into the public sphere, where, as Lori Ginzberg (1990) points out, their efforts to achieve moral reform encountered serious obstacles, centered on the political impotence of women as a disfranchised group. Confronting this handicap, radical women pushed for the right to vote at the Seneca Falls Convention in 1848.

Working-class women may have enjoyed a measure of independence denied middle-class women (because of their income) but the ideals of an increasingly bourgeois northern society denied working-women's claim to virtue on account of their very involvement in the market nexus, a sphere assigned by bourgeois mores to men and women of loose morals. As Christine Stansell (1987) argued, however, working-class women hardly saw themselves in this light. Women who left the New England countryside to work in Lowell factories often did so to help their households fulfill traditional notions of household competence. But later these women learned to enjoy the autonomy that came with their wages; they often sought and found husbands among the men of factory towns. Women in artisan households also found themselves hard at work with little time for escape from the traditional household economy. When the "putting out" and related part-time labor systems evolved, these city women often had to work harder for outside bosses whose very success undermined the workshop system which had sustained artisan life for several generations.

The position of women in an Old South where a powerful cross-class male alliance apparently formed to insure their subordination is the subject of Michele Gillespie's stimulating chapter. Gillespie's historiographical inquiry addresses the question, raised by the important work of Elizabeth Fox-Genovese (1988), of whether or not southern plantation women remained outside the "cult of domesticity" which characterized the lives of middle-class women in the antebellum North. Fox-Genovese maintained that slavery slowed the development of a strong bourgeoisie in the pre-Civil War South, while the influence of slaveholding and plantation agriculture perpetuated an older, Old Testament ideal of the patriarchal household as the fundamental unit of society. The patriarchal ideal circumscribed the place of women in southern society even more severely than the concept of separate spheres limited women in the North. The role of the plantation mistress, though, ironically resembled that of the domestic manager in the North. The patriarchal ideal, as practiced in the Old South, placed household activity under the firm control of the plantation mistress, a charge which included management of some slaves. Fox-Genovese posits that the plantation mistress benefited enormously from the slaveholding system and lived as part of antebellum America's most privileged class, despite the limitations on their civil and political rights. And as Stephanie McCurry (1995) has maintained, even non-elite women in the Old South, influenced by the teachings of evangelical religion from scattered southern pulpits, tended to accept patriarchal values. Initially, more southern women than men were drawn to evangelical teachings, and the radical potential of evangelicalism as a social leveler posed a threat to patriarchy, but, following Christine Heyrman's argument, Gillespie notes that "white men confronted clergymen, pressing them to limit women's roles and embrace a more muscular Christianity," pushing the southern church in a more conservative direction. Other scholars, however, have suggested that extended kinship networks helped diminish the oppressiveness of southern patriarchy by increasing interaction and female bonding across class lines. On many issues, as Gillespie points out, developments among southern women tended to follow national patterns. Southern women readily accepted the transformation of their role from that of republican mother and protectors of public virtue to that of teachers of Christian piety and the stewards of private morality. Companionate marriages, an emerging nineteenth-century convention, appear to have thrived in the Old South. Still, Catherine Clinton and others have forcefully argued for the existence of an horrific "double standard" for sexual conduct in the Old South, as masters and, indeed, virtually all white men roamed free to seek sexual pleasure with slave women, while white women were expected to remain virgins before marriage and faithful thereafter (Clinton and Gillespie 1997). Apart from its manifest unfairness, this double standard often shielded male cruelty and violence, not only against slave and free black women but also against susceptible white women, and it created a rage among white women in slaveholding households that often found expression against ever-vulnerable slave women.

Gillespie also evaluates the scholarship on the position of yeomen and poor white women in the Old South. In an influential study, Stephanie McCurry (1995) argued that while yeoman women often ordered plain folk households internally, often inculcating these households with the values of evangelical Christianity, they enjoyed little or no economic or political power despite their economic and social contributions to the household. In a sense, the male household head's commitment to patriarchy and the broader social commitment to slavery produced the subordination of women across class lines. Moreover, as McCurry points out, the growing commitment to evangelical religion and patriarchal values reinforced support for the slaveholding order, among not only yeoman men but yeoman women as well, producing an intense conservatism on social issues which outlasted slavery in the region.

A number of authors have noted that interracial sex presented a challenge to white identity and hence to the organizing motif of whiteness in the Old South. Work by Cynthia Kierner (1998) advanced the idea, consistent with much of the post-Fox-Genovese literature, that women in the Old South developed their own notions of domesticity and separate spheres, concepts which flourished in the North during the same period but which often extruded a modicum of southern distinctiveness due to their peculiar manifestations on slaveholding farms and plantations where the "family" often meant not simply those in the Big House or farmstead but those in the slave quarter and scattered cabins as well. As Gillespie's chapter reveals, Kierner's argument that "evangelicalism and domesticity served southern women as well as northern women" mounts an effective challenge to Fox-Genovese's (1988) contention for an exceptional world of southern women unaffected by the cult of domesticity or the concept of separate spheres. Gillespie also noted that since the 1990s, historians, led by Laura Edwards (2000), have begun to look at ways women influenced politics, not simply by whispering, or even yelling, in their husbands' ears but through appearances at campaign events and other public ceremonies, and through letters to husband-politicians away serving in Congress or state legislatures.

Gillespie also assesses the valuable spate of recent works studying slave women, who often faced the double jeopardy of mistreatment on the basis of both race and gender. Recent scholarship has sustained the view that slave marriages, slave families, and slave communities served as important "invisible institutions," which helped slaves cope with their plight and resist further exploitation with whatever meager means they had at their disposal. Yet some recent work also suggests that slave children faced an especially bleak childhood in which coming of age was complicated by possibility of sale, sexual exploitation, and the almost certain exploitation of their labor at an early age. Gillespie highlights the important work of Brenda Stevenson (1996), who argues that slave men and women, though themselves often the victims of capricious violence and constant exploitation, too often took their frustration out on their children in the form of abuse.

The study of the slave family also looms large in Larry Hudson's chapter on the historiography of antebellum slavery. In fact, Hudson concluded that "two features of slavery in the Old South distinguished it from slavery elsewhere in the Americas: the family and the relative absence of large-scale servile rebellion." Hudson's chapter analyzes how the complex pattern of slave resistance to bondage so well documented by the scholarship of the period since the late 1970s helped the enslaved carve out vital "living space" for themselves while enduring systematic oppression. One product of the "living space" slaves created by their various modes of resistance was the possibility for an active and vibrant family life despite the hardships and inhumanity of slavery. Ironically, Hudson argues, the very strength of these family ties, both nuclear and extended, and the larger community life which constellations of slave families generated, produced commitments and affections which militated against the most extreme form of slave resistance–organized insurrection. With spouses, children, friends, and extended family to consider, slaves proved reluctant to participate in open rebellions, where punishment likely consisted of execution or exile. Citing work by Loren Schweninger and John Hope Franklin (1999), Hudson notes that even the "risky acts" of running away became largely the province of the "young, male, and single," while "for the remainder, the vast majority of enslaved African Americans, therefore, life was characterized not by flight, but by purposeful, 'watchful waiting.'" This emergence of such strategic caution among slaves, Hudson insists, in no way implied acceptance of the permanence of slavery as an institution or the legitimacy of the masters' authority, but rather that slaves preferred to wait until the odds favored a successful bid for freedom.

Following the pioneering work of Ira Berlin and others, Hudson discusses the need to consider slavery as an evolving institution with significant regional variations

(Berlin and Rowland 1992; Berlin and Morgan 1993). Recent scholarship suggests, according to Hudson, that perhaps the most important factor in determining regional variations was the dominant staple crop. Cotton, rice, tobacco, and sugar cultivation all created different work routines and working conditions for slaves and through these influences on slave work helped to shape local slave cultures as well. Hudson also recounts the voluminous recent literature on how slaves themselves participated in a sort of petty local market economy in which they bought, sold, and bartered goods and services on their own account, sometimes even amassing significant property. Hudson suggests that masters generally accepted slave participation in these emerging "slave economies" as yet another way of enmeshing the enslaved in a web of local relationships that tied slaves to the community and militated against insurrection.

Despite the presence of slavery, as Charles C. Bolton's chapter points out, the market revolution in the Old South pushed yeomen and poor whites toward increased involvement in the market economy. Historically isolated from large-scale market activity, and either priding themselves on their independence (yeomen) or striving to achieve it (poorer whites), common whites in the Old South often viewed market expansion with suspicion even as they grew more heavily involved in it. The focus of Bolton's chapter is on the nature of social and economic relations between planters, yeomen, and propertyless whites in the Old South. He concludes that while yeomen and landless whites dominated the region numerically, planters held the preponderance of economic power and social prestige and at least tried to control the political process (though they enjoyed very mixed success in this regard). Bolton's survey of the literature emphasizes the poverty and plight of landless whites in a region where they were destined to compete with slave labor for their livelihood. Bolton also suggests that the literature indicates that the seemingly intransigent conservatism of the Old South owed much to a common desire among white male heads of household, regardless of class, to preserve the subordination of women, a subordination comparable, at least at the conceptual level, to their desire to keep African Americans enslaved. Following Stephanie McCurry's (1995) argument, Bolton suggests that a common interest in the continued subordination of "others" cemented the interests of common white men to those of elite planters.

The themes of market revolution, slavery, and the influence of slaveholders come together in Michael Morrison's chapter on antebellum politics. Morrison traces the emergence of the Civil War from the disintegration of the Second American Party system and the intensifying debate over the future of slavery in the western territories. Morrison argues that positions on the expansion of slavery emerged along partisan lines, and often as much for partisan as sectional motives. As tension over the expansion of slavery opened fissures in the existing parties, it opened the door to the intense sectional wrangling that led to Civil War. Morrison rightly insists that recent scholarship overwhelmingly affirms Lincoln's contemporary suggestion that slavery was "somehow" the cause of the Civil War. Yet a good deal of disagreement remains over exactly how slavery caused the war and why it caused it when it did. Morrison skillfully traces Michael Holt's (1978) argument that while slavery produced competing sectional ideologies with the potential to sever the ties of the Union, the disintegration of the Second American Party, a disintegration driven to a significant degree by issues unrelated to slavery or its expansion, unleashed them.

Nevertheless, Morrison makes it clear that the ideological combat over slavery in the territories ultimately produced two dramatic new strains of political ideology in the United States, one in the North and one in the South, that quickly reshaped the terms of political debate during the 1850s. In the North, a robust critique of slavery as a labor system emerged in the form of the free-labor ideology so well analyzed by Eric Foner in 1970. Free-labor ideology claimed that freedom and opportunity for free laborers hinged on the avoidance of direct competition with slaves. This conclusion led free-labor Republicans to an unyielding stand against the expansion of slavery. The free-labor ideology, with its emphasis on the virtue of work and the possibility of upward social mobility, appealed to opponents of slavery on economic as well as moral grounds. It also drew adherents from those who simply wanted to maximize the access of free white farmers and workers to western lands. A parallel reaction occurred in the South, where radical southern rights advocates increasingly identified the freedom and opportunity of white southerners as the product of a leveling upward sustained by slavery. According to southern rights advocates, slavery guaranteed the civic equality of white men and protected the southern social system from the radical tendencies of a free proletariat.

John Ashworth's chapter evaluates scholarship on the triumph of the Republican party in the North in still greater detail. Ashworth reminds us that Republicans self-consciously defined themselves in contradistinction to the slave-labor economy of the South. Republicans viewed the South as oppressive, backward, and a drag on the larger national economy. At the same time, the free-labor ideology hardly represented a prescription for industrialization and a rapidly centralizing economy but instead offered a passionate ideological defense of small farms and small shops. William Gienapp (1987) has argued that the rise of the Republican party owed much to the cultural issues such as nativism and temperance which helped alienate northern voters from existing parties. Gienapp also saw Republican success emerging not only from the party's ability to define itself in opposition to the South, but also from its ability to blame northern social problems on the so-called "slave power" conspiracy, a northern label for the political clout wielded by the slaveholding states. Buttressed by the three-fifths compromise, the "slave power" allegedly foisted proslavery policies on the rest of the nation through its disproportionate influence in Congress and on the presidency. Ashworth also emphasizes that the Republican party included factions with significantly different degrees of antislavery sentiment. The most radical advocates of racial equity in antebellum America tended to support Republicans, who took a firm stand against the expansion of slavery. But many Republicans held more moderate antislavery views and simply focused on the issue at hand: stopping the westward expansion of slavery and the augmentation of the slave power in the United States Senate.

Daniel Crofts analyzes the emergence of the Civil War by focusing on why the center failed to hold when moderates in both North and South seemed to out-number radicals. Southern Rights radicals, Crofts insists, increasingly imposed "suicidal demands" on the national Democratic party, ironically if not intentionally undermining the party's ability to protect slavery through maintaining a national Democratic majority. These southern demands prompted growing alarm in the North, even among Democrats, and constantly refreshed northern fears of an aggressive slave power. Once Lincoln was elected, radical secessionists knew they could wait no longer; slavery on the southern periphery would only grow weaker by the year. Secessionists demanded immediate action. This appeal fell on receptive ears in the lower South where many yeomen already believed that antislavery Republicans were trying to fasten second-class citizenship upon themselves and their neighbors, and that many abolitionists, a group they scarcely distinguished from Republicans, would willingly unleash the terror of slave insurrection on the South. In the upper South, where party competition sustained hope for a reversal of course at the next election, the appeal rang hollow. Moreover, precisely because the upper South's defense of slavery remained linked to maintaining influence within the Union, the secession of the lower South produced furious upper South action to knit the Union back together again, albeit on terms that would safeguard slavery. Crofts also highlights literature pointing to Republican bungling when the party assumed power in 1860. Republicans, including President Lincoln, repeatedly underestimated the extent of popular support for secession in the South. Even in the North, sentiments differed over whether the Union should be maintained by force. Crofts suggests that possibly only the northern belief that a majority of white southerners preferred to remain in the Union persuaded northerners to support the use of force to suppress the rebellion. As Crofts' survey points out, northern reluctance to use force to suppress the southern rebellion evaporated into "patriotic indignation" once the Confederacy fired on Fort Sumter. As Lincoln told the nation on July 4, 1861, saving the Union "would demonstrate to the world" that minorities could not overturn a decision "fairly, constitutionally Decided" at the ballot box, and northerners responded to Lincoln's call for volunteers in full force.

In Part II, the voluminous literature on Lincoln and his wartime presidency is the focus of Kevin Gannon's chapter on "Saving the Union." Gannon points out that over the years the much-admired Lincoln has received his share of criticism from scholars who argue that his policies needlessly pushed the nation into war during the spring of 1861. Especially during the 1930s, with the carnage of World War I and the bitter fruits of the Treaty of Versailles all too evident, advocates of the "needless war" hypothesis argued that savvy politicians, like those of the Clay, Webster, Calhoun generation, could have used their skill to prevent war altogether. During the 1950s and 1960s, however, liberal scholars influenced by the Civil Rights Movement pointed out such moderation carried the price of prolonging slavery, and perhaps even risking its survival into the twentieth century, where it might have led to substantial support in the American South for a conservative, Prussian-style modernization program. Gannon's chapter concedes the charge that Lincoln consistently overestimated Unionist strength in the South and underestimated the popularity of secession among southern whites, but he also reminds readers that many southerners failed to recognize the popularity of Lincoln's free-labor ideology and its moderate antislavery message in the North. Lincoln and the Republicans appealed to northern voters, not because Democrats failed to refashion their coalition, but because northerners had come to embrace the free-labor Republican message. Gannon traces the massive literature on Lincoln as commander-in-chief and architect of Union military policy, finding him a spur to cautious generals, a leader who knew how to strike when the iron was hot and yet show patience when tempted by quixotic action. Gannon also reviews the recent scholarship maintaining that the process of "self-emancipation," driven by slave resistance and rebellion and flight to Union lines intensified once the war began. Without denying the role that African American agency played in emancipation, Gannon concludes that Lincoln's role as the "Great Emancipator" remains important. He quotes approvingly James McPherson's assessment:

> [B]y pronouncing slavery a moral evil that must come to an end and then winning the presidency in 1860, provoking the South to secede, by refusing to compromise on the issue of slavery's expansion or on Fort Sumter, by careful leadership and timing that kept a fragile Unionist coalition together in the first year of war and committed it to emancipation in the second, by prosecuting the war to unconditional victory as commander-in-chief of an army of liberation, Abraham Lincoln freed the slaves. (McPherson 1996: 207)

In the second chapter on the Civil War, Carol Reardon explores the reasons for the Union victory in the Civil War and why it took historians so long to develop a sustained interest in the question. As Reardon points out, studies of "Why the South Lost the War" had been a hardy historical perennial for decades before the question of how the Union won the war attracted significant attentions from scholars. Like studies of Civil War causation, stories of the epic political and military conflict in American history have often centered on the Confederacy, the rise and fall of its military fortunes, and the internal strife which some scholars believe undermined the Confederate war effort. But comparatively little attention has been paid to how the Union handled its own military and political challenges. Reardon's analysis recounts a body of scholarship which quickly idolized Lincoln as the savior of the Union but was slow to perceive of Grant as a brilliant general who conceived and executed a strategy to vanquish a clever but outmanned enemy by taxing its ability to sustain the fight over the long haul. Yet Reardon also points out that many scholars argue that Grant's "strategy of exhaustion" should not be confused with the kind of all-out assault on an enemy's (civilians included) ability to wage war necessary to categorize the strategy as one of "total war." In addition to offering an excellent analysis of the surfeit of Civil War battle histories, Reardon also examines in detail the role played by ideology and home front morale on the Union war effort before concluding her chapter with an assessment of recent scholarship on the motivation of Union soldiers. In summing up, Reardon points out that when former Confederate General Pickett was asked after the war why his famous charge at Gettysburg failed, the much-criticized commander laconically replied, "I think the Union Army had something to do with it." Reardon agrees, noting that while "historians have been slow to give the Union military effort the detailed examination it deserves, the truth behind General Pickett's words cannot be mistaken."

In the counterpart to Reardon's chapter, Steven Woodworth ably discusses the vast literature on the Confederacy's military effort. Woodworth concludes that the Confederates suffered from bungling military leadership, President Jefferson Davis' indecisiveness, and Robert E. Lee's penchant for strategic audacity and tactically aggressive moves. According to Woodworth, Lee's battlefield boldness produced some rousing and impressive Confederate victories, but over time his impetuous approach cost the Confederate army valuable troops and still failed to cow the Union into seeking peace. On the western front, Confederate generals were regularly out-maneuvered by their Union counterparts, and the triumph of the Union army in the West divided the Confederacy and allowed Sherman's decisive march through Georgia and the Carolinas to trap Lee between Grant and himself. Before Sherman could arrive to cut off a prospective Lee retreat, however, Grant had worn Lee down and cut off his retreating army at Appomattox. Nine days after Lee's surrender, Johnston surrendered to Sherman at Durham Station, North Carolina, and, in Woodworth's words, "with that, though other surrenders followed piecemeal over the next few weeks, the war, for all practical purposes, was over."

The rich and growing literature on the southern home front during the Civil War and the impact of home front morale on the war effort receives a fresh analysis in Mary DeCredico's chapter which traces the changing assessments of Jefferson Davis as a war leader and his role in the ultimate "failure of Confederate nationalism." Highlighting the "brother's war" aspect of the conflict in the upper South, DeCredico carefully chronicles the burgeoning literature on internal conflict there, an area where pro-Union sentiment remained strong in many areas. She discusses the question of Confederates in North Carolina and Tennessee, and to a lesser extent in Georgia and Alabama, who remained decidedly lukewarm, and sometimes openly hostile, toward the Confederate war effort. Turning her attention to the growing literature on the changing role of women during the war, which a number of scholars argue led to a significant if temporary change in gender roles in the region, DeCredico examines Drew Faust's (1996) contention that women's roles evolved rapidly under the pressures and hardships of war, often placing women in a difficult practical and ideological position. Forced by the exigencies of war to depart from their "dependent" status to manage household and plantation affairs, southern women nevertheless tended to remain ideologically committed to traditional social values and beliefs. DeCredico also evaluates recent work on the role of children in the war, and details the voluminous recent literature on how the institution of slavery began to crumble under the pressures of war as slaves pushed for autonomy, and ultimately freedom, as Confederate military fortunes sagged.

Lincoln, other nineteenth-century contemporaries, and many modern historians point to the "new birth of freedom" that emancipation gave the American republic as justification of the war's terrible carnage. Fueled by interest in history from the "the bottom up," formally known as the "new social history," and the new interest in African American history spawned by the Civil Rights Movement, studies of the emancipation of the Old South's nearly 4 million slaves have proliferated since the early 1960s. Joseph P. Reidy's important chapter evaluates this explosion of literature. He examines recent scholarship that has focused on the agency of slaves in pushing for emancipation, not only through their long-term resistance to slavery but also through enhanced levels of resistance and rebellion during the war itself, and on the role played by African American troops in the Union military effort. Reidy highlights the importance of Leon Litwack's Pulitzer Prize-winning *Been in the Storm So Long* (1979) in creating a broad scholarly appreciation of the role the freedpeople played in giving meaning to their freedom. As Reidy points out, Litwack resisted focusing "narrowly on the transformation of labor relations or of African American families or of the southern body politic, although he offered insightful commentary on all those topics," instead emphasizing "personal encounters – between former masters and former slaves, African American soldiers and their

Confederate counterparts, freedmen and freedwomen, Klansmen and their victims." With "graceful and moving prose, his analysis ranged across the complex terrain between two poles: the bitter resentment that most white southerners harbored and the daunting struggle that freedpeople waged for freedom, dignity, and equality."

Reidy's chapter effectively recounts the literature documenting the dramatic role the freedmen played in creating the politics of Reconstruction and the complex web of economic arrangements that emerged after the Civil War. In assessing the literature on the role of freedmen in the postbellum southern economy, Reidy covers scholarly debates over the persistence of planter power in the New South and the degree to which new labor arrangements involving freedpeople, including tenancy and sharecropping, reflected the emergence of a new capitalist agriculture in the rural South. Reidy points out that while "freedpeople lacked the wealth and other productive resources that their former owners possessed, their ability to work gave them leverage in the struggle over the labor arrangements to replace slavery." Reidy notes that the work of Eric Foner (1988) and others revealed "considerable variation" in labor arrangements "from plantation to plantation within the same neighborhood, from state to state, and from one crop region to another." Based on his review of the literature, Reidy concludes that arrangements varied widely during the early postwar years but eventually settled into clearer and more stable patterns. For example, in the cotton South, gang labor survived for several years after the war, particularly in plantation areas, but family-based labor arrangements also developed within the first few postwar years. "From those beginnings," Reidy argues, "fully articulated systems of tenancy and sharecropping later emerged," and whenever possible, "freedpeople used the political process, and particularly their newfound right of suffrage to help influence the evolution of these labor arrangements."

Moving to different historiographical terrain, Reidy discusses the recent spate of works examining emancipation "through the prism of gender." Reidy notes Peter Bardaglio's (1995) contention that southern defeat weakened the standing of the household as the effective unit of social control, causing conservative white southerners to turn to the state as a new source of authority. He also highlights the work of Laura Edwards (1997) and its analysis of how postbellum southern women, and especially African American women, used the blow to patriarchal authority delivered by Confederate defeat to improve their position in postbellum society.

A chapter co-authored by O. Vernon Burton, David Herr, and Matthew Cheney begins Part III on Reconstruction with a discussion of the many difficulties involved in defining the Reconstruction period. According to this chapter, the political, economic, and social dimensions of Reconstruction proceeded on very different timetables. Political Reconstruction, the authors agree, had been overturned everywhere in the former Confederacy by 1877, and much earlier in some places, justifying the traditional dating of the end of political Reconstruction to the so-called "Compromise of 1877." This Compromise smoothed the way for the election of Republican Rutherford B. Hayes as president and secured a Republican promise to remove all federal troops supporting Republican administrations from the southern states. Yet, as the authors point out, the economic reconstruction of the South took much longer, and many economic historians argue that the region did not return to the national economic mainstream until the post-World War II national economic boom and the formal desegregation of southern society ended the isolation of southern labor markets and opened the capital-starved region fully to outside investment. Social historians tend to define Reconstruction differently still, seeing it as a period which began with emancipation but ended dismally with the white supremacist imposition of segregation and disfranchisement of African Americans in the late nineteenth and early twentieth centuries. In the rest of their essay, the authors skillfully review a broad range of historiographical issues, setting the stage for the more specialized chapters that follow.

In his contribution on the "Politics of Reconstruction," Michael Perman insists that this era was "concerned, above all, with politics." In Perman's view, the problem which defined the era was "how to reorganize the politics of the former Confederate states in such a way as to enable them, without undermining the gains achieved by the Union victory on the battlefield, to return to Congress and become reincorporated into the political life of the nation." And, at least in terms of politics, Perman marks the end of Reconstruction with the federal government's decision in 1877 "to terminate its decade-long involvement in the South." Perman recounts approvingly the massive revision in the political history of Reconstruction that has occurred since the early 1960s. Long discredited are the racist interpretations of the Dunning School, which characterized Reconstruction as an era of political corruption and incompetence, an "era of good stealing," as coalitions of recently freed blacks and opportunistic Yankees looted southern treasuries and railroad corporations and anarchy ruled the southern economy. New studies of the Republican-dominated state governments in the Reconstruction South posit regimes that were hardly perfect. Nevertheless, they grappled seriously with overwhelming problems and groped their way toward policies which would ensure basic civil rights and promote economic development. These regimes tried to establish basic civil and political rights against fierce opposition from the defeated but bitterly hostile southern white majority. The earlier portrayal of Reconstruction southern Republicans as extremists eager to inflict providential vengeance on a prostrate South collapsed under an impressive array of state political studies showing sharp divisions within the Republican party, including strong factions of moderates within the party. Republican policies appeared harsh to many whites because white southerners tended to think of federal terms for Reconstruction not as dictates emerging from military victory but as political proposals open to negotiation.

Perman's chapter also highlights his own work on the collapse of centrist politics in the South during the Reconstruction era. During the first part of Reconstruction, Perman argues, both Republicans and Democrats moved to the center to build winning coalitions. Later, as racial polarization sharpened in the region, both parties adopted an expressive politics in which each party appealed to its base with ideological and cultural hard lines. The latter appeals produced a divided and polarized electorate in 1876. Perman also evaluates a growing literature on the role of violence and intimidation in ending the Republican rule in the postwar South. Highlighting the contribution of George Rable's (1984) *But There Was No Peace*, Perman concludes that Reconstruction violence emerged as a "critical ingredient" in the white South's ultimate ability to win the peace. The often mentioned "failure" of Reconstruction, Perman insists, had less to do with the inadequacies of Republican leadership than with the "immense" obstacles and difficulties which stood in its way. In Perman's view, the revisionist writing on Reconstruction "confirms the suspicion" that the problems which thwarted Reconstruction efforts were "intractable," and that the Reconstruction era was not so much a "failure" as a "tragedy."

Peter A. Coclanis and Scott Marler assess the literature of Reconstruction largely from a macroeconomic perspective. Coclanis and Marler note that the traditional scholarship over-emphasized the Civil War as a cause of postbellum southern poverty. Using institutional economics as way of looking at the structural problems of the New South economy, Coclanis and Marler develop their chapter as an extended analysis of Roger Ransom and Richard Sutch's (1977) influential *One Kind of Freedom*, a study in which two accomplished econometricians argued that African American incomes grew slowly in the postbellum South because institutionalized racism thwarted the free market mechanisms which would otherwise have made more progress possible. Coclanis and Marler, however, question whether Ransom and Sutch identified the right institution – the postbellum southern credit market – as the chief culprit in the perpetuation of southern economic backwardness. Ransom and Sutch maintained that the postbellum credit market was dominated by scattered supply merchants. These merchants allegedly enjoyed a territorial monopoly that allowed them to charge the bloated interest rates that choked economic progress in the postwar South. But an abundance of impressive evidence on town development in the New South revealed that supply merchants tended to cluster in railroad towns where they competed rather vigorously for the supply trade while speculating in staple crops rather than scattering geographically through a thinly populated countryside in search of the advantages of geographic isolation.

Also reexamining the literature on the seemingly intractable economic problems of the late nineteenth-century South, R. Tracy McKenzie focuses on the microeconomic decisions of postbellum southern farmers and workers, white and black. McKenzie skillfully recounts the debate over whether black workers, especially African American women and children, withdrew from the labor force once slavery was abolished, triggering what whites accustomed to the forced labor of slavery perceived as a labor shortage. McKenzie also assesses the complex historiography addressing the emergence of sharecropping and tenant farming in the late nineteenth century. The creation of a complex postbellum labor system which relied heavily on sharecropping and tenant farming emerged from the confluence of a variety of factors, including a credit crunch, the inexperience of former masters and former slaves with free labor, the determination of landowners and federal authorities to restore aggregate agricultural output as quickly as possible, and the freedpeople's desire to shape the meaning of freedom by providing for their own subsistence. In connection with the emergence of tenant farming on a widespread basis among whites, McKenzie assesses recent scholarship on the decline of the white yeoman farmer in the postbellum South. Forced into the market by wartime deprivation, credit shortages, and population pressures, yeomen lost much of their antebellum self-sufficiency as they produced more and more for the cash economy. Caught by the high price of credit and fluctuation in staple yields, yeomen accumulated debts and often lost property to foreclosure or the sheriff's hammer. Even more commonly, sons of propertied families spent longer and longer terms as tenants before acquiring property of their own. McKenzie also highlights his own findings that, at least in Tennessee, rising tenancy rates owed more to the movement of landless white laborers into the tenant farming ranks than to the decline of the yeomanry.

Jeannie Whayne's chapter examines the position of southern women during the "Age of Emancipation," with a focus on how much any wartime alteration in women's roles sustained itself into the postwar era. Whayne is persuaded that the roles of African American women changed the most, as emancipation opened opportunities for freedwomen to reduce their labor force participation to suit their family circumstances and preferences. In a sweeping survey of the sometimes contradictory historiography on this subject, Whayne notes that some scholars insist that whenever possible, and to whatever extent possible, African American freedwomen reduced their labor market participation in favor of the traditional white model of doing household chores and raising children, while doing a little extra field, garden, or domestic work on the side for wages. Other scholars counter that African American women in the post-emancipation years resisted the attempted inculcation of bourgeois family values and continued to participate aggressively in the labor force. The latter group argues that the formation of the postbellum southern agricultural labor force as a constellation of tenants and sharecroppers owed much to the desire of African American women to work with other members of their family as household units. Such an arrangement, they believed, secured as much autonomy as possible from landowners. At the same time, it allowed freedwomen to do agricultural work to augment their household income and help their families crawl up the so-called agricultural ladder. Whayne also examines the literature on how white women responded to emancipation, focusing particularly on how elite white women reshaped the strictures of *Herrenvolk* democracy to retain their dominance as a class. Recent scholarship suggests that while the antebellum legal system hesitated to limit the prerogatives of patriarchy, the postbellum years saw southern courts move quickly to assert class, race, and gender authority through the legal system. Whayne highlights Laura Edwards' (1997) argument that elite white women recognized the importance of the public sphere, and especially the ballot box and the court room, even as they styled themselves as "paragons" of the private sphere and used their acumen to help elite white men restore white supremacy. Whayne also notes that Beth Barton Schweiger's (2000) scholarship on the emergence of women in leadership roles in postbellum southern church bureaucracy paralleled roles played by middle-class women in voluntary reform organizations in the antebellum North.

Paralleling Whayne's effort, Nina Silber's chapter provides a careful assessment of the historiography on women in the postbellum North. Silber addresses the literature's attention to the question of whether or not the Civil War represented a watershed for northern women. The answer, according to Silber's assessment of the literature, remains ambiguous. Wartime exigencies clearly forced women into new roles in the labor force, but they quietly returned to more traditional female occupations after the war ended. Northern women rushed to support the war effort as nurses and providers of relief for the poor and needy, but women had long been active in volunteer benevolent societies, and their wartime activities scarcely represented a major departure from antebellum practice. Some women had been active in abolition and the women's rights movement but the war represented a hiatus in the latter. Apart from abolition, reform zeal, and particularly the drive for the suffrage, waned during Reconstruction. The success of women writers, Silber concludes, may have allowed the feminization of the Civil War, as female war efforts were celebrated and the civic participation of women was tacitly endorsed as a valued part of the federal cause. In the end, Silber suggests, "this impression of a transformation was itself evidence of a real turning point for northern women," as they began not only to "imagine a new relationship with the nation state" but also "to forge one as well."

In the volume's penultimate chapter, Gaines M. Foster evaluates the literature on the legacy of the Civil War for the South. Southern defeat evolved, as Robert Penn Warren (1964) suggested in the 1960s, into a "Great Alibi" for all the region's failures during the late nineteenth and early twentieth centuries. For at least 75 years after the end of Reconstruction, segregation, disfranchisement, and the South's distinctive legacy of poverty and economic backwardness made the South a "land apart" from the rest of the nation. Foster points out that for many economic historians, the South's distinctiveness is rooted in the peculiarities of its nineteenth-century economy. As economic historian Gavin Wright (1978, 1986) emphasized, emancipation abruptly changed southern agriculture from a system controlled by labor lords (slaveholders) interested in maximizing output per hand and in maintaining the value of their peculiar capital (slaves) into a system centered on landlords interested in maximizing output per acre and strapped for capital by the abolition of slavery. With the end of slavery, the emergence of a credit system that depended heavily on the local reputation of borrowers slowed the geographic mobility of laborers and isolated the South from national labor markets. As C. Vann Woodward (1951) suggested years earlier, this isolation produced the long-term economic stagnation that turned the rural New South into a vast pawn shop. David Carlton's (1990) work on southern entrepreneurs emphasized that the slow building of a so-called New South depended on town- and city-based entrepreneurs who, apart from those along North Carolina's Tobacco Road, were plagued by capital shortages and a large but relatively unskilled labor supply. At the same time, these entrepreneurs worked in a national market they did not control, and often could scarcely influence. Hence southern entrepreneurs, lacking capital and concerned about vulnerability to outside competition, remained an unreliable and often short-sighted group unable to drive the southern economy rapidly toward the national mainstream.

Foster also examines the notion that the South lost the war but won the peace through the overthrow of Republican Reconstruction and the disfranchisement and segregation of African Americans by the late nineteenth century. The national embrace of white supremacy found strong support in the southern black-belt, where the restoration of white control outweighed economic progress in the minds of most whites. Foster notes that the dominant mode of southern white conservatism, deeply rooted in the black-belt regions, often faced challenges from a variety of southern dissenters, including redneck populists and liberals in the hillcountry. These dissenters from conservative orthodoxy generally supported federal aid to the region, both to provide relief and stimulate sagging farm and mill communities. And, across the South, progressives urged moderation and compromise on racial issues in the interest of enhanced economic development for the region and enjoyed occasional success.

Foster concludes that the so-called Lost Cause ideology perpetuated a sense of provincial defiance and regional resentment in the white South. Noting its origins in Confederate military camps, Foster nevertheless emphasizes the renewed livelihood the Lost Cause gained from politicians on the stump once the genuine pain and anguish of defeat wore off. Assessing the work of a number of writers who found a loss of southern self-confidence and collective self-worth a problem, Foster finds that defeat left white southerners lacking confidence in their American identity and looking for ways to reassert it. The Lost Cause redefined and uplifted the southern memory of the war, turning it from a shameful defeat into an honorable sacrifice, one that ignored slavery, and placed the vanquished on a par with the victors in heroism and patriotism. Over time, the Lost Cause helped heal scars and facilitate national reconciliation (among whites only) and partially through the national embrace of white supremacy during the so-called Progressive era. Of course, even after this putative spirit of reunion triumphed, images of backwardness and intolerance pervaded national portrayals of the South well into the late twentieth century. The lingering interest in southern separatism, evidenced by the still avowedly pro-secession plat-form of the League of the South, and the recent resurgence of Scottish or Celtic identity movements have nonetheless gained only marginal appeal among southern whites. Perhaps, as Foster observes wryly, the limited popularity of the Celtic revival may arise from no larger a consideration than the fact that "not too many good ol' boys will embrace a movement that might require that they wear a skirt."

In the volume's final chapter, Heather Richardson surveys the historical literature on the impact of Reconstruction on northern labor. Richardson suggests that the absence of southern political influence in national councils, with its chronic suspi-cion of accruing federal power, paved the way for more aggressive assertion of the class agenda of northern capitalists. Hence, outside the South, the Reconstruction era and the late nineteenth century proved a period of accelerating conflict between free but propertyless labor and increasingly concentrated capital. This burgeoning class conflict in postbellum America, Richardson claims, remains a too often over-looked aspect of Reconstruction history. During the 1870s, Richardson argues, moderate northern Republicans became increasingly wary of the power of organized labor, and with a eye on the Paris communes, frightened of its radical potential. Yet, despite the sounding of a radical voice here and there, the American labor movement as a whole, and especially the dominant National Labor Union (NLU), appeared more interested in defending, or perhaps restoring, the economy of small producers which had characterized the economy of the early Jacksonian era than in joining a worldwide socialist movement. The NLU mounted a somewhat nostalgic defense of a petty producer economy in which control of productive property or possession of a prized job skill defined its owner as an independent person worthy of republican citizenship and capable of rising up the economic ladder through hard work and accumulation. As Richardson points out, the rise of the American Federation of Labor in the 1880s initiated the gradual replacement of the restorationist utopianism of the NLU with the practical but hardly radical demand of "more" from Samuel Gompers. But reaction to a labor movement increasingly strengthened by immi-grants flocking to its ranks drove capital and corporations toward a defiant posture which often resulted in the violent confrontations that became characteristic of labor tensions during the Gilded Age. In their struggle to win this pitched battle with labor, capitalists regularly sought and usually received the aid of federal and state governments eager to protect property and curry favor with wealth. Ultimately, according to Richardson, a government-assisted suppression of radical dissent helped define both the socialism and syndicalism outside the mainstream of American pol-itics. "The question of what America would become after the Civil War was certainly not settled in 1877," Richardson concludes. "Indeed, in that year the Great Railroad Strike indicated that the eventual nature of the American nation was more in doubt than ever. The direction of America was settled only by the disfranchisement of those who seemed to deny individualism in favor of class organization and government aid. By 1900, they had been effectively purged from the electorate." Yet rather than reactionary conservative hegemony, the defeat of radicalism in the United States produced an era of centrist reform, movements which sought to meliorate industrial capitalism's shortcomings without threatening the system itself. At the dawn of the twentieth century, progressive reformers across the nation were poised to "use the government to address the inequities of corporate capitalism with confidence that America was a nation in which socialism could never destroy individualism."

Richardson's concluding chapter reminds us that perhaps the final yet most subtle irony of the American Civil War remains that the new social order the war helped create reflected the ambitions of neither the victors nor the vanquished. Indeed, if the contributions to this *Companion* are any indication, recent scholarship suggests that both free-labor, free-soil Republicans in the North and proslavery secessionists in the South yearned to defend a disappearing world of Jeffersonian producers steadily being caught up in the vortex of a market revolution they sometimes embraced, sometimes shunned, but seldom understood. Through the ideologically colored and partisan-focused political lens of the antebellum era, voters in both North and South came to blame the other for menacing internal changes in their society. In the North, where commerce and industry steadily created a permanent if fluid working class, free-labor Republicans developed a searing critique of the slaveholding South. They indicted the allegedly backward slave-based southern economy as a drag on national prosperity and blamed the slave power for the exertion of its disproportionate political influence to the detriment of national freedom and prosperity. In the popular northern imagination, southern slavery put shackles on northern opportunity and progress. In the South, both radical and moderate secessionists saw the abolition movement, and its free-soil allies, as a threat to white freedom and progress as antebellum white southerners understood the terms. In the minds of white southerners, slavery for blacks guaranteed white independence and provided an avenue for upward social mobility. At the very least, slavery prevented the spread of widespread dependence among whites and prevented the emergence of a white proletariat in the region. Abolition threatened to turn this world upside down, and deluge whites in a flood of free blacks angry from years of exploitation. The restriction of slavery in the territories seemed to suggest that southerners were second-class citizens. In the popular southern white imagination, the abolition and free-soil movements loomed as threats to the republican independence and equality of white southerners.

After the Civil War, neither the free-labor vision of the Republican party nor the proslavery vision of pro-secession southerners emerged from the war's four years of bloodshed and agony, or from the emancipation of nearly 4 million slaves, intact. Instead, the postwar years nationally were characterized by the steady but nonetheless dramatic emergence of a modern industrial economy sustained by concentrated capital and a heavily immigrant working class. By 1920, an America transformed by industrialization, urbanization, and immigration looked far different from the nation that emerged from a bloody war in 1865.

In 1968, the historian David M. Potter, working with a far less rich body of historiography than currently exists, concluded that the great triumph of the Civil War was Lincoln's success in marrying the cause of nationalism to that of liberalism (largely through emancipation). As Potter all too accurately noted, this "conjunction" of liberalism and nationalism was "by no means inevitable," as ample late nineteenth and twentieth-century examples indicate. Potter admitted that this marriage of nationalism and liberalism has not always lived up to its potential. The marriage, Potter contended, "gave nationalism a sanction, which frequently since then, it has failed to deserve" and "gave to liberalism a strength which, since then, it has frequently not known how to use" (1968: 298). Since Potter wrote, not only has historians' understanding that the worldview of neither the victor nor the vanquished triumphed grown more nuanced, but also the historiography has broadened in productive and salutary ways. As this volume abundantly shows, no longer is the study of the coming of the Civil War, the war itself, and the Reconstruction era chiefly the study of the political campaigns, issues, military battles, and strategies (though those are still important issues), as was generally the case when Potter wrote. Rather, it is also the study of slavery (and slave family, community, religion, and resistance), of emancipation, of women of all regions and classes, of gender roles, of yeoman farmers and workers, of the home front, of reform, of the cultural legacies of victory and defeat, and, of course, of the economy in all its changes. Thus, since Potter penned his interpretation, the historiography on the Civil War and Reconstruction has grown more diverse and inclusive in a variety of ways, as this *Companion* details, especially in exploring the depths (and shallows) of the "new birth of freedom" that emancipation and Union victory gave the nation, a gift that redeemed the sacrifice, if anything could.

At the same time, little in this explosion of fine scholarship directly contradicts Potter's conclusion that the success of Lincoln and the Union cause "vindicated government of the people, for the people, and by the people" and "proved that democracy, with all its weaknesses, can withstand the shocks of war" (Potter 1968: 298). But at its best and in its breadth, recent middle period historiography not only rightly acknowledges the Civil War era's success in sustaining "government of the people, by the people, and for the people" as the world's "best hope" for freedom, but also calls our attention away from Lincoln's eloquent paean to democracy at Gettysburg to the great national commission he issued in his Second Inaugural Address just a month before his death. When Lincoln gave this address in March of 1865, he was only a few weeks away from finally bringing the American Civil War to a successful conclusion. So, as he prepared his inaugural remarks, Lincoln held unprecedented political capital and military power at his disposal. He stood before his audience in the mud and muck of Washington on that late winter day as savior of the Union, emancipator of nearly 4 million slaves, and commander-in chief of the most powerful army the world had ever seen. But at that moment of destiny, he chose not to celebrate the Union's power, but to define its future mission. He reflected on the 600,000 Americans dead – 350,000 on his side, 250,000 on the other – all Americans in Lincoln's eyes, and offered a social and political challenge. Lincoln charged Americans, then and now, to make the lasting legacy of the Civil War one of "binding up the nation's wounds," of caring for those on society's margins (its "widows and orphans"), and of cherishing "a just and lasting peace among ourselves and with all nations." The rich and suggestive historiography summarized in this volume represents the best scholarly efforts of the period since the early 1960s to inform, and perhaps even inspire, current and future citizen-custodians of Lincoln's legacy.

REFERENCES

Bardaglio, Peter W. (1995) *Reconstructing the Household: Families, Sex, and the Law in the Nineteenth-Century South.* Chapel Hill, NC: University of North Carolina Press.

Berlin, Ira and Morgan, Philip (eds.) (1993) *Cultivation and Culture: Labor and the Shaping of Slave Life in the Americas.* Charlottesville, Va.: University of Virginia Press.

Berlin, Ira and Rowland, Leslie (1992) *Families and Freedom: A Documentary History of African-American Kinship in the Civil War Era.* New York: New Press.

Carlton, David L. (1990) "The Revolution from Above: The National Market and the Beginnings of Industrialization in North Carolina," *Journal of American History* 77: 445–75.

Clinton, Catherine (1982) *The Plantation Mistress: Women's World in the Old South.* New York: Pantheon.

Clinton, Catherine (1984) *The Other Civil War: American Women in the Nineteenth Century.* New York: Hill and Wang.

Clinton, Catherine and Gillespie, Michele (eds.) (1997) *The Devil's Lane: Sex and Race in the Early South.* New York: Oxford University Press.

Clinton, Catherine and Silber, Nina (eds.) (1992) *Divided Houses: Gender and the Civil War.* New York: Oxford University Press.

Edwards, Laura F. (1997) *Gendered Strife and Confusion: The Political Culture of Reconstruction.* Urbana, Ill.: University of Illinois Press.

Edwards, Laura F. (2000) *Scarlett Doesn't Live Here Anymore: Southern Women in the Civil War Era.* Urbana, Ill.: University of Illinois Press.

Faust, Drew Gilpin (1996) *Mothers of Invention: Women of the Slaveholding South in the American Civil War.* Chapel Hill, NC: University of North Carolina Press.

Foner, Eric (1970) *Free Soil, Free Labor, Free Men: The Ideology of the Republican Party before the Civil War.* New York: Oxford University Press.

Foner, Eric (1988) *Reconstruction: America's Unfinished Revolution, 1863–1877.* New York: Harper and Row.

Fox-Genovese, Elizabeth (1988) *Within the Plantation Household: Black and White Women of the Old South.* Chapel Hill, NC: University of North Carolina Press.

Gienapp, William E. (1987) *The Origins of the Republican Party, 1852–1856.* New York: Oxford University Press.

Ginzberg, Lori (1990) *Women and the Work of Benevolence: Morality, Politics, and Class in the Nineteenth Century United States.* New Haven, Conn.: Yale University Press.

Haskell, Thomas (1985) "Capitalism and the Origins of Humanitarian Sensibility, Parts I and II," *American Historical Review* 90 (April and June): 339–61 and 457–566.

Heyrman, Christine Leigh (1997) *Southern Cross: The Beginnings of the Bible Belt.* New York: Alfred A. Knopf.

Hobsbawm, Eric J. (1975) *The Age of Capital, 1848–1875.* New York: Charles Scribner's Sons.

Holt, Michael F. (1978) *The Political Crisis of the 1850s.* New York: Wiley.

Kierner, Cynthia (1998) *Beyond the Household: Women's Place in the Early South, 1700–1835.* Ithaca, NY: Cornell University Press.

Litwack, Leon F. (1979) *Been in the Storm So Long: The Aftermath of Slavery.* New York: Alfred A. Knopf.

McCurry, Stephanie (1995) *Masters of Small Worlds: Yeoman Households, Gender Relations, and the Political Culture of the Antebellum South Carolina Low Country*. New York: Oxford University Press.

McPherson, James M. (1996) "Who Freed the Slaves?," in McPherson, *Drawn with the Sword: Reflections on the American Civil War*. New York: Oxford University Press.

Melish, Joanne Pope (1998) *Disowning Slavery: Gradual Emancipation and "Race" in New England, 1780–1860*. Ithaca, NY: Cornell University Press.

Potter, David M. (1968) *The South and the Sectional Conflict*. Baton Rouge, La.: Louisiana State University Press.

Rable, George C. (1984) *But There Was No Peace: The Role of Violence in the Politics of Reconstruction*. Athens, Ga.: University of Georgia Press.

Ransom, Roger L. and Sutch, Richard (1977) *One Kind of Freedom: The Economic Consequences of Emancipation*. Cambridge: Cambridge University Press.

Schweiger, Beth Barton (2000) *The Gospel Working Up: Progress and the Pulpit in Nineteenth-Century Virginia*. Oxford: Oxford University Press.

Schweninger, Loren and Franklin, John Hope (1999) *Runaway Slaves: Rebels on the Plantation*. New York: Oxford University Press.

Stansell, Christine (1987) *City of Women: Sex and Class in New York, 1789–1860*. Urbana, Ill.: University of Illinois Press.

Stevenson, Brenda E. (1996) *Life in Black and White: Family and Community in the Slave South*. New York: Oxford University Press.

Warren, R. P. (1964) *The Legacy of the Civil War: Meditations on the Centennial*. New York: Vintage.

Woodward, C. Vann (1951) *Origins of the New South, 1877–1913*. Baton Rouge, La.: Louisiana.

Wright, Gavin (1978) *The Political Economy of the Cotton South: Households, Markets, and Wealth in the Nineteenth Century*. New York: Norton.

Wright, Gavin (1986) *Old South, New South: Revolutions in the Southern Economy since the Civil War*. New York: Basic Books.

PART I

Sectional Conflict and the Coming of the Civil War

CHAPTER ONE

Slavery and the Union, 1789–1833

DOUGLAS R. EGERTON

Once upon a time – and it was not so very long ago – studies of American slavery invariably meant studies of slavery as a system of labor, or slavery and its connection to politics. Now, 140 years after the firing on Fort Sumter, monographs on unwaged labor tend to focus on such topics as resistance and rebellion, the black family and community culture, or enslaved women and the internal economy. Each year brings so many new specialized studies and articles on the varieties of unfree labor in North America that even scholars who pretend to specialize in the field can scarcely keep up. This development is as welcome as it is problematical, for many earlier studies on slavery as a form of labor organization tended to ignore the role that bondpeople played in the creation of southern society and culture. But the historiographical trends since the late 1970s have often tended to obscure the role that politics played in shaping the black community – or that slavery played in shaping the nature of the American Union. Elizabeth Fox-Genovese and Eugene D. Genovese (1983: 212) put it best, if perhaps a bit bluntly: history "is primarily the story of who rides whom and how." As a good many early national politicians rode to fame and political fortune precisely because labor on their estates was performed by enslaved and unwaged workers, any study that ignores the relationship between political ideology and slavery presents at best an incomplete picture.

This chapter seeks to explore the interconnections between slavery and the American political system during the early national years. As such, this unhappy saga presents modern readers with a cautionary tale. While scholars no longer accept the old view that slavery was all but moribund as an economic system in the wake of the American Revolution, there is also little doubt that the chaos of the war, together with the emergence of natural rights philosophy, damaged unfree labor considerably, especially in the North. Yet the 44 years covered by this chapter proved to be one long, if decidedly unsteady, retreat from liberty. Students tend to regard the story of history as a steady march from darkness to daylight, but no simple hosanna to progress may be found here. Instead, as the years turned into decades, American politicians in the North and South sought to refasten the chains of slavery more often than they tried to sever the links. In 1789, it was difficult – although by no means impossible – to find a political theorist who defended American slavery as anything but a necessary evil. But by 1833, and in some areas even before, white southern leaders were quite nearly unanimous in defending their peculiar institution as a positive good, and far too many northern statesmen were content to sit by and watch as this grim counter-revolution unfolded.

Curiously, a first-rate study of slavery and its tangled relationship to the federal constitution remains to be written. Permanent servitude – although not the term "slavery" itself – appeared at least three times in the original document, in clauses pertaining to runaway slaves, the importation of Africans, and taxation and apportionment (the infamous three-fifths clause). Yet classic studies and law school casebooks on the constitutional convention by Carl Van Doren (1948) and Gerald Gunther (2001) mentioned slavery only in passing; Van Doren's influential monograph contains fewer than 20 scattered references to unfree labor. Until a comprehensive study appears, two collections of essays and documents remain indispensable for understanding decisions made at the Philadelphia meeting. The first, *Slavery and the Law*, edited by legal scholar Paul Finkelman (1997), contains 14 original essays that explore the relationship of bondage to the constitution. The second, John Kaminski's (1995) *A Necessary Evil?*, is an equally massive collection of primary documents that reveals the founders' innermost thoughts on the greatest contradiction to the ideals of the Declaration. Neither collection offers much support to the popular notion that the revolutionary generation did all they could to eradicate slavery from the land of liberty.

Even law students who are dimly aware that the constitution contained veiled references to slavery probably have no idea of just how central unfree labor was to American organic law. The delegates who met in Philadelphia, Finkelman (1997) observes, "talked frankly about slavery." They only decided "not to use the term in the final document because they feared it would undermine support for ratification in the North," where laws for gradual manumission had already been passed in several state assemblies. But despite their preference for euphemistic terms, such as "other Persons" or "person[s] held to Service or Labor," the men who wrote the constitution were careful to insure against federal emancipation (Finkelman 1997: 17–18). The requirement that it take three-quarters of the states to ratify an amendment all but gave the slaveholding states a veto over any future attempts to alter the protections granted in the constitution. As Jack Rakove (1986) writes in his examination of the ideas behind the constitution, even Virginia delegate Edmund Randolph, who publicly "lamented that such a species of property existed," agreed that the constitutional "security" southern states "sought for slavery was legitimate" (p. 85).

Modern defenders of the Philadelphia convention accuse its historical critics of presentism, and indeed it would be both acontextual and unreasonable to insist that the men who fashioned the constitution – a roster that included *northern* slaveholders like Alexander Hamilton – should have eradicated slavery by constitutional fiat. Even had the delegates expressed any desire to do so, such a radical course would have doomed ratification to failure. But the present-day debate should not be about what the founders did *not* do, but rather what they did. Viewed in this light, the documents collected by Kaminski (1995) are damning. For every delegate like Virginia slaveholder George Mason, who argued that "[s]lavery discourages arts and manufactures" and teaches "the poor [to] despise [manual] labor," two voices from the lower South denounced those "who carried their ethics beyond the mere *equality of men*, extending their humanity to the claims of the whole animal creation" (Kaminski 1995: 59–60, emphasis in original). Nor was this a simple debate between northern and southern delegates. Because many slave ships sailed from New England ports – Captain Joseph Vesey's slaver, the *Prospect*, was fitted out and insured in Boston – it was rare for a northern voice to criticize the Atlantic trade, which in fact continued for at least 20 more years. In Newport, one writer even heard it said that Quaker Moses Brown was "going into this trade in Middletown and Norwich" (Kaminski 1995: 95). The currently fashionable defense of presentism, it seems, covers a multitude of sins. After all, it was not the sons or daughters of the founding fathers who were being sold into bondage in a foreign land; nor, to be blunt, was it the ancestors of those historians now most inclined to embrace the presentism defense.

Just as the definitive monograph on slavery and the constitutional convention remains to be written, so too does the topic of unfree labor and the Federalist party during its heyday require a new writer. Admittedly, fiscal and diplomatic issues dominated the rhetorical landscape throughout the 1790s, yet an historiographical consensus is beginning to suggest that the two emerging parties were divided by more than whiskey taxes and federal banks. According to Fritz Hirschfeld (1997), whose *George Washington and Slavery* is as close as one can come to a study of federal policy toward unwaged labor during the first half of the decade, the president consistently if quietly urged his correspondents to support gradual emancipation on the state level. Typical of his writings on this matter was a 1796 letter to an English correspondent. "[T]here are laws here [in Pennsylvania] for the gradual abolition of Slavery," Washington wrote, "which neither [Maryland nor Virginia] have, at present, but which nothing is more certain than that they must have, and at a period not remote" (Hirschfeld 1997: 190). Washington's strong feelings regarding manumission, however, were characteristically made to a foreign national; as Robert McColley (1973) once observed, early national Virginians tended to sound most like abolitionists when writing to European acquaintances.

Encouraging plans for gradual emancipation in the Chesapeake states was all to the good, but private letters hardly substituted for aggressive federal action. As Hirschfeld (1997) admits, Washington, like far too many modern presidents, consistently delayed action on race relations in the name of sectional harmony and the larger (white) national good. Having listened at the Philadelphia convention as South Carolina delegates threatened to leave the meeting if the further importation of Africans was not allowed, Washington never used his considerable power or prestige "to muster the necessary votes" in Congress "to cripple effectively the commerce in human cargoes." Worse yet, his only official action pertaining to slavery was to affix his signature on the federal Fugitive Slave Act 1793. Here too, of course, context is critical. Early national presidents never vetoed legislation they regarded as constitutional on policy grounds. Still, thousands of young black men and women undoubtedly shared Hirschfeld's judgment that Washington "cannot escape his share of the blame for the pain and suffering inflicted on future generations of African Americans" by putting his signature to this law (Hirschfeld 1997: 190–1).

The high water mark of Federalist antislavery activity, if such a term may be applied to such a moderate policy, came during the single term of President John Adams. The second president's numerous biographers have consistently failed to emphasize this point, beyond the routine observation that the Massachusetts

Calvinist regarded unfree labor as immoral and economically wrongheaded. Yet buried within Alexander DeConde's (1966) classic *The Quasi-War* is the little-studied fact that Adams pursued a policy of détente with Saint Domingue's Toussaint Louverture that not only was free of racial bias but also quite nearly altered the course of slavery's westward expansion. For a variety of obvious reasons, from New England trade to the desire to deny France its crucial privateering base during the last years of the eighteenth century, Adams and Secretary of State Timothy Pickering made peace with the French colony the centerpiece of their Caribbean diplomacy. In early 1799, the administration dispatched Edward Stevens to Le Cap François with promises that America would end its naval blockade of the colony in exchange for promises that General Louverture would quietly pull free of Parisian control. The result, partly negotiated in Philadelphia between Adams and Louverture's agent Joseph Bunel (talks that included the first-ever formal dinner between an American president and a man of color), was the secret treaty of amity and commerce of June 23, 1799, which was signed by Louverture, Stevens, and English diplomat Thomas Maitland (DeConde 1966: 206–12).

At length, Pickering openly encouraged Louverture to drop the façade of loyalty to the Directory and declare independence, which was to be guaranteed by both the English and American navies. According to biographer Gerald H. Clarfield (1980), Pickering worried that as a French subject, Louverture might help to "arouse and organize the slaves of the [American] South for a bloody revolution." But a President Louverture safely within the American orbit could serve to quell slave unrest throughout the Caribbean. To that end, Adams dispatched four frigates to support Louverture in his struggle with mulatto General André Rigaud, who remained loyal to France (Clarfield 1980: 198). Thomas Ott's (1973) study of *The Haitian Revolution* adds that Pickering, for his part, dispatched a model constitution for Louverture's consideration, which was penned by Alexander Hamilton. When Rigaud and the colonial agents loyal to Paris were defeated, Stevens assured Pickering, "[a]ll connection with France will soon be broken off" (Ott 1973: 119).

The failure of Adams to achieve reelection in 1800 put an end to the growing understanding between the American government and the all but independent French colony. Despite modern efforts to suggest that the election of Thomas Jefferson ushered in an "empire of liberty" (Boyd 1948), it is hard not to conclude that for Americans of African descent, the Republican victory meant a diminution of liberty both in the Caribbean and on the western frontier. As is suggested below, because French imperial schemes wedded the reenslavement of Saint Domingue to the reacquisition of Louisiana, a continuing détente between the federal government and General Louverture might well have left New Orleans in the weak hands of Madrid. Certainly, a Federalist victory would have left Atlantic diplomacy in the staunchly anticolonial hands of young John Quincy Adams and William Vans Murray, both of whom were deeply sympathetic to Louverture. The younger Adams hoped to "protect [Haitian] independence" with the American and British navies, while "leaving them as to their government totally to themselves" (Egerton 2002: 323).

The single term of John Adams also coincided with the passage of a gradual Emancipation Act in the important state of New York. The ideology of revolutionary republicanism, combined with the impact of mercantile capitalism and a relatively smaller number of slaves in the northern states, had led to a series of gradual emancipation laws in the North, starting with Pennsylvania in 1783. But conservative as these laws were – most bondpeople born after the passage of these Acts received their freedom only in their mid-twenties – they were especially difficult to pass in those states where unwaged labor remained important to regional economies. Dutch farmers on Long Island were bitterly critical of even the smallest steps toward gradual manumission, and several attempts to pass emancipation laws in the 1790s failed. As Graham Russell Hodges (1997, 1999) demonstrates in a series of monographs on New Jersey and New York, legislation finally achieved a measure of liberation in those states in, respectively, 1804 and 1799, but only after pacifying masters who charged that the states were robbing them of their property. In New York, black men born at the dawn of the new century remained enslaved until their twenty-eighth birthday (at a time when average life expectancy for black males was 33). In New Jersey, where approximately six African Americans remained enslaved as late as 1861, the Democratically controlled state assembly initially defeated ratification of the Thirteenth Amendment.

Even less promising was the way in which many white northerners hoped to eliminate slaves at the same time as they eradicated slavery. In New England especially, whites quickly forgot their involvement in the Atlantic slave trade, and many people, as Joanne Pope Melish (1998) suggests in *Disowning Slavery*, made "an easy leap from the erasure of the experience of slavery to the illusion of the historical absence of people of color generally" (p. xiv). Leonard Bacon of New Haven bristled at suggestions that the poverty of African Americans in Connecticut had anything to do with northern racism. "On the contrary," he wrote, "it would seem far otherwise; inasmuch as slavery never existed here to any considerable extent." Even John Quincy Adams, who had good cause to know better, tried to rewrite New England's history in such a way as to imply that it had always stood as a beacon of individual liberty (Melish 1998: 214–20).

Such comforting untruths to the contrary, the fact remains that by 1804, slavery had become the peculiar institution of the South alone, and that was hardly all to the good. Moreover, if the Adams years may be regarded as a momentary hiatus in the Union's long march toward a national defense of slavery, the election of Virginia planter Thomas Jefferson returned the young republic to its unhappy path toward civil conflict. The extant scholarship on Jefferson and slavery is enormous, and of late tends to focus on personal events at Monticello, most notably his relationship with Sally Hemings, his enslaved sister-in-law. For the purposes of this chapter, however, the proper focus should be on the relationship between Jefferson's administration and slavery as a national issue. Curiously, until the mid-1970s and publication of John Chester Miller's (1977) *The Wolf by the Ears: Thomas Jefferson and Slavery*, no monograph paid much attention to the role that slavery played in the political activity of the third president. (As late as 1961, Thomas P. Abernathy could write a lengthy chapter entitled "Jefferson and the South" in his magisterial *The South in the New Nation, 1789–1819* and mention slavery exactly *once*.) Although Miller's 29 chapters examined Jefferson and unfree labor from every possible angle and over the course of the Virginian's long life, several chapters dealt specifically with Jefferson the president.

Although Miller defended Jefferson on several private issues, he was quick to criticize Jefferson as chief executive. His failure to support proposed legislation in

1806 – at a time when his popularity was at its peak – that would have excluded slavery from Washington City drew Miller's fire. "Had the president exerted himself on this issue," Miller wrote, "he might have spared the country the spectacle of a slavemarket in the shadow of the Capitol and gangs of manacled slaves being driven through the streets of the nation's capital" (Miller 1977: 132). It was certainly not the case that Jefferson favored the internal slave trade. Rather, as Joseph J. Ellis observed, "[m]oral pronouncements aside, Jefferson had also left a long and clear record of procrastination and denial on the slavery issue" (Ellis 1998: 264).

As to the Louisiana Purchase, typically regarded by scholars as Jefferson's greatest accomplishment while president, Miller (1977) takes an equally dim view. Although some writers have argued that the president voiced support of Napoleon Bonaparte's plans to invade Saint Domingue in hopes of persuading the first consul to sell his recently acquired New Orleans and West Florida, Miller suggests that the Virginian was painfully slow to grasp the French connection between the Caribbean sugar colony and the Louisiana breadbasket. Only after informing Paris of his support for a French invasion did Jefferson come to understand "that St. Doming[ue] and Louisiana were part of a master plan so inimical to the interests of the United States that it must be thwarted at all costs" (Miller 1977: 137). More recently, Robert L. Paquette has been even more blunt. Had Bonaparte succeeded in reenslaving the Haitian people, his army was to sail across the Caribbean and take control of New Orleans, which the Treaty of San Ildefonso allowed France to do. "At the very least," Paquette (1997: 211) charges, the "bargaining that might have resulted many months or several years later with Napoleon developing Louisiana from an entrenched position would have looked quite different from that which resulted in the sale of all of Louisiana."

The late Dumas Malone would have none of that. Jefferson's leading biographer conceded – with considerable understatement – that in his conversations with the French charge, Jefferson "appears to have gone farther than was wise or necessary" in commenting that his administration would be happy to help "reduce Toussaint to starvation." Yet scholars who regard the third president as an unusually intelligent leader have a hard time accepting Malone's assertion that Jefferson "could hardly have been aware" that Bonaparte wished to use the American Midwest as a granary for his Haitian laborers (Malone 1970: 251–2). Either Jefferson was particularly obtuse when it came to agrarian policy – and he certainly was not – or his hatred and fear of black rebels in the Caribbean blinded him to French policy. As Robert Tucker and David C. Hendrickson (1990: 301) have written, Jefferson's confused policy toward French designs makes sense only if "he felt obliged to respond to the mounting fears of the southern slaveholders over the spread of the black rebellion" in Saint Domingue.

Malone was on firmer ground, however, in praising Jefferson for moving decisively against the international slave trade. The constitution guaranteed the lower South, as well as New England traders, a 20-year window during which they might import more Africans, but that hardly meant that Congress was compelled to close that window in 1807. In a message to Congress dated December 2, 1806, Jefferson urged an end to "those violations of human rights which have been so long continued on the unoffending inhabitants of Africa." Unhappily, following this rather promising declaration, the president grew silent and totally abstained from the debate that followed. Malone suggested that Jefferson's refusal to join the dispute "can be readily attributed to political prudence and his desire to maintain the unity of his [sectional] party." Never much given to argument under any circumstances, Jefferson even declined to say whether he still believed, as he had written in 1776, that the Atlantic trade was "piratical," which would have made the smuggling of humans a capital crime. At length, Congress outlawed the trade but refused to establish any mechanism for the enforcement of the Act, which was left to Albert Gallatin and the Treasury Department. Given Jefferson's notorious dislike of federal power, of course, it is hardly "surprising," to borrow Malone's droll term, "that the record of federal action was essentially negative" (1970: 544–7).

Even so, the federal ban on the Atlantic slave trade was a promising new beginning, in that it reinforced the long-dormant idea that the government had the power to move against slavery in at least some areas. Unhappily for the few anti-slavery activists in Washington – exactly none of whom embraced the term "abolitionist" – the 1807 law proved to be an ending rather than a fresh start. To the contrary, as Steven Deyle (1992) observed in an important article, the end of the Atlantic trade only gave rise to an interstate commerce in black bodies designed "to satisfy the frontier planters' insatiable demand for labor" (Deyle 1992: 62). In a much under-appreciated study, *Speculators and Slaves*, Michael Tadman (1989) demonstrates that a small army of buyers worked established rural routes they developed over time. Paying in cash, buyers preferred to purchase bondpeople between the ages of 15 and 25 years of age. For slaves who lived in the upper South, the cumulative chances of being sold away was, over the first 40 years of their lives, nearly 40 percent. Contrary to myth, most sales stemmed not from "special [financial] emergencies" but from the "racist insensitivity" of Chesapeake masters (Tadman 1989: 11–46). Perhaps as few as 5 percent of upper South sales resulted from the death of an owner or a public sale for debt. Instead, savvy planters sold surplus humans during boom times, when they knew labor prices would be high. Most masters, unlike those pictured in antebellum novels, were not in the clutches of cruel traders. They were simply greedy.

The larger importance of this trade was not merely the forced migration of "two-thirds of a million people," a figure that does not include the even larger number of bondpeople who were sold locally, from neighbor to neighbor, or the destruction of countless black families and communities. Politically speaking, this thriving interstate commerce helped to shape both federal and state policies over the decades, from the removal of southern Native Americans in 1830 to Virginia's 1861 vote for secession. Writing in 1999, Walter Johnson suggests that the trade generated "something close to half a billion dollars" before its end during the war. Johnson's figure includes not only the sale price for black Americans, but also the cash spent on transportation, food, clothing, and insurance. "Their sales had to be notarized and their sellers taxed" (1999: 6–9). Not surprisingly, this amount of wealth could hardly fail to attract the attention of southern politicians (as well as northern bankers), who represented districts chronically short of hard currency. Slavery might have been in a state of decline in the Chesapeake, but the sale of black bodies made it abundantly clear to Virginia and Maryland politicians where their loyalties and interests lay.

Even as young bondpeople marched west, some politicians in Washington hoped to ship other slaves east. Seven years after Jefferson began his Monticello retirement, an idea he first had proposed as a young member of the Virginia Assembly resurfaced in the nation's capital: the idea of colonizing liberated bondpeople on the western shores of Africa. Suspicious scholars doubt that Jefferson was ever serious about this proposal. Joseph Ellis suspects that the Duc de La Rochefoucauld-Liancourt was not far wrong when he criticized Jefferson for chaining gradual emancipation to removal so that liberation was "reduced to the impossible" (Ellis 1998: 175). But the fact remains that in Jefferson's day, the possibility of colonizing the entire African American population was every bit as feasible as it was despicable. White colonizationist Philip Slaughter observed in 1855 that the removal of several million slaves hardly posed a problem to politicians who had watched just over 1 million Irish men and women flood into American ports in a single five-year period (Ellis 1998: x). To that, historian William Freehling (1994: 154) adds that a federal government that herded Native Americans west into Oklahoma was quite capable of herding black Americans out of the republic. "In an age of forced exoduses, forced Americanization, and massive movements of people," Freehling writes, "a purifying federal migration experiment with blacks looked as pragmatically American as the Trail of Tears."

Seen in that light, the American Colonization Society may be regarded as, to borrow the words of Daniel Walker Howe, an "awesomely ambitious [and] rigorously logical" plan to rid the nation of enslaved labor by a "ruthless . . . manipulation of humanity" (1979: 136–7). Founded by border state moderates in December 1816, the Society was the *only* antislavery organization that hoped to receive federal assistance. As Philip J. Staudenraus (1961) argued in what has become the standard treatment of the Society, *The African Colonization Movement*, the group's members established their base in Washington so that they could be "close to the national vaults." Early founders Henry Clay and Congressman-elect Charles Fenton Mercer well understood that their massive undertaking would require national assistance to become reality. Just as he hoped to allocate federal revenues to tie the nation together in an "American System" of roads and canals, Clay and his allies hoped that their "undertaking shall be adopted and patronized by the Government, so as to become essentially national in its means and objects" (Staudenraus 1961: 23–35, 50).

In just three years, the Society, as John Quincy Adams put it, got "their fingers into the [federal] purse." On January 13, 1819, Congressman Mercer introduced legislation requiring the president to remove "beyond the limits of the United States" any Africans illegally imported into the country in violation of the 1807 Act. Mercer also urged President James Monroe to appoint a colonial agent "residing upon the coast of Africa" to receive the slaves. The bill, which was signed by Monroe in early March, authorized the appropriation of 100,000 dollars "to carry this law into effect" (Egerton 1997: 144). Although Monroe probably never knew that the Society's agents used a portion of this money to purchase land in what became Liberia, he was certainly aware that virtually none of the black settlers who sailed for Africa were natives rescued from illegal slavers. The president, according to Staudenraus (1961: 51–3), often repeated the Society's claims that free blacks constituted "a class of very dangerous people" who endangered southern stability (pp. 51–3). The prospect of mass removal, he hoped, might encourage masters to manumit their slaves and thus relocate the entire black population of Virginia.

Because Monroe was "deeply sympathetic with the aims of the Colonization Society," notes biographer Harry Ammon, the colony was "largely sustained from funds allocated to the federal agents resident in Liberia" (1971: 522–3). In gratitude, the directors of the organization named the first settlement Monrovia.

For all of its political clout in Washington, the Colonization Society failed to remove many free blacks from the nation. Somewhat more seriously, it failed to motivate many planters to liberate their labor force so that they might be freed in the continent of their ancestors. Ultimately, the organization must be understood to be the most conservative of all solutions to the young republic's racial problem. The "humanitarian proclamations" of young politicians like Clay and Mercer, observes Donald R. Wright, "could not hide [the racism that] was at the heart of the society's existence." Rather than striving to end the racism that supported slavery in America, "the society preferred to remove the objects of the racism" (Wright 1993: 176–7). In the end, the group's moderate approach served only to unite its sectional enemies. As Peter Kolchin writes, both black Americans, who were naturally "hostile" to being sent "back" to a land they had never known, and deep South planters, who regarded *any* federal involvement with their unfree labor force, no matter how mild, as a frighteningly dangerous precedent, refused to cooperate with the Society (Kolchin 1993: 185).

In March 1820, 86 free black colonists – exactly none of them illegally imported Africans – landed on the coast of what would become Liberia. By that date, many of the Society's founders were deeply embroiled in the Missouri debates, a controversy that forced slavery and its westward growth back into the national dialogue. As Glover Moore (1953) described the affair half a century ago in his still-definitive *The Missouri Controversy, 1819–1821*, the debates in Congress forced the white South to put aside their hoary assertions that slavery was an unfortunate, if necessary, evil and articulate a more positive defense of their culture and society. After years of ignoring the issue, or talking around it in the guise of colonization, northern politicians like Congressman James Tallmadge, Jr, of New York lit "the fuse" of sectionalism by refusing to play any further part in an implicit agreement to leave emancipation in the hands of southern moderates. Moore observed that leaders like Jefferson had not only failed to eradicate unfree labor in their own states, they now defended its migration into the northern sections of the Louisiana Purchase territory on the grounds that "diffusion" was the best way to achieve an end to enslaved labor. Even Henry Clay, an avid supporter of removal to Africa, professed to believe "that the condition of the Negroes would be improved if they were spread over a larger area" in the American West (Moore 1953: 47).

Perhaps no better indication of the southern failure to resolve their labor problem existed than the man reading the debates in his Monticello study. That Jefferson, who as a young man had advocated restricting slavery from the public domain – North and South – could now recommend that it be allowed to spread beyond the Mississippi so as to better kill, serves as a sad reminder of how badly the enlightened southern men of the revolutionary generation had bungled this issue. As Joseph Ellis bluntly writes, the "political dimensions of [Jefferson's] thinking are fuzzy" on this issue. "Slavery would migrate into the West and simply disappear in the vastness of empty space" (1998: 269). According to John Chester Miller, when the Marquis de Lafayette heard Jefferson explain how spreading slavery across the frontier would hasten its extinction, he sadly concluded that his old friend had fallen "victim to a grand illusion" (1977: 239).

Jefferson, unhappily, was hardly alone in defending this latest rationalization for state and federal inactivity regarding slavery. Worse yet, having twisted themselves into the position that the good of the republic demanded the spread of slavery into Missouri, southern politicians found that it was but a short step to the next, and sadly logical proposition: that it was in fact a good thing for slavery to be there. When the aged Nathaniel Macon rose in the Senate in late January 1820, to invite his northern brethren to visit his plantation "and witness the meeting between the slaves and the owner, and see the glad faces," he was not merely defending unwaged labor in his native North Carolina. Macon was defending it in the West as well. Here was the "beginning of the defense of slavery," wrote George Dangerfield (1952: 220) in his masterpiece, *The Era of Good Feelings*, "not as an evil which could not be remedied, but as a positive good." Like Jefferson, James Madison and President Monroe continued to advocate diffusion as a means to emancipation, but Macon's reverse logic was impeccable, and Ellis caught the contradiction. If "diffusion over a greater surface would make [slaves] individually happier," to use Jefferson's words, why bother to eliminate this allegedly benign institution at all (Ellis 1998: 268)?

For many scholars, Madison's support for this dubious proposition is particularly troubling. As Drew R. McCoy put it in his thoughtful *The Last of the Fathers*, if Madison "truly deplored slavery," why did he not at least advocate its geographical restriction, "especially since he had done so earlier in his career" (1989: 266)? McCoy suspects that Madison, unlike his celebrated mentor, quietly harbored grave doubts about the theory that diffusion would somehow bring about the eradication of slavery. What he was quite sure of, however, was that further congressional wrangling over this issue "would most certainly have catastrophic consequences." Faced with the harsh realization that his region, and indeed perhaps his country, could never resolve the matter peacefully, he rather naively chose to remain "a prisoner of his republican idealism and the optimistic temperament that sustained it" (McCoy 1989: 266–7, 272). When faced with the impossible, Madison, like Jefferson before him, embraced the pleasant fiction that time and distance would do away with unfree labor.

For his part, Jefferson had few doubts as to who was behind this unprecedented attack on the southern way of life. Northern voters had been "fanaticized" by Clintonians like Tallmadge – and, thus, closet Federalists in Jefferson's mind – and Federalist stalwarts like Rufus King, who had taken up the issue following Tallmadge's retirement from Congress. Writing without editorial comment, Malone noted that Jefferson stubbornly "denied that morality was at issue" in what he insisted "was really a struggle for [political] power" (1981: 329). Malone's footnotes, of course, reveal that he based much of his analysis on Glover Moore's (1953) richly detailed study. But if Moore's half-century-old monograph now appears somewhat dated, those signs of age may be due to his willingness to accept the charges of partisan politics leveled by southern men like Jefferson. Northern activists who wished to restrict slavery to the Old South were labeled "Anti-Missourian zealots," and Moore praised "the considerable body of Northern Democrats" who came to understand "that the Federalists and Clintonians were seeking to make political capital out of the Missouri question." By employing terms like "zealots," which implied mindless fanaticism, Moore cast his rhetorical vote with those who denied that Tallmadge and King might have been motivated by any sentiments finer than a desire to escape the political wilderness (Moore 1953: 172, 177–8).

Certainly Moore was correct, however, in his assessment that the rancorous Missouri debates served to silence those moderate southern voices who persisted in regarding unfree labor as a necessary evil. Like George Dangerfield, Moore regarded 1821 as a political dividing line, not merely between North and South, but within the southern states as well. "The Missouri Controversy marked the end of the liberal phase of antebellum Southern history," he wrote, "during which the thinking of Southern statesmen had been dominated by the philosophy of the Age of Enlightenment," even if, he conceded, "that philosophy had not been put into practice." Over the next four decades, southern men would polish and refine their proslavery arguments, but nothing was said after 1821 that had not already been uttered during the previous two years. The republic had witnessed positive good theory on display, together with threats of disunion and civil war should the planter class not be allowed to carry their peculiar institution into the western territories. At the very least, Tallmadge's failed amendment allowed many leading politicians to rationalize their defense of a system they professed to dislike. As the eccentric John Randolph of Roanoke put it: "These Yankees have almost reconciled me to negro slavery" (Moore 1953: 347–9).

Randolph was right to be concerned. On the day that Rufus King delivered his second speech on the Missouri question, the Senate gallery was crowded with African Americans who came to hear the one-time presidential candidate announce that he felt degraded at having to sit in the same chamber as slaveholders. Reading the debates in far-off Charleston, free black carpenter Denmark Vesey came to understand that America was two countries; perhaps, he thought, northern whites might prove a bit tardy in riding to the defense of the southern planter class. According to Edward A. Pearson's (1999) comprehensive new collection of documents, *Designs Against Charleston: The Trial Record of the Denmark Vesey Slave Conspiracy of 1822*, Vesey used the debates "to convince other men to join" his plot. By (disingenuously) interpreting the compromise solution as "an emancipation proclamation," Pearson argues, "the rebel leader held out a promise of liberation that may have ameliorated the subordination of some slaves" (1999: 120). Certainly there can be no doubt that the old abolitionist was a close student of events in Washington. "Mr. King was the black man's friend," Vesey told one slave, as the New Yorker had publicly pronounced slavery "a great disgrace to the country" (Egerton 1999: 131).

In the same way that the Missouri controversy played a role, however small, in inspiring Denmark Vesey to plan for black freedom, the Charleston slavery conspiracy played a role, probably very large, in the nullification controversy of the early 1830s. According to William W. Freehling, whose prize-winning study of nullification, *Prelude to Civil War*, begins in 1816, Vesey's massive conspiracy convinced the South Carolina planter class that they needed to find a method to keep antislavery activism at bay while yet keeping "the distressing subject buried." By using the increasingly high federal tariff – which the planter class indeed regarded as a tax on their way of life – as a test case, lower South politicians could develop a strategy of single-state nullification as "a weapon" to "check the abolitionists without discussing slavery" (Freehling 1965: 85–6). It was, Freehling argues, no coincidence that many of the leading nullifiers, including James Hamilton (who used the Vesey affair to rise from mayor to state governor), were veterans of the two Charleston tribunals that blamed slave unrest on congressional interference in Missouri.

For the nullification crisis to have an impact on the course of proslavery disunionism, it had to be, at bottom, about slavery. Biographer Robert V. Remini, whose five superb volumes on Andrew Jackson (1977–84), Henry Clay (1991), and Daniel Webster (1997) require 11 inches of shelf space in every research library, suspects that it was not. The postwar tariffs of protection, he suggests, were largely responsible for South Carolina's economic woes. Proto-industrial tariffs may not have driven down cotton prices, as most nullifiers liked to argue, but they undoubtedly made it more expensive to run a plantation and purchase products manufactured abroad. Whereas Freehling (1965: x) argues that a defense of slavery was the "hidden reason motivating these events," Remini believes that Freehling "overstates his thesis" (Remini 1984: 535). Echoing Paul Bergeron's (1976) influential article Remini regards the Tariff of Abominations 1828 as *the* central issue here. In this view, the thesis that the need to advance a theoretical defense against the rising tide of militant antislavery, or indeed "that slavery motivated much of the politics of the South" or the Democratic party, is simply "to take a totally wrong tack on the question" (1988: 83).

For many deep South politicians, however, the tariff question was inseparable from a range of related issues – from African colonization to economic modernization – that all implied federal intrusions into their plantation world. As evidence for what he calls "the indirect defense of slavery," Freehling quotes the *Winyaw Intelligencer* at length: "[I]t ought to be understood, that the Tariff is only one of the subjects of complaint at the South. The Internal Improvement" and "the interference with our domestic policy – most especially the latter – are things" that will, "if necessary, be met with something more than words." For more than a decade prior to the nullification crisis, Carolina statesmen, Freehling observes, emphasized that "the problem of public confidence in slavery seemed in part a crucial economic question" (1965: 87, 110–11). In short, modern attempts to identify the *single* greatest cause of nullification are probably doomed to failure. Since the Missouri debates, states' rights advocates fretted about northern antislavery, just as hardpressed upcountry yeomen complained about the impact of tariff laws passed for the benefit of free state industrialists. The memory of Denmark Vesey haunted lowcountry planters and Charleston residents, most of whom already feared the capitalist market revolution implicit in federally supported internal improvements and national banking systems. The possibility of employing single state nullification as a weapon to maintain the southern status quo, in short, unified most white Carolinians in a common cause.

In recent years, even Freehling has modified his decades-old thesis, although he continues to maintain – and no doubt with considerable justification – that the "fallout from Denmark Vesey put the coastal gentry on the road to nullification" (1990: 599). But as William J. Cooper, Jr, noted in 1978, outside "of South Carolina, few saw nullification as a necessary protection for slavery," although after Nat Turner's bloody uprising, most whites were concerned about slave insurrections (Cooper 1978: 46). Certainly the precise relationship between proslavery ideology and political activity is both difficult to prove and "murky" at best, to borrow the words of Richard E. Ellis. But even as critics nibble away at the edges of Freehling's much-debated theory, a consensus of sorts has emerged that lower South politicians like John C. Calhoun came to understand "that planter insecurity over the future of slavery could be put to political use." Certainly Calhoun and the nullifiers were not the first southerners to recognize that states' rights might protect slavery. But as Ellis (1987) argues in his *The Union at Risk*, Old Republicans like John Taylor or even John Randolph of Roanoke "never made the defense of slavery a central political concern the way Calhoun and his followers began to do after 1833." Initially, Andrew Jackson might have thought that the tariff and its constitutionality was the central question on the minds of the nullifiers, but by the end of the congressional debates in 1833, the Jacksonians finally understood "that the slavery question had indeed been very much involved" (Ellis 1987: 189–94).

What remains beyond dispute is that all of these factors produced what Lacy K. Ford, Jr (1988) calls "an unusual" level of "political unity among white South Carolinians" in the immediate post-nullification era. Although almost all southern states had counties dominated by plantation agriculture and unfree labor, in the Carolina lowcountry "the size of the black majorities was overwhelming." As Ford observes in *Origins of Southern Radicalism*, the coastal parishes from Georgetown to Beaufort boasted an African American population of roughly 85 percent. "Indeed, the population distribution in a number of the Lowcountry parishes resembled that of the West Indies and other parts of the Caribbean slave empires far more than it did that of the Southern black belt." Such demographic realities made Carolina planters suspicious of any reform movement, black revolutionary, or tariff that might endanger their way of life. But certainly "fears that a racial bloodbath along the lines of the Haitian revolution might occur" explains much about the lowcountry's growing estrangement from a federal government they believed cared too little about either their livelihood or their lives (Ford 1988: 123).

As Ford notes, South Carolina's "uniquely radical response" to northern challenges was largely "shaped by the towering political presence of John C. Calhoun" (1988: 123). As author of the historic *South Carolina Exposition and Protest*, Calhoun could hardly escape, as biographer Irving H. Bartlett (1993) puts it, "being known as the mastermind of nullification." In the most balanced study yet available of the cast-iron man, Bartlett clearly admires Calhoun's intellectual abilities – as well as his determination to find some middle ground between unionist and "fire-eater" in South Carolina. But he is blunt as to the danger that nullification posed to both the republic and Calhoun's own political career. While his abandonment of his youthful nationalist tendencies saved his career in his native state, Calhoun's adoption of nullification ruined his reputation as a national leader. How such an extreme, regional position "could have taken him to the presidency defies comprehension," Bartlett writes. "Not even a man of iron can be sustained forever on reason" (1993: 183). More to the point, if Calhoun regarded the implied threat of disunion as the formula by which the republic might hold together, he was sadly mistaken. As George Dangerfield observed of the *Exposition*'s curiously dated nature, the "Hartford Convention had taught the lesson that the compact theory of the Constitution was something people pulled out of its pigeonhole when they were disgruntled," only to turn their back on it "when times got better and feelings were less exacerbated." If South Carolina never returned the concept to its "pigeonhole," it was only because their seigneurial way of life, and the modern world's growing assaults upon it, never allowed them to do so (Dangerfield 1952: 411).

By 1833, as Andrew Jackson's shrewd combination of a lower tariff and the Force Bill led an isolated South Carolina to back down, white southerners began to pull together – even as they began to pull away from the federal Union. As northern activists increasingly abandoned the conservative solution of African American colonization in Liberia, militant antislavery remained as the only answer to the republic's rising number of slaves. Black abolitionists like Vesey and Turner refused to distinguish between planters and yeomen in their struggles to liberate their followers, which served to further unify the region behind a Democratic party that hoped to avoid further sectional animosity. In short, the truce of 1833 was not only the end of one era, but also the beginning of another, during which the Old South stood unified on the importance of defending its peculiar institution. On this steely new determination, last words go to editor and author John B. Boles. When South Carolina rescinded its Ordinance of Nullification on March 15, a possibly calamitous national crisis was averted. "But South Carolina did not feel chastised and perhaps learned too well another lesson: nullification was no option for discontented states, which left only secession" (Boles 1995: 257).

BIBLIOGRAPHY

Abernathy, Thomas P. (1961) *The South in the New Nation, 1789–1819*. Baton Rouge, La.: Louisiana State University Press.

Ammon, Harry (1971) *James Monroe: The Quest for National Identity*. New York: McGraw-Hill.

Bartlett, Irving H. (1993) *John C. Calhoun: A Biography*. New York: Norton.

Bergeron, Paul (1976) "The Nullification Controversy Revisited," *Tennessee Historical Quarterly* 35: 263–75.

Boles, John B. (1995) *The South through Time: A History of an American Region*. Englewood Cliffs, NJ: Prentice-Hall.

Boyd, Julian P. (1948) "Thomas Jefferson's Empire of Liberty," *Virginia Quarterly Review* 24: 549–50.

Clarfield, Gerald H. (1980) *Timothy Pickering and the American Republic*. Pittsburgh, Pa.: University of Pittsburgh Press.

Cooper, William J., Jr (1978) *The South and the Politics of Slavery, 1828–1856*. Baton Rouge, La.: Louisiana State University Press.

Dangerfield, George (1952) *The Era of Good Feelings*. New York: Harcourt.

DeConde, Alexander (1966) *The Quasi-War: The Politics and Diplomacy of the Undeclared War with France, 1797–1801*. New York: Charles Scribner's & Sons.

Deyle, Steven (1992) "The Irony of Liberty: Origins of the Domestic Slave Trade," *Journal of the Early Republic* 12 (1): 37–62.

Egerton, Douglas R. (1997) "Averting a Crisis: The Proslavery Critique of the American Colonization Society," *Civil War History* 43: 142–56.

Egerton, Douglas R. (1999) *He Shall Go Out Free: The Lives of Denmark Vesey*. Madison, Wis.: Madison House.

Egerton, Douglas R. (2002) "The Empire of Liberty Reconsidered," in Peter Onuf and Jan Lewis (eds.) *The Revolution of 1800*. Charlottesville, Va.: University of Virginia Press.

Ellis, Joseph J. (1998) *American Sphinx: The Character of Thomas Jefferson*. New York: Alfred A. Knopf.

Ellis, Richard E. (1987) *The Union at Risk: Jacksonian Democracy, States' Rights and the Nullification Crisis*. New York: Oxford University Press.

Finkelman, Paul (ed.) (1997) *Slavery and the Law*. Madison, Wis.: Madison House.

Ford, Lacy K., Jr (1988) *Origins of Southern Radicalism: The South Carolina Upcountry, 1800–1860*. New York: Oxford University Press.

Fox-Genovese, Elizabeth and Genovese, Eugene D. (1983) *Fruits of Merchant Capital: Slavery and Bourgeois Property in the Rise and Expansion of Capitalism*. New York: Oxford University Press.

Freehling, William W. (1965) *Prelude to Civil War: The Nullification Controversy in South Carolina, 1816–1836*. New York: Harper and Row.

Freehling, William W. (1990) *The Road to Disunion: Secessionists at Bay, 1776–1854*. New York: Oxford University Press.

Freehling, William W. (1994) *The Reintegration of American History: Slavery and the Civil War*. New York: Oxford University Press.

Gunther, Gerald (2001) *Constitutional Law*, 3rd edn. New York: Foundations Press.

Hirschfeld, Fritz (1997) *George Washington and Slavery: A Documentary Portrayal*. Columbia, Mo.: University of Missouri Press.

Hodges, Graham Russell (1997) *Slavery and Freedom in the Rural North: African Americans in Monmouth County, New Jersey, 1665–1865*. Madison, Wis.: Madison House.

Hodges, Graham Russell (1999) *Root and Branch: African Americans in New York and East Jersey, 1613–1863*. Chapel Hill, NC: University of North Carolina Press.

Howe, Daniel Walker (1979) *The Political Culture of the American Whigs*. Chicago: University of Chicago Press.

Johnson, Walter (1999) *Soul by Soul: Life Inside the Antebellum Slave Market*. Cambridge, Mass.: Harvard University Press.

Kaminski, John P. (ed.) (1995) *A Necessary Evil? Slavery and the Debate over the Constitution*. Madison, Wis.: Madison House.

Kolchin, Peter (1993) *American Slavery, 1619–1877*. New York: Hill and Wang.

McColley, Robert (1973) *Slavery and Jeffersonian Virginia*, 2nd edn. Urbana, Ill.: University of Illinois Press.

McCoy, Drew (1989) *The Last of the Fathers: James Madison and the Republican Legacy*. New York: Cambridge University Press.

Malone, Dumas (1948–81) *Jefferson and his Time*, six vols. Boston, Mass.: Little, Brown.

Melish, Joanne Pope (1998) *Disowning Slavery: Gradual Emancipation and "Race" in New England, 1780–1860*. Ithaca, NY: Cornell University Press.

Miller, John Chester (1977) *The Wolf by the Ears: Thomas Jefferson and Slavery*. New York: Free Press.

Moore, Glover (1953) *The Missouri Controversy, 1819–1821*. Lexington, Ky.: University Press of Kentucky.

Ott, Thomas (1973) *The Haitian Revolution, 1789–1804*. Knoxville, Tenn.: University of Tennessee Press.

Paquette, Robert L. (1997) "Saint Domingue and the Making of Territorial Louisiana," in David Barry Gaspar and David Patrick Geggus (eds.) *A Turbulent Time: The French Revolution and the Greater Caribbean*. Bloomington, Ind.: Indiana University Press.

Pearson, Edward A. (ed.) (1999) *Designs against Charleston: The Trial Record of the Denmark Vesey Slave Conspiracy of 1822*. Chapel Hill, NC: University of North Carolina Press.

Rakove, Jack N. (1986) *Original Meanings: Politics and Ideas in the Making of the Constitution*. New York: Alfred A. Knopf.

Remini, Robert V. (1984) *Andrew Jackson and the Course of American Democracy, 1833–1845*, 3 vols. New York: Harper and Row.

Remini, Robert V. (1988) *The Legacy of Andrew Jackson: Essays on Democracy, Indian Removal, and Slavery*. Baton Rouge, La.: Louisiana State University Press.

Remini, Robert V. (1991) *Henry Clay.* New York: Norton.

Remini, Robert V. (1997) *Daniel Webster: The Man and His Time.* New York: Norton.

Slaughter, Philip (1855) *The Virginian History of African Colonization.* Richmond, Va.: MacFarlane.

Staudenraus, P. J. (1961) *The African Colonization Movement, 1816–1865.* New York: Columbia University Press.

Tadman, Michael (1989) *Speculators and Slaves: Masters, Traders, and Slaves in the Old South.* Madison, Wis.: University of Wisconsin Press.

Tucker, Robert W. and Hendrickson, David C. (1990) *Empire of Liberty: The Statecraft of Thomas Jefferson.* New York: Oxford University Press.

Van Doren, Carl (1948) *The Great Rehearsal: The Story of the Making and Ratifying of the Constitution of the United States.* New York: Viking.

Wright, Donald R. (1993) *African Americans in the Early Republic, 1789–1831.* Arlington Heights, Ill.: Harlan Davidson.

CHAPTER TWO

The Market Revolution

JOHN LARSON

At the end of the revolutionary era, the United States comprised 13 colonial provinces on the coast of North America. Nearly all of 3.9 million people extracted a living through agriculture while a small merchant class traded staple crops and foodstuffs for tropical goods, useful manufactures, and luxuries in the Atlantic commercial community. By the time of the Civil War seven decades later, the United States sprawled across the continent with nearly 32 million people laboring, not just on farms, but in factories making iron and steel products, boots and shoes, textiles, paper, packaged foodstuffs, firearms, farm machinery, furniture, tools, and all sorts of housewares, borrowing money from banks, buying insurance, traveling on steamboats and railway carriages, and producing between \$2–3 billion dollars' worth of goods and services, including exports worth \$400 million (Wattenberg 1976: 239, 885). This dramatic transformation was the "market revolution," and it stood for antebellum Americans – as it does for modern historians – near the center of all explanations of what happened to the United States during its grand experiment in republican self-government.

Two sustaining myths – one liberal and triumphant, the other sinister and tragic – compete in the American mind as explanations for the market revolution. In the triumphal tale, ordinary people, once freed from the tyranny of Old World institutions, aligned themselves with natural forces in the marketplace, exercised their liberty, stayed the hand of government, followed their instincts, and made themselves into a "people of plenty" (Potter 1954). Represented most favorably in our literature by works of Louis Hartz (1955), David Potter (1954), and Daniel Boorstin (1965), to name but three, this liberal narrative finds deep roots in the dominant American culture as well as in cherished ideas of the "self-made man" and the "land of opportunity." In the darker story, capitalists hijacked the promise of American democracy, rigged politics and captured governments, imposed market values over human relations, and ushered in an economic system that gratified the interests of the few at the expense of the many. Never dominant (although perhaps believed by a majority of working-men and women throughout American history), this more conspiratorial account underlies much critical, left-wing scholarship and, quite recently, Charles G. Sellers' (1991) *The Market Revolution*.

The truth of what happened in the antebellum economy doubtless lies somewhere between these myths, yet it remains sufficiently elusive and contested that historians cannot find a ready solution. We can describe *what* happened, but no language of consensus has been found to specify the causes or characterize the consequences of this great transformation. Small wonder, then, that the pre-Civil War generation failed to negotiate these wrenching changes with either grace or generosity. This transformation in the American economic system sprang from widely shared causes and conditions; but the first fruits and tangible evidence of capitalist modernization seemed to collect disproportionately in cities and towns of the North, giving rise among contemporaries to frankly sectional interpretations. However much the Civil War was fought over slavery, states' rights, and the power of the Union, it was caused as well by tensions that derived from the market revolution.

The market revolution began with a convergence of conditions and opportunities at the close of the Revolution. A youthful population spread thinly on a bountiful land, Americans at independence enjoyed a relatively high standard of living and a reproductive rate that approached the biological maximum. Doubling in number every 25 years, these colonists-turned-citizens now controlled their own destiny and (as far as European powers were concerned) the eastern half of central North America. The last important acts of the confederation Congress – the Land Ordinance of 1785 and the Northwest Ordinance of 1787 – profoundly democratized real estate transactions and guaranteed civil rights to westering pioneers. Equally aggressive policies under the new constitution, aimed at extinguishing the claims of Native Americans, promised by 1795 that young Americans could expect to continue their habits of breeding, moving west, and snatching an easy subsistence from undeveloped Indian land. Almost everyone saw the new United States as a treasure house of opportunity, a great poor man's country. As George Washington put it: "I wish to see the sons and daughters of the world in Peace and busily employed in the more agreeable amusement of fulfilling the first and great commandment, *Increase and Multiply*" (quoted in Larson 2001b: 14).

Abundant resources, personal freedom, and a young energetic population virtually guaranteed the extension of Anglo-American agriculture across the mountains to the Mississippi, but the market revolution would not transform anything until engines of intensification began to reorder this rural agrarian paradise. Transportation improvements were needed to "vent" the surplus product of interior settlements lest ambition decay into indolence. Home manufactures were wanted to reduce the nation's appetite for European imports before the new nation sank into neocolonial dependency. Somebody – governments or private businesspeople – must mobilize capital, generate a currency, reactivate trading connections, and stimulate markets, especially for the staple crops grown by African slaves throughout the southern states. Thus conditions were right for the market revolution to begin, but policy decisions and positive actions were required to set the process in motion. This purposeful feature gave purchase to fantastic charges of conspiracy whenever significant and unwanted changes took place, and they help sustain critical explanations today.

Alexander Hamilton's fiscal policies, adopted by Congress in the early 1790s, established the public credit of the United States, created a securities market and investment-grade stocks and bonds, and launched the first Bank of the United States to mobilize capital and circulate paper money (Perkins 1994: chs. 10–11). By design

Hamilton's policies favored commercial interests, creditors, and contracts: such were the engines of economic development. But if the future prosperity of Americans depended on these policy initiatives (and it is hard to imagine otherwise), they apparently effected a tremendous transfer of wealth and power away from the real producers of goods into the hands of speculators and stock-jobbers – as critics said, the "paper interest." From the very beginning political debates swirled with arguments, not over prosperity itself, but over what it would take to produce the wealth and comfort Americans automatically associated with their rights as free men. Governments could not avoid playing a role in infant American economies, if only by coining money, protecting property, and setting up courts of justice. Furthermore, fresh from life under British mercantilism, few Americans yet imagined truly free markets of the kind proposed in that new book just making the rounds in 1776 – Adam Smith's *Wealth of Nations.*

In addition to these first federal initiatives, state governments and private citizens contributed to the framework of institutions that would launch the market revolution. In Philadelphia, Stephen Girard opened a private commercial bank that set local standards for discount and exchange. States chartered their own central banks or limited numbers of incorporated banks, sometimes filling their vaults with paper state securities in lieu of specie. By 1815 over 200 separate banks contributed to the American money supply, an institutional chaos soon to be augmented (although not significantly improved) by the creation of the Second Bank of the United States (Chandler 1977: 30).

Land speculation soaked up a great deal of this newly minted capital. Real farm- and plantation-making quickly backed up the value of these paper claims, but sometimes panics, such as occurred in 1819, suddenly squeezed out exuberance before productivity could catch up, punishing the innocent (or so it seemed) with crashing prices while leaving bankers and other high-flyers inexplicably unscathed. People harbored deep resentments toward banking, speculation, and all kinds of paper investments, yet simple pioneer farmers could not move themselves to Kentucky without converting their current assets into some kind of cash, purchasing a farm, and making immediate improvements to bring it into production – a process estimated to cost several hundred dollars. Subsistence farming was an illiquid enterprise (ask any European peasant), and American yeomen could not enjoy their rights or pursue their ambitions without certain instruments of exchange that would become the tools of capitalist transformation.

Agricultural expansion drove American economic growth, and just as soon as credit and currency were adequate to marketing the surplus, demands for internal improvements – roads, bridges, turnpikes, and canals – stirred the imaginations of dreamers, schemers, and entrepreneurs. In 1785, in response to burgeoning markets for food and firewood in the city of Boston, the Commonwealth of Massachusetts contracted with certain wealthy "incorporators" to build a bridge over the Charles River. In return for constructing this public convenience (and relieving the government of its obligation to do so), the corporation received certain privileges including the right to collect tolls on the bridge for the coming 40 years. Except for the most common roads and bridges, responsibility for which lay with local town or county authorities, early American governments typically employed chartered companies to develop bridges and turnpikes, clear waterways, dredge harbors, and build docks, piers, and wharves (Handlin and Handlin 1947; Hartz 1948, ch. 2; Kutler 1971; Larson 2001b). In this way local taxes were held to a minimum, private wealth was directed toward public service, and the costs of improving the infrastructure fell on the beneficiaries most directly. Those who objected to "extravagant" new facilities remained free to use the old roads and ferries, or to sneak around tollbooths on the illegal bypass loops that invariably appeared on incorporated turnpikes.

Money also found its way very early into manufacturing ventures, sometimes with, sometimes without, the state's encouragement through bounties or incorporation. In 1791, for example, hoping to honor his newfound Quaker convictions and get out of the African slave trade, Providence merchant Moses Brown hired Samuel Slater to build the first water-powered cotton textile mill in America. A tiny affair with nine women and children tending the machinery, Slater's first Pawtucket mill nevertheless produced a supply of cotton that overwhelmed the local market and threatened (as Brown complained) to spin up all his assets into yarn. This experiment launched the industry that completely transformed the region. Within a few years small, cheap copycat mills sprang up on streams all over southern New England, financed by local merchants or wealthy farmers, commonly in partnership with "mechanicks" who could tend and repair the equipment. Local tool-makers evolved into machinery manufacturers, and anyone who owned a hand loom put aside everything to manufacture cloth from yarn "put-out" on consignment by the owners of the spinning mills (Coleman 1963; Tucker 1984). North of Boston, with the aid of a corporate charter, Francis Cabot Lowell and his associates spent much larger sums on the Merrimack River, exploiting their grander power source to drive an integrated complex of machines for spinning, weaving, and finishing, all in one establishment. In the 1820s, with the opening of huge factories at Lowell, industrialization in America acquired both an icon and a permanent force. But neither the integrated operations at Lowell was nor the small, rural, Slater-style mills were intended to transform society in dramatic, irreversible ways. In fact, the paternalistic boardinghouse system adopted at Lowell was specifically intended to protect the country girls from industrial exploitation and prevent the rise of a landless working class (Dublin 1979; Prude 1983).

Before 1815 almost everything new in the American economy, no matter how hotly it may have been debated, could be seen as a response to genuine needs that had promised widespread benefits for all kinds of people. And while we can see in retrospect the separate "gears" of a modern capitalist economic machine, they had not yet locked together in system of engagement that would become self-perpetuating. But in the decade after 1815, even more rapid growth and westward migration, continuing innovations, rising competition among American communities in a booming domestic market, and a major panic and depression beginning in 1819 both fostered and exposed the emergence of this interlocking capitalist market system. By the mid-1820s most Americans recognized that fundamental changes in political economy were pending or already taking place. Therefore, by the time of the election of Andrew Jackson in 1828, the market revolution had become both an engine of social change and a self-conscious topic of public debate concerning the health of the republic.

Growth itself seemed to be the prime force behind the articulation and integration of interlocking capitalist elements within the American domestic economy. The burgeoning agricultural surplus fed spiraling demands for roads, turnpikes, wagons, teamsters, and finally major interregional canals to bring this bounty to market. New York's initiative in building the Erie Canal (begun 1817, finished 1825) linked the Atlantic with the "western waters" and opened a spectacular interior breadbasket along the Mohawk River and the Great Lakes. Grain and flour poured into New York City, stimulating all kinds of business and innovations among that city's merchants and artisans. Meanwhile, along the canal itself, Americans discovered the magic of the multiplier effect as hamlets grew into cities overnight. First the digging itself, then the transport and handling business brought new money into rural communities. Farmers produced more wheat for export, millers threw up dams and began grinding flour, coopers arrived to make barrels (farmers profiting again in winter by making barrel stave blanks for the coopers), house carpenters labored frantically to accommodate the swelling population.

Rochester, New York, exploded from a village of 1,500 in 1821 into a city of 10,000 by 1830. The town was awash in crafts-workers, salespeople, laborers, speculators, lawyers, crooks, and clergymen, most of them strangers. By one 1826 account over 100 new people arrived each day, and another 100 moved on – net gain, 10–15 (Johnson 1978: 13, 17, 37). In such a marketplace, supply never outstripped demand and economic rewards showered anyone with a "better idea" for meeting their neighbors' needs. Carpenters adopted quick-and-dirty "balloon-frame" construction techniques; coopers and shoemakers routinized and subdivided traditional skilled crafts, inventing jigs, tools, and frames that allowed less experienced (less expensive) hands to do more work; in the case of shoemakers even putting out pieces for needle assembly to low-paid women all over town, turning apprentices from would-be artisans into runners and errand boys (Johnson 1978: 38–42; Rilling 2000). Certain master craftsmen climbed *up* the ladder to become merchant-manufacturers, and once they had all the local people shod, these high-output shoemakers began exporting cheap brogans in barrels for sale to planters in the South, who eagerly snapped up the product to "give" to their slaves each Christmas.

In New York City, the rising volume of business had been driving innovation since before the canal was begun. British "dumping" at the end of the war of 1812 had stimulated wholesalers who perfected New York's famous system of dockside auctions. Warehouses filled up everywhere as ships' cargoes were off-loaded, broken and sorted into lots, and resold for domestic distribution or directly to local retailers. The canal in effect closed a commercial loop by funneling agricultural commodities into the hands of these same merchants while ferrying imports back up the canal into the hinterland. Bankers and insurance underwriters further institutionalized their services; brokers cared less *who* their customers were than whether they paid with good money and fast. Robert Fulton's steamboats first plied the waters of New York harbor in 1807, then soon pushed upstream against the Hudson's currents to help make the Erie Canal not just a downstream "vent" but a two-way highway. After 1815 steam navigation quickly spread to interior rivers like the Mississippi and Ohio, fed by New York expertise and investment capital (Albion 1939: chs. 4, 5, 8; Hunter 1949).

In January 1818 the Black Ball Line of packet ships advertised the world's first scheduled service, and a new standard of dependability began transforming all sorts of business transactions. Buyers and sellers flocked to New York port because it was becoming the best place to do business – and because they flocked there, it *was* the best place to do business. Coastal traders from New England, the South, and New Orleans congregated there to get the freshest European goods, the lowest prices on imports, and the best contracts for outgoing produce. Some 20 years after that first daring Black Ball departure, New York merchants had virtually engrossed American domestic commerce, and the cotton export trade that logically "belonged" to Charleston and Savannah passed through the hands of Manhattan brokers and speculators (Albion 1939: chs. 3, 6).

The staggering rise of New York port sparked an urgent competition in rival Atlantic cities such as Boston, Philadelphia, Baltimore, and even fledgling Washington City (which harbored pretensions of becoming the emporium of the republic). From the beginning a city of artisans, Philadelphia focused its attention on expanding and retaining its hinterland commerce and especially on preventing easy transportation down the Susquehanna River from pouring into Baltimore's lap the riches of central Pennsylvania. Baltimore and Boston both developed niche markets in the China trade, developing fast "clipper ships" to trim down the length of the voyage, carrying California hides and Middle Eastern opium to Canton, and bringing to American stores non-British supplies of tea, ceramics, and luxury textiles. The persistent demands of Caribbean sugar planters for food, lumber, and livestock fueled booms in mid-Atlantic flour, New York packed beef, Rhode Island horses and cattle, and (in a case Daniel Boorstin celebrated as proof of Yankee liberal enterprise) Boston ice (Boorstin 1965: 10; Gilchrist 1967; Lindstrom 1978; Browne 1980).

None of this commercial excitement in the seaport cities kept pace with the growth of New York, and in the 1820s and 1830s, as the impact of the Erie Canal became apparent, frantic interests demanded transport improvements deep into the interior as the only way to level this new playing field. Philadelphia pinned its hopes on canals winding along and between the Schuylkill, Susquehanna, and Allegheny rivers, trying to replicate over a 3,000-foot mountain ridge what New York had done across its "water-level route." The effort was heroic, but the results have been ridiculed (unfairly) in textbooks ever since. Richmond, Virginia, thrust new life into the languishing James River waterway and tried to improve at least export navigation as far up as Lynchburg if not beyond. Dusting off another dream from the Confederation era, Washington City revived the old Potomac Canal and launched (with federal charter and financial assistance) the Chesapeake and Ohio (C & O) Canal. In desperate self-defense, Baltimore turned to experimental technology, hurriedly pushing its Baltimore and Ohio (B & O) Railroad up the same narrow valley as the C & O Canal, destined for the Ohio River and the commerce of the Old Northwest. Boston likewise threw its efforts into railroads instead of canals. Responding on the other side of the Appalachian barrier, the infant states of Ohio, Kentucky, Indiana, Illinois, and even Michigan Territory, launched internal improvement programs to link the Great Lakes to the Ohio, Wabash, and Illinois rivers and improve local export navigation (Larson 2001b: chs. 3, 6).

Uneven and imperfect as these state and local projects were, taken together, by the 1840s, American turnpikes, canals, and steamboats had revolutionized transportation even before the arrival of steam railroad trains. Freight rates for commodities fell dramatically, on land from 30 cents per ton-mile to 7 or 8, on water from 10 cents to less than a penny! Travel times shrank as well: according to Alan Pred's calculations, in 1840 information and passengers spread out from New York City between five and 20 times as fast as they had 50 years before (Pred 1973: 64, 74).

Distances seemed to be dissolving, and for the first time New Yorkers could reach their countrymen on the Mississippi more quickly than they could reach Liverpool or Le Havre. Still profoundly disintegrated, this relatively "low-tech" transportation network comprised hundreds of separate routes, conveyances, and facilities and employed thousands of independent forwarding merchants, livery agents, wagonmasters, stagedrivers, steamboat captains, canalboaters, mule skinners, warehousemen, teamsters, dock workers, cartmen – individual sellers of services knit together by market transactions the complexity of which absolutely boggles the modern mind. Nevertheless, the volume and velocity of domestic trade carried out in this manner mushroomed and literally created a demand for the faster, cheaper, and more dependable integrated services that would be offered within a decade by the railroads.

While commercial interests assembled the framework for this burgeoning domestic marketplace, American manufacturers steadily increased their own contributions to American economic growth. All the major cities in the early republic harbored traditional "man-u-factories" of every description: shoemakers, tanners, hatters, tailors, carpenters, joiners, cabinetmakers, coopers, wagonmakers, wheelrights, blacksmiths, silversmiths, gunsmiths, watchmakers – the list goes on. Smaller country towns boasted more limited arrays of local artisans, but even in rural backwaters one could find farmer-crafts-workers capable of putting shoes on the children, beds in the loft, and chairs beneath the weary pioneer's behind. Deprived of foreign manufactures off and on by turmoil in Europe, and then by the war of 1812, American producers had stepped up their output with positive results. With the return of peace in 1815 the British dumped huge stocks of goods on American markets, and the highly capitalized American industries – cottons and woolens, iron and steel – begged for protection by import tariffs from the "unfair" competition of European producers. The next year Congress obliged, and the United States began to encourage (albeit feebly) domestic manufacturing. What really stimulated production in American workshops, however, was the relentless surge in demand produced by the growth and extension of the domestic marketplace itself (Chandler 1977: ch. 1).

Given the structure of the system of manufacturing that had prevailed since colonization, rising demand typically was met by replicating whole workshops with new masters, journeymen, and apprentices turning out custom orders on demand. And so it was throughout the urban frontier from Pittsburgh to St. Louis (Wade 1959; Ross 1985). But the relentless growth of demand in antebellum America, coupled with the assembly of commercial networks capable of delivering goods and services across previously unimaginable distances, gave rise to innovations within these workshops that fueled the great transformation from artisanal to industrial production. As we saw in the case of Rochester's shoemakers, ambitious master craftsmen in every line looked for ways to routinize and subdivide the work, often embedding knowledge or technique in jigs and simple machines that allowed untrained (read *cheaper*) employees to do skilled work and do it faster. Interchangeable parts first appeared among the makers of cheap wooden clocks and were adopted by gun manufacturers and other makers of small machines, eventually gaining worldwide notice (rightly or not) as the "American System of manufacturing" (Rosenberg 1972: 87–90).

In larger cities, forward-looking masters increased the size and productivity of their shops, adapting accordingly their procedures for purchasing materials, hiring and training hands, and selling their wares. By the 1830s certain masters had taken off their aprons because they spent their days buying and selling, supervising, planning, and arranging for transport, insurance, or financing. Where appropriate – especially in textiles, metal fabricating, and wood products – machines multiplied the labor of men. Where available, waterpower further intensified the output of machinery. Steam engines gradually brought into the heart of the city the kind of supplemental power previously available only on rural streams (Hunter 1979: ch. 4; Hunter 1985: chs. 1–2). Soon traditional workshops resembled modern "factories" and master crafts-men became capitalistic manufacturers. Furnace tenders learned how to light and burn Pennsylvania's heat-rich anthracite coal, and steam-driven industries (not to mention mining and transportation) gained another round of relative advantages. At every stage, productivity rose, prices fell, and consumers generally benefited; but artisans-in-training – apprentices and journeymen – found themselves trapped in new roles without hope of independent places in the economy of the future. Work-men hated these "bastard workshops." According to Sean Wilentz (1984: 48–52), in New York as early as 1815, 52 percent of journeymen were over 30 years of age, often heads of households with wives and children, laboring for life at wages meant for youngsters.

The cumulative effect of all these developments was the emergence and articula-tion of what we recognize as the modern capitalist economic system. Almost imper-ceptibly structural changes knit themselves in interlocking combinations. Face-to-face commercial transactions, so typical of rural village life in the late eighteenth century, evolved into institutional exchanges dependent more on cash and facilitating mid-dlemen. Where villagers once exchanged eggs, butter, and firewood for yarn, shoes, or furniture directly from the spinner, cobbler, or carpenter, they soon passed all produce through the books of the country storekeeper and eventually bought their shoes, chairs, and yardgoods from craft workers they never met who worked in factories in unimaginable eastern or northern cities. Without delay, the overworked pioneer housewives hung up their spinning wheels and purchased ready-made woolens and cottons as soon as supplies became available. Not for a moment did they think that by dropping the extraordinary tedium of spinning, knitting, weaving, and sew-ing all of their family's textiles they would usher in a new economic system that profoundly restricted their liberty, autonomy, and independence. Yet such was the effect of the encroaching web of market transactions that characterized their lives.

One of the earliest signs of market penetration was the rising export of surplus crops. Early subsistence farmers produced their immediate needs at home and raised cash with exports only to pay taxes or purchase coffee, powder, lead, and window glass. However, as their accounts at the store began to mount, farmers raised more chickens for sale in town, more wheat for sale at the local flour mill, more hogs and cattle that could walk to distant markets, in order to balance their purchases. Farm women made butter and cheese for the nearest urban community where folks had no cows of their own. Some farmers brought the storekeeper firewood or forest products like barrel staves. Others worked together to drive large herds of livestock to regional cities such as Cincinnati, where animals were slaughtered and processed for further export in national or international markets. Storekeepers, like it or not, found themselves wholesaling produce for export in order to stock their shelves with retail merchandise, and these primitive entrepreneurs often promoted industry and transportation improvements in desperate efforts to move out commodities brought to them by customers eager to purchase their wares. What stood out in the frontier progression from subsistence to export economy was the invisibility of the process and the relative innocence of each individual whose choices drove the transformation forward (Wade 1959; Rohrbough 1978: ch. 4).

Further up the chain of entrepreneurial innovation, "likely" young men (and this *was* mostly a man's business) took positions as clerks where they learned elementary commercial skills. Some became managers of branch stores capitalized by their employers; some saved enough from their wages to buy a stock of goods and go out on their own. In larger towns and cities the burgeoning volume of trade fostered specialization, and wherever transactions became numerous the need for paperwork and records multiplied. Institutional procedures replaced family connections or personal acquaintance among buyers, sellers, employers, and employees. Banks replaced family, friends, and local notables as the primary sources of business capital, and by the 1850s Lewis Tappan's credit reporters were making formal ratings of merchants in Chicago, Cincinnati, or Cleveland for the benefit of lenders and vendors in Boston, New York, and Philadelphia (Chandler 1977: 220). Partnerships remained the preferred instrument for larger businesses, but in most states general incorporation laws made the once-scarce corporate charter readily available for groups interested in manufacturing, mining, turnpikes, insurance, sometimes banking, and experimental railroad development.

Without anybody wishing it so, the increasing scope of commercial transactions, the increasing distance between buyers and sellers, the institutionalization of relations, and the proliferation of intermediaries disembedded individual transactions from contexts in which the common welfare or "commonwealth" of whole communities once had seemed self-evident. Not that folks were any more (or less) inclined to abuse their neighbors, but how were they to know who *was* their neighbor in a complicated nexus of actors and agents they never saw or knew by name, where prices, commissions, and the terms of trade seemed always to be set by somebody else? This was, of course, the genius of the free commercial marketplace: it depersonalized transactions, stripped them of all but economic information, and opened the game to anyone with something to sell or the wherewithal to buy. The result, overall, was a decline of what we might call "diseconomies" or wasteful transaction costs, but this rationalization came at a price in terms of community welfare and social relations. Individuals who bore their neighbors no ill will now found themselves required to raise prices, call in loans, lower wages, or fire employees because competitive forces left them no choice. Once the market revolution had produced a certain level of complexity and interdependence, the most moral or ethical of entrepreneurs found themselves powerless to stand against a panic or a boom.

Nowhere was the progress of this capitalistic ethos more unanticipated or insidious than in New England, where the textile revolution fueled economic growth for two generations after 1800. Much of the industry took the form of small Slater-style mills built at rural waterpower sites that required the owner to install not just a factory but a town as well. To recruit a workforce of women and children, Slater himself found that he often had to lure whole families with promises of farm work for the men, convenient rental housing, company stores, churches, and Sunday schools. Marginal farmers traded agrarian poverty for real cash wages and the promise of a rising standard of living. But as competitive markets squeezed Slater, once-independent yeomen found their women and children working longer hours for lower rates while their own agricultural employment – a luxury peripheral to Slater's interests – disappeared (Tucker 1984: 141–62). Indebted to the mill-owner for store credit and past rent, such families could neither bargain nor protest, nor even escape their employers' grasp. Competition, not community standards, set the price of yarn or cloth. Lord and master of everything in town, Samuel Slater could no more go on producing textiles at a loss than could his workers return to farms long sold or abandoned. How could a system evolve where not even the owners of everything could have their way? And how could a people be free or independent when they owned nothing and owed everything to employers who could not (or would not) guarantee them even a subsistence?

Market forces subverted designs at the Lowell mills as well. The incorporators at Lowell initiated women's employment and the boarding house system with the explicit intention of avoiding the social degradation and working-class dependency that critics already had seen in the Arkwright mills of England. A paternalistic environment designed to guarantee the virtue of young, unmarried girls (complete with housemothers and sewing circles) was supposed to render factory employment safe, enjoyable, and above all *temporary* for young women of rural New England. Unfortunately, markets forced the Lowell group to press down wages, speed up machinery, maximize workdays, and otherwise squeeze their "wards" in order to remain competitive against English suppliers of cheap cotton cloth. Diminishing wages left no surplus income to fatten dowries or send home to support younger brothers and sisters; longer hours and harder conditions took their toll on health, spirits, eyesight, and physical beauty, until more and more "mill girls" had missed the window of opportunity for marriage (Dublin 1979). Like journeymen in bastard workshops, such female operatives struggled to live forever on wages first pegged at a temporary level, and their futures grew as dim as the lighting at dawn and dusk in their wintry New England factory workrooms.

Even in the countryside the market revolution generated problems for families engaged in the once-timeless and uncomplicated business of farming. Even before the Erie Canal was built, farmers along the Hudson River north of New York City worried that their "natural" advantage as suppliers to a fast-growing urban population would be erased by cheap transportation reaching into the Genesee valley. So it was, after 1830, that the breadbasket shifted westward, forcing farmers nearer the city into meat, dairy, and vegetable production: more valuable enterprises, perhaps, but far more dependent on immediate market forces, transportation costs, and innovative competition. Within a generation (by the 1850s), Genesee farmers felt the same displacement as foodstuffs from Michigan, Ohio, and Indiana rode eastward on discriminatory railroad rates that favored long over short hauls. Caught in the middle, upstate New York farmers found themselves too far from the city for butter and meat but not far enough to sell flour and corn in competition with new western sources (Benson 1955: ch. 1). Butchering, traditionally a decentralized local enterprise (and an asset to the neighborhood), became "meat packing" as it grew in scale, transforming locales – sometimes whole towns – into nearly unlivable scenes of carnage and offal. Cincinnati became known as "Porkopolis," a city in which the odds stood "five hundred to one" (said English tourist Frances Trollope) that a women could not cross the street without "brushing by a snout fresh dripping from the kennel" (Trollope 1993: 53). Even rural marriages felt the strain of accommodating the capitalist system as dairying, traditionally women's work and supplemental to household income, began to surpass grain farming as the primary source of support for many families in regions hard by major cities (Jensen 1986).

Falling together in the 1850s with a suddenness that startled most observers, all these disparate changes and adaptations seemed to assemble themselves into a giant, interlocking network of institutions, expectations, and behaviors that all found their legitimacy in market forces. With prices set by impersonal market mechanisms, vendors no longer dickered with their customers. Market quotations from New York, New Orleans, or even London seemed to establish the value of everything in the most remote country villages. Banks, transportation companies, insurers, and large mercantile houses seemed to hold all the cards in whatever bargaining went on in these complex commercial networks, leaving individual entrepreneurs on the defensive, afraid of being bested, and determined to recover their losses from the next most vulnerable "chump" in the game. Whatever mutuality may have existed in the "moral economy" of traditional networks of community exchange (and there clearly was some, however bitterly historians dispute its importance), it disappeared from the commercial culture of the antebellum North as the sectional conflict drew nearer.

Almost none of this narrative is in dispute among historians. It happened. People talked and wrote about what happened in the ways that have been cited above. What remains fiercely contested is why it happened and whether anybody or any class of persons caused it to happen that way. Some historians join Sellers (1991) on the left, lamenting the rise of a market-driven capitalist system and finding agents of its construction lurking in the historical record. Others on the liberal right (economic liberalism now sustains political conservatives) share something of Hartz's (1955) appreciation for the release of energy that resulted and tend to celebrate, not denigrate, those same agents. A few attempt to pose as agnostics, typically locating agency, not in the hands of any one group of actors, but in the very liberation of the common people – and satisfying nobody in the process. These arguments all seem to stand well on their own terms, but each can be toppled by removing the foundations upon which it was built, and this makes the problem endlessly fascinating.

Much of present historiography on the early United States rests in one way or another on the works of Gordon Wood. First by recovering the importance of classical republican ideals in the minds of America's founders (Wood 1969), and then later by locating that dynamic American revolutionary experience in an evolving Atlantic world context (Wood 1992), he portrays an almost utopian starting point from which the new United States might have developed in more than one direction. Deeply suspicious of government, Wood is not himself appalled to find that the emerging liberal democracy that resulted unleashed entrepreneurial freedom and ultimately a market revolution. Similarly, economic historians such as Winifred Rothenberg (1992) have argued that the capitalist economy evolved naturally out of the fragmentary or primitive marketplaces of colonial America, emphasizing a continuity in economic structures and principles that lay beneath the superstructural upheaval of national republican liberation. Joyce Appleby's (2000) study of the first generation of independent Americans traces the remarkably successful experience of liberation to roughly 1825; Daniel Feller (1995) continues her optimistic story into the 1840s, rightly calling attention to the confidence and sense of promise with which so many in the Jacksonian generation faced the world.

Drawing on a contrary historiography, although they often ring changes on agrarian, artisanal, or commonwealth republicanism, a number of historians reprise the same events in a minor key. Collections of essays by Alan Kulikoff (1992) and James A. Henretta (1991) nicely introduce pictures of a colonial political economy fundamentally different from that which emerged in the nineteenth century. In these accounts something more like E. P. Thompson's (1971) "moral economy" prevailed in colonial America, where family preservation, community welfare, and material security – not profit maximization, acquisitive calculation, and abstract market forces – guided economic behaviors that remained deeply embedded in cultural systems. Christopher Clark (1990) develops a similar thesis in a booklength study spanning almost a century of development after 1780 in rural Massachusetts.

John Ashworth (1995) offers the most frankly Marxian interpretation of American political economy in the first of two projected volumes that promise to explore the connections between slavery and capitalism before the American Civil War. Tony Freyer (1994) attempts to sort Jacksonian Americans into "capitalists" and "producers," categories presumed to be distinct and culturally (if not morally) incompatible. A collection edited by Jonathan Prude and Steven Hahn (1985) pursues the critique into the later antebellum decades and into the countryside of the yeoman farmers who still made up the bulk of America's population. Charles Sellers' (1991) *Market Revolution* promises a comprehensive explication of this critical tradition, but its date of publication obscures the author's reliance on a literature mostly published before 1975.

Between contending parties on the left and right, many historians prefer to embrace contemporary language with its ambiguities intact rather than explicate and sort it into abstract categories of analysis (passing the buck, in effect, to their readers). Daniel Walker Howe's (1979) study of the ideology of American Whigs rescues Andrew Jackson's primary opponents from the slanderous labels Jacksonians had fixed on them. The result, while sympathetic to the Whigs, remains agnostic on the merits of the capitalist transformation for which they are (wrongly) thought primarily responsible. Harry Watson (1990) synthesizes the long "Jacksonian period" from presidents Monroe to Tyler with only a trace of nostalgia for what Jackson's liberals *said* they were doing. My own *Internal Improvement* (Larson 2001b) laments not so much agrarian simplicity as the promise of quality governance that was lost in the conflation of political and economic freedom between the Jefferson and Jackson eras. By far the most balanced introduction to the literature before 1995 can be found in Paul Gilje's introductory essay in *Wages of Independence* (1997).

Legal historians contributed powerful voices to the conversation about the market revolution, beginning famously with James Willard Hurst two generations ago. In *Law and the Conditions of Freedom*, Hurst (1956) first characterized the "release of energy" that liberal historiography continues to celebrate in the antebellum story. Morton J. Horwitz (1977) published a critical, almost conspiratorial challenge to Hurst's liberalism, claiming for state and federal judges an activist role in tearing down common law traditions and wielding law instrumentally on behalf of clamorous entrepreneurs. Horwitz in turn has been attacked from many quarters. Contextualization, embeddedness, and attention to ideology continue to distinguish ever more sophisticated legal studies: for example, William Novak's (1996) study of local public welfare law neatly situates regulatory traditions within the specific contexts of liberalizing American communities in what seems to be a durable synthesis of liberal and radical perspectives.

Historical geographer D. W. Meinig explains America within a provocative Annales-like framework, especially in Volume 2 of *The Making of America* (1998). Alan Pred (1973) has done marvelous things with maps and information flow charts, blending cartography, statistics, economics, and history. For individual agency in bringing about the market revolution, see Alan Taylor's (1996) *William Cooper's Town* or my own *Bonds of Enterprise* (Larson 1984, rev. edn. 2001a), as examples of detailed studies that expose individual decision-makers, the impact of their purposeful actions, and the unanticipated consequences that so often magnified the importance of particular lives. In the end, historiographical trends remain inconclusive, and historians will continue to divide over the causes of the market revolution depending on what it is they wish to explain (as well as what they think of the resulting world in which we live).

Finally, why approach the market revolution as a sectional phenomenon? It was born of conditions that prevailed in all of the original 13 states, and the staple-crop planters of the antebellum South sold their cotton and bought supplies in the same developing capitalistic markets, profiting handsomely in good years and suffering like everybody else when financial stringency or overproduction depressed commodity prices. Yet by 1850 there was no doubt in people's minds, North and South, that the economic cultures of the sections had diverged, creating in the North disproportionate growth, wealth, and power to control economic structures and placing the most fundamental social values and institutions at risk. Yankees – overwhelmingly converted by this time to an orthodox liberal conviction that free markets rewarded free men and that political liberty existed inseparable from entrepreneurial independence – tended to explain the transformation as the inevitable result of natural forces (supply and demand) within a free society unencumbered, as theirs was, by antiquated institutions (read "slavery"). Southerners, of course, could not embrace that interpretation and nursed instead a simmering resentment that the Union and its policies somehow had produced this result, and that their good will and participation in the constitutional experiment since 1789 had been used to destroy their future.

Such precisely was the burden of the last argument John C. Calhoun composed in 1850 for delivery in the United States Senate (*Congressional Globe*, 1850: 451–5). "What is it," he asked, "that has endangered the Union?" An "almost universal discontent" in the southern states caused, not by the recent agitation against slavery, but by the destruction of the sectional "equilibrium" that had prevailed at the adoption of the constitution. Citing census statistics from 1790 and 1840, Calhoun showed how the North had grown in population and extent until it enjoyed a "predominance in every part of the Government." Had this predominance come about naturally, "without the interference of Government," he admitted, the South would have no complaint. But such was not the case: "It was caused by the legislation of this Government," erected as the agent of all but in effect captured by northern hands. With this assertion, Calhoun began perhaps the most portentous history lecture ever heard in the Senate chambers.

Three "series of acts" had produced the injustice. The first series barred the South from all but a fraction of the common lands in the West; the second raised and disbursed revenue in ways that grossly favored the North; the third produced political reforms that "radically changed" the "original nature of the Government." To an audience grown weary of watching federal policies and federal politics held hostage (as they saw it) by a southern "slave power conspiracy," Calhoun's audacity must have seemed breathtaking. But history is a malleable servant, and Calhoun's interpretation unfolded like a scripture revealed for people predisposed to see the story just that way.

Before the constitution even had been written, Calhoun began, the Northwest Ordinance excluded slavery – and thus the South – from access to the territory north of the Ohio. In 1820 the Missouri Compromise further limited access to a fraction of the lands acquired in 1803 from Louisiana. Northern auditors doubtless remembered the Missouri crisis as ending in a victory for the slave states: forbearance by northern interests in the face of a national apportionment scheme that "artificially" enlarged the southern body politic by counting 60 percent of the slaves. That original concession gave Virginia practical control over national politics into the mid-1810s, but Calhoun now dismissed the "three-fifths clause" as a trick to disable the South. The recent (1848) acquisitions of land from Mexico brought the total land area acquired since independence to 2,373,046 square miles, of which Calhoun accused the North of engrossing (or intending to engross) for itself about three-fourths.

As to revenues and disbursements, Calhoun alluded to policies toward which his opposition had been legendary. The reliance on tariffs for revenue, he claimed, automatically drew wealth from the exporting states because they purchased most of the imports. Additional tariffs since 1816, raised specifically to protect American industries, he counted as so much cash "into the pockets of the manufacturers" – Yankees all. Finally, federal disbursements – especially internal improvement subsidies but also national banking, payments to Indians, and military contracts – had transferred "a vast amount" of this southern treasure directly to the North. (The truth of this claim is still debatable.) Combined with exclusion from the territories, this capital transfer (rather than any natural, regional, or entrepreneurial advantage) explained the wealth and growth of the northern states. If such policies had not existed "it scarcely admits a doubt" that the South would have retained fully half the antebellum immigrants and its rightful share of national wealth and power.

The third and greatest series of crimes against the federal equilibrium had transformed the original "Federal Republic" into one "great national consolidated Democracy," arrogating unto itself unlimited authority over policies of every description. Between Congress bribing local voters en masse with tariff protection and internal improvements, and the Supreme Court assuming the final right to judge the limits of its own charter, Calhoun saw no effective means for states to protect their rights (and peculiarities) against a nationwide majority. South Carolinians had tried in 1831 during the nullification crisis, and Andrew Jackson sent the army to compel their surrender. Just as the North gained a preponderance that guaranteed "absolute control" over the national government, that government laid claim to a power "as absolute," said Calhoun, "as that of the Autocrat of Russia, and as despotic in its tendency as any absolute Government that ever existed."

One final step completed Calhoun's logic of doom. Northern control of a despotic government would hurt the South only if there existed some "question of vital importance" on which the two sections disagreed. Of course, the recent agitation against slavery proved that northern people "considered themselves under the most sacred obligation" to destroy African slavery. Time and again, for two generations, Americans had renewed a covenant of compromise that protected slavery in the states and – despite assurances by slaveholding founders that the "curse" *must* pass away – allowed it to spread into southwestern territories. Time and again, at least since the Missouri debates, Congressmen thought they had conceded everything to southern sensitivities, gagging themselves and their constituents, tolerating auctions at the foot of the Capitol steps even when they had the votes to abolish the slave trade in the District of Columbia. Now they were gathered in 1850 to broker one more compromise – to extend the tradition of forbearance that had sustained the Union six decades running – and here stood Calhoun (actually he lay dying on a pallet while someone read his speech) denouncing it all as a sham and an impasse (Knupfer 1991: ch. 5).

Calhoun's final declamation, however tortured as history, proved absolutely brilliant as polemical analysis. Northern politicians indeed could dream of sectional control of the federal government, but as yet they shared no intention to abuse the South or emancipate the slaves. Northern people felt as buffeted as southerners by changes set in motion by the market revolution, and there was nothing like a single point of view that could be tapped on anything beyond the narrowest commitment to "free soil" – the exclusion of slaves (and blacks) from states and territories where they did not already reside. More than once in the past quarter-century, Calhoun himself had rallied the voters of the West, slave and free, on behalf of states' rights against the threat of Washington's consolidated reach. On matters of banking, tariff protection, and internal improvements (the last of which they desperately desired) western interests always had divided and usually had sided with the South against what Jackson called a "monied aristocracy" residing in the eastern states.

The market revolution – like a Cheshire cat, just coming into view as Calhoun's words were read – clearly fed the prosperity and growth of the northern states, but hardly anyone was ready yet in 1850 to believe there had grown up within the Union two distinct and hostile systems of political economy. Now Calhoun planted the seed of a fateful interpretation, and while exchanging insults over the next 10 years, commentators North and South would generate a literature (dare we say a liturgy?) that affirmed the very worst of that dark vision. By casting the North as the *intentional* architect of the modern, liberal, capitalistic system, Calhoun polarized the options and made enemies of men and women who still questioned banks and corporations and the money power, but who knew the difference between slavery and freedom.

In the end, what we make of the market revolution that so dramatically transformed the antebellum North depends on what it is we wish to explain about the United States, the rise of modern capitalism, the evolution of popular democracy, the success (or failure?) of American constitutionalism, or the mounting sectional crisis and impending Civil War. Claiming freedom from the restraints of the British class system, material scarcity, European tradition, and legal inequality, early Americans reached for wealth and power in whatever ways they found congenial. Given a fluid field for innovation and creativity, some prospered more than others, some innovated more than others, some consolidated their winnings and reached for bigger and bigger things. If there is anything "natural" about the capitalist system it is that, absent restraint and regulation, free enterprise and market exchanges will produce big winners, growth, innovation, and an ever-quicker circulation of goods and money. Yet Adam Smith (1993 [1776]) admitted in *The Wealth of Nations* that this is not the *intended* result but the *unintended consequence* of individual purposeful actions. Herein lies the key to our confusion (and theirs): good or bad intentions had little to do with the market revolution.

If there is anything else "natural" about the capitalist system it is the tendency of the winners in a free market system to seek ways to protect their success and prevent the erosion of their winnings due to further competition and innovation. Part of this is inherent in complex system designs: early solutions to problems always yield pathways or components that are built into future generations of solutions. Both technological hardware and cultural software, including personal habits and conventional wisdom, become locked in and more or less invulnerable (like the Microsoft operating system producing this text). Part of this is beneficial, but part of it results from nefarious, greedy, and monopolistic behavior (Microsoft again), and it serves more to lock out new contenders for wealth and power than to develop the system or improve the efficiency of transactions. This aspect Adam Smith did not foresee; in fact, he so associated market interference with governmental favor that he fancied the free market to be immune to other such distortions. But early Americans saw it plenty, and this was the evidence that fostered Jackson's antibank and anticorporation sentiments, labor's anticapitalist rhetoric, and historians' persistent search for the agents of infection who first introduced this pathological behavior.

In retrospect we tend to see the market revolution as inevitable because it happened, because it made the world the way we recognize it at the present time, and because winners always tend to adjust our working ideology to support the outcomes they enjoy. Contemporaries, less sanguine about their own futures and far less certain about the source of their own prosperity, looked for more proximate threats to the conditions that sustained their freedom. Whether drawn by positive experiences with entrepreneurial liberty or driven by fear of Africans, immigrants, and bewildering change, northerners in the 1850s came to see liberty, democracy, and capitalism as so intertwined as to be inseparable. Competitive individualism had replaced virtuous republicanism as the template for American success, and northerners – even those still limited in means and opportunities – began to think in terms of a formulation made famous by Eric Foner (1970): "Free soil, free labor, free men." After 1848, as the apparent "slave power" that ruled the South placed ever-more threatening demands on federal politics and federal policies, the northern children of the market revolution finally threw down the gauntlet, not against the agents of modern capitalism but against its howling critics in the planter class, who seemed willing to obstruct all progress in order to defend their own "peculiar institution."

BIBLIOGRAPHY

Albion, Robert G. (1939) *The Rise of New York Port, 1815–1860.* New York: Charles Scribner's Sons.

Appleby, Joyce Oldham (2000) *Inheriting the Revolution: The First Generation of Americans.* Cambridge, Mass.: Belknap Press.

Ashworth, John (1995) *Slavery, Capitalism and Politics in the Antebellum Republic.* Volume 1: *Commerce and Compromise, 1820–1850.* Cambridge: Cambridge University Press.

Benson, Lee (1955) *Merchants, Farmers, and Railroads; Railroad Regulation and New York Politics.* Cambridge, Mass.: Harvard University Press.

Boorstin, Daniel J. (1965) *The Americans: The National Experience.* New York: Random House.

Browne, Gary L. (1980) *Baltimore in the New Nation.* Chapel Hill: University of North Carolina Press.

Chandler, Alfred D., Jr (1977) *The Visible Hand: The Managerial Revolution in American Business.* Cambridge, Mass.: Belknap Press.

Clark, Christopher (1990) *The Roots of Rural Capitalism: Western Massachusetts, 1780–1860.* Ithaca, NY: Cornell University Press.

Coleman, Peter J. (1963) *The Transformation of Rhode Island, 1790–1860.* Providence, RI: Brown University Press.

Congressional Globe (1850) 31st Congress, 1st Session, US Senate, Washington, DC.

Dublin, Thomas (1979) *Women at Work: The Transformation of Work and Community at Lowell, Massachusetts, 1826–1860.* New York: Columbia University Press.

Feller, Daniel (1995) *Jacksonian Promise.* Baltimore, Md.: Johns Hopkins University Press.

Foner, Eric (1970) *Free Soil, Free Labor, Free Men: The Ideology of the Republican Party Before the Civil War.* New York: Oxford University Press.

Freyer, Tony A. (1994) *Producers Versus Capitalists: Constitutional Conflict in Antebellum America.* Charlottesville, Va.: University Press of Virginia.

Gilchrist, David T. (ed.) (1967) *The Growth of the Seaport Cities, 1790–1825.* Charlottesville, Va.: University Press of Virginia.

Gilje, Paul A. (1997) *Wages of Independence: Capitalism in the Early American Republic.* Madison, Wis.: Madison House Publishers.

Handlin, Oscar and Handlin, Mary Flug (1947) *Commonwealth: A Study of the Role of Government in the American Economy: Massachusetts, 1774–1861.* New York: New York University Press.

Hartz, Louis (1948) *Economic Policy and Democratic Thought in Pennsylvania, 1776–1860.* Cambridge, Mass.: Harvard University Press.

Hartz, Louis (1955) *The Liberal Tradition in America.* New York: Harcourt Brace.

Henretta, James A. (1991) *The Origins of American Capitalism: Collected Essays.* Boston, Mass.: Northeastern University Press.

Horwitz, Morton J. (1977) *The Transformation of American Law, 1780–1860.* Cambridge, Mass.: Harvard University Press.

Howe, Daniel Walker (1979) *The Political Culture of the American Whigs.* Chicago: University of Chicago Press.

Hunter, Louis C. (1949) *Steamboats on the Western Rivers.* Cambridge, Mass.: Harvard University Press.

Hunter, Louis C. (1979, 1985) *A History of Industrial Power in the United States, 1780–1930,* three vols. Volume 1: *Water Power in the Century of Steam.* Volume 2: *Steam Power.* Charlottesville, Va.: University Press of Virginia.

Hurst, James Willard (1956) *Law and the Conditions of Freedom in the Nineteenth-Century United States.* Madison, Wis.: University of Wisconsin Press.

Jensen, Joan (1986) *Loosening the Bonds: Mid-Atlantic Farm Women, 1750–1850.* New Haven, Conn.: Yale University Press.

Johnson, Paul E. (1978) *A Shopkeeper's Millennium: Society and Revivals in Rochester, New York, 1815–1837.* New York: Hill and Wang.

Knupfer, Peter B. (1991) *The Union As It Is: Constitutional Unionism and Sectional Compromise, 1787–1861*. Chapel Hill, NC: University of North Carolina Press.

Kulikoff, Alan (1992) *The Agrarian Origins of American Capitalism*. Charlottesville, Va.: University Press of Virginia.

Kutler, Stanley I. (1971) *Privilege and Creative Destruction: The Charles River Bridge Case*. New York: W. W. Norton.

Larson, John Lauritz (2001a [1984]) *Bonds of Enterprise: John Murray Forbes and Western Development in America's Railway Age*. Iowa City, Iowa: University of Iowa Press.

Larson, John Lauritz (2001b) *Internal Improvement: National Public Works and the Promise of Popular Government in the Early United States*. Chapel Hill, NC: University of North Carolina Press.

Lindstrom, Diane (1978) *Economic Development in the Philadelphia Region, 1810–1850*. New York: Columbia University Press.

Meinig, D. W. (1998) *The Making of America: A Geographical Perspective on 500 Years of History*, four vols. Volume 2: *Continental America, 1800–1867*. New Haven, Conn.: Yale University Press.

Novak, William J. (1996) *The People's Welfare: Law and Regulation in Nineteenth-Century America*. Chapel Hill, NC: University of North Carolina Press.

Perkins, Edwin J. (1994) *American Public Finance and Financial Services, 1700–1815*. Columbus, Ohio: Ohio State University Press.

Potter, David M. (1954) *People of Plenty, Economic Abundance and the American Character*. Chicago: University of Chicago Press.

Pred, Alan R. (1973) *Urban Growth and the Circulation of Information: The United States System of Cities, 1790–1840*. Cambridge, Mass.: Harvard University Press.

Prude, Jonathan (1983) *The Coming of Industrial Order: Town and Factory Life in Massachusetts, 1810–1860*. New York: Cambridge University Press.

Prude, Jonathan and Hahn, Steven (eds.) (1985) *The Countryside in the Age of Capitalist Transformation*. Chapel Hill: University of North Carolina Press.

Rilling, Donna J. (2000) *Making Houses, Crafting Capitalism: Builders in Philadelphia, 1790–1850*. Philadelphia, Pa.: University of Pennsylvania Press.

Rohrbough, Malcolm J. (1978) *The Trans-Appalachian Frontier: People, Societies, and Institutions, 1775–1850*. New York: Oxford University Press.

Rosenberg, Nathan (1972) *Technology and American Economic Growth*. New York: Harper & Row.

Ross, Steven J. (1985) *Workers on the Edge: Work, Leisure, and Politics in Industrializing Cincinnati, 1788–1890*. New York: Columbia University Press.

Rothenberg, Winifred Barr (1992) *From Market-Places to a Market Economy: The Transformation of Rural Massachusetts, 1750–1850*. Chicago: University of Chicago Press.

Sellers, Charles G. (1991) *The Market Revolution: Jacksonian America, 1815–1846*. New York: Oxford University Press.

Smith, Adam (1993 [1776]) *The Wealth of Nations: An Inquiry into the Nature and Causes of the Wealth of Nations*. Oxford: Oxford University Press.

Taylor, Alan (1996) *William Cooper's Town: Power and Persuasion on the Frontier of the Early American Republic*. New York: Random House.

Thompson, E. P. (1971) "The Moral Economy of the English Crowd in the Eighteenth Century," *Past & Present* 50: 76–136.

Trollope, Frances (1993) *Domestic Manners of the Americans*. Edited and with an introduction by John Lauritz Larson. St James, NY: Brandywine Press.

Tucker, Barbara M. (1984) *Samuel Slater and the Origins of the American Textile Industry, 1790–1860*. Ithaca, NY: Cornell University Press.

Wade, Richard C. (1959) *The Urban Frontier: The Rise of Western Cities, 1790–1830*. Cambridge, Mass.: Harvard University Press.

Watson, Harry L. (1990) *Liberty and Power: The Politics of Jacksonian America*. New York: Noonday Press.

Wattenberg, Ben J. (ed.) (1976) *The Statistical History of the United States*. New York: Basic Books.

Wilentz, Sean (1984) *Chants Democratic: New York City and the Rise of the American Working Class, 1788–1850*. New York: Oxford University Press.

Wood, Gordon S. (1969) *The Creation of the American Republic, 1776–1787*. Chapel Hill, NC: University of North Carolina Press.

Wood, Gordon S. (1992) *Radicalism of the American Revolution*. New York: Alfred A. Knopf.

CHAPTER THREE

Slavery and the Old South

LARRY HUDSON

> . . . if it be not now, yet it will come
> – the readiness is all.
> Hamlet 5:3:212

Two features of slavery in the Old South distinguished it from slavery elsewhere in the Americas: the family and the relative absence of large-scale servile rebellion. It is not by accident that the two are related: where and when enslaved family forms became an integral component of the slave community, the occurrence of overt and violent acts of resistance declined markedly. It should come as no surprise that both enslaver and enslaved had a vested interest – fundamentally different but mutually beneficial – in the well-being of a productive, stable black family. The story of the Old South describes the decline in overt black resistance to the institution of slavery, and the black community's deepening commitment to the family.

Long before the American Revolution, there was a noticeable decline in aggressive acts of resistance. As John Boles (1984: 70) writes, "with wives and children to think about, black males were less willing to risk open rebellion." By the end of the antebellum period, the wide array of tactics used by the enslaved to establish and maintain a stable family life became the primary counter-revolutionary force in American slavery. Given the obstacles they had to overcome, these people were successful. Enslaved African Americans tended to look to the amelioration of their day-to-day lives while patiently waiting for the freedom they knew would come. Unlike earlier generations, for these slaves the fight against slavery would be the struggle toward a different kind of freedom.

Throughout much of the seventeenth and part of the eighteenth centuries, there were frequent attacks against the institution of slavery, often led by men born in Africa who were determined to rise in order to end their enslavement, slavery itself, and establish free societies. Ira Berlin (1998) suggests that one result of the "creolization" or Americanization of the enslaved populations, as they made the cultural transition from Africans to African Americans, was the shift away from direct and violent attacks on slavery. Not only did the size and frequency of slave insurrections decline, but also that of departures from the plantation. As Loren Schweninger and John Hope Franklin (1999) have reconfirmed, the decision to flee slavery was no simple matter. Motivated by a complex array of factors, it was always accompanied by acute risk to the individual, his or her family, and to the whole slave quarters community. Furthermore, those participating in these risky acts of resistance tended to be overwhelmingly young, male, and single. For the remainder, the vast majority of enslaved African Americans, therefore, life was characterized not by flight, but by purposeful "watchful waiting." Sound instincts, born from experience and combined with their religious faith, confirmed in them the belief that freedom would come through patience and preparedness, and not through a mad, headlong dash for the "Promised Land."

Their goal was to one day live as free men and women. Their strategy, in a word, was "readiness." These were not passive beings simply waiting for freedom in a celestial tomorrow; readiness demanded a constant and deliberate struggle against an evil institution, while preparing themselves for freedom. They would look to the institutions necessary for their survival and their preparedness for freedom. Of primary importance were the strength and stability of the family, their religious beliefs and practices, and the opportunity to materially improve the quality of their lives. For enslaved black Americans in the Old South, family and community were both the means and the measurement of their survival under slavery and their readiness for freedom. While no less desirable, physical freedom from slavery remained a distant goal. More immediate, and to be pursued no less aggressively with countless visible and less visible attacks on the slavery, was a freedom "in" slavery.

Historians of slavery continue to struggle to find the right balance between the picture of the all-powerful slaveowner and the debased, docile slave, on the one hand, and the ingenious, resilient, and autonomous slave, on the other. An earlier generation of historians provided the foundations that would culminate in the Stanley Elkins' (1959) image of the "Sambo" – the happy-go-lucky, master-loving slave. Most of them allowed that slavery not only stunted the development of the enslaved, but also left them ill-prepared to make a successful transition to freedom. No institution had suffered more from the brutal callousness of human slavery than the black family. In the mid-1960s, Daniel Moynihan, a member of the Lyndon B. Johnson administration, drew on the work of these historians and observed that "At the heart of the deterioration of the fabric of Negro Society is the deterioration of the Negro family" (1967: 5), and the problems faced by black families in American cities were clear legacies of their ancestors' enslavement. According to Moynihan, American slavery was the most awful the world has ever known and "it was by destroying the Negro family under slavery that white America broke the will of the Negro people" (1967: 30). The black family, he concluded, was caught in "a tangle of pathology" from which it could not extricate itself "without assistance from the white world" (1967: 47).

Coming in the midst of the Civil Rights Movement and the specter of black rebellion, Moynihan's report created an academic maelstrom, yet, as one of his strongest critics, Herbert Gutman (1976), points out, Moynihan had not created a "fictive history." He had simply reported what was then "conventional academic wisdom." Nonetheless, what followed would be both an attack on Moynihan and a challenge to the work of earlier historians. In the forefront of this new scholarship were John Blassingame, Eugene Genovese, and Robert Fogel and Stanley Engerman, and, of course, Gutman. These historians would rely on new approaches, sources, methodologies, and technologies. Previously, much of what we learned about slavery and slaves had been provided by documentation left us by slaveholders. The 1970s saw a new direction in slavery studies that drew heavily on a wide variety of plantation records, and, almost for the first time, sources that included the voice and perspectives of the enslaved. The best example of the latter is the 1930s Work Progress Administration interviews of former slaves.

What emerged was a picture, best presented by John Blassingame (1976), of black people under slavery who were culturally connected to their African past, sufficiently adept to avoid the more damaging effects of American slavery. Able to build a life of their own under slavery, they stepped into freedom relatively unscathed. The primary institution that made black survival possible, and slave life so culturally vibrant, was a ubiquitous two-parent slave family structure. In his attack on Moynihan's most damaging claims, Gutman's (1976) *The Black Family in Slavery and Freedom*, presented compelling evidence of long-lasting, two-parent families on plantations throughout the Old South. Slavery, it seems, had not seriously impaired the black family.

Among Eugene Genovese's many contributions to this new scholarship was *Roll, Jordan, Roll: The World the Slaves Made* (1974). As the subtitle suggests, it exposed the world of the enslaved and offered a brilliant discussion of a paternalistic relationship that bound together slaveowner and slave. Accepted by both, paternalism, he argues, "afforded a fragile bridge across the intolerable contradictions inherent in a society based on racism, slavery, and class exploitation that had to depend on the willing productivity of its victims" (1974: 5). Here was a mechanism with which scholars could begin to reveal and better understand the operation and meaning of the intimate world of the enslaved. As most of us accepted, slaveowners dealt the cards and kept the best for themselves. What *Roll, Jordan, Roll* made clear, however, was that powerful as they were, slaveholders could not keep all the best cards for themselves. And, armed even with only the poorest cards, the enslaved sometimes gained the upper hand because they had the ability to elicit from owners privileges which soon became rights that could be rescinded without some risk to the good order and morale of the plantation.

Despite abolitionists' success in painting slaveholders as both evil and incompetent, Fogel and Engerman (1974), with the tools of the cliometric, have shown us that slaveholders were not fools, and that human slavery was a profitable (if not entirely efficient) means of exploiting southern agriculture. In *Time on the Cross*, slaveholders appear to be rational and pragmatic beings who were not afraid to use positive incentives to encourage satisfactory behavior among their black labor force.

Individually and collectively, these scholars have shifted conventional academic wisdom and revealed a very different picture of the slave past: a system of slavery that was not so closed, slaveowners not so powerful, and slaves not so powerless that no choices were available to them. Enslaved African Americans were able to squeeze out a modicum of autonomy – a "living space" within a cruel and brutal institution to make a life and a world for themselves. Gutman went so far as to suggest that the social and cultural practices of the slaves did not even require scholars to have much knowledge of their owners. Accordingly, the story about slavery, slave life, and culture is about what the enslaved did, not what was done to them. These historians have not only altered the way we look at the past and its influence on our world today, but also changed the very questions we formulate about slavery and the Old South.

As the 1990s drew to a close, some historians began to question the accuracy of these pictures of the slave past. In his excellent synthesis of the literature, for example, Peter Kolchin (1993: 137) observes that some of our arguments for the "slave autonomy have been overstated and eventually will be modified on the basis of future evidence." More recently, Colin Palmer opined:

> We have come so far that the image of broken traumatized Samboes has been replaced with that of the resilient, Teflon-coated person who endured much but also created much, and who walked away from his/her oppression . . . relatively unscathed psychologically. (Palmer 1996: 74)

The work of Genovese and Gutman has especially informed much of the scholarship since the 1970s. Genovese has been taken to task for his use of paternalism, and some have doubted the chances of the millions of enslaved who lived on farms and small plantations to find suitable partners with whom to begin, much less maintain, a two-parent family. Despite these concerns, the picture of busy, hardworking, family-centered slaves has become a compelling vision of the past. Our lens on the slave past has shifted a long way since the mid-1970s. Like the institution itself, it defies easy categorization.

If nothing else, Philip Morgan's (1998) *Slave Counterpoint* describes the very breadth, depth, and variety of the institution of slavery and, even with the similarities that abound, there are huge differences that render it changeable and different. His overriding aim is to demonstrate that slavery was no monolithic, unchanging institution; that it varied immensely over time and place. In successfully doing so, he has removed some of the obstacles that render it difficult or impossible for us to view slavery as anything but an evil and morally unsound system or to draw any moral distinction between "slaveries."

Slavery took shape differently in the many regions of the South. Even within the same community one could identify variations, each with important consequences for the growth and development of black culture and society. The efforts of Ira Berlin and Philip Morgan (1993) have done much to undermine the lingering tendency among historians of slavery to view the institution as a monolithic system, static and unchanging. Although it was an institution organized for the primary purpose of exploiting the labor of a group of people, American slavery was continually in flux. As the institution developed as a means to exploit the widespread availability of land on which to grow tobacco and alleviate a chronic shortage of willing laborers, it was never automatically or originally racial. American slavery took some time to develop and did so in a relatively haphazard fashion, beginning with a period that still remains murky. Before the 1660s, for example, the exact distinctions between the treatment and status of white European indentured servants, Native Americans, and African servants is unclear. Edmund Morgan (1975) marks the rebellion led by Nathaniel Bacon in 1676 as a significant moment in American racial adjustment and the confirmation of black slavery. The advantages of racial slavery, as a means of maintaining white cohesion and thus minimizing the risk of class tensions, he suggests, proved irresistible for the Virginia elite.

It was not until the eighteenth century, however, that Americans, white and black, established the broader patterns of racial slavery. Always changing in response to external factors such as access to the international slave trade, and internal ones such as mortality and fertility rates, the institution was seldom static. Less easily quantified factors such as "creolization" or "Americanization" also influenced the form, function, and viability of slavery. These factors would shape the life experiences of the enslaved. While the basic philosophy of slavery would remain unchanged – maximum exploitation of the enslaved black labor at minimum expense to the enslaver – African Americans developed an array of techniques to create a dynamic cultural and spiritual life of their own under slavery.

By 1808, the official closing of the slave trade, a number of events had ensured a rapid process of creolization – Africans became African Americans. Most noticeable was the religious fervor that resulted from the First Great Awakening in the 1730s; added to this was the spread of the post-revolutionary antislavery sentiment, especially in the northern states, and, in the South, the maturity of the plantation communities. These factors, and many others, combined and, sometimes imperceptibly, altered the relationship between enslavers and the enslaved. In this climate, the importance placed upon the *de jure* laws of slavery (which in many ways were becoming more harsh) declined as slaveholders, increasingly adamant about their property rights, independence, and liberty, determined to become masters of their households. These men made and acted upon their own rules – often more lax than the law allowed – jealously guarding their authority on the home place. They decided which rights their enslaved workers could enjoy. Only when the latter's conduct threatened the good order of society were they obliged to resort to the rigid and harsh firmness of the law.

Most scholars agree that important as were the formal rules of slavery, it was the rules and regulations operating within the slaveholders' domain that most concerned and shaped the world of slavery in which both the owners and the owned lived their lives. For example, although the enslaved could not legally marry, own property, read, write, trade their goods, carry arms, hunt, manage plantations, and so on, to varying degrees they did all of the above. Human slavery, as Orlando Patterson (1982) shows, has always been an interpersonal relationship at the mercy of forces not always easily controlled by enslaver or enslaved. In America this was also the case. Often, what took place on the home place was the result of constant struggle between an owner who often lacked either the interest or the energy necessary to fight slave quarters communities determined to wrest for themselves some small concession from reluctant owners. An exception, of course, was the South Carolina planter, James Henry Hammond, who had to endure his share of defeats at the hands of his slaves. Drew Faust (1982) describes the travails of a slaveholder who desired a more complete mastery over his black workers, the nature of which could only follow from some reciprocal arrangement beneficial to the enslaved. Hammond, like many of his ilk, had to concede a great deal to his black workers in order to "master" his black workforce. On his plantation, and many others throughout the Old South, enslavers and enslaved struggled, often within a paternalist understanding, to dominate and control important areas of their lives.

These constant contests produced a battery of encounters, some of which were clear victories for the enslaved, as slaveholders, in the name of moral and good order, were obliged to make more and more concessions to their enslaved populations. As Eugene Genovese makes clear in *Roll, Jordan, Roll*, paternalism with its "insistence upon mutual obligations – duties, responsibilities, and ultimately even rights" (1974: 5) held open the possibility of victory for the enslaved, minuscule at times, but power did sometimes shift from enslaver to enslaved. The cumulative effect of slaveowner concessions to their workers was the creation of a social and cultural space between the lives and the worlds of these two antagonists. While never entirely separate or discrete, given an ever-present, constant, and volatile interdependency, both sides learnt what could be expected from the other, and how far the other might safely be pushed. Until either side overstepped acceptable practice, there could exist a tentative peace – "a living space" between them. The relationship between enslavers and enslaved, always fraught, was never without dramatic moments of violence and passion. By the late eighteenth century, accommodation and rebelliousness were no longer "two poles of behavior." Enslaved African Americans fought an ongoing war with their enslavers to make a life of their own under slavery. In their daily battles against the dehumanizing potential of human slavery, there were many thousands of acts of successful rebellion.

Like other Americans, there were factors that determined the life experiences of the enslaved. Among these were their place of birth, demographics, gender, location, and, importantly, the crop or industry in which they were bound to labor. These variables were important predictors of their social and cultural development. Historians now anticipate significant dissimilarities in the life and work style of enslaved people in northern slave systems, or in urban settings, when compared with those living and working on southern farms and plantations. Furthermore, communities where crops such as tobacco, rice, cotton, or sugar predominated all appear to have produced some unique social arrangements the nature of which determined how the enslaved organized and viewed their world.

Available evidence suggests that enslaved black people in the Old South were neither foolish nor reckless people. The relative absence of large-scale revolts and other acts of overt resistance should not be mistaken for an "accommodation" – the gradual wearing down by a cruel system that turned grown men and women into docile, obedient, dependent creatures. This was not generally the case. The attention these people devoted to their families and communities demonstrated a determination, strength, and enduring patience that incorporated a focus on the immediate, daily concerns of their lives. They also had an eye to a not-too-distant future when they would live their lives unburdened by the physical and emotional demands of slavery.

Perhaps the most crucial variable touching all areas of the lives of the enslaved, and others who lived and worked in agricultural communities, was the crop they were obliged to cultivate. Gavin Wright (1978) assigns a good deal of power to the Old South's primary crop. It was the very nature of cotton cultivation that gave the South a prosperity, growth, and unity that it could not otherwise have had. He contends that as long as there remained the opportunity for upward social mobility – the possibility of owning land and slaves – class relations would remain stable and fairly harmonious despite the large-scale economic inequality. Enslaved African Americans are yet to be fully incorporated into this organic, interdependent, and essentially democratic picture of the Old South. By the 1820s, most enslaved

Americans were working in cotton-producing areas, and an increasing number of them were actively engaged in producing small amounts of cotton for their own benefit. As such, they too were exposed to the cultural power of the "fleecy staple."

Given that some slave families could produce anything from a few pounds to a half or a whole bale of cotton, they clearly had "a stake in slavery." As John Campbell (1993) shows, the contest between cotton-producing masters and cotton-producing slaves extended beyond the home place and into the wider arena of international cotton prices as the latter looked to market their crops to the highest bidders. Enslaved workers took advantage of their opportunities to add to the quality of their lives under slavery.

In the South Carolina and Georgia lowcountry, a system of labor developed where slaveowners assigned their workers a particular area of land to be worked – typically a quarter of an acre for most planting operations. Once the "task" was satisfactorily completed the worker could use the remainder of the day to his or her benefit. Coupled with the task system of labor was the provision of a small garden – anything from the small area around their cabins to several acres somewhere else on the plantation. The benefits to both enslavers and enslaved soon became clear as the task and garden system promised to instill discipline in the enslaved, while allowing the enslaved the opportunity to produce crops and foodstuff for themselves which they could barter or sell. Several recent publications have brought a great deal of attention to the operation of the task system and the extent to which lowcountry slaves were able to accumulate property and with it improve the quality of their lives under slavery. Not surprisingly, historians have tended to identify these opportunities exclusively with the rice-producing regions of the lowcountry, and exclude the vast majority of the enslaved from the potential economic and social benefits of a work system that allowed them some control over the length of the work day and the opportunity to produce goods for their own use. In fact, the overwhelming majority of enslaved workers in the Old South had some access to "extra-work" activities. Paying their workers for extra weekend work, allowing them the occasional day or half-day off to work their gardens, and purchasing the products of their gardens, enslavers used a range of work and garden systems to encourage their workers to "grab a stake in slavery."

The collection of conference papers published under the title *Cultivation and Culture: Labor and the Shaping of Slave Life in the Americas* (Berlin and Morgan 1993) is a testament to the efforts of the enslaved to use a variety of work and garden systems to create a life for themselves and their families under slavery. For example, in the South Carolina upcountry where the task system was subordinated to workers operating not individually but in gangs, John Campbell shows that they found time to work their gardens and to participate in the internal economy "to better themselves materially" (1993: 244). These upcountry bondsmen and women used their opportunities to "assert greater control and independence in their lives, create and strengthen social relationships." Even farther north in the Piedmont regions of northern Virginia described by John T. Schlotterbeck (1991), the absence of a sophisticated task system, and the mixed farming practices of the region with its limitations on the amount of land slaveowners could make available to their black workers, the enslaved showed their determination and ability to accumulate extra goods for exchange or sale. Even on Louisiana sugar plantations, as Roderick

McDonald (1993) shows, the enslaved workers produced crops for themselves and accumulated property that they used to improve the quality of life and make their houses, gardens, and ground the "focus for their family and community life" (McDonald 1993: 15). Although the work and garden system was widespread, the task system should not be seen as peculiar to the lowcountry, but simply the most sophisticated expression of work and garden systems familiar to enslaved workers throughout the South.

Much to slaveowners' satisfaction, the growing economic activity on the part of the enslaved led to an increased involvement in the economy of slavery as well as a deepening commitment to family, community, and place. As Rufus King, overseer and slaveholder, summed up so neatly in 1828: "every means be used to encourage [enslaved workers] and impress on their minds the advantage of holding property and the disgrace of idleness." Old South slave managers exercised these and a wide range of other measures to encourage their workers to develop what they identified as good, regular, and productive habits. As Larry Hudson (1997: XX) points out, "if they could be taught the value of industry and enterprise through the management of their own piece of land, then, so the argument went, these qualities would be reflected in the work they did for their owner and in their feelings both for him and for the home place."

The work that the enslaved performed in their own time, earning cash money from owners or neighbors, or more typically in small garden patches around their cabins where they produced crops and raised livestock for sale or exchange, increased the amount of money, goods, and services at their disposal. This expansion of goods and services created an internal economy wherein they established and maintained a regular commercial traffic between themselves and others. The ensuing economic activity of the enslaved provided a foundation for their domestic and community life, and shaped the social institutions in the quarters.

It was only a matter of time before the family and work activities of the enslaved resulted in the construction of self-imposed obstacles to any mass flight from slavery. The investment in the family, in their work gardens, and community life, not only discouraged risky escape attempts, but also rendered fundamentally different the day-to-day experience of slavery. Under slavery, adults, parents, and grandparents whenever possible, had to be responsible for their dependants, and increasingly to their community. Running away and other overt acts of resistance threatened the very institutions they held more dear than freedom.

The stability of the black family under slavery, often precarious, obliged the enslaved to channel much of their physical, emotional, and economic resources to its mainten-ance. To better understand their world and the achievements they made under slavery, scholars now focus their attention on the contributions the enslaved made to protect the institution of the family. Previously, their primary focus had been on the enslaver, but this has shifted to members of the family themselves. As John Boles (1984: 70) suggests, "attention should focus on what slave owners . . . did not do and how slaves in large measure controlled their own lives." Whether we like it or not, the decisions made by large numbers of enslaved African Americans in the late eighteenth and early nineteenth centuries profoundly shaped the institution of slavery. For better or worse, slaveowners were in no position to create a system entirely of their own design. The prioritizing of family, community, and religion by the enslaved assured the enslavers that even short-term defeats could bring about medium- and long-term benefits. For the enslaved, this was the price they would have to pay if they were to have any hope of realizing their immediate needs. Longer term, as DuBois (1992[1935]) suggested, they would prepare themselves and wait. They would ready themselves. Nothing was of more importance to enslaved communities than the familial ties that bound them together into families and communities.

The social and political cohesiveness of the white South, as Gavin Wright argued so persuasively in *The Political Economy of the Cotton South*, was made possible by the very nature of cotton cultivation. It was cotton, he argues, that gave the South "a prosperity, growth and unity that it could not otherwise have had . . . despite the large scale economic inequality" (Wright 1978: 15).

The most crucial variable touching all areas of the lives of the enslaved was the crop they were obliged to cultivate, and, by 1820, the most enslaved Americans were working in cotton-producing areas. Furthermore, an increasing number of them were actively engaged in producing small amounts of the cotton for their own benefit. As such, they too were part of the organic world facilitated by the fleecy staple. When families could expect to produce anywhere from a few pounds to a half sometimes even a whole bale of cotton, they had reasonable cause to look to a more immediate amelioration of their life situation rather than to flee to what Frederick Douglass termed a "doubtful freedom" (1986: 123). Until Union troops approached the farms and plantations of the South, mass flight was as uncommon as it was irresponsible.

The recent work on the operation of plantation labor systems, and their shaping of black life under slavery, has returned our attention once again to the "task system." Most prevalent in the rice-producing regions of lowcountry South Carolina and Georgia, black workers there could accumulate property and improve the quality of their lives under slavery. Historians, however, have tended to associate the task and garden labor system exclusively with rice production. Thus the vast majority of the enslaved, who worked neither in the rice fields nor in the lowcountry, were denied the opportunity to engage in the sometimes lucrative enterprise of "extra-work" activities. In fact, the overwhelming majority of enslaved workers in the rural South had some access to "extra-work" activities with all their monetary and psychological promise. Once proven as a satisfactory work system in rice cultivation, tasking soon spread to a wider variety of labor activities on the plantation, and then well beyond the lowcountry to other parts of the Old South, taking with it a degree of trust and mutual responsibility on the part of enslaver and enslaved. Clearly, the benefits that accrued to the enslaved – work, family, and community – resulted in self-imposed obstacles to any widespread violent resistance to their enslavement.

Work and garden systems, of which the task and garden system should be seen not as peculiar but as the most sophisticated expression, were familiar to most of the southern enslaved workers. The internal economy that it fueled allowed the enslaved a real opportunity to aspire to the provision and maintenance of stable, hardworking, healthy families. The stability of the black family under slavery, precarious at best, obliged the enslaved to channel much of their physical, emotional, and economic resources to its protection. To better understand their world and the achievements they made under slavery, scholars now focus their attention on the contributions made by individuals to maintain its integrity. Previously, their primary focus had been on the enslaver, but this has shifted to members of the family themselves.

Recent departures in the field of family and gender studies have opened a wider window onto the more intimate life of enslaved men and women. They present these folks in their many and varied roles of husbands, wives, parents, grandparents, children, providers, consumers, hard workers as well as shirkers. These studies reveal multilayered familial relationships that present complex family structures where previously the dominant image of the slave family was that of the dependent mother and child.

One unforeseen result of the work and garden system was its favoring of able-bodied workers, particularly male workers. Any suggestion, however, that enslaved males enjoyed more independence and autonomy than their female counterparts did not sit easily with slaveowners. As Genovese (1974) points out, in his various roles as artisan, hunter, fisherman, market gardener, and musician, the male was, along with the planter, a major provider for his family. Those who found this gender behavior acceptable sometimes used it to discipline black males. By having to work with women labor gangs in the fields or being compelled to wash the family's clothes and attend to house cleaning, these men were forced to perform "women's work." The humiliation that these men felt suggests that slave quarters communities embraced these gender distinctions. Without much consideration, most enslavers probably constructed management strategies for their farms and plantations on what one scholar terms "patriarchal and capitalist assumptions" (Jones 1985: 12). If not quite a wholesome picture of male patriarchy, it is a long way from the dependent, irresponsible Sambo image sketched by Stanley Elkins. Falling somewhere between the two is the egalitarian relationship described by Deborah Gray White. In *Ar'n't I a Woman?* White (1985) examines the various stereotypes with which the black slave woman had to cope. Her discussion of the family unit, however, shows husbands and wives sharing the responsibilities for family maintenance and support. The work of other women historians sheds additional light on this question of gender relations and the slave family.

Brenda Stevenson (1996), whose work is as much a contribution to black and white family history as it is to southern history, provides a cautious note. *Life in Black and White* highlights the similarities and differences in this crucial human institution brought about by race and life in the Old South. The family and work experiences of the enslaved people she describes differs from those of Genovese (1974) and Gutman (1976a). Although she argues that the stable black family was not pervasive under slavery, she does concede that "in most families . . . men who had physical or emotional access to their families wielded some manner of control even if they did not provide much financial attention or other kinds of traditional patriarchal 'protection'" (Stevenson 1996: xii). Betty Wood's (1995) work provides a much-needed link between the revolutionary and the antebellum periods, important decades often ignored by colonialists and nineteenth-century historians alike. For Wood, the enslaved were positioned to help themselves and to shape their family life. *Women's Work, Men's Work* demonstrates how their garden produce contributed significantly to the material comfort and health of enslaved families and provided family members with a profoundly significant degree of autonomy in the organization of at least one area of their lives. Although a dilemma for slaveholders,

few had the desire, energy, or ability to challenge the developing patterns of patriarchy fueled in part by work and garden systems, a burgeoning internal economy, and
two-parent families. Where the benefits outweighed the costs, slaveholders were not
averse to letting the forces of nature and the market run their course, particularly
when they stood to benefit from family arrangements that provided them with the
means to discipline and punish younger family members through the male heads of
family. What redounded to the enslaved, of course, was a measure of social and
economic control – a "living space" wherein they could shape important elements of
their lives. As two works, Marie Jenkins Schwartz's (2000) *Born in Bondage* and
Sharla Fett's (2002) *Working Cures* suggest, there is still much to learn about black
people's life under slavery.

During the antebellum period, enslaved black people shaped and protected institutions of their own making. Of growing importance to them were the family, work
opportunities that strengthened family bonds, participation in an internal economy
that provided them with opportunities to add markedly to the quality of their lives,
and a growing faith in God. All of these combined to produce the kind of men and
women who knew the value of an aggressive but deliberate patience. Although they
were convinced that deliverance would come, they did not know when or how
it would come, but individually and collectively they knew they had to be ready.

Until the day of Jubilee arrived, enslaved African Americans were always going
to be at pains to protect the integrity of their institutions, particularly the family,
which was entirely without legal protection. Frequently broken by factors out of
their control, family stability was sometimes even out of the control of the enslavers
themselves. All too often the sudden demise of a slaveholder resulted in the breakup
and scattering of black families. Available figures for the arbitrary breakup of
enslaved families, although still inconclusive, show that the practice continued up
to the Civil War. There is some evidence, however, that the practice was declining.
Kenneth Stampp (1956) in *Peculiar Institution* suggests that slave buyers often
purchased their workers in family groups and promised not to divide them. Whether
"to win good will or to quiet the conscience of sellers," as Stampp (1956: 257)
surmised, we do know that some enslavers, particularly after the birth of radical
abolitionism in the 1830s, felt pressured to give more attention to the welfare of
their black workers. Despite these burgeoning reforming efforts, black families continued to be ripped apart by slaveowners or traders unable or unwilling to respect
the integrity of the slave family. Although Fogel and Engerman (1974) calculate
that some 13 percent of interregional slave sales resulted in marriage separations,
Michael Tadman's (1989) study allows that sentiment as well as economic benefits
could have combined to encourage enslavers and traders to sell their property in
family groups. He agrees that interregional sales resulted in marriage separations
among the enslaved that averaged about 13 percent, but estimates that it might have
been as high as 20 percent for lower South residents. What is clear, however, is that
as the antebellum period wore on, enslaved African Americans were not struggling
entirely alone to establish and maintain a stable family life.

Embraced by the reforming spirit of evangelicalism, and strongly supported by a
recently independent Southern Church determined to reform the institution of
slavery, antebellum slaveholders turned their attention to the spiritual and family life
of their enslaved workers. They increased their efforts to encourage family life among

the enslaved, to keep their black families together, and to lift the moral and religious tone of the slave quarters. These "pious" masters of men looked to model their management style not on their parents and grandparents, but on the great slave masters of biblical times.

Although the techniques that slaveholders applied in the religious education of their black workers tended toward the coercive and self-serving, the power of the Christian doctrine reached the slave quarters community and quickly became a major force in the life of the enslaved. Notions of brotherhood, marital fidelity, and the rewards of self-sacrifice began to influence the institutions in the quarters.

While the religious techniques that slaveowners used to teach their workers to behave well, accept their punishment, and to "love Master" drove many discerning slaves into their own "brush arbor" churches, few were insulated from the white churches and the lessons taught to congregations all over the South. Typically, as Boles (1984) explains, the black members sat through the whole service and heard the "same theology the whites heard"; and only at the conclusion of the service would the minister turn his attention to the slaves and address them in what was an "addendum to the main sermon." To reinforce the appropriate lessons and to spread them throughout the slave quarters, slaveowners and white ministers had to rely upon a very small cadre of pious slaves who served as the eyes, ears, and voices of the church. Although no more than 25 percent of slaves were members of white churches in 1860, the influence of religion on enslaved African Americans went far beyond these pious few.

A deepening faith increased their ability to respond to and protect themselves emotionally and spiritually against the vicissitudes of their enslavement. If nothing else, as Albert Raboteau (1978) is at pains to demonstrate, "religious slaves kept in touch with . . . an inner world where they could develop a scale of values and fixed points of vantage from which to judge the world around them and themselves." Within this "inner world" the enslaved may have found a "contentment" that "stifled outward political resistance, but it may also be argued that it represented a symbolic inward resistance, a testing of will and a victory of the spirit over brutality" (Raboteau 1978: 308). Sterling Stuckey makes a reluctant concession to the powerful effect of Christianity on the slave quarters. According to him, "the great bulk of slaves were scarcely touched by Christianity, their religious practices being vastly more African than Christian" (1987: 35). He does allow, however, that when the appeal of Christianity was combined with African practices as within the circle of the African "ring shout," "new life was breathed into Christianity" (Stuckey 1987: 37). The crucial point here is that the practice of outlawed African rituals could only safely take place under cover of Christianity. Thus, in order to avoid (and be alert to) the possibility of detection, the slaves had to familiarize themselves with the outer signs of white Christianity. At the very least, a growing number of enslaved African Americans were behaving, living and organizing their world as if they were God-fearing Christians.

Until 1861, when Union troops approached the farms and plantations of the South, mass flight was as uncommon as it was irresponsible. Typically, runaways had been male, young, and unburdened by the emotional weight of family and community. When hundreds and thousands of enslaved people fled their farm and plantation homes during the Civil War, therefore, this was of a profoundly different character.

The arrival of Union troops in the slave South altered the entire context of black escape efforts. Running ceased to be a solitary endeavor. It was a chance to gain liberty for themselves and their kindred. This was no temporary vacation from slavery, no blind rush for the northern Promised Land. This was a direct attack on the institution of slavery. Furthermore, as Ira Berlin and Leslie Rowland (1992) point out, the decision to flee slavery was a family concern. Like their revolutionary foreparents over a century earlier, their action was intended to destroy their owners' interest in slavery, and to remove themselves forever from its confines. They took with them their family, their property, and all the accumulated provisions they could carry. They turned their backs on slavery and looked forward to freedom.

Not all of those who had the opportunity to flee slavery after the outbreak of hostilities in 1861 did so. No doubt some of those who had the opportunity to flee remained on the home place, loyal to their owners or simply disinclined to risk all they had accumulated under slavery. Other factors determined the size and timing of the flight to freedom. For example, those from the border states, or those areas where fighting took place early and continued for a time, were more likely to learn quickly that the war and Union presence meant that they had a real shot at freedom. However, enslaved men and women in parts of the Confederacy removed from the fighting and Union presence were less well placed to strike for freedom. Exactly how many fled their enslavement is not clear. Irving Jordan (1995) estimates that about 15 to 20 percent reached safety within the Federal lines, but Clarence Mohr (2001 [1986]) estimates that as many as 80 percent of fugitives were probably not recorded in official documents. Those who were ready and able to flee took their opportunity and fled to the relative safety of Union lines. While many others continued to wait for clearer signs, as James Roark (1977) suggests, their altered relationship with owners did much to hasten the demise of slavery as an institution.

The absence of large-scale revolts or mass departures from the plantation should not imply "accommodation" although these people were not reckless fools. There had occurred, nonetheless, a profound adjustment in their perspective. It would take more than the moral violence, the brutal work regime, and the other by now familiar deprivations of life under slavery to bring about mass flight or collective violence. These people waited, strengthened by their expanding and deepening faith and an investment in family and community. As Berlin writes, "while slaveowners held most of the cards in the meanest of contests, slaves held cards of their own" (Berlin and Rowland 1992), the least appreciated of which was their enduring, aggressive patience – their readiness.

BIBLIOGRAPHY

Berlin, Ira (1998) *Many Thousands Gone: The First Two Centuries of Slavery in North America*. New York: Oxford University Press.

Berlin, Ira and Morgan, Philip (eds.) (1993) *Cultivation and Culture: Labor and the Shaping of Slave Life in the Americas*. Charlottesville, Va.: University of Virginia Press.

Berlin, Ira and Rowland, Leslie (1992) *Families and Freedom: A Documentary History of African-American Kinship in the Civil War Era*. New York: New Press.

Blassingame, John W. (1976) *The Slave Community: Plantation Life in the Antebellum South*, rev. edn. New York: Oxford University Press.

Boles, John B. (1984) *Black Southerners*. Lexington, Ky.: University Press of Kentucky.

Breeden, James O. (ed.) (1980) *Advice Among Masters: The Ideal in Slave Management in the Old South*. Westport, Ct: Greenwood Press.

Campbell, John (1993) "As 'A Kind of Freeman?': Slaves' Market-Related Activities in the South Carolina Upcountry," in Ira Berlin and Philip Morgan (eds.) *Cultivation and Culture: Labor and the Shaping of Slave Life in the Americas*. Charlottesville, Va.: University of Virginia Press.

Douglass, Frederick (1986 [1845]) *Narrative of the Life of Frederick Douglass: An American Slave, written by Himself*. New York: Penguin.

DuBois, W. E. B. (1992 [1935]) *Black Reconstruction: An Essay toward a History of the Part which Black Folk Played in the Attempt to Reconstruct Democracy 1860–1880*. New York: Harcourt Brace.

Elkins, Stanley (1959) *Slavery: A Problem in American Institutional and Intellectual Life*. Chicago, Ill.: University of Chicago Press.

Farmer, James O. (1986) *The Metaphysical Confederacy: James Henley Thornwell and the Synthesis of Southern Values*. Macon, Ga: Mercer University Press.

Faust, Drew Gilpin (1982) *James Henry Hammond: A Design for Mastery*. Baton Rouge, La.: Louisiana State University Press.

Fett, Sharla M. (2002) *Working Cures: Healing, Health, and Power on Southern Slave Plantations*. Chapel Hill, NC: University of North Carolina Press.

Fogel, Robert and Engerman, Stanley (1974) *Time on the Cross: The Economics of American Negro Slavery*. Boston, Mass.: Little, Brown.

Genovese, Eugene (1974) *Roll, Jordan, Roll: The World the Slaves Made*. New York: Pantheon.

Gutman, Herbert G. (1976) *The Black Family in Slavery and Freedom, 1750–1925*. New York: Pantheon.

Hudson, Larry E., Jr (1997) *"To Have and to Hold": Slave Work and Family Life in Antebellum South Carolina*. Athens, Ga.: University of Georgia Press.

Johnson, Walter (1999) *Soul by Soul: Life Inside the Antebellum Slave Market*. Cambridge, Mass.: Harvard University Press.

Jones, Jacqueline (1985) *Labor of Love, Labor of Sorrow: Black Women, Work and the Family from Slavery to the Present*. New York: Basic Books.

Jordan, Ervin L., Jr (1995) *Black Confederates and Afro-Yankees in Civil War Virginia*. Charlottesville, Va.: University of Virginia Press.

Kolchin, Peter (1993) *American Slavery, 1619–1877*. New York: Hill and Wang.

McDonald, Roderick (1993) *The Economy and Material Culture of Slaves: Goods and Chattels on the Plantations of Jamaica and Louisiana*. Baton Rouge, La.: Louisiana State University Press.

Mathews, Donald (1977) *Religion in the Old South*. Chicago, Ill.: University of Chicago Press.

Mohr, Clarence L. (2001 [1986]) *On the Threshold of Freedom: Masters and Slaves in Civil War Georgia*. Baton Rouge, La.: Louisiana State University Press.

Morgan, Edmund S. (1975) *American Slavery, American Freedom: The Ordeal of Revolutionary Virginia*. New York: Norton.

Morgan, Phillip D. (1998) *Slave Counterpoint: Black Culture in the Eighteenth-Century Chesapeake and Lowcountry*. Chapel Hill, NC: University of North Carolina Press.

Moynihan, Daniel P. (1967) "The Negro Family: The Case for National Action," in Lee Rainwater and William Yancey, *The Moynihan Report and the Politics of Controversy*. Cambridge: MIT Press.

Palmer, Colin A. (1996) "Rethinking American Slavery," in Alusine Jalloh and Stephen E. Maizlish (eds.) *The African Diaspora*. College Station, Tex.: Texas A & M University Press.

Patterson, Orlando (1982) *Slavery and Social Death: A Comparative Study.* Cambridge, Mass.:
    Harvard University Press.
Piersen, William D. (1993) *Black Legacy: America's Hidden Heritage.* University of Massa-
    chusetts Press.
Raboteau, Albert J. (1978) *Slave Religion: "The Invisible Institution" in the Antebellum South.*
    New York: Oxford University Press.
Roark, James L. (1977) *Masters without Slaves: Southern Planters in the Civil War and
    Reconstruction.* New York: Norton.
Schlotterbeck, John T. (1991) "The Internal Economy of Slavery in Rural Piedmont," in Ira
    Berlin and Philip D. Morgan (eds.) *The Slaves' Economy: Independent Production by Slaves
    in the Americas.* London: Frank Cass.
Schwartz, Marie Jenkins (2000) *Born in Bondage: Growing up Enslaved in the American
    South.* Cambridge, Mass.: Harvard University Press.
Schweninger, Loren and Franklin, John Hope (1999) *Runaway Slaves: Rebels on the Planta-
    tion.* New York: Oxford University Press.
Stampp, Kenneth M. (1956) *Peculiar Institution: Slavery in the Antebellum South.* New York:
    Knopf.
Stevenson, Brenda E. (1996) *Life in Black and White: Family and Community in the Slave
    South.* New York: Oxford University Press.
Stuckey, Sterling (1987) *Slave Culture: Nationalist Theory and the Foundations of Black America.*
    New York: Oxford University Press.
Tadman, Michael (1989) *Speculators and Slaves: Masters, Traders, and Slaves in the Old South.*
    Madison, Wis.: University of Wisconsin Press.
White, Deborah Gray (1985) *Ar'n't I a Woman? Female Slaves in the Plantation South.* New
    York: Norton.
Wiley, Bell Irvin (1938) *Southern Negroes, 1861–1865.* New Haven, Conn.: Yale University
    Press.
Wood, Betty (1995) *Women's Work, Men's Work: The Informal Slave Economies of Lowcountry
    Georgia.* Athens, Ga.: University of Georgia Press.
Wright, Gavin (1978) *The Political Economy of the Cotton South: Households, Markets, and
    Wealth in the Nineteenth Century.* New York: Norton.

CHAPTER FOUR

Planters, Plain Folk, and Poor Whites in the Old South

CHARLES C. BOLTON

Popular remembrances of the Old South typically focus on the world of majestic plantations, and the white gentlemen, belles, and black slaves who populated that realm. While wealthy planters living on large estates controlling the lives and work of hundreds of bondspeople were indeed an important part of the antebellum South's landscape, planters represented only a small percentage of southern slave-holders and a mere fraction of the total white population in 1860. Until quite recently, popular notions merely reflected the state of historical scholarship, for most of white society beyond the plantation remained virtually invisible to scholars. Even when historians began in the 1960s to look at non-elites in all societies, students of the Old South turned their attention primarily to the black slave population, a focus that has greatly enriched our understanding of the slave experience. Only since the early 1980s have historians begun to explain the diversity of white social and eco-nomic groups. Although the complexities of white society in the antebellum South are increasingly apparent, debates continue on how best to describe the white social structure in the decades before the Civil War.

Questions about the nature of white society in the Old South commenced even before the Civil War began, as antebellum Americans hotly debated the topic. Northern abolitionists and travelers, such as Frederick Law Olmstead, claimed that slavery had created two classes of whites in the South: aristocratic slaveowners and degraded poor whites. This view flowed naturally from northern conceptions of a slave power that undermined American democratic ideals. White southerners, on the other hand, did not perceive slavery and democracy as necessarily incompatible, and they countered the northern portrayal of their world with a slightly more com-plicated taxonomy. For example, Daniel R. Hundley (1860), in *Social Relations in Our Southern States*, identified seven white social groups in the South: the southern gentlemen, the middle classes, the southern yeomen, the southern Yankees, cotton snobs, the southern bullies, and poor white trash. In Hundley's classification scheme, the first three groups were defined in economic terms, while the latter four were characterized by cultural attributes. According to Hundley, the South's economic hierarchy consisted of an economic elite (southern gentlemen); a middle class, which included everyone from farmers to small planters to artisans to the professional class;

and a yeomanry comprised of poorer farmers, some who might own a few slaves. Thus, Hundley claimed, slavery enriched white southerners economically. He did admit that the region had a number of "degraded" members, though this condition did not spring from economic poverty caused by slavery, as northerners suggested; rather, the lack of economic achievement and status resulted from Yankeeness, ignorance, drunkenness, or laziness.

Modern historians of the Old South have found both of these contemporary portraits to be overdrawn, though they have not necessarily agreed on a suitable replacement scheme of classification. At the same time, even as scholars have offered a variety of increasingly sophisticated and complex portrayals of the antebellum South's white society, the heart of the contemporary debate among antebellum Americans has continued to inform more recent discussions: understanding what effect slavery had on the structure of white society. Did slavery create a society in the antebellum South dominated politically and economically by slaveholders, especially the wealthiest planters? Or did the antebellum South, despite slavery, develop as a society where wealth was distributed fairly wide among whites? In other words, did slavery create white poverty or a general condition of basic prosperity for all whites, slaveowners and nonslaveholders alike? If the latter is the case, then what role did nonslaveholders play in the historical development of the region? How did they view their position in a slave-based society? All of these questions about the Old South's economic and social structure are important, for they impact on our understanding of antebellum southern politics, and thus interpretations of the coming of the Civil War. Indeed, much of the recent effort to uncover the nature of the white society in the antebellum South has been driven, on some level, by a belief that a clearer understanding of this issue perhaps holds the key to answering the question of why the South went to war in 1861.

Any examination of white society in the Old South has to begin with the slaveowners, and with the planters among them who controlled at least half of the slave population. In 1860, only approximately one-quarter of white families in the region owned slaves. Planters, typically defined as individuals owning 20 or more slaves, were even scarcer, about 12 percent of all slaveholders and 4 percent of the total white population in 1860. The true aristocrats of the Old South, those who held 50 or more slaves, represented a mere 3 percent of slaveholders and less than 1 percent of white society on the eve of the Civil War. Despite their relatively small numbers, slaveholders played a pivotal role in the South, the only US region during the first half of the nineteenth century in which the "peculiar institution" not only persisted but continued to expand. Slavery, and slaveowners, made the South distinctive from other parts of the United States, so understanding both the institution of slavery and those who were directly involved with and typically benefited from black bondage obviously is a key concern for anyone trying to comprehend the essential nature of the Old South.

Two competing interpretations have dominated recent scholarship on southern slaveholders. The first was originally put forward by Eugene Genovese (1965) in *The Political Economy of Slavery*. Genovese described the antebellum South as a society dominated by a planter class (or by slaveowners, for the two groups remain interchangeable in Genovese's description) with a unique worldview forged through a divergent labor system. In the Old South, masters developed a paternalistic relationship with their bound workers, in contrast to the impersonal, market-driven conduct that characterized owner–worker relations in the North's free-labor, capitalist system. Southern slaveowners bought and sold black laborers but not their labor. For Genovese, this distinction was crucial. Because of their reliance on slave labor, southern planters had an aristocratic, precapitalist, anti-bourgeois outlook, with "values and mores emphasizing family and status, a strong code of honor, and aspirations to luxury, ease, and accomplishment" (Genovese 1961: 28). In addition, the paternalistic ethos that characterized master–slave relationships permeated all other social relations. As the dominant economic and political group in the South, slaveowners succeeded in imposing their unique values and perspective on all of southern society, including black slaves and white nonslaveholders, largely by convincing them that slaveholder rule was entirely natural and legitimate. Genovese's interpretation provided a plausible explanation for the coming of the Civil War. He claimed that conceiving of planters as capitalists, similar to northerners in their economic orientation, left one to wonder what the fighting was all about. However, if southern planters, defenders of a precapitalist island in an emerging capitalist world, believed that the North threatened slavery, and thus the institution that supported their prized and unique way of life, the struggle for southern independence began to make sense.

Genovese, along with his wife Elizabeth Fox-Genovese, later modified and augmented this original thesis. In a jointly authored work, *Fruits of Merchant Capital* (1983), the Genoveses conceded that the Old South was indeed part of the capitalist world, intimately involved in the world cotton market, but they still maintained that slave relations of production precluded slaveholders in the antebellum South from adopting the outlook of a capitalist bourgeoisie. Instead, they harbored a precapitalist mentality, which infected all of southern society. In *Within the Plantation Household*, Fox-Genovese (1988) further demonstrated how the Old South remained different from the capitalist North through her study of slaveholding women. She argued that slavery led to a different set of experiences for southern and northern women because slavery precluded capitalism, which was changing the nature of northern households during the antebellum years. In the North, the functions of the household, and consequently gender relations, were increasingly transformed by the market and the state. The household became the home, a separate sphere for women, in which they developed an "ideology of domesticity," as well as women's clubs and associations, thoughts and spaces that spawned both feminism and abolitionism (Fox-Genovese 1988: 81). In the South, by contrast, slavery ensured that the household remained the center of both production and reproduction, a realm dominated completely by men. Slaveholding women accepted this patriarchy, for like all other dependants, slaveholding women saw the hierarchies controlled by their husbands as part of an organic universe.

Genovese's (1965) portrait of southern slaveholders as premodern aristocrats who hegemonically determined the character of the South was challenged by James Oakes (1982) in his *The Ruling Race*, which convincingly pointed out some flaws in Genovese's argument. For one thing, Oakes' work suggested that Genovese's account had a certain static quality to it. Oakes acknowledged the existence of the paternalistic master, but he also showed that such individuals were, by 1860, a small fringe of the slaveholding class concentrated in the oldest and richest parts of the South. During the colonial period, paternalistic slaveholders were quite prominent, but with the cotton boom beginning in the early nineteenth century, the American dream of prosperity became linked with slavery in the South. Even most of the established planters of the South Atlantic seaboard did not shun the opportunity to seek material advancement in the fresh cotton lands of the Old Southwest. Comfortable, stable patriarchs had become few and far between by the eve of the Civil War. Another important aspect of Oakes' study was his focus on the majority of slaveowners who were not planters but owners of five or fewer slaves, part of what he labeled a slaveowning "middle class." Genovese's planter hegemony apparently did not take root among these individuals, whose lives were characterized by "demographic restlessness," "economic insecurity," and "grasping materialism" (Oakes 1982: 40–1, 57). In other words, the vast majority of southern slaveholders resembled their middle-class, capitalist counterparts in the North.

Like Genovese, Oakes also later modified his original position. In *Slavery and Freedom* (1990), Oakes moved beyond his portrayal of southern slaveholders as simply a regional version of the American liberal capitalist. He also conceded that masters and slaves often did develop a non-market relationship. Oakes suggested that southern slaveowners were conflicted members of the capitalist world. They recognized that the slavery that allowed them to prosper implicitly contradicted the liberal bourgeois values to which they subscribed, eventually leading to internal friction with nonslaveholders and external discord with northerners who had a more traditional conception of liberal capitalism. The debate between the Genoveses and Oakes cannot ultimately be resolved because of their irreconcilable definitions of capitalism. For the Genoveses, capitalism, above all, requires free labor. Fox-Genovese described capitalism as a system that:

> depends upon the divorce of labor from the land, the transformation of labor-power (not labor) into a commodity, and the political recognition of both land and labor as entities of absolute property that can be freely exchanged on the market. (Fox-Genovese 1988: 53)

Oakes, on the other hand, believes that any group of people enmeshed in the world of capital and markets have to be considered capitalists in some sense, whatever their system of labor. Oakes' position seems the more sensible one. After all, in the Old South, slaveholders were certainly involved in using their capital, much of it invested in slave laborers, to produce commodities for distant markets to create additional capital. They were slaveowning capitalists.

The antebellum South undoubtedly did have its slaveowners who could be considered aristocratic lords, especially those living on established estates in the most settled parts of the region, men who considered paternalism in all social relations a matter of principle, the linchpin in the ordering of an organic, hierarchical world. Applying this characterization to the slaveholding class as a whole, however, remains problematic. To begin with, the existence of a paternalistic master–slave relationship cannot necessarily be assumed to have created a premodern ideology and behavior among slaveowners, for the paternalistic treatment of slaves by masters was not necessarily incompatible with capitalist behavior. In fact, economic self-interest could just as easily explain paternalism among slaveowners. As Shearer Davis Bowman (1993) has noted in his *Masters and Lords*, a comparative study of mid-nineteenth-century planters in the American South and Prussia, most slaveholders did not have to cleave to premodern values to understand that their own economic self-interest was often served by treating their bondpeople with a certain measure of decency. Thus, whatever degree of paternalism defined master–slave relationships, those attitudes were the result of the calculating economic decisions (and Christian ethical notions) of US slaveowners, and Bowman sees little reason why American slaveowners, like their Prussian Junker counterparts, should not be characterized as agrarian capitalists, though capitalists with a conservative rather than a liberal outlook. It is also important to question whether paternalistic treatment of slaves was actually practiced as much as it was talked about. Paternalistic rhetoric certainly abounded in the Old South, especially after northern abolitionists by the 1840s began to portray slaveowners as sadistic monsters, and southerners fashioned a proslavery response focusing on the benefits of slavery to both bondpeople and the South's white citizenry. As Oakes (1982) noted, however, during the cotton booms of the early nineteenth century and the late 1840s and 1850s, many slaveowners, even planters, were on the move and looking to advance economically. Slaveowners had to separate slave families; masters had to work slaves hard to create plantations and farms out of the seeming wilderness of the Old Southwest. As they scrambled to get ahead, many slaveowners surely trimmed on whatever paternalistic ideals they may have held or whatever standards of treatment for bondpeople they may have followed during calmer times.

If the antebellum South did have a significant class of aristocratic, premodern slaveowners dedicated to preserving and encouraging paternalistic social relations throughout southern society, one would expect the wealthiest masters to be in the vanguard of this group. A number of detailed studies of the slaveholding elite, however, have failed to confirm the existence of such a crowd. For example, Jane Turner Censer's (1984) analysis of the largest planters in North Carolina (those who owned more than 70 slaves in 1830) and their relationship with their children specifically examines what values these planters passed on to their children. Rather than transmitting premodern, paternalistic notions to the entire society, as Genovese (1965) suggested, Censer found that the Tar Heel State's largest planters did not even imbue their own children with such values. Rather, planters instructed their offspring in the middle-class, Victorian values embraced by other elites in nineteenth-century America: "hard work, frugality, self-control, and success," as well as the importance of education and material achievement (Censer 1984: 53). William K. Scarborough's (2003) study on the Old South's elite slaveowners (those who owned more than 300 slaves in 1850 or 1860) also offers little support for Genovese's position. In his detailed look at all aspects of life among the slaveholding elite, Scarborough agrees with Censer (1984) that, in both attitude and behavior, the South's largest planters differed little from northern elites. Indeed, Scarborough underscores that some of the South's wealthiest planters, most notably those in Natchez, were themselves from the North and that almost all elite planters maintained intimate personal and business relationships with that region, a fact that calls into question the development of any separate worldview for the South's slaveholders. The slaveholding elite in backcountry districts appear to be even more unlikely candidates for the title of premodern ruler. John Inscoe's (1989) study of slaveholders in the North Carolina mountains, a region with few slaveowners and even fewer large planters, found that slaveowners there were a "stable elite" who ruled their neighborhoods, both economically and politically, through a combination of slave-holder hegemony, a dense web of contacts among whites of all classes, and a shared white racism (Inscoe 1989: 116). Even so, these North Carolina slaveowners were not a premodern elite; rather, they could best be characterized as a "prosperous, ambitious, and progressive middle class of business and professional men" (Inscoe 1989: 7).

If the elite among slaveholders did not have an aristocratic, anti-bourgeois out-look, then that characterization certainly could not be applied to the great majority of slaveowners, especially those trekking to the frontiers of the Old Southwest for the chance to augment or make their fortunes, or to the numerous population of slaveowners who owned a handful of slaves and who populated every district through-out the antebellum South. We still know relatively little about the latter group, partly because, like nonslaveholders, the documentary sources about their lives are relatively sparse. Despite Oakes' (1982) focus on small slaveholders, there have been few follow-up efforts by historians to examine the lives of the South's most typical slaveowners. What is known is that small slaveowners lived spartan and simple lives compared to the slaveowning gentry and had a different relationship with the few slaves they held. These slaveowners obviously came into closer contact with their bondpeople – even working alongside and living with them at times – and had little chance to develop the paternalistic attitudes that only physical separation and eco-nomic wealth could promote. Indeed, some historians have suggested that the lives of small slaveholders resembled those of nonslaveholders more than wealthier slaveowners. As Edward Baptist's (2002) detailed examination of middle Florida's plantation frontier shows, even the wealthiest migrants to the Old Southwest fron-tier could not simply reproduce the stable hierarchies of the South's more settled locales; indeed, "they found upon arrival in new districts that older verities of political and cultural power became open questions" (Baptist 2002: 8).

While the debate will surely continue on the nature of the antebellum South's slaveowning class, historians have really just begun the effort to uncover the lives of the other 75 percent of the Old South's white population, the nonslaveholders, and what role they might have played in the history of the region. The earliest historians of the antebellum South barely noticed any whites who were not slaveowners. Until quite recently, the lone exception to this scholarly neglect was the work in the 1940s of Frank L. Owsley, his wife Harriett C. Owsley (a sometimes uncredited co-author of her husband's work), and his students, Herbert Weaver and Blanche H. Clark. The Owsleys and their students made unprecedented use of census manuscripts and county records from Louisiana, Alabama, Mississippi, Georgia, and Tennessee to paint a portrait of what they called the "plain folk." This group included all whites:

> who were neither rich nor very poor.... The group included the small slaveholding farmers; the nonslaveholders who owned the land which they cultivated; the numerous herdsmen on the frontier, pine barrens, and mountains; and those tenant farmers whose agricultural production, as recorded in the census, indicated thrift, energy, and self-respect. (Owsley 1949: 7–8)

Economically, this southern middle class was not part of the plantation economy but strove for self-sufficiency in their agricultural pursuits. The Owsley school suggested that in the lower South, 80–85 percent of these plain folk owned land, which was easily available at low prices. At the same time, plain folk farmers and herders generally sold any surplus crops and animals for high prices. Like Daniel Hundley (1860), the Owsley group believed that almost all whites in the Old South's slave society achieved a significant measure of economic success. Frank Owsley (1949) argued that given such economic realities, along with progressively democratic political institutions, the plain folk did not view the planters as their oppressors. Rather, many of the plain folk remained quite satisfied with their self-sufficient lifestyle, and for those who did aspire to planter status, such a goal was easily attainable in a society in which widespread economic mobility prevailed, at least during the 1850s. Owsley also emphasized that the plain folk – and many planters – shared cultural connections, which sprang from their common ethnic heritage as descendants of migrants from the British Isles. This culture was reflected in the group's folkways: close-knit families, strong kinship ties, similar religious beliefs, and neighborliness (house-raisings, log-rollings, and various forms of communal entertainment).

Criticism of the Owsley thesis appeared simultaneous with its dissemination. In 1946, Fabian Linden, a graduate student at the University of North Carolina, raised questions about the statistical sampling methods of Owsley and his students and suggested that the group had not proved that economic wealth was widespread in the South rather than concentrated in the hands of planters. Linden (1946) faulted the plain folk scholars for ignoring almost one-quarter of the southern population in their calculations, especially the urban population and the rural population who were not listed on census records as farmers (including those designated as laborers, woodcutters, and ditchers). Thus, Owsley and his students disregarded the existence of the poorest whites, which inflated the claims of widespread land-ownership and underestimated the extent of economic concentration. Among other criticisms, Linden also pointed out that the Owsley group's calculation of upward economic mobility in the 1850s looked only at individuals who persisted within a single county, a formula that neglected the large number of individuals who moved to new locales between 1850 and 1860 and perhaps overstated the extent of economic progress. Despite this lively debate between the Owsley school and its lone graduate student critic, the argument did not spark any sustained investigation of the antebellum South plain folk.

Thirty years later, when scholars began to examine the world of white non-slaveholders once again, the work of the Owsley school provided a useful starting point. Early on, however, a central tenet of the Owsley group's economic contentions was undermined. A study by Randolph B. Campbell and Richard G. Lowe (1977), *Wealth and Power in Antebellum Texas,* employed a quantitative analysis of the distribution of wealth and power in Texas in 1850 and 1860 to test the Owsley notion that the antebellum South was a region of economic and political democracy and found the thesis lacking. This statistical examination of Texas's four major geographical regions suggested that throughout the state, "all important forms of wealth – real and personal property, slaves, and total wealth – were concentrated in the hands of a small group constituting less than 10 percent of all free Texans" (Campbell and Lowe 1977: 135). As for Texas politics, Campbell and Lowe did find Owsley's democratic institutions, but they also showed that the leadership of these political entities was decidedly in the hands of wealthy elites. Writing a year later in

The Political Economy of the Cotton South, the economist Gavin Wright (1978) agreed that a huge economic gap existed between a small group of slaveowners and the much larger group of nonslaveholders in the antebellum South; moreover, he showed that the chasm between the two groups was widening, not narrowing, in the 1850s.

If economic democracy did not exist in the antebellum South, and slaveowners held the reins of political power in the region, why did nonslaveholders accept and support the rule of slaveowners? One answer might be that all whites were fundamentally united by a shared racism. While earlier historians had suggested such an idea, George Fredrickson (1971) in *The Black Image in the White Mind*, offered the fullest explanation of this notion. Fredrickson's examination of white thinking on race suggested the importance of the concept of *Herrenvolk* democracy for the antebellum South, essentially democracy for the master race of whites. Fredrickson noted that whether or not wealthy slaveowners held aristocratic notions, they were likely to keep them to themselves when seeking political office in the Old South. The region, especially the newer states of the Old Southwest, had some of the most democratic political structures in antebellum America. Slaveowners had to stake their claims to public power in ways that would capture broad approval from the entire white male population, which was fully enfranchised in many southern states. Whites were already united by their shared belief in white supremacy, so wealthy slaveowners acquired and maintained their power by appealing to the racist fears that haunted the white mind to convince poorer nonslaveholders that the existence of black slavery allowed all whites to occupy the same level of basic equality.

Another approach to this question of why the white South appeared so united politically in the face of significant economic disparities was suggested by Frank Owsley's idea that nonslaveholders were largely self-sufficient yeoman farmers who lived in a world quite distinct from that of the plantation districts. Gavin Wright (1978) expanded on this view when he suggested that, unlike planters who sought to maximize profits by acquiring more land and slaves to produce as much cotton as possible, yeoman farmers practiced a "safety-first" economic policy. They calculated how to ensure the self-sufficiency of their households before devoting any land or labor to cotton production. Thus, for Wright, the antebellum South's political economy consisted of a market economy for planters and a primarily subsistence economy for the yeomanry. This idea of a dual political economy in the Old South offered a plausible explanation of how yeoman farmers and wealthy planters might coexist in a polity nominally committed to white equality yet riven with serious economic inequalities between various segments of white society. Both James Oakes (1982) and Eugene Genovese (1965), as part of their divergent explanations of the slaveholder class, incorporated a similar view of nonslaveholders: they largely occupied a different physical space than planters, with a different outlook on what constituted economic success. For example, Genovese suggested that one reason nonslaveholders accepted slaveholder hegemony was that most nonslaveholders lived in backcountry districts, where planters granted them a large measure of autonomy in dealing with local issues and concerns. Physical separation thus allowed for a separate political development, one that might subscribe to more egalitarianism than planters permitted in their own neighborhoods.

This portrait of a separate, backcountry yeoman world, largely self-sufficient and able to evolve in a separate milieu to that of the planters, was fully developed in

Steven Hahn's (1983) innovative and thorough study of the Georgia upcountry, *The Roots of Southern Populism*. The Georgia upcountry – that area between the Georgia mountains and the state's plantation belt – had its planters and poor whites, but the yeomanry dominated life in these counties. Utilizing an inventive research design that connected a variety of local records and manuscript sources from the entire upcountry region with census samples from two of the upcountry counties, Hahn suggested that the antebellum plain folk, or yeomen, of this region developed their own unique anti-bourgeois worldview, not at the behest of planters but rather because of the region's relative isolation from the plantation economy. Yeoman farmers in the Georgia upcountry strove to maintain and reproduce a life that guaranteed the independence of individual households. They relied on their own labor or that of their families to produce much of what they needed to live. They generally had limited contact with the cotton export market, and they formed primarily local networks of exchange to secure what they could not produce themselves. "Habits of mutuality" defined economic and social relations among the upcountry's petty producers and "imparted to their culture a communal, prebourgeois quality whose egalitarian proclivities sharply distinguished it from that of the planters" (Hahn 1983: 52). Even though the upcountry saw growing commercialization of agriculture during the 1850s, upcountry folk remained committed to their precapitalist lifestyle. Although an increasing number of upcountry farmers entered the cotton economy during the 1850s (in Carroll County the percentage of farmers producing cotton rose from 41 to 87 during the decade), Hahn explains that many of these new entrants into the world of cotton agriculture were not emergent capitalists but the typical yeomen of earlier years who simply saw cotton farming "as a convenient means of establishing themselves in general farming, acquiring material comforts, and accumulating property to pass on to their children and thereby reproduce their experiences" of the independent household (Hahn 1983: 47–8). Politically, conflicts between whites in the upcountry, while not eliminated, were muted, as whites across the economic spectrum typically subscribed to a political philosophy of preindustrial republicanism, which stressed the value of independent producers to the success of republican government. In both economic and political orientation, the Georgia upcountry differed markedly from the state's plantation districts, but much as Genovese had argued, Hahn suggested the two areas could coexist as long as planters did not intrude on the prerogatives of yeoman society. Such a peace prevailed during the antebellum period but began to unravel during the Civil War and culminated with the Populist revolt of the late nineteenth century.

If the Georgia upcountry was indeed a place where a backcountry yeomanry remained committed to preserving their isolation and avoiding entanglement with the growing market economy – even through the boom times of the late 1840s and 1850s that increasingly transformed southern agriculture – nonslaveholders in other locales apparently did not share this experience. Lacy K. Ford's (1988) examination of the South Carolina upcountry, *Origins of Southern Radicalism*, portrayed the region as one in continual transformation from the time of the American Revolution to the Civil War, an area by the latter date "no longer truly backcountry but never entirely a plantation region" (Ford 1988: 44). The main factor reshaping the upcountry during this period was the spread of short-staple cotton production. By 1850, all farmers in the South Carolina upcountry, where 80 percent of farmers owned land, were enmeshed in the cotton economy. At the same time, slavery produced economic inequalities. While 15 percent of the region's farmers held more than 20 bondpeople, another 20 percent owned between six and 19 slaves, and another 15 percent possessed at least one slave. Nevertheless, a majority of upcountry farmers were yeomen, which, according to Ford's definition, were all the nonslaveholding farmers and those small slaveholders with five or fewer bondspeople. While some yeomen worried that relying on producing cotton for the commercial market threatened the loss of personal independence, they still succumbed to the lures of cotton, while also generally maintaining production to satisfy self-sufficiency needs. Thus, while yeomen (and planters) practiced what Gavin Wright (1978) had labeled "safety-first" agriculture, there was no dual economy in the South Carolina upcountry, planters producing for the market and the plain folk focusing only on self-sufficiency. Although Ford demonstrated that upcountry yeomen did not necessarily have any unshakeable antipathy to market agriculture, he did agree with Hahn (1983) that yeoman farmers remained devoted to an ideology of republicanism that valued personal economic independence. Ford (1988), however, argued that planters also shared these republican beliefs, and both groups believed that black slavery guaranteed the best way to ensure that most whites could qualify for republican citizenship; in other words, a *Herrenvolk* republicanism prevailed in South Carolina's upcountry.

Studies of antebellum Tennessee and Mississippi have also suggested that non-slaveholders in these areas were not necessarily backcountry agrarians steering clear of the market economy. Robert Tracy McKenzie's (1994) quantitative study of both the plantation areas and the nonplantation districts of antebellum and postbellum Tennessee, *One South or Many?*, discounts the notion that the nonslaveholding yeomanry lived in a separate world with their own unique economic development and mentality. McKenzie found that the only clear distinction between plantation districts, the upcountry, and the mountains in Tennessee was that slavery increased as one moved east to west across the state. In all regions of the state, however, farmers both produced enough food to remain self-sufficient and raised cotton, foodstuffs, or livestock for sale in commercial markets. In fact, in all parts of antebellum Tennessee, the only farmers not involved with the market were the poorest ones. The more obvious economic distinctions were those that existed within each region, such as "the gross income disparities that separated market and subsistence-oriented farmers within all three sections" (McKenzie 1994: 56). Despite the wealth inequalities that characterized all regions of Tennessee, enough upward mobility existed (at least among those who persisted in a single county between 1850 and 1860) for notions about white equality to have some basis in fact.

Likewise, Bradley Bond's (1995) study of nineteenth-century Mississippi, *Political Culture in the Nineteenth-Century South*, found that white Mississippians of all economic classes valued both independence and participation in the market. They did not recognize the apparent anomaly between market production and a desire for self-sufficiency. In fact, "a broad-based consensus on the place of slavery in society obscured the contradictions inherent in Mississippians' retention of communal and market-oriented values" and helped bind all white citizens "in a good republic" (Bond 1995: 13). In a separate investigation of the nonslaveholding livestock tenders of south Mississippi in *Plain Folk of the South Revisited*, Bond (1997) argued that south Mississippi's nonslaveholders eagerly embraced the market economy. Historians have often portrayed the herdsmen of Mississippi's Piney Woods as people who sought escape from the vagaries of the cotton economy, the epitome of Owsley's (1949) isolated, self-sufficient yeomen. A closer look at their economy, however, showed that the Piney Woods plain folk did not come to the pine forest to recapture some pastoral ideal; rather, they came to seek profits, though from livestock rather than cotton. Bond's examination of census records and the scant documentary record available indicated that south Mississippi's herders did not plant enough grain to cover family subsistence needs. Even so, throughout the 1850s, they sought to acquire additional land and raise larger herds, apparently hoping to make up the shortfall in food through profits from selling livestock. Rather than practice a safety-first strategy of agriculture, the Piney Woods livestock tenders adopted an accumulation-first approach in their economic actions. As Bond suggests, the safety-first model of economic production perhaps represented a poor strategy for people who had uprooted themselves to move to the Old Southwest in search of a better life. Such people were likely the individuals from the older states who had the most gumption and did not mind taking a few risks for the possibility to get ahead.

The more recent studies of nonslaveholders have proved that Frank Owsley (1949) and his students were wrong about the Old South's wide distribution of wealth. There was no economic democracy in the antebellum South; slaveowners controlled the bulk of the region's economic resources. The early plain folk scholars also misjudged the degree to which nonslaveholders were isolated from the planters' world of the market economy. Most antebellum plain folk did not live in self-sufficient havens from the market economy; rather, most produced cotton, food-stuffs, or livestock that they sold to distant markets. One aspect of Owsley's economic argument that has been preserved (though reworked) in recent studies of the Old South's yeomanry is that most nonslaveholders – and many slaveowners – were dedicated to an ideal of economic independence, whatever their involvement in market production. This belief in the reality, or at least the possibility, of white economic independence was linked to the idea that slavery represented the best way to secure white economic freedom.

The lack of documentary evidence generated by nonslaveholders, and the exist-ence of detailed census information about nonslaveholding households and their production, has often forced historians to focus a good deal of their attention on the economic experiences of nonslaveholders. Most students of white nonslaveholders, however, have also suggested other reasons beyond shared economic experiences for why nonslaveholders showed little interest in opposing the wealthy slaveowners who controlled economic and political life in the Old South. J. William Harris' (1985) *Plain Folk and Gentry in a Slave Society* expertly details all the factors that came together to promote white unity across class lines, and ultimately led whites to join together in a war to defend slavery. Harris' study focuses on the rural areas sur-rounding Augusta, Georgia, three Georgia counties and one South Carolina district, where nonslaveholders ranged from more than 60 percent to less than 20 percent of the farming population. In all these areas, slaveowners and nonslaveowners shared similar economic experiences. Most of the largely landowning farming population were involved in the cotton economy, despite the fact that many did not achieve household self-sufficiency. While these basic economic experiences fundamentally united whites across class lines, Harris also argued that slavery helped stoke the fires of class resentment. White leaders argued that black slavery represented an ideal base for whites-only republicanism. In a society with at least some social mobility, such claims reflected reality and further promoted white harmony. Even so, because of the concentrated wealth slavery encouraged, the peculiar institution also created internal enemies to the southern republic among nonslaveholders. For Harris, slavery ensured that class tensions were ever-present in the hinterlands of antebellum Augusta, although they were generally kept under wraps because of the various "ligaments of community" that tied the white classes together: wealthy aid to the poor in difficult times, face-to-face relationships, religion, and politics and elections.

Other historians have placed even more stress than Harris on the "ligaments of community" as the crucial factor linking white slaveowners and nonslaveholders in a community of interest. Orville Vernon Burton's (1985) intensive study of the South Carolina plantation district of Edgefield, *In My Father's House Are Many Mansions*, found that despite dramatic disparities in the distribution of wealth, class conflict or antagonism did not appear. In the Edgefield district, half of the households owned slaves, but the other half was almost as likely to be landless. The top 10 percent of households owned 73 percent of personal wealth, while the poorest 25 percent owned practically no personal property. Burton argues that despite these economic cleavages, large planters and small farmers "were in much agreement on values, goals, and modes of interaction, all of which proceeded from a society based on complex kinship, religious, and social ties" (Burton 1985: 46). Any conflict that did break out in Edgefield, even between the classes, was easily contained by this general agreement. In *Kinship and Neighborhood in a Southern Community*, an examination of a different kind of Old South community, the primarily nonslaveholder world of Orange County, North Carolina, Robert C. Kenzer (1987) also found that kinship was a strong bond that easily trumped any class divisions that may have separated residents. Though on a smaller scale than Burton's Edgefield district, Orange County had its own disparities in wealth. The small group of farmers with slaves had different economic fortunes than the majority without. Two-fifths of the households did not even own land, and most of these who stayed in Orange County during the 1850s (about 60 percent) failed to secure real property during the decade. Even so, "the caste division based on race, together with the network of kinship, prevented class antagonisms and promoted social cohesion" (Kenzer 1987: 29). All whites were invested in the slave system because of their ties to slaveholding families, and the landless were linked to the landed through family relationships; indeed, many frequently worked on the land of kinfolk.

Examinations of the cultural world of nonslaveholders have generally confirmed Owsley's contention that cultural bonds united white nonslaveholders (and planters), and these ties played an important role in muting the economic disparities in white society. At times, however, the claims for a common plain folk culture have been overly ambitious. Take for instance Grady McWhiney's (1988) study, *Cracker Culture*, which builds on Owsley's (1949) belief that the plain folk's common culture could be traced to their shared ethnicity as migrants from the British Isles. McWhiney claims that a Celtic, or cracker, culture permeated the antebellum South, especially the ranks of the plain folk. This culture defined the South as different from the North and consisted of a set of shared beliefs and behavior that included an aversion to hard work, a tendency to favor herding over farming, a desire to extend hospitality, a willingness to resort to violence, and a distrust of formal education and other forms of "progress." These traits developed because the vast majority of migrants to the antebellum South hailed not just from England, but from the Celtic regions of the British Isles (Ireland, Scotland, and Wales). McWhiney's argument certainly has some merit, especially considering that even now the overwhelming majority of white southerners trace their roots to a Scots-Irish heritage. Cultural practices from that part of the world surely found their way into the Old South, just as African cultural legacies also survived in the region years after the African slave trade ended. But McWhiney's argument that this cracker culture defined the South as different from the North downplays the importance of other factors, such as the institution of slavery, which must have played an important role in shaping a distinctive white culture, even among nonslaveholders. In addition, McWhiney's southern particularity argument is weakened by the fact that the very same crackers of the South could be found in parts of the North (and presumably were carriers of the same culture). For example, the nonslaveholders who left the North Carolina backcountry between 1830 and 1850 were as likely to go to Indiana, Iowa, and Illinois as they were to relocate to Mississippi or Alabama. At the same time, McWhiney's reliance on travelers' accounts for evidence of this culture at times results in little more than unsubstantiated characterizations of white nonslaveholders. Relying largely on this literature, McWhiney (1988) describes the plain folk as too lazy to worry about much more than basic survival. Such a conclusion, however, seems unlikely in the face of other studies of the plain folk, relying on other documentary and quantitative evidence, that have portrayed them as active participants in the emergent market economy of the antebellum South.

A more evidentially impressive attempt that also makes sweeping claims for the centrality of a common plain folk culture can be found in Bill Cecil-Fronsman's (1992) *Common Whites*. He argued that 90 percent of North Carolinians, all the nonslaveholders and the slaveowners who owned fewer than 10 slaves, shared a folk culture that stressed their position in society as non-elites, or common whites. Utilizing a wide array of sources, including several that tap directly into nonslaveholder voices, such as petitions and letters to North Carolina governors and legislatures, and folktales, Cecil-Fronsman describes this common-white culture as one that accentuated the values of economic self-sufficiency, devotion to kin and local communities, and an intense egalitarianism, which led to class resentments but never class struggle, primarily because the common white folk culture proved no match for the more solidly established hegemony of the planter class. Cecil-Fronsman does not see this culture as static and unchanging; in fact, he notes that the increasing development of a commercial economy in the 1850s had already begun to weaken the strength of this common white world in the years before the Civil War. Despite this recognition, Cecil-Fronsman's common whites, like McWhiney's (1988) plain cracker folk, are too flat and homogenous. A common culture has erased almost all differences within the group. Did small slaveowners and landless tenants really share the same experiences and the same sense of their place in a slave society? Or what about the livestock tender supposedly practicing the Celtic ideal and his neighbor laboring on the farm of a slaveowner?

The most original analysis of the relationship between nonslaveholders and slaveholders in the Old South moved beyond the parameters established by the

Owsley school and looked at an important and essential aspect of life basically unnoticed by other students of the plain folk. In *Masters of Small Worlds*, Stephanie McCurry (1995) argues that to understand why the yeomanry in South Carolina supported secession, one has to first understand the politics within yeoman households. McCurry's focus is the South Carolina lowcountry, an area where substantial and notable plantations dotted the landscape but where yeoman households were most common; for McCurry, yeomen were farmers who provided most of the labor to work their farms, or those farmers with less than 150 acres of improved land and fewer than 10 slaves. As owners of land, the yeomanry of the lowcountry were masters over their property and all the dependants of their household: slaves, wives, and children. So, even if they did not own slaves, or not enough bondpeople to allow them to forgo working their own crops, they were "masters of small worlds." This essential understanding affected all aspects of life, from social relations to religion to politics. McCurry (1995) agrees with the bulk of plain folk scholars that the yeomanry were interested in maintaining and reproducing independent households, but she adds an interesting twist to this argument by stressing that in order to achieve the yeoman ideal, independent men had to command the labor of their dependants, including women, who provided important and basic labor to the primary project of yeoman households. As McCurry put it, "Dependence was the stuff of which independence – and manhood – were made" (McCurry 1995: 72). While McCurry agrees with Eugene Genovese (1965) that class hegemony united slaveowners and nonslaveowners, she offers a different reason for why the yeomanry accepted planter leadership so readily: the two groups were held together by a gendered vision of class solidarity. Both yeomen and planters agreed that owning land and controlling dependants gave them the prerogatives accorded to masters. Yeomen used this common understanding of the sanctity of the independent household and the independent male to wage various battles with planters, such as disputes over the uses of common land and conflicts over slave discipline and yeoman interactions with slaves. Yeomen and planters, however, were "unequal masters," and "yeoman farmers most often found themselves overmatched" in battles with planters (McCurry 1995: 92–3). Ultimately, the gendered conception of class solidarity meant that the yeomanry had to accept the right of planters to control and protect their households and dependants, including the slave members.

Evangelicalism bolstered the yeomanry's worldview, according to McCurry. Although evangelical Christianity had the potential to encourage egalitarianism by stressing the equality of all believers before God, it did not always develop that way. In the lowcountry, yeomen who embraced evangelicalism in the years after the American Revolution invested it with "a largely conservative and nascent proslavery shape that shored up their own claims to power and authority at home and abroad" (McCurry 1995: 147). When evangelicalism later attracted a following among lowcountry planters in a series of revivals during the early 1830s, about the same time as the yeomanry secured political rights previously reserved for planters, religion and politics in the lowcountry became part of a single orthodoxy, "a conservative Christian republicanism" that viewed slavery as an organic part of society's hierarchy, in much the same way that women were naturally seen as dependants in the secular household (McCurry 1995: 209). So when northerners attacked slavery, the yeomanry viewed the move as an assault on the independent household, an institution they wished to preserve, along with all the attendant prerogatives that entity assured for them.

McCurry's (1995) analysis is a powerful one, soundly based on a wide range of census and archival sources, and suggests the need for some dramatic reshaping of how the Old South's economy and social structure are conceived. Even so, her argument is not without flaws. For one thing, her claim for the centrality of evangelical Christianity in South Carolina society may be overstated. Lacy K. Ford (1988), in his study of the South Carolina upcountry, also noted the importance of evangelicalism to life in that region, but concluded that evangelical Christianity became more important in South Carolina after the Civil War, a claim that probably applies to the antebellum South as a whole. In short, the South as a solid Bible Belt did not always exist; this defining characteristic of southern life was emerging only in the antebellum years. McCurry (1995) also has a broad definition of the yeoman class, and it remains unclear if her arguments apply equally to the owner of nine slaves and a nonslaveholding farmer eking out an existence on a few acres. Nevertheless, McCurry offers perhaps the most plausible explanation of how Genovese's planter hegemony might have actually worked. All men were agreed on the subordinate position of women in society. The world they lived in provided them with tangible benefits, even if they did not own slave property. Other factors, of course, may have also bolstered planter hegemony, such as a shared racism among whites, or just a simple willingness to accept society as one finds it, what might be called the inertia principle of human nature. People born into any society generally accept that world and its institutions, and only a relative few ever seek to challenge the existing norms. Nonslaveholders, raised in a world where slavery was a fact of life, were undoubtedly predisposed to accept the institution's legitimacy on some level. Unraveling the exact source or sources of the yeomanry's ideology remains an inexact undertaking, for the documentary record they left behind is relatively minuscule. Even so, McCurry's analysis demonstrates that future efforts to understand the world of non-slaveholders must consider the impact of gender relations, as well as those of race and class.

One shortcoming of the detailed local studies of nonslaveholders to date is that most have focused on the yeomanry in the older, settled states of the Atlantic seaboard. One notable exception is Edward Baptist's (2002) examination of the development of the frontier counties of Jackson and Leon in the panhandle of Florida. Baptist examines how the lives of planters, non-elite white men, enslaved African Americans, and women intersected in the creation of a plantation society in this corner of the Old Southwest frontier. Seeking to move beyond the limitations of the existing terminology used to describe nonslaveholders, Baptist labels his non-elite white men "countrymen," a term middle Florida planters used to describe their non-planter neighbors. Baptist convincingly argues that the term reflects both the uncertain and changing economic status of non-elite men on the Old Southwest frontier and their efforts "to claim and assert manhood," contentions that, during the early decades of settlement, placed countrymen in conflict with the area's planters, who unsuccessfully sought to reserve the prerogatives of manhood for members of their own social class (Baptist 2002: 39).

Overall, historians who have focused on studying the plain folk in the antebellum South have tended to agree that, despite class divisions arising from the great disparities in wealth created by slavery, nonslaveholders were ultimately yoked to their white, slaveholding neighbors, because of either common cultural connections or a shared belief in the ideals of white supremacy, white independence, or male domination, all secured through the maintenance of slavery. One group of whites in the Old South who complicate this portrait of white unity, yet who have received little attention from scholars, are the poor whites. The antebellum observer Daniel R. Hundley (1860) described poor whites in purely cultural terms, as social misfits, primarily because he refused to allow the possibility of northerners' claims that a slave economy created white poverty. Modern historians have also been reluctant to admit that the southern economy, dominated by plantation agriculture, not only created an economic system that explicitly eliminated the possibility of black advancement but also created a significant amount of white poverty and dependence. Who can be characterized as poor among whites in the Old South? Certainly, individuals who could not acquire land or slaves in an overwhelmingly agricultural society relying on enslaved labor have to be considered impoverished on some level, unable to sustain the independence recent studies of the yeomanry have attributed to that group.

A broad range of researchers looking at a variety of locales have noted the existence of a large number of landless, slaveless whites in the antebellum South, comprising anywhere from 20 to 40 percent of white households during the 1850s. Historians, however, have disagreed on how to characterize these people. Most of the yeoman studies have downplayed the differences between landless and landed nonslaveholders, suggesting that the landless (at least those who remained in the area of study between census years) were linked to their landed neighbors by kinship ties or were merely younger sons waiting for their opportunity to move up the agricultural ladder. Such a characterization undoubtedly bolsters arguments that focus on the centrality of notions of personal independence as key to understanding the world of nonslaveholders and no doubt certainly describes at least a part of the Old South's landless population. However, a study by Charles Bolton (1994), *Poor Whites of the Antebellum South*, which concentrated specifically on examining landless poor whites in two nonplantation districts, central North Carolina and northeast Mississippi, found that more than one-half of the landless households that persisted in the central Piedmont of North Carolina remained permanently mired in poverty over time. Most worked at a shifting number of jobs – tenant farmer, farm laborer, sawmill worker, miner, railroad hand – filling temporary labor needs in an economy dominated by landowning yeomen, who used family labor whenever possible, and slaveholding farmers, who relied on slave labor whenever feasible. These poor whites were not all young men either; for some casual labor and persistent poverty were lifetime callings. Bolton's (1994) work suggest that despite the claims of white antebellum southerners and some later historians, slavery did not guarantee middle-class self-sufficiency or comfortable wealth for all whites. Black slavery, combined with the increasing commercialization of agricultural production and a credit system that did not always operate according to the "habits of mutuality" described by Steven Hahn (1983), ensured the existence of a landless, poor white class that failed to advance economically.

The landless, poor white population that remains most difficult to see is actually the largest group, those poor whites who constantly moved around to search for work; to seek better opportunities; or to flee from family, enemies, or the law. Early on, Fabien Linden (1946) pointed out how looking only at the persisting nonslaveholders in a county overestimated the economic success of yeoman farmers and livestock tenders. Most of our knowledge about nonslaveholders, however, has come from focused local studies, a research plan that permits the accretion and combination of sources necessary for studying people who left a scant documentary record but one that cannot trace one of the central aspects of life for the poorest of the antebellum South's plain folk – their frequent geographical mobility. Oftentimes, historians have followed Frank Owsley's (1949) lead and merely assumed that poor whites who moved into the expanding Old Southwest could take advantage of cheap land and find the economic success that had eluded them in the older, settled regions of the Atlantic seaboard. In his study of poor whites, Bolton (1994) tried to determine what happened to poor whites as they moved westward across the cotton South during the antebellum years. He discovered that for those moving to north-east Mississippi, prosperity was not assured. Probably less than 10 percent of those who arrived without land managed to secure real property, although most of those who failed to secure a farm in northeast Mississippi did not remain but kept on moving, continuing the quest for economic success in other locales.

If poor whites had different economic experiences than the more affluent plain folk, they also often failed to form secure connections to the common antebellum white culture noted by historians. Economic necessity dictated that poor whites move around quite frequently, not only to distant lands but also to the next neighborhood or county. As a result, although some poor whites did become firmly enmeshed in antebellum communities, their frequent migrations meant that very often poor whites did not establish the firm kinship and religious ties that character-ized the lives of most antebellum yeomen. The nature of poor white economic life also led to different kinds of contacts between poor whites and blacks in the Old South, perhaps even resulting in different views about the institution of slavery than more prosperous whites. Timothy J. Lockley's (2001) monograph, *Lines in the Sand*, investigated how poor whites – whom he defines as not only landless whites but also poor artisans, shopkeepers, and farmers – interacted with African Ameri-cans, both enslaved and free, in the Georgia lowcountry. He found that relations between the two groups were complex. While at times antagonistic, poor whites and blacks also worked, played, and worshiped together as equals; engaged in clandes-tine but mutually beneficial trade networks; and even on occasion, joined in "crimi-nal" actions that directly challenged the institution of slavery. Lockley's (2001) work suggests that poor whites were obviously the weak link in any kind of shared racism that united whites across class lines.

If the existence of poor white men challenged the idea that a shared experience of economic independence or a common attitude toward antebellum blacks united all white nonslaveholders, the presence of poor white women challenged the Old South's traditional gender boundaries. As Victoria Bynum (1992) explained in *Unruly Women*, a study of poor and yeoman women in three North Carolina Piedmont counties before and during the Civil War, "to be poor was even more shameful for white women because it violated norms of white femininity" (Bynum 1992: 6). Poor white women who violated established sexual or social mores, most of whom lived in households without a male head, were seen as particularly "dangerous" to those who had a vested interest in preserving the status quo. As a consequence, North Carolina officials vigorously prosecuted women for bastardy, prostitution, and fornication offenses and used the apprenticeship laws to remove children born to unattached poor white women. These leaders recognized that "to maintain traditional relations of race, class, and power required not only racial and class subordination but also the ordering of women's social and sexual behavior" (Bynum 1992: 34).

Our understanding of the contours of white society in the antebellum South has increased dramatically since the early 1980s. No longer seeing just a world of planters or slaveowners, we now have a new sense of the lives of the white majority of nonslaveholders and the role they played in shaping southern society. This new knowledge, however, has complicated the efforts to easily describe the shape of white society in the years before the Civil War. To be sure, the Old South had planters, plain folk, and poor whites, but precise definitions of just who belonged to each group and how different classes of whites interacted with each other remain difficult questions, without clear-cut answers.

BIBLIOGRAPHY

Baptist, Edward E. (2002) *Creating an Old South: Middle Florida's Plantation Frontier before the Civil War*. Chapel Hill, NC: University of North Carolina Press.

Bolton, Charles C. (1994) *Poor Whites of the Antebellum South: Tenants and Laborers in Central North Carolina and Northeast Mississippi*. Durham, NC: Duke University Press.

Bond, Bradley G. (1995) *Political Culture in the Nineteenth-Century South: Mississippi, 1830–1900*. Baton Rouge, La.: Louisiana State University Press.

Bond, Bradley G. (1997) "The Vernacular Architecture of the South: Log Buildings, Dog-Trot Houses, and English Barns," in Samuel C. Hyde Jr (ed.) *Plain Folk of the South Revisited*. Baton Rouge, La.: Louisiana State University Press.

Bowman, Shearer Davis (1993) *Masters and Lords: Mid-Nineteenth Century US Planters and Prussian Junkers*. New York: Oxford University Press.

Burton, Orville Vernon (1985) *In My Father's House Are Many Mansions: Family and Community in Edgefield, South Carolina 1848–1889*. Chapel Hill, NC: University of North Carolina Press.

Bynum, Victoria E. (1992) *Unruly Women: The Politics of Social and Sexual Control in the Old South*. Chapel Hill, NC: University of North Carolina Press.

Campbell, Randolph B. and Lowe, Richard G. (1977) *Wealth and Power in Antebellum Texas*. College Station, Tex.: Texas A & M University Press.

Cecil-Fronsman, Bill (1992) *Common Whites: Class and Culture in Antebellum North Carolina*. Lexington, Ky.: University Press of Kentucky.

Censer, Jane Turner (1984) *North Carolina Planters and their Children, 1800–1860*. Baton Rouge, La.: Louisiana State University Press.

Ford, Lacy K., Jr (1988) *Origins of Southern Radicalism: The South Carolina Upcountry, 1800–1860*. New York: Oxford University Press.

Fox-Genovese, Elizabeth (1988) *Within the Plantation Household: Black and White Women of the Old South*. Chapel Hill, NC: University of North Carolina Press.

Fox-Genovese, Elizabeth and Genovese, Eugene D. (1983) *Fruits of Merchant Capital: Slavery and Bourgeois Property in the Rise and Expansion of Capitalism*. New York: Oxford University Press.

Fredrickson, George M. (1971) *The Black Image in the White Mind: The Debate on Afro-American Character and Destiny, 1817–1914*. New York: Harper and Row.

Genovese, Eugene D. (1965) *The Political Economy of Slavery: Studies in the Economy and Society of the Slave South.* New York: Pantheon.

Hahn, Steven (1983) *The Roots of Southern Populism: Yeomen Farmers and the Transformation of the Georgia Upcountry, 1850–1890.* New York: Oxford University Press.

Harris, J. William (1985) *Plain Folk and Gentry in a Slave Society: White Liberty and Black Slavery in Augusta's Hinterlands.* Middletown, Conn.: Wesleyan University Press.

Hundley, Daniel R. (1860) *Social Relations in our Southern States.* New York: H. B. Price.

Inscoe, John C. (1989) *Mountain Masters, Slavery, and the Sectional Crisis in Western North Carolina.* Knoxville, Tenn.: University of Tennessee Press.

Kenzer, Robert C. (1987) *Kinship and Neighborhood in a Southern Community: Orange County, North Carolina, 1849–1881.* Knoxville, Tenn.: University of Tennessee Press.

Linden, Fabian (1946) "Economic Democracy in the Slave South: An Appraisal of Some Recent Views," *Journal of Negro History* 31: 140–90.

Lockley, Timothy James (2001) *Lines in the Sand: Race and Class in Lowcountry Georgia, 1750–1860.* Athens, Ga.: University of Georgia Press.

McCurry, Stephanie (1995) *Masters of Small Worlds: Yeoman Households, Gender Relations, and the Political Culture of the Antebellum South Carolina Low Country.* New York: Oxford University Press.

McKenzie, Robert Tracy (1994) *One South or Many? Plantation Belt and Upcountry in Civil-War Era Tennessee.* New York: Cambridge University Press.

McWhiney, Grady (1988) *Cracker Culture: Celtic Ways in the Old South.* Tuscaloosa, Ala.: University of Alabama Press.

Oakes, James (1982) *The Ruling Race: A History of American Slaveholders.* New York: Alfred A. Knopf.

Oakes, James (1990) *Slavery and Freedom: An Interpretation of the Old South.* New York: Alfred A. Knopf.

Owsley, Frank L. (1949) *Plain Folk of the Old South.* Chicago: Quadrangle.

Scarborough, William K. (2003) *Masters of the Big House: The Elite Slaveholders of the Mid-Nineteenth Century South.* Baton Rouge, La.: Louisiana State University Press.

Wright, Gavin (1978) *The Political Economy of the Cotton South: Households, Markets, and Wealth in the Nineteenth Century.* New York: Norton.

SUGGESTED FURTHER READING

Bode, Frederick A. and Ginter, Donald E. (1986) *Farm Tenancy and the Census in Antebellum Georgia.* Athens, Ga.: University of Georgia Press.

Bolton, Charles C. and Culclasure, Scott P. (1998) *The Confessions of Edward Isham: A Poor White Life of the Old South.* Athens, Ga.: University of Georgia Press.

Clark, Blanche H. (1942) *The Tennessee Yeoman, 1840–1860.* Nashville, Tenn.: Vanderbilt University Press.

Genovese, Eugene D. (1975) "Yeoman Farmers in a Slaveholders' Democracy," *Agricultural History* 49: 331–442.

Hyde, Samuel C., Jr (ed.) (1997) *Plain Folk of the South Revisited.* Baton Rouge, La.: Louisiana State University Press.

Olmsted, Frederick Law (1856) *A Journey in the Seaboard Slave States in the Years 1853–1854, with Remarks on their Economy.* New York: Dix and Edwards.

Weaver, Herbert (1945) *Mississippi Farmers, 1850–1860.* Nashville, Tenn.: Vanderbilt University Press.

CHAPTER FIVE

Humanitarian Reform and Antislavery

JAMES B. STEWART

When abolitionist feelings first began to circulate in Great Britain and North America in the 1770s, the institution of slavery had been exerting enormous power over a wide expanse of the globe for many centuries. From Greco-Roman times onward, the exploitation of unfree humans had shaped economies and social orders throughout the western world. Slaves by the hundreds of thousands had built the civilizations of the classical era. Throughout the Middle Ages, the Renaissance and well into the eighteenth century, landed aristocrats commanded the unfree labor of millions of their fellow Europeans through the practices of villeinage and serfdom. As historian David Eltis (1999) emphasized in his in-depth analysis of the African slave trade on a global scale, *The Rise of African Slaves in the Americas*, by the seventeenth century western Europeans had all abandoned the idea of enslaving one another even as they turned to Africa as a source of unfree labor. By the eighteenth century, the power of slavery and the African slave trade to generate massive wealth and to forcibly redistribute African-born peoples throughout the western hemisphere had become a proven fact. Spain, Portugal, the Netherlands, France and England, bastions of "freedom" with respect to the treatment of their own peoples, nevertheless developed immense slavery-based empires stretching from Brazil and the Caribbean through British North America.

Thus when the American patriots first asserted the revolutionary claim of equality in 1776, they did so in a world in which systems of slavery had become deeply entrenched and extraordinarily productive. That the author of the Declaration of Independence, Thomas Jefferson, owned close to 200 slaves symbolized as few other facts could the tangled relationships that Edmund Morgan, Winthrop Jordan, and other histor-ians have established between the birth of American "freedom," the ongoing tragedy of racial exploitation, and the rise of the abolitionist spirit. Jordan (1965), in *White over Black*, presents a deep analysis of the origins of racial prejudice in the British North American colonies. Morgan's (1975) *American Slavery/American Freedom* delineates slavery's pervasive influence on revolutionary ideology and social relations in the South. These historians illustrate that, even as British North Americans asserted the right of revolution, every colony, North and South, maintained a system of slavery.

Though rural New Englanders had few uses for slaves, rich Yankees confirmed a high status by owning them as personal "servants." In Rhode Island, New York, New Jersey, Delaware, and Pennsylvania, by contrast, slaveholders profited in large-scale farming. In major northern cities, slaves labored in manufacturing and construction. The findings of historians Ira Berlin (1998) and William McManus (1970) have confirmed that though the total number of African Americans living in the North, free or enslaved, was only 4 percent of the total population, slavery clearly contributed to the development of the region's economy. In the southern colonies, meanwhile, slavery exercised an infinitely more pervasive influence. In Berlin's words, the northern colonies constituted "societies with slaves." In the South, by contrast, there were only "slave societies" (Berlin 1998: 11).

In every southern colony, as much fine scholarship has demonstrated, elite slaveholders directed politics, shaped the economy, and defined social norms. From the rice-growing coasts of South Carolina and Georgia to the tobacco plantations of Virginia, North Carolina, and Maryland, these "first families" derived their power from their command over their numerous slaves, who, by 1776, constituted 35 out of every 100 of the colonial South's inhabitants. The majority of the South's whites, small slaveholders and middling subsistence farmers, often resented those claiming to be their "betters." Yet when they could not isolate themselves from the influence of these elites, they more often deferred to them than opposed them, for this was a society based on clear ordering of privilege, the cultural and social implications of which have been masterfully explained by Bertram Wyatt-Brown (1982) in *Southern Honor* – the strong (and therefore honorable) over the weak (and therefore despised), the rich over the middling and the poor, men over women – and, above all, white over black.

For this reason, southern whites of all social classes generally concurred that "inalienable rights" and claims of equality did not apply to people of African ancestry. Moreover, from the beginning, nearly all English settlers from Georgia to Massachusetts had harbored deep prejudices against dark-skinned Africans that had justified the process of enslavement as a proper one, for it not only compelled work from the "naturally lazy" blacks, but also kept control over a "dangerously degraded race," two characteristics imputed to African-descended peoples to mark their disqualification from republican citizenship. Thus, by 1776, the strength of slaveowning and white racial prejudice posed enormous challenges to those patriots who began linking independence from England with abolitionist goals. Nevertheless, the colonists' revolt against England inaugurated the crusade against slavery.

Several influences explain this development; all of them can be traced to the colonists' revolutionary beliefs – beliefs that David Brion Davis (1975) has examined so richly in his work, *The Problem of Slavery in the Age of Revolution, 1776–1823*. Some revolutionary leaders such as Benjamin Franklin, Thomas Paine, Patrick Henry, and Benjamin Rush developed strong abolitionist conclusions from enlightenment rationalism and Scottish "common-sense" philosophy – both of which fueled their hatred of monarchy and aristocracy. Believing the enlightenment axiom that environmental conditions determined people's intellectual and moral development, not their color or inherited status, such leaders concluded that the contradictions between patriots' demands for liberty and their oppression of black slaves were too enormous to ignore. According to this logic, emancipation would relieve African

Americans of their "degraded" circumstances and allow them to "rise" to respectable citizenship, even as white Americans cast off their own corrupting attachments to "corrupting" slaveholding. Other patriotic spokesmen drew their abolitionism from evangelical religion. As scholars such as James Essig (1982), Christine Heyrman (1984), and Jean Soderlund (1985) have emphasized, Calvinist revivalists such as Samuel Hopkins and Jonathan Mayhew joined with Quaker evangelicals, such as John Woolman and Anthony Benezet, and Methodists, such as Francis Asbury, to condemn slavery as the arrant defiance of God's will, and the principal obstacle to the achievement of independence. Imbibing such sentiments, some prominent planter politicians in the upper South, such as St. George Tucker and Peyton Randolph, gradually emancipated their own slaves, calling on others to follow their examples. As emphasized by historians Gary Nash (1990) in *Race and Revolution*, and Woody Holton (1999) in *Forced Founders*, much of the motivation for these slaveholders' antislavery derived from their (not ungrounded) fears that the South's rapidly expanding black population harbored insurrectionary inclinations and stimulated the reproductive "mixing of the races." For this reason, such planters supported the closing of the African slave trade as well as the principle of very gradual, and well-compensated, emancipation. Inspired by a powerful mixture of fearful self-interest and high ideological principle, the logic of the Revolution challenged slavery's moral legitimacy as never before.

Most crucially, however, the struggle for independence led African Americans, enslaved and free alike, to revolt wholesale against their oppressors, transforming the Revolutionary War into what historians now recognize as North America's largest slave insurrection. In both North and South, as scholars such as Sylvia Frey (1993), Sidney Kaplan (1989), and William D. Pierson (1996) have all demonstrated, slaves fought on both sides in exchange for promises of freedom. Numerous others used the disruptions of warfare to escape to northern cities. In all, it is estimated that perhaps as many as 25,000 African Americans succeeded in freeing themselves between 1776 and 1783, while all across the North they asserted their claims to citizenship by petitioning state legislatures to enact bills of emancipation, negotiating with their masters to secure their freedom, and filing emancipation suits in courts. In all these ways, African Americans not only secured their individual liberty, but also stepped forward collectively into the world of active citizenship, establishing in every northern city communities supported by church and civic organizations which offered economic opportunity, education, and leadership in struggles against discrimination and slavery.

Such unprecedented activity, in turn, forced white northerners to argue among themselves as never before about whether these irrepressible African Americans constituted a "degraded race" that threatened the values of the emerging republic, or whether, instead, they merited full citizenship. As David Gellman (2000) and Dickson D. Bruce (1982) have demonstrated, debates on such questions filled the pages of urban newspapers, with whites attempting to speak for, as well as against, the interests of the enslaved, even as black writers, for the first time, spoke comprehensively for themselves. In this manner, African American voices, projected by white writers as well as by blacks, secured their permanence in the political cultures of the northern states. More important still, this same process fostered the emergence of an extraordinary group of elite African American community leaders: formidable personalities such as Philadelphia's James Forten, who rose to prominence as an entrepreneurial sail-maker, and his close associate, Richard Allen, founder of the African Methodist Episcopal Church. Their equivalents in Boston included Prince Hall, founder of the African American Masonic movement, and James Easton, a highly successful manufacturer, while in New York, John Teasman pioneered in developing public education for African Americans.

This unprecedented prominence of African American leaders, issues and advocacy in the "public sphere" soon made its influence felt in the workings of revolutionary governments. By the late 1790s, every state legislature north of Virginia and Maryland had enacted bills of gradual emancipation, with Massachusetts leading the way in 1780, and New York State the last to follow suit in 1798. But liberation itself was a slow, unjust and partial process. By extending the age threshold required for emancipation to 21 or higher, slaveholders often exploited their slaves through their most productive years before releasing them, and then exploited them further by requiring extended apprenticeship. Exactly how many slaves were sold to southern buyers by their northern owners prior to emancipation deadlines remains uncertain, but historians agree that the number was not inconsiderable.

Hence, by the mid-1820s, though every northern state save New Jersey and Delaware had rid itself of slavery, it is hardly surprising (though nevertheless tragic) that African Americans found their political and civil rights being strictly limited in these new post-emancipation regimes. Simultaneously, harsh patterns of daily discrimination and terrifying moments of white mob violence increasingly blighted their lives. Though, as abolitionists always knew, freedom for African Americans in the post-emancipation North had little to do with equality, most white northerners failed utterly to grasp this vital truth. Instead, by the 1830s, they had repressed all memory of the North's long history of slavery and discrimination, preferring instead to condemn their free black neighbors as a "degraded race" while drawing self-satisfied contrasts between their own presumably benevolent free states, where slavery had been ended peacefully, and the backward, despotic South where slavery held perpetual sway. By thus "disowning slavery" as part of their regional history, as Joanne Pope Melish (1998) has demonstrated in *Disowning Slavery*, whites in the North created a racial tyranny of the majority that was, in its own perverse way, as terrifying to combat and as impervious to change as southern slavery itself.

As if to reinforce these strong white supremacist trends, the new federal constitution of 1787 also worked towards racially reactionary goals when guaranteeing powerful protections for slavery in the southern states. Here, despite an impressive wave of private manumissions involving some of the upper South's most esteemed politician-statesmen, George Washington foremost among them, emancipation ultimately made no permanent inroads. Several features of the new federal constitution further buttressed the planters' interests by counting slaves as three-fifths of a full person when apportioning representation, guaranteeing the use of federal power to quell slave insurrection, extending the African slave trade for two decades (until 1808), and providing for a federally enforced fugitive slave law. All these provisions confirmed that slavery had been granted formidable legitimacy by the Founding Fathers, who envisioned a strong national government which of necessity must be able to suppress divisive attempts to weaken or abolish slavery. As fine constitutional scholarship such as Paul Finkelman's (1996) *Slavery and the Founders* has demonstrated, the constitutional convention's deliberations over slavery thus amounted more to a capitulation than to a compromise. Though the 1790s Northern Federalist party luminaries such as John Jay, Alexander Hamilton, Fisher Ames, and Josiah Quincy expressed deep opposition to southern slavery on moral as well as political grounds, the ineffectiveness of their dissent only documented the success of the new constitution in protecting what were now clearly becoming the well-understood interests of the South's planter class. As historian Leonard D. Richards (2000) has cogently documented in his work, *The Slave Power*, here were found the roots of the "slave power conspiracy" that ultimately galvanized opposition from antislavery northerners in the decades preceding the outbreak of the Civil War.

With slavery unchallenged throughout the plantation South, abolished but also "disowned" in the white supremacist North, and nationally protected by the federal constitution, the abolitionist spirit of 1776 had all but vanished as the eighteenth century closed. By 1820, the "cotton revolution," inaugurated by Eli Whitney's gin, sustained Britain's insatiable demand for cheap clothing and stimulated an explosive westward expansion of the southern frontier. As a consequence, several new slave states such as Kentucky, Tennessee, Louisiana, Mississippi, and Alabama entered the Union. As Michael Tadman (1989) and Walter Johnson (1999) have demonstrated in their works *Speculators and Slaves* and *Soul by Soul* respectively, the sprawling domestic slave trade, now thriving as never before, expanded rapidly into these newly opened and highly profitable markets. By 1830, the total property value embodied in slavery had grown to exceed all other forms of investment within the United States, except for investment in land itself. In the face of this explosive growth, white abolitionist numbers shrank to a quiet handful – mostly isolated Quakers such as Benjamin Lundy, Jessie Torrey, and John Rankin, who restricted the publishing of small newspapers and broadsides in the upper South. Only those energetic free black leaders living in northern cities (as mentioned earlier) continued to speak for abolitionism as a coherent social movement.

Abortive insurrection led by free blacks, in Virginia by Gabriel Prosser (in 1800) and in South Carolina by Denmark Vesey (in 1822), as well as the remarkably violent black revolution that succeeded in Haiti in the 1790s, added immeasurably to the nation's reactionary racial mood. Besides extinguishing any residual interest in manumission among upper South slaveholders, these frightening auguries of race war heightened planters' fears of slave revolt, their worries about the rapidly expanding number of southern free blacks, and their interest in the American Colonization Society, founded in 1816. Raising the banner of "benevolent reform," this Society proposed the voluntary repatriation to Liberia of free blacks and emancipated slaves, a program that also appealed strongly to reform-minded northern whites, who regarded it as a moderate way to address their cautious though genuine moral concerns about slavery. Most free blacks in the North, however, denounced colonization as a wholesale negation of their demands for full citizenship, based, as it clearly was, on the assumption that even the most accomplished free blacks had no viable prospects while remaining in the United States.

Judged in retrospect, colonization appears a chimerical project since the mass transport of over 2 million people as well as compensation for the entire planter class would have been required were it to have been successful in solving the problem of slavery. But in the 1820s, free blacks had every good reason to fear and condemn it, for the Society rapidly received endorsements from every northern state legislature and drew the glowing support of some of the nation's most powerful politicians, Henry Clay, James Madison, and James Monroe among them. By the later 1820s northern free blacks also were deeply aware that the forced expulsion of southern Indian peoples at the behest of slaveholding politicians gave awful premonitions about the colonizationists' deeper plans for them, specifically. Though strong political disagreements split southern and northern Congressmen over the admission of the slave state, Missouri (1819–21), such sectional tensions did nothing to hearten either the North's black activists or its few white activists since, from their perspectives, Missouri's admission only proved again that slavery ruled over national politics, just as colonization defined the limits of "benevolent" reform.

Indeed, throughout the North, the decade of the 1820s witnessed an unprecedented spread of anti-black bigotry that greatly strengthened that region's support for southern slavery. Massive immigration from the British Isles suddenly put economically insecure English, Scottish, and Irish workers into competitive proximity with northern free blacks, stimulating fears about the possibility of subjecting European-descended people to "white slavery" and thereby creating deep new levels of white working-class prejudice. Indeed, the historian David Roediger (1991) analyzed the development of white supremacist ideology and identity in the new republic in *The Wages of Whiteness*, as did Eric Lott (1993) in *Love and Theft*, and Alexander Saxton (1989) in *The Rise and Fall of the White Republic*. Among "respectable" middle-class whites, the belief meanwhile grew that free blacks represented a "naturally degraded race" that needed policing rather than assistance. Free African Americans grew ever more anxious and defensive as large-scale anti-black riots erupted for the first time in major northern cities, and as state and local governments passed harsh new discriminatory legislation, even while broadening the right of the franchise to include all adult white males. In newly admitted western "free" states such as Illinois and Ohio, for example, specific constitutional provisions either prohibited blacks from immigrating or explicitly denied them most civil rights. In 1827, the New York State legislature restricted suffrage to black males possessing more than 200 dollars in taxable property, while two years later the white residents of Cincinnati rioted so viciously that many local blacks sought permanent residence elsewhere.

In response to these menacing developments, besieged black leaders throughout the North gathered their collective strength by founding their own newspaper, *Freedom's Journal* (in 1827), and their own organization, the Colored Convention Movement (in 1830), each a vehicle for protesting against discrimination, denouncing colonization, and debating the possibility of voluntary emigration to Haiti or lower Canada. In 1829, when Boston's David Walker first published his extraordinary pamphlet, *An Appeal to the Colored Citizens of the World, and Most Particularly to Those of the United States*, his beleaguered black readers understandably embraced his revolutionary call for the use of defensive violence, his unflinching condemnation of Thomas Jefferson's racial bigotry, his scathing condemnations of black Americans' apathy and ignorance, and his unsparing condemnations of the American Colonization Society. Clearly, as free blacks in the North understood it, the end of the 1820s was forcing them to confront a compounding racial crisis of extremely dangerous proportions.

By 1831, however, this crisis no longer impended. Instead, as Louis Masur's (2001) work *1831: The Year of Eclipse* has emphasized, it exploded, as four nearly simultaneous events set off fundamental struggles over slavery and racial oppression unparalleled in the nation's history, conflicts that ultimately presaged Civil War. In addition to the discovery that Walker's *Appeal* was circulating among slaves in the South's coastal cities, the year 1831 brought with it Nat Turner's bloody insurrection in Southampton County, Virginia, where 57 whites were slaughtered, and a slave revolt of unprecedented size in British Jamaica; dangerous secession threats from South Carolinian "nullifiers" who feared the federal government threatened their right to hold slaves; and, perhaps most portentous of all, the publication by white Bostonian William Lloyd of a new abolitionist newspaper, the *Liberator*, which espoused a radical new doctrine – "immediate emancipation." To slaveholders and free northern blacks, to white reformers of all types, and to politicians everywhere, it was suddenly clear that slavery constituted an explosive moral question that was impossible to ignore.

Garrison's demand for "immediate emancipation" all but foreordained this result since it quickly became the rallying cry of a broad-based, white-dominated movement for the destruction of slavery. The imperative that the "God-defying sin" of owning fellow humans be swept from the Earth as rapidly as possible was adopted by northern reformers from Great Britain's abolitionist movement which, at that time, was demanding that Parliament legislate compensated emancipation throughout the Empire's colonies, a goal accomplished in 1833. Soon after Garrison adopted immediatism, dozens of influential white reformers throughout New England joined him to form the nucleus of a vibrantly radical white-led crusade that was to continue for at least four decades, even after the Civil War had ended slavery. As they mounted their initial crusades, they eagerly encouraged participation by leaders of the North's African American communities: men like James Easton and James Forten, who responded with great enthusiasm, thereby suddenly creating the nation's first biracial social movement. In the atmosphere of mounting racial intolerance so prevalent in the 1820s and 1830s, this eagerness on all sides to "mix" black people with white was undoubtedly immediate abolitionism's most controversial and disturbing feature.

Modern historians such as Robert Abzug (1995) and Anna Spreicher (2000), who have examined the deeper beliefs and motives of white immediatists, have followed the classic expositions of Gilbert Hobbes Barnes (1950 [1933], 1965 [1934]) and Whitney Cross (1950), completed in the 1930s and 1940s, which emphasized the importance of the religious spirit in inspiring a commitment to "the Cause." During the 1820s a popular resurgence of evangelical Protestantism known as the "Second Great Awakening" swept the nation, and for certain New Englanders its impact had deep abolitionist implications. Powerful revivalist preachers such as Lyman Beecher and Charles G. Finney propounded doctrines that stressed the individual's free-will choice to turn away from sin, to seek personal holiness, and then, once "saved," to bring God's truth to the "unredeemed" and to combat the social evils that "sin" inevitably fostered – drunkenness, greed, impiety, sexual license, and the exploitation of the weak and defenseless. To the ears of certain Beecher and Finney devotees – such as the pious millionaire merchant brothers from New York City, Arthur and Lewis Tappan, Theodore Dwight Weld, evangelical Protestantism's most charismatic prophet, and Elizur Wright Jr, mathematical genius turned religious zealot, as well as "primitive" Baptists like Garrison, neo-Calvinists like Samuel Sewall Jr and William Jay, and radical Quakers like Lucretia Mott, Angelina and Sarah Grimke, and John

Greenleaf Whittier – these doctrines made clear that slavery was the most heinous and God-defying of all sins. In what other society did exploitation of the weak and defenseless take place more brazenly? Where was sexual wantonness more rampant than in the masters' debauchery of their female slaves? Where was impiety more openly encouraged than in the masters' refusals to permit their slaves' freedom of religious expression? Where was brutality more evident than in the masters' heavy use of the whip and branding iron, or their callous disregard for the slaves' ties of family? Who needed more desperately than the slaveowners to respond to the challenge of God's truth that they repent and immediately emancipate those whom they abused so vilely? The response to all these urgent questions, of course, required preaching the truth of "immediate emancipation" by means of what was termed "moral suasion," that is, by making peaceful Christian appeals that would awaken the slumbering consciences of southern slaveholders and their bigoted northern accomplices.

Embedded in these abolitionist appeals were attitudes and values that marked the movement as an unprecedented step in the direction of ideological modernity. Foremost among these were sensibilities of empathy upon which abolitionists so deeply relied when imagining the silent sufferings of the powerless and exploited slaves and responding to their plight with deep humanitarian concern. As Elizabeth Clark (1995) argues in her insightful article, "The Sacred Rights of the Weak," the immediatists' constant emphasis on the sexually exploitative, violent and even mur-derous impact of slavery upon its presumably helpless victims clearly prefigures contemporary crusades on behalf of the "unborn," victims of torture, the homeless, those condemned to capital punishment and so forth. For the first time in the nation's history, overpowering white concern for the plight of "the suffering stranger" had become sufficiently widespread to sustain a powerful social reform movement. Abolitionism was tinctured with other elements of modernity as well, some racial and others involved with the development of the nation's capitalist economy. In regard to race, as I have argued elsewhere, by the later 1830s most abolitionists, whatever their skin color, had come to define the goal of their struggles as that of making the "black race" equal to the "white" (Stewart 1997). While on one level this expectation confirmed the abolitionists' egalitarian belief that all dark-complexioned persons must be treated exactly as were all with light complexions, on another, it fully embraced the unquestioned assumption that biologically determined "races" and no other human characteristics were what truly defined fundamental human reality. In this crucial respect, the most egalitarian social movement the nation had yet produced was nevertheless deeply involved, albeit unconsciously, in the much broader national process of constructing racial categories as unquestionable "facts" of nature, a modern view of "race" that held sway well into the later twentieth century. Only quite recently, with the advent of "postmodern" approaches to the study of "race," have such assumptions been effectively challenged.

Abolitionism's relationship to the spread of western capitalism and the onset of the industrial revolution also has marked the movement as a powerful vehicle for social and economic modernization. While the work of Eric Williams (1994 [1944]) first linked the abolition of British slavery in the Caribbean to the economic interests of England's rising manufacturing economy, American historians also have long made such equations, beginning with the writings of Charles Beard in the 1920s.

More recently, however, scholars such as Eric Foner (1988), Paul Johnson (1978), Amy Dru Stanley (1998), and others have stressed that abolitionists' deep beliefs in economic individualism, moral self-control, and long-range personal goals fostered attitudes toward the individual's freedom to work and toward problems of poverty and class exploitation that meshed beautifully with the development of modern industrial capitalism. That view, however, has also provoked considerable dissent not only from those like Paul Goodman (1998) and Vernon Volpe, who see in abolitionism implacable hostility to modernizing capitalism, but also from scholars like James Huston (1987), Jonathan Glickstein (1991), and myself, who find abolitionists deeply ambivalent. Making matters all the more complicated have been scholarly responses to the work of Thomas Haskell (Bender 1992), who has argued that capitalist modes of problem solving provided the initial impetus for abolitionist thought and action. Extended rebuttals to this view put forth by David B. Davis (1975), John Ashworth (1995), Seymour Drescher (1977), and others make clear that capitalism's relationship with abolitionism, though complicated, was certainly real, and closely related to a modernizing nation.

Whatever its long-term connections to modernity, however, the cause of immediate abolitionism was, from the very first, immensely unpopular in the North as well as in the South. Nevertheless, it also initially grew at a spectacular rate as its leaders busied themselves in the early 1830s. Bankrolled principally by the Tappans, grassroots organizers created hundreds of anti-slavery societies across New England, New York, and Pennsylvania. Further west, particularly in Ohio, Theodore Weld, Elizur Wright Jr, Beriah Green, and their many co-workers likewise helped to establish hundreds of abolitionist organizations. The contents of Garrison's *Liberator* were quickly amplified by dozens of pamphlets and newspapers that circulated widely throughout the free states, with titles such as *The Slaves' Friend*, *The Emancipator*, and *Human Rights*. Salaried agents traversed the free states organizing meetings and denouncing the sins of slaveholding in public speeches. The American Anti-Slavery Society, founded in 1833, sponsored all these activities and, in addition, implemented a "great postal campaign" in 1835, using the United States Mail Service to goad the consciences of slaveholders by flooding the South with abolitionist literature. It also set in motion a "Great Petition Campaign" starting in 1836 that sent the United States Congress thousands of petitions, accompanied by tens of thousands of signatures, each praying that Representatives enact specific pieces of antislavery legislation. In cities across the North, meanwhile, white abolitionists joined with local African American activists in daring efforts to "uplift the black race" by founding schools, moral reform societies, manual labor academies, and Sunday school groups. The most enduring of these, Oberlin College, established in 1835, represented the nation's first example of multiracial coeducation.

As this and many other examples made clear, immediatism was, from the first, a racially "amalgamated" enterprise that welcomed women as well as men, a practice that violated heavy national proscriptions against females taking part in political actions and against blacks becoming personally involved as equals with whites. Instead, prominent black leaders such as James Forten, Hosea Easton, Charles B. Ray, and James Barbadoes visibly attached themselves to the largely white American Anti-Slavery Society; Garrison and the Tappans, in turn, entered openly into the deliberations of the National Colored Convention. The undeniable power of women of both races in the immediatist ranks – people like the white Lydia Maria Child or the black Sarah Forten – further reinforced the impression that abolitionism sought to undermine every traditional relationship, particularly those which placed masters over slaves, men over women, and whites over blacks. By attracting the support of what ultimately turned out to be, in Julie Roy Jeffrey's (1998: 1) apt phrase, a "vast, silent army" of ordinary women of both races, abolitionism did, indeed, defy practically every prevailing political norm. Given all this, it seems all but inevitable in retrospect that the abolitionists' efforts provoked politicians, slaveholders, and ordinary citizens almost everywhere to acts of unprecedented repression and organized violence.

In the South, the "Great Postal Campaign" was quickly quelled by mobs organized by angry slaveholders that ransacked post offices, burned abolitionist pamphlets, and hung Garrison and the Tappan brothers in effigy – all with the approval of Postmaster-General Amos Kendall and his patron, President Andrew Jackson. In Congress, the petition campaign also met with repression, resulting in the passage of a controversial "gag rule" that prevented antislavery memorials from being debated at all. Meanwhile, in the free states, between 1834 and 1838, major cities exploded in racial violence as white mobs attacked African American communities and abolitionist meetings in cities such as Boston, Philadelphia, Utica, New York City, Hartford, Pittsburgh, and Cincinnati. Leonard D. Richards (1971), in "*Gentlemen of Property and Standing*", and Paul Gilje's (1996) work, *Rioting in America*, demonstrated that those encouraging the mobs were commercial and business elites, "gentlemen of property and standing" as abolitionists sneeringly termed them, who sensed in immediatism wide-ranging, conspiratorial assaults and threats against their locally based authority. Leading the attacks on black churches and abolitionist meeting halls were unskilled and semi-skilled laborers – often recent immigrants – who feared deeply that slave emancipation and the empowerment of their free black neighbors would lead to their own social and economic "enslavement." Condoning the violence and blaming the abolitionists for causing it were spokesmen for the nation's two great political parties, the Whigs and the Democrats, both of which required support from southern slaveholders as well as from anti-black voters in the free states. By the late 1830s both political parties, nearly all the nation's leading business and church figures, the vast bulk of the northern working class, and the entire white South had arrayed themselves as one against the abolitionists. As a means to rapidly abolish slavery, "immediate emancipation" had plainly failed.

To be sure, repression did bring abolitionism some gains, particularly through new leaders such as the magnificent orator/agitator Wendell Phillips and the millionaire/philanthropist Geritt Smith, who were spurred to immediatism by their disgust with proslavery mobs. The suppression of civil liberties, such as the rights to petition and peaceful assembly, also began leading northerners in increasing numbers to suspect that slaveholders and their free state allies conspired against white people's constitutional freedom and political interests. Russel B. Nye (1949), in *Fettered Freedom*, discussed the mingling of civil liberty concerns with antislavery feeling in the North. Similarly, Eric Foner's (1970) *Free Soil, Free Labor, Free Men* and Richard H. Sewell's (1976) *Ballots for Freedom* have also demonstrated that these powerful feelings spread rapidly in the 1840s and 1850s, linking political controversies between northern and southern politicians over slavery's role in westward expansion to the still more fateful questions regarding the destiny of African people within the framework of the republic.

The impact of repression also shattered the immediatist movement forever as warring factions drew conflicting meanings from their dismaying trials by violence during the late 1830s. For the abolitionists who followed William Lloyd Garrison, such as Wendell Phillips, Henry C. Wright, and Sarah and Angelina Grimke, repression by church, state, and the political process fostered a deep alienation from all such institutions, as well as a deepening reverence for the sanctity of non-coercive relationships and a belief in the possibility of human perfectibility. Such axioms, as Lewis Perry (1973) and Aileen Kraditor (1967) have explained, also led most Garrisonians to reject church and state authority, endorse radical pacifism, embrace women's rights, and demand the dissolution of a presumably proslavery Union. These were creeds that most Garrisonians maintained until the eve of the Civil War which, as Ellen DuBois (1978) confirmed in *Feminism and Suffrage*, also directly inspired the founding of the first women's rights movement by feminist-abolitionists in Seneca Falls, New York (in 1848).

Garrison's opponents vehemently rejected these novel doctrines, yet divided among themselves. Some, following Lewis Tappan, attempted to persevere with original "moral suasion" by founding the American and Foreign Anti-Slavery Society, designed to compete with the Garrison-dominated American Anti-Slavery Society. Others, following Joshua Leavitt and Henry B. Stanton, became engaged in encouraging the rising anti-southern resentments among northern voters over such issues as the "gag rule" and the possible annexation of new frontier slave territories such as Texas. To these anti-Garrisonians, abolitionist duty dictated the plunge into politics by founding an emancipationist third party, the Liberty party, which, in one form or another, campaigned in presidential contests through Lincoln's election in 1860.

For the next two decades, from 1840 until 1861, these competing sects of abolitionists pursued their preferred political strategies with few measurable results while creating among themselves what historian Lawrence Friedman (1984), in *Gregarious Saints*, has termed "sacred communities" which gave them personal support as they continued their efforts to challenge the nation's white supremacist polity. Meantime, however, the focus of national conflicts over slavery shifted to Congress, where Whigs and Democrats struggled with growing sectional discord over slavery's westward expansion. In the complex process of sectional estrangement that developed in politics in the1840s and 1850s over whether or not newly acquired western territories should open to slavery or instead be reserved as "free soil," immediate abolitionists played only limited roles. The Texas annexation and the Mexican War (1845–8) first raised this sectional issue, which then exploded in the North in the later 1850s after the Kansas-Nebraska Act (1854–7) and the Dred Scott Decision (1857), which seemingly guaranteed the unlimited expansion of slavery. As the Whig party dissolved, the Democratic party split along North–South lines, a new Republican party emerged in the free states that pledged to arrest any further expansion of slavery, and abolitionists exercised little immediately observable power. When explaining the massive collapse and realignment of parties that took place in the later 1850s, political historians with otherwise quite divergent views such as Joel Silbey (1977), John Ashworth (1995), Michael Morrison (1997), and Michael Holt (1978) suggest little role for immediate abolitionists. These reformers did, however, wield significant influence of an indirect sort because of their close relationships with antislavery-minded United States Senators and Representatives, all of whom maintained strong abolitionist associations throughout their careers. Ohio Senators Salmon Chase and Benjamin Wade, for example, traced their antislavery roots to the early 1830s and the compelling abolitionist "witness" of Theodore Dwight Weld. So did Ohio Congressman Joshua R. Giddings, unquestionably slavery's most radical political foe throughout his unequaled two decades in the House of Representatives. Illinois Representative Owen Lovejoy's brother, the immediatist Elijah, was murdered in 1837 by a proslavery mob, while Massachusetts Senators Charles Sumner and Henry Wilson collaborated openly with Boston's Garrisonians. Though this list could easily be extended, the larger point should be clear. While the abolitionist movement had little measurable effect on rollcall votes or congressional legislation, its many ties to prominent northern politicians gave its ideas publicity and currency in the highest of political circles. Just as important, this same process led southern Congressmen quickly to suspect (with good reason) that some of their "Yankee" counterparts were actually covert abolitionists and, therefore, uncommonly dangerous to the South's position within the Federal Union.

On state and local levels, abolitionist engagement in the politics of race and slavery was far more obvious, lacking in subtlety and directly supported by the "sacred communities" they had fashioned for themselves. For example, white and black abolitionists sometimes created significant alliances to challenge segregation and political disenfranchisement. In Boston, suspicions turned into amply substantiated fears. Leading immediatists such as Wendell Phillips, Thomas Wentworth Higginson, and Frederick Douglass gladly became implicated in the frontier bloodshed, especially when supporting the abolitionists most responsible for spilling it – John Brown and his sons, who slaughtered several unoffending settlers during the Kansas "wars" of 1855–6. In this, however, such immediatists were hardly alone, since prominent members of the North's just-emerging Republican party also proved eager to "save" Kansas from slavery by sending arms to Kansas "free-staters." Though Republicans forswore all intention to dismantle slavery in the South, and often affirmed their dedication to white supremacy, their party platforms consistently registered hostility to slavery's expansion westward. This position won them much abolitionist sympathy, clear northern majorities in 1856 elections, and a victorious national plurality for Abraham Lincoln in 1860. By this time, Brown had been hanged for his incendiary attempt (secretly financed by six prominent immediatists) to provoke slave insurrection by seizing and distributing weapons from the federal arsenal at Harpers Ferry, Virginia, and slaveholders were now well satisfied that Lincoln and his party were fundamentally no different than Brown, Douglass, and Garrison – "black Republican abolitionists" all. Though three decades of immediatist crusading had produced few measurable results, the abolitionists had exercised an undeniable influence on frightened slaveholders' decision to leave the Federal Union and commence a Civil War.

Though a few pacifist abolitionists opposed the onset of war, the vast majority of the original immediatists enthusiastically supported hostilities against the South. Until late 1862, President Lincoln, like most Republicans, understood the war as an effort to restore the Union rather than abolish slavery, a view that abolitionists hotly contested. As James McPherson (1965) explained, Massachusetts in particular witnessed successful biracial efforts by Garrisonians to desegregate public education, while in New York State, white and black Liberty party members campaigned (unsuccessfully) to repeal unequal suffrage restrictions against black men. During these struggles, well analyzed by James and Lois Horton (1997), Julie Winch (1988), Carleton Mabee (1970), Jane and William Pease (1974), and others, African American activists developed their own independent crusades against slavery and discrimination, partly in reaction to expressions of racially tinged superiority directed toward them by their white abolitionist coworkers. Impressive new leaders – some escapees from slavery, others free northerners, such as Frederick Douglass, Henry Highland Garnet, James McCune Smith, and Sojourner Truth – came to the fore in the 1840s and 1850s to testify eloquently against slavery and white supremacy and to infuse black abolitionism with rich new ideological visions. Such visions sharpened acutely after Congress passed a stringent new Fugitive Slave Law in 1850 that threatened not only escapees but also free northern blacks with reenslavement. In response, black and white abolitionists united in acts of defiance which sometimes turned to violence, as in Christiana, Pennsylvania, in 1851, where a slaveholder was shot and killed by resisters when attempting to recapture a fugitive. Syracuse, Boston, Oberlin, and Detroit also witnessed such confrontations in the 1850s, with the risk of bloodshed always high. By embracing confrontation, abolitionists of both races did exercise one surprisingly influential type of political influence in the decade before the Civil War, specifically among the South's slaveholders. Because of resistance to the Fugitive Slave Law, as southern planters judged it, the North in the 1850s seemed to be overrun with lawbreaking abolitionists whom authorities could not or would not put down. When protracted guerrilla warfare between southern and northern settlers broke out in Kansas in the mid-1850s over the possible introduction of slavery, their 30-year crusade against slavery gave them the status of vindicated prophets in the eyes of many northerners, a fact they exploited to mold public opinion in favor of emancipation. Douglass, Phillips, and Garrison suddenly became the North's most sought-after public speakers and, in their orations, they castigated Lincoln's failure to emancipate and urged the mobilization of African American fighting units. In private, they cultivated political alliances with abolitionist-minded Republican Congressmen. But when ever-larger numbers of slaves took advantage of the chaos of war by abandoning their masters and following the Union armies, they advanced the abolitionists' cause as no Congressman or immediatist could.

To have forced these refugees to return to their masters – traitorous slaveholders who had taken up arms against the Union – was, to Republican party members, politically unthinkable. The logic of emancipation thus became impossible to deny. But as soon as President Lincoln's Emancipation Proclamation came into force, on January 1, 1863, Phillips, Douglass, and the rest next began demanding constitutional amendments that would outlaw slaveholding permanently and secure full citizenship to those emancipated. Abolitionists also took advantage of massive Union Army conquests in coastal South Carolina by sending into that region ministers, schoolteachers and businesspeople, whose task it became to prepare the emancipated for political and social equality. Thanks to the combined efforts of northern abolitionists, black soldiers, and self-liberated slaves, when the war ended in 1865 it initiated a social revolution in the South, a full "dress rehearsal for reconstruction," as historian Willie Lee Rose (1964) has termed it. No matter how badly hobbled by illiteracy, poverty, and the lack of political rights, every former slave was incontestably free.

It was a revolution that many defeated southern whites immediately attempted to suppress, violently if necessary. In 1865–6, following Lincoln's assassination, former Confederate states recognized the permanence of emancipation by ratifying the Thirteenth Amendment, but then put so many harsh restrictions on the rights of those who had been liberated as to suggest, to even dispassionate observers, that they were reinstating slavery in another form. Such intransigence, however, played directly into the hands of abolitionists such as Phillips and Douglass and radical Republicans such as Thaddeus Stevens, Charles Sumner, and Benjamin Wade, who truly wished to reconstruct the nation as a biracial democracy, and supported granting freed people farm lands confiscated from leading Confederates. Since many northerners feared that their hard-won victory would be lost if former Confederates were allowed to return to power, the idea of enfranchising former slaves as voters and protecting them as free laborers seemed not only just, but politically imperative. Thus, most Republicans finally threw their support behind the idea of black enfranchisement.

Though Garrison and some of his supporters argued that the abolitionist mission had been fulfilled with the passage of the emancipationist Thirteenth Amendment, Phillips, Douglass, Elizabeth Cady Stanton, and many other veterans adamantly disagreed, insisting that the real struggle was only beginning. Until 1870, when Congress and two-thirds of the states had ratified the Fourteenth and Fifteenth Amendments guaranteeing equal legal protection to all citizens and enfranchising all adult black men, these aging radicals kept up an incessant agitation for complete, federally enforced black equality, dividing among themselves only on the question of extending voting rights to women of both races. In the process, they led the unsuccessful battle in 1867 to impeach and try Lincoln's successor President Andrew Johnson because of his adamant opposition toward radical Reconstruction. But when the Fifteenth Amendment did become a reality, abolitionists concluded that they had at last redeemed the commitments they had made decades earlier, to sweep away the tyranny of slaveholding and to construct instead a society secured by just, uniform principles of racial equality.

In retrospect, the abolitionists' legacy can appear to be far less hopeful. By the 1890s, white reactionaries had overturned Reconstruction governments throughout the South. Disenfranchisement, terrorism and sharecropping, chain gangs and segregation, all justified in the name of white supremacy supported and sustained the new order. So, in the long run, as Merton Dillon (1959) has argued, it is difficult to believe that the abolitionists, for all their idealistic persistence, actually succeeded in forcing the nation to confront its deeper racial tragedy. Even with the overthrow of legalized segregation and the rise of a large new black middle class, thanks largely to the Civil Rights Movement of the 1950s and 1960s, far too much evidence of that tragedy remains embedded in our nation today to easily justify some more hopeful conclusion.

But by drawing on studies of historical memory, more heartening assessments of the abolitionists' enduring significance will emerge. It was no accident, in other words, that young African American activists of the early twentieth century such as W. E. B. DuBois and James Weldon Johnson derived deep personal inspiration from abolitionist models exemplified in the lives of James McCune Smith, Henry Highland

Garnet, and Frederick Douglass. In like manner, scholars and activists in the 1960s discovered the abolitionists anew as the Civil Rights Movement forced the nation once again to confront the tragedies of "race" embedded in its history. The result has been a spectacular renaissance of African American history, as well as an energetically sustained, continuing initiative over more than three decades by historians and literary scholars to study of abolitionism. But the lengthy lists of fresh biographies, revealing monographs, and compilations of primary sources suggest only parts of this more affirming (and challenging) abolitionist legacy. In addition, its spirit sustains the work of public agencies such as the National Park Service's program to develop "underground railroad" sites, the ever-closer relationships between abolitionist scholarship and efforts to combat slavery's current global resurgence, and the work of very generous private foundations to underwrite new scholarship, curriculum development, and collaborations between historians of slavery and abolitionism throughout the world.

So although the abolitionists' legacies are, in one sense, whatever we decide to make of them, there is a far more important historical truth to be remembered. Whatever their strengths and deficiencies, these disruptive reformers once dared, over and over, to teach bitter but essential lessons about social injustice to their contemporaries, whether their contemporaries wished them to do so or not. As their official interpreters, and as citizens too, historians have compelling reason to uphold their example.

ACKNOWLEDGEMENTS

An abbreviated version of portions of this chapter appeared in Beverly McMillan (ed.) (2002) *Captive Passage: The Transatlantic Slave Trade and the Making of the Americas,* Washington, DC: Smithsonian Institution Press. I am grateful to Ms McMillan and to the Smithsonian Institution Press for permitting me to expand on this earlier essay.

BIBLIOGRAPHY

Abzug, Robert (1995) *Cosmos Crumbling: American Reform and the Religious Imagination.* New York: Oxford University Press.
Ashworth, John (1995) *Slavery, Capitalism and Politics in the Antebellum Republic.* Cambridge: Cambridge University Press.
Barnes, Gilbert Hobbs (1950 [1933]) *The Anti-Slavery Impulse, 1830–1844.* New York: Harcourt, Brace and World.
Barnes, Gilbert Hobbs (1965 [1934]) (eds.) *Letters of Theodore Dwight Weld, Angelina Grimke and Sarah Grimke, 1822–1844.* Gloucester, Mass.: P. Smith.
Bender, Thomas (1992) *The Antislavery Debate: Capitalism and Abolitionism as a Problem in Historical Interpretation.* Berkeley, Calif.: University of California Press.
Berlin, Ira (1998) *Many Thousands Gone: The First Two Centuries of Slavery in North America.* New York: Oxford University Press.
Bruce, Dickson D. (1982) *The Rhetoric of Conservatism: The Virginia Convention of 1829–30 and the Conservative Tradition in the South.* San Marino, Calif.: Huntington Library.
Clark, Elizabeth (1995) "'The Sacred Rights of the Weak': Pain, Sympathy, and the Culture of Individual Rights in Antebellum America," *Journal of American History* 82: 463–93.

Cross, Whitney R. (1950) *The Burned-over District: The Social and Intellectual History of Enthusiastic Religion in Western New York, 1800–1850.* Ithaca, NY: Cornell University Press.

Davis, David Brion (1975) *The Problem of Slavery in the Age of Revolution, 1770–1823.* New York: Oxford University Press.

Dillon, Merton L. (1959) "The Failure of the Abolitionists," *Journal of Southern History* 25: 159–77.

DuBois, Ellen (1978) *Feminism and Suffrage: The Emergence of an Independent Women's Movement in America, 1848–1869.* Ithaca, NY: Cornell University Press.

Drescher, Seymour (1977) *Econocide: British Slavery in the Era of Abolition.* Pittsburgh, Penn.: University of Pittsburgh Press.

Eltis, David (1999) *The Rise of African Slaves in the Americas.* New York: Cambridge University Press.

Essig, James D. (1982) *The Bonds of Wickedness: American Evangelicals Against Slavery, 1770–1808.* Philadelphia, Pa.: Temple University Press.

Finkelman, Paul (1996) *Slavery and the Founders: Race and Liberty in the Age of Jefferson.* Armonk, NY: Sharpe.

Foner, Eric (1970) *Free Soil, Free Labor, Free Men: The Ideology of the Republican Party before the Civil War.* New York: Oxford University Press.

Foner, Eric (1988) *Reconstruction: America's Unfinished Revolution, 1863–1877.* New York: Harper and Row.

Frey, Sylvia (1993) *Water from the Rock: Black Resistance in the Revolutionary Age.* Princeton, NJ: Princeton University Press.

Friedman, Lawrence J. (1984) *Gregarious Saints: Self and Community in American Abolitionism.* New York: Cambridge University Press.

Gellman, David N. (2000) "Race, the Public Sphere and Abolition in Late Eighteenth Century New York," *Journal of the Early Republic* 20: 607–36.

Gilje, Paul A. (1996) *Rioting in America.* Bloomington, Ind.: Indiana University Press.

Glickstein, Jonathan A. (1991) *Concepts of Free Labor in Antebellum America.* New Haven, Conn.: Yale University Press.

Goodman, Paul (1998) *Of One Blood: Abolitionism and the Origins of Racial Equality.* Berkeley, Calif.: University of California Press.

Heyrman, Christine Leigh (1984) *Commerce and Culture: The Maritime Communities of Colonial Massachusetts, 1690–1750.* New York: Norton.

Holt, Michael F. (1978) *The Political Crisis of the 1850s.* New York: Wiley.

Holton, Woody (1999) *Forced Founders: Indians, Debtors, Slaves and the Making of the Revolution in Virginia.* Chapel Hill, NC: University of North Carolina Press.

Horton, James and Horton, Lois (1997) *In Hope of Liberty: Culture, Community and Protest among Northern Free Blacks, 1700–1860.* New York: Oxford University Press.

Huston, James L. (1987) *The Panic of 1857 and the Coming of the Civil War.* Baton Rouge, La.: Louisiana State University Press.

Jeffrey, Julie Roy (1998) *The Great, Silent Arm of Abolitionism: Ordinary Women in the Abolitionist Movement.* Chapel Hill, NC: University of North Carolina Press.

Johnson, Paul E. (1978) *A Shopkeeper's Millennium: Society and Revivals in Rochester, New York, 1815–1837.* New York: Hill and Wang.

Johnson, Walter (1999) *Soul by Soul: Life Inside the Antebellum Slave Market.* Cambridge, Mass.: Harvard University Press.

Jordan, Winthrop (1965) *White over Black: American Attitudes toward the Negro, 1550–1812.* Chapel Hill, NC: University of North Carolina Press.

Kaplan, Sidney (1989) *The Black Presence in the American Revolution.* Amherst, Mass.: University of Massachusetts Press.

Kraditor, Aileen (1967) *Means and Ends in American Abolitionism: Garrison and his Critics on Strategy and Tactics, 1834–1854.* New York: Random House.

Lott, Eric (1993) *Love and Theft: Blackfaced Minstrelsy and the American Working Class.* New York: Oxford University Press.

Mabee, Carleton (1970) *The Non-Violent Abolitionists.* New York: Harper and Row.

McManus, William (1970) *Black Bondage in the North.* New York: Oxford University Press.

McPherson, James M. (1965) *The Struggle for Equality: The Abolitionists during the Civil War and Reconstruction.* Princeton, NJ: Princeton University Press.

Masur, Louis (2001) *1831: The Year of Eclipse.* New York: Hill and Wang.

Melish, Joanne Pope (1998) *Disowning Slavery: Gradual Emancipation and "Race" in New England, 1780–1860.* Ithaca, NY: Cornell University Press.

Morgan, Edmund S. (1975) *American Slavery, American Freedom: The Ordeal of Revolutionary Virginia.* New York: Norton.

Morrison, Michael A. (1997) *Slavery and the American West: The Eclipse of Manifest Destiny and the Coming of the Civil War.* Chapel Hill, NC: University of North Carolina Press.

Nash, Gary (1990) *Race and Revolution.* Madison, Wis.: Madison House.

Nye, Russel B. (1949) *Fettered Freedom: The Slavery Controversy and Civil Liberties.* Ann Arbor, Mich.: University of Michigan Press.

Pease, William H. and Pease, Jane H. (1974) *They Who Would be Free: Blacks' Search for Freedom.* New York: Oxford University Press.

Perry, Lewis C. (1973) *Radical Abolitionism: Anarchy and the Government of God in Antislavery Thought.* Ithaca, NY: Cornell University Press.

Pierson, William D. (1996) *From African to African American: From the Colonial Era to the Early Republic, 1526–1790.* New York: Twayne.

Richards, Leonard D. (1971) *"Gentlemen of Property and Standing": Anti-abolition Mobs in Jacksonian America.* New York: Oxford University Press.

Richards, Leonard L. (2000) *The Slave Power: The Free North and Southern Domination, 1780–1860.* Baton Rouge, La.: Louisiana State University Press.

Roediger, David (1991) *The Wages of Whiteness: Race and the Formation of the American Working Class.* London: Verso.

Rose, Willie Lee (1964) *Rehearsal for Reconstruction: The Port Royal Experiment.* Indianapolis, Ind.: Bobbs-Merrill.

Saxton, Alexander (1990) *The Rise and Fall of the White Republic: Class Politics and Mass Culture in Nineteenth-Century America.* London: Verso.

Sewell, Richard H. (1976) *Ballots for Freedom: Antislavery Politics in the United States, 1848–1865.* New York: Oxford University Press.

Silbey, Joel H. (1977) *A Respectable Minority: The Democratic Party in the Civil War Era, 1860–1868.* New York: Norton.

Soderlund, Jean R. (1985) *Quakers & Slavery: A Divided Spirit.* Princeton, NJ: Princeton University Press.

Speicher, Anne M. (2000) *The Religious World of Antislavery Women: Spirituality in the Lives of Five Abolitionist Lecturers.* Syracuse, NY: Syracuse University Press.

Stanley, Amy Dru (1998) *From Bondage to Contract: Wage Labor, Marriage, and the Market in the Age of Slave Emancipation.* New York: Cambridge University Press.

Stewart, James Brewer (1997) *Holy Warriors: The Abolitionists and American Slavery.* New York: Hill and Wang.

Tadman, Michael (1989) *Speculators and Slaves: Masters, Traders, and Slaves in the Old South.* Madison, Wis.: University of Wisconsin Press.

Williams, Eric Eustace (1994 [1944]) *Capitalism and Slavery.* Chapel Hill, NC: University of North Carolina Press.

Winch, Julie (1988) *Philadelphia's Black Elite: Activism, Accommodation, and the Struggle for Autonomy*. Philadelphia, Penn.: Temple University Press.
Wyatt-Brown, Bertram (1982) *Southern Honor: Ethics and Behavior in the Old South*. New York: Oxford University Press.

SUGGESTED FURTHER READING

Ford, Lacy K., Jr (1991) *The Origins of Southern Radicalism: The South Carolina Upcountry, 1800–1860*. New York: Oxford University Press.
McCurry, Stephanie (1995) *Masters of Small Worlds: Yeoman Households, Gender Relations, and the Political Culture of the Antebellum South Carolina Low Country*. New York: Oxford University Press.
Nash, Gary and Soderlund, Jean (1991) *Freedom by Degrees: Emancipation and its Aftermath in Pennsylvania*. New York: Oxford University Press.
Newman, Richard S. (2002) *The Transformation of American Abolitionism: Fighting Slavery in the Early Republic*. Chapel Hill, NC: University of North Carolina Press.
Price, George and Stewart, James Brewer (eds.) (1999) *To Heal the Scourge of Prejudice: The Life and Writings of Hosea Easton*. Amherst, Mass.: University of Massachusetts Press.
Stadenraus, Philip (1961) *The African Colonization Movement*. Ithaca, NY: Cornell University Press.
Stewart, James Brewer (1998) "The Emergence of Racial Modernity and the Rise of the White North, 1776–1840," *Journal of the Early Republic* 18: 181–217.
Walters, Ronald (1976) *The Antislavery Appeal: American Abolitionism after 1830*. Baltimore, Md.: Johns Hopkins University Press.
Zilversmidt, Arthur (1967) *The First Emancipation: Gradual Emancipation in the North*. Chicago: University of Chicago Press.

CHAPTER SIX

Women in the Antebellum North

Teresa Murphy

The market and industrial revolutions transformed the lives of women as well as men in the North during the antebellum period. However, scholars have debated the precise nature of these changes since women's history first exploded as a field in the 1970s. The earliest of these scholars focused on the ideals of "true womanhood," a domestic ideology that set women off from the new rough-and-tumble world of economic competition and democratic politics. Particularly important was the ideology of separate spheres that structured both the gender relations and gender hierarchy of the period. To what extent were women simply oppressed by this separate sphere and to what extent did they manipulate its shape to exercise influence within and far beyond the thresholds of their homes?

Later scholarship has questioned the usefulness of the separate spheres paradigm from a variety of perspectives. Its boundaries were shown to be so permeable as to be almost meaningless. More important was the recognition that class and race divided women as much as or more than a separate sphere united them. Thus the power relations between women have provided important sites of investigation. Scholars have also focused on the ways in which wage-earning women and women of color in the North led lives very different from those of middle-class women, facing the double burden of heavy labor and contempt because they failed to live up to middle-class ideals of domesticity.

These differences among women and power relations between them have also been important in more recent investigations of the reform activities and political agitation of women that swept the North during the antebellum period. While earlier scholarship focused on the way in which many voluntary associations were an extension of women's sphere, later scholarship has demonstrated the different female networks that underlay these efforts as well as the ways in which racism and class bias surfaced in reform activities.

The "cult of true womanhood" was explored by the historian Barbara Welter (1966) in her pioneering assessment of ideals laid out for women in the ladies' magazines of the antebellum period. The true woman was pious, pure, submissive, and domestic (Welter 1966: 152). These characteristics presumed a woman who focused her activities on the home: rearing her children in Christianity and virtue, providing a comfortable moral retreat for her husband, cooking and cleaning as necessary or supervising servants. She recognized her husband as both the spiritual and economic head of the family, though she saw her special mission in providing religious instruction. Women might leave their homes to pay visits to friends and to attend church, but these were the only social arenas they entered with complete propriety. Their separation from the worlds of business and politics was part of a delicate balance being struck in the antebellum period as women were expected to be moral anchors in a sea of raucous democratic politics and hard-nosed business competition. This was a role that circumscribed the tradition of political activism created by women during the revolutionary period and supported a gender hierarchy in which men were at the top.

The domestic virtue associated with the cult of true womanhood completed an important transition in ideas about virtue that had begun in the eighteenth century. Eighteenth-century notions of virtue had encompassed public virtue as well as private. Ideals of the republic were rooted in the notion of a virtuous citizenry, capable of judging what was in the best interests of the whole commonwealth. Women were not considered particularly virtuous, nor were they considered capable of exercising public virtue. However, their extensive participation in religious activities and the growing moral significance of their domestic responsibilities combined with a movement in political and economic thought to remove virtue from calculations of appropriate public behavior. Thus, the feminization of virtue became a means for privatizing virtue as well. Women were the repositories of virtue and virtue resided in the home and heart of individuals (Bloch 1987). This new gender ideology of virtue served the interests of a growing market economy and a political system increasingly comfortable with competing parties by displacing moral constraints from the public world into the home.

Early scholarship in women's history explored the ways in which the separate spheres elaborated by this cult of true womanhood provided bonds of sisterhood for women who shared the same experiences. Most important here was the work of Nancy Cott (1977), which demonstrated the ways in which women in New England developed a shared consciousness about their condition of womanhood. As Cott observed, most women were content with their place in society as women and proud of the roles they played. While they might be excluded from many of the activities of men, they were conscious of their own values and capabilities as women. They recognized the importance of their childrearing and domestic activities. On the other hand, regardless of their pride in their accomplishments, this consciousness of themselves as a group was also an important precondition for creating the early movement for women's rights. Without recognizing what they shared, it would be impossible for them to advocate for themselves (Cott 1977: 194).

While housekeeping was central to the ideology of true womanhood in the antebellum period, it came to be viewed more as a moral activity than an economic one. The woman who kept a clean house, a cheerful kitchen, and an active spinning wheel could be assured of a happy family. The ideology of the nineteenth century downplayed the economic aspects of housework that had been more clearly present in the colonial period. With productive activities moving to shops and even factories, both of which were increasingly removed from the home, and with the home increasingly viewed as a haven from the economic world rather than a part of it, housework was increasingly viewed as a non-economic activity. Yet as Mary Ryan (1981) pointed out, middle-class women did engage in cash-producing activities such as taking in boarders, and this was a critical element in family strategies to solidify or achieve middle-class position. Women worked so that boys could attain schooling, for example. Jeanne Boydston (1990) demonstrated how housework retained its economic value in other ways throughout the nineteenth century. In the unpaid labor of cooking, cleaning, sewing, and childcare, women in middle-class households provided a significant financial benefit for their families. Many women provided additional direct cash income for their families not only by taking in boarders but also by selling extra foods produced in their kitchens, or in some cases, through more unusual activities such as writing for the emerging literary market. The "pastoralization" of housework during this period, in which housework was constructed as a non-economic undertaking, was an important part of the move toward an industrial economy in which the value of labor was attached to the cash produced rather than the work accomplished. Women's work was not becoming easier, it was simply not being recognized as labor in the same way because most housework did not produce cash (Boydston 1990: 133, 158).

Working-class families derived an even larger percentage of their family wealth from the provision of these services by women. Women of these families were even more likely than middle-class women to take on additional activities for generating real cash income for their families by taking in laundry as well as boarders or sewing at home for merchants. However, the more visible participation of working-class women in a market economy was precisely why they were seen as failing to live up to the standards of true womanhood. African American women, most of whom had to work for wages, felt this exclusion even more keenly. Some of the most important scholarship in women's history has analyzed the ways in which working-class women and women of color were excluded from the cult of true womanhood as they struggled to support themselves and their families.

Wage-earning women in the North were far from being a monolithic group. Their working and domestic lives varied by age, city, and occupation. Industrialization created a variety of systems of production for distant markets. This meant that some women stayed in their homes stitching shoes and sewing shirts, while other women worked for wages in the factories of Lowell, Massachusetts, and Manchester, New Hampshire, and still other women worked as domestic servants or shop assistants. In one way or another, most of these women were explicitly drawn into the new market economy of the North that was rooted in profits rather than personal relationships. Their wages, often paid to them directly, conferred a degree of independence. Scholars have been particularly interested in analyzing the nature of that independence, assessing to what extent it was a reality, as well as how it varied depending on the type of work, family circumstances, and marital status of the female worker. In addition, scholars have examined how patriarchal assumptions continued to structure important aspects of the wage relationship.

Women who worked in their homes, stitching shoes and sewing shirts, tended to be married, or at least to be mothers. Their wages were lower than they might get if they left their homes to work, but most of these women had household duties to attend to and children to supervise so that such jobs were not really possible. Female shoe-binders, who stitched shoes throughout the New England countryside, were

part of the changing organization of labor in shoemaking. As merchants took control of the shoemaking process from artisans, they introduced a division of labor that
allowed for greater profits. Skilled men were retained to cut the shoe leather, but the
leather was then given in large lots to women, who were considered far less skilled,
for detailed stitching to create the upper part of the shoe. Women were usually paid
from 2 to 5 cents for binding a pair of shoes, depending on how crude or refined
the product was supposed to be, a price that was approximately half what a man
would be paid. Merchants thus used assumptions of gender hierarchy, paying women
less than men, to increase their profit margins. While most women took up household chores in addition to shoe-binding, even the most dedicated worker would not
be able to produce more than 10 pairs of shoes per day. At that rate, it is clear that
even the most productive women could not survive solely on their wages from shoe-
binding (Blewett 1988: 30–2). While some of the shoe-binders were widows trying
to support themselves and/or children, most were part of a larger family economy in
which the men farmed, fished, and/or made shoes. Sometimes the wages were paid
to their husbands or fathers, but in most cases the women were paid directly.
However, regardless of the independence that was implied in such payments, these
women were usually contributing to a family income and were thinking in those
terms.

Young single women who went to work in the textile factories such as Lowell had
a much stronger sense of independence as a result of their wages. These young
women lived in dormitories, free from family demands. They came from farm
families throughout New England that were not necessarily thriving but that were
far from destitute. They were by and large better paid than shoe-binders. While a
newcomer might make only about $0.44 per day, more experienced workers made
from $0.66 to 0.78 per day (Dublin 1979: 66). Some women contributed their
wages to family needs, such as a brother's education or parent's mortgage, and all
were responsible for paying for room and board at their dormitories, but most
managed to save some of their wages for their own goals: for education, dowries,
and new clothes. Combined with the educational and cultural opportunities that
Lowell offered with its various churches, lyceums, and lectures, young women found
Lowell an important opportunity for personal development and independence before
settling down as wives and mothers.

For wage-earning women in cities such as New York, domestic servitude was the
most common form of employment. Although wages in 1835 averaged only $1.50
per week, servants were provided with room and board, so that they might have
an opportunity to save some of their wages. Still, domestic work was an unpopular
alternative as young women found their social independence curtailed by long hours
and strict supervision (Stansell 1987: 272). Young single women might also find
employment in book binderies and dress shops or in the other small manufactories
that existed throughout the cities. For women who could not leave their children,
there was also the work of sewing, though these wages were particularly meager.
During most of the antebellum period, seamstresses in New York earned between
$0.75 and $1.50 per week (Stansell 1987: 111). A single woman might get by on
this amount, but a woman trying to support her family could not. Again, it is clear
from the wages they paid that employers assumed that women were not the family
breadwinners, though in many cases this assumption was simply incorrect.

Just as young women in Lowell were able to create an active social life for themselves through churches, lyceums, and other activities, young single women in cities such as New York found an active social life as well. They socialized on weekends in boisterous crowds on the Bowery, for example, wearing clothes that were more revealing and bold in coloring than that of the bourgeois woman. In this instance, they were not so much excluded from the sphere of bourgeois woman-hood as scornful of it.

However, if some of these young women were willing to flout the principles of middle-class propriety, they were more concerned about racial boundaries. In most wage-earning occupations of the North, from textile work to shoe-binding to sewing, native-born white women were the predominant form of early labor. African American women were often excluded from these positions – in Lowell factories, native-born women refused to work with them, for example. Instead, African American women often were found in the least desirable occupations, taking in laundry and working as domestic servants in cities (Stansell 1987: 13, 157). As immigration increased during the antebellum period, Irish women, in particular, began to replace African American women as servants and eventually also began to find their way into New England factories, a move that native-born white women often abhorred. As a result, the Irish were often introduced into mills one room at a time, usually being concentrated in the lower-paying rooms, resulting in a continuing wage differential between native born and immigrant women (Dublin 1979: 153–5; Stansell 1987: 157).

Market transformations occurred in the countryside as well as in urban areas. Farm women in rural areas remained a clear part of the production unit. Their work in producing garden goods, raising poultry, and dairying had been a significant component since the eighteenth century, but these activities took on increased market value as urban areas grew. As Joan Jensen (1986) has demonstrated, during the early eighteenth century butter-making became a particularly important commodity activity of farm women, who were able to expand their businesses as a result of technological innovations in the production process. Although butter seldom fetched cash, it allowed families to barter at local markets and with local merchants for a wide variety of other foodstuffs, cloth, shoes, pottery, and the like.

Women who participated in this kind of rural economy did not embrace ideals of domesticity in the same way as their more urban counterparts did. Their kitchens were more important than their parlors, emphasizing the importance of the productive activ-ities that occurred rather than leisure ones. And while childrearing gained attention, just as it did in more urban areas, children's roles as producers within the family were of greater importance than in urban areas (Jensen 1986: 126–7).

Many of the same splits and contradictions that showed up between the cult of true womanhood and the real lives of women were evident in their cultural lives as well. During the antebellum period, female literacy increased tremendously, particularly in the North. Women became avid readers and active producers of much of the literature circulating in the broadening cultural marketplace. In novels, spiritual biographies, and poetry, sentimentalism became the most common form of expression, privileging the heart over the mind as women were encouraged to weep for the sorrows and misfortunes of those less fortunate in life. This emotional outpouring was most intense in the sentimental novel, one of the most successful commodities in the growing cultural marketplace, and its political implications have been the object of intense debate in recent years.

By 1850, almost all native-born white women in the North were literate. This literacy was in large part due to the growing public school system in the North, which educated both boys and girls at the primary level. While few women achieved higher levels of education, it was common during the antebellum period for native-born white women to read the popular novels, biographies, spiritual tracts, and journals that were becoming readily accessible in the early nineteenth century. Technological improvements in printing presses made cheap copies of books a reality and an extensive system of lending libraries allowed women (who had enough time) to read a wide variety of books for a small fee.

Throughout the North, reading societies and lyceums were established. While some included both men and women, many were gender specific. Many literary societies were composed of white women, but in most major cities African American women formed literary societies also. By 1831, there were 27 African American female literary societies in Philadelphia alone (McHenry 2002: 57). African American women not only shared their readings, but also like most of their white counterparts, wrote for their societies as well. Moreover, they chose readings that allowed them to engage important political questions related to slavery.

Girls also began to receive increased educational opportunities. The idea that girls should receive a more extensive education had been promoted since the revolutionary period. At the very least, a well-educated mother would be better able to produce well-educated children, including boys who would one day be citizens of the new republic. The move for female education drew support from men and women of many political persuasions and with many different agendas. Although not receiving the same level of public education as boys, girls in the antebellum North increasingly received some elementary school education. As agitation increased to educate girls to a higher level in the same subjects as boys, private academies began to flourish. Catherine Beecher, for example, instituted a rigorous curriculum for the girls at her seminary in Hartford, Connecticut, stressing usefulness rather than decorative qualities in her students and introducing topics such as moral philosophy. She saw the home as woman's sphere, but had an expansive view of that sphere, which certainly included teaching as an occupation for women. The home could be an influential component of society only if its mistress was well educated (Sklar 1973: 96–7). Emma Willard also trained teachers rigorously at her Troy Female Seminary. A few women were even able to obtain college degrees for the first time at coeducational Oberlin College and at the all-female Mount Holyoke Seminary.

With increased education, women became a larger part of the popular reading audiences and female authors also began to produce more, writing many of the most popular books on the market. Authors such as Catherine Sedgewick, Lydia Maria Child, Sarah Josepha Hale, Harriet Beecher Stowe, Fanny Fern, and Susan Warner were only a few of the best-known authors producing for a national audience. While they were openly criticized by some for their lack of talent (most famously by Nathaniel Hawthorne), their popularity remained high and their work has been approached with increasing respect by serious scholars.

Collectively, these authors, and others like them, are most famous for the sentimental novel. The sentiment they promoted among readers was empathy for the trials and tribulations of the heroes and heroines of their stories. Readers felt the sufferings of a widow, a dying child, a deserted lover. Because these stories appealed to the emotions, they were coded feminine, though men might read them as well. But it was women, in particular, who viewed them as their literature. There has been considerable debate about the underlying politics of this literature, whether it reinforced female stereotypes of difference, or provided a covert yet effective way for female political expression, or exploited and reinforced racial and class hierarchies. Ann Douglas (1977), for example, criticized the sentimental culture of this period as a kind of straitjacket that kept women from truly facing the political issues around them, dulling the intellectual analyses that might be possible by turning problems into more easily consumable emotional outbursts. Jane Tompkins (1985), on the other hand, argued that sentimental novels were popular precisely because they provided a way to work out complicated social and political issues. Cathy Davidson (1986) argued that novels of this period could provide subversive ideas for many of the women who read them. All may be true to some extent, Shirley Samuels (1992) has argued, pointing out that this is a complex literature in which the logic of both power and powerlessness can be elaborated simultaneously (Douglas 1977: 12–13, Tompkins 1985: 146, Samuels 1992: 4).

The sentimental structure was particularly effective at conveying the atrocities of slavery – the separated lovers or parents, the child without family, the brutality of masters and mistresses. Antislavery literature was awash with the sentimental as a way of evoking outrage and compassion among northerners. Some of the authors who engaged in this tactic, such as Lydia Maria Child, have been criticized for creating "the tragic mulatto," a sentimental figure more white than black. This racial characterization might lead northern whites to identify with the sufferings of slaves, but it undermined sympathy for real African Americans and effectively denied them the same feelings in antebellum literature (Sánchez-Eppler 1993: 31). As Hazel Carby pointed out, African American females were more likely to be portrayed as outside the boundaries of true womanhood in these sentimental novels, particularly as their sexuality was emphasized, often in counterpoint to the passionlessness of white women (Carby 1987: 32).

There was also a voyeuristic side to this sentiment. Readers could feel the sufferings of others without actually having to endure the consequences and they could appropriate their sufferings for their own uses. Moreover, the readers who consumed this literature might share the feelings of the characters they read about, but they also could feel superior to them as they felt sorry for them.

Most recently, Amy Kaplan (1998) has explored the cultural logic of women's sentimental and domestic literature to argue that it legitimized imperialist conquest and westward expansion. The civilizing functions of the home could be extended across the frontier, giving female influence an imperial reach. Moreover, the nation could be imagined as a home, and those conquered as charges to be cared for (Kaplan 1998).

In all of these analyses, the permeability of boundaries between the separate spheres of home and world is clear. Just as women transgressed the boundaries regularly in real life, so did they also in their cultural representations. Literature was thus a way for women to engage the public and political issues around them in an indirect manner.

While literature was one way in which women actively engaged issues beyond their homes, religion was another. Continuing a trend that had begun in the eighteenth century, women increasingly became a larger proportion of the membership in Protestant churches throughout the United States. As revivals swept region after region in successive waves of religious fervor, women were more likely than men to have conversion experiences. This religious fervor reinforced their role as spiritual guardians and moral leaders within their homes and encouraged them to broaden this role in voluntary societies outside their homes. Both evangelical and non-evangelical women formed a variety of societies to promote the well-being of those around them. In almost all cases they focused on spiritual well-being, but they also tended to the poor, eventually began to attack alcohol usage and prostitution, and in some cases took on more political issues such as Indian removal, abolitionism, and labor reform. Not all women took on all reforms. They created distinct social networks that were bounded not only by specific issues or beliefs, but also by class, race, and ethnicity.

Throughout the antebellum period, the United States was a predominantly Protestant country and the revivals of that time brought an increasing number of people within the churches. Mary Ryan (1981) has documented the growing proportion of women who joined those churches, bringing their children and sometimes their husbands with them. In the revivals she examined in Oneida County, New York, she found the percentage of female converts in varying revivals to range from a low of 52 percent to a high of 72 percent (Ryan 1981: 79). As Ryan has argued, the women who participated in the religious and reform activities of their cities were central to the creation of bourgeois ideology and middle-class formation during this period. They educated and shaped their sons to be "self-made men" in the new world and they trained their daughters to follow in their footsteps. However, for Ryan, these activities were a temporary station for women on the way to the creation of their bourgeois families – once their task was complete, they returned to their more private sphere rather than demanding expanded rights. Although women altered traditional patterns of authority through their religious and reform activities, they were not seeking a change in their own status or to obtain a more permanent, public life.

However, religious revivals not only inspired large numbers of women to join churches, but also inspired a surprising number to preach. Although women in the South were barred from the pulpit, some women in the North created a female ministry. Women had preached during the eighteenth century, but during the nineteenth century women asserted their role as spiritual guardians to legitimize their activities. Quakers and Shakers had always allowed female leaders, but new evangelical sects that were growing in prominence during the early nineteenth century such as the Freewill Baptists, Christians, African Methodists, and Methodists also began to welcome female preachers (Brekkus 1998: 144–5). This was one way in which they demonstrated their critique of established churches and cultures. Because these religions opened themselves to the poor and uneducated, and because they preached a religion of the heart, conceivably anyone could be a preacher – slave, day laborer, or woman. Camp meetings were a particularly inviting spot for women to try their preaching as normal social rules were suspended. Women who took on these roles compared themselves to the prophetesses of the Old Testament who had a special mission to preach the word of God. Those who wrote about their experiences in spiritual autobiographies were proud of their preaching and constructed clear public personas that were quite different from the narratives of domesticity that were found in the traditional spiritual biographies of women. However, according to Catherine Brekkus, as these sects became more established during the 1830s and 1840s, they became increasingly hostile to female preaching (Brekkus 1998: 262–306).

In addition to propelling religious fervor, many women in the North took on the activities of one or more reform associations. Reform associations had begun before the heyday of revivals and always encompassed women of a variety of religious experiences. Anne Boylan (2002) has demonstrated that Catholic and Jewish women as well as non-evangelical Protestant women formed a variety of societies. However, these societies were usually limited by religion, race, and to some degree class. Catholic and Jewish women had their own societies for ameliorating the conditions of the poor, as did African American women (Boylan 2002: 38–43). Moreover, even among Protestant women there were different networks of reformers, influenced partly by their religious affiliation, but also by their class. Class background was particularly important for the success of a group as wealthier women's organizations had the best access to halls of political and economic power in pushing their agendas (Boylan 2002: 218).

Nancy Hewitt (1984) closely analyzed many of the class distinctions inherent in women's organizations in her study of female reform in Rochester. She divided the white Protestant reformers into three groups: first, benevolent women interested in ameliorating the social conditions of their society; second, perfectionist women who were interested in cleansing the world of moral evil through various forms of moral reform focused on the individual; and third, ultraist women who actively critiqued institutions of their society such as slavery and actively campaigned for social and political change. These women were divided not just by their ideologies, but also by their social background. The women committed to amelioration came from the established and solid upper class of Rochester, while the women committed to perfectionism came from a prosperous but more unstable social class of merchants and professionals who had more recently attained their wealth and were a bit more insecure in it. Ultraist women were the least affluent, often of farming rather than commercial backgrounds or married to artisans, living on the outskirts rather than the downtown of the city, and largely Hicksite Quakers. Ultraists were the group that was most likely to engage in collaborative work with African American women and working-class women, who represented the two other reform networks in town and who were more focused on improving the circumstances of their own group rather than outreach to others less fortunate (Hewitt 1984: 38–63).

The ameliorative activities of wealthier women tended to focus on the poor: providing food or medical care to the sick or housing and educating orphans with no resources. Reflecting their privileged place in the social order, they were not so much interested in changing society as they were in providing relief to those in need. Perfectionist women were more likely to translate their evangelical zeal into attempts to perfect human character. Many of them supported the temperance movement, and encouraged a move toward total abstinence, in an attempt to create a more perfect society. However, they were quite clear that this perfection came through individual moral transformation. The temperance movements that their enthusiasm inspired achieved widespread acceptance during the middle decades of the nineteenth century. These movements to control and eventually eliminate the consumption of alcohol were a critical factor in the creation of bourgeois morality and upward mobility. Ultraist women who supported more radical causes such as antislavery challenged the social, political, and economic order surrounding them. Their demands for an end to slavery challenged the constitution and the economic prosperity of white southerners, not to mention the racial fears of white northerners. As radicals, their numbers were far smaller than the other groups, though in helping to bring about an end to slavery, their impact has been far reaching.

As Hewitt (1984) suggests, working women also organized, though their efforts were focused more on labor issues related to their own working conditions. Women in industrial towns and cities throughout the North organized during the 1830s and 1840s to combat speed-ups, pay cuts, and long workdays. In all areas of wage work, pay was declining and working conditions deteriorating. When mill-owners in Lowell reduced wages by 25 percent in 1834, female factory workers signed petitions of protest and 800 of them turned out and paraded through the streets. They stressed the importance of their independence from both their families and their employers, claiming their rightful heritage as "daughters of freemen." In 1836, they turned out again when mill-owners tried to raise the rates at boarding houses (Dublin 1979: 89–98). Shoemakers in Lynn also organized during 1834 to protest a reduction in their wages. Forming the Female Society, these women met in local churches and justified their demands not only in terms of independence, but also with reference to the value of their household work (Blewett 1988: 35–7). Their place as workers living with their families shaped their sense of being workers in ways that were different from women in Lowell, and their meeting within the churches rather than in the streets suggests that these women had more concerns about public demonstrations than did the young women in Lowell. Seamstresses in New York had turned out in 1825, and in 1831 the tailoresses went on strike. The tailoresses stressed their need to support themselves, independent of a male breadwinner, as did book-binders in 1835 (Stansell 1987: 135).

As women organized during the 1830s, the response of male working-men was conflicted. Male shoemakers in Lynn supported the demands of the Female Society because they recognized the impact of women's wage cuts on their family economies (Blewett 1988: 39). But the National Trades Union, made up of artisans from cities throughout the North, felt that women's wage work, in the long run, injured working-class families because women undercut the wages of men and were unable to take up their rightful place supervising their homes. In this sense, the working-men showed support for the domestic ideals that were defining the bourgeoisie but were becoming beyond the reach of the laboring classes. They were concerned not only with domestic ideals but also with the moral purity of women, a virtue that they felt factory girls might surrender when away from the protection of their families (Stansell 1987: 137–8).

Issues of morality and moral reform surfaced in the 1840s as women organized primarily around issues of time rather than pay in the 10-hour movement. Stansell has argued that the presence of moral reform rhetoric in the labor protests of New York seamstresses was the result of middle-class meddling that undercut the efficacy of the working-women's activities (Stansell 1987: 147–9). However, in New England, moral reform rhetoric emanated from working-men and women who had been caught up in revivals and temperance campaigns during the previous decades. Working-women expressed concern for their salvation as much as their independence in the labor struggles of the 1840s. Male suspicion continued about the moral dangers inherent in the independence of female factory workers, but women's use of language that demonstrated their commitment to moral improvement and referenced their roles as mothers and sisters went a long way toward facilitating interaction (Murphy 1992: 212). These working-women from New England joined with men in submitting petitions to the state legislature demanding a 10-hour day, and in doing so they not only agitated in public, but also entered the world of politics.

The petitions submitted by working-women in the 1840s continued an important political tradition begun by women active in the anti-removal and antislavery campaigns of the previous decade. These movements have been of interest to historians of women not only because of their impact on important traditions of reform but also because they raised issues of women's involvement in politics that would become important in the women's rights movement.

Mary Hershberger (1999) has argued for the significance of the anti-removal petitioning campaigns that began in 1829 as a precursor to later antislavery activities. Women as well as men submitted numerous petitions to Congress opposing Andrew Jackson's policy of Indian removal. Catherine Beecher and Lydia Sigourney in Hartford spearheaded the campaign for female signatures, though they did so with some secrecy, refusing to sign their appeal or to publicly acknowledge their role. Women such as Angelina Grimke were powerfully affected by this political activity and returned to it as part of their antislavery work (Hershberger 1999).

The most controversial reform activities undertaken by women were those connected with antislavery. A range of actions were carried out by women committed to this cause, just as in other campaigns, but by any standard, this was a radical activity because of the financial and political implications of antislavery demands. African American women, like African American men, had been among the earliest citizens to begin agitation for the end of slavery. Maria Stewart of Boston was particularly well known for her fiery speeches attacking slavery and her demands of other African Americans that they rise up against the system. Stewart retired from public agitation in 1833, however, as members of the black community became increasingly uncomfortable not only with her public speaking but also with her criticisms of African Americans for failing to challenge slavery more.

Both white and black women began to organize their own antislavery associations in 1833 after they were barred from joining the newly formed American Anti-Slavery Society. African American women in Boston formed the first female antislavery organization in the country and African American women in Philadelphia joined with white women to form the Female Anti-Slavery Association. Some of the associations were racially integrated, but not all, and African American women continued to maintain all-black associations as well, sometimes participating in both. Indeed, in New York City, white antislavery women were opposed to allowing African American women any position of leadership and few African American women joined.

These antislavery organizations did, however, foster the creation of a political culture for women. The antislavery petitioning campaigns of the 1830s garnered the support of thousands of women in the North. Women signed petitions on a variety of questions, from abolishing slavery in the District of Columbia to opposing the annexation of Texas. And as they did so, they faced growing criticism about the impropriety of their activities. The submissive plea of an individual for help from the government, which had been the nature of petitions in the revolutionary era, had been transformed into a mass movement of political protest.

The public meetings and public speaking drew even greater criticism and violent attacks from anti-abolitionist mobs. Many of the most effective leaders of the movement were women who spoke powerfully in public. These included Abby Kelley as well as Sarah and Angelina Grimke. The Congregational ministers of Massachusetts publicly rebuked the Grimke sisters for their behavior in a published pamphlet. Catherine Beecher also condemned the public activities of the Grimkes and the petitioning activities of women against slavery, provoking a spirited debate. Critics roundly condemned female antislavery speaking as promiscuous behavior and argued that their lack of decorum proved the socially unacceptable nature of the antislavery movement. Catherine Beecher argued that women should confine their attempts at political change to influencing their husbands within the sanctity of their homes. As criticism of female antislavery activity grew, some of the more conservative members of the Anti-Slavery Society urged the women to stop speaking publicly. Indeed, they were reluctant to allow women to participate in any way in the organization, for fear of giving up even one ounce of respectability. As a result, when Lucretia Mott attended the World Anti-Slavery Convention in London in 1840, she was barred from participating. The following year, the American Anti-Slavery Society split. More conservative antislavery advocates retained an all-male organization and moved toward political involvement. The more radical group, under the leadership of William Lloyd Garrison, quickly appointed women to its executive committee and affirmed its support for the rights of women as well as slaves.

The reform activities of women in the North had raised the "Woman Question" in a variety of ways, but none more dramatically and influentially than the antislavery movement. Through their public and political agitation and their attacks on both the financial and constitutional underpinnings of the country, antislavery women had clearly transgressed the domestic boundaries of their sphere. Faced with criticism not only from their opponents but also from many of their male colleagues, it is not surprising that many antislavery women began to advocate rights for women as well as slaves. Sarah Grimke made the case forcefully in her *Letters on the Equality of the Sexes*, published in 1838. After Lucretia Mott and Elizabeth Cady Stanton confronted the exclusion of women at the World Anti-Slavery Convention, they contemplated the need for a convention on women's rights. Antislavery had been a radicalizing experience for these women in a variety of ways. Ellen DuBois (1978), in examining the impact of antislavery activism on demands for women's rights, has argued that women developed an anti-institutional and anti-clerical stance as a result of their participation in the antislavery movement. Thus repositioned, women were able to focus on their equality with men rather than their differences (DuBois 1978: 36).

More recently, Lori Ginzberg (1990) has argued that women in reform movements took up the most controversial tenet of the women's rights movement, suffrage, only after facing the practical limits of their moral reform strategies. Many women in the antislavery movement were particularly uncomfortable with the idea of political participation for men as well as women – after all they viewed the United States as having been founded on a corrupt bargain that preserved slavery. They took up petitioning with reluctance, developing an extensive grassroots form of protest, and recognizing the political nature of their activities. But they eventually had to confront the growing importance of electoral politics over moral suasion in movements for social change. They also had to confront the fact that they could not exercise the same informal influence over men as wealthier and more conservative women could. Their social networks did not grant them the same access to men of power in the country. These factors pushed antislavery activists toward women's rights as a necessary means to abolitionist ends as well as an end in itself (Ginzberg 1990: 97). As Susan Zaeske has demonstrated, petitioning had become a more socially acceptable form of female political expression by the 1850s, and even Catherine Beecher, who had earlier attacked the practice, signed one in 1854 (Zaeske 2003: 172).

Antislavery agitation was an important impetus in the growth of the women's rights movement, but it was far from the only one. Nor was suffrage the only demand. Education, property rights, even dress reform were addressed throughout the ante-bellum period as important means for improving the status of women. These broader issues of women's rights have been analyzed by Nancy Isenberg (1998), one of the strongest proponents for decentering the significance of suffrage in the women's rights movement. As Isenberg points out, questions of family organization and religion were central to debates on women's rights.

Reformers raised questions about a broad range of issues stemming from the legal subordination of women within their families. They demanded protection from spousal abuse, equal rights with their husband in child custody cases, and control of their property and wages. Although many states began to pass married women's property laws beginning in the 1830s, the change was more to protect family property than to provide women with increased independence. The laws were by and large narrowly focused on protecting a woman's inheritance from seizure should her husband become bankrupt, rather than altering her subordinate status within marriage. However, it was quickly realized that these property laws could encourage further ideas of female independence. Women's rights activists began to push for a broader interpretation of the property laws to include a married woman's right to control her wages as well as her right to make independent contracts (Isenberg 1998: 161–90). In addition to demanding equality with men in their families, they also began to demand greater equality in their churches. They criticized the customs that kept women from being ordained as ministers and from exercising control over church property.

Education also became a key demand. While some colleges were open to women, most were not. Postgraduate training was virtually unheard of. Medical, legal, and theological training were closed to women. Yet, as women obtained college degrees, some wished to push the boundaries of their education further. Antoinette Brown was denied admission to the divinity school at Oberlin. Elizabeth Blackwell managed to graduate from Geneva Medical College in 1849, before it stopped matriculating women, an experience that led her to found her own medical college for women in New York two decades later. Other medical schools for women were founded in major urban centers throughout the Northeast. As these women pushed for higher levels of education, their demands were not so much to take on the traditional duties of women with better education, but to be allowed to work as equals with men in every profession.

Beginning with the convention of Seneca Falls in 1848, women in the North began to meet regularly to demand not only the right to vote, but also to control their bodies and their property, to be paid the same as men, to have equal access to education and to be treated as equal partners in marriage and equal citizens in the republic. Those who demanded full equality for women were a small group. Most women in the North rooted their social identity in a belief in gender differences and separate spheres. While they might cross the boundaries of those spheres regularly, or debate the extent to which the women's sphere could be extended, they were not willing to attack it with demands for equality.

Even though most women in the antebellum North were reluctant to attack the ideal of separate spheres, that does not mean it was a monolithic reality. The experiences and identities of women in the antebellum North, like those of men, varied widely. Women's identities and activities were shaped not only by their gender, but also by other social factors such as race and class. As a result, the ideas and activities of white middle-class women often reinforced class and racial hierarchies even as these women sought to assert a common female identity and to ameliorate suffering. To a certain extent, an interest in these power relations has been provoked by critiques that emerged within the women's movement, arguing that factors such as race and class divided women as much as gender united them. As a result, a much more nuanced view of women's history has emerged that can be integrated into larger historical debates about how power was constructed and exercised in antebellum America. At this point, however, the integration of women's history into the larger narrative of American history still remains more of a goal than a reality.

BIBLIOGRPAHY

Blewett, Mary (1988) *Men, Women, and Work: Class, Gender, and Protest in the New England Shoe Industry, 1780–1910*. Urbana, Ill.: University of Illinois Press.

Bloch, Ruth (1987) "The Gendered Meanings of Virtue in Revolutionary America," *Signs* 13: 37–58.

Boydston, Jeanne (1990) *Home and Work, Housework, Wages, and the Ideology of Labor in the Early Republic*. New York: Oxford University Press.

Boylan, Anne (2002) *The Origins of Women's Activism, New York and Boston, 1797–1840*. Chapel Hill, NC: University of North Carolina Press.

Brekkus, Catherine A. (1998) *Strangers and Pilgrims: Female Preaching in America, 1740–1845*. Chapel Hill, NC: University of North Carolina Press.

Carby, Hazel (1987) *Reconstructing Womanhood, The Emergence of the Afro-American Woman Novelist*. New York: Oxford University Press.

Cott, Nancy (1977) *The Bonds of Womanhood, "Woman's Sphere" in New England, 1780–1835*. New Haven, Conn.: Yale University Press.

Davidson, Cathy (1986) *Revolution and the Word: The Rise of the Novel in America*. New York: Oxford University Press.

Douglas, Ann (1977) *The Feminization of American Culture*. New York: Alfred A. Knopf.

Dublin, Thomas (1979) *Women at Work: The Transformation of Work and Community at Lowell, Massachusetts, 1826–1860*. New York: Columbia University Press.

DuBois, Ellen (1978) *Feminism and Suffrage: The Emergence of an Independent Women's Movement in America, 1848–1869*. Ithaca, NY: Cornell University Press.

Ginzberg, Lori (1990) *Women and the Work of Benevolence: Morality, Politics, and Class in the Nineteenth Century United States*. New Haven, Conn.: Yale University Press.

Grimke, Sarah Moore (1838) *Letters on the Equality of the Sexes, and the Condition of Women: Addressed to Mary S. Parker*. Boston, Mass.: I. Knapp.

Hershberger, Mary (1999) "Mobilizing Women, Anticipating Abolition: The Struggle against Indian Removal in the 1830s," *Journal of American History* 86: 15–40.

Hewitt, Nancy (1984) *Women's Activism and Social Change: Rochester, New York, 1822–1872*. Ithaca, NY: Cornell University Press.

Isenberg, Nancy (1998) *Sex and Citizenship in Antebellum America*. Chapel Hill, NC: University of North Carolina Press.

Jensen, Joan (1986) *Loosening the Bonds: Mid-Atlantic Farm Women, 1750–1850*. New Haven, Conn.: Yale University Press.

Kaplan, Amy (1988) *The Social Construction of American Realism*. Chicago, Ill.: University of Chicago Press.

McHenry, Elizabeth (2002) *Forgotten Readers: Recovering the Lost History of African American Literary Societies*. Durham, NC: Duke University Press.

Murphy, Teresa (1992) *Ten Hours' Labor: Religion, Reform, and Gender in Early New England*. Ithaca, NY: Cornell University Press.

Ryan, Mary (1981) *The Cradle of the Middle Class: The Family in Oneida County, New York, 1780–1865*. New York: Cambridge University Press.

Samuels, Shirley (ed.) (1992) *The Culture of Sentiment: Race, Gender, and Sentimentality in Nineteenth-Century America*. New York: Oxford University Press.

Sánchez-Eppler, Karen (1993) *Touching Liberty: Abolition, Feminism, and the Politics of the Body*. Berkeley, Calif.: University of California Press.

Sklar, Kathryn (1973) *Catherine Beecher: A Study in American Domesticity*. New York: Norton.

Stansell, Christine (1987) *City of Women: Sex and Class in New York, 1789–1860*. Urbana, Ill.: University of Illinois Press.

Tompkins, Jane (1985) *Sensational Designs: The Cultural Work of American Fiction, 1790–1860*. New York: Oxford University Press.

Welter, Barbara (1966) "The Cult of True Womanhood: 1820–1860," *American Quarterly* 18: 151–74.

Zaeske, Susan (2003) *Signatures of Citizenship: Petitioning, Antislavery, and Women's Political Identity*. Chapel Hill, NC: University of North Carolina Press.

SUGGESTED FURTHER READING

Dorsey, Bruce (2002) *Reforming Men and Women: Gender in the Antebellum City*. Ithaca, NY: Cornell University Press.

Epstein, Barbara (1981) *The Politics of Domesticity: Women, Evangelism, and Temperance in Nineteenth-Century America*. Middletown, Conn.: Wesleyan University Press.

Halttunen, Karen (1982) *Confidence Men and Painted Women: A Study in Middle-Class Culture in America, 1830–1870*. New Haven, Conn.: Yale University Press.

Kelley, Mary (1996) "Reading Women/Women Reading: The Making of Learned Women in Antebellum America," *Journal of American History* 83: 401–24.

Kelly, Catherine (1999) *In the New England Fashion: Reshaping Women's Lives in the Nineteenth Century*. Ithaca, NY: Cornell University Press.

Kerber, Linda (1988) "Separate Spheres, Female Worlds, Woman's Place: The Rhetoric of Women's History," *Journal of American History* 75: 9–39.

Painter, Nell (1996) *Sojourner Truth, a Life, a Symbol.* New York: Norton.
Smith-Rosenberg, Carroll (1985) *Disorderly Conduct: Visions of Gender in Victorian America.* New York: Oxford University Press.
Solomon, Barbara (1985) *In the Company of Educated Women: A History of Women and Higher Education in America.* New Haven, Conn.: Yale University Press.
Zagarri, Rosemarie (1988) "The Rights of Man and Woman in Post-Revolutionary America," *William and Mary Quarterly* 3rd ser., 55: 203–30.

CHAPTER SEVEN

Women in the Old South

MICHELE GILLESPIE

Southern women's history has transformed the study of antebellum southern history since the late 1970s. The field's path-breaking employment of sources, approaches, themes, and arguments has forced all historians to rethink old assumptions about power and resistance in the Old South, to pay attention to a host of voices hitherto ignored, and to revise our fundamental understanding of southern society. This body of scholarship reveals that the lives of all women in the slave South proved diverse, transitory, and profoundly different from men's lives. At the same time, the latest scholarship suggests that women's concerns and experiences, and southern society's ideas about what constituted women's roles and their larger meanings, were intricately woven into the public world as well as the private one. Consequently, all southern historians must apply the work of women's historians to their larger debates about the structure of the planter family, the nature of master–slave relations, and the evolution of southern political discourse. Yet despite the richness of these contributions and the stunning impact they have made upon the discipline, women's history in the Old South in some respects remains "unfinished business," as pioneering southern women's historian Ann Firor Scott (1993 [1970]) has been wont to say.

There is no more enduringly popular image of southern womanhood than the plantation mistress as southern belle, pale perfection in her hoop skirts and bonnet, piously fulfilling her domestic duties at every turn. Yet the earliest work on southern women in the antebellum period did not investigate the historic roots of this romanticized ideal. That analysis would come much later. Instead, Julia Cherry Spruill (1938) and Eleanor Miot Boatwright (1994 [1941]), representing a mere handful of historians during the first half of the twentieth century committed to southern women's history, culled through plentiful source material to document southern white women's economic realities, social attitudes, religious beliefs, class differences, legal status, and varieties of work. Reflecting the time in which they lived, these historians paid limited attention to race and slavery, but their work conveys a critical understanding of the daily difficulties encountered by white women across class, and merits our continued attention. Unfortunately, their scholarship lay fallow for many decades, even with the publication of Mary Elizabeth Massey's (1966) *Bonnet*

Brigades, a significant book because it demonstrated the centrality of women's experiences on the home front and the battlefield for understanding the Civil War. Despite these important early works, southern women's history as a field of inquiry, just like women's history in general, had yet to be accepted as mainstream scholarship.

It was Ann Firor Scott's (1970) *The Southern Lady* that first put southern women's history on the scholars' map, while it was Catherine Clinton's (1982) *The Plantation Mistress* that kept it there. Scott argued that contrary to the popular image of the antebellum southern lady as submissive paragon of virtue, elite and middle-class southern white women were in fact strong, resilient, hard-working and not always happy with their subordinate status as the planter's helpmeet. Indeed some plantation mistresses were covertly critical of slavery. The Civil War, Scott (1970) contended, marked a critical transition in these women's lives, for while forced out of necessity to take over the management of homes and farms, they discovered in the process they were far more capable than their patriarchal world had ever permitted them to realize. Scott's scholarship was part of a larger shift in academe as a whole, as a new generation of scholars asked fresh questions about the past that reflected their own coming of age in the midst of the Civil Rights and women's movements in the 1960s and 1970s.

As graduate students began to examine American history in the wake of these transforming social movements, they focused on groups of people whose histories had generally been forgotten. Women's history was one of the new fields they inaugurated as a result. The subsequent outpouring of dissertations and monographs that explored women's past soon made clear the significance of women's history as a discipline, and helped reshape the contours of US history in the process. The bulk of this new work, however, was regionally specific. It concentrated largely on the experiences of eighteenth- and nineteenth-century women in New England. It reflected an almost exclusive perusal of northeastern archives and used that narrow framework to generalize about all women's experiences throughout America.

In 1982, Catherine Clinton challenged these limitations in *The Plantation Mistress*. Unlike antebellum New England women, Clinton argued, antebellum southern women found no collective identity upon which they could build a feminist movement. Her conclusions also challenged Anne Scott's (1970) premise that a self-conscious feminism had begun to take root among southern women on the eve of the Civil War. Clinton's trail-blazing book set the standard for southern women's history by asking critical questions about every aspect of elite white women's lives and by insisting upon the uniqueness of the slave society in which they lived. After reading some 500 manuscripts by elite women living in households with 20 or more slaves, Clinton (1982) concluded that plantation mistresses were trapped within the very patriarchal world that cultivated their romanticization. She found that these women worked extremely hard at managing the household, whether they were worrying about the state of the larder or a newborn slave infant's health. Despite all their work and their sacrifices, however, these women had no real authority or power. Nor did they have an economic stake in their contributions, for under common law their husbands claimed their property. Finally, these women could not even consider their bodies as their own, given the cultural imperative of producing heirs, especially male ones, to preserve family inheritance and vouchsafe a patriarch's manhood.

In the end, Clinton (1982) argued, slavery produced a complicated set of sexual dynamics that proved key to sustaining the oppression of slaves and white women in this patriarchal world. She cited evidence attesting to the exploitation and dehumanization of female slaves through rape and concubinage by planters. She suggested that these acts of sexual violence also exploited and dehumanized male slaves by emasculating them, even as cultural ideals desexualized plantation mistresses by placing them on their proverbial pedestals. Clinton (1982) urged, and has continued to do so in her subsequent work, that scholars pay careful attention to the history of sexuality, the construction of power and the use of violence as critical tools in the perpetuation of this oppressive slave society.

Clinton's insistence on the power of the planter patriarch to shape all personal and social relations reflects a larger argument that has long dominated southern history. It is steeped in the pioneering work of Eugene Genovese, especially in *The Political Economy of Slavery* (1965) but also in *Roll, Jordan, Roll* (1974), books which did not deal with women or gender explicitly. Genovese depicted elite southern families as anything but loving, permissive, and egalitarian. Instead, planters were premodern authoritarians who ruled supreme, but mediated their power through a quasi-benevolent paternalism. Enlarging in important ways upon Genovese's original framework, the majority of women's historians, beginning with Scott (1970) and Clinton (1982), understood that the institution of slavery rested on planters' patriarchal power, which justified not only the exploitation of enslaved African Americans, but also the subordination of women within planter families and by extension within southern society.

This argument received its fullest theoretical explication in Elizabeth Fox-Genovese's (1988) *Within the Plantation Household*. The author contended that while the southern economy was heavily invested in a developing world market system, the social relations of slavery were not in the least capitalistic. The central characteristic of the slave South, then, was not so much plantation agriculture, but the patriarchal household, in which nuclear family members, extended kin, hired hands, and slaves were all viewed as the dependants of the male household head. Unlike the North, where production had moved out of the household and into the factory, the plantation household was the key production unit in the antebellum South. The plantation mistress had authority within this household based on her ability to juggle two critical and seemingly opposed roles. On the one hand, the mistress was valued for her mothering, her piety, her graciousness, and her "ornamentation," all abstracted, passive duties. On the other hand, she was expected to take firm control over household production, managing the making of food and clothing, and controlling the tasks and behavior of slaves. In this latter role, the plantation mistress's efforts and authority were instrumental to the functioning of the plantation household.

Fox-Genovese (1988) pressed her analysis further, however, by challenging Clinton's (1982) depiction of plantation mistresses as victimized and isolated. Rather than being exploited and repressed under this arrangement, Fox-Genovese suggested, the planter's wife benefited from the slave system that sustained the plantation household. Elite white women's work and intellect were integral to the success of the planter patriarch and the larger society in which he prevailed. Under these circumstances, plantation mistresses could not be (and were not) proto-feminists. Indeed, Fox-Genovese stressed, these women absolutely failed to grasp the underlying repressiveness of a patriarchal order that pitted white women against black women. There were limited exceptions. Civil War diarist Mary Chesnut compared women's status in marriage to slavery not so much to caricature the peculiar institution of slavery as to indict a world where white wives and black concubines, along with black men, all existed in subjugation to white men. Unfortunately, Chesnut simply could not imagine an alternate way to order the world and ultimately benefited from the privileges awarded her as an intelligent woman within this ruling elite.

Fox-Genovese, like Clinton, compelled southern historians to pay attention to the gendered as well as the racial dimensions of power in the slave South, and to acknowledge their inextricability. Moreover, in viewing the household as the locus of production, Fox-Genovese helped scholars explain why this society remained in some respects so removed from the swirling tide of transatlantic change that was reshaping society in Europe and the North. The rural, isolated setting of the plantation where production took place, imbuing patriarchs with an awesome kind of authority, made the slave South as a whole more impervious to capitalism's modernizing nudges and kept women, white and black, in thralldom, but for elite women it was a thralldom that they benefited from maintaining. Hence Fox-Genovese's book marks one of the first efforts to take conservative slaveholding women's writings seriously. Her discussion of Louisa McCord, which emphasizes McCord's intelligence as well as her insistence upon white women's assumption of their rightful (and subordinate) place alongside their men as protectors of (white) Christian civilization, turned this largely forgotten nineteenth-century author into a veritable household name, at least among southern historians. If Fox-Genovese is somewhat sympathetic to McCord's sensibilities, it must be because she appreciates the completeness of McCord's defense of patriarchy. Louisa McCord does indeed make a more compelling argument for proslavery than even the infamous George Fitzhugh in that she articulates the importance of gender as well as race and class in defending the virtues of slavery. The publication of Richard Lounsbury's (1996, 1997) edited volumes of McCord's writings reveals just how well developed McCord's thoughts on the moral need for a social hierarchy in the slave South really were, confirming Fox-Genovese's original premise.

Christie Farnham (1994) extends Fox-Genovese's analysis by looking at the education of the elite daughters of the antebellum South. Farnham's *The Education of the Southern Belle* argues that girls' schools trained their students to handle the gendered power that came with their privileged class. By 1830, growing numbers of girls' academies insisted upon young women's intellectual capabilities by providing them with a traditionally male curriculum that included the classics, mathematics, and the sciences. Yet these schools also indoctrinated these young women in the gendered rules of socializing within their milieu. This training included proper moral deportment for young women who were expected to be southern society's exemplars of virtue and chastity. The tension for these students then was how to balance the rigorous academic learning they received, which nurtured their intellect, with the deeply conservative and gendered expectations of their social class and the power it wielded. Ultimately, these young women were expected to delight in their special role as southern ladies, and not use their serious education to challenge their place or pursue other ambitions. Farnham's (1994) valuable analysis also reminds us that we know too little about the education of literate white women in less privileged circumstances, what they read and why, and what values, gendered or otherwise, were nurtured in the process.

While his book does not address southern women's history explicitly, Steven Stowe's (1987) graceful *Intimacy and Power in the Old South* shows southern historians how the planter class used writing, as much as family expectations within the household and the formal education of planter children, to reinforce its right to rule at the apex of the southern social hierarchy. Planter family correspondence, Stowe finds, reveals how elite southerners knitted their personal and social lives together, using linguistic forms to explore the tensions between the individual and society, intimacy and power, and the feminine and masculine. Elite southerners' ability to maintain self-control at all costs, and to move gracefully within southern gendered expectations, confirmed authority and power among their own class and in the wider society in which they lived. Constructing this seamless and idealized self through writing was as important for women as it was for men.

Sally McMillen (1990), in her intriguing book, *Motherhood in the Old South*, affirms the distinctiveness of elite southern women's experience from a perspective few scholars have pursued. She examines southern white women's experiences with pregnancy, childbirth, and breastfeeding within the larger context of southern medical practice. While southern mothers shared experiences with mothers elsewhere in the country, southern women viewed motherhood as their sacred female duty within this particular social order. Carrying out that responsibility was challenged by the high infant mortality rates that plagued the southern clime as well as the traditional and often risky practices doctors employed, such as bleeding and the use of powerful laxatives. This work raises important questions. How did mothering as ideal and as experience compare across classes? Did poorer white women rely more exclusively on midwives and therefore benefit from a women's community or suffer from a dearth of professional medical care? What did mothers teach their daughters about sex, reproduction, and mothering and how did those lessons change over time, and across class, not to mention race? Although McMillen (1990) suggests that her findings apply to the middle and upper classes of the South, her sources largely reflect the interests and experiences of the wealthiest planter families, and in doing so, affirm the importance of mothering to the southern ladyhood ideal and the physical hardships and emotional sadness elite women encountered in the process of raising their children.

The outpouring of scholarship that consistently confirms the distinctiveness of antebellum southern white women's experience remains impressive. This work not only uses plantation correspondence and writings extensively, but also covers the entire antebellum period and attempts to spread out across the whole geography of the South as well. Yet within this body of work, one debate in particular continues to rage: the debate over elite women and their power, or lack of it, within this white male-dominated ruling elite framework. Jean Friedman (1985) added significantly to that debate by placing religion at the center of elite women's lives in *The Enclosed Garden*. She argued that the demands of evangelical Protestantism made southern women's experiences with religion profoundly different from those of northern women, who were able to use the moral sensibility of the Second Great Awakening, along with middle-class women's separation from men, to construct a public role for themselves as reformers and feminists. In the antebellum South, Friedman insists, southern women could never isolate themselves from the rest of society. They secured their identity not only from the slavery system and patriarchy, but also from requisite membership in local evangelical churches. Evangelicalism, then, represented another critical arena in which patriarchal authority was reinforced. As in their private lives, elite women, as well as lower-class white women and slaves, witnessed a double standard, this time through church discipline. Although other scholars acknowledged the importance of piety for the plantation mistress ideal, and the degree to which women looked to religion for comfort, Friedman stressed how pivotal evangelical religion proved in reinforcing even elite women's subordinate status and power in this society.

Christine Heyrman (1997) and Cynthia Lynn Lyerly (1998) represent the handful of scholars who have followed up on Friedman's (1985) important lead by looking at women's relationship to evangelicalism. Both Heyrman and Lyerly complicate Friedman's picture by showing that southern women were highly visible and active participants in early Methodism. Heyrman points out that many women converted despite the objections of their fathers and husbands. Lyerly stresses that these women found sustenance and even a measure of independence in their personal relationship with a feminized Jesus, which seems truly subversive of the patriarchal ideal. Threatened by the growing female majority, however, white men confronted clergymen, pressing them to limit women's roles and embrace a more muscular Christianity, Heyrman contends. This insightful work asks historians to take women's spiritual concerns and changing role in the evangelical church seriously. It invites more studies on the relationship between southern religious identity and women and power, especially across class, race, and time. Were evangelical churches, which existed beyond the reach of the household, one of the most important institutions for forging white female culture in the Old South?

Friedman (1985) also argues that extended kinship networks played a critical role in reinforcing the discipline of the evangelical church and the circumscribed roles of women in this preindustrial world. These later studies of evangelical religion in the antebellum South bring even more nuance to this key point. They show how the changing structure of this society, where this extended community of family and church predominated, made it virtually impossible for women to avoid carrying out their expected duties and roles – maternity, domesticity, piety, self-denial – without serious social sanction by the late antebellum period. As a result, women in this period who failed to meet their responsibilities did not blame the gendered limitations of the slave society in which they lived, but turned upon themselves in humiliating self-denigration. Scholars of southern religion believe that these powerful links between regional kinship networks and evangelical religion help explain why patriarchy proved so impervious.

Yet Joan Cashin (1991) in *A Family Venture*, another slim, intelligent study, takes umbrage at this portrayal of the extended southern family as repressive for women. While she too agrees that kinship networks fostered a web of interdependent and reciprocal relationships, she suggests that women found comfort, independence, and a separate female world within their supposed confines. This world was torn apart, she argues, by a rising generation of young men eager to leave their established families on the seaboard South and make their own way in the new southwest.

By combining the history of the plantation family with the history of westward migration, Cashin (1991) finds new ways to understand how gender functioned in the ordered, traditional world of the southeast versus that of the frontier isolation of the southwest. Heading west for young men represented an act of manhood and independence, an opportunity to escape the imprisonment of family and community. But heading west for women was not liberating in the slightest, Cashin contends, for to do so was not an act of their own volition, but the decision of their husbands and fathers. In their new rough-hewn world, women were pitiful creatures, isolated in nuclear families, and absolutely bereft without the kin, church, and community networks that had sustained them back east. The paternalism that planter culture cultivated among men in the established southeast was abandoned on the trek west, producing a class of men who were brutish, bad-tempered, and prone to excessive drink and violence, and a class of women who were victimized and isolated, unable to find any comfort whatsoever in their role as southern ladies. Cashin's study was based largely on reading the personal correspondence of these planter families, and self-perceptions do not always ring true to history when put to the test. But by asking how the dynamics of planter families changed across time and place, even within the antebellum period, Cashin has added a more critical and sophisticated level of analysis to southern women's history.

If Cashin's work, along with that of scholars of women and southern religion, builds upon Clinton's original conceptualization of women's isolation within the plantation household, the efforts of scholars like Kirsten Wood (2004) and Jane and William Pease (1999) remind us that some mistresses found ways to maneuver for power within their patriarchal world, and not simply as proslavery advocates like Louisa McCord. Wood, whose work examines the lives of slaveholding widows in the southeast, and is modeled on recent scholarship on women, gender, and status in early modern Europe, argues that her subjects understood the power of interdependent kin and community networks so well that they manipulated them to their best advantage. Although technically powerless as single women, for they could no longer claim their special role within the planter family following their husband's death, widows used the ideals of familial relationships not only to guarantee their own security but to acquire a more powerful voice in extended family concerns as well.

The Peases, who researched the lives of three generations of women in an aristocratic South Carolina family in *A Family of Women* (1999), found like so many other scholars that elite women's lives were structured by rigid patriarchal roles in which marriage and motherhood determined women's individual choices as well as their societal value. But what emerges from the Peases' willingness to look carefully at these women over time is how the Petigru sisters found avenues for nurturing their individual identities within this repressive environment. One strategy was relatively simple: offering emotional support to each over the course of a lifetime, despite living in distant households. Another strategy was to master the demands of the mistress role and the plantation. Excellent management skills, as well as knowledge about medicine, disease, and childbearing, made Adele Allston a powerful partner of her husband Robert Allston at Chicora Woods plantation. Robert, in fact, left Adele in control of Chicora Woods so he could pursue his own political career. Thus, while Adele Allston had no choice but to accept these duties, for as a woman she herself was not free to pursue a political life, her intelligence and hard work gave her more than a modicum of authority within her limited world. Melanie Pavich-Lindsay's (2002) edited volume on Anna Matilda Page King, another intelligent, hard-working wife of an ambitious absentee planter-cum-politician, masterfully highlights that fine line between empowerment and imprisonment that elite southern women navigated throughout their lifetimes.

Compelling as the patriarchal paradigm and the complicated place of white elite women within it has proven, one group of scholars has insisted that it bears serious limitations. These historians have been less willing to emphasize the uniqueness of the slave South and its telling impact on southern women. Informed by the French Annales school with its *histoire sociale*, and by the work of family historians such as Lawrence Stone, John Demos, and Phillip Greven, this group has argued that the planter family had become decidedly "modern" by the early nineteenth century. Jan Lewis (1983), in *The Pursuit of Happiness*, suggested that the public expectations and ambitions of Virginia's finest families were transformed into private, personal ones over the course of the revolutionary era. Whereas obligation, manly virtue, and honor were all requisite measures of worldly success among the pre-revolutionary generation, post-revolutionary Virginians, struggling with financial loss, the spread of evangelical religion, and the democratization of society, placed new value on individualism and the private world of love and emotion, nurtured best within the bosom of one's family.

Similarly, Jane Turner Censer (1984), in *North Carolina Planters and their Children*, found strong evidence that planter families favored companionate marriages and made extensive emotional and economic investments in their children as early as 1800. Unlike the gender-determined parental behavior emphasized by those scholars who identify the planter household as patriarchal, the North Carolina parents in Censer's study did not punish their children. Instead, their offspring apparently had internalized parental expectations and behaved appropriately. Moreover, parents showed equal interest in children of either sex, provided daughters as well as sons with fine educations, and bequeathed equally to male and female children, regardless of birth order, in their wills.

These two books argue that the internal dynamics of planter family life, including the division of gender roles and the wielding of power and emotion, can be read as responses to the beginnings of capitalism. Their work pays less attention to slavery and racial dynamics in the construction of the modern family within the planter class because the market revolution ultimately challenged the very premise of a slave society. Accordingly, this argument does not consider the planter family and the gendered dimensions within it as a dynamic force capable of shaping society in its own right. Instead these historians found that the planter family, in all its privilege, civility, and internal equality, marks the best locale from which to chart the effects of sweeping economic and social transformations upon a premodern slave society.

Anya Jabour (1998) reminds us of the value of this approach in *Marriage in the Early Republic*. Jabour plumbs the inner workings of an allegedly companionate marriage. What intrigues here is not simply the honest commitment of these two loving people to each other's emotional fulfillment, but why that commitment failed over the course of their long lives together. Jabour suggests that it is the maturation of the plantation South, with its hardening expectations about patriarchal roles and behavior, that dooms the egalitarian desires of the Wirts. What comes to constitute success for William Wirt and the men of this class in the new Old South was not a loving family, but professional and economic power, which generated new tensions and pressures for Elizabeth Wirt and women of her class, undermining the companionate marriage ideal that had emerged in the early republic. Although new national cultural values nurtured heightened expectations for love and intimacy within marriage, the extraordinary demands of the planter's world reinforced patriarchy in practice. In the end, capitalism's cultural impact on the early South was diluted by the spread of the cotton economy, which rejuvenated not only the plantation system but also the patriarchal household and gender inequity.

It is readily apparent that elite slaveholding women, and attendant questions about their power and status, have generated the greatest scholarly attention over the past several decades. This can be blamed in part on the wonderful abundance of archival sources about planter families, made even more accessible with two fine microfilm series, *The Records of Antebellum Southern Plantations*, edited by Kenneth Stampp, and *Southern Women and their Families*, edited by Ann Firor Scott, both from University Publications of America. Scholars are fortunate that this well-educated ruling elite documented so much of its public and private life, leaving a rich cache of information on the world the slaveholders made. But this emphasis on the plantation class also highlights a significant problem. The majority of antebellum southern women have had to stand in the shadow of their more glamorous and lettered sisters, patiently waiting their turn for scholarly acknowledgement and analysis.

Certainly southern women's historians recognized early on that they could not study slaveholding women's lives without examining their relationships with slaves, and especially with slave women. Catherine Clinton's (1982) work insisted that plantation mistresses recognized the similarities between the enslavement of African Americans and their enslavement as women, and pointed out opportunities for slave women and elite women to form close bonds despite the profound differences in their circumstances. Indeed, mistresses and slaves understood that there was little they could do to prevent masters from embracing a sexual double standard. Planters could publicly maintain a white family while privately pursuing sexual relationships with slave women, consensual or not, with little or no public censure. Elizabeth Fox-Genovese (1988) and others have suggested that the predominance of this unfair double standard made elite women all the more likely to practice extreme forms of violence and cruelty toward slave women under the guise of deserved punishment. Still, even as this work made clear how important slave women's experience was to women's history and to the history of the antebellum South, slave women's perspective was being given short shrift, even as scholars tried to write a southern women's history that was more inclusive.

Jacqueline Jones (1985) began to rectify that imbalance in her wide-ranging history of black women in America, *Labor of Love, Labor of Sorrow*. Her book shows slave women struggling to meet whites' expectations and still care for their own families. Jones also highlighted planters' insistence on labeling all women as workers, regardless of age, physical ability or family status, even as these same planters all too often sexually exploited them. Deborah Gray White (1985), in her important book *Ar'n't I a Woman?*, the first full-length study of antebellum slave women, focused her analysis more closely on the double jeopardy that slave women faced as a result of racial and sexual discrimination. White examined the daily experiences of slave women within the context of longstanding myths about black womanhood, weaving her analysis from traditional sources like slave narratives and demographic evidence with less conventional sources like literature and folk culture. Her work explicitly examined relationships within the slave community, between men and women, and between women, and offered a powerful critique of those historians of the 1970s who failed to consider slave women and gender in their otherwise compelling work on slave culture and community. As a result of Jones' and White's important work, no historians of American slavery can write about slave men without writing about slave women any longer.

White (1985) made especially clear that slave women's experiences differed greatly from those of slave men. She stressed that slave women may well have been the most exploited, neglected, and abused social group in American history. She conveyed the power of cultural stereotypes – including the loyal "Mammies" who served as selfless surrogate mothers for elite white children and the fiery, sex-starved "Jezebels" who drove otherwise innocent planters into their slaves' beds – and how they were used to justify whites' blindness to slave women's real plight. Not only did White document slave women's vulnerability to sexual abuse by white men, but also she recorded the economic value white men placed upon slave women because of their reproductive capacity. Bearing children put slave mothers in a terrible bind. It enhanced their value in the master's eyes, for slave children meant more work performed and more profit in their pockets over the long haul. For slave mothers, children required a degree of protection that they could never truly provide within the slave system. Having children also signified the loss of physical mobility. Mothers did not want to leave their children to visit husbands on other plantations or sell garden produce in the city market. Most certainly, mothers did not want to run away, for taking their children increased the likelihood of capture, and running away without them meant their abandonment.

Whereas Jacqueline Jones (1985) emphasized the importance of family in sustaining slave women's lives, a fact White would never deny, *Ar'n't I a Woman?* suggests that slave women may have been happiest and felt safest among other slave women. This community of women was a by-product of white work expectations, although whites never anticipated their social repercussions. Slave women often toiled as field hands in sex-segregated groups. They worked together within the slave quarters to finish the laundry, shuck corn, and make quilts. They shared in childcare. Skilled slave women often passed their knowledge of cooking or sewing or healing to the next generation of slave women. White (1985) suggests that the bonds forged through these work relationships were often more stable and sometimes even more intimate than those between husbands and wives, given the precariousness of marriage within the plantation system.

White (1985) also raised another challenging point. Because slave men lacked authority within this world, for they could not provide for their families, own property, have protection under the law, or prevent their wives and children from being abused or sold, their relationships with women may have been more equitable and mutually supportive. White presses this position because she considers traditional depictions of black male–female relationships, whether as matriarchal or patriarchal, too simplistic. Still, the egalitarian label the author attempts to apply seems problematic as well. As long as slave women remained vulnerable to rape by white men, equality within slave marriage could never be realized. On the other hand, White's evidence shows us that slave women benefited from relationships with other slave women *and* slave men. They were mutually supportive even if neither slave men nor slave women could prevent the domination of the slaveholder.

The questions that White (1985) and Jones (1985) posed transformed the study of American slavery as much as they transformed the study of southern women. Brenda Stevenson (1996), who studied enslaved and slaveholding families in Loudoun County, Virginia, following their lead, used gendered analysis to examine such topics as courtship, marriage, divorce, and parenting in white and black families. Her conclusions paint a bleak picture of the slave community, where the violence masters wrought upon slaves could in turn be wrought upon slave children by their tortured parents. Stevenson also demonstrates the terrible impact of mass sales of slaves, bound for markets in the new southwest, on marriage and family. Although men, women, and children were all victims of the increased willingness of planters to profit from slave sales, it is the women – as mothers and wives – who emerge from this work as the most bereft. Not only did they witness the disintegration of their family, but also they then had to continue their lives with only the memory of their loved ones to sustain them. Stevenson's (1996) use of the case study, like that of Ann Malone (1992), Vernon Burton (1985), and others, is extremely valuable because it serves historians a deep slice of antebellum society and culture across time but within a very specific context.

Maria Jenkins Schwartz's (2000) *Born in Bondage*, one of two more recent books on slave childhood, not only reiterates the terrible destruction that slavery wrought, but also uses this case study approach to especially good advantage by analyzing three different regions within the South to make her case. This book, along with Wilma King's (1995) *Stolen Childhood*, presents important arguments about the stark world that slave children encountered and the struggles between slave parents and white owners to raise them. Implicit in this scholarship is the centrality of slave family and community to slave children's sense of self. Yet the evidence in these studies suggests that childrearing, most certainly out of necessity, given the way whites constructed slavery, proved to be largely women's purview, even if the authors do not address this point explicitly. If this is indeed the case, then we need a whole new set of studies that look at how slave women helped construct their children's gendered identities and the implications for their ability to endure slavery. How did young girls come to understand their roles as workers, and their future roles as wives and mothers in this society under such difficult constraints? How did girls think about their sexual maturation and its meanings in a society where they were prone to sexual violence at the hands of their masters? What was their mothers' role in that process? What about slave boys and their coming of age? How did mothers shape their sons' conceptions of manhood in a larger society that largely denied slave men their masculinity?

The study of slave women is such a fruitful field to pursue that two essay collections perhaps best convey its promise. The essays in Gaspar and Hine's (1996) *More than Chattel* and Morton's (1996) *Discovering the Women in Slavery*, when taken as a whole, move beyond looking at slavery through the lenses of slave community and slave family to put women at the center of their analysis. In doing so, these essays insist that historians consider the tremendous burden that slave women bore as workers, for they were both producers and reproducers in this society. They ask us to think comparatively about women in slavery, making connections and differentiations between North American, Caribbean, and Brazilian slavery, and under French, Spanish, and Anglo-American regimes. They press us to look at women and gender in West Africa and the degree to which gendered Africanisms shaped slave culture and slave women's roles in the Americas. They raise questions about women's experience with and perceptions of pregnancy, childbirth and childrearing, disease, healing and mortality, sexual violence, and resistance and how they differed across place and time. The very breadth of this work reminds us of how much remains to be explored.

While casting the net widely is important, thematically focused monographs can also transform the ways we think about gender and slavery. Sharla Fett's (2002) *Working Cures*, with its emphasis on the social, cultural, and political implications of healing in the slave community, does precisely that. Not only does she examine the conflicts between slaveholders' conceptions of slave health and those of African Americans, which were relational and drew from community relationships, spiritual power, and African practices, but she also shows how medicine on plantations represented an important battleground for determining power relations between slaveholders and slaves. Those tensions were especially evident in conflicts over child-bearing, childcare, and women's work. Slave women, who performed the bulk of plantation health work, gained considerable – although all too often overlooked – authority from their alternative constructions of medicine and healing.

Important insights about a dominant culture can often be gleaned by examining the people at its margins. Studying free blacks, and especially free black women, provides critical perspectives about the nature of lived experience as opposed to formal laws and systems in the antebellum South. Adele Logan Alexander (1991) in *Ambiguous Lives* and Kent Leslie (1995) in *Woman of Color* have written fascinating biographies of free women of color and their families in the Georgia Piedmont over the course of the nineteenth century. Susan Hunt, a free woman of color because of her female Cherokee forebears, and Amanda America Dickson, the daughter of a slave mother and a wealthy white planter and businessman, managed to circumnavigate the seemingly deeply rooted racial ideology of the antebellum South that defined who was slave and free and black and white by virtue of their color, their access to wealth and power, and their kinship bonds. Dickson's father ignored law and convention, acknowledging Amanda as his daughter, arranging her marriage to his nephew, and bestowing his fortune upon her at his death. Hunt was the mistress of a white lawyer, and raised their children hidden away in a series of rooms in the bachelor's mansion. Whereas Dickson lived publicly as a free black woman and the daughter of a well-known white man, Hunt and her children lived a largely secret life. Both these free women of color, light-skinned, protected by white men, and leading lives of relative privilege compared with most free blacks and slaves, none-theless confronted innumerable social and cultural barriers, as well as legal and economic ones. Their stories, so painstakingly researched and reconstructed, tell us about a world that historians are only beginning to recognize, one where social relations defied all legal and social prescriptions. At the same time, they underline a central truth about gender and race in the Old South. White men could cross the social boundary of race not only to father children with black women, consensually or not, but also to challenge social sanction even further by living with an African American woman, slave or free, as their "wife."

Yet the unique worlds revealed by the lives of Dickson and Hunt do not look quite so unusual when viewed in a more comparative framework. The work of a new generation of scholars, including Gwendolyn Midlo Hall (1992), Kimberly Hanger (1997), Virginia Gould (1998), and Jane Landers (1999), shows us that both slave women and free women of color experienced relative freedom and substantial social mobility as late as the early nineteenth century in the Gulf South, although these experiences were not without their hardships and constraints. Unlike Dickson and Hunt, however, the majority of free women of color in these port cities along the Gulf were working-women, who supported themselves and their families through their labor as servants, laundresses, seamstresses, and even as entrepreneurs and shopkeepers. Although a number of new studies about free black communities in the Atlantic South have appeared since the early 1990s, for the most part they do not pay close attention to women and gender. Given the compelling work on the Gulf South, it seems all the more reasonable to expect more careful studies of free black women throughout the region, in rural and urban environments, in the upper South as well as in the deep South. Diane Batts Morrow (2002) sets the new standard for such welcome scholarship in writing the history of the Oblate sisters of antebellum Baltimore, Maryland, free black religious women who educated the mulatto daughters of southern planters and who had to find a delicate balance between their relative autonomy as free people, their religious identity and institutional demands, and their place in this world as free women of color.

While plantation mistresses and slave women have garnered the bulk of scholarly attention and theoretical frameworks, Native American women in the slave South are beginning to receive their due. Theda Perdue (1998), in *Cherokee Women*, argues that Cherokee women sustained their communities with their strength and their commitment to cultural persistence. In exemplary fashion, Perdue weaves together methods and insights gleaned from a variety of interdependent disciplines: history, archeology, ethnology, women's studies, and anthropology. Tracing the history of women's roles in Cherokee society from the seventeenth century to removal, Perdue argues that it was women's adaptability that ensured Cherokee survival at the precarious edges of whites' ever-expanding "frontiers."

Although she agrees with traditional scholars that by the early nineteenth century, male-dominated political forms had begun to prevail in Cherokee society, Perdue insists that Cherokee women remained the "conservators of traditional values" and retained a special authority of their own. Despite the federal government's efforts to "civilize" the Cherokee – forcing them to adopt European-American gender roles, with men as farmers and women as housewives – Cherokee women resisted, guarding their tradition of matrilineality in the face of white patrilineality, maintaining land communally despite pressures by whites to hold land individually, and protesting removal to Indian Territory.

In *Weaving New Worlds*, Sarah Hill (1997) relies on material culture as well as oral and written history to convey a complementary history of Cherokee women's influence. Their production of intricately woven river cane and later white oak baskets for harvests and ceremonies and mats for covers and shrouds had been a cultural mainstay of Cherokee life for several hundred years. By the early nineteenth century, the period in which the federal government imposed new regulations and institutions on Cherokee culture, women had begun to trade baskets for supplies to sustain their vulnerable communities. Thus women's production not only preserved cultural myths and traditions but also connected the Cherokees to the beginnings of the market revolution on the southern frontier. Together Perdue's and Hill's findings, supported by wide-ranging sources and thoughtful interdisciplinary analysis, remind us of what can be gained from using gender to scrutinize the history of southern Indian societies, including the Choctaw, Creek, and Seminole, before the Civil War. It would be equally useful to look more closely at Indian women's and white women's interactions with each other, their perceptions about their differing social roles, the impact of Christian mission work in building reciprocity between them, and their relative influence on political discourse based on their understanding of white patriarchal authority and each other.

While scholars have begun to add African American and Native American women into the mix of southern women's history, and to complicate that history in the process, white non-elite women, the majority of women in the South, have only recently begun to receive the attention they are warranted. This lingering class bias is not limited to southern women's historians but reflects a short-sightedness among southern historians in general. While Clinton, Fox-Genovese, and many other southern women's historians came to understand what elite white women thought of themselves and of slavery through these women's voluminous writings, other scholars turned to more objective and wide-ranging evidence, and in doing so, discovered a whole host of other historical actors, white and black women, middle-class and poor women, small slaveholding and nonslaveholding women.

Victoria Bynum's (1992) *Unruly Women* marks an important contribution to the study of those women deemed deviant because their behavior challenged the mores of antebellum southern society. By examining three North Carolina counties in great detail, using court records, civil complaints, newspapers, divorce cases, and other public records, Bynum recreates these communities and the lives of three groups of marginal women in them. On one hand, Bynum uncovers a diverse world in which mostly poor white women challenged southern patriarchy. When seeking divorce these women spoke publicly against the violent behavior of abusive husbands; they pursued sexual liaisons that defied socially understood barriers of color and class; and they even protested the political ideology of the Confederacy. In bringing these women and their actions to light, Bynum makes clear the integral relationship between family and politics, between public and private in the Old South. Many of Bynum's women lived beyond the reach and the "protection" of white men, but in doing so, and in transgressing the racial code that prevented white women's association with black men, these "unruly" women and their children had to pay the price: social ostracism and the hypocritical imposition of the law. While these women resisted the confines of southern patriarchy, it ultimately ensnared them. The ruling elite benefited from the subordination of all women, not just elite women, to sustain slavery. Unruly women, whose children could not be enslaved, nor would ever become heirs of planter families, had to be kept in line.

This insistence on the power of southern patriarchal authority to prevent most southern women from public engagement and political action found its most sophisticated defense in Stephanie McCurry's (1995) *Masters of Small Worlds*. Rather than make women the center of her study, McCurry relies on gender to illuminate yeoman households, their complicated relations with the planter aristocracy, the limitations of republican democracy, and the powerful influence of evangelical churches in shaping social, cultural, and political relations across class. Using the antebellum South Carolina lowcountry as her backdrop, McCurry reminds readers that yeoman farmers, not rich rice planters, formed the majority of the white population. They owned few or no slaves, and relied on their own labor and that of their family members, including their wives and daughters, to produce crops. Within the yeoman household, the male head ruled supreme, not only over his slaves, but also over his other dependants, white women, and children. This authority secured the male head not only economic independence, but political and social independence too. In theory, every yeoman shared this independence with every planter, despite startling discrepancies in wealth and power. This social ordering of the household was heavily reinforced within the evangelical church, where members across race, class, and gender were reminded that they were part of a hierarchical family with its requisite if unequally distributed duties. These beliefs about family and religion not only reinforced slavery, but also empowered the planter aristocracy, who were assured of the yeomen's tacit participation in their politics.

This argument builds in important ways upon the arguments of those historians who contend that elite southern women had no real influence beyond the house-hold, for McCurry shows that women in yeoman households had little power either. Economic, cultural, and political exigencies were threaded together to sustain the peculiar institution, and white women's subordination across class was critical to the proslavery defense. Thus, McCurry and other southern women's historians have been quick to point out that patriarchal authority became more repressive over the course of the antebellum era, rather than less so, in part as a result of the maturation and spread of the plantation economy, but also in response to antislavery politics and the influence of the abolition movement.

As Catherine Clinton (1982) argued in the *The Plantation Mistress*, sex in the Old South was a highly politicized act, especially when it transcended race – see also Clinton and Gillespie (1997), *The Devil's Lane* – and interracial sex did undermine the key arguments for the prevailing racial ideology. But only when patriarchal authority was shaken by national politics and northern threats in the 1850s did controlling sex between white women and black men became supremely important in southern society, as Martha Hodes (1997) explains in *White Women, Black Men*. Like Diane Somerville (1995), Hodes debunks the old saw that southern whites had wrought physical and legal vengeance on black men who had sex with white women since time immemorial. Hodes finds that the desire for race control only partially explained social responses to interracial sex. Just as important were perceptions about women's sexuality, protecting economic interests, reinforcing patriarchy, con-trolling class, and even ideas about justice, in shaping white responses to the knowl-edge of sex between a black man and a white woman. Thus, when a white husband accused his white wife of a longstanding affair with a neighbor's slave, the commun-ity, aware of the affair, remained silent and the husband was denied his appeal. Breaking up the white family because of the failure of the social hierarchies of race and gender to prevent the illicit affair, Hodes argues, only served to reveal the inherent weaknesses in white patriarchy. Therefore, the adulterous wife was pro-tected by law in order to shore up what was perceived to be a weak social structure. In the end, Hodes contends, it was the children of such interracial liaisons, living symbols of defiance against the rules of race and patriarchy, who exposed the southern social world's true vulnerability. Hodes' study is valuable because it examines the interconnectedness of black and white lives, and teases out whites' perceptions of these interracial liaisons and their context. But what remains to be done, in what will be an admittedly difficult task, is to tease out blacks' perceptions of these liaisons and their meanings. To what extent did African Americans view black men's sex with white women as anything but consensual within the broader parameters of a world shaped by white authority, regardless of gender?

While Hodes looked at white communities' perceptions of sex across the color line, Peter Bardaglio (1995) in *Reconstructing the Household* looked at the southern legal system, as evidenced in appellate court records, and found consistent regulation of family and sexuality to reinforce the institution of slavery. While family law in the North had begun to embrace a more egalitarian and liberal domestic order, the South clung to a hierarchical, corporatist ethos that preserved slavery. While Hodes discovered that white communities generally looked the other way when it came to illicit interracial sex until the 1850s, Bardaglio revealed that southern courts did not, censuring sex between black men and white women whenever possible. The courts, however, did ignore sex between white men and black women, and the sexual exploitation that accompanied such relations. Any children produced from such liaisons were legally slaves, and not a threat, whereas the mulatto children of white women and black men, because they were born free, challenged the very notion of a race hierarchy upon which southern society depended; this explains the court's rulings. While one looks closely at communities, and the other at the court system, both bold books confirm the power of patriarchal authority in the Old South, and the degree to which even the most personal choices always had political repercussions.

Suzanne Lebsock (1984), in *The Free Women of Petersburg*, moves us past the power of patriarchal authority and the limitations it could impose on black and white women and black men to provide us with a more complex and perhaps even subversive picture. Her book remains a pioneering biracial study of southern women's public and private behavior based on quantitative analysis and public records. She argues that southern free women, white and black, actually gained autonomy from southern men, not as a result of feminist sensibilities similar to those of women in the North, but through their own increasing economic independence. It was free white and black women's choices in work, marriage, and inheritance that secured them this financial freedom, although these choices were made in some cases by men eager to protect their wives and daughters from future uncertainties. Lebsock's analysis is insightful in other ways too. She finds that companionate marriage among middle-class white women brought with it a measure of marital discord as roles and authority began to be rearranged. She discovered that while some women worked because they had to, other middle-class women continued their careers after marriage to maintain their economic autonomy and the subsequent power it secured for them. White women also established authority through their work in voluntary associations, which were more often secular than religious in origination. Lebsock concluded that white female authority in the Old South hinged on women's "personalism," the degree to which women typically worked to fulfill the needs of deserving individuals, including meritorious slaves. Thus, suggests Lebsock, in what is an especially important conceptualization, personalism made white women's benevolent work an inherently subversive influence on slavery, even if these female organizations and their female leaders entertained absolutely no abolitionist sensibilities whatsoever. Lebsock's study received high praise for her use of local history and social history methods to ask much larger questions of wide-ranging historical importance, but the degree to which she insisted upon the public visibility of women, including free black entrepreneurial and property-owning women as well as white women, was more often than not dismissed as exceptional because her evidence and arguments were based on an urban setting and therefore deemed unrepresentative of the Old South.

Lebsock's (1984) challenge to look at southern women as public actors has more recently received revived attention. Several significant new books explore the role of southern women in antebellum political life and their influence on political culture. In doing so, this exciting new scholarship asks historians to rethink their understanding of what constitutes political life, "the public," and power relations. Although Cynthia Kierner's (1998) *Beyond the Household* focuses mainly on women and gender in the eighteenth-century South, she argues for the increasing inextricability of the defense of slavery with the defense of patriarchal relations in marriage over the course of the antebellum era. Marriages and the nature of power within them were becoming public territory, Kierner posits, as proslavery defenders likened the "natural" inequality of husband and wife to that of slaveholder and slave.

Kierner's (1998) study, based on the writings of white women in North Carolina and Virginia, emphasizes the critical work that southern elite women performed, as well as their increasingly public roles over the course of the eighteenth and into the nineteenth centuries. Moreover, Kierner finds that these women were not stunted by the construction of the southern lady ideal, in all its passivity and dependency, at the height of the Old South. Defining participation in the public sphere as participation in informal civil and social life, the world of literature and letters, economic transactions, and religious and benevolent work, Kierner shows not only how developing gender ideology in the South honored domesticity and women's moral influence in the household, but also how it paved the way for elite women's "genteel" influence on public culture. Although Kierner argues that evangelicalism and domesticity served southern women as well as northern women in the early antebellum period, women did not romanticize marriage and domesticity as men did. Nor was the leap from the domestic sphere to the public sphere as big as historians once suggested. Southern women in the countryside and the city needed moral instruction and a good education to fulfill their domestic duties. They also learned moral piety and virtue through the evangelical church. Together, the church and the school provided women with an opening into public life, as teachers and headmistresses, as Sunday school teachers, as missionaries, and as organizers of charitable organizations and reform associations. Kiener's study invites others like it elsewhere in the South. How much latitude were women allowed in public life in the deep South, for example, when the slave economy was in its heyday? What did female participation in public culture look like in Appalachia? Or in the thriving port cities of the Gulf South? Moreover, what did female participation in public culture by elite and middle-class women mean for poor and working-class white and free black women? To what extent were their interests and needs compromised by these charitable efforts, or were these efforts as subversive as Suzanne Lebsock (1984) suggested in *Free Women of Petersburg*?

Elizabeth Varon (1998) finds even stronger evidence of white women's main-stream involvement in antebellum southern political life in *We Mean to Be Counted*. Elite and middle-class women in Virginia, conservative in their political and social outlook, worked in charitable associations, embraced the colonization movement, expressed their views as writers, and participated in the Whig party's many campaign events. As self-proclaimed Female Citizens, these women's new civic roles evolved alongside the rise of the second party system, sectionalism, and secession. By the 1840s, practitioners of "Whig womanhood" argued that women must help shape party politics by acting as partisans and facilitators in the public sphere. Because they were such selfless patriots and moral arbiters, women had a duty to monitor the political process. By the 1850s, the Democrats recognized the value of women's participation and welcomed them to their circle too. The rise of secessionist senti-ment transformed the idea of female civic duty in the South. White women's purity of spirit made them better southern patriots than men, and hence gave them the authority to lead the battle to defend the South. The attack on Harpers Ferry and the 1860 election only underlined the significance of Virginia women's anti-Union voice, and helped launch an even fiercer female southern nationalism that Varon labels "Confederate womanhood."

Varon (1998) ably demonstrates the high degree of politicization among well-to-do Virginia women in the late antebellum era. Like all fine work, Varon's raises new questions. One wonders, again, about poor and wage-earning white women's political views and influence, and black women's perceptions and actions. One also wonders whether "Whig womanhood" took shape in other parts of the South and under similar or different circumstances.

The best work on antebellum southern women's history looks beyond the stand-ard periodization of the Old South (1800–60) to better document permanence and change in women's roles and identity. Gendered examinations of southern colonial history by such scholars as Mary Beth Norton (1996), Kathleen Brown (1996), and Kirsten Fischer (2002) have begun to influence studies of gender in the nineteenth century in important ways, whether tracing the origins of the antebellum southern lady ideal or looking at how and why political leaders manipulated expectations about gender roles and slavery to their own ends. Likewise, understanding what happened during the Civil War and the demise of the Old South better illuminates both the norms and the changing functions of women and gender. Scholarship on Confederate womanhood by Rable (1989), Clinton and Silber (1992), Whites (1995), Faust (1996), and Edwards (2000) has not only revealed the degree to which women's and men's experiences transformed women's roles, but also has insisted that women "made" the history of the Civil War as much as men. In *The Civil War as a Crisis in Gender*, Whites (1995) reminds us, like McCurry (1995), that white men's authority over the household confirmed their independence and status as public men on the eve of secession. White women accepted their subordin-ate role in return for white men's protection as well as their race privilege.

The Civil War was waged to protect white men's independence and white women's dependence, but Whites (1995) shows that it had the reverse effect. Con-federate men lost almost everything, including their independence and privilege. As a result white women redefined the meaning of the household, making it the central symbol of the war, ignoring the role of slavery and class conflict in the process. Faust (1996), in *Mothers of Invention*, looks principally at elite slaveholding women and their reluctance to accept the changes wrought by war, even as they learned to cast aside ladyhood to nurse wounded soldiers or publicly proselytize on behalf of the Confederacy. Faust's most profound contribution to southern history, however, is her argument that elite women gradually gave up the struggle at home. As slavery deteriorated on the home front, disillusioned elite women were increasingly unwilling to shore the peculiar institution back up, and saw themselves as victims of the cause itself. Women's subsequent criticisms of the Confederate leadership and their unwillingness to endure more wartime sacrifices ultimately undermined wartime morale. The lessons that elite women learned in wartime, moreover, would be reflected in their political attitudes and demands in the late nineteenth century.

It is crucial to recognize that this latest scholarship asks southern historians not only to include women in their work, but also to redefine politics and even rewrite political history. Government, for far too long, has been too narrowly and in the end wrongly defined as free white men's dealings with each other and ultimately as white men making history. Adding gender, along with race and class, to the analysis of politics broadens and deepens our understanding of power relations and public life. It gives us a richer and more complex picture of the past, one that makes explicit the critical connections between family and state. It invites close studies that not only take the relationship between women's domestic roles and public roles seriously, but also explore how the relationship between gender and power in individual households and gender and power in politics is conveyed, and the degree to which the overriding need to sustain slavery as an institution affected those relationships.

But redefining politics is not the only new direction in southern women's history. Unfortunately, too little scholarship explores women and economic transformation in the Old South. Although scholars acknowledge that plantation mistresses indeed labored, and that slave women performed every manner of task, from the most backbreaking field labor to fine embroidering, we know almost nothing about how the majority of white and free black women juggled reproductive and productive labor, whether paid or not, and how that balancing act changed over the course of the antebellum period when the market revolution was transforming American society and culture. Forthcoming monographs must flesh out the myriad ways women navigated their own economic needs and those of their families within the parameters of a slave society. Certainly the majority of women's work has been unacknowledged but how did that work shape relations within the household and within the community? How important were prevailing cultural attitudes about women's proper role to these women at work? Do they help explain the invisibility of women in certain trades and professions, even as careful study of the historical record shows there were women at work in the iron industry in the Tennessee mountains and in the silk factories in western Virginia? How did ethnicity and class shape gender and race conventions? Was it easier for Irish American women to compete with slave and free black women for work as nannies and laundresses, for example, because the prevailing southern lady stereotype was applied only to white Protestants? In general, it seems clear that southern historians have overlooked the entrance of southern women into the market. Yet the latest scholarship, as in Delfino and Gillespie's (2002) *Neither Lady nor Slave*, suggests that poor and middle-class black and white women workers, paid and unpaid, paved the way for the expansion of commerce and industry to the rural as well as the urban South. On one hand, women's paid occupations, which grew out of the gendered expectations of the household, from washing and cooking, to sewing for hire, to millwork, were all deemed permissible because they were extensions of women's roles in the preindustrial household and not a threat to the white male-dominated social order. But to what extent did these women resist their personal circumstances as a result of their working experiences, and vice versa? In what ways did women's work, paid or unpaid, politicize women's understanding of power within the household? Within this society? What kinds of social orderings and ideals, including not only racialized ones but also class and gendered ones, were fundamentally challenged when black and white women worked next to each other in the earliest textile mills, sold their produce together at the local market, or offered their bodies at the same bawdy house for profit? In what ways did these ordinary women benefit from the intrusion of the new market economy and in what ways did they endure new sets of hardships as they entered into paid work? Were wage-earning women perceived as yet another threat to white patriarchal and racial slavery in the late antebellum era? The sources are difficult to locate and harder to tease out, but the answers to such questions will help us understand the power of patriarchal authority and gender conventions in the Old South, and their limitations too.

Southern women's history, like all women's history, is undergoing a transition in the early twenty-first century. This transition ultimately reflects the tremendous impact this field has had upon southern history as a whole, not so much as measured by the sheer numbers of books and articles published, which are nonetheless impressive, but even more compellingly by the big debates and the transforming arguments wrought by this scholarship. Historians worth their salt can no longer write a book about any aspect of the Old South without knowing the historiography of southern women's history and without applying gendered analysis to their work. What was once scholarship at the margins has now become the center. It is this new set of realities that the current generation of southern historians must ponder. Have the contributions of southern women's historians proved so instrumental in shaping how we understand the Old South that southern women's history as a *separate* area of inquiry has become virtually obsolete? The answer is probably "yes" in theory, but "not yet" in practice. While southern women's history has done more than any other field to hone the cutting edge of southern history over the past quarter of a century, not all historians have yet acknowledged this reality, or have trained their graduate students to understand its implications. Until that time comes, women's history in the Old South remains at the very least the most influential field in nineteenth-century southern history.

BIBLIOGRAPHY

Alexander, Adele Logan (1991) *Ambiguous Lives: Free Women of Color in Rural Georgia, 1789–1879.* Fayetteville, Ark.: University of Arkansas Press.

Bardaglio, Peter W. (1995) *Reconstructing the Household: Families, Sex, and the Law in the Nineteenth-Century South.* Chapel Hill, NC: University of North Carolina Press.

Boatwright, Eleanor Miot (1994 [1941]) *Status of Women in Georgia, 1783–1860.* Brooklyn, NY: Carlson.

Brown, Kathleen M. (1996) *Good Wives, Nasty Wenches, and Anxious Patriarchs: Gender, Race, and Power in Colonial Virginia.* Chapel Hill, NC: University of North Carolina Press.

Burton, Orville Vernon (1985) *In my Father's House are Many Mansions: Family and Community in Edgefield, South Carolina 1848–1889*. Chapel Hill, NC: University of North Carolina Press.

Bynum, Victoria E. (1992) *Unruly Women: The Politics of Social and Sexual Control in the Old South*. Chapel Hill, NC: University of North Carolina Press.

Cashin, Joan (1991) *A Family Venture: Men and Women on the Southern Frontier*. New York: Oxford University Press.

Censer, Jane Turner (1984) *North Carolina Planters and their Children, 1800–1860*. Baton Rouge, La.: Louisiana State University Press.

Clinton, Catherine (1982) *The Plantation Mistress: Women's World in the Old South*. New York: Pantheon.

Clinton, Catherine and Gillespie, Michele (eds.) (1997) *The Devil's Lane: Sex and Race in the Early South*. New York: Oxford University Press.

Clinton, Catherine and Silber, Nina (eds.) (1992) *Divided Houses: Gender and the Civil War*. New York: Oxford University Press.

Delfino, Susanna and Gillespie, Michele (eds.) (2002) *Neither Lady nor Slave: Working Women of the Old South*. Chapel Hill, NC: University of North Carolina Press.

Edwards, Laura F. (2000) *Scarlett Doesn't Live Here Anymore: Southern Women in the Civil War Era*. Urbana, Ill.: University of Illinois Press.

Farnham, Christie Anne (1994) *The Education of the Southern Belle: Higher Education and Student Socialization in the Antebellum South*. New York: New York University Press.

Faust, Drew Gilpin (1996) *Mothers of Invention: Women of the Slaveholding South in the American Civil War*. Chapel Hill, NC: University of North Carolina Press.

Fett, Sharla M. (2002) *Working Cures: Healing, Health, and Power on Southern Slave Plantations*. Chapel Hill, NC: University of North Carolina Press.

Fischer, Kirsten (2002) *Suspect Relations: Sex, Race, and Resistance in Colonial North Carolina*. Ithaca, NY: Cornell University Press.

Fox-Genovese, Elizabeth (1988) *Within the Plantation Household: Black and White Women of the Old South*. Chapel Hill, NC: University of North Carolina Press.

Friedman, Jean F. (1985) *The Enclosed Garden: Women and Community in the Evangelical South, 1830–1900*. Chapel Hill, NC: University of North Carolina Press.

Gaspar, David Barry and Hine, Darlene Clark (eds.) (1996) *More than Chattel: Black Women and Slavery in the Americas*. Bloomington, Ind.: Indiana University Press.

Genovese, Eugene D. (1965) *The Political Economy of Slavery: Studies in the Economy and Society of the Slave South*. New York: Pantheon.

Genovese, Eugene D. (1974) *Roll, Jordan, Roll: The World the Slaves Made*. New York: Pantheon.

Gould, Virginia Meacham (ed.) (1998) *Chained to the Rock of Adversity: To be Free, Black and Female in the Old South*. Athens, Ga.: University of Georgia Press.

Hall, Gwendolyn Midlo (1992) *Africans in Colonial Louisiana: The Development of Afro-Creole Culture in the Eighteenth-Century*. Baton Rouge, La.: Louisiana State University Press.

Hanger, Kimberly S. (1997) *Bounded Lives, Bounded Places: Free Black Society in Colonial New Orleans, 1769–1803*. Durham, NC: Duke University Press.

Heyrman, Christine Leigh (1997) *Southern Cross: The Beginnings of the Bible Belt*. New York: Alfred A. Knopf.

Hill, Sarah H. (1997) *Weaving New Worlds: Southeastern Cherokee Women and their Basketry*. Chapel Hill, NC: University of North Carolina Press.

Hodes, Martha (1997) *White Women, Black Men: Illicit Sex in the Nineteenth-Century South*. New Haven, Conn.: Yale University Press.

Jabour, Anya (1998) *Marriage in the Early Republic: Elizabeth and William Wirt and the Companionate Ideal*. Baltimore, Md.: Johns Hopkins University Press.

Jones, Jacqueline (1985) *Labor of Love, Labor of Sorrow: Black Women, Work, and the Family from Slavery to the Present*. New York: Basic Books.

Kierner, Cynthia (1998) *Beyond the Household: Women's Place in the Early South, 1700–1835*. Ithaca, NY: Cornell University Press.

King, Wilma (1995) *Stolen Childhood: Slave Youth in Nineteenth-Century America*. Bloomington, Ind.: Indiana University Press.

Landers, Jane (1999) *Black Society in Spanish Florida*. Urbana, Ill.: University of Illinois Press.

Lebsock, Suzanne (1984) *The Free Women of Petersburg: Status and Culture in a Southern Town, 1784–1860*. New York: Norton.

Leslie, Kent Anderson (1995) *Woman of Color, Daughter of Privilege: Amanda America Dickson, 1849–1893*. Athens, Ga.: University of Georgia Press.

Lewis, Jan (1983) *The Pursuit of Happiness: Family and Values in Jefferson's Virginia*. Cambridge: Cambridge University Press.

Lounsbury, Richard C. (ed.) (1996) *Louisa S. McCord: Poems, Drama, Biography, Letters*. Charlottesville, Va.: University of Virginia Press.

Lounsbury, Richard C. (ed.) (1997) *Louisa S. McCord: Selected Writings*. Charlottesville, Va.: University of Virginia Press.

Lyerly, Cynthia Lynn (1998) *Methodism and the Southern Mind, 1770–1810*. New York: Oxford University Press.

McCurry, Stephanie (1995) *Masters of Small Worlds: Yeoman Households, Gender Relations, and the Political Culture of the Antebellum South Carolina Low Country*. New York: Oxford University Press.

McMillen, Sally G. (1990) *Motherhood in the Old South: Pregnancy, Childbirth and Infant Rearing*. Baton Rouge, La.: Louisiana State University Press.

Malone, Ann Patton (1992) *Sweet Chariot: Slave Family and Household Structure in Nineteenth Century Louisiana*. Chapel Hill, NC: University of North Carolina Press.

Massey, Mary Elizabeth (1966) *Bonnet Brigades: American Women in the Civil War*. New York: Alfred A. Knopf.

Morrow, Diane Batts (2002) *Persons of Color and Religious at the Same Time: The Oblate Sisters of Providence, 1828–1860*. Chapel Hill, NC: University of North Carolina Press.

Morton, Patricia (ed.) (1996) *Discovering the Women in Slavery: Emancipating Perspectives on the American Past*. Athens, Ga.: University of Georgia Press.

Norton, Mary Beth (1996) *Founding Mothers and Fathers: Gendered Power and the Forming of American Society*. New York: Alfred A. Knopf.

Pavich-Lindsay, Melanie (ed.) (2002) *Anna: The Letters of a St. Simons Island Plantation Mistress, 1817–1859*. Athens, Ga.: University of Georgia Press.

Pease, Jane H. and Pease, William H. (1999) *A Family of Women: The Carolina Petigrus in Peace and War*. Chapel Hill, NC: University of North Carolina Press.

Perdue, Theda (1998) *Cherokee Women: Gender and Culture Change, 1700–1835*. Lincoln, Nebr.: University of Nebraska Press.

Rable, George C. (1989) *Civil Wars: Women and the Crisis of Southern Nationalism*. Urbana, Ill.: University of Illinois Press.

Schwartz, Marie Jenkins (2000) *Born in Bondage: Growing up Enslaved in the American South*. Cambridge, Mass.: Harvard University Press.

Scott, Ann Firor (1970) *The Southern Lady: From Pedestal to Politics, 1830–1930*. Chicago: University of Chicago Press.

Somerville, Diane Miller (1995) "The Rape Myth in the Old South Reconsidered," *Journal of Southern History* 61: 481–518.

Spruill, Julia Cherry (1938) *Women's Life and Work in the Southern Colonies*. Chapel Hill, NC: University of North Carolina Press.

Stevenson, Brenda E. (1996) *Life in Black and White: Family and Community in the Slave South*. New York: Oxford University Press.

Stowe, Steven (1987) *Intimacy and Power in the Old South*. Baltimore, Md.: Johns Hopkins University Press.

Varon, Elizabeth (1998) *We Mean to Be Counted: White Women and Politics in Antebellum Virginia*. Chapel Hill, NC: University of North Carolina Press.

White, Deborah Gray (1985) *Ar'n't I a Woman? Female Slaves in the Plantation South*. New York: Norton.

Whites, LeeAnn (1995) *The Civil War as a Crisis in Gender: Augusta, Georgia, 1860–1890*. Athens, Ga.: University of Georgia Press.

Wood, Kirsten E. (2004) *Masterful Women: Slaveholding Widows from the American Revolution through the Civil War*. Chapel Hill, NC: University of North Carolina Press.

SUGGESTED FURTHER READING

Bernhard, Virginia, Brandon, Betty, Fox-Genovese, Elizabeth, and Perdue, Theda (eds.) (1992) *Southern Women: Histories and Identities* [Southern Women Series]. Columbia, Mo.: University of Missouri Press.

Bleser, Carol (ed.) (1990) *In Joy and in Sorrow: Women, Family, and Marriage in the Victorian South*. New York: Oxford University Press.

Boswell, Angela (2001) *Her Act and Deed: Women's Lives in a Rural Southern County, 1837–1873*. College Station, Tex.: Texas A & M University Press.

Clark, Emil (2003) *Masterless Mistresses: The New Orleans Ursulines and the Development of a New World Society, 1727–1834*. Chapel Hill, NC: University of North Carolina Press.

Clinton, Catherine (ed.) (1994) *Half Sisters of History: Southern Women and the American Past*. Durham, NC: Duke University Press.

Cole, Stephanie (2003) *Servants and Slaves: Domestic Service in Antebellum North/South Border Cities*. Urbana, Ill.: University of Illinois Press.

Coryell, Janet L., Swain, Martha H., Treadway, Sandra G., and Turner, Elizabeth H. (eds.) (1998) *Beyond Image and Convention: Explorations in Southern Women's History* [Southern Women Series]. Columbia, Mo.: University of Missouri Press.

Coryell, Janet L., Appleton, Thomas H., Jr, Sims, Anastatia, and Treadway, Sandra G. (eds.) (2000) *Negotiating Boundaries of Southern Womanhood: Dealing with the Powers That Be* [Southern Women Series]. Columbia, Mo.: University of Missouri Press.

Edwards, Laura F. (1999) "Law, Domestic Violence, and the Limits of Patriarchal Authority in the Antebellum South," *Journal of Southern History* 65: 733–70.

Farnham, Christie Anne (ed.) (1997) *Women of the American South: A Multicultural Reader*. New York: New York University Press.

Fraser, Walter J., Saunders, R. Frank, Jr, and Wakelyn, Jon L. (eds.) (1985) *The Web of Southern Social Relations: Women, Family, and Education*. Athens, Ga.: University of Georgia Press.

Gillespie, Michele and Clinton, Catherine (eds.) (1998) *Taking Off the White Gloves: Southern Women and Women's History* [Southern Women Series]. Columbia, Mo.: University of Missouri Press.

Hagler, D. Harland (1980) "The Ideal Woman in the Antebellum South: Lady or Farmwife?," *Journal of Southern History* 46: 405–18.

Hall, Jacquelyn Dowd and Scott, Ann Firor (1985) "Women in the South," in John B. Boles and Evelyn Thomas Nolen (eds.) *Interpreting Southern History: Historiographical Essays in Honor of Sanford W. Higginbotham*. Baton Rouge, La.: Louisiana State University Press.

Hawks, Joanne V. and Skemp, Sheila (eds.) (1983) *Sex, Race, and the Role of Women in the South*. Jackson, Miss.: University Press of Mississippi.

Hine, Darlene Clark and Thompson, Kathleen (1988) *A Shining Thread of Hope: The History of Black Women in America*. New York: Broadway Books.

Jacobs, Harriet A. (1987) *Incidents in the Life of a Slave Girl, Written by Herself*, ed. L. Maria Child, new edn. ed. by Jean Fagan Yellin. Cambridge, Mass.: Harvard University Press.

Jones, Ann Goodwyn and Donaldson, Susan V. (eds.) (1997) *Haunted Bodies: Gender and Southern Texts*. Charlottesville, Va.: University of Virginia Press.

Lerner, Gerda (1967) *The Grimke Sisters from South Carolina: Rebels against Slavery*. Boston, Mass.: Houghton Mifflin.

McLaurin, Melton (1991) *Celia: A Slave*. Athens, Ga.: University of Georgia Press.

Moynihan, Daniel P. (1981) "The Negro Family: The Case for National Action," in Lee Rainwater and Elisabeth Muhlenfeld, *Mary Boykin Chestnut: A Biography*. Baton Rouge, La.: Louisiana State University Press.

Raimy, Daina L. (1998) "'She Do a Heap of Work': Female Slave Labor on Glynn County Rice and Cotton Plantations," *Georgia Historical Quarterly* 82: 707–34.

Schwalm, Leslie A. (1997) *A Hard Fight for We: Women's Transition from Slavery to Freedom in South Carolina*. Urbana, Ill.: University of Illinois Press.

Scott, Ann Firor (ed.) (1993) *Unheard Voices: The First Historians of Southern Women*. Charlottesville, Va.: University of Virginia Press.

Smith, Margaret Supplee and Wilson, Emily Herring (1999) *North Carolina Women: Making History*. Chapel Hill, NC: University of North Carolina Press.

Weiner, Marli F. (1998) *Mistresses and Slaves: Plantation Women in South Carolina, 1830–1880*. Urbana, Ill.: University of Illinois Press.

Weisenburger, Steven (1998) *Modern Medea: A Family Story of Slavery and Child Murder from the Old South*. New York: Hill and Wang.

Wolfe, Margaret Ripley (1995) *Daughters of Canaan: A Saga of Southern Women*. Louisville, Ky.: University Press of Kentucky.

Wood, Betty (1995) *Women's Work, Men's Work: The Informal Slave Economies of Lowcountry Georgia*. Athens, Ga.: University of Georgia Press.

Woodward, C. Vann (ed.) (1981) *Mary Chestnut's Civil War*. New Haven, Conn.: Yale University Press.

CHAPTER EIGHT

The Road to Secession

MICHAEL MORRISON

The American Civil War remains one of the two great events in the nation's history (the Revolution being the other) and was, as Shelby Foote had it, "the crossroads of our being." Yet although the body of knowledge about the impending crisis has increased greatly, historians have not been able to agree on a precise route that the nation took to that historic crossroad. In his second inaugural address in March 1865, Abraham Lincoln looked back at the beginning of the Civil War four years earlier. "All knew," he said, that slavery "was, somehow, the cause of the war" (Basler 1953–5, vol. 8: 332). Few historians would doubt the basic truth of his statement, and no plausible interpretation of the conflict can ignore slavery. Nonetheless, scholars remain sharply divided. Questions of inevitability, the precise role of the institution of slavery, and cultural and economic differences between and within the sections continue to baffle and intrigue historians of the middle period.

Contemporary observers North and South came to the conclusion that by the late 1850s, sectional conspirators were dragging their constituents and, by extension, the federal Union down the road to destruction. After the war, northern partisans such as Henry Wilson of Massachusetts appealed to the moral absolutes of freedom and national unity (as Republicans had done in 1860), charging that secession was the result of a slave power conspiracy that was intent on breaking up a Union it could not control. "By means illegitimate and indefensible," he asserted, "reckless of principle and of consequence, a comparatively few men succeeded in dragooning whole states into the support of a policy the majority condemned, to following leaders the majority distrusted and most cordially disliked" (Wilson 1877: 127). Northerners had fought to preserve the Union and a system of free labor against the aggressive designs of southern slaveholders who had plotted their treason as early as the outbreak of the Mexican–American war in 1846 and pursued it steadily throughout the 1850s. (For a more recent version of this interpretation see Richards (2000) *passim.*)

Southerners such as the former vice-president of the Confederacy, Alexander Stephens, flatly denied that they had broken any "sacred compact." They claimed that Republicans like Wilson had stirred up sectional conflict with the intent to incite war between the states in order to abolish slavery. Although northern politicians and capitalists had built a majority in Congress on the pretext of restricting the spread of slavery, the real object was to destroy the rights of the southern states and undermine the constitution's guarantee of minority rights. Republicans wished to seize national political power, exploit the slave states like colonies, and promote their own personal and sectional wealth. Southern states withdrew from the Union to protect their people from destruction by a hostile majority.

The question of inevitability was raised in the late nineteenth century when historians such as James Ford Rhodes, Edward Channing, and John Back McMaster identified slavery as the central and virtually only cause of the Civil War. In their view irreconcilable moral differences over slavery – the North detesting it, the South embracing it – fostered sectional alienation and an irrepressible conflict over the extension of the institution. "If the Negro had not been brought to America," Rhodes wrote, "the Civil War would not have occurred" (Rhodes 1919, vol. 3: 148).

The centrality of the moral dimension to the sectional conflict would again resonate during the Civil Rights Movement; Arthur M. Schlesinger, Jr, claimed that it was the "moral issue of slavery that gave the [political] struggles of the period their significance" (Schlesinger 1949: 978). More recently historical analyses of sectional tension that emphasize the centrality of slavery to southern politics and culture continue to resonate through the scholarship of, among others, William J. Cooper (2000), William W. Freehling (1990), Bertram Wyatt-Brown (1982), John McCardell (1979), and, most recently, Manisha Sinha (2000).

Progressive historians, who were themselves influenced by the conflict between capital and labor in the late nineteenth and early twentieth centuries, subsequently pursued the question of whether the sectional conflict was irrepressible and the war was inevitable. The road to secession was paved by a series of clashes between southern free-trade agrarians and northern capitalists who supported high tariffs to protect American manufacturers. Emphasizing northern industrialization, population growth in the free states, and the centralization of political power in the North and, by extension, Washington, Charles Beard (1933) and others concluded that the Civil War was a sectional conflict produced by each section trying to protect its economic interests and increase its share of the national wealth. Slavery in their view was not so much a cultural or social institution as it was an economic institution – a labor system, nothing more, nothing less. Principles were rationalizations; power was real.

Economic determinism and the inevitability of sectional conflict were resuscitated in the 1960s, when historians stressed the dissimilarities between a modernizing North and a premodern South. Emphasizing factors such as urbanization, population growth, the emergence of a working class, the growth of a market economy, and industrialization (which was used interchangeably with modernization), these scholars viewed the war as the means by which the South was integrated into a modern, industrial economy.

Cultural and social conflicts between the sections continued to remain central to the question of the inevitability of the Civil War. Allan Nevins (1947) argued that by 1857 the North and South were rapidly becoming "separate peoples." Though the root of their differences was slavery, Nevins went on to argue that "differences of thought, taste, and ideals gravely accentuated the misunderstandings caused by the basic economic and social differences" (Nevins 1947: 553, 554).

Eric Foner (1970) emphasized the importance of "free-labor" ideology to northern opposition to slavery. That is, the crisis was one that pitted the value systems of a northern industrial society against the South's agrarian, anticapitalist way of life. The moral concerns of abolitionists were not the dominant sentiments of the North. Rather the free-labor ideology of Republicans constituted a yardstick by which to measure the South's society and economics. "The Republican critique of southern society thus focused on the degradation of labor," Foner observed; "the result was not only regional economic stagnation, but a system of social ethics entirely different from that of the North" (Foner 1970: 50). Taking a somewhat different tack, John Ashworth (1995) contends that the American Civil War should be understood as a "bourgeois revolution" and that the conflict between the sections "can only be understood in terms of the differences between capitalist and slave modes of production." The growth of wage labor, Ashworth concludes, "was crucial in generating new and more militant forms of antislavery" (Ashworth 1995: ix).

Though these historians disagree over whether moral, economic, cultural, social, or ideological issues were the primary cause of the Civil War, they have been in general agreement that the conflict between North and South was deeply embedded in the nature of the two societies. As such, the sectional crisis and war were virtually inevitable. Writing in the shadow of World War I and II, revisionist historians, aware of the inept diplomacy and politics of Clemenceau and Wilson, Chamberlain, Roosevelt, and Hitler, begged to differ. They argued that the sectional conflict was "repressible" and that the Civil War was needless. Inept politicians from Douglas to Buchanan and Seward to Davis inflamed public sentiment over irrelevant issues. J. G. Randall, for example, wrote that "to see the period as it is, is to witness uninspired spectacles of prejudice, error, intolerance, and selfish grasping." The war was fought over an abstraction ("an imaginary Negro in an impossible place [the West]", Randall 1940: 7).

Although each of these schools of interpretation dilates on the origins of sectional tensions, a generally acceptable explanation for the Civil War remains elusive. What is more, a larger, more critical question remains: why did sectional tensions, which had existed from the earliest days of the republic, increase so rapidly in the second half of the 1850s? Although historians may strongly disagree about the origins of the sectional crisis, most would concur that by the late 1850s there was widespread disagreement between parties and between sections over the nature of the threat to republican government and the Union in which it was enshrined. The conflict over the extension of slavery into the West, which began in earnest with the introduction of the Wilmot Proviso in 1846, the failure of the Compromise of 1850 to provide a comprehensive and final solution to the territorial issue, the collapse of the second party system, and the rise of the Republican party had engendered a struggle between the free and slave states for the power to shape the character of the territories and thus control the national government.

However, a series of events beginning in early 1857 – the *Dred Scott* decision which seemed to prove the existence of a slave power conspiracy, the Lecompton fiasco and Douglas' Freeport doctrine which vitiated popular sovereignty as a solution to the territorial solution, John Brown's raid at Harpers Ferry which reified the specter of an abolitionist conspiracy, southern demands for a federal slave code and the consequent rupture of the Democracy, and Lincoln's election – each linked as it was to the territorial question would constitute the circuitous and precipitous road that led the nation to the abyss of civil war. By 1860, free-soil northerners and states' rights southerners believed each other to be engaged in a plot or conspiracy to control America and to deny the other a role or participation in the national government. Thus, the territorial issue would become for Americans a way of identifying and destroying the subversive elements in American democracy. And in so doing, they would destroy themselves.

Some historians maintain that Texas annexation in 1845 first raised the issue of slavery expansion (see Merk 1972; Cooper 1978: 206–13, 217–19; Freehling 1990: 402–25; Ashworth 1995: 418, 434; and Sinha 2000: 65–6). Perhaps. But it was the Wilmot Proviso, introduced in 1846 which would have banned slavery from all territory acquired from Mexico, and the southern response to it that fashioned the "blades of a pair of shears" that would sever the bonds of Union in 1860 (Potter 1976: 62). Eric Foner (1969) has astutely pointed out that although free-state resentment and alienation from what they believed to be a pro-South Polk administration lurked behind the proviso, northern Democrats supported it as a means to allay growing opposition in the North to the Mexican conflict and prospective expansion. Restriction, moreover, allowed northerners to express and act on their antislavery sentiments without, so they believed, jeopardizing the Union. Heretofore, their love of Union restrained antislavery activism. Restriction allowed them "to oppose slavery and to cherish a Constitution and Union which protected it" (Potter 1976: 46).

But the appeal of the proviso went deeper yet. Wilmot and his supporters denied that Congress had the power to legalize slavery, a creature of state and local laws, in any territory directly under federal jurisdiction. More to the point, they concluded that the Union itself rested on the principle of individual freedom: to extend slavery would contravene that fundamental tenet. Additionally, they asserted that personal liberty lay at the heart of meaning of the American Revolution and, by extension, the republic. As it resolved itself in the minds of these restrictionists, therefore, the question was not whether black slaves would become free (as abolitionists demanded), but whether white men would remain free.

Southerners agreed that Congress's power over slavery was limited: it could not restrict the spread of slavery. To do so would violate the due process clause of the Fifth Amendment. They replied hotly to the charge that they were unAmerican. If individual liberty constituted one of the animating objects of the American political system so, too, did the principle of equality: the equality of slaveholders under the constitution and of the slave states within the Union. Restriction, they contended, would reduce southern citizens – slaveholders and nonslaveholders alike – to a second-class, degraded status. It would be the means of their enslavement within the Union. And, they rejoined, the history of the Revolution was one of a struggle by British colonists against the oppression of inferiority. The proviso, then, not only marked an abandonment of the principles of the Revolution and an abrogation of the constitution but also signaled the beginning of another epochal struggle between a tyrannical majority and an abused minority (Morrison 1997: 53–63).

Southern rights legislators brought the territorial issue to the homes and hearths of their nonslaveholding constituents by linking restriction to the constituents' future progress – or degradation. They believed that slavery promoted equality by meliorating

class conflict and ensured liberty by making exploitation of white workers and independent agriculturalists unnecessary. Supporters of the proviso argued that restriction would only affect slaveholders. But if, as southerners believed, the northern
free-labor system generated hierarchy, oligarchy, conflict between capital and democracy, and relationships founded on economic dependency, inviting southerners to
emigrate to such a society was to ask them to move to an alien, unAmerican world
(Thornton 1978: 204–26; Ford 1988: 184–6; Carey 1997: 86–7; Morrison 1997:
6–7, 116; cf. Foner 1970: *passim*).

The hypothetical conflict over slavery restriction became real with the Mexican
cession in 1848. Compromise remained elusive. Though some advocated the extension of the Missouri Compromise line to the Pacific (including President Polk and
James Buchanan), the admission of Oregon as a free state in 1848 rendered this
solution too advantageous to the South. Moderate Democrats then advanced the
position of non-interference or, as it became known, popular sovereignty. It had
many distinct advantages. It was sufficiently ambiguous to ensure widespread appeal.
Popular sovereignty also would remove the contentious territorial issue from the
halls of Congress. Most important, limited government and non-interference in the
local affairs of citizens resonated with the longstanding principles of the Democratic
party and the meaning of the American Revolution. Stephen Douglas maintained
that self-government was "the principle in defense of which the revolution was
fought. It is the principle to which all our free institutions owe their existence, and
upon which our entire republican system rests" (Morrison 1997: 146–7).

The territorial provision of the Compromise of 1850 seemed to embrace that
solution. Non-interference was written into the bills for New Mexico and Utah. The
sectional gap was bridged – or glossed over – by extending the constitution over all
territories and allowing for appeals on the slavery question to the Supreme Court.
And the further that northern Democrats moved away from the settlement, the
less they focused on the legislation itself. The Compromise, especially its territorial
provisions, appeared to be an endorsement of Democratic orthodoxy. Put in other
terms, the dynamic elements of the sectional conflict had not been slavery versus
antislavery but consolidation versus limited government. Operating on that conviction,
Stephen Douglas made popular sovereignty the organizational principle of the Kansas-
Nebraska Act. Ensuring that the Act was consistent with popular sovereignty, the
bill repealed the Missouri Compromise ban on slavery north of the line 36° 30′.

If moderate Democratic support of the popular sovereignty reflected an enduring
and deeply held belief in the capacity of the people not only to govern themselves
but also to do right, events in Kansas proved them wrong. By 1856, any semblance
of constitutional government, law, and order had wilted on the dusty plains of
Kansas. Politics there had come to embrace the same controversy over slavery extension so lately heard in Congress. Vote fraud led to the election of a proslavery
legislature, which proceeded to enact a series of laws (some draconian) that legalized
slavery. Enraged free-soil settlers adopted their own constitution that established a
shadow government that excluded slavery. Political turmoil in the territory had the
effect of dividing the settlers into warring camps. Bushwhacking, intimidation, the
return of "border ruffians" from Missouri, the sack of the free-soil government at
Lawrence, and John Brown's murder and mutilation of five innocent settlers near
Pottawatomie Creek seemed proof that a civil war had begun in Kansas. The middle

ground of popular sovereignty provided the context for a battleground. The final crisis of the Union was at hand.

On March 6, 1857, two days after the inauguration of James Buchanan, the Supreme Court of the United States announced its decision in the case of *Scott* v. *Sanford*. Beyond denying the slave Scott's claim that residency in free territory made him a free man, the Court repudiated the power of Congress to outlaw slavery. Although the story of the Buchanan administration is the story of the disruption of the Democratic party, Republican attacks on the decision had the effect of uniting the party behind the Court. Democrats North and South understood the decision to be an endorsement of the party's principles that they had championed since the age of Jackson. Simply put, the decision was another check against the unwarranted and unconstitutional centralization of power in the federal government. More immediately, it vindicated the Kansas-Nebraska Act, which had repealed the Missouri Compromise ban on slavery. It also appeared to endorse the Democracy's solution of non-interference in the territorial issue.

Initially, at least, *Dred Scott* had a much greater effect on the Republican belief in a slave power conspiracy. In a single stroke, the Court declared that the major concrete policy of the Republican party – the restriction of slavery – was unconstitutional. Republicans mounted an intense vituperative attack on the Court's southern members. But damning the members of the Court fell a good deal short of a solution to their dilemma. Having aroused the suspicions of the rank and file, party members then declared that the decision was not binding. That is, once the Court had decided that Scott, as either a black or a slave, had no recourse to the federal courts, the Court had resolved the problem before it. Put in yet other terms, Republicans asserted (one would hardly say they proved) that the Court took up a political issue and ruled on a question not properly before it.

But it was precisely because the Court had exceeded its authority that the *Dred Scott* decision was so threatening. In the first place the Supreme Court had taken the constitution – the greatest document ever devoted to human liberty, so Republicans argued – and made it the bulwark of slavery and, worse, slave extension. It also gave the lie to the South's defense of states' rights. Those who had historically opposed a strong national government now reveled in the Court's defense of slavery. But most importantly, the decision fueled the party's belief in a slave power – working through the Democratic party – conspiring to extend slavery into the territories of the West. Abraham Lincoln told an audience in Springfield, Illinois, that:

> when we see a lot of framed timbers different portions of which we know have been gotten out at different times and places and by different workmen – Stephen [Douglas], Franklin [Pierce], Roger [Taney], and James [Buchanan], for instance – and we see these timbers joined together . . . in *such* a case we find it impossible to not *believe* that Stephen and Franklin and Roger and James all understood one another from the beginning, and all worked upon a common *plan* or *draft* drawn up before the first lick was struck. (Basler 1953–5, vol. 2: 465–6, emphasis in original)

Like the Compromise of 1850, which was intended to put the sectional conflict to rest once and for all, and the Kansas-Nebraska Act that was to enshrine the principle of non-intervention as the definitive solution to the territorial issue, the *Dred Scott* decision failed to accomplish what was expected of it. It annulled a law that had been repealed three years earlier and denied freedom to slaves in an area in which there were no slaves. The decision also placed obstacles in the way of sectional adjustment by stiffening southern extremist demands for constitutional protection. It also strengthened the arguments of those in the South who claimed that territorial popular sovereignty – the ability of a territorial legislature to prohibit slavery – was unconstitutional. That is, Congress cannot delegate a power which is unconstitutional and which it does not possess to the territorial legislature, itself a creature of Congress (Fehrenbacher 1978: 456–7).

Most importantly, *Dred Scott* reinforced a belief among northern restrictionists that an aggressive slaveocracy was conspiring to impose slavery first on the territories and ultimately on the nation. By essentially declaring that freedom was local to those states that had abolished it and that slavery could expand anywhere it was not specifically banned, the Court put itself in the indefensible position of pitting the constitution against the basic American values of liberty and equality. Simply put, under the whip of slaveholders the Court had converted the charter of freedom into a safeguard of slavery.

Despite the constitutional implications of the *Dred Scott* decision for popular sovereignty, pro-Nebraska Democrats and moderate southern former Whigs were still convinced that their formula could yield a solution to the territorial imbroglio. Members of the Republican party considered continued Democratic confidence in popular sovereignty laughable if not insane. Affairs in Kansas proved that it was one of the greatest humbugs of all time. Not only were political affairs in Kansas a disgrace, but also events there too plainly proved that the slave power would stop at nothing to take practical advantage of the repeal of the Missouri Compromise line. Political domination of slaveholders, operating through the Democratic party, undermined the principles of free government – in Kansas and Washington – and, as *Dred Scott* had seemed to indicate, menaced constitutional checks and balances. Although sectional tensions had increased steadily since 1846, what alarmed Republicans was the naked arrogance and rapid progress of the tyranny. By 1857, Republicans began moving away from specific indictments of the institution itself. Instead, they used slavery to define broadly the meaning and limits of freedom not only within the North's free-labor economy but also, more importantly, within the nation's republican state.

To most Republicans, a slave power conspiracy had assumed a specific shape by 1857 and, equally significant, its aggressive designs were developing in identifiable, coordinated, and inexorable phases. From the Louisiana Purchase to the Kansas debacle, the litany of the slave power's advances had become part of the Republican canon. Only the acquisition of new territory in the 1840s brought the North and South into open, direct, and immutable conflict. From the Democracy's first flirtation with territorial aggrandizement to the latest agonies in Kansas, events seemed to demonstrate the concert of action derived from a deliberate plan.

James Buchanan also had a plan. Just before Franklin Pierce left office, the proslavery legislature in Kansas called for the election of delegates to a convention that would frame a state constitution for the territory. Buchanan, hoping to make popular sovereignty work and desperate to remove the territorial question as a bone of sectional contention, sent Robert J. Walker to the territory as governor. Walker was to impose order and to secure an impartial and fair election. He had little chance of success. Walker alarmed slave-state men with his free and easy-going attitude toward free-state settlers in Kansas. For their part, free-state men refused to participate in June elections to the constitutional convention, claiming that the voting procedure was a fraud. Although the proslavery delegates to the convention did not represent the free-soil sentiments of the majority of settlers, they were elected legally. The Lecompton delegates drafted a proslavery constitution. Instead of submitting the entire document to the voters as Walker had demanded (and Buchanan had promised), the delegates offered them a Hobson's choice. Settlers were given the option of voting for a constitution "with slavery" or "without slavery." If they voted "without slavery," it meant the end of the importation of slaves into Kansas. In either case, those slaves already in the territory (and their descendants) would remain. Kansas would be a slave state.

Stephen Douglas led the attack on Lecompton and the administration. He rejected the claim that submission of the slavery question alone complied with the meaning and intent of popular sovereignty. He contended that the Kansas legislature had exceeded its authority and denied that the Lecompton convention had the power to establish a state government. Not only was the constitution a swindle and a violation of Democratic practice, but also the administration and slave-state Democrats were attempting to force statehood on the people of Kansas against their will. If Kansas was admitted, Douglas warned, it would mean that organic law was not to be the embodiment of popular will. Imposing Lecompton on the people of Kansas, he and others maintained, would be tyrannical, and it would rest on an assumption of despotic power by the national government.

This southerner Democrats denied. As they viewed the issue, the status of Kansas as a free or slave state was less important than the principle of state equality. They realized that the slave population in Kansas was limited and that the viability of the institution was problematic. (The census of 1860 would show only two slaves being held in Kansas.) If northerners rejected the Lecompton constitution, they would not only abridge the equality of the states but also deny to the South its equal rights on a historically vital point. With Douglas clearly opposed to Lecompton and in open rebellion against the Buchanan administration, extreme states' rights Democrats concluded that their alliance with the northern wing of the party was a sham. Lecompton, not *Dred Scott*, was the beginning of the end for the Democracy (Stampp 1990: 266–331).

If Lecompton seemed to be fraudulent, the solution to the deadlock in Congress was an outright swindle. With the administration's blessing, Congressman William English of Indiana proposed a bill that would have reduced the public land in Kansas from 23 million acres to 4 million. The voters in Kansas would then vote whether to accept the state constitution with the reduced acreage. If they rejected the bill, Kansas would remain a territory and could not again apply for statehood until the census showed a population of 90,000. Put in other terms, this face-saving maneuver would allow the citizens of Kansas to vote on the amended Lecompton constitution but would avoid the principle of resubmission, which southerners strongly opposed. Voters in Kansas rejected the land grant reduction (and, by extension, the constitution) by 11,300 to 1,788. Kansas would remain a territory until 1861, at which time it was admitted as a free state.

In the aftermath of the Lecompton fiasco, states' rights southerners turned their backs on the northern wing of the Democracy. Many believed that the South needed to confront openly the Republican party. Three events between 1858 and 1860 made confrontation imperative and inevitable: Douglas' Freeport Doctrine, John Brown's raid on Harpers Ferry, and southern Democrats' demand for a federal slave code. The effect of these episodes was finally and fatally to disrupt the Democratic party, leave the Union hanging by a thread, and eventually bring together the two blades of the territorial shears.

If southerners expressed little confidence in Douglas' support for southern rights and less in popular sovereignty as a guarantor of those rights, his Freeport heresy simply confirmed their contempt for both. In August 1858 in their debate at Freeport, Lincoln asked Douglas whether, in the light of *Dred Scott*, citizens of the territories could lawfully exclude slavery prior to the formation of a state constitution. Douglas replied that slavery could not "exist a day or an hour anywhere, unless it is supported by local police regulation" (Basler 1953–5, vol. 3: 114–15). He denounced slavery agitation as unnecessary and an impediment to national expansion and the spread of free institutions. To this Lincoln responded that the issue was not states' rights or the rights of the citizens of the several states but the preservation of republican institutions. The sectional conflict was simply a struggle between right and wrong, freedom and slavery. Like southern Democrats, Lincoln, too, was for open confrontation on the slavery extension issue.

Lincoln's unyielding restrictionism and his attack on southern institutions were not unexpected by southerners, though they were unwelcome. And in the aftermath of the Lecompton debacle, neither was Douglas' apostasy. Southern Democrats had already concluded that popular sovereignty was but another means to deny the slave states equal, unfettered access to the territories. Worse, it was far more disingenuous and thus more threatening than the Republican demand for restriction. However taken one with another, Lincoln's demand that slavery be excluded from the territories, his desire to make issue with the slave states on restriction, and Douglas' Freeport heresy evinced a widespread antislavery consensus in the free states. Though free-state antislavery sentiment had long existed, now it seemed that a minority party – a faction – could command the votes of a majority of northern voters by playing on their prejudices and sectional hostilities.

Overweening sectional majorities threatened the complex matrix of constitutional guarantees that had protected southern rights. And to 1858, most moderate southerners insisted that the most fundamental southern right was the right to be left alone. John Brown's raid on Harpers Ferry raised the question of whether that limited demand was even possible. On October 16, 1859, Brown left a rented farm in Maryland with 20 men, crossed the Potomac, and seized the federal arsenal at Harpers Ferry. His goal was to arm the many slaves that would rush to his cause, set up a black stronghold, and provide a nucleus of support for slave insurrections. The raid failed utterly. He cut the telegraph lines, seized the arsenal, took a few prisoners, and sat. Armed citizens quickly confronted him, and a detachment of United States Marines led by Robert E. Lee soon reinforced them. With most of his men dead and himself wounded, Brown surrendered.

Brown was put on trial for his life for treason against the state and conspiracy to incite slave insurrections. Brown conducted a spirited defense, which inspired admiration in the North and fear and loathing in the slave states. In the course of the trial Brown's connection to the "Secret Six" – prominent, well-educated northern Republicans – was made public. Southerners could accept, though surely not condone, the actions of a man they considered insane. They could not tolerate the support of well-to-do, well-educated northern reformers. Discovery of the Secret Six lent emotional and intellectual credence to the existence of an abolitionist conspiracy (that was itself a mirror image of the slave power conspiracy engendered by the *Dred Scott* decision). Southerners were no longer disposed to distinguish between abolitionists like Brown and Republicans who provided the antislavery rhetoric and financial and emotional support to such sectional extremists. Republicanism and abolitionism became a distinction without a difference.

Antislavery sentiment that sustained sectional politics and engendered raids like Brown's suggested to southern rights advocates that moderate northern Democrats were unable to arrest the growth of fanaticism in the North. Lecompton's defeat, Douglas' desertion, and free-state hostility demonstrated by Brown's raid led southern Democrats to look to the federal government for protection of their rights. On February 2, 1860, two months before the opening of the Democratic nominating convention in Charleston, Jefferson Davis of Mississippi introduced in the Senate a set of resolutions asserting that it was the duty of the federal government to provide the necessary protection of slave property in the territories if the judiciary could not ensure its safety. Southern Democrats charged with some truth that Republicans were hiding behind states' rights in order to justify the passage of personal liberty laws, which were in clear violation of the constitution and the fugitive slave law passed in 1850. Moreover, non-interference had proven inadequate to the defense of southern rights. Southern Democrats insisted that Davis' measures provided for the protection of slaves as property, not for the protection of the institution.

The rift within the Democracy was complete. Douglas hotly denied that he had deceived anyone about the principles of popular sovereignty. Douglas and other moderate northern Democrats maintained that while he remained consistent to the party's principles as expressed in 1850, 1852, 1854, and 1856, southern Democrats had altered their position; they were now the centralizers. Southerners were in favor of non-interference when the people of the territory wanted slavery, they concluded. The moment they made clear that they did not want it, southerners were willing to use the power of the federal government to intervene in local affairs and force the institution on them. With Davis' resolution and the northern attack on it, another chord of the Union snapped. The last remaining national party had split along sectional lines.

That division was reified at the Charleston convention when lower South delegates withdrew after the delegates rejected the majority report endorsing the *Dred Scott* decision and adopted a minority platform standing by congressional non-interference with slavery in the territories. Although the convention had adopted a platform, it had not nominated a candidate. The remaining delegates agreed to adjourn and reconvene in Baltimore in June. When they reassembled, lower South delegates refused to participate. The rump convention proceeded to nominate Douglas for president. The Charleston bolters joined by administration supporters met in Richmond and nominated John C. Breckinridge of Kentucky on a platform endorsing *Dred Scott* and calling for congressional protection of slavery in the territories.

The Republicans met in Chicago. They passed over prominent party leader William Seward, nominating instead Abraham Lincoln (or as the Republican press initially had it, "Abram" Lincoln). Hoping to broaden their electoral base, the party chose a virtual political unknown who was strong enough on slavery restriction to satisfy some of the more radical antislavery members, and moderate and obscure enough to have made few enemies. They also attempted to move beyond the slavery extension issue by endorsing a protective tariff for manufacturers, more liberal naturalizations laws, and a program of internal improvements, which included a transcontinental railroad.

There was yet a fourth party that doddered off into the presidential fray. Old Whig conservatives met in Baltimore and organized the Constitutional Union party. They nominated John Bell of Tennessee. Denouncing sectional agitators of all stripes, they placed Bell's nomination on the sufficiently bland and broad platform of "The Constitution, the Country, the Union of the States, and the Enforcement of the Laws."

Like the parties themselves, the campaign unfolded along sectional lines, with Lincoln and Douglas squaring off in the North and Breckinridge and Bell in the South. Throughout the campaign the slave states never learned to distinguish between Lincoln and more radical Republicans. (The mistrust was made worse by Lincoln's stubborn refusal to make assurances to the South or to amplify his position.) For their part, northern Republicans failed to take full measure of southern intransigence and, especially, their fear and loathing of Lincoln.

The four-way race indicated the extent to which the country had become sectionalized by the slavery extension issue. Free soil, positive protection, and popular sovereignty demonstrated that there was no common vision of, or mutually acceptable solution to, the territorial imbroglio. Taken one with another, these positions reflected a fragmented, sectionalized political system. However, the system was functioning exactly as it was supposed to: representing the will of the people. Douglas and Bell wanted to remove the issue from national politics either by leaving it with the people of the territories or ignoring it altogether. Lincoln and Breckinridge wished to engage the question of slavery extension, agitate it, and resolve it. Lincoln's election in November genuinely reflected irreconcilable differences in the electorate.

Because the salient issue in the campaign was the territorial question and because the South defined that question in terms of its equal rights in the Union, Lincoln's election was unacceptable. Not that it was illegal. Rather the North had succeeded in organizing a wholly sectional party essentially without a single supporter in the slave states. With Lincoln's election the party had seized the machinery of government with the avowed intent of destroying the limitations and conditions under which a constitutional government operated. The election of Lincoln had produced a settled conviction in the minds of southerners that there was no longer any security for them and their rights under the constitution and within the Union. As the lower South began to secede from the Union in late 1860 and early 1861, literally every slave state Senator who resigned his seat concluded that democracy had failed in some real way. A man not even before the deep South electorate would now rule over the slave states.

Although some historians (and the League of the South) have defined the sectional struggle and secession as a conflict between states' rights and an indivisible Union, secessionists would have maintained that this was to mistake process for substance. Secession was, of course, a right. But they viewed it as a means to protect the essence of equality and self-government that had until Lincoln's election been guaranteed by the constitution and embraced in the Union. All could agree with R. M. T. Hunter of Virginia when he asserted that the Republicans' intent was to implement policies "to ends and purposes not only different from, but hostile to those for which this political organism was created. They destroy the Union as it was framed by the fathers, and seek to substitute another for it" (Ambler 1918: 344–5). Determined to preserve these rights for themselves and their posterity, the South seceded.

Clearly Lincoln was correct in maintaining that slavery was the cause of the war. But precisely how? The conflicting (and conflicted) views of a slave power thesis and an abolitionist conspiracy seem antediluvian today. The weight of historical evidence argues that there was no conscious conspiracy in either the free or slave states to deny the other section a role in the national government. This fact clearly did not prevent political leaders, such as Lincoln, and constituents in both sections from operating on that assumption. Moreover southerners, too, saw the sectional conflict as a question of freedom versus slavery. Finally, neither section pursued a consistent position on states' rights. Northerners who supported Congress's power to restrict the extension of slavery into the West also maintained the power of a state to pass personal liberty laws that negated the federal slave code. By 1859 southerners were for their part ready to use the power of Congress to protect their slave property in the territories.

Those historians that stress the inevitable clash of cultures and irrepressible conflict that stemmed from it implicitly deny the South's integration into the antebellum political system. However, they underestimate commonalities of language, religion, and especially political heritage. They also beg the question of whether regional social and cultural differences were of a sufficient magnitude to produce a civil war. Furthermore, historians such as J. Mills Thornton (1978), Lacy K. Ford (1988), and Michael F. Holt (1978) have affirmed the importance of a revolutionary ideology embraced by the South and shared with the North that both paid homage to, and was defined by, the tenets of liberty and equality.

Historians have also pointed out and documented the deep-seated racial prejudice of northerners, especially in the Old Northwest. Paul Finkelman (1989) has shown that slavery continued in the region for decades after the passage of the Northwest Ordinance that banned the institution north of the Ohio River. Slavery continued in Indiana after statehood, and Illinois did not abolish slavery until 1848. Eugene Berwanger (1967) has amply demonstrated that Midwesterners could be both antislavery and racist. Indeed Democrats there attempted to neutralize the Republican appeal by declaring that the Republicans aimed "to elevate the African race in this country to complete equality of political and economic condition with the white man" (Holt 1978: 187). A Republican editor countered that:

> the party which favors the preservation of the territories for the white settler, that takes the ground against the extension of slavery, that does not wish to extend niggerdom and niggers, is certainly the white man's party. . . . Persons who oppose this party must be the nigger or black party. (Morrison 1997: 230)

The focus of restrictionists was not on blacks who were in thrall to slaveholding southerners, but on white northerners who might be enslaved if the slave power, working through the Democratic party, captured the free territories of the West and seized control of the government. One party member asserted that the Democracy's policies consistently tended "to degrade free labor [and] give the slave power the control of the government" (*Address of the Cameron and Lincoln Club* 1860: 1). On the other hand, since the colonial period slavery had been a graphic reminder to southerners of the reality of degradation, impoverishment, and despotism. And, as Mills Thornton (1978) and Lacy Ford (1988) have amply demonstrated, southerners also contended that it was a mechanism for encouraging independence and social mobility.

The Progressive School analysis ignores the fact that both sections were industrializing and that the economy of the Old Northwest (which Progressive historians had tied to the economic interest of the Northeast) resembled more closely that of the slaveholding Southwest than it did New England. Furthermore, although per capita income in the Old Northwest and Southwest was somewhat lower than in the East, wealth on both frontiers was more evenly distributed. More to the point, farmers of Indiana and Alabama, Illinois and Mississippi were anxious about economic change and saw the fate of the western territories as critical to their own well-being.

Although Mark Summers (1987) has amply made plain the political corruption that permeated politics in the 1850s, it does not follow that the territorial issue was an abstraction, as revisionists claim. Slavery and the extension of the institution to the West were central to political life in the 1850s and especially after 1857. All politicians from Lincoln to Davis conceived of their work as principled, responsible, and even noble. The sectional crisis could have been avoided only if they had struck compromises that each would have regarded as immoral and cowardly. Benjamin Wade argued that threats of secession notwithstanding, "The day of compromise is past." War, an Indiana Republican asserted, would be preferable "than to degrade ourselves by yielding one iota of our principles." An Ohio party member agreed, concluding that "*right* and *truth* & eternal *justice*" hung in the balance (Morrison 1997: 273–4).

As these varied interpretations of the Civil War indicate, the relationship of slavery to the sectional crisis is complex. As an institution and a trope, slavery subverted liberty, gave the lie to self-determination, and flatly opposed liberty. The conflict between slavery and freedom reflected fears of the public that encroaching power would usurp their liberty. In the early days of the republic, these tensions were between the center and periphery: the power of the national government and the rights of the states and the liberties of their citizens. The ascendancy of Jacksonian democracy and a concomitant emphasis on states' rights and the growth of a market economy reconfigured these tensions. Social and cultural dissimilarities within sections and class-based conflicts over economic agendas issued in a national polity in which the lines of tension were urban and rural, East and West.

Beginning with Wilmot's Proviso, and increasingly after the *Dred Scott* decision, the axis of political conflict began to shift. Political conflict between the periphery and center over the shape and power of the national government which had structured and reverberated through the Bank War in 1832 was replaced by a sectional conflict to shape the character of the territories and thus to control the national government. Politicians agitating on the territorial question eventually engendered the conviction that each side had become the negation of what the other side stood for. The North and South each fought to keep the American experiment alive. Lincoln again had it right – or half-right – at Gettysburg. The Civil War was understood to be a test of whether any nation conceived in liberty and dedicated to equality could long endure.

BIBLIOGRAPHY

Address of the Cameron and Lincoln Club of the City of Chicago, Il., to the People of the North West (1860) Chicago, Ill.: The Club.

Ambler, Charles H. (ed.) (1918) "The Correspondence of Robert M. T. Hunter, 1826–1876." *Annual Report of the American Historical Association for the Year 1916*, 2 volumes. Washington: Government Printing Office.

Ashworth, John (1995) *Slavery, Capitalism and Politics in the Antebellum Republic.* Volume 1: *Commerce and Compromise, 1820–1850.* Cambridge: Cambridge University Press.

Basler, Roy P. (ed.) (1953–5) *The Collected Works of Abraham Lincoln*, eight vols., plus index. New Brunswick, NJ: Rutgers University Press.

Beard, Charles A. and Beard, Mary R. (1933) *The Rise of American Civilization*, two vols. New York: Macmillan.

Berwanger, Eugene H. (1967) *The Frontier against Slavery: Western Anti-Negro Prejudice and the Slavery Extension Controversy.* Urbana, Ill.: University of Illinois Press.

Carey, Anthony Gene (1997) *Parties, Slavery and the Union in Antebellum Georgia.* Athens, Ga.: University of Georgia Press.

Cooper, William J., Jr (1978) *The South and the Politics of Slavery, 1828–1856.* Baton Rouge, La.: Louisiana State University Press.

Cooper, William J., Jr (2000) *Jefferson Davis, American.* New York: Alfred A. Knopf.

Fehrenbacher, Don E. (1978) *The Dred Scott Case: Its Significance in American Law and Politics.* New York: Oxford University Press.

Finkelman, Paul (1989) "Slavery and the Northwest Ordinance: A Study in Ambiguity," *Journal of the Early Republic* 6: 343–70.

Foner, Eric (1969) "The Wilmot Proviso Revisited," *Journal of American History* 56: 267–79.

Foner, Eric (1970) *Free Soil, Free Labor, Free Men: The Ideology of the Republican Party before the Civil War.* New York: Oxford University Press.

Ford, Lacy K., Jr (1988) *Origins of Southern Radicalism: The South Carolina Upcountry, 1800–1860.* New York: Oxford University Press.

Freehling, William W. (1990) *The Road to Disunion: Secessionists at Bay, 1776–1854.* New York: Oxford University Press.

Holt, Michael F. (1969) *Forging a Majority: The Formation of the Republican Party in Pittsburgh, 1848–1860.* New Haven, Conn.: Yale University Press.

Holt, Michael F. (1978) *The Political Crisis of the 1850s.* New York: Wiley.

Holt, Michael F. (1999) *The Rise and Fall of the American Whig Party: Jacksonian Politics and the Onset of the Civil War.* New York: Oxford University Press.

McCardell, John (1979) *The Idea of a Southern Nation: Southern Nationalists and Southern Nationalism, 1830–1860.* New York: Norton.

Merk, Frederick (1972) *Slavery and the Annexation of Texas.* New York: Knopf.

Morrison, Michael A. (1997) *Slavery and the American West: The Eclipse of Manifest Destiny and the Coming of the Civil War.* Chapel Hill, NC: University of North Carolina Press.

Nevins, Allan (1971 [1947]) *Ordeal of the Union.* New York: Charles Scribner's Sons.

Potter, David M. (1976) *The Impending Crisis, 1848–1861*, completed and ed. Don E. Fehrenbacher. New York: Harper and Row.

Randall, J. G. (1940) "The Blundering Generation," *Mississippi Valley Historical Review* 27: 3–28.

Rhodes, James Ford (1892–1918) *History of the United States from the Compromise of 1850.* 7 vols. New York: Harper.

Richards, Leonard L. (2000) *The Slave Power: The Free North and Southern Domination, 1780–1860.* Baton Rouge, La.: Louisiana State University Press.

Schlesinger, Arthur M., Jr (1949) "The Causes of the Civil War: A Note on Historical Sentimentalism," *Partisan Review* 16: 968–81.

Sinha, Manisha (2000) *The Counter-revolution of Slavery: Politics and Ideology in Antebellum South Carolina.* Chapel Hill, NC: University of North Carolina Press.

Stampp, Kenneth M. (1990) *America in 1857: A Nation on the Brink.* New York: Oxford University Press.

Summers, Mark W. (1987) *The Plundering Generation: Corruption and the Crisis of Union, 1849–1860.* New York: Oxford University Press.

Thornton, J. Mills, III (1978) *Politics and Power in a Slave Society: Alabama, 1800–1860.* Baton Rouge, La.: Louisiana State University Press.

Wilson, Major L. (1974 [1877]) *Space, Time, and Freedom: The Quest for Nationality and the Irrepressible Conflict, 1815–1861.* Westport, Conn.: Greenwood Press.

Wyatt-Brown, Bertram (1982) *Southern Honor: Ethics and Behavior in the Old South.* New York: Oxford University Press.

SUGGESTED FURTHER READING

Barney, William L. (1974) *The Secessionist Impulse: Alabama and Mississippi in 1860.* Princeton, NJ: Princeton University Press.

Channing, Steven A. (1970) *The Crisis of Fear: Secession in South Carolina.* New York: Simon and Schuster.

Cooper, William J., Jr (1983) *Liberty and Slavery: Southern Politics to 1860.* New York: Alfred A. Knopf.

Gienapp, William E. (1987) *The Origins of the Republican Party, 1852–1856.* New York: Oxford University Press.

Greenberg, Kenneth S. (1985) *Masters and Statesmen: The Political Culture of American Slavery.* Baltimore, Md.: Johns Hopkins University Press.

Nichols, Roy Franklin (1967 [1948]) *The Disruption of the American Democracy.* New York: Free Press.

Olsen, Christopher J. (2000) *Political Culture and Secession in Mississippi: Masculinity, Honor, and the Antiparty Tradition, 1830–1860.* New York: Oxford University Press.

Sewell, Richard H. (1976) *Ballots for Freedom: Antislavery Politics in the United States, 1848–1865.* New York: Oxford University Press.

CHAPTER NINE

The Republican Triumph

JOHN ASHWORTH

Ever since the Civil War has been studied, historians have been aware of the role of the Republican party in not merely leading the northern armies and the northern people to victory but also in helping bring the war about (Pressly 1954). The initial wave of secession, on the part of the seven states of the lower South, was, of course, precipitated by the election of the first Republican president, Abraham Lincoln, and the new president's refusal to allow those states to "depart in peace" then triggered the secession of four more states. These undeniable facts have seemed to many historians to demonstrate Republican complicity in, if not responsibility for, the most spectacular political crisis in the nation's history.

Nevertheless, until a generation ago there was no single volume devoted to the ideology or the institutional structure of the antebellum Republican party (see, however, Crandall 1930). This was perhaps because of the way in which the war was itself seen. Although the origins of the Civil War had been, almost from the moment of its conclusion (if not even earlier), a subject of enormous interest and one to which many hundreds of volumes were devoted, few felt compelled to study the Republicans systematically. Without doubt this was largely because of the nature of the debate over the war's origins.

For virtually a century historians were preoccupied with the question of inevitability. Could the war have been averted, or was there instead, as William H. Seward had put it in 1858, an "irrepressible conflict" (Craven 1960) between North and South? This question reverberated through Civil War historiography. Those who agreed with Seward as to the war's inevitability often followed Charles and Mary Beard (1933) in insisting that the conflict was the product of a fundamental clash between North and South which was simply not amenable to compromise. Unlike Seward, however, the Beards tended to see economic interests as the motor of history and accordingly they minimized the role of ideas and of ideals. In their view slavery was of little importance in accounting for the war (Beard and Beard 1933). Rather the struggle pitted an industrializing North against an agrarian South. This made the role of the Republicans an important one but did not seem to require the historian to look too closely at the party itself. Since Republicans spent a good deal of time discussing slavery, their formal utterances should, it followed, be ignored except when they disclosed their real priorities. These were to promote northern economic development by means of banks, tariffs, internal improvements, and homestead laws, all measures which threatened the agricultural order of the South and against which southerners ultimately rebelled. Since the Republicans were merely the bearers of northern economic interests, their party did not require close scrutiny, their beliefs did not merit close examination.

A variant of the "irrepressible conflict" argument, and one which Seward himself might have found more congenial, stressed not the economic aspects of the slavery question but rather its moral dimension. In the aftermath of World War II a number of historians claimed that slavery posed a moral dilemma of the first magnitude, one which only those historians gripped by "historical sentimentalism" could ignore (Schlesinger 1949). But whereas this approach perhaps helped to rehabilitate the abolitionists, whose reputation was also being enhanced by the contemporary concern with civil rights, it did little for the Republicans, to whom moral issues were, it seemed, less central. Indeed the concern for civil rights in the 1950s and 1960s inspired a search for racism in earlier decades of American history and here the record disclosed that not merely southerners, and not merely Democrats, but also northern Republicans were tainted by racial prejudice (Durden 1965). The result was a reemphasis of Republican limitations, but no systematic examination of the party's beliefs or behavior.

Meanwhile, those who had argued that the war was instead "repressible" also viewed the Republicans with scant sympathy. Most of these "revisionist" scholars had, since the 1930s, stressed not the intractability of the slavery question, nor the divergent economic interests of the two sections, but instead the failures of a "blundering generation" of statesmen. While these historians certainly condemned southern extremists, they reserved their major criticisms for northern antislavery militants. Of course the abolitionists received most censure but Republicans, and especially radical Republicans, were not far behind. Their party was accused of having artificially whipped up a crisis over slavery, and then being unable to resolve it. To these historians it seemed, once again, that there was little need for a detailed examination of such a party.

Thus by the end of the 1960s historians had still not given the Republican party the attention that it clearly deserved. The emergence of any new major party in American history is, of course, a rare event and one might have thought that on those grounds alone it merited close scrutiny. The immediate effects of the party's first national triumph were so cataclysmic that the historiographical gap seems, in retrospect, to have been a yawning one.

Into this gap stepped Eric Foner in 1970 with the first modern book-length study of the antebellum Republicans. Foner's volume was entitled *Free Soil, Free Labor, Free Men: The Ideology of the Republican Party before the Civil War*. The 1960s had seen a rediscovery of the role of ideas in American politics, beginning perhaps with the work of Bernard Bailyn (1967) on the American Revolution, and Foner's (1970) book, with its insistence that the ideas of the Republicans be taken with the utmost seriousness, was almost certainly a part of this movement. Foner also drew upon the work of his own dissertation supervisor and mentor, Richard Hofstadter (1948), who had contributed an incisive essay upon Abraham Lincoln to his classic work, *The American Political Tradition and the Men Who Made It.*

Foner argued that the Republicans possessed a clearly articulated and reasonably coherent ideology or worldview, at the heart of which was a celebration of the free labor economy and society of the North. The concept of "free labor," he declared, "lay at the heart of the Republican ideology" (Foner 1970: 11). This entailed a matching disapprobation of southern society, which was seen as a virtual negation of everything that Republicans held dear. Whereas the northern economy was dynamic and progressive, the South was languishing, unable to compete in the race to industrialize and urbanize. While northern society, in Republican eyes, offered un-paralleled opportunities to the free laborer to rise in the social scale, southerners were weighed down by the incubus of slavery. And whereas northern society was egalitarian, democratic, and largely classless, the South was in the grip of a "slave power" which rode roughshod over the rights of nonslaveholders as well as slaves and which made a mockery of the nation's democratic heritage.

For Foner the struggle over slavery in the territories was absolutely central. Anxious to recreate northern society in the West, and, by occupying the free or cheap land available there, to prevent the emergence of class divisions in the East, Republicans insisted that the territories be reserved for free men and not southern slaves or slaveholders. For Foner the Republicans were essentially a free-soil party.

Foner's book had many strengths. Indeed it should be regarded as a classic work of political history. Foner (1970) carefully assessed the role of each of the various groups – radicals, moderates, conservatives, and former Democrats – who made up the new party. He also offered a balanced view of the Republican attitude to race, acknowledging that some party spokesmen were indeed guilty of making utterances that were, even by the standards of the time, unusually virulent, but nevertheless arguing persuasively that recent historians had probably exaggerated this point. Foner also gave some attention to the concept of the slave power in Republican thought and assessed the role of nativism in the political upheaval that brought the party to prominence. These and other issues have been taken up by scholars since the publication of Foner's volume and they have been given more prominence than he afforded them. Yet it is clear that the modern controversy over the Republican party dates from the publication of *Free Soil, Free Labor, Free Men*.

There are several questions which the historian of the antebellum Republican party needs to address. Most of them are the questions which Foner (1970) addressed, though some have become more rather than less controversial in the intervening years. First, we need to ask what the role of slavery was in the formation and the ideology of the new party. Some historians have sought to revise Foner by claiming that nativism played a key role in the political upheaval of the mid-1850s or even that the party embodied certain religious or denominational values to a greater degree than it represented antislavery. Second, it is necessary to look closely at antislavery itself, in order to demonstrate the relative importance of its different strands. Slavery attracted opposition on moral grounds, on the grounds that it gave disproportionate political power to a southern elite, and on the grounds that it retarded economic growth and development. Which of these indictments was upper-most? Third, it is noteworthy that Foner gave little attention to the views of the principal enemies of the Republicans in the North, the Democrats, and, in his 1970 volume at least, did not seek to explain the emergence of the free labor outlook. It is therefore important to situate Republican ideology both within the political debates of the 1850s and with reference to the nation's evolving political culture. Finally it will be instructive to return to the issues raised by earlier scholars who were preoccupied with the statesmanship of Republicans (and other political figures of the late antebellum era). To what extent can Republicans be charged with having blundered into war?

The role of slavery in the emergence and rise to power of the Republican party continues to attract considerable attention. As we have seen, for the Beards and their disciples, the antislavery of Republicans seemed little more than window-dressing. The real priority of the party was the economic policies to which it was committed. Banks, tariffs, homesteads – these were at the top of the Republican agenda and they were the means by which an industrializing North would subordinate the values and interests of the slaveholding South. Not the least of Foner's achievements was to lay this rather crude reductionism to rest. He was able easily to demonstrate that the Republican party was not in fact fully committed to a protective tariff or a national bank. Foner paid considerable attention to the role of the various factions within the Republican party and this enabled him to show conclusively that when they abandoned their former colleagues, the Democrats who joined the new party took with them their commitment to limited government and to states' rights. Thus prominent former Democrats (or Democratic Republicans as they might be termed), like William Cullen Bryant in New York City, were doctrinaire free traders. Meanwhile other Republicans, and especially those of a radical persuasion, took precisely the opposite view to that claimed by Beard and Beard (1933). For them the tariff was a distraction from the main issues which concerned slavery and the slave power. Some former Whigs in the new party were, to be sure, committed to the principle of protection, but it was simply not an issue upon which the party could unite.

Much the same could be said of the banking and currency question, which again pitted former Whigs in the party against erstwhile Democrats. (In the 1860s, of course, the party would find a new unity on these measures but it is important not to read back into the 1850s the political configurations that were created by the exigencies of war.) The Homestead issue, on the other hand, did indeed command more widespread, if not universal, support within Republican ranks, but the Democrats too in the North favored this measure. It is thus impossible to claim that the Republican party before the Civil War was, in the sense that the Beards claimed, the party of northern industrial capitalism.

This does not mean, however, that historians now agree that slavery was the central issue in either the creation of the Republican party in the mid-1850s or its rise to power in the final years of the decade. As far as the creation of the party is concerned, the crucial years were between 1853 and 1856. The traditional view, virtually unchallenged for more than a hundred years after the events themselves, was that the introduction of the Kansas-Nebraska Act destroyed the unity of the Whig party by making it impossible for its northern wing, always more committed to antislavery than northern Democrats, to remain within the party. These northern Whigs, it was held, were then joined by a significant minority of northern Democrats who were similarly unable to stomach the introduction of slavery into territory from which it had previously been excluded. The defectors from both parties then joined forces with antislavery radicals, many of whom had previously supported the Liberty and Free Soil parties, and founded the Republican party.

This traditional interpretation has been strongly challenged. The reasons for the challenge are many. In the first place, the older view placed heavy, almost exclusive, emphasis upon federal rather than state or local politics and many historians have in recent decades argued that this is a distortion of the antebellum reality. Before the Civil War, it has been suggested, Americans were far more likely to respond to the issues that affected them most immediately; more often than not such issues were local rather than national.

Closely linked with this discounting of federal politics has been the claim that ethnocultural issues were the primary source of political divisions at least in the North. (The relative ethnic homogeneity of the South has made it difficult to advance similar claims for that region.) Such issues, it is argued, were far more likely to arise at local and state level than in Washington, DC. But the emphasis upon ethnocultural issues does not derive simply from the renewed attention given to local and state politics. In a sense it was a part of a larger movement that emphasized consensus in the American past.

Although the work dealt with the Jacksonian era rather than the 1850s, it is impossible to deal with the ethnocultural historians without giving attention to Lee Benson's (1961) pioneering study *The Concept of Jacksonian Democracy*. Benson argued that those who had found deep economic or class divisions underlying the partisan struggle in the 1830s and 1840s had seriously misjudged the politics of the era. Instead the parties were agreed upon the fundamentals of capitalism and democracy. The division was instead along ethnic and religious lines, with the Whigs the party of evangelical, native-born Protestants and the Democrats the party of the immigrant, the Roman Catholic, the non-evangelical, and the Free Thinker (Benson 1961).

Other historians followed in Benson's footsteps and studied the politics of other eras. Not surprisingly, the 1850s received considerable attention. While traditional historians had kept their gaze firmly upon events in Washington (or at least upon events set in train in Washington) the so-called "new" political historians who stressed ethnocultural factors were now at least equally conscious of the controversies raging within some of the northern states over temperance, and, following the unprecedented surge in immigration of the late 1840s, over nativism. Some historians have claimed that it was these controversies that destroyed the second party system which had previously pitted Democrat against Whig and thus played a vital role in the creation of the Republican party.

The scholars most closely identified with this viewpoint are Michael Holt and William Gienapp. Both have claimed that the collapse of the second party system and the rise of the Republican party should be understood as different, if related, processes. In a sense they are willing to concede that the latter owed much to the sectional controversy, and in particular to the passions aroused in 1856 by "Bleeding Kansas" and "Bleeding Sumner." But the earlier process, by which the second party system was undermined, they attribute to other issues, frequently local or state-wide in character and frequently connected with immigration or temperance (see also Formisano 1971).

Holt in two extremely important works, *The Political Crisis of the 1850s* (1978) and *The Rise and Fall of the American Whig Party* (1999), looked in considerable detail at events within the states prior to the collapse of the Whig party and the emergence of the Republicans. He concluded that a growing consensus between the major parties was a profound danger to the continuation of the second party system. This consensus had many different roots. In some states the growing economic prosperity made the traditional Jacksonian economic issues – banks, tariffs, internal improvements – increasingly irrelevant. In others constitutional revisions robbed the parties of issues over which they could disagree. But it was, for Holt, the temperance and immigration issues that were decisive. Although the Whigs had traditionally displayed some suspicion of immigrants and had traditionally favored moral reforms like temperance, their failure to pursue these policies opened the way for the emergence of temperance and nativist parties. And it was these which, more than anything else, destroyed the second party system.

Many of Holt's conclusions received powerful support from the work of William Gienapp. In Gienapp's (1987) *The Origins of the Republican Party*, he too stressed that nativism and temperance played a crucial role in destroying the second party system. He also emphasized that this process was well underway even before Stephen A. Douglas introduced his Kansas-Nebraska Act. "By the end of 1853," he concluded, "*before* the Kansas-Nebraska bill had been introduced, ethnocultural issues, by powerfully stimulating party decomposition, had already precipitated the beginning of realignment in a number of northern states" (Gienapp 1987: 67, emphasis in original).

What are we to make of these claims? Both *Origins of the Republican Party* and *Rise and Fall of the American Whig Party* were based on a prodigious amount of research into the primary sources. Both scholars had acquired an enviable familiarity with politics in most, if not all, the states of the Union and both were able to move with ease from federal to state level politics in a way that was scarcely even attempted by most practitioners of the "old" political history. Some significant interpretive gains have undoubtedly been achieved. There is now no doubt that from the early 1850s through to 1855 voters in many northern states were extremely receptive to the appeals of the Temperance and/or the Know Nothing parties. But were they more receptive to these appeals than to those of antislavery spokesmen? Prior to the introduction of the Kansas-Nebraska Act there can be little doubt that they were but we should note that this has rarely been denied even by those most committed to the traditional interpretation. The question is whether the intrusion of these issues destroyed the party system and whether the slavery controversy itself lacked the power to achieve this.

As far as the first of these questions is concerned, it is still not entirely clear that the party system was beyond redemption in 1854, or at any rate prior to the controversies unleashed over Kansas. The events of 1853 and early 1854 certainly weakened it but it has not been demonstrated that the blows received were necessarily fatal. Parties have, after all, staged recoveries and it would be ironic if Holt and Gienapp, both of whom are confirmed antideterminists, were to insist that recovery was impossible. Moreover, although there is no doubt that many voters and leaders did not go directly from the Whig to the Republican party but instead reached their destination via the Know Nothings, this discovery may be of rather less importance than is sometimes claimed. After all, Holt and Gienapp both acknowledge that sectional issues, in the form of the furore over "Bleeding Kansas" and "Bleeding Sumner," had risen to the top of the political agenda by the time of the presidential election of 1856. In this sense, the traditional view in fact requires only a minor modification. It was not simply the passage of the Kansas-Nebraska Act, but also its consequences in Kansas ("Bleeding Kansas") and the consequences of those consequences ("Bleeding Sumner"), which transformed politics and allowed the Republicans to take over as the major anti-Democratic party in the North.

Much depends, therefore, on the role of slavery within Republican ideology. If nativism can be shown to have been a central feature of Republican ideology even after the demise of the Know Nothings then this would indeed constitute a major revision of the established view. Holt and Gienapp have both stressed the links between Republicans and nativists and they have been joined in this by Joel Silbey (1985) who has, if anything, made the case even more strongly. In a justly influential article entitled "The Surge of Republican Power" Silbey argued not that slavery was unimportant as an issue but rather that it "was part of the larger matter of cultural hegemony." Silbey deliberately focused upon a question largely neglected by other new political historians: the origins of the Civil War itself. The Republicans, he suggested, were not so much an antislavery or free-soil party but rather were the party of Yankee cultural imperialism. They wished to impose, by law if necessary, the values of their section. Some of these were the values of antislavery and of free labor but others were more closely related to the older ethnocultural issues – temperance, anti-Catholicism, hostility to immigrants. The Democratic party had traditionally opposed the attempt to impose these values on the nation and many Democrats continued to view the threat posed by the Republicans in precisely these terms. Silbey quotes one Democratic editor whose views perfectly encapsulate his interpretation of the Republican appeal: "abolitionism is but a small part of their programme and probably the least noxious of their measures." Their mission was to stir up hostility to immigrants, to launch crusades against liquor, to fan the flames of religious discord – as well as to promote antislavery. For Silbey the slavery issue could and should be subsumed under the larger heading of cultural politics (Silbey 1985: 186).

This view has its strengths. There is no doubt that many of their opponents insisted that antislavery was only one of the evils with which the Republican party was tainted. Some northerners (but few southerners) also claimed that temperance and nativism were more important than slavery. There is no doubt too that these various issues were, as Silbey has emphasized, interlinked. Yet it is claiming too much to suggest that in the nation as a whole, and in the 1850s overall, these other issues were as important as those where slavery was directly involved.

What was the Republican commitment to temperance, sabbatarianism and especially to nativism? Fortunately a full-length treatment of the relationship between Republicans and Know Nothings has now been provided. In *Nativism and Slavery* Tyler Anbinder (1992) in effect resuscitated the Foner view with some minor qualifications. He showed that while many Republicans had originally been Know Nothings, their commitment to nativism even before 1856 should not disguise their often still-deeper commitment to antislavery. And after 1856 although some concessions were offered in terms of policies and platforms, these were limited in scope and impact. Many Republicans were willing to require a literacy test for voting, and some were prepared to countenance a short period between the naturalization of immigrants and their enfranchisement. But the main nativist policy, a lengthening of the naturalization period to 14 or even 21 years, never came close to becoming

Republican orthodoxy. This should surprise no one. The former Democrats in the party came from a political tradition that welcomed immigrants wholeheartedly while radical Republicans viewed nativism as, at best, a diversion from the real issue of slavery. Former Whigs were, in general, more likely to be nativist but here it is important to note that Abraham Lincoln, for example, was both publicly and privately anti-nativist, while upon William Seward, unquestionably the party's leading statesman before 1860, nativists poured more vitriol than upon any other antebellum statesman. In other words the Republican commitment to nativism (and still more to temperance and sabbatarianism) was far more tentative and ambiguous than Silbey allows. The simple fact is that the new party was profoundly divided on all the ethnocultural questions that did not involve slavery.

A majority of historians would probably accept that, however important nativism and anti-Catholicisim might have been to some Republicans in some states on some occasions, their party was defined above all by its attitude to slavery. But even here there has been considerable disagreement. Some historians have emphasized that antislavery was above all motivated by hostility to African Americans (whose presence in the territories, it is claimed, Republicans were determined to prevent). In a sense this is the opposite view to the one which claimed that antislavery in the North was motivated essentially by a concern for the welfare of the slaves.

Both these attitudes were present in the Republican party. Some Republicans, and especially those who had formerly been Democrats, did not hesitate to declare that they were quite indifferent to the plight of the African American, whether slave or free, and that their concern was exclusively with the detrimental effects of slavery upon whites and white society. But at the same time, there was an element within the party that was far more sympathetic to African Americans. Almost all radical Republicans voiced such concerns but it is important to note that someone like Abraham Lincoln, who was a moderate within the party and who occupied what might be called its ideological center of gravity, insisted that the moral question of slavery must not be ignored. Although Lincoln did not believe that blacks were the equals in all respects of whites, he did insist that they had important rights which whites were bound to respect. But the moral question was not for Lincoln uppermost.

Nor was it uppermost within the party as a whole. Neither racism nor humanitarianism lay at the heart of Republican ideology. Most scholars probably now accept that far more frequently voiced than either the moral or the racist indictment of slavery were the economic and political critiques. There is no agreement, however, as to which of these should be accorded precedence.

The economic critique of slavery stressed its adverse effects upon growth and development in both the South as it then was and the West, as it might become, if slaveholders were allowed to migrate there. As we have seen, this was for Foner (1970) the primary Republican concern. But this view has been disputed by Holt (1978, 1999) and Gienapp (1987), who have instead insisted that primacy be accorded to the political indictment, centering on the claim that slavery promoted a slave power that rode roughshod over the political and civil liberties of whites as well as blacks, in the federal government as well as in the states of the South.

Foner himself had been by no means unaware of the political indictment of slavery and in fact devoted a full chapter of *Free Soil, Free Labor, Free Men* to Salmon P. Chase's articulation of the "slave power" thesis. But he did give primacy to the demand for free soil, and to the matching insistence that free labor was superior in the West and in the nation as a whole.

Who is right? This is by no means an easy question to answer. Few Republicans dissented from the political critique of slavery. Although Eli Thayer of Massachusetts ridiculed the apocalyptic fears of the slave power voiced by his colleagues, he was very much a maverick figure and few if any Republicans followed his example. But equally few (if any) dissented from the view that slavery damaged a region economically: all agreed on the superiority of free labor. As Foner himself pointed out, a staple of Republican speeches was a lengthy comparison between pairs of states, one northern, one southern, often chosen because they had entered the Union at the same time, and invariably demonstrating the superiority of the North in terms of schools, churches, banks, cities, population, and the rest.

It is therefore very difficult to resolve this controversy. One apparent advantage accruing to those who emphasize the slave power is that while virtually all northerners, whether Republicans, Democrats, or Know Nothings, agreed on the superiority of free labor, the slave power was a distinctively Republican (and abolitionist) construct. Democrats did not employ this rhetoric. We shall return to this matter later. But it should be noted that the slave power thesis has its own dangers. As currently articulated it tends to sunder the political history of the 1850s from its social roots. For whereas the Foner view located Republican ideology in the burgeoning northern economy which inspired a confidence in the superiority of free labor, the slave power thesis, as currently advocated, instead implies a more narrowly political approach, not merely to Republican ideology itself, but also, given the central role of the Republican electoral triumph, in precipitating the break-up of the nation, in the origins of the Civil War itself.

Here it is important to supplement and modify the work of Holt and Gienapp by looking, as it were, behind the slave power argument. The political critique of slavery in fact acquired its importance only because of two underlying factors. One of these was the danger of slave rebellion, which fueled southern fears and which, slaveholders reasoned, required a restriction of the civil liberties of whites as well as blacks, non-slaves as well as slaves, in the face of antislavery pressure from the North. The southern response to this pressure produced a counter-response in the North in the form of the slave power thesis. In other words, although scholars have ignored this point, to stress the slave power is to stress the vulnerability of slavery in the South (as compared with the much greater stability of free labor in the North) (Ashworth 1995).

Yet slavery had had this vulnerability since its beginnings in the Americas. This should remind us of the importance of the second factor which explains the emergence of the slave power critique in the final antebellum decades. It was the attacks from the North (and from Britain) that convinced slaveholders that they needed to tighten their grip over their own states and over the federal government. So in other words the idea of a slave power and the political arguments against slavery generally acquired their potency only because of, first, the vulnerability of the slave regime to insurrection, and second, the other attacks on the institution from outside – that is to say, the economic and moral arguments. Thus the political arguments, *even if we found that they were made more frequently than any other*, are in this sense derivative of the other arguments – and of the inherent weakness of slavery itself. In this sense a purely empirical approach, which counts up the number of references to the slave power and compares it with the number of references to "free labor" or "free soil," cannot resolve the controversy. There are other reasons for, in effect, preferring the Foner (1970) view.

Yet this approach itself needs modification. Perhaps the most telling criticisms of the Foner thesis have to do with questions he did not himself consider. These are concerned with the timing and the prevalence of the free labor critique of slavery and the South. As for timing, it is not entirely clear why northerners should have become committed to a free-labor ideology only in the 1850s, since slavery had been eradicated from the North many decades earlier. Similarly, and partly as a consequence of its eradication, virtually all northerners were committed to free labor. Northern Democrats, in particular, never advocated the reintroduction of slavery into the North no matter how sympathetic they might be to southerners and tolerant of the institution in the South. As we have seen, scholars have pointed out that the slave power was a distinctively Republican construct whereas the celebration of free labor was not.

Foner (1996) himself has addressed some of these concerns in an excellent discussion of "Free Labor and Nineteenth-Century Political Ideology." Here he adopted a highly nuanced approach to the understanding of free labor and observed that in the nineteenth century there were two partly competing versions of "free labor." One envisioned an economy of small independent producers, more often than not farmers but in some cases small-scale craftsmen, whereas the other insisted that wage workers too were, at least potentially, involved in "free labor." Those involved in this kind of free labor were said to benefit from contractual freedoms enjoyed by the wage laborer, as opposed to the slave. According to Foner, with the Republicans the two definitions of free labor "coexisted in uneasy tension, only partly reconciled by the insistence that free society offered every industrious wage earner the opportunity to achieve economic independence" (Foner 1996: 111).

Elsewhere I have also suggested that what might be called the "free labor" interpretation of Republican ideology could be strengthened if more account were taken of the growth of wage labor within the North (Ashworth 1996). For most of human history, wage-earners have been viewed with considerable suspicion and they have, in particular, been thought to lack the independence necessary for enfranchisement. However, I sought to show that some Republicans revised or even entirely rejected this approach. Thus Lincoln himself, although convinced that the worthy would ultimately cease to work for wages, nevertheless argued that the wages system was an essential mechanism for social mobility. And just as wages were essential to social mobility, so social mobility was essential to American democracy. Northern Democrats, however, did not view the wages system in this light. In this way, therefore, a refinement of the Foner thesis might help answer one of the criticisms levelled against it.

Similarly, it might be suggested that the development of the wages system did much to create the disparity between North and South that so struck northerners and that so clearly informed their indictment of slavery. Whereas by mid-century the North had had a free-labor economy for at least a generation, the 1850s, it has been argued, more than any other decade "saw the emergence of the wage earner" (Taylor 1951: 270–300). In other words if we accord a special place to the development of wage, rather than merely free, labor then the problems of timing and prevalence which have prompted criticisms of the Foner thesis may be largely overcome.

There is additional reason to look more closely at the wages system in the North. One consequence of the development of wage labor (rather than merely of free labor) was the growing separation between home and work. As employment moved out of the home a new veneration for the family as a refuge from the evils of the world began to take hold of the northern middle class. In a society which venerated the family antislavery was given a new impetus. This fed into the moral critique of slavery which so influenced abolitionists and those on the radical wing of the Republican party.

Nevertheless, more work needs to be done on the contrasts and similarities between the ideology of the Republicans in the 1850s and that of their main rivals, the northern Democrats, in the same decade and also their immediate predecessors in the 1830s and the 1840s. The northern Democrats remain woefully understudied and although Daniel Walker Howe (1979) has offered some extremely perceptive comments on the differences between Whigs and Republicans, further study is probably required here.

There is, however, a further problem confronting historians of the antebellum Republican party. Ironically it has to do with perhaps the oldest issue in Civil War historiography: the question of the "needless war" brought about by a "blundering generation." Few historians have discussed these, the principal tenets of Civil War revisionism, in recent decades yet ironically their work has, usually without their realizing it, given considerable support to the revisionist thesis.

This is certainly true of those who have stressed the importance of the slave power construct. Many historians might well agree that the South wielded a disproportionate amount of power within the federal government and few would deny that slaveholders wielded a disproportionate amount of power within the state governments of the South. Nonetheless Republicans pressed this line of attack to lengths (Davis 1969) which most scholars have found rather embarrassing. The most extreme contemporary accusation leveled against the slave power was that it actually sought to spread slavery into the North. In the aftermath of the *Dred Scott* decision, no less a statesman than Abraham Lincoln, while admitting that there was no direct evidence to confirm the existence of a conspiracy, nevertheless took pains to explain that the circumstantial evidence was conclusive:

> When we see a lot of framed timbers, different portions of which we know have been gotten out at different times and places and by different workmen – Stephen [Douglas], Franklin [Pierce], Roger [Taney], and James [Buchanan], for instance – and when we see these timbers joined together . . . or, if a single piece be lacking, we can see the place in the frame exactly fitted and prepared to yet bring such a piece in – in such a case we find it impossible to not believe that Stephen and Franklin and Roger and James all understood one another from the beginning and all worked upon a common plan or draft drawn up before the first lick was struck. (Current 1967: 100)

There is not the slightest reason to doubt that Lincoln (and others) sincerely believed this. Most scholars have found equally little reason to believe that they were correct. In fact hardly any southerners actually expected to be able to establish slavery in the North and most, including ardent secessionists, ridiculed the idea. But if this were indeed a misperception, how significant was it? During the secession crisis Lincoln refused to compromise on the question of slavery expansion. If, as seems highly likely, this refusal was based, in part, on the fear of slavery spreading ultimately into the North, and if, as is still more likely, the refusal played a key role in precipitating the war, then the misperception was of enormous importance. Although some revisionists wished to exculpate Lincoln and acquit him of the charge of irresponsibility or blunder, one might press their arguments further and convict, along with the rest of the statesmen of the 1850s, Abraham Lincoln too. He too can be cited as a member of the "blundering generation."

To the extent that historians claim that the slave power was the key tenet of the Republican faith, therefore, they apparently confirm the role of misperceptions and blunders in the coming of the Civil War. But the same problem is present in the work of Eric Foner (1970). At first glance Foner's thesis suggests a strong anti-revisionism since he traces policy to ideology and links ideology with material forces. Thus Republicans acted in conformity with their free-labor outlook and, in so doing, were "*merely* reflecting the experiences of millions of men who had 'made it' and millions of others who had a realistic hope of doing so" (Foner 1970: 34, emphasis added). Yet even here, there was an unrecognized slippage towards revisionism and an emphasis on accident and blunder.

Some concrete examples may illustrate this point. Though he did not dwell upon them, in fact Foner's (1970) analysis confirmed that the Republicans made one error after another, some of them not so important, others quite catastrophic. Thus he too noted that Republicans believed in a slave power and he found "puzzling" the claim that southerners wished to spread slavery into the North and destroy civil liberties there too. Here was a misperception. Similarly Lincoln and probably most other Republican leaders wildly exaggerated the extent of unionist sentiment in the South on the eve of the war. Here was a disastrous error, since it led Republicans to underestimate the danger they faced. And if Lincoln's view of the South was grossly distorted, his view of his own section was scarcely more accurate. Indeed, according to Foner he misperceived northern society in a variety of respects: he hopelessly underestimated the extent of wage labor in the North; he made claims for the extent of social mobility which were far wide of the mark; he believed, quite erroneously, that the West was an effective safety valve for eastern discontent. Thus Foner stressed that Lincoln and the Republicans were going to war to preserve the northern social system but since they could not even see it clearly, let alone take adequate steps to ensure its survival, one might indeed question their statesmanship. It is true that many or even all of these opinions or misperceptions grew out of an ideology or worldview but to this the revisionist could reply that this was itself an ideology of blunder; the fact that the blunders may have been related one to another scarcely makes them less reprehensible or less important. The Republicans were, it would seem, indeed part of the "blundering generation" (Foner 1970: 100, 119–20, 32).

It would appear therefore that Civil War revisionism has ironically enjoyed its greatest successes at a time when it has fewest avowed adherents. Yet the revisionist case must be challenged and an analysis of Republican ideology suggests the means by which this can be achieved. The critique of revisionism might proceed as follows. Revisionism is correct in stressing the errors made by leading Republicans (as well as southerners). It is also correct in its assertion that there was no economic interest, narrowly understood, that was not open to compromise. As Eric Foner (1970) has shown, it was the ideologies that were in conflict rather than the underlying economic interests, narrowly defined. But the crucial final step needed to vanquish revisionism – not taken by Foner – is to demonstrate that the errors, north and south of the Mason–Dixon line, flowed from ideologies which had crucial effects at home, in promoting the interests of certain groups at the expense of others. Thus though errors were critical, they were not the product of defective statesmanship; rather the need to promote or contain certain interests at home so constrained the freedom of action of the statesmen that no error-free attitude to the other section or the sectional conflict was actually possible. Misunderstanding and misperception were endemic in the conflict. Rather than being random or attributable to misfortune or poor judgment, many of the statesmen's misperceptions, on both sides of the Mason–Dixon line, functioned to maintain cohesion and stability in their respective social systems.

Thus, as I have argued, the elites of the North were confronted by a growing class of wage workers, whose role in the sectional controversy has been almost entirely ignored (Ashworth 1996). The problem here was that the wage worker had traditionally, in Europe as well as in the United States, been seen as akin to a slave and therefore quite unfit to enjoy political freedoms. However, economic developments in the North had produced a rapid increase in the number of wage workers, particularly in the 1850s, and the problem was to integrate them into a society where economic independence, not wage labor, had been the traditional badge of republican freedom, but where they nevertheless now had the vote.

This task had been largely achieved by 1860. By then wage labor was deemed honorable or at least quite acceptable for a variety of reasons. One was that there were – or were thought to be – simply not enough wage workers to constitute a problem. This was a claim made by Abraham Lincoln and it is in this context that his hopeless underestimate of the number of wage laborers (noted by Foner) should be viewed. Lincoln's error was in part attributable to another error (also noted by Foner): his excessive reliance upon the West as a safety valve. As the critics of Frederick Jackson Turner pointed out long ago, eastern laborers could scarcely go West in large numbers since they lacked both the skills and the necessary capital; these criticisms, however, could be leveled at Lincoln as much as at Turner.

But more important in Lincoln's time was the notion that social mobility would carry enough wage laborers into the ranks of the self-employed – and then ultimately make them employers in their turn – to remove the danger posed by what would otherwise become a permanent proletariat. Hence Lincoln's exaggeration of the prospects for social mobility in the antebellum North (once again as noted by Foner). Moreover, many northerners now stressed that wage workers, even if they did not escape their dependence on wages, were still honorable citizens, deserving of freedom and political rights. For, unlike the slaves, they were in possession of that precious gift, "a family not marketable." Finally, the incentives placed before the wage workers, but not before the slaves, would impel them to labor, not only to their own advantage but also to that of the economy as a whole.

Republicans did not, however, merely argue that northern society benefited from the presence of wage laborers and the opportunities they were afforded. Instead they insisted that the glory of the northern economic system, with its foundation in free (and wage) labor, was that it gave expression to innate human qualities, qualities which it was the nation's role and destiny to promote. As I have argued elsewhere, Lincoln, for example, believed that democracy, the Union, freedom, equality, even the Declaration of Independence could not be understood except in terms of mobility, of free labor and of wages. Thus while in reality the wage worker had traditionally been seen – in the United States as well as in Europe – as a most unsuitable candidate for membership of a democratic citizenry, Lincoln and other Republicans instead constructed an ideology in which he embodied and facilitated basic and timeless human aspirations, aspirations which it was the nation's particular genius to be able to foster. Indeed Lincoln now held that the presence and role of the wage worker confirmed that northern society was natural and in harmony with fundamental human qualities and aspirations (Ashworth 1996).

But the reasoning that labeled the northern social system "natural" made the South an anomaly or aberration. Since slavery denied incentives to the laborer, a slave economy was doomed to stagnation. Since southern slavery did not allow marriage it promoted gross immorality among slaves and masters alike. Above all, since slavery went against the grain of human nature, it could only be sustained by a tyranny. The tyranny was the slave power. Forced to repress the stirrings of the human heart, the slaveholders were compelled to suppress the dissent that everywhere threatened them, from slaves, slaveholders, and nonslaveholders. Such was the enormity of their task that it might ultimately require them to plant slavery in the North. So unless action were taken the result would be a violation and betrayal of the ideals for which the nation was founded.

Republicans thus concluded that the South was weak and the North strong, provided only that northerners would stand firm against aggression. Yet the South had the power to divert the nation from its true path, as the history of the slave power and its aggressions showed. But if resistance were offered then the enfeebled southern economy would be no match for the North. Meanwhile, the ultimately irrepressible wishes and aspirations of the nonslaveholding whites of the South would, if the control of the slaveholders were removed, burst forth in a crescendo of unionist fervor. Republicans were confident that their own social system was ultimately impregnable; but they insisted that the North must resist the external forces – demands for more slave territory, restrictions on free speech and freedom of the press, the political ostracism of all antislavery statesmen – that alone could threaten it.

In this sense, therefore, there was indeed an irrepressible conflict and it was a conflict over the values of the nation. The Republican triumph in 1860 represented the formal enshrinement in the federal government of the notion that freedom was both natural and national and slavery merely a sectional aberration. In this context it was little wonder that the South refused to accept a Republican victory and that the bitterest political struggle in the nation's history rapidly ensued.

BIBLIOGRAPHY

Anbinder, Tyler (1992) *Nativism and Slavery: The Northern Know Nothings and the Politics of the 1850s.* New York: Oxford University Press.

Ashworth, John (1995) *Slavery, Capitalism and Politics in the Antebellum Republic.* Volume 1: *Commerce and Compromise, 1820–1850.* Cambridge: Cambridge University Press.

Ashworth, John (1996) "Free Labor, Wage Labor, and the Slave Power: Republicanism and the Republican Party in the 1850s," in Melvin Stokes and Stephen Conway (eds.) *The Market Revolution in America: Social, Political and Religious Expressions, 1800–1880.* Charlottesville, Va.: University Press of Virginia.

Bailyn, Bernard (1967) *The Ideological Origins of the American Revolution.* Cambridge, Mass.: Harvard University Press.

Beard, Charles A. and Beard, Mary R. (1933) *The Rise of American Civilization*, two vols. New York: Macmillan.

Benson, Lee (1961) *The Concept of Jacksonian Democracy: New York as a Test Case.* Princeton, NJ: Princeton University Press.

Crandall, Andrew W. (1930) *The Early History of the Republican Party, 1854–1856.* Boston, Mass.: R. G. Badger.

Craven, Avery (1960 reprint) *The Coming of the Civil War.* Chicago, Ill.: University of Chicago Press.

Current, Richard N. (ed.) (1967) *The Political Thought of Abraham Lincoln.* Indianapolis: Bobbs Merrill.

Davis, David Brion (1969) *The Slave Power Conspiracy and the Paranoid Style.* Baton Rouge, La.: Louisiana State University Press.

Durden, Robert F. (1965) "Ambiguities in the Antislavery Crusade of the Republican Party," in Martin B. Duberman (ed.) *The Antislavery Vanguard: New Essays on the Abolitionists.* Princeton, NJ: Princeton University Press.

Foner, Eric (1970) *Free Soil, Free Labor, Free Men: The Ideology of the Republican Party before the Civil War.* New York: Oxford University Press.

Foner, Eric (1996) "Free Labor and Nineteenth-Century Political Ideology," in Melvin Stokes and Stephen Conway (eds.) *The Market Revolution in America: Social, Political and Religious Expressions, 1800–1880.* Charlottesville, Va.: University of Virginia Press.

Formisano, Ronald P. (1971) *The Birth of Mass Political Parties: Michigan, 1827–1861.* Princeton, NJ: Princeton University Press.

Gienapp, William E. (1987) *The Origins of the Republican Party, 1852–1856.* New York: Oxford University Press.

Hofstadter, Richard (1948) *The American Political Tradition and the Men Who Made It.* New York: Vintage.

Holt, Michael F. (1978) *The Political Crisis of the 1850s.* New York: Wiley.

Holt, Michael F. (1999) *The Rise and Fall of the American Whig Party: Jacksonian Politics and the Onset of the Civil War.* New York: Oxford University Press.

Howe, Daniel Walker (1979) *The Political Culture of the American Whigs.* Chicago: University of Chicago Press.

Pressly, Thomas J. (1954) *Americans Interpret their Civil War.* Princeton, NJ: Princeton University Press.

Schlesinger, Arthur M., Jr (1949) "The Causes of the Civil War: A Note on Historical Sentimentalism," *Partisan Review* 16: 968–81.

Silbey, Joel H. (1985) *The Partisan Imperative: The Dynamics of American Politics before the Civil War.* New York: Oxford University Press.

Taylor, George R. (1951) *The Transportation Revolution, 1815–1860.* New York: Rinehart.

SUGGESTED FURTHER READING

Gienapp, William E. (1986) "The Republican Party and the Slave Power," in Robert H. Abzug and Stephen E. Maizlish (eds.) *New Perspectives on Race and Slavery in America.* Lexington, Ky.: University Press of Kentucky.

Nevins, Allan (1950) *The Emergence of Lincoln*, two vols. New York: Charles Scribner's Sons.

Potter, David M. (1976) *The Impending Crisis, 1848–1861*, completed and ed. Don E. Fehrenbacher. New York: Harper and Row.

Richards, Leonard L. (2000) *The Slave Power: The Free North and Southern Domination, 1780–1860.* Baton Rouge, La.: Louisiana State University Press.

Sewell, Richard H. (1976) *Ballots for Freedom: Antislavery Politics in the United States, 1848–1865.* New York: Oxford University Press.

CHAPTER TEN

And the War Came

DANIEL CROFTS

Secession continues to puzzle. The person who best understood the potential dynamics of the secession movement, Edmund Ruffin, never played any significant political role and was hardly renowned for his political perspicacity (Ruffin contended that several deep South states could, by themselves, initiate a process that would result in an independent South: Dumond 1931: 50–5; Crofts 1989: 91–2). By contrast, the person now generally considered the most astute politician of the era, Abraham Lincoln, could not have won the presidential election of 1860 had he or his supporters suspected that Ruffin's vision had substance ("The people of the South have too much of good sense and good temper to attempt the ruin of the government," Lincoln wrote in August 1860; "At least so I hope and believe": Basler 1953–5, vol. 4: 95).

The conventional wisdom about secession among present-day historians, well summarized by Eric Foner (1970), assumes that profound North–South dissimilarities enabled "conflicting sectional ideologies" to take root in the 1840s and 1850s, "each viewing its own society as fundamentally well-ordered, and the other as both a negation of its most cherished values and a threat to its existence." White southerners increasingly insisted that slavery was "the very basis of civilized life," but northerners saw the slave South as "backward and stagnant," the "antithesis of the good society." Northern Republicans coalesced in the 1850s to displace an insidious "slave power" that had, in their view, secured control of the federal government. Republicans wanted to open new avenues for "free labor" by restricting the expansion of slavery to the territories. They anticipated too that nonslaveholding southern whites would before long awaken to challenge a system that blighted their own opportunities. Matters came to a head in 1860. In Foner's view, the South's effort to secede from the Union and establish an independent government was "a total and logical response to the situation which confronted it in the election of Lincoln" (Foner 1970: 9, 41, 316). Eugene Genovese complements Foner, seeing secession as the predictable outcome to a long history of southern separateness, grounded in North–South material differences and led by a farsighted planter class that bid for independence rather than submit to slow strangulation (Genovese 1965: 243–74).

Genovese (1965) and Foner (1970) see a logic to events that most contemporaries did not see. Majorities of whites in the 15 slave states initially rejected the idea that Lincoln's election, by itself, justified disunion. Majorities in the free states stood ready to amend the constitution to affirm the safety of slavery where it already existed. Moderates both North and South outnumbered the antagonistic minorities in each section who fed on each other, gradually eroding the center. Majorities preferred that the center hold and expected it to do so. Its sudden collapse in mid-April 1861 occasioned widespread astonishment. Much therefore depends upon how one assesses secession. Was it foreordained? Or was it a freak occurrence spurred by panic and fear, and bound to dissipate unless secessionists struck while the "iron was hot" (Potter 1976: 501)? Was the war inevitable? Or was it a product of timing, chance, and circumstance?

This survey of secession crisis historiography will probe the complexities suggested by the preceding paragraphs. First, it will examine the original secessionists and the states of the deep South where they gained control during the weeks after Lincoln's election. Second, it will assess the reaction of northerners – a kaleidoscope of disbelief, dismay, finger-pointing, and anger – to the startling turn of events in the deep South. Finally, it will explore the last phases of the crisis in early 1861, best understood in triangular terms – the deep South speedily creating an independent government; the North blinking with amazement and momentarily paralyzed; the nonseceding states of the upper South scrambling to avert a showdown and preserve the peace.

Historians seeking to understand secession have typically looked first at the deep South. They have asked whether a conspiratorial nucleus of malcontents somehow managed to spellbind or overawe the wider public, and whether secession was in some sense a coup. The absence of mainstream political leadership among original secessionists would seem to point in this direction, as would the depressed levels of turnout for convention elections won by secessionists. As keen a scholar as David M. Potter concluded that secessionists capitalized on "an atmosphere of excitement approaching hysteria" to ram through a program that lacked majority support (Potter 1976: 500; Potter 1995: 207–18). Others contend that deep South secession had genuine popular roots, reflected and reinforced by Southern Rights control of governorships and legislatures throughout the region. How else, asks William L. Barney, could one explain the "carnival atmosphere," the "frantic enthusiasm," and the seemingly spontaneous displays of "joyous celebration" that accompanied secession (Barney 1972: 184–205, quotes on pp. 188–9)? The Confederacy's subsequent ability to mobilize manpower and to absorb dreadful losses also suggests an abundance of patriotic ardor.

Eric Walther (1992) provides biographical sketches of the leading original secessionists or fire-eaters – William L. Yancey, Robert Barnwell Rhett, and seven others. Of the nine, four were South Carolinians and three others had important ties to that uniquely estranged state. What stands out is their marginality: none was a politically influential insider, although Yancey gained prominence in 1860 as a Southern Rights absolutist. Nor were they conspiratorial revolutionary masterminds; there was no Lenin among them. Only Ruffin, "the evangelist of disunion," made any systematic effort to spread the "gospel." Secessionists sensed correctly that the 1860 election offered them a unique opportunity. In other respects they were blind: eight of the nine fire-eaters discussed by Walther believed that secession risked neither danger nor sacrifice; that "southern military might would bring easy victory over a cowardly North" (Walther 1992: 185, 255, 262).

For secessionist ideas to flourish, the ground first had to be prepared by others. The leaders of the southern Democratic party created a situation that was ripe for trouble. They were transfixed with resentment at Illinois Senator Stephen A. Douglas for daring to assert that slaveholders would not take slaves to the federal territories without support from other settlers. Accordingly, Southern Rights Democrats insisted that Congress pass a law protecting the territorial rights of slaveholders. They spurned common-sense rebuttals by moderates, who pointed out that slave labor was most profitable in "the cotton and sugar States," that only a "fit subject for a lunatic asylum" would take valuable slaves to the arid territories, and that the whole matter was therefore a "useless and foolish abstraction." Some made lame efforts to argue that something practical or tangible might be involved, but the Southern Rights fallback position had it that honor, or equal rights, or equality in the Union were at stake (see Dumond 1931: 40–50; Crofts 1989: 123, 125). Roy Franklin Nichols' masterwork captures the rule-or-ruin outlook of deep South Democrats, who refused to recognize that their power in the nation depended upon the ability of northern Democrats to continue winning elections (Nichols 1967 [1948]). The Democratic party offered a minority region the means to exercise power nationally, but only if certain limitations or restraints were observed. In the late 1850s and 1860, however, Southern Rights Democrats lost sight of this key reality and instead attempted to impose suicidal demands on the northern Democracy. Ultimately, they split the party and ran John C. Breckinridge for president on a separate Southern Rights ticket. During the campaign, they kept up a hysterical drumbeat about the dangers of a "Black Republican" president. These alarms were generally coupled, however, with reassurances that Breckinridge was a good unionist (he said so himself) and that the South hoped and expected to stay in the Union. But if Lincoln were elected? Most Breckinridge supporters preferred to insist that Lincoln could not or would not emerge victorious, even though the wounds they inflicted on the northern Democracy made that result ever more probable.

It remains unclear why Southern Rights Democrats should have behaved so self-destructively. If one assumes that violent conflict was logical and foreordained, the question is not likely even to be asked, but it should be. Charles G. Sellers made a brief stab in the right direction in the mid-1960s, starting with the idea that the South became "aggressively defensive" during the 1850s and made "a series of constantly mounting demands for symbolic acts by which the North would say that slavery was all right." What happened, of course, was that the quest for "symbolic Northern approval of slavery" boomeranged, because southern demands provoked increased northern alarm "at the encroachments of an 'aggressive slavocracy'" (Sellers 1965: 88–9). By 1860, the South had painted itself into a corner, and it would either have to eat its words or it would have to act on its threats, something that a majority of northerners considered impossibly irrational. On the whole, Southern Rights Democrats were guilty of gross political ineptitude rather than deliberate sabotage; only a small minority appear to have welcomed or anticipated a political breakdown that would set the stage for disunion.

A series of monographs written during the 1970s and 1980s focus on particular states in the deep South. South Carolina, the most aggrieved southern state which of course led the secession movement, was described by Steven A. Channing as obsessed about the maintenance of white hegemony and fearful of racial apocalypse. Channing (1970) faulted white South Carolinians for exaggerating "Northern unity and fanaticism" and depicting the Republican party as hell-bent on abolition. William L. Barney (1974) found comparable anxieties in Alabama and Mississippi, brought to a head by the presumption that a Republican president would close off the territories and implement a slow strangulation of the slave system. According to Barney, younger upwardly mobile supporters of Breckinridge, the Southern Rights presidential candidate, led the drive for secession. They downplayed any danger of war and acted with "exuberance and confidence." Michael P. Johnson contended that Georgia's planter elites pushed for secession because they feared that heretofore quiescent nonslaveholders would threaten their political dominance once Lincoln held power in Washington; thus, "the internal crisis of the South necessitated secession" (Johnson 1970: 87). Although Johnson propounded his interpretation with a boldness that his statistics hardly warranted, he did show that many privileged Georgians worried about the loyalties of ordinary whites and he called attention to anti-secession proclivities in the upcountry that proved more salient in parts of the upper South. By contrast, J. Mills Thornton III asked why ordinary folk came "to perceive events through the eyes of the extremists" (1978: 451). His imaginative and idiosyncratic tale, widely regarded as the most original of the modern books about lower South secession, centered on the idea that white Alabamians, already alarmed by the way state government had become a cat's paw for railroad promoters, saw the Republican victory in 1860 as an insulting threat to their equality in the Union. Thornton called attention to something of first importance: fire-eaters made an impact only because white yeomen could be persuaded to embrace their cause; a standard bearer's power results from the readiness of other soldiers to follow. As can happen, however, the scholar with an arresting insight overstated his case; Thornton would not have impaired his main argument had he said that the upcountry acquiesced in secession once it happened, rather than led it. Lacy K. Ford (1988) demonstrated that Thornton's insights applied nicely to upcountry South Carolina. There during the 1850s landowning white yeomen came to share the outlook of extremists. Ordinary whites concluded that white liberty, independence, and equality all hung in the balance, and that only drastic remedies would suit. Texas, the western frontier state of the deep South, was initially divided, as explained in a capable study by Walter Buenger (1984). East Texas was part of the plantation South and eager to embrace the secession cause, but the "other Texas" was populated by upland southerners, Germans, and Mexicans, all of whom were less disposed to close ranks. An anti-secession governor, Sam Houston, also slowed the move for independence. In the end, however, Texas did join the Confederate cause with the same "joyous spirit" manifest elsewhere in the lower South. J. William Harris wrote an especially persuasive brief analysis of secession in the Piedmont region of Georgia and South Carolina bordering on the Savannah River, where racial and class fears interacted explosively at the moment when control of the federal government appeared to have fallen into hostile hands (Channing 1970: 77–93, 286–93; Barney 1974: 234–5, 313; Johnson 1977: 87; Thornton 1978: 451, 456–7; Ford 1988: 349–60; Buenger 1984: 148; Harris 1985: 125–39. For new evidence that Thornton exaggerated pro-secession proclivities in northern Alabama, see Storey 1999).

Several important conclusions may be drawn from the modern studies of secession in the deep South. First, it now appears beyond dispute that secession met with popular approval. These books, Johnson (1977) excepted, place fresh emphasis on the irresistible secessionist groundswell in the lower South during the weeks after Lincoln's election. Whatever hesitancy existed before that point unraveled with remarkable speed, setting the stage for the Confederate nation's rapid emergence. The readiness of ordinary whites to follow the fire-eaters astonished many politicians, who struggled to reposition themselves at the head of the new order. In some areas pro-secession candidates ran without opposition, and turnout sagged because the result was a fait accompli. Pro-secession mobs also persecuted isolated individuals who challenged the imperatives of community unanimity. In the face of such evidence, Potter's idea that "secession was not basically desired even by a majority in the lower South" must be questioned; although probably accurate before November 6, it paid insufficient heed to the rapid changes of the secession winter (Potter 1995 [1942]: 208).

Second, secession can only be understood in a specific political context. The partisan dynamics of the six-year period from 1854 to 1860 antagonized North and South in ways that previously would have been unthinkable. By 1860, as Foner (1970) noted, two mirror-opposite sectional ideologies had taken shape: Republicans promised to curb a "slave power conspiracy" that denigrated "free labor" and allowed the South to exercise disproportionate power in the Union; they proposed, ambiguously, to place slavery (in Lincoln's words) "where the public mind shall rest in the belief that it is in course of ultimate extinction" (Basler 1953–5, vol. 2: 461; Foner 1970). Modern scholarship on the lower South, just summarized above, repeatedly demonstrates an ideologically charged furor about the menace of northern "fanaticism." These stereotypes were plainly exaggerated for political effect. Potter contended that northerners and southerners developed "distorted mental image[s]" of each other, losing sight of "how much alike they were" (Potter 1976: 43).

Third, once Lincoln was elected and secession actually started to take place, it was implemented with a desperate sense that time was of the essence, that the opportunity to act was fleeting and would disappear if not seized. Secessionists insisted that "delay is dangerous"; they blasted as suicidal "the fatal delusion that there yet is hope"; were the South to "linger" in the Union it would face "inevitable ruin" (Dumond 1931: 288–90). In part, this attitude reflected the reality of continued slave redistribution within the South: slaves from the upper South were moved to the cotton states of the gulf South and the Mississippi delta. By 1860, 61.3 percent of slaves lived in the deep South, compared to only 19.5 percent in 1790 (Kolchin 1993: 242). By 1860 slavery was no more than incidental in Delaware, northwestern Virginia, and Missouri, and it was eroding in Maryland and Kentucky. If the South were ever to bid for independence, it needed to do so while the upper South still had some commitment to slavery. That was the long-term spur to action; however, the short-term one was plainly more pressing. Secessionists bent every effort to secure southern independence in advance of Lincoln's inauguration. Why the rush? Why not wait for some "overt act"? Some secessionists argued that the South could, by confronting Lincoln with a fait accompli, achieve independence without having to fight. Others thought symbolic pride was at stake; it would be humiliating to live "even for an hour" in a country with a Republican president (Scarborough 1972–89, vol. 1: 407, 410, 424, 557–9, 633–5). Also involved was a dread that secessionist nightmares would prove true. The South had not yet been "disgraced or ruined" one newspaper reasoned, but "the Abolitionists intend to do it, and they have just received the power to do it." Why then "shall we wait till they do it?" (Dumond 1931: 381). Comparably worrisome was the possibility that ordinary white southerners might adjust themselves to the new power arrangements in Washington, DC. Secessionists denounced the "misguided friends of the Union in the South" for talking as if "the stray sheep of the South will return and bleat for admission into the original fold" (Dumond 1931: 491). Secessionists feared that their "ascendancy was transient" and considered delay "almost worse than opposition." As will be explained more fully in Part III of this book, the upper South initially refused to follow the deep South out of the Union, and anti-secessionists there ridiculed precipitators for perpetrating a mass delusion. David Potter has wisely questioned whether the atmosphere of extreme crisis could have been long sustained had the South "waited until Lincoln had come to office and been given a chance to show his Whiggish moderation" (Potter 1976: 500–1; Crofts 1989: 114–17).

Fourth, it has become increasingly difficult to depict secession as the consequence of irreconcilable cultural or economic differences. One cannot easily make the case for North and South as two incompatible peoples or civilizations, separated by divergent material interests. Potter acknowledged that the South was more rural, hierarchical, and clan-oriented than the North but he judged that claims for the South's "wholly separate culture" by the 1850s had the ring of special pleading (Potter 1968: 69; Potter 1976: 30–2). So too, North–South economic differences certainly did exist and were becoming more pronounced over time. The major unit of production in the South remained the plantation, supplemented by the farm; the North turned increasingly to factory mechanization, which produced equipment that made family farms more productive (McPherson 1983). However, regional economic dissimilarities may complement national economic self-sufficiency, and such was indeed the case in the United States in the mid-nineteenth century (Potter 1976: 32–4). Moreover, such differences as did exist had for many years proven compatible with a shared sense of American nationality. Even a cursory examination of the sectionalized rhetoric of the 1850s will show that all discussion of cultural and economic differences was dwarfed by a single topic: slavery in the territories.

Sectional polarization in the 1850s resulted far less from longstanding cultural or economic differences and far more from an ideological polarization that was directly rooted in the political breakdown of the 1850s and consequent sectional polarization of the party system. The controversy regarding slavery in the territories became irreconcilable only because it defined the sectionally antagonistic parties that arose after 1854. Republicans united around territorial restriction as a least common denominator to hold together an anti-"slave power" coalition. Although only a symbolic way to show that the party intended to "contain" slavery, because no slaveholders actually intended to take slaves to the Rocky Mountains or the deserts of the Southwest, the symbol produced an uproar in the South, all the more so after the Supreme Court's *Dred Scott* case of 1857 appeared to guarantee slaveholders the same "right" that Republicans proposed to extinguish. Consequently, Southern Rights absolutists insisted that the Democratic party go on record supporting passage by Congress of a territorial slave code, that is, a law to protect slavery in the territories; they split the party when northern Democrats refused to commit political suicide by doing so and they threatened to split the Union if a Republican who favored territorial restriction was elected president (Crofts 1989: 95–100, 122–6). It is difficult to make the case that secession resulted from a "thirst for territorial expansion." Michael F. Holt has concluded, I believe correctly, that secessionists cared primarily about the symbolic "humiliation" and "disgrace" of "submitting" to Republican power (Holt 1978: 223, 241–2). Thornton made the same point: "The essence of the case was not what would happen to southerners when they were excluded from the territories but was the fact that they were to be excluded" (1978: 226). Bertram Wyatt-Brown's compelling essay, "Honor and Secession," contended that fears about tampering with "southern property rights" (1985: 184) explained much less about secession than what was perceived as an insulting denial of southern equality in the Union. Christopher J. Olsen's recent book notes that white Mississippians, stung by Republican accusations that they were barbarous and morally defective, resolved upon "manly action" to avenge a "personal attack" (Thornton 1978: 218–27; Wyatt-Brown 1985: 183–213, esp. 184, 201; Olsen 2000: 9, 14). Those historians who contend that the South had a direct material interest in taking slaves to new territories have overstated their case (Genovese 1965: 3–10, 243–74; Barney 1972: 6–21; Barney 1974: 14–16, 19–24).

Fifth, the sudden transformation of the lower South from disaffected region to independent country needs to be analyzed in the context of other nationalist movements. As has been seen elsewhere and in very recent times, national awakenings often coalesce rapidly and acquire a momentum of their own. They may be sparked by a "crisis of fear," or in reaction to some provocation that undermines loyalty to or acceptance of a larger national entity. Peoples who previously shared a sense of national commonality may become bitterly estranged (Potter 1968: 34–83). Secessionist spokesmen often complained that northern contempt for the South made continued political fellowship impossible. Because a majority in the North considered the South "degraded and unworthy" for holding slaves, "virtually they are two separate nationalities" (Dumond 1931: 315–17). It must be emphasized that secessionist editors and orators were hard-pressed to identify provocations remotely comparable to the national catalysts that mar the bloodstained history of the twentieth century. By any reasonable standard, southern grievances were paltry, and were for the most part no more than anticipated. There was, of course, a good bit of ill-substantiated rhetoric about how a Republican president would unleash more John Browns, stir slave insurrections, and subject the white women of the South to unimaginable peril. These fanciful nightmare specters probably did good service out on the rural stump, but they could hardly be made compelling for an informed or cosmopolitan audience. Something more plausible had to be invented. One of the most famous and widely reprinted specimens of Southern Rights demonology thus predicted that a Republican president would use a "gradual and insidious approach" to entice native white southerners with "federal office, contacts, power and patronage." The South could thus suffer "ruin and degradation" even though "no act of violence may ever be committed" and "no servile war waged" (Dumond 1931: 141).

Surprisingly little has been written during the past half-century about the North and the secession crisis. This is to be regretted, because the response of the North ultimately dictated the course of events. Two paramount questions must be asked, one about the South and one about the North. First, why did the South secede? Answers to that question, at least for the lower South, have just been surveyed;

consideration of the upper South will wait until the next section. Second, however, and of equal importance, why did the North refuse to let the South secede?

The imbalance of interest in the northern and southern sides of the story is in some respects predictable. The overt challenge to national authority came from the South, and the historian of secession is likely to look first in that direction. One other matter has dissuaded historians of the secession crisis from investigating the North. Kenneth M. Stampp's (1950) book on the North and the secession crisis, published over half a century ago, quickly became conventional wisdom on the subject. The book itself may be only dimly remembered but it lives on in a hundred textbooks (Stampp is actually better known for a subsequent book, which pioneered the ongoing effort to better understand slavery in light of modern sensibilities regarding race and culture). His history of the secession crisis depicted North and South as fundamentally antagonistic, anticipating Foner (1970) and Genovese (1965). Stampp dismissed all talk of compromise as "fraudulent" and celebrated the northern public's refusal to appease disunionists. His sympathies lay with stiff-backed northerners who stood ready to fight – and who soon fought for emancipation as well as for reunion. He viewed the sectional crisis as one that could be resolved only by war. Given his preconceptions, Stampp adopted a circular logic: those who best understood the crisis recognized its irreconcilable nature, and that included not just antislavery northerners but also southern secessionists. From the first paragraph of his book, Stampp asserted the fire-eaters were right to say that the South must either seek independence or lose slavery (Stampp 1950: 1–3). As it turned out, of course, they did both, and that was because the North fought back and ultimately prevailed.

Could matters be viewed differently? Stampp's book begins in November 1860, following Lincoln's election. Had he set the stage by examining the pre-election period, he would have needed to address David Potter's riveting account of the way that many northerners sleepwalked into the crisis, notwithstanding abundant evidence of "impending catastrophe." For Republicans, threats of secession, "like the ticking of a familiar clock, had . . . ceased to be audible." They had been made cynical by previous versions of a repeatedly staged drama in which southerners threatened disunion, their northern partisans posed as "Union-savers" – and both then walked off "arm in arm, dividing the spoils." In 1860 Republicans told their supporters to ignore the latest version of something that had "all the earmarks of a political confidence game" (Potter 1995 [1942]: 9, 15). Even after the election, most Republicans continued to underestimate the extent of southern disaffection. They belittled the secession movement as "bluff," "brag," or "bluster," likely to subside only if ignored. Those who suggested doing something "to arrest the secession stampede" met with a cold response. Rather than attempt to placate the "wild delirium of the secession epidemic," one advised, the party should "stand firm." Lincoln privately cautioned against any "surrender to those we have beaten." To do so would set an ominous precedent, whereby disgruntled losers could subvert the electoral process (Crofts 1989: 216–34, quotes on pp. 216, 230, 233–4).

About half the chapters in Stampp's (1950) book focus on northern public opinion. His "North" was narrowly defined: his heroes are the ideologically committed Republicans who refused to compromise and refused also to acquiesce in secession, and who realized increasingly that they must fight. There is good reason to think that there is more to the story. Stampp made some use of Howard C. Perkins'

(1942) sprawling two-volume anthology of northern newspaper editorials written during the secession crisis, but Potter (1968) noted that "Perkins' materials have not yet been adequately used" and that judgment still remains true (Potter 1968: 142). The Perkins volumes reveal a good deal of discussion about various possible compromise measures, primarily but not exclusively in non-Republican newspapers. Republicans considered the Crittenden Compromise a "total surrender" but displayed some willingness to consider other measures (Perkins 1942, vol. 1: 316–17; cf. pp. 310–12, 317–22). Even more striking is Perkins' discovery that a significant minority of Republican newspapers considered peaceable separation a lesser evil than war. For example, the *Indianapolis Daily Journal* feared that civil war would defeat "the very objects it was intended to secure," that it would ruin rather than preserve the Union. The influential *Springfield Republican* editorialized on February 22 that "a Union that can only be maintained by force is not worth the cost." The similarly influential *Cincinnati Commercial* on March 23 approved the administration's supposed decision to abandon Fort Sumter and allow "peaceful separation," on grounds that there was "no province in the world conquered and held by military force, that is not a weakness to its master." Two days later the *Newark Mercury* noted that many "merchants and manufacturers" preferred to abandon Sumter and acknowledge Confederate independence rather than go to war; it reluctantly entertained the possibility that such a course had become "necessary and inevitable" though it continued to hope for a different result. As late as April 12 the *Hartford Courant* declared that northern public opinion was "gradually settling down in favor of the recognition of the New Confederacy by the Federal Government" because war would transform "the present alienation" into "deadly hostility and incurable hate" (Perkins 1942, vol. 1: 331–4, 357–9, 371–5, 658–60, 377–9; see also Current 1963: 88, 92–3). The editor of the Indianapolis paper changed his views about use of force between December 22 and January 17 (see pp. 343–4). I have written about an incipient tendency among upper South unionists to consider peaceful separation in March without emphasizing the extent to which similar patterns of thought were occurring in the North, even among some Republicans (Crofts 1989: 285–8). None of these Republican statements just mentioned fully paralleled the well-known position of the *New York Tribune*, which gave top priority to avoiding any "compromise with slavery," and pretended rhetorically to endorse "peaceable secession" as a lesser evil (Potter 1968: 219–42, quote on p. 233). Instead, the evidence cited by Perkins appears prompted primarily by a horror of war, together with the hope that voluntary reunion remained ultimately possible so long as existing estrangements were not made irreconcilable by bloodshed. John T. Hubbell's (1969) enlightening dissertation explored the role of northern Democrats in the secession crisis: they too eagerly championed conciliatory overtures toward the upper South, including abandonment of Sumter, and they regarded war as a greater calamity than peaceful separation (Hubbell 1969: 174).

The division of opinion in the North reflected continued eleventh-hour efforts to find a peaceful path out of the impasse. A hastily constructed and mutually suspicious alliance of conciliatory Republicans, Douglas Democrats, and upper South unionists coalesced in January and February 1861. Realizing that they could do nothing in the short term to satisfy the seceding states of the lower South, the would-be peacemakers attempted to hold the eight slave states of the upper South in the Union, while also preventing any resort to arms. Even Stampp, who indignantly pointed out that "the whole movement was doomed from the start" so long as the deep South wanted independence, recognized that a majority of northerners (albeit a minority of Republicans) "favored some kind of an adjustment" (Stampp 1950: 131–2, 141). Large majorities in the upper South were similarly disposed. Indeed, the need to help anti-secessionists in the upper South became the key justification for the conciliatory campaign. The *New York Times*, for example, decided on February 12 that "conciliation and compromise become now acts of friendly arrangement, instead of surrender to open and defiant enemies" (Crofts 1989: 240). What could be done? Various ideas percolated – to issue reassuring statements, to appoint a southerner to Lincoln's cabinet, to call a constitutional convention, or to pass a constitutional amendment reaffirming the safety of slavery in the states. Efforts continued to remove the theoretical nettle long at the core of the crisis, the future of slavery in the territories. By March, more urgent and immediate questions took priority. How could the allegiance of the nonseceding slave states be made more unconditional? Did any possible way remain for the federal government to regain the allegiance of the seceding states? Above all, was peaceful reunion still possible?

The secession of the deep South placed the slave states of the upper South in an exposed position. They were caught in the middle, both figuratively and literally. The upper South resented Lincoln's victory but majorities there did not see it as a sufficient cause to break up the Union. Only an "overt act" in violation of the constitution could justify such extreme remedies. The upper South was dismayed by the deep South's precipitous and unilateral decision to secede. Instead of a Union with 15 slave states and 18 free states, secession threatened to diminish the number of slave states to eight of which Delaware had only the most tenuous commitment to slavery, while Maryland and Missouri had slave populations comparable to revolutionary-era New York and New Jersey, which had enacted gradual emancipation. Slaveholders remaining in a nation that included only the free states and the upper South had reason to worry about the erosion of constitutional sanctions for slavery.

More immediately, secession threatened the upper South with invasion from both directions, should war break out between the federal government and the deep South. Fearing that they would "bear the brunt" in any conflict, upper South unionists ridiculed as "absurd" secessionist predictions that the North would be too cowardly and irresolute to fight. They sensed too, however, that any clash of arms would drive the upper South into the arms of the Confederacy, creating a situation "as when a brother is assailed," and "all his brethren rush to his rescue," not stopping to inquire whether "he be right or wrong." Alarm that the country stood on the brink of civil war, and that the war would prove to be a bloodbath, was much more widespread during the secession winter in the upper South than in the North or the deep South (Crofts 1989: 121, 125–7).

Under the circumstances, the upper South attempted to interpose as a peace-maker, assisted by Stephen A. Douglas and many other northern Democrats. Henry Clay of Kentucky had performed such a role in 1820, 1833, and 1850; heirs to his tradition of sectional accommodation were both numerous and influential in the upper South. Would-be compromisers there included almost all former Whigs, National Democrats who had voted for Douglas in 1860, and a significant increment of Breckinridge Democrats who did not regard their presidential vote as an endorsement of secession. At first these elements agreed to support Kentucky Senator John J. Crittenden, who proposed to amend the constitution to prevent Congress from interfering with slavery in all territories south of 36° 30′ either now held or "hereafter acquired," while specifying that territorial legislatures there must protect it. The Crittenden Compromise was designed to arrest the secession movement in the deep South; its architect and most of its supporters had not before favored any sort of territorial "protection." They acted as they did out of a cold fear that the choice had narrowed to territorial compromise or civil war (Crofts 1989: 125–7, 195–214).

It became apparent in January and February 1861 that the Crittenden Compromise could not prevent deep South secession, even had Republicans been willing to accept it, which they were not. Secessionists repeatedly insisted that no terms would be acceptable. Instead, they organized an independent government and selected Jefferson Davis as its president. The conciliators thereupon attempted to gain Republican support for lesser remedies that did not include "protection," but which might provide a basis to reassure the upper South that it could safely remain in the Union. Anticipation of some such palliative contributed to decisive anti-secession majorities when Virginia, North Carolina, and Tennessee voted in February. Ultimately, no formula regarding the future of the territories could be agreed upon, but other things did happen as Congress sputtered to the end of its lame duck session. First, two-thirds majorities of both the House and the Senate passed a constitutional amendment protecting slavery where it already existed. This would have become the Thirteenth Amendment had it ever been ratified by the states. Five years (and one civil war) later, a very different Thirteenth Amendment was enacted. Second, Congress organized territorial governments in Dakota, Colorado, and Nevada without reference to slavery. In effect, Republicans quietly conceded the point that Stephen A. Douglas had been making for several years – that "popular sovereignty" would limit slavery just as effectively as overt prohibition. Republicans also chose to let stand the New Mexico territorial slave code, which had failed to attract slaveholders to that distant, arid region (Crofts 1989: 113–14, 255–6).

A behind-the-scenes struggle of epic proportions developed in late 1860 and early 1861 to shape the southern policy of the incoming administration. A majority of Republicans, well described by Stampp (1950), insisted that secession would self-destruct if not appeased. Should it become necessary to use force, they believed that the loyal masses of the South would join hands with the federal government to overthrow the conspirators. A conciliatory minority within the Republican party warned against any use of force and called, instead, for concessions to keep the upper South in the Union. They recognized that the upper South's loyalty was by no means assured, but they calculated that Unionism there could be made more firm and unconditional. The leader of the conciliators was New York Senator William H. Seward, Lincoln's principal rival for the presidential nomination, who carried a somewhat undeserved reputation as an antislavery zealot. Seward, who had been offered the position of secretary of state in Lincoln's cabinet, worked surreptitiously throughout the winter to move Lincoln away from the hard-line no-compromise orthodoxies that remained widespread within the party. The classic account of these developments, written in 1942 by David Potter, tended to blur the differences separating the two principal protagonists, depicting Seward as Lincoln's "agent" rather than as spokesman for an outlook on the crisis that differed from mainstream Republican thinking (Potter 1995 [1942]: xx–xxvi, 249–314, "agent" on p. 169).

The responsibility for managing the crisis fell to the new president on March 4. Lincoln insisted in his inaugural address that the Union remained "unbroken," and that he was bound by his oath of office to faithfully execute the laws "in all the States." He also stated, however, that he would for the present "forgo" appointment of federal officials and enforcement of the laws wherever "the attempt to do so" would be "irritating" or "impracticable." He also included several rhetorical overtures suggested by Seward, anticipating a "peaceful solution" of the crisis and "the restoration of fraternal sympathies and affections" (Basler 1953–5, vol. 4: 254–5, 265–6; Potter 1995 [1942]: 318–29). All evidence suggests that Lincoln still hoped and expected to preserve the peace. It is often forgotten that the booby prize in his cabinet was the post of secretary of war, and that it went by default to a presumed incompetent, Simon Cameron, who soon proved that these suspicions were all too true. Lincoln had also authorized Seward to offer a cabinet seat to a southern non-Republican, but the would-be nominee, John A. Gilmer of North Carolina, proved unwilling to accept. Had he decided otherwise, Gilmer would likely have been secretary of the navy (Crofts 1989: 221–9, 245–7).

During the six weeks between the inauguration and the outbreak of war in mid-April, matters of utmost gravity hung in the balance. A self-proclaimed independent nation, the Confederate States of America demanded the surrender of all remaining federal outposts in the deep South, most prominent among them Fort Sumter in the harbor of Charleston, South Carolina. At the same time, eight slave states in the upper South remained in the Union and responsible spokesmen there warned that any use of federal force against the deep South would have a disastrous effect in their states. For several weeks Lincoln wavered. Ultimately, he concluded that peaceful reunion was out of the question, that the Confederacy must be challenged, and that he would attempt to hold Sumter.

The interpretation of Lincoln's decision-making process in March and April summarized in the paragraph above is most fully developed in books by Richard Current (1963) and Daniel Crofts (1989). The accounts there largely parallel earlier work by Kenneth Stampp (1950) and Allan Nevins (1959). All four disagree with Potter (1995 [1942]), who emphasized Lincoln's continued hopes for peaceful reunion even as he prepared to resupply Sumter. (A popular history of the Sumter crisis reflects the near-consensus among scholars: Klein 1997.)

Current vividly explicated Lincoln's crisis management during his first weeks in office, arguing that the new president intended throughout to hold and if possible reclaim all federal property in the seceded states. Whatever hesitation he exhibited during March was only temporary (Current 1963: 43–70, 202–3). The alternative approaches put forward by Seward were castles in the sand, based on unrealistic overconfidence in the strength of southern Unionism. In Current's view, the great majority of Virginians were "either moderate or extreme secessionists" and by March the state was on the verge of leaving the Union (Current 1963: 31, 53). Current, Stampp, and Nevins share an interpretation of the Civil War – and the secession crisis that preceded it – very similar to that held by patriotic northerners in the late nineteenth century. Any "appeasement" would have been both wrong and ineffectual.

Lincoln's only valid option was to bring force to bear against the secession challenge, and he did so (see Crofts 1989: 474–5).

Current may be correct to say that Lincoln always hoped to hold and even reclaim forts, but the evidence seems to me overwhelming that he came to Washington also expecting to preserve the peace. Only at the end of March did Lincoln fully recognize that holding Sumter meant going to war. Current also projected to an earlier moment what certainly did happen after mid-April in Virginia and the upper South: it was not simply Seward's imagination that the men who dominated the Virginia Convention in March hungered to preserve the peace and remain in the Union. Current was on much more solid ground, however, in challenging Potter's view that Lincoln and Seward were equally committed to a non-confrontational approach and that Lincoln continued to expect a peaceful resolution of the crisis. After deciding on March 29 to make an effort to reprovision Sumter, Lincoln knew that hostilities were probable (Current 1963: 190–9).

By late March two very different assessments of the available choices had emerged. Seward and the southern unionists said that only a non-confrontational Federal policy offered any chance of reversing deep South secession and stimulating voluntary reunion. They feared that war would unite the South and make reunion impossible. To avert an armed collision at Fort Sumter, they would have yielded the outpost. But a growing body of Republican opinion had come to suspect that voluntary separation would be the inevitable result of Seward's policy. Rather than acquiesce in permanent disunion, Seward's critics were prepared to use force to protect Sumter, the symbol of federal authority in the deep South. In short, Seward and the southern unionists saw war as the greatest danger to reunion, while growing numbers of Republicans, and most important, Lincoln himself, saw fear of war as the greatest danger to reunion (Current 1963: 65–86; Crofts 1989: 290, 355–9).

These contending viewpoints depended upon divergent assessments of the southern political climate. Seward's policy reflected his continuing contacts with upper South unionists, and his confidence that their position remained firm. To that extent, his policy had a more solid basis than has often been recognized. Even though influential northern newspapers such as the *New York Tribune* and the *New York Herald* both decided in March that secession was spreading to the upper South, Seward believed correctly that it would not, so long as peace could be preserved. Unfortunately for Seward and his hopes for peaceful reunion, the other half of his calculations were farfetched: no unionist stirrings could be detected in the seceding states. Instead, by late March several candid upper South unionists privately recognized that the choice had probably narrowed to peaceable separation or war. Of the two, they considered peaceable separation the lesser evil. In order to prevent war they advised surrender of Forts Sumter and Pickens, the two installations in the deep South remaining in federal hands. This policy was hardly one, however, that they reasonably could have expected Lincoln to accept (Crofts 1989: 283–95).

And he did not. Continued toleration of Confederate pretensions threatened Lincoln with increasingly grave diplomatic, economic, and political dangers: the European powers soon might have offered to mediate the crisis or even to recognize the Confederacy; the commercial and financial consequences of secession appeared potentially ruinous; and restlessness within the Republican party could have burst into open revolt. Lincoln decided, probably on March 29, that "he must try to relieve Sumter," even though "relief meant war" (Nevins 1959, vol. 1: 55). As Don E. Fehrenbacher has elegantly summarized: "Lincoln was prepared to accept war rather than acknowledge the dissolution of a Federal Union which in Davis's eyes had ceased to exist; Davis, in turn, was ready to make war for the territorial integrity of a Southern Confederacy which in Lincoln's eyes had never begun to exist" (Potter 1976: 581, segment written by Fehrenbacher).

Lincoln's decision to resupply Sumter, and his subsequent call for 75,000 troops once the Confederacy attacked the fort, propelled four additional states of the upper South out of the Union. Virginia, North Carolina, Tennessee, and Arkansas together contained almost half the white population of the area that became the Confederacy and an even larger share of the resources the South needed to fight a war. Had the Confederacy not grown to include the four states from the upper South, its claim to independence would have been far less impressive, as would its ability to make good that claim (Crofts 1989; for a full modern assessment of secession in Arkansas see Woods 1987). When asked in February 1861, whether it would leave the Union because Lincoln had been elected president, the upper South answered, *no*. But when asked two months later to support the federal government in a war against the seceded states, Virginia, North Carolina, Tennessee, and Arkansas rebelled. The upper South found itself, as Potter wrote, "in a position similar to that of a moderate and powerful nation which has made an unlimited alliance to protect a weak but belligerent neighbor, and which has thus placed its own peace at the discretion of its trigger-happy ally" (Potter 1976: 512).

No hard evidence exists, nor is any ever likely to be found, to suggest what impact Lincoln expected war would have on the upper South. He may have underestimated the latent pro-Confederate sympathies of states that had only recently rejected secession. Or he may have concluded that the Union could be restored only by fighting against an enlarged Confederacy and that it was better to fight sooner than later. At the same time, there is abundant evidence that Seward worried all the time that war would unite the South. He did not foresee that the passions generated by the attack on Fort Sumter would produce an outburst of patriotic unanimity in the North, such as to make forced reunion ultimately possible, though at a ghastly price in blood and treasure (Crofts 1989: 357–8).

In the days and weeks after the outbreak of fighting and Lincoln's call for 75,000 troops, two intensely rival nationalisms sprung forth North and South. Except in the deep South, where excitement had been building all winter, these eruptions of national feeling remained latent so long as the eleventh-hour maneuvering to preserve the peace continued. Suddenly it was as if a dam had broken. Across the upper South, huge numbers of former Union supporters became instant secessionists, and the torrent pulled four additional states loose from their previous moorings. In the words of two astute North Carolina unionists, Lincoln's proclamation "as by a stroke of lightning, made the North wholly North and the South wholly South," resulting in a "United North against a United South and both marching to the field of blood" (Crofts 1989: 333, 340; see also Dumond 1931: 505–6). In the free states all hesitancy suddenly evaporated amid a blaze of patriotic indignation. The Confederate firing on the flag at Fort Sumter "aroused the popular fury to an intense degree" and made the North "a unit." Northerners struggled to find the right words to describe "an outpouring of volcanic lava" that obliterated former party lines as volunteer soldiers "rushed to arms." They confidently predicted a "swift and overwhelming" war that would vindicate national honor and put "traitors" to the sword (Perkins 1942, vol. 2: 735–41, 755–7, quotes on pp. 735, 755–7). Relatively few either North or South understood that the "two *alien* sections" were much alike and that both were animated by similarly intense patriotism (Perkins 1942, vol. 2: 744–6, quote on p. 744). The result was a civil war of "peculiarly intense destructiveness," waged in pursuit of "notably absolute objectives." Civil wars by their very nature are zero-sum games, and this was to be the first such conflict in world history in which each rival could enlist a broad cross-section of its citizenry and tap the ever-increasing base of material resources made possible by mechanized industry (Weigley 2000: xv–xvi).

Because the lapse of time was short, it is tempting to project back into the prewar months the fiercely aroused nationalisms that appeared in mid-April. To do so would not be entirely in error, but it invites distortion. The irreconcilably antagonistic North and South described by historians such as Foner and Genovese were much easier to detect after April 15. Then and only then could northerners start to think in terms of a conflict waged on behalf of "the general cause of self-government" and the "hopes of humanity and the interests of freedom among all peoples and for all ages to come." Dire warnings appeared: "the world's best promise in the success of popular government is in jeopardy!" From this perspective, southerners were fighting "not only to overthrow a government but to turn back the stream of human history" (Perkins 1942, vol. 2: 758, 947). Of course southerners saw matters very differently; they liked to think of themselves as heirs to the patriots of 1776, resisting tyrannical oppression in order to secure liberty and independence. Each side invoked universalistic principles, and James M. McPherson makes an effective case that the common soldiers on both sides consciously fought to sustain these principles (McPherson 1997: 14–29, 90–116).

Only under the changed circumstances that followed the outbreak of fighting could Lincoln start to articulate his uniquely influential rationale for the Union war effort. In his message to Congress on July 4, 1861, Lincoln justified his actions in terms that linked the fate of the American nation to what has since come to be called the "free-labor ideology" of the North:

> This is essentially a People's contest. On the side of the Union, it is a struggle for maintaining in the world, that form, and substance of government, whose leading object is, to elevate the condition of men – to lift artificial weights from all shoulders – to clear the path of laudable pursuit for all – to afford all, an unfettered start, and a fair chance, in the race of life.

He judged that "the plain people" understood and appreciated "that destroying the government, which was made by Washington, means no good to them," and that they would "demonstrate to the world" that discontented minorities could not use bullets to overturn a decision "fairly, and constitutionally, decided" by ballots (Basler 1953–5, vol. 4; 438–9). He returned to these themes in the Second Inaugural:

> Both parties deprecated war, but one of them would *make* war rather than let the nation survive; and the other would *accept* war rather then let it perish. And the war came. (Basler 1953–5, vol. 8: 332)

Two anthologies of newspaper editorials, which have already been cited extensively above, belong on any short list of important books about the secession crisis. Dwight L. Dumond's (1931) *Southern Editorials on Secession* is both indispensable and flawed. Some industrious scholar should compile and publish a comparable volume that overcomes some of its defects. Over one-third of Dumond's selections (72 of 183) deal with the period before Lincoln's election and only a small handful (17) with the period after his inauguration. Plainly the editor judged that he was obligated to provide a great deal of information about the pre-November 6 background to secession, and he did indeed locate some memorable materials. For example, one may find a fascinating spectrum of opinion about Southern Rights Democrats, from their own ambiguous assurances that they were not disunionists to warnings from Bell and Douglas partisans that "Jacobin conspirators" would welcome Lincoln's election as a pretext to split the Union (Dumond 1931: 140–2, 162–4, 184–7, 191–9). Dumond gave fullest coverage during the secession crisis itself to the month of December (38 editorials – over one-fifth of the book) with diminished coverage thereafter once secession had become a fait accompli in the lower South. For him, the "last phase of the secession movement" began when Major Robert Anderson transferred his forces to Fort Sumter in late December. Dumond paid little attention to the upper South's initial refusal to join the seceding states: Virginia's call for the Peace Conference only temporarily "arrested a rapid trend of popular sentiment in favor of immediate secession." By then, in any case, most prominent journals had "raised the banner of resistance" (Dumond 1931: xx–xxii).

Dumond's base of evidence for the lower South diminished sharply at the New Orleans city limits. Fully 66 of his 98 editorials on the lower South came from newspapers published in that single city. The book includes only four editorials published by Alabama newspapers, one from Mississippi, and none from either Florida or Texas. The book has somewhat better geographic balance for the upper South with a mix of editorials from Virginia (28), Kentucky (25), and Tennessee (19), but there is nothing from Maryland, Delaware, Arkansas, or northwestern Virginia, and only three from Missouri. The coverage of Virginia is topheavy with editorials from two secessionist newspapers in Richmond, both of which were far out of step with majority opinion in the state until Lincoln's call for troops. Almost three-quarters of the editorials published in the book came from only five cities: New Orleans, Louisville, Richmond, Nashville, and Charleston, South Carolina.

By contrast, Howard C. Perkins' (1942) *Northern Editorials on Secession* was compiled far more deliberately and systematically. Unlike Dumond, who opted for a purely chronological approach, Perkins organized his editorials into 27 topical segments, while using chronology within each chapter. He published 495 editorials, almost three times as many as Dumond. Perkins also cast a remarkably wide net, with significant entries from every free state except California and Oregon, which were not yet connected by telegraph to the rest of the country. He also included material from northwestern Virginia and Washington, DC. Perkins quite properly included a cross-section of items from New York City (70), Philadelphia (39), Boston (28), and Chicago (21), but he reached far beyond the metropolitan centers. Fully 101 different towns and cities are represented in the two-volume anthology, as are 190 different newspapers.

Perkins' editorial selection process gave heaviest priority to northern reactions once it became plain that the deep South seriously intended to disrupt the Union. Whereas Dumond judged his task substantially done by midwinter, Perkins gave greatest attention to late winter and spring. Fully 12 of his 27 chapters deal entirely or in significant part with the period after Lincoln's inauguration, and there is extensive coverage post-Sumter. By contrast, Perkins devoted only a single introductory chapter to the 1860 presidential campaign.

Perkins believed that newspaper editors both reflected and created public opinion, and that they performed essential roles in mediating between politicians and the mass public. "They were certainly far better spokesmen of their times than the editors of modern newspapers," he wrote, "and the conclusion seems warranted that they were the best spokesmen of their day" (Perkins 1942, vol. 1: 5). He marveled at the astonishing sequence of events packed into a short interval of time. In the fall of 1860 "nobody in the North bought a gun or refused a southern order for goods." Much less than a year later an enormous groundswell of northern opinion was resolved to use armed force to subdue the South. "We have lived a century in six months," one editor realized (Perkins 1942: 4). Several more centuries lay just ahead.

BIBLIOGRAPHY

Barney, William L. (1972) *The Road to Secession: A New Perspective on the Old South.* New York: Praeger.

Barney, William L. (1974) *The Secessionist Impulse: Alabama and Mississippi in 1860.* Princeton, NJ: Princeton University Press.

Basler, Roy P. (ed.) (1953–5) *The Collected Works of Abraham Lincoln,* eight vols., plus index. New Brunswick, NJ: Rutgers University Press.

Buenger, Walter L. (1984) *Secession and the Union in Texas.* Austin, Tex.: University of Texas Press.

Channing, Steven A. (1970) *The Crisis of Fear: Secession in South Carolina.* New York: Simon and Schuster.

Crofts, Daniel W. (1989) *Reluctant Confederates: Upper South Unionists in the Secession Crisis.* Chapel Hill, NC: University of North Carolina Press.

Current, Richard N. (1963) *Lincoln and the First Shot.* Philadelphia, Pa.: Lippincott.

Dumond, Dwight L. (ed.) (1931) *Southern Editorials on Secession.* New York: Century Co. for the American Historical Association.

Foner, Eric (1970) *Free Soil, Free Labor, Free Men: The Ideology of the Republican Party before the Civil War.* New York: Oxford University Press.

Ford, Lacy K., Jr (1988) *Origins of Southern Radicalism: The South Carolina Upcountry, 1800–1860.* New York: Oxford University Press.

Genovese, Eugene D. (1965) *The Political Economy of Slavery: Studies in the Economy and Society of the Slave South.* New York: Pantheon.

Harris, J. William (1985) *Plain Folk and Gentry in a Slave Society: White Liberty and Black Slavery in Augusta's Hinterlands.* Middletown, Conn.: Wesleyan University Press.

Holt, Michael F. (1978) *The Political Crisis of the 1850s.* New York: Wiley.

Hubbell, John Thomas (1969) "The Northern Democracy and the Crisis of Disunion, 1860–1861," unpublished PhD dissertation, University of Illinois.

Johnson, Michael P. (1977) *Toward a Patriarchal Republic: The Secession of Georgia.* Baton Rouge, La.: Louisiana State University Press.

Klein, Maury (1997) *Days of Defiance: Sumter, Secession, and the Coming of the Civil War.* New York: Alfred A. Knopf.

Kolchin, Peter (1993) *American Slavery, 1619–1877.* New York: Hill and Wang.

McPherson, James M. (1983) "Southern Exceptionalism: A New Look at an Old Question," *Civil War History* 29 (Sept.): 230–44.

McPherson, James M. (1997) *For Cause and Comrades: Why Men Fought in the Civil War.* New York: Oxford University Press.

Nevins, Allan (1959) *The War for the Union.* Volume 1: *The Improvised War, 1861–1862.* New York: Charles Scribner's Sons.

Nichols, Roy Franklin (1967 [1948]) *The Disruption of the American Democracy.* New York: Free Press.

Olsen, Christopher J. (2000) *Political Culture and Secession in Mississippi: Masculinity, Honor, and the Antiparty Tradition, 1830–1860.* New York: Oxford University Press.

Perkins, Howard C. (ed.) (1942) *Northern Editorials on Secession,* two vols. New York: Appleton-Century for the American Historical Association.

Potter, David M. (1968) *The South and the Sectional Conflict.* Baton Rouge, La.: Louisiana State University Press.

Potter, David M. (1976) *The Impending Crisis, 1848–1861,* completed and ed. Don E. Fehrenbacher. New York: Harper and Row.

Potter, David M. (1995 [1942]) *Lincoln and his Party in the Secession Crisis.* New Haven, Conn.: Yale University Press; reissued with new introduction by Daniel W. Crofts. Baton Rouge, La.: Louisiana State University Press.

Scarborough, William K. (ed.) (1972–89) *The Diary of Edmund Ruffin,* three vols. Baton Rouge, La.: Louisiana State University Press.

Sellers, Charles G., Jr (1965) "Comment on Avery O. Craven, 'Why the Southern States Seceded'," in George H. Knoles (ed.) *The Crisis of the Union, 1860–1861.* Baton Rouge, La.: Louisiana State University Press.

Stampp, Kenneth M. (1950) *And the War Came: The North and the Secession Crisis.* Baton Rouge, La.: Louisiana State University Press.

Storey, Margaret (1999) "Southern Ishmaelites, Wartime Unionism and its Consequences in Alabama, 1860–1884," unpublished PhD dissertation, Emory University, Atlanta, Ga.

Thornton, J. Mills, III (1978) *Politics and Power in a Slave Society: Alabama, 1800–1860.* Baton Rouge, La.: Louisiana State University Press.

Walther, Eric H. (1992) *The Fire-Eaters.* Baton Rouge, La.: Louisiana State University Press.

Weigley, Russell F. (2000) *A Great Civil War: A Military and Political History, 1861–1865.* Bloomington, Ind.: Indiana University Press.

Woods, James M. (1987) *Rebellion and Realignment: Arkansas's Road to Secession.* Fayetteville, Ark.: University of Arkansas Press.

Wyatt-Brown, Bertram (1985) *Yankee Saints and Southern Sinners.* Baton Rouge, La.: Louisiana State University Press.

PART II

The Civil War and American Society

CHAPTER ELEVEN

Saving the Union

KEVIN GANNON

Several decades ago, David M. Potter – in a statement destined to become replete with irony – made the flat declaration that "at last it begins to look as though the tremendous amount of literature available on Lincoln is pretty adequate without the addition of constant new studies" (quoted in Donald 1956: ix). Future historians, however, have not heeded Potter's admonition, and the volume of Lincoln studies, especially those centering on the Civil War era, has become immense – a trend that is likely to continue with the approach of the 2006 bicentennial of Lincoln's birth. Certainly fascination manifested toward the Civil War by both scholars and the general reading public accounts for part of this phenomenon. However, the central role of Lincoln's presidency in the wartime "birth" of the modern United States has attracted the interest of numerous scholars across a variety of disciplines. During the presidency of Abraham Lincoln, the American Union was not only preserved, but fundamentally remade as well. The Civil War's implications for the American polity were so sweeping that Charles and Mary Beard (1933) called it the "Second American Revolution." As president for the duration of the conflict, Abraham Lincoln utilized a personal initiative and an array of executive powers to a degree beyond even that of other wartime presidents in the history of the American republic. What made this possible was the fact that the Civil War was an unprecedented crisis – politically, constitutionally, culturally – in which novel and hitherto unimagined measures would have to become standard operating procedure for the federal government. Lincoln was the principal architect of these measures and the most active agent in the Union's transformation. Because of these roles, Lincoln became a lightning rod for opposition and criticism, both during his presidency and in later assessments of that period.

Historians have divided sharply over numerous aspects of Lincoln's wartime presidency. His abilities and performance as a wartime leader, military strategist, advocate for emancipation, defender of the constitution and civil liberties, and principal architect of a new breed of nationalism are but some of the subjects in the robust historiography of the Lincoln presidency. Certain areas emerge, however, which have occupied significant attention and thus become the most active and important areas of this historiography. Historians have addressed the somewhat amorphous issues of "character" and principle in assessing Lincoln's presidency. Lincoln's performance as commander-in-chief of the Union army and his home front policies during the war (as well as their political efficacy) have garnered extensive treatment. His grappling with the issues of slavery and emancipation – and the larger considerations of "Union," "liberty," and reconstruction – has been the subject of numerous scholarly inquiries as well. An assessment of the literature surrounding these themes reveals both the fault lines within different historiographical camps and the continuing relevance of this debate over Lincoln's saving and remaking of the American Union. This chapter, then, is intended as an introduction to the massive corpus of literature surrounding a few of these key themes of Lincoln's wartime presidency.

Assessments of Abraham Lincoln's "nature," as well as his character and principles, form the essential backdrop for considerations of more specific issues associated with his presidency. Thus, these traits of Lincoln's have become contested terrain among historians, and their discussions of them reflect in large part the ways in which they viewed the war, Reconstruction, and Lincoln's role in them. As one might expect, interpretations of these events are representative of larger intellectual patterns within the profession. For example, the so-called "revisionist" school of Civil War historiography, defined largely by post-World War I disillusionment with warfare in general, argued that the Civil War was an eminently "repressible" conflict (Craven 1939). The most representative figure of this period of the historiography was James G. Randall (1947), who argued that the war was the product of a "blundering generation" of statesmen who fell prey to the "extremists" on either side of the sectional debate; thus, irresponsible politicians were to blame for the carnage, rather than the force of irreconcilable ideals between North and South. Thus, Randall's (and the revisionists') Lincoln was a moderate figure, driven – for example – by no crusading zeal for the abolition of slavery. Instead, Lincoln the temperate political leader was pushed to the revolutionary policies of warfare and emancipation by the radical elements of his own party, who were in turn informed by abolitionists and other "extremists." Randall's sympathy for political moderation, and his explicit preference that it would have prevailed in 1861, leads his biography of Lincoln (1945) to read almost as a paean to Stephen A. Douglas and James Buchanan, whom Randall characterized as exemplars of judicious statesmanship. But this revisionist interpretation suffered from significant drawbacks, as pointed out by subsequent generations of scholars. Perhaps most egregiously, the revisionists' eagerness to downplay ideological commitment, and even fervor, as legitimate causes for war led them to discount slavery as a fundamental cause of the sectional crisis; Avery Craven (1942: 93), for example, made the incredible assertion that slavery "played a rather minor part in the life of the South and of the Negro." This tendency is representative of the fundamental weakness of the revisionist interpretation as a whole. As Thomas Pressly (1954) pointed out in his mid-century historiographical survey *Americans Interpret Their Civil War*, the revisionists' standard "was not whether the people of the 1860s considered the issues of their day important enough to quarrel over, but whether twentieth-century historians considered them important" – which, if Craven was reflective of this school of thought, they most certainly did not (Pressly 1954: 314). Therefore, the revisionists' definition of Lincoln as an ultimately moderate leader who fell prey to wily agitators and the machinations of "blundering" politicians reflects not so much the reality of the Civil War generation as that of the post-World War I generation.

Yet elements of this interpretation have persisted in subsequent historians' interpretations of Lincoln within the larger context of the coming and course of the Civil
War. David Donald (1956) characterized Lincoln the president as one who had a
special "talent for passivity." Given this passivity, letting events define him rather
than actively seeking the opposite, Lincoln's tendencies in this regard, especially
concerning vigorous prosecution of the war and the advancement of emancipation,
continually frustrated the press, the public, and other political leaders. Only his
political dexterity kept him and his party in power beyond 1864 (Donald 1956: 68,
65). Thus, Lincoln's chief trait as a wartime leader was, in this earlier estimation
by Donald, the *absence* of leadership. Donald's fullest statement of this argument
appeared in his magisterial biography of the president, simply titled *Lincoln* (1995).
Serving as the volume's epigraph is Lincoln's famous declaration that "I claim not to
have controlled events, but confess plainly that events have controlled me." According to this perspective, Lincoln came late to such radical ideals as the abolition of
slavery, pushed along by inexorable political pressure and public opinion. These
ideals had certainly not been part of his early make-up or political lexicon, Donald
asserts, but began to emerge only in the 1850s. Lincoln's presidency was thus
marked chiefly by a passivity that reacted to events, rather than attempting to
proactively shape them. "He did not come to conclusions quickly, and he was temper-
amentally averse to making bold moves" (Donald 1995: 285–6). Emancipation –
formally enunciated as a war aim in the preliminary Emancipation Proclamation of
September, 1862 – emerged only after Lincoln's wrestling with the issue produced
no verdict, causing him "to leave the decision to a Higher Power" (Donald 1995:
374). Yet Donald's overarching characterization of Lincoln as primarily passive in
nature leads to an internal contradiction in his work – not just in *Lincoln*, but
in some of his earliest essays as well (especially the essay "A. Lincoln, Politician," in
Donald 1956). According to Donald, Lincoln possessed significant political skill,
and more importantly, an almost insatiable ambition. These traits propelled his
political career forward, Donald declares; but this begs the question as to how
Lincoln could be so active in advancing his own political career, yet display essentially passive qualities upon reaching the apex of that career.

A bit more digestible than Donald's attempt to reconcile ambition with passivity
is Michael Holt's (1986) argument in "Abraham Lincoln and the Politics of
Union." According to Holt, Lincoln reacted to events, not completely passively,
but rather in decided contrast to the vocally activist congressional bloc of radical
Republicans. Indeed, this contrast accounted for the friction between these two
branches of the government for the duration of Lincoln's presidency. Holt argues
that, reflecting his qualities as the quintessential politician, Lincoln sought to create
a coalition of conservative and moderate Republicans, as well as border-state unionists and northern "war" Democrats, which was to become the basis of a new "Union
Party." Certainly Lincoln was mindful of the potential for this type of movement –
he generously (over)estimated the unionists' strength in the South during the
"secession winter," the Republican party actually went by the appellation of Union
party in the 1864 election, and Lincoln's running mate in that contest was Tennessee Unionist and former Democrat Andrew Johnson. But the *meaning* of a postwar
Union for Lincoln and his potential allies is a subject outside the purview of Holt's
analysis, which does not move beyond an analysis of politics defined by structure and
form only. Holt underestimates, just as his revisionist forebears did, the way in

which Lincoln's ideological views appealed to northerners during the Civil War. Holt's corpus of work addresses the question of why northerners did not support (defined by casting a vote for) another anti-Democratic coalition during the political breakdown of the 1850s (Holt 1978: 3–4, 179–81). The way to understanding Lincoln's personal ideals and the degree of public support they received while he was president is to turn the question around, and ask why northerners voted Republican, as opposed to allowing another anti-Democrat coalition to survive and flourish. This conclusion is shared by a number of historians concerned not only with the forms of politics, but their ideological underpinnings as well.

Partly reacting to the Randall–Donald–Holt line of argument, then, other historians have stressed Lincoln's ideological convictions, their force in the larger political culture of the North, and the active approach of Lincoln the wartime president within that milieu. In decided contrast to the portrayal of an essentially passive Abraham Lincoln, roused to action and commitment only by the exigencies of partisan politics, a significant body of scholarship has portrayed Lincoln as a dynamic and committed president, driven by firm and remarkably consistent ideological imperatives. Phillip Shaw Paludan (1994), in a volume written for the American Presidents series, argues that Lincoln's faith in the essentially republican nature of the United States' political and constitutional system was the driving principle behind his presidency. Against the larger ideal that the inexorable logic of the nation's constitutional framework and documentary heritage pointed toward freedom and equality, Lincoln's specific policies took shape, according to Paludan. Lincoln's presidency thus both reflected and saved these principles; the Union's victory was the result in part of "the president's devotion to and mastery of the political-constitutional institutions of his time" (Paludan 1994: 319). According to Paludan, these traits of Lincoln's were the defining features of a presidency which in turn defined the ultimate triumph of the Union's military and ideological forces. Paludan posits the Union's embrace of "positive liberty," a concept which can be most easily understood by contrasting it with its opposite, "negative liberty." The former, simply put, implies freedom *to*, while the latter might be summed up as "freedom *from*." The ideology defined by the positive conception of liberty steered the Lincoln presidency, as it had steered Lincoln himself as he evolved from Whig to Republican in the 1850s. Agreeing with Eric Foner's (1970) landmark study of Republican party ideology, Paludan identifies Lincoln's creed of equality of opportunity, and the government's role in fostering that creed, as the ideological glue holding the Union's war effort together. In "the crucible of war," Paludan argues, "[a]n older idea of liberty from government being transformed into a vision of liberty because of government. The government's new responsibility was to assist, to enable, to provide an environment for liberty" (Paludan 1994: 230). Abraham Lincoln's significance, in Paludan's view, was to orient the government to fulfill this role of fostering and nurturing a new definition of liberty which he himself had done so much to propagate.

Covering similar terrain, but from a more personal as opposed to a political or institutional perspective, is Brian R. Dirck's *Lincoln and Davis: Imagining America* (2001). Dirck compares Abraham Lincoln and Jefferson Davis as wartime leaders, with regard not so much to their specific policies and actions as to their "understanding of national identity – American, Confederate, Union" – in short, the "national imaginations" of the two (Dirck 2001: 2). Drawing on Benedict Anderson's (1981) conceptual framework of the nation as an "imagined community," Dirck posits that Lincoln's America was a "community of strangers" (as opposed to the "community of friends" envisaged by Davis). Immigration and slavery had made the sections of the Union and their inhabitants somewhat alien to one another, but Lincoln was comfortable with that reality, according to Dirck. Whereas Davis defined his nationalism in sentimental and communal terms, Lincoln saw a heterogeneous Union whose diverse elements could be accommodated within the Republican credo. Dirck notes that during his 1858 debates with Stephen A. Douglas, Lincoln called the Declaration of Independence the "electric chord" that ran throughout the Union, implying that a common ideological heritage defined a Union of increasingly diverse and impersonal elements (Dirck 2001: 123). Here, Dirck provides a complement to Paludan's (1994) characterization of Lincoln's faith in a larger set of constitutional ideals, though Dirck would call this commitment one to a sort of national vision. "Lincoln did not draw sharp distinctions between North and South, retaining a sense of the American nation as a unified whole," Dirck contends. However, this vision of Union, while providing a larger rallying point for the war to preserve it, had "a price to be paid for [this] unbifurcated national imagination," Dirck continues; perhaps Lincoln might have imitated Jefferson Davis, "who understood quite well the value of defining and using the 'enemy' in creating the negative spaces of nationalism, in creating a viable national community" (Dirck 2001: 225). One might question just how well this "negative" nationalism worked in creating a truly "viable national community" for the Confederacy, but Dirck's emphasis on Lincoln's transcendent "national imagination" provides an important illustration of the larger principles which animated Lincoln as president. Both Paludan's and Dirck's arguments agree in that they see these beliefs, whether manifested personally or through the instruments of office, as defining elements of Lincoln's wartime presidency as it unfolded against a backdrop of truly revolutionary transformations.

This type of backdrop has also provided fodder for historiographical debate. Historians who classify Lincoln as essentially conservative (e.g., Randall and Donald) or at the very least pragmatic (e.g., Holt) have a difficult time viewing him as an active proponent of what became the revolutionary transformations of the Union and its government during his presidency. But as James M. McPherson points out, stated purposes that might seem conservative on the surface actually carried fundamentally radical undertones:

> To *preserve* the Union and *maintain* the republic: these verbs denote a conservative purpose. If the Confederacy's war of independence was indeed a revolution, Lincoln was most certainly a conservative. But if secession was an act of counterrevolution to forestall a revolutionary threat to slavery posed by the government Lincoln headed, these verbs take on a different meaning and Lincoln's attempt to conserve the Union becomes something other than conservatism. (McPherson 1991: 29)

Southern secession, as McPherson argues in his major work *Battle Cry of Freedom* (1988), was indeed a "pre-emptive counterrevolution," bent upon preserving slavery and the norms of the white society dependent upon that institution (McPherson 1988: 861). Confederate leaders well understood this counter-revolutionary nature of their undertaking; Alexander Stephens's "cornerstone" speech is but the most prominent evidence of this understanding, mirrored by Jefferson Davis' flat declaration that the Confederacy disavowed any revolutionary intent – that, according to Davis, was the province of the "Black Republicans" just ascending to power. So preserving the Union, as the central goal of Lincoln's presidency, actually meant much more than just the mere act of maintaining a status quo. Preserving the Union, according to McPherson, also "ended seventy years of southern domination of the national government and transferred it to Yankee Republicans who controlled the polity and economy of the United States for the next seventy years" (McPherson 1991: 38). The Republicans' control of the apparatus of the state ensured that a much different Union emerged out of the war than the one envisioned and cherished by Confederate counter-revolutionaries. Lincoln played the central role in this transformation, McPherson argues. Lincoln was truly a "revolutionary statesman," as "it was his own superb leadership, strategy, and sense of timing as president, commander in chief, and head of the Republican party that determined the pace of the revolution and ensured its success" (McPherson 1991: 42). In this line of argument, Lincoln emerges as an ideologically committed and active leader both cognizant and approving of the momentous changes for which his presidency served as catalyst.

"The powers Lincoln exercised were breathtaking in their extent and significance," according to William E. Gienapp in his *Abraham Lincoln and Civil War America* (2002). "He spent money without congressional authorization, suspended the writ of habeas corpus throughout the Union, authorized military trials of civilians, dictated the terms of peace, and abolished slavery by presidential edict" (Gienapp 2002: 192). What type of man was able to embrace this tremendous range of powers, while remaining what Harriet Beecher Stowe called "the *safest* leader a nation could have" (quoted in Gienapp 2002: 192)? Gienapp elaborates a definition of Lincoln that attempts to answer this fundamentally important question. Lincoln, he asserts, was able "to grow into the office" he held through such qualities as "knowledge of and faith in ordinary people," the ability to "manage men" to accomplish political goals, the possession of "an extraordinary patience," and a self-confidence which made Lincoln "[p]reeminently his own man" (Gienapp 2002: 189–90). Thus, Gienapp's Lincoln was a president who possessed a profoundly effective intersection of personal qualities and political attributes. Yet Gienapp retreats from his position at certain points within the work. Having asserted that Lincoln exercised an unprecedented range of powers to equally unprecedented effect, he does not make the step that McPherson and other historians have made regarding the revolutionary proclivities held by Lincoln as the driving force for this exercise. According to Gienapp, Lincoln was a "fundamentally conservative" president who was consistently preoccupied with attempts "to control the revolutionary forces the war had unleashed" and "displayed a gradualist approach to social change" (Gienapp 2002: 124, 167). Where the arguments of the type advanced by Gienapp and McPherson differ, then, is not in their detailing of the revolutionary changes of the era, but rather in where they assign the impetus for those changes: in the larger course of events of the war itself, or in the actions and decisions of an active wartime president. Indeed, the seeming verity of the first of these might actually mask the more subtle reality of the second. This remains an unresolved, but fundamentally important, question within the historiography of the Lincoln presidency.

Another avenue of historians' attempts to define Abraham Lincoln lies in the realm of psychohistory. This particular branch of the discipline has attracted its share of debate; much of the controversy centers on whether one attaches as much legitimacy to observations informed by psychoanalytic theory as one would to more conventional source material. It is undeniable that psychologically informed observations can offer unique insights into the character and motivations of historical agents – it is also undeniable that this particular methodology has its own set of pitfalls. Despite his being the product of a much different cultural milieu, given Abraham Lincoln's complex personality and the equally complex conditions he encountered as president, historians have used psychologically informed analysis in addressing the Lincoln presidency on a number of occasions, despite the standard objections which have accrued to their doing so. The result has been an array of provocative insights that have both enhanced and challenged commonly held assumptions about Lincoln's presidency.

Charles B. Strozier (1988) places Lincoln's wartime presidency within the context of his larger "quest for union." According to Strozier, "public and private concerns blended in creative ways" for Abraham Lincoln. After 1854, when he reached his point of awakening as a politician, Lincoln found "that his private concerns found reflection in the country as a whole. His own ambivalent quest for union – with his dead mother, his bride, his alienated father – gave meaning to the nation's turbulence as it hurtled toward civil war" (Strozier 1988: 235–6). Dwight G. Anderson (1988), however, ascribes Lincoln's motives not to a need to realize both personal and societal union, but to a burning desire to realize the dictates of his own ambition. This realization, in Anderson's analysis, came with a degree of guilt – for in assuming preeminence as a national leader, Lincoln had figuratively assassinated George Washington by superseding him in the republic's pantheon. Washington, according to Anderson, "provided Lincoln with an imaginary father whom he both emulated and defied," and over whom Lincoln ultimately won a "symbolic victory." Guilt accompanied this process, but it "provided the psychological basis for Lincoln's refoundation of political authority in the United States" (Anderson 1988: 254). This authority, though, is for Anderson a negative aspect of Lincoln's presidency; allusions to Shakespeare's *Macbeth* run through Anderson's work, both in the Lincoln texts he analyzes and his own commentary. For Anderson, Lincoln is the Macbeth who (metaphorically, at least) assassinated Washington's Duncan. Like Macbeth, Anderson asserts, Lincoln was a "tyrant" whose ultimate aim was to distinguish himself for both his own time and posterity (Anderson 1988: 261). Anderson's Lincoln appears as the prototype for more modern US interventionism, justified by noble-sounding rhetoric, throughout the world; Anderson implies a connection between Lincoln's ambition and a larger – but similar – American ambition which formed much of the rationale for the war in Vietnam (see Boritt 1988: xviii).

Probably the two best-known psychologically informed studies of Lincoln and his presidency are George B. Forgie's *Patricide in the House Divided* (1979) and Michael Burlingame's *The Inner World of Abraham Lincoln* (1994). For Forgie, Lincoln's ultimate consideration was the preservation of liberty as handed down from the founding generation's efforts to construct the American polity. Drawing upon Oedipal analysis, Forgie alludes to Lincoln's efforts to prevent the rise of "tyrants" (and unlike Anderson 1988, Forgie does not place Lincoln in this category) who might undo the work of the revolutionary "fathers." Similar to the arguments of Paludan (1994) and Dirck (2001) cited earlier, then, Forgie points toward a deeper ideological commitment within Lincoln which drove his presidency and its actions; Forgie, though, looks not to the external political culture in which Lincoln cut his teeth as a publicly oriented citizen and leader, but to inner-directed definitions of self and identity which provided the fundamental, even subconscious, basis for Lincoln's actions when confronted with Confederate efforts at "patricide." Michael Burlingame's (1994) study, though, is concerned with the sources of Lincoln's personal drive from within rather than the type of externally enforced values with which Forgie is concerned. Informed by Jungian psychoanalytic theory, Burlingame's argument centers on an assessment of how Lincoln became renewed as a committed politician in the 1850s. Traditional explanations tend to focus on the corrosive fallout from the Kansas-Nebraska Act 1854 and its galvanizing effect on proto-Republicans, Lincoln included (see, for example, Gienapp 2002: 49–51). Burlingame, though, puts this external stimulus in a secondary position; it was but a part of a larger personal event – perhaps the archetypal midlife crisis – through which Lincoln went around the same time. (A caveat: Burlingame attributes some of Lincoln's restlessness to a poor marriage to Mary Todd Lincoln, as do many of the other psychologically oriented historians.) Yet this characterization might not be accurate; an important reassessment of Lincoln's marriage is Jean H. Baker's (2001) essay, which should be read in conjunction with the studies discussed in this portion of this chapter. As the debate raged over the Kansas-Nebraska Act, Lincoln contemplated the particular point he had reached in life, according to Burlingame, and he found it wanting in terms of his keenly felt ambition (Burlingame 1994: *passim*). Thus, Lincoln the rejuvenated politician reentered the fold not only as a representative of the Whig discontent over Kansas-Nebraska, but also from a more intense personal desire to make good in a society which ultimately defined its most worthy citizens by their public – and political – accomplishments. Like Forgie (1979), Burlingame defines Lincoln as an inner-directed individual, and like Anderson (1988), Burlingame points toward Lincoln's ambition as a driving force behind his public life and its accomplishments. But Burlingame is not so quick to assign cynical motives of self-aggrandizement to Lincoln's acting upon the urges of his ambition; rather, Burlingame realizes, more than Anderson, the significant public and civic frames of reference which informed the construction of a politician such as Lincoln's very sense of self-worth.

More recently, some assessments of Lincoln as both man and president have addressed a previously neglected aspect of Lincoln's worldview: his philosophical and religious beliefs and how they shaped the course of his presidency. Alan C. Guelzo, in *Abraham Lincoln* (1999), claims that much of the modern Lincoln historiography has attempted "to read Lincoln seriously as a man of ideas" (Guelzo 1999: 19). Lincoln, Guelzo maintains, "was not a mere politician"; rather, his political views incubated in an outlook built upon three elements. First was a worldview built upon the "ingrained" Calvinism of his youth, which Lincoln tended to reject intellectually, even if its deterministic and fatalist tendencies remained deeply rooted in his psyche. Second was the "Lockean enlightenment," which contributed to Lincoln's religious skepticism. This skepticism was not liberating, however, but the source of at least some sense of loss and unhappiness. In this, Lincoln was a proto-typical Victorian. Third was the "classical liberalism," especially in the realm of economic thought, which contributed mightily to Lincoln's enunciation of the free-labor ideal (Guelzo 1999: 20). In the crucible of his wartime presidency, Guelzo continues, Lincoln saw a transformation of his religious perspective which would have dramatic consequences regarding specific wartime measures, such as emancipation. His "notion of providence was softening under the pressure of the war and its losses into something more personal and perhaps more inscrutable and infinitely less routine," Guelzo asserts. Lincoln held the war to be one to vindicate an ideal of liberty and progress, yet the course of the war through late 1862 was certainly not supporting that conception. Therefore, in Guelzo's nuanced argument,

> Lincoln had to confront the unsettling possibility that providence was guided by more than mere cause and effect, that a more mysterious and unpredictable purpose guided human events . . . Lincoln had come, by the circle of a lifetime and the disasters of the war, to confront once again the Calvinist God . . . who possessed a conscious will to intervene, challenge, and reshape human destinies without regard for historical processes, the voice out of the whirlwind speaking to the American Job. (Guelzo 1999: 325, 326–7)

Calvinist influences from Lincoln's youth had combined with adult-learned ideals of enlightenment and progress to form a unique fusion which would be the all-important backdrop for the course of his presidency.

The most recent biographer of Lincoln, Richard Carwardine (2003), refers to this fusion as a "hybrid religious faith" which, among other things, "helped shape Lincoln's approach to slavery as a morally-charged political issue" (Carwardine 2003: 37). This blend of the moral and political, according to Carwardine's (also an historian of antebellum religion) interpretation, was the defining characteristic of Lincoln's presidency. As president, Lincoln articulated a "largely consistent political program, reflecting a clear philosophy and ethical stance" (Carwardine 2003: 11). According to Carwardine, this "ethical stance" and the "political program" it guided accounted for one of the most important elements explaining the support and approval for his definition of the war's purpose and the policies directed toward enacting it: Lincoln's "remarkable success in reaching out to what was the most powerful of all the era's subcultures, evangelical Protestantism," in addition to his core Whig–Republican constituency (Carwardine 2003: xiii). In this vein, according to Carwardine, "[o]ne of Lincoln's great political achievements was so to define . . . national ideals and elevate the Union cause as to harness the energizing forces of Yankee Protestant radicalism, without at the same time frightening off more conservative Unionists." In other words, Lincoln matched the description proffered by Pennsylvania Congressman William Kelley – "the wisest radical of them all" (Carwardine 2003: 296). By fusing the inner spiritual ideals with the less abstract but equally important political skills, Carwardine's portrait of Lincoln is able to account for both the vast scope of Lincoln's actions as wartime president, and the manner in which he was able to acquire a legitimacy for those actions within the larger context of northern public opinion. In this regard, Carwardine synthesizes the two major strands of historians' definitions of Abraham Lincoln: the works that emphasize the "public" persona and policy-oriented features of his presidency, and those treatments that focus upon the "inner" Lincoln to explain those features.

The Civil War was most immediately, after April 12, 1861, a military crisis. To be sure, there were the larger political and constitutional dimensions to the crisis as well, not to mention the now-violent debate over slavery's place in the American republic. But Lincoln believed that military success mattered the most; without victories on the battlefield, the rebellion of southern states could not be suppressed and the Union and constitution that he had sworn to protect would therefore cease to exist. Thus, Lincoln's activities in the realms of military strategy and personnel loomed large throughout his presidency. The record was not one of uninterrupted successes, especially in the early stages of the war. As T. Harry Williams pithily observed in *Lincoln and his Generals* (1952), "[s]ome readers may say that they could do with less of McClellan and more of Grant. So could have Lincoln" (Williams 1952: viii). Williams' study was one of the earliest efforts to focus on Lincoln "as a director of war" (Williams 1952: vii), an active agent in the formulation of strategy and command decisions for the Union effort. In this regard, William asserts, Lincoln's overall performance was outstanding. What difficulties existed early in the war, he argues, lay more at the feet of George McClellan than the president. The misguided and overly cautious strategies of the general, most significantly the ill-fated Peninsula Campaign of early 1862, were ones that Lincoln acceded to only "grudgingly" and "against his judgment" (Williams 1952: 66–7). As incompetents such as McClellan and (to an extent) Halleck were replaced by generals more in tune with the needs and circumstances of a total war, Lincoln was also refining his considerable grasp of the intricacies of military strategy and the art of war. This understanding, Williams asserts, played a significant role in the concluding phases of the conflict. Even though Lincoln played less of a direct role in formulating strategy and operations during Grant's tenure than he did with his earlier generals-in-chief, Williams finds the presidential imprint upon the major decisions in the war's final stages. In particular, "Lincoln's influence upon Grant's thinking was clearly evident" in the 1864 eastern campaign (Williams 1952: 306). This assessment is part of Williams' larger (and highly favorable) conclusion that "Lincoln stands out as a great war president . . . and a great natural strategist, a better one than any of his generals . . . by his larger strategy, [Lincoln] did more than Grant or any general to win the war for the Union" (Williams 1952: vii).

This favorable assessment received probably its most classic statement in David Potter's (1960) article. Wars are, after all, military actions attempting to impose a particular set of political ideals upon a resistant people, and this was especially true in the case of the Civil War. Potter's conclusion was that Lincoln was infinitely better suited to this reality than was his Confederate counterpart Jefferson Davis. In Potter's estimation, "it hardly seems unrealistic to suppose that if the Union and the Confederacy had exchanged presidents with one another, the Confederacy might have won its independence" (Potter 1960: 112). This has been the prevailing assessment of the historiography since, though the case is perhaps not as cut and dried as

Potter suggests. James McPherson points out that though Lincoln's "superiority" to Davis as a war leader might seem "indisputable," the truth is that "Lincoln made mistakes as a war leader":

> He went through a half-dozen failures as commanders in the eastern theater before he found the right general. Some of his other military appointments and strategic decisions could justly be criticized. And as late as 1864 . . . Lincoln came under enormous pressure to negotiate peace with the Confederacy . . . If the election had been held in August 1864 instead of November, Lincoln would have lost. He would thus have gone down in history as an also ran, a loser unequal to the challenge of the greatest crisis in the American experience. (McPherson 1992: 39)

Yet this was not the case; events on the battlefield – most notably Sherman's capture of Atlanta in September – would vindicate Lincoln's course and contribute mightily to his reelection. But this serves to underscore the fundamental reality which dictated perhaps above all else the ultimate course of Lincoln's presidency: Lincoln the wartime leader was only as good as the Union's armies and their leadership on the fields of battle. It is no wonder, then, that Kenneth Williams (1949–59) titled his five-volume military study of the Civil War *Lincoln Finds a General* – this seemed to be the predicating factor for wartime success. The title emphasizes both the need for the "right" battlefield leadership and Lincoln's pivotal role in bringing it to the fore.

Lincoln's relationships with his various commanding generals have been the objects of historians' attention. Perhaps the most controversial – and least successful – of the Union commanders was General George B. McClellan, who was everything, it seemed, that Lincoln was not: a pro-southern Democrat, arrogant to the point of pomposity, yet irresolute and indecisive when the stakes were at their highest. McClellan's biographer, Stephen W. Sears (1988), though objective in his treatment of the controversial general, still sees McClellan causing numerous problems for Lincoln through both his personal and military shortcomings. "George McClellan," Sears argues, "was marked by a streak of willful, self-destructive obstinacy" which prevented full communication and efficient cooperation with his civilian superiors, whom he disdained anyway (Sears 1994: 23). Sears sees "the most intensely focused period of Lincoln's partnership with General McClellan," the period from early January to March 1862, where president and commanding general pulled back and forth over matters of grand strategy, as a contest which culminated in McClellan's launching of the ill-fated Peninsula Campaign (Sears 1994: 24). What prodded McClellan to formulate his design for a landing on the York River peninsula and subsequent march on Richmond were two "general war orders" Lincoln issued in January and February 1862. Earlier pro-McClellan historians (and McClellan himself in his later memoirs) decried these orders for a "general advance" of all Union forces in the east as the misguided blundering of a perhaps well-intentioned, but incompetent, armchair strategist. Sears, though, points out that these orders, rather than mandating specific strategic movements, were meant by Lincoln to do no more than "signal his impatience," and in doing so, "[t]hey served their purpose very nicely" (Sears 1994: 27).

Sears' argument points toward a larger evolution of Lincoln's abilities in the realm of military science; forced by McClellan's inaction and obstreperousness to assume more of an active role in the formulation of military aims and strategy, Lincoln rose to the task. He had become knowledgeable enough by early 1862, for example, to have serious reservations about McClellan's plans for the Peninsula Campaign. But Lincoln was also a relative newcomer to the science of war – as Gabor Boritt (1992) points out, Lincoln was essentially a "pacific man" throughout most of his career. He abhorred violence on a personal level (displayed most evidently by his distaste for hunting, a prevalent masculine activity of the era), had only limited military experience during the Black Hawk War of the 1830s (where he did not see combat), and opposed the war with Mexico (Boritt 1992: 200; see also Paludan 1994: 100). Lincoln's confidence in his own capabilities, then, was not strong enough to override the judgments of the more experienced McClellan, despite his strong misgivings. It was ironic then, according to Sears, that Lincoln – through his general war orders – became "the moving force behind the implementation of the Peninsula Campaign – a campaign he never approved of" (Sears 1994: 49). But Lincoln's letters to McClellan – framed as suggestions rather than orders – during the course of preparations for the campaign revealed, according to Sears, a "remarkably apt" grasp of military matters; they were "Abraham Lincoln at his best, full of common sense and sound military judgments" (Sears 1994: 48). The problem, for both Lincoln and McClellan, was that "Lincoln could do everything for this general but make him fight – and in the end, that is the measure of the general" (Sears 1994: 50). Lincoln's final dismissal of McClellan after the general's failure to pursue Robert E. Lee after Antietam underscores this fundamental military defect in McClellan's generalship; it also hints at a president who took a fair amount of time to achieve enough confidence in his own military knowledge and acuity to be able to take such action.

When he had done so, however, Lincoln displayed a more sure-footed grasp of what James McPherson (1991: 66) identified as the two crucial elements of the Union's war aims: "military strategy" and "national strategy" (or, in other words, operational strategy and grand strategy). This was evidenced by Lincoln's increasing willingness to actively intervene in military affairs; indeed "[s]ome of the most dramatic events in Lincoln's presidency grew out of his direct intervention in strategic and command decisions" (McPherson 1991: 66) – for example, his personal orders in an 1862 visit to the Peninsula which led to the Union occupation of Norfolk, and the September 1863 decision to send four divisions of the Army of the Potomac west to reinforce General William Rosecrans at Chattanooga. After Ulysses S. Grant was appointed commanding general of Union forces in the spring of 1864, however, Lincoln's direct interventions in military matters nearly stopped, a change which most historians of the war recognize (e.g. Williams 1952; McPherson 1991). An important caveat to this, though, is offered by John Y. Simon (1994). Initially, Simon argues, "Lincoln saw Grant as a potential political rival, as possibly another McClellan, that former military savior headed toward the Democratic nomination for president." Therefore, before Lincoln was comfortable with fully entrusting Grant with the degree of authority the lieutenant general was eventually given, he "needed abundant reason to believe that Grant posed no political threat" (Simon 1994: 176). For his part, Grant would also have misgivings as his working relationship with Lincoln grew closer. According to Simon, "Grant needed equal assurance that Lincoln posed no military threat," in other words, that he would not become another McClellan. Only after they were secure in these realizations were Lincoln and Grant able to create "an effective partnership in a turmoil of clashing authority" which characterized the nation's most significant military and political conflict. The final result of this partnership, in Simon's view, was one where "Lincoln redefined the concept of commander-in-chief," while "General-in-Chief Grant had to act vigorously within the military sphere, tread softly in the political sphere, and understand as well the politics of command." Simon's conclusion is that "[u]nder Lincoln's guidance, sometimes oblique, sometimes imperious, Grant succeeded" (Simon 1994: 176, 198). Thus, Simon's examination of Lincoln and Grant mirrors the generally favorable assessment of his performance as commander-in-chief that Lincoln has received in the historiography.

One of the fundamental reasons why Lincoln has received such credit for the success of the Union war effort in latter-day assessments of his presidency, indeed as he did at the time as well, is that he – more than any other figure, military or civilian – was identified with that effort. "This was his war," Phillip S. Paludan argues, and "[h]e kept close watch on the warmaking he was asking Union generals to direct" (Paludan 1994: 100). Numerous details of his conduct as president stand out for their illustration of just how closely involved Lincoln was as commander-in-chief – the constant late-night visits to the War Department's telegraph office, the personal intercessions in disciplinary cases, and the highly involved manner with which Lincoln formulated military policy in the early years of the war are just a few of them. But the third of these, direct involvement in day-to-day operations, as has been mentioned, declined significantly by early 1864. In indirect variation to this trend, however, was Lincoln's involvement in, and indeed control of, what McPherson (1991) calls the "national strategy" of the war effort. Yet the success of this larger "national strategy" hinged upon military successes, and more than any other individual, Abraham Lincoln as president was responsible for bringing about the conditions for the eventual military success of the Union war effort. In doing so, William Gienapp argues, Lincoln "redefined the nature of the president's role as commander-in-chief" (Gienapp 2002: 191). One of the most visible features of this redefinition was the stature that Lincoln held among the rank and file of the Union army.

A fundamental truth of the Union effort in the war was, in the words of Lincoln's advisor Francis P. Blair, that "[w]e must look to the Army as a great political, as well as war machine" (quoted in Carwardine 2003: 274). Lincoln's efforts at forging a "national strategy" – which would ultimately include such revolutionary elements as emancipation – were bolstered by the support he received from the ranks of the army. Lincoln's personality and sentiments were such that Union soldiers saw him as an accessible leader who did not put on airs or act the part of anything but the virtuous republican citizen. In this manner, Richard Carwardine asserts, "Lincoln became a powerful virtual presence amongst his men." This had specific consequences which could be quite significant. Since, as Carwardine puts it, "Lincoln thus came to be personally loved and admired, as Jefferson Davis never was," even potentially inflammatory decisions had their impact softened by the ever more common image of Lincoln as "Father Abraham." When Lincoln dismissed McClellan from command for the final time in September 1862, for example, worries about how a popular general's ouster might sit with the rank and file were mitigated by the assurances deriving from Lincoln's support from within that same constituency.

Lincoln could thus take the militarily necessary step of sacking McClellan because "he was confident that he enjoyed the trust of the rank and file, even if his stock was low amongst the Democrats in the general's officer corps" (Carwardine 2003: 275–6; for further treatment of Lincoln's rapport with the Union soldiers see Davis 2000). Additionally, Lincoln's stature within the Union army legitimized his urgings for support and sacrifice among the general population of the North. As Melinda Lawson (2002) shows in her study of what she calls "a new American nationalism" forged during the war, "the sacrifice and obedience that Lincoln demanded were for the perpetuation of a moral order that offered generous rewards to ordinary people" (Lawson 2002: 165). That hundreds of thousands of these "ordin-ary people" were currently engaged in protecting that moral order on the battlefield, and explicit in their allegiance to Lincoln while doing so, made the legitimacy of Lincoln's "demands" virtually unquestioned in the mainstream of northern public opinion. This would have crucial consequences when it came to some of Lincoln's most controversial wartime decisions.

None of the policies enacted during the presidency of Abraham Lincoln was as controversial or potentially revolutionary as emancipation. Yet, as has been pointed out numerous times, the Emancipation Proclamation of 1863 technically freed no slaves, as it applied only to areas currently under Confederate military control and nowhere else. This limited scope of Lincoln's formal statement of emancipation policy has served to convince many historians that Lincoln was only half-hearted in his support for emancipation and that events and political exigencies dictated his policies in this regard rather than the reverse. "Lincoln tried to face political reality as it was," according to David Donald, "not as he would have it become" (Donald 1956: 133). According to Robert Johannsen, this had been the case for Lincoln's attitudes toward the institution of slavery in his pre-presidential career as well, setting the context for his presidency. Lincoln certainly disliked slavery personally, according to Johannsen, but the depth of this dislike was not always evident. It was not until the fallout from the Kansas-Nebraska Act 1854 that Lincoln articulated a firm antislavery position, and even then, Johannsen argues, this position was developed in response to external political, rather than internal moral or personal, concerns. With regard to the issue of slavery during his rise to prominence, "Lincoln, in the fashion of a true politician, issued mixed signals," aimed at reassuring southern-ers while encouraging northern Republicans as well (Johannsen 1991: 98). Taking a different stance is James McPherson (1991), who sees more of a long-term moral commitment in Lincoln's classic definition of republican equality as "the right to eat the bread, without leave of anybody else, which his own hand earns" shared by all men. "Lincoln did not consider this a new definition of liberty," according to McPherson. "He believed that Thomas Jefferson and the other founders had meant to include the Negro in the phrase 'all men are created equal' . . . for they were stating a principle that they hoped would eventually become a reality" (McPherson 1991: 52). The primary questions here revolve around how consistent Lincoln's attitudes toward slavery were, and the particular motivations – external or internal – that prompted Lincoln to elaborate upon these beliefs.

This tension over Lincoln's prewar attitudes toward race and slavery is evident in an even larger degree in the historiography of Lincoln's presidency. Historians who have recognized the limited and formal nature of the Emancipation Proclamation characterize Lincoln as the most reluctant of emancipators. Lincoln's repeated declarations that he was no abolitionist and his continued, even tenacious, support for the idea of colonization also inform the interpretation of Lincoln as essentially conservative on the matters of race and slavery. In the estimation of William Gienapp, for example, the "scheme of compensated emancipation . . . revealed how fundamentally conservative Lincoln was, and how he hoped to control the revolutionary forces the war had unleashed" (Gienapp 2002: 124). Gienapp's characterization of Lincoln as a reluctant emancipator, at best, is an echo of earlier arguments by both T. Harry Williams (1941) and James G. Randall (1947). Williams argued, for example, that Lincoln "surrendered" to the radical Republicans (who Williams actually referred to as the "conquering Jacobins") because of his overweening concern for political favor. According to Williams' argument, Lincoln was not "blind to the mounting Jacobinism among the people whose tribune he always considered himself to be. If they demanded that the Union be saved through emancipation, Abraham Lincoln would save it that way" (Williams 1941: 170–1). But the problem with this interpretation is that it posits a false dichotomy: either Lincoln was for emancipation personally, *or* he responded to external political pressures in formulating this policy. No room is left for a blending of the two, or for a consideration that Lincoln's personal views might well have been accommodated and strengthened by the larger climate of public opinion. Lincoln was a politician as much as he was anything else, and politics is above all else the art of the possible. There is nothing within this definition of politics which precludes one's personal proclivities from becoming political policy without being somehow corrupted in the process. The historians who characterize Lincoln's emancipation policy as being exclusively politically rather than morally driven are unable to reconcile themselves to the fact that both elements existed. For example, Gienapp's assertion that Lincoln's emancipation policy displayed a fundamental conservatism seems belied by his assertion on the next page of the same work that "[w]ith a stroke of the pen, Lincoln had changed the nature of the war. Both sides understood that the war had been fundamentally transformed, that the Union was no longer fighting to restore the old Union *but to create a new one*" (Gienapp 2002: 125, emphasis added).

This transformation of the very nature of the Union's war effort was certainly not without its political risks. James McPherson (1997), in his study of the soldiers of the Civil War armies, devotes considerable attention to the effects of Lincoln's emancipation policies within the Union forces. By linking the preservation of the Union with the abolition of slavery, McPherson argues, Lincoln was able to tap into what Union soldiers saw as a chief war aim to support a new, more revolutionary policy. What guarantee was there, the rhetorical question seemed to ask, that should southern slavery not be abolished, there would not be yet another conflict within the space of a decade at most? The Emancipation Proclamation triggered a brief surge of dissent within a large minority of anti-emancipationists within the army during the winter of 1862–3, McPherson concedes, but in the long run, "the evidence seems to indicate that pro-emancipation convictions did predominate among the leaders and the fighting soldiers of the Union army." This sentiment would only increase, McPherson concludes, with the army's backlash against the "copperhead" peace movement, and the troops' actual experience with "contraband" slaves moving into Union lines – and the tangible damage these movements accomplished in terms of the Confederacy's manpower and unity of purpose (McPherson 1997: 124; on the actions of fugitives and the damage they caused the Confederacy, see Freehling 2001: esp. 132–5, 145–7). A more recent assessment of Lincoln's emancipation policy concludes, along the lines of McPherson's argument, that "[t]he unified political purpose Lincoln encouraged amongst his troops by arousing their 'slumbering patriotism' . . . was challenged but not fundamentally compromised by his role as the Great Emancipator" (Carwardine 2003: 277). As far as the army was concerned, the majority opinion in the ranks seemed to be summed up nicely by an Indiana sergeant who proclaimed "'he was for emancipation subjugation extermination and hell and damnation if they would bring the war to a speedy end.'" According to Carwardine, Lincoln's emancipation did not provoke a crisis of morale in the Union ranks because "[p]ragmatic calculation fused with abolitionist idealism" to create a large degree of support for emancipation as a policy which would both redefine the purpose of the war while offering the chance to shorten the conflict as well, by inflicting significant damage upon the Confederacy's military capabilities (Carwardine 2003: 278).

The most complete examination of Lincoln's policies and views toward race, slavery, and emancipation is LaWanda Cox's *Lincoln and Black Freedom* (1981). Probably the most signal contribution of Cox's work is its refusal to embrace the artificial divide between principle and pragmatism that is evident to some degree in much of the historiography. Cox instead sees Lincoln's political proclivities and well-honed pragmatism as essential components that ultimately assured the success of the larger principle. Lincoln's own words provide the theme for this component of Cox's thesis: "It is not 'can *any* of us *imagine* better?' but 'can we *all* do better?'" (Cox 1981: 11, emphasis in original). Even the most noble of principles has no power without practical results, and Lincoln understood this vital fact. The governing element in this regard was the constitutional limitations Lincoln saw placed upon him by the delineated powers and obligations of the national executive:

> Lincoln clearly recognized as president that he had no legal power to act against slavery because it was a moral wrong. That he struggled to subordinate his antislavery convictions to his conception of the powers and duty of the presidency cannot be doubted. To those who opposed his antislavery initiatives, or found them difficult to support, Lincoln was quick to defend his motives as those of commander in chief rather than of moralist by earnestly affirming his "good faith" and arguing the [military] "necessity" of emancipation. (Cox 1981: 14)

This *modus operandi* was not one calculated to please all constituencies within the Union; radicals within Lincoln's own party and committed abolitionists (not necessarily mutually exclusive groups) decried the president's seeming slowness and reluctance to address the issues of slavery and emancipation as genuine moral necessities. Yet Cox points out that the differences between Lincoln and the congressional radicals have been exaggerated. Viewed through the lens of Lincoln's pocket veto of the Wade–Davis Bill 1864, the assumption that a gulf existed between the president and the congressional radicals seems plausible, and has been accepted largely at face value in the historiography. Cox points out, though, that later tensions over reconstruction policy have obscured the earlier closeness of Lincoln's and the radicals' positions. The Second Confiscation Act 1862, for example, granted freedom only to "contrabands" within Union lines, while the Emancipation Proclamation covered the whole of the Confederacy. The first might have had more effect in the short term, but the second was certainly the more far-reaching and revolutionary of the two – even if those qualities were revealed more slowly (Cox 1981: 15–19). This blend of far-reaching policies couched in pragmatic and astute terms characterized much of Lincoln's leadership style, and nowhere was this more evident than with emancipation.

Cox's argument that Lincoln and the radical Republicans agreed upon more things than they disagreed over is instructive. Hans Trefousse (1969) described the radical Republicans as "Lincoln's vanguard for racial justice." If Lincoln might not have always kept pace with the forwardmost elements of this vanguard, he did move far ahead of general public opinion in the Union. By a thorough examination of the implementation of Lincoln's reconstruction policies in occupied Louisiana during the final year or so of the Civil War, Cox is able to clear up what she sees as misconceptions regarding Lincoln's beliefs and aims as they had evolved to that point. "The Louisiana story . . . confirms that president and the radicals of his party shared an identity of purpose, if not of rhetoric and tactic, in seeking basic rights, citizenship, and political participation for former slaves" (Cox 1981: 142). Cox's argument thus anticipates that of Carwardine (2003) in its emphasis on Lincoln's skill for blending the pragmatic with the ideal to enact significant policies and at least attempt to provide for their efficacy.

This insight is also shared by Gabor Boritt (2001), who addresses Lincoln's repeated advocacy of colonization of free blacks as a solution to the problems of race and slavery within the Union. Other historians have pointed toward this consistent avowal of colonization as proof that Lincoln was handcuffed by the prevailing racial ideology of the time, and was therefore fundamentally conservative on the issue of emancipation. Probably the most firm statement in this vein is that of Robert F. Engs (1991), who calls the image of Lincoln as the catalyst for emancipation a "fiction." Engs argues that this type of enshrinement of Lincoln was a postwar creation of whites to rob blacks of their rightful place as the actual agents of their own freedom. "The poor, uneducated freedmen fell for that masterful propaganda stroke," Engs asserts, "But so have the rest of us, black and white, for over a century!" (Engs 1991: 13). Other historians (see esp. Harding 1981; Freehling 2001) have argued that the process was overwhelmingly one of "self-emancipation," as southern blacks essentially voted with their feet during the war, crossing over into Union lines to achieve practical freedom while hesitant politicians debated formal emancipation in the halls of government. Boritt, though, points to Lincoln's grasp of politics as the art of the possible above all else, and thus is able to characterize Lincoln's use of colonization not as a sign of Lincoln's reluctance regarding emancipation, but "as a way to allay his own uncertainties, and more importantly the fears of the vast majority of whites, concerning the eventual place of the free black people in the United States" (Boritt 2001: 12). Colonization was thus a "lullaby," meant to soften the impact of emancipation; "[o]nce emancipation was a *fait accompli,* the lullaby had served its purpose," and indeed was heard no more (Boritt 2001: 14). By 1863, according to Boritt, "[c]olonization was dead and Lincoln did not mourn." "Did Lincoln move forward fast enough?" he continues. "Many reformers thought not, but their job was relatively easy: agitate, tell the truth. The politician had to bring people along" (Boritt 2001: 17–18). One of the clearest pieces of evidence as to the skill with which Lincoln performed his duties as president and thus figured prominently in rescuing the Union from rebellion and permanent schism, and in rescuing slaves from bondage, is the fact that in the end he did "bring people along."

The "self-emancipation" argument is a valid one, but one must also be mindful that it was Union forces invading slaveholding territory that made self-emancipation a viable possibility. So to answer the rhetorical question, "Who freed the slaves?," the conclusion of James McPherson summarizes the reality of wartime emancipation:

> . . . [B]y pronouncing slavery a moral evil that must come to an end and then winning the presidency in 1860, provoking the South to secede, by refusing to compromise on the issue of slavery's expansion or on Fort Sumter, by careful leadership and timing that kept a fragile Unionist coalition together in the first year of war and committed it to emancipation in the second, by prosecuting the war to unconditional victory as commander in chief of an army of liberation, Abraham Lincoln freed the slaves. (McPherson 1996: 207)

Though McPherson's chain of events might strike the reader as perhaps an overly simplistic interpretation of cause and effect, the overall argument is a reasonable one. Because emancipation was a wartime occurrence, Lincoln – as the individual who had more power than any other individual to shape that wartime context – played the largest (but not the only) role in not only bringing about the conditions in which emancipation could realistically occur, but also ensuring those conditions would endure long enough to make that occurrence an irrevocable one.

Despite David Potter's (1960) confident assessment decades ago that the field of Lincoln studies was saturated, historians have not slowed down noticeably in their efforts to continually reinterpret and redefine the wartime presidency of Abraham Lincoln. Because the Civil War so profoundly reshaped the American Union, Lincoln's seemingly larger-than-life role in the war's course remains a powerful attraction to those concerned with understanding the conflict in its manifold dimensions. A multitude of specific areas of inquiry, a number of them outside the scope of this essay, have flourished in Lincoln historiography. Areas of disagreement and different emphases continue to exist, but that is what gives the historiography an element of continuing dynamism. The one area of common agreement, though, is the degree of importance and prominence accorded to Lincoln. In the modern historical understanding, this does not simply mean a return to the "great man" school of history, but rather a realization of one of the fundamental truths of his-tory: the power of contingency. Abraham Lincoln's personal and political qualities intersected with the public duties he accepted on the eve of the greatest conflict in the history of the American republic. Lincoln did not save the Union alone – that was also accomplished by, among others, hundreds of thousands of ordinary men who served in the Union army and millions of African Americans whose individual acts of resistance added up to a significant undermining of the Confederacy's ability to wage war. But more than any other individual, Lincoln contributed to not only saving the Union in a general sense, but to giving it the particular character with which it emerged out of the destruction of the Civil War.

BIBLIOGRAPHY

Anderson, Benedict (1981) *Imagined Communities: Reflections on the Origins and Spread of Nationalism.* London: Verso.

Anderson, Dwight G. (1988) "Quest for Immortality: A Theory of Abraham Lincoln's Political Psychology," in Gabor S. Boritt (ed.) *The Historians' Lincoln: Pseudohistory, Psychohistory, and History.* Urbana, Ill.: University of Illinois Press.

Baker, Jean Harvey (2001) "Abraham and Mary: A Marriage," in Gabor S. Boritt (ed.) *The Lincoln Enigma: The Changing Faces of an American Icon.* New York: Oxford University Press.

Beard, Charles A. and Beard, Mary R. (1933) *The Rise of American Civilization,* two vols. New York: Macmillan.

Boritt, Gabor S. (ed.) (1988) *The Historians' Lincoln: Pseudohistory, Psychohistory, and History.* Urbana, Ill.: University of Illinois Press.

Boritt, Gabor S. (1992) "War Opponent and War President," in Boritt (ed.) *Lincoln the War President: The Gettysburg Lectures.* New York: Oxford University Press.

Boritt, Gabor S. (2001) "Did He Dream of a Lily-White America? The Voyage to Linconia," in Boritt (ed.) *The Lincoln Enigma: The Changing Faces of an American Icon.* New York: Oxford University Press.

Burlingame, Michael (1994) *The Inner World of Abraham Lincoln.* Urbana, Ill.: University of Illinois Press.

Carwardine, Richard J. (2003) *Lincoln* [Profiles in Power Series]. London: Pearson Education.

Cox, LaWanda (1981) *Lincoln and Black Freedom: A Study in Presidential Leadership.* Columbia, SC: University of South Carolina Press.

Craven, Avery O. (1939) *The Repressible Conflict, 1830–1861.* Baton Rouge, La.: Louisiana State University Press.

Craven, Avery O. (1942) *The Coming of the Civil War.* New York: Charles Scribner's Sons.

Davis, William C. (2000) *Lincoln's Men: How President Lincoln Became Father to an Army and a Nation.* New York: Free Press.

Dirck, Brian R. (2001) *Lincoln and Davis: Imagining America.* Lawrence, Kan.: University Press of Kansas.

Donald, David Herbert (1956) *Lincoln Reconsidered: Essays on the Civil War Era.* New York: Alfred A. Knopf.

Donald, David Herbert (1995) *Lincoln.* New York: Simon and Schuster.

Engs, Robert F. (1991) "The Great American Slave Rebellion," lecture delivered to the Civil War Institute at Gettysburg College, June 27.

Foner, Eric (1970) *Free Soil, Free Labor, Free Men: The Ideology of the Republican Party before the Civil War.* New York: Oxford University Press.

Forgie, George B. (1979) *Patricide in the House Divided: A Psychological Interpretation of Lincoln and his Age.* New York: Norton.

Freehling, William W. (2001) *The South vs. the South: How Anti-Confederate Southerners Shaped the Course of the Civil War.* New York: Oxford University Press.

Gienapp, William E. (2002) *Abraham Lincoln and Civil War America: A Biography.* New York: Oxford University Press.

Guelzo, Alan C. (1999) *Abraham Lincoln: Redeemer President.* Grand Rapids, Mich.: William B. Eerdmans.

Harding, Vincent (1981) *There is a River: The Black Struggle for Freedom in America.* New York: Harcourt Brace.

Holt, Michael F. (1978) *The Political Crisis of the 1850s.* New York: Wiley.

Holt, Michael F. (1986) "Abraham Lincoln and the Politics of Union," in John L. Thomas (ed.) *Abraham Lincoln and the American Political Tradition.* Amherst, Mass.: University of Massachusetts Press.

Johannsen, Robert W. (1991) *Lincoln, the South, and Slavery: The Political Dimension*. Baton Rouge, La.: Louisiana State University Press.

Lawson, Melinda (2002) *Patriot Fires: Forging a New American Nationalism in the Civil War North*. Lawrence, Kan.: University Press of Kansas.

McPherson, James M. (1988) *Battle Cry of Freedom: The Civil War Era*. New York: Oxford University Press.

McPherson, James M. (1991) "Abraham Lincoln and the Second American Revolution," in *Abraham Lincoln and the Second American Revolution*. New York: Oxford University Press.

McPherson, James M. (1992) "American Victory, American Defeat," in Gabor S. Boritt (ed.) *Why the Confederacy Lost*. New York: Oxford University Press.

McPherson, James M. (1996) "Who Freed the Slaves?," in McPherson, *Drawn with the Sword: Reflections on the American Civil War*. New York: Oxford University Press.

McPherson, James M. (1997) *For Cause and Comrades: Why Men Fought in the Civil War*. New York: Oxford University Press.

Paludan, Phillip Shaw (1994) *The Presidency of Abraham Lincoln*. Lawrence, Kan.: University Press of Kansas.

Potter, David M. (1960) "Jefferson Davis and the Political Factors in Confederate Defeat," in David Donald (ed.) *Why the North Won the Civil War*. Baton Rouge, La.: Louisiana State University Press.

Pressly, Thomas J. (1954) *Americans Interpret their Civil War*. Princeton, NJ: Princeton University Press.

Randall, James Garfield (1945) *Lincoln the President: Springfield to Gettysburg*, two vols. New York: Dodd Mead.

Randall, James Garfield (1947) *Lincoln the Liberal Statesman*. New York: Dodd Mead.

Sears, Stephen W. (1988) *George B. McClellan: The Young Napoleon*. New York: Ticknor and Fields.

Sears, Stephen W. (1994) "Lincoln and McClellan," in Gabor S. Boritt (ed.) *Lincoln and his Generals*. New York: Oxford University Press.

Simon, John Y. (1994) "Grant, Lincoln, and Unconditional Surrender," in Gabor S. Boritt (ed.) *Lincoln and his Generals*. New York: Oxford University Press.

Strozier, Charles B. (1988) "Lincoln's Quest for Union: Public and Private Meanings," in Gabor S. Boritt (ed.) *The Historian's Lincoln: Pseudohistory, Psychohistory, and History*. Urbana, Ill.: University of Illinois Press.

Trefousse, Hans L. (1969) *The Radical Republicans: Lincoln's Vanguard for Racial Justice*. New York: Alfred A. Knopf.

Williams, Kenneth P. (1949–59) *Lincoln Finds a General: A Military Study of the Civil War*. New York: Macmillan.

Williams, T. Harry (1941) *Lincoln and the Radicals*. Madison, Wis.: University of Wisconsin Press.

Williams, T. Harry (1952) *Lincoln and his Generals*. New York: Alfred A. Knopf.

CHAPTER TWELVE

Civil War Military Campaigns: The Union

CAROL REARDON

Nearly a century after the end of divisive conflict of 1861–5, the bibliographical note to David Donald's essay collection *Why the North Won the Civil War* (1960) began with a curious comment: "Studies devoted primarily to explaining the reasons for Northern victory in the Civil War are not numerous." A short list of suggestions for further reading on this topic seemed to validate that observation, each successive title containing explicit reference to the collapse, failure, or defeat of the Confederacy rather than the success of the war effort of the Union.

The title of that short volume accurately summarizes the single most important critical question Civil War historians have asked about the northern military effort: why did the North win? Equally interesting, however, we must consider why so few have devoted their scholarly attention to the question.

Several reasons suggest themselves. First and foremost, and in reverse of usual practice, the defeated South stole a march on the victorious North and won early decisive victories in the literary war for the history books. Most Civil War historians now understand how the Southern Historical Society, the so-called "Lee cult," Lost Cause partisans, and other former Confederates wrote – or rewrote – the history of the conflict to their liking. Regardless of political agendas that colored individual commentaries on the causes and consequences of the war, nearly all southerners wondered how their able and devoted soldiers lost the war. In a rapidly reached consensus, they offered a first explanation for Union success: the North prevailed because it enjoyed a preponderance of numbers and resources that simply overwhelmed the men in gray and butternut.

Few northerners felt compelled to challenge the South's dearly held notion. Most had come to embrace the moral superiority of their cause – which they identified as the preservation of the Union, and only secondarily the end of slavery – and that sufficiently explained the inevitability of their success. The 1865 observation of George Bancroft in the *New York Herald* that "Heaven has willed it that the United States shall live" rang true to them. In that light, examining just how they won seemed somehow superfluous, self-serving, or even irrelevant.

While those who remembered the Civil War as moral crusade did not need detailed battle narratives, they did require leaders of character to represent their cause. Thus, two key personalities emerged early on as the singular individuals without whom the North might have lost: President Abraham Lincoln and General Ulysses S. Grant. Merrill D. Peterson's *Lincoln in American Memory* (1994) describes in detail how Americans preserved and enhanced the Great Emancipator's image, but the elevation of Ulysses S. Grant as the greatest northern general of the war deserves greater attention.

Grant's image was not purposefully and conspiratorially constructed as was Lee's postwar evolution into the "marble man." Nonetheless, despite the legacy of a scandal-ridden presidency, portrayals of Grant the General rested first and foremost on his strength of character. Shortly after Grant died in 1885, a Union veteran explained that his former commander deserved his place at the head of "the world's roll of honor of greatest soldier of his day" because his moral character demanded it: "*In trials*, patient and silent; *in battle,* watchful and determined; *in reverses*, active, cheerful, hopeful; in victory, merciful, modest and magnanimous." The veteran mused further, "I ask you, was there not something grand, bordering on the divine influencing the conduct of Grant toward Lee, as they sat together at Appomattox, indicating a sublimity of character and superhuman power that freed him from the common sentiment of the masses?" (Powell 1892: 401–2).

Real substance of military competence underpinned all this sentiment, of course, so Grant and his fellow soldiers, men comfortable with the complex terminology and theories of the art of war, helped to develop a second interpretation for Union success.

General Grant's own memoirs remain essential reading for all serious students of the Civil War. Usually a modest man, Grant painted an interesting picture of his first meeting with his commander-in-chief in 1864, when Lincoln told him:

> he had never professed to be a military man or to know how campaigns should be conducted, and never wanted to interfere in them . . . All he wanted or had ever wanted was some one who would take the responsibility and act, and call on him for all the assistance needed, pledging himself to use all the power of the government in rendering such assistance. (Grant 1885–6, vol. 2: 122)

At that first meeting, Grant recalled, "the President told me he did not want to know what I proposed to do" (vol. 2: 123). Thus, Grant did not immediately communicate his plans for the simultaneous movement of all Union armies. A few weeks later, when the two met again, the president "had of course become acquainted with the fact that a general movement had been ordered all along the line, and seemed to think it a new feature in war" (vol. 2: xxx). After explaining that troops usually assigned to guard captured territory or prevent rebel moves northward could do their jobs just as well by moving forward and engaging southern armies wherever they might be found, Lincoln answered, "Oh, yes! I see that. As we say out West, if a man can't skin he must hold a leg while somebody else does" (vol. 2: 143).

Grant's narrative suggested two things. First, he – not Lincoln – designed the Union's military strategy that finally won the war. Second, he operated with a minimum of civilian interference. Neither point was entirely true, of course. But Grant's brothers-in-arms certainly reinforced that perception. As General Philip Sheridan wrote in his own memoirs, Grant discharged successfully "the stupendous trust committed to his care." Little Phil believed that that when Grant's "military history is analyzed after the lapse of years, it will show . . . he was the steadfast centre about and on which everything else turned" (Sheridan 1888, vol. 2: 204).

Grant's interpretation colored the works of the first generation of university-educated historians such as James Ford Rhodes, John Bach McMaster, Frederick Jackson Turner, and John Codman Ropes, but not to the detriment of Lincoln. The historians admired both the president and the general who set the stage for future American greatness. They also placed greater emphasis on understanding the causes and the consequences of the great conflict rather than the military affairs of the war itself. But beyond a relatively cursory retelling of the military events that had inflicted such deep and painful loss, few showed much interest in analyzing the great campaigns of that war. In interpreting the conflict as the moral crusade that secured the continuation of the republic, that first great generation of professional historians working between 1890 and the eve of World War I did not need to probe deeply into the reasons why the Northern armies won.

Nonetheless, two important works from unlikely authors established the foundation for future discourse on this question. Two American soldier-scholars contended that the study of military history helped army officers master the theory and nature of the art of war and turned to the Civil War rather than the traditional Napoleonic campaigns to teach important lessons. Lieutenant John Bigelow, Jr (1890), emphasized the art of war on the national and theater levels. Major Matthew Forney Steele (1909) paid greater attention to executing campaign plans and fighting battles.

In 1890, Lieutenant Bigelow published *The Principles of Strategy Illustrated Mainly from American Campaigns*. Bigelow argued that mastery of the art of war at the strategic level best prepared a professional soldier to serve his country. "Tactics," all soldiers knew, was "the art of conducting war in the presence of the enemy," but strategy, "the art of conducting it beyond his presence" (Bigelow 1890: 17). Thus, all those entrusted with the preservation of the nation, military and civilian alike, had to master it. He drew upon several campaigns from the Revolutionary War, and upon Shiloh, Jackson's Shenandoah Valley Campaign, Second Bull Run, Chancellorsville, Gettysburg, Vicksburg, Grant's 1864 Overland Campaign, Atlanta, Sherman's March to the Sea, and the naval blockade of southern ports in the Civil War to describe three kinds of strategy.

The first, "strategy proper, or regular strategy," he wrote, "aims at depriving the enemy of his supplies" (Bigelow 1890: 105). All armies needed three things, Bigelow wrote: men, ammunition, and provisions. Citing Washington as the Union's most important base – giving it legitimate military importance beyond its status as a national capital – and Richmond serving the Confederacy in the same manner, Bigelow explained in detail why he considered the conduct of Grant's 1864 Overland and Petersburg campaigns to cut the Confederacy's lines of communications and supply while closely guarding his own lines of operation to be models of soundly executed "regular strategy."

A second kind of strategy, "tactical strategy," he described as overmatching the enemy on the field of battle. He discussed Napoleonic-era military theories about the superiority of adopting interior lines of operation that allowed an army to concentrate its own combat power and the consequent advantage of maneuvering against or attacking fragments of an enemy forced to operate on exterior lines. As an example, Bigelow examined in detail the Battle of Gettysburg. Lee's smaller force fought on exterior lines, and when neither Union flank folded under individual Confederate attacks, Lee assumed they had been strengthened, and massed instead in the center for an assault made famous as "Pickett's Charge." The numerically superior Union army, working on interior lines, shuttled troops from quiet sectors to the crisis point and easily repulsed the attack.

Then Bigelow introduced "political strategy," designed to "embarrass" an enemy's government. This could be done by "impairing, destroying, or blocking the machinery of the enemy's government" to carry the war "home to the enemy's people." It could also be accomplished by "coercing his government, under penalty of dissolution or overthrow," by destroying popular will. The 1864 campaigns of Sherman and Sheridan provided many of Bigelow's examples, but he even considered the effectiveness of the blockade to support his belief that, in modern war, conditions might well exist for the proper consideration of "the people as a military objective" (Bigelow 1890: 105).

As Bigelow developed his own theories about strategy, he also created much of his own specialized military vocabulary. Since the US Army did not write doctrine or define its key terms until World War I, Bigelow could use the term "strategy" and its different forms in his own unique ways. He also limited his concept to those forms that include the application of military force, and he did not extend it to include non-military elements of national power that would, in time, become part of any discussion of "strategy." Over time, as both Bigelow's precise meanings and as the concept itself evolved in the twentieth century to take more complex forms, the term "strategy" became vulnerable to confusion and oversimplification. Still, Bigelow forced Civil War historians to consider objectively and theoretically the strategic level of war fighting and to see the conflict as more than simply a series of battles. Indeed, since Bigelow's time, most Civil War scholars who consider the northern war effort have tended to adopt his approach.

In 1909, Major Matthew Forney Steele, an instructor at the US Army's officer schools at Fort Leavenworth in the early twentieth century, compiled his lectures into *American Campaigns*, the first military history textbook the War Department officially approved. Like Bigelow, Steele resisted the influence of sectional bias. He visited the major battlefields of the war to familiarize himself with the key terrain over which the armies fought. He also applied a critical eye to first-hand accounts and published memoirs to adhere to the canons of historical scholarship of his day. Unlike Bigelow, Steele paid more attention to the tactical level of war fighting.

Steele's most insightful commentary described armies jockeying for advantage as they moved to contact or in the fighting on the battlefield itself. The Union's Vicksburg campaign particularly impressed him, Steele asserting that "there has been no more brilliant series of military operations in American history, and none that conformed more closely to the principles of the military art" (1909, vol. 1: 417) than Grant's operations from Port Gibson to Vicksburg. Indeed, the campaign offered many lessons, "the Union side, full of examples to be followed; on the Confederate side, full of examples to be avoided" (1909, vol. 1: 417). But Steele still could view critically even those he admired. After condemning the poorly designed Confederate attack formations at Shiloh, he then added, "On the Federal side the tactics were, if possible, worse. With no prearranged plan, there was want of cohesion and concert of action between the various units" (1909, vol. 1: 188). Unlike Grant's contemporaries who praised the general for keeping his composure that day, Steele hammered him for his poor use of reserves and cavalry, inattention to security matters, and inability to stop the flight of demoralized troops.

Steele could look beyond the battlefield to give "political strategy" a place in modern war. "It is as much the province of strategy to dishearten the hostile people, – to make them appreciate the hopelessness of continuing the war – to make them crave peace – as it is to defeat and destroy their armies" (Steele 1909, vol. 1: 167). Interestingly, Steele included this comment in his discussion of the impact of the fall of Forts Henry and Donelson on southern morale, and not at a more predictable point in his narrative, such as Sherman's march to the sea. But Steele's greatest legacy to military history rests on his skill at describing armies in contact on the field of battle.

Because they were soldiers writing primarily for other soldiers, the works of Bigelow (1890) and Steele (1909) remain underappreciated. Not long after they wrote, the antiwar and isolationist tendencies in post-World War I America, plus the emergence of economic and social history schools, redirected the attention of most Civil War historians toward the causes and consequences of the war, once more at the expense of military conduct of the war itself. When "drums and trumpets" military history fell out of fashion in the academic world, the best Civil War military history of the 1920s and 1930s written in the United States tended to flow from the pens of non-academicians, many, such as Douglas Southall Freeman, with unabashed southern biases that rarely addressed northern issues.

While American historians remained quiet on the subject during this period, British military officers entered the literary lists. In 1929, J. F. C. Fuller published *The Generalship of Ulysses S. Grant*. Fuller argued a strong case for Grant's special status as the unequivocal savior of the Union, invariably at Lincoln's expense. He accepted at face value many pronouncements in Grant's memoirs. Then, after noting – as Grant had – that Lincoln possessed no military experience, he blasted the president for allowing political opponents to influence both the Union's war aims and the conduct of campaigns. He criticized Lincoln's early reliance on General Winfield Scott, and he considered the president's practice of making generals out of volunteers representing key political and ethnic constituencies to be "a grand-strategical mistake of the first order." The North did not find a way to win until March 1864 when Lincoln made Grant the general-in-chief of the Union army. With a clear plan to win the war, Grant simply went out and did it. But to understand the dimensions of the challenges Grant faced, Fuller insisted that a serious student of the Civil War had to understand northern politics, or "it is not possible justly to appreciate his work" (Fuller 1929: 40, 46).

Fuller did not speak for all his countrymen, or even for all his brother officers. A British artillery officer Alfred H. Burne (1938), in his less well-known but very astute commentary entitled *Lee, Grant, and Sherman*, argued that the two Union generals, in particular, possessed both talent and flaws. Sherman avoided risk too often and would not go in for the kill. Although Burne praised Grant's "broadness of conception and singleness of aim," the general still "failed to exploit situations that by his skill he had created," especially at the North Anna and at the crossing of the James River; his willingness to accept a siege at Petersburg also struck Burne as "unimpressive" (Burne 1938: 201, 202). He found Lee, too, an admirable yet flawed leader, but, as in his consideration of the northern generals, Burne based his critique on their military decisions alone. In so doing, he broke with the notion of commenting on the generals' "moral qualities," leaving that to their own contemporaries. Burne's work suggested that much good history remained to be written by scholars willing to view "givens" with a critical eye.

After World War II, three American writers began to reverse the longstanding trend of writing about Civil War military history from a southern perspective to consider the conflict from a northern point of view. In the process, all three reinstated Lincoln as the primary architect of Union military victory, with Grant now his key swordbearer.

Bruce Catton, a midwesterner fond of boasting of his fellow midwesterners' contributions to victory, considered Lincoln essential to Union success. In the years after World War II, it was not difficult to make comparisons between the conflagration just ended and the Civil War, as Catton (1958) did in *America Goes to War*, when he wrote that "it was all or nothing." "The distinguishing mark of modern war" had become simply "anything goes." Such unique conditions required a special leader, and Lincoln filled the bill. Catton argued that Lincoln ultimately began to shape the war effort with postwar goals in mind. Thus he named Grant as the commander of all Union armies to ensure the South was soundly beaten and hence eager to accept Union terms of peace.

The last book in Allan Nevins' eight-volume *Ordeal of the Union* entitled *The War for the Union* also delved into the special relationship between Lincoln and Grant that led the North to victory. They both came from the Midwest and "had long seemed without heroic traits" (Nevins 1971: 15). Opportunity and hard-won experience had brought them together by 1864. Nevins admired both men, and accorded Grant much of the credit for the Union military strategy that won the war. Still, among the long list of positive character traits Nevins accorded Grant, he included "his strong instinct for obedience to the civil arm. . . . He knew when the President and Congress ordered, he must obey" (1971: 17).

T. Harry Williams, however, did not equivocate. He secured Lincoln's place as the Union's great savior. In *Lincoln and his Generals*, Williams (1952) argued, first and foremost, that Lincoln was the key to Union victory. "Judged by modern standards," Williams wrote, "Lincoln stands out as a great war president, probably the greatest in our history, and a great natural strategist, a better one than any of his generals. He was in actuality as well as in title the commander in chief who, by his larger strategy, did more than Grant or any general to win the war for the Union" (Williams 1952: vii). While Lincoln found a kindred spirit in Grant, the president never gave him free rein to run the war to the degree that the general and his earliest biographers suggested. Williams found Grant's memoirs to be "wide of the truth" and the general quite capable of giving a "characteristic misleading account" of events on occasion (Williams 1952: 305, 308). To those historians who bought into Grant's claim that Lincoln let him run the war unfettered, Williams argued that "What Lincoln really said to Grant in their various interviews was that he did not want to know *the details* of Grant's plan" (Williams 1952: 306, emphasis added). Since Lincoln already knew the grand plan – Grant had told him – and since it conformed to his own, he simply got out of the way and let the general execute it.

In *Lincoln and his Generals*, Williams made a second major contribution to Civil War military history when he inspired scholarly interest in understanding the way in which nineteenth-century armies functioned on their highest levels. He wanted both to restore Lincoln to his preeminent place in the northern war effort and to consider his influence in creating a modern command system for the US Army. Arguing as Catton and others would that the Civil War was the "first of the modern total wars," he noted that the US Army was remarkably unprepared for war on the grand scale and that Lincoln had to function as his own "chief of the general staff or as the joint chiefs of staff" (Williams 1952: 8). If he interfered with the plans of McClellan and other generals, if he gave out commissions to help create more broad-based popular support for the war effort, if he settled arguments between his generals or bore the brunt of popular criticism about their performance, he did so because he had no other options. A modern command system finally emerged in the winter of 1863–4, and Lincoln and the Congress became its primary architects. "The arrangement of commander in chief [Lincoln], general in chief [new Lieutenant General US Grant], and chief of staff [Major General Henry Halleck] gave the United States a modern system of command for a modern war" (Williams 1952: 302). Beyond Catton, Nevins, and Williams, however, few others devoted much attention to how the Union won.

These authors' description of the Civil War as the "first modern war" – especially in light of World War II and the growing threat of the Cold War – focused special attention on what appeared to be substantive changes in Union military strategy in 1864–5 after Grant took command that finally forced the South's capitulation. Historians discussed the issue for over two decades when Russell Weigley (1973) distilled much of the argument into his influential work *The American Way of War*. "Grant accepted a Napoleonic strategy of annihilation as the prescription for victory in a war of popular nationalism" (Weigley 1973: 141). The two main southern armies under Lee and Johnston had to be destroyed, and since that was not likely to happen "in a single battle in the age of rifled firearms," Grant planned to "fight all the time" and give his enemy "no opportunity for deceptive maneuver" (Weigley 1973: 142, 143). The loss of life in doing so must be high, so Grant sought a second, indirect means that might hasten the South's fall. By the time of the Civil War, Weigley argued, "the logistical requirement so armies had become large enough and complex enough that making war against the enemy's resources did begin to appear a tempting prospect" (1973: 146). Sherman did this in Georgia, of course, but he also developed "a deliberate strategy of terror directed against the enemy's people's minds" (1973: 149). The impact of these closely argued ideas convinced many military historians of the Cold War era that the Civil War had become a "total war."

On the eve of the Civil War centennial, to inspire deeper discussion about the roots of northern victory and to encourage consideration of both the military and non-military factors that shape modern wars, David Donald edited *Why the North Won the Civil War* (1960a). Its five essays – authored by Donald, Richard N. Current, T. Harry Williams, David M. Potter, and Norman A. Graebner – presented five very different perspectives on how the Union won.

Richard Current seemingly set himself apart from the others from the start, accepting the southern argument that northern resources proved so overwhelming that its victory was inevitable. Indeed, he suggested that perhaps historians should ask: "How did the South manage to stave off defeat so long? Or perhaps the question ought to be: Why did the South even risk a war in which she was all but beaten before the first shot was fired?" (Current 1960: 15). The South believed that the odds facing the Americans in 1776 and in 1812 were "as bad or worse" than those the Confederacy faced in 1861, Current asserted, and since they defended their homes, the South also held an important psychological edge. But, the South sorely lacked the economic infrastructure to win. "For the North to win, she had only to draw upon her resources as fully and as efficiently as the South drew upon hers; or, rather, the North had to make good use of only a fraction of her economic potential" (Current 1960: 30). The North's vast "productive ability made the Union armies the best fed, the best clothed, the best cared for that the world ever had seen." In short, "God was on the side of the heaviest battalions" (Current 1960: 31, 32).

The four other contributors accepted the notion that Confederate victory was at least possible. T. Harry Williams compared the military leadership of both sides, an intriguing subject since the generals on both sides "were products of the same educational system and the same military background" (Williams 1960: 35). Since most of them had learned about the art of war from West Point Professor Dennis Hart Mahan – a disciple of Swiss military theorist Antoine Henri Jomini – they worked from the same set of premises. Even though Bigelow (1890) and Steele (1909) had plowed this ground before, Williams introduced the wider Civil War community to Jomini's ideas, stressing his emphasis on the superiority of the strategic offensive and his four strategic principles: first, targeting decisive points in a theater of war, maneuvering the bulk of one's own force against them, and protecting one's own communications and threatening those of the enemy; second, maneuvering to engage portions of the enemy with the bulk of one's own force; third, on the field of battle, identifying the key points and overwhelming them with the bulk of one's own force; and fourth, using concentrated forces speedily and simultaneously. Since West Point graduates commanded both armies in 55 of the Civil War's 60 greatest battles and led one of the armies in the other five, Jomini's impact on Civil War generalship could not be doubted.

In Williams' mind, however, Jomini's legacy may have left one discordant note: he wrote as if war fighting was simply a professional military exercise. Perhaps this explained why "Lincoln's first generals did not understand that war and statecraft were parts of the same piece" (Williams 1960: 49). But Grant's common sense allowed him to see beyond mere theory, however, and, Williams concluded, "It was this ability of Grant's to grasp the political nature of modern war that marks him as the first of the great modern generals" (1960: 52). The Grant–Lincoln team proved to be unbeatable, but Lincoln remained the key. As Williams (1960: 53) wrote forthrightly, "Lincoln was an abler and a stronger man than Davis."

Norman Graebner believed that "Even limited European power, thrown effectively into the scale against the North, could have rendered the Southern cause successful" (Graebner 1960: 55). Graebner considered Secretary of State William H. Seward the underappreciated hero of the northern war effort. Using both threats and good-faith promises and an unparalleled understanding of the traditions that underpinned Old World diplomacy, Seward managed to convince England and France early on that extending quick diplomatic recognition to the Confederacy, or even a declared neutrality, could lead to a costly maritime war that might prove financially devastating even in victory. Significantly, Graebner suggested, moral arguments held little sway, noting that "Lincoln's Emancipation Proclamation, although designed, at least partially, to influence European attitudes toward the Union cause, had little effect on European sentiment and none on European actions" (Graebner 1960: 65). The fall of 1862 was the key period for diplomatic efforts, but Northern military success in repulsing Lee from Maryland and Bragg from Kentucky won the diplomatic war for the Union.

David Donald's own essay proclaimed that the Confederacy "died of democracy." The southern soldiers' dislike of regimentation and their insistence that they elect their own officers stemmed from strong beliefs that in any struggle between the rights of the state and personal rights, the latter must win. Even though soldiers on both sides came from similar stock, Donald (1960: 83) noted, "in the Northern armies the respect for soldiers' individual rights never quite led to chaos." While the southern soldier was "a democratic liberty-loving individualist," Union soldiers "became a cog in a vast machine" (Donald 1960: 84), and that machine won the war.

In the volume's final essay, David Potter compared the senior political leadership of both sides. Jefferson Davis "failed in three important ways," Potter argued. He botched his relations with other Confederate leaders and with the people, he misunderstood his job as president, and he did not handle well "his politico-military role as commander-in-chief" (Potter 1960: 101). Lincoln understood what it took to win, including cooperating with military and political leaders he disliked or who disliked him, something Davis simply could not do. In the end, Potter argued, "Lincoln thought of the war as something to be fought, but Davis thought of it as something to be conducted" (Potter 1960: 109).

Military historians have picked away at ideas in one or more of these essays for years, but the first truly sweeping reappraisal that required all Civil War historians to revisit their assumptions appeared in 1983 when Herman Hattaway and Archer Jones published *How the North Won*. Implicitly rejecting Current's "larger battalions" notion from the start, the authors asserted that "Strategy, management, and execution weigh more than superior numbers and resources in dictating the outcome of wars. The weaker side can win: the South almost did" (Hattaway and Jones 1983: ix). Eschewing generations of historical interpretations that cited various turning points, they pointed instead to a factor related to the perceived modernity of Civil War: "an important key to northern success lay not in specific battles as much as in the North's development of superior managerial systems among both soldiers and civilians" (Hattaway and Jones 1983: x).

Clearly, they followed trails that T. Harry Williams (1960) had blazed, but Hattaway and Jones (1983) explicitly took on at least one of Williams' most central points and stood it on its head. They attributed the Union's slow start to victory – at least through 1863 – not merely to conservative Union generals who resented the meddling of radical Republican politicians but to the generals' own resistance against being pushed to do things that their understanding of military theory suggested they should not do. Unlike Williams who had stressed the strength of the strategic offensive, Hattaway and Jones argued that Union generals also embraced a part of contemporary military theory that taught the superiority of the tactical defensive. Unfortunately, many northern leaders – including Lincoln – compared any Union general who lacked aggressiveness on the battlefield to "a dreadful reminiscence of McClellan," whose strong anti-administration political leanings bred such a deep mistrust of his motives that they obscured his legitimate military concerns. Northern political leaders came to believe that "decisive victories eluded the[ir] generals because they did not really want them" (Hattaway and Jones 1983: 489).

As Weigley (1973) and many others had asserted, the Union army's plan for 1864 rested on a strategy of annihilation bent on destroying southern armies. Hattaway and Jones viewed the scheme differently. Grant actually adopted "a strategy of exhaustion." He did not plan primarily "to decimate, much less destroy, the man-power of the enemy's armed forces," but intended first and foremost "to destroy their logistical support" (Hattaway and Jones 1983: 489). Grant decided upon a series of coordinated raids, conducted by large armies of infantry that would prevent the Confederates from concentrating against them and thoroughly destroy the South's war-making resources. While they still considered Grant to rank among the first modern generals, Hattaway and Jones viewed his policy of raids as "a reversion to older methods of warfare made necessary, in part, by the pre-existing hostility of civilians in an essentially national war" (Hattaway and Jones 1983: 694). But those old methods aimed at new targets: railroads and factories. Grant expected to make his most decisive strokes through multiple offensives – a coordination made possible by the 1864 reorganization of the army's senior leadership – in the west. In the east, however, Grant kept Richmond as his goal to allay the potential political and psychological damage that Lee might inflict if he moved north yet again. Grant even accepted a siege at Petersburg to tie Lee down and to help the Union win through Sherman's great successes in the west and deep South.

In the end, "Halleck generals" from the West accomplished what the eastern generals focused on Richmond could not. But the eastern generals were right about something, too. "Much of the civilian-military tension in the Civil War revolved around a civilian demand for direct offensive action and a military insistence that the defense was too strong," Hattaway and Jones noted, and the lengthy casualty lists convinced them that "The soldiers were correct" (Hattaway and Jones 1983: 694).

Certainly the specter of Sherman and Sheridan taking the war to the southern people in 1864 – at Grant's orders, with Lincoln's approval – suggested that the North had won in part because they changed the rules of warfare. The Union had begun to fight, as Catton (1958) had suggested, by breaking those rules to make civilians and their property acceptable targets. But a strategy of exhaustion is implicitly not a strategy of annihilation, and, to Hattaway and Jones (1983), this was not a total war, at least not in a military sense.

As Hattaway and Jones started a reconsideration of some of the most accepted ideas of the historians of the 1960s, other challengers took on other long-enduring notions about how the Union won the war. Mark Grimsley's *The Hard Hand of War* (1995) not only provided valuable insights into the political side of military strategy but also made a most convincing argument against the notion that the Union turned to a "total war" strategy to win. Grimsley first traced northern military strategy through the summer of 1862, when it rested on a conciliatory approach to lure seceded states back into the Union; at that point, McClellan on the Peninsula and other Union generals respected – even guarded – southerners' private property where their armies operated. Beginning in the summer of 1862, shown best through the policies of General John Pope in Virginia, field commanders protected less private property and began confiscating materials with military utility. The Emancipation Proclamation ended the conciliatory policy for good in 1863, but the "hard war" policy as demonstrated by Sherman, Sheridan, and others did not emerge full bloom until 1864–5. "Hard war" possessed two attributes, Grimsley argued. First, actions taken against southern civilians and property were "made expressly in order to demoralize the southern civilians and ruin the Confederate economy, particularly its industries and transportation infrastructure." Second, these operations "involved the allocation of substantial military resources to accomplish the job" (Grimsley 1995: 3).

But Grimsley made a second point clear, as well. Despite the popular mythology and historical discussion about Sherman "making Georgia howl" or Sheridan's crow carrying its rations on its back over a burned-out Shenandoah Valley, the Union's "hard war" policy had limits. Delving deeply into Sherman's campaigns after Atlanta, Grimsley explained the general's policy for dealing with the southern civilians as being "squarely in line with previous Federal policy," with "a directed severity to be visited upon surplus crops and livestock, but not private homes, and against open, avowed secessionists, and not those who were neutral or loyal." This guidance shaped Sherman's official policy as his army marched to the sea and turned north into the Carolinas. As Grimsley asserted, "A prescription for indiscriminate, all annihilating total war this emphatically was not" (Grimsley 1995: 174).

Grimsley's work, painstaking in its detail, provided an interesting counterpoint to Charles Royster's *The Destructive War*, which considered the Civil War's grand "scale of destruction to which the participants committed themselves" (Royster 1991: xi). With different visions of the future driving each side and a willingness to fight to the death for what they believed, the resulting destruction did not particularly surprise Royster. Those who took part in it may have "surprised themselves, but the surprise consisted, in part, of getting what they had asked for" (Royster 1991: xii). No one could have predicted the depths of the hatred, the violence of released passions, the arbitrariness of the actions of enraged human beings. While the war generation showed "a widespread penchant for sentimentalizing violence" for moral inspiration, generals such as William Tecumseh Sherman had to learn that "the God of special providences or the God of impersonal universal laws governed the armies' conflict" and, when they could not control those forces, they "developed an undertone of desperation" resolved only by "throwing themselves unreservedly into war" (Royster 1991: xii).

No discussion of Union military success can be considered complete if discourse remains only on the strategic level, however. Even though "drums and trumpets" history seldom has gained much intellectual credibility in the academic history community, the Civil War's campaigns, battles, tactics, and the individual soldier's experience all provide important insights into understanding other dimensions of military history that illuminate why the North won the Civil War.

While the Civil War generation lived, objective examination of any major battle proved to be nearly impossible. Moreover, until the completion of the publication of official records of the war, research on military topics that satisfied the historical canons of the day remained difficult. Nonetheless, setting the early standard for campaign and battle history was, once more, John Bigelow, who, in 1912, published *The Battle of Chancellorsville*. Relying on after-action reports and drawing critically on the published memoirs of veterans of both armies, Bigelow (1912) produced a model of campaign analysis that still stands up well today. He divided his work into the planning phase and the execution phase. In the first, a strategic overview established the political and military context of the Chancellorsville campaign, described the geography of the theater of war, provided a comparative assessment of military resources available to both sides, and outlined both armies' organization, logistics, and planning. Only then, Bigelow considered in detail the move to contact and the battles of May 1–6, 1863, often down to brigade and regimental level. Bigelow relied on the principles of war, the terrain of the battlefield, and official reports to guide his work. He neither began with nor reinforced the assumption that Chancellorsville was Lee's greatest battle, nor did he find Hooker's performance uniformly poor. And he provided maps – lots of them.

Unfortunately, not many authors – soldiers, scholars, or talented writers without scholarly credentials – followed Bigelow's path until the Civil War centennial of the 1960s spawned new popular interest in the conflict's greatest campaigns and battles. Some studies written during that decade, especially Edwin B. Coddington's magisterial *The Gettysburg Campaign* (1968), still remain the classic scholarly work on a key battle. Like Bigelow, Coddington worked without partisan prejudice; for once, this was not Lee's battle to win or lose. The much maligned General George G. Meade fared well in Coddington's hands. Coddington also gave the new social history a place in Civil War military history by adding the private soldier's voice to the narrative. Delving deep into the previously unused interviews and correspondence of John B. Bachelder, the unofficial "first historian" of Gettysburg, Coddington produced a campaign study that covered the full spectrum of military experience from Lincoln and Davis, through Meade and Lee, to the privates in blue and gray.

The mere fact that it took over a century for the first truly outstanding history of Gettysburg to appear should suggest that, despite the frequent charge that there is nothing new to write about the Civil War, the reality is quite the reverse. Only a few of the war's major campaigns have benefited from the same depth of analysis as Coddington (1968) gave Gettysburg. The decade between 1990 and 2000, however, saw the publication of a number of superb works to indicate that the writing of objective, thorough, and thought-provoking battle studies is not a lost art. Gordon C. Rhea's four volumes on the 1864 Overland campaign – *The Battle of the Wilderness* (1994), along with *The Battles for Spotsylvania Court House and the Road to Yellow Tavern* (1997), *To the North Anna River* (2000), and *Cold Harbor* (2002) – have entirely illuminated the complex and confusing clash of armies as Grant jockeyed for position to take Richmond in May and early June 1864 and Lee deftly deflected each move. Albert Castel's painstakingly detailed *Decision in the West* (1992) explores Sherman's efforts to maneuver three separate Union armies against this key Georgia rail center during that spring and summer, and John Hennessy's masterly *Return to Bull Run* (1993) examines concisely what may really deserve to be considered Lee's greatest campaign. Both works benefit from their authors' keen critical eye and prodigious research efforts that uncovered great masses of previously unused archival materials. The same can be said of Francis Augustin O'Reilly's *The Fredericksburg Campaign* (2002) which forces scholars to consider the complex interaction of military and political events in Virginia in late 1862, effectively eradicating the battle's single enduring and gory image of waves of Union troops breaking against the Confederate earthworks on Marye's Heights. Richard Hatcher and William Garrett Piston (2000) most clearly expanded the traditional battle study in *Wilson's Creek*, infusing their military narrative with threads of social history that examine the demographic and ethnic composition of the two new armies of citizen soldiers that fought over control of southwest Missouri in the summer of 1861.

Informing these battle studies are a number of more specialized works that relate to the experience of combat and shed light on why the North won. The interplay of tactics and technology has fascinated many historians who marveled at the high cost of this war. As Fuller (1929: 65) noted in his study of Grant's generalship, for instance, "The rifle bullet ruled the field, and in each battle its power created some new and unexpected situation," including the increased use of entrenchments, mortars to fire into them, balloons to see over them, and grenades and booby traps to prevent their easy capture. Since northern armies adopted the rifle more generally and earlier than the southern army did, and since northern industry could produce more and better weapons – including breechloading and repeating rifles – Union battlefield success ultimately owed something to this important innovation.

Until the 1980s, the central role of the rifled musket in reshaping Civil War tactics remained unchallenged, when Paddy Griffith, in *Battle Tactics of the Civil War* (1989), denied that this weapon dramatically changed the clash of arms on the battlefield. Most Civil War battles, he noted, took place in wooded and hilly country with restricted fields of fire where the increased range of rifled weapons could not be employed to greatest advantage. Moreover, these new rifles worked best in the hands of skilled men, and most Civil War commanders largely ignored marksmanship and combat training. Citing some interesting (and controversial) statistical evidence, Griffith estimated that, over the course of the entire war, from a sampling of 113 references to range, he found 70 instances (or 62 percent) where the opposing armies opened fire at 100 yards or less, 96 (or 85 percent) at 250 yards or less, and none that engaged each other at 500 yards or more.

Those clashes at close quarters during the Civil War have been called "soldier's battles." The final element to explaining northern success has taken historians into the world of the individual Union soldier, to examine key questions about why he enlisted, why he stayed under arms once he understood the realities of military service, and how he dealt with the trauma of combat until victory blessed his cause.

Both the rise of social history and experience of the Vietnam War have inspired historians to dig more deeply into what motivated Civil War soldiers to fight in America's deadliest war. James M. McPherson's *For Cause and Comrades* (1997) examined three interrelated questions: first, why did Union soldiers enlist? Second, what made them stay the course once they had experienced the sacrifice of a soldier's life? Third, what sustained them in battle? Drawing on thousands of soldiers' letters and diaries, McPherson concluded that many soldiers responded to the call to arms from strong belief in the political ideals – especially the preservation of the Union – for which the war was waged. The strength of their political views continued to sustain them through the war's darkest days, even as they bonded with their brothers-in-arms and marched, camped, fought beside, and buried them.

In addition to the fruits of his prodigious research effort into primary sources, McPherson (1997) built his analysis as well on arguments advanced by Earl J. Hess and Reid Mitchell. In *Liberty, Virtue and Progress*, Hess (1988: 1) argued for "ideology and culture as major – if not key – motivations for any society engaged in a war that is large enough to demand the support of a majority of its citizens." Northerners fought in support of and to protect values that served as "the basis of American identity," including "self-government, democracy, individualism, egalitarianism and self-control." In *The Vacant Chair*, Mitchell (1995: xiii) argues that community, home, and family – and the values they represented – all "shaped the way in which northern soldiers experienced the Civil War." McPherson (1997) also challenges some of the key arguments in *Embattled Courage*, in which Gerald F. Linderman (1987) argues that the trauma of combat created an ever-growing gap between soldiers and civilians, and that, as the war progressed, the ability of political ideology to inspire soldiers waned sharply, and, thus, Union soldiers fought on chiefly for each other. In turn, in *The Union Soldier in Battle*, Hess (1997) – while not discounting that the "touch of elbow" with their comrades helped some northern soldiers to stay the course – argued that family, the moral and social values of their homes and communities, and the public school system that reinforced those values played an even more important role in sustaining Union morale. Religion and political ideology never lost their appeal either, Hess argues, and, collectively, "the variety of supports for morale were impressive" and "they connected the fate of the individual soldier to that of thousands of other soldiers in Union service and to the fate of the nation itself" (Hess 1997: 109).

Weigley (2000) distilled many of the most current ideas about the conduct of the Civil War on the strategic level, tactical level, and personal level in his *A Great Civil War: A Military and Political History, 1861–1865*. As the subtitle suggests, Weigley views political and military affairs as inextricably intertwined in this great conflict about values that continually inspired combatants and civilians alike. In this bitterly fought war, he still attributes to Grant and the Union a strategy of annihilation, but his explanation sounds much like that Hattaway and Jones (1983) used to describe their strategy of exhaustion. When Grant could not maneuver Lee into an untenable position and compel his surrender – as he had done at Vicksburg – he "turned to much grimmer methods of annihilating it through attrition" (Weigley 2000: 328–9) by locking Lee in constant combat and, ultimately, a draining siege.

Additionally, Weigley (2000) examines the conduct of the war from an additional dimension, the operational level. As the concept of "strategy" expanded over time to include national war aims and the use of both military and non-military elements of national power on the grand scale, the US Army began in the 1980s to apply the concept of the operational art to its considerations of military actions within a theater of war that rely upon the coordinated use of multiple forces or the successive actions of a single force. In an innovative way, he linked together seemingly disparate military actions in the spring of 1862 at Shiloh, at Island No. 10 and Memphis, and even the battle at Pea Ridge in Arkansas into a larger western-theater operation to accomplish one key goal in the North's early-war strategy: the control of the Mississippi River and its key tributaries. Similarly, in his consideration of Grant's plans for 1864, Weigley argues that the Union general personally orchestrated the actions of three armies against Lee in Virginia and provided Sherman with three more armies to take on General Joseph E. Johnston in Georgia. "Even though the concept of the operational art remained imperfectly grasped" (Weigley 2000: 329), he argued, Grant's dispositions in each theater forced the southern commanders to contend with far more formidable threats than they had ever done before. The unrelenting pressure on multiple fronts finally broke Confederate military resistance.

After the war, General George Pickett was asked why his famous charge at Gettysburg failed. In answer, he replied, "I think the Union Army had something to do with it" (Pickett 1908: 569). While historians have been slow to give the Union military effort the detailed examination it deserves, the truth behind General Pickett's words cannot be mistaken. Many of the war's major campaigns – most notably Shiloh, Tullahoma, Chickamauga and Chattanooga, and Petersburg – remain understudied. While many Confederate brigade commanders already have become grist for biographers, the careers and contributions of many far more senior and important northern generals – including such leaders as Joseph Hooker, William Rosecrans, and George G. Meade – still remain lightly examined. The entire subject of civil–military relations in the Civil War era, when the requirements of war fighting and the political goals of civilian leaders mesh or clash, offers many opportunities for deeper study. Few scholars have taken up detailed studies of recruiting and officering the northern armies, especially as it occurred on the state and local levels. Thus, the study of the Civil War's military affairs from the Union perspective remains one of the most potentially fruitful areas for future research.

BIBLIOGRAPHY

Bigelow, John, Jr (1890) *The Principles of Strategy Illustrated Mainly from American Campaigns*. New York: Lippincott.

Bigelow, John, Jr (1912) *The Battle of Chancellorsville: A Strategical and Tactical Study*. New Haven, Conn.: Yale University Press.

Burne, Alfred H. (1938) *Lee, Grant, and Sherman: A Study in Leadership in the 1864–65 Campaign*. New York: Charles Scribner's Sons.

Castel, Albert (1992) *Decision in the West: The Atlanta Campaign of 1864*. Lawrence, Kan.: University Press of Kansas.

Catton, Bruce (1958) *America Goes to War*. Middletown, Conn.: Wesleyan University Press.

Coddington, Edwin B. (1968) *The Gettysburg Campaign: A Study in Command*. New York: Charles Scribner's Sons.

Current, Richard N. (1960) "God and the Strongest Battalions," in David Donald (ed.) *Why the North Won the Civil War*. Baton Rouge, La.: Louisiana State University Press.

Donald, David M. (ed.) (1960a) *Why the North Won the Civil War*. Baton Rouge, La.: Louisiana State University Press.

Donald, David M. (1960) "Died of Democracy," in David Donald (ed.) *Why the North Won the Civil War*. Baton Rouge, La.: Louisiana State University Press.

Fuller, J. F. C. (1929) *The Generalship of Ulysses S. Grant*. New York: Dodd Mead.

Graebner, Norman (1960) "Northern Diplomacy and European Neutrality," in David Donald (ed.) *Why the North Won the Civil War*. Baton Rouge, La.: Louisiana State University Press.

Grant, Ulysses S. (1885–6) *The Personal Memoirs of Ulysses S. Grant*, two vols. New York: Charles H. Webster.

Griffith, Paddy (1989) *Battle Tactics of the Civil War*. New Haven, Conn.: Yale University Press.

Grimsley, Mark (1995) *The Hard Hand of War: Union Military Policy toward Southern Civilians, 1861–1865*. New York: Cambridge University Press.

Hatcher, Richard and Piston, William Garrett (2000) *Wilson's Creek: The Second Battle of the Civil War and the Men Who Fought It.* Chapel Hill, NC: University of North Carolina Press.

Hattaway, Herman and Jones, Archer (1983) *How the North Won: A Military History of the Civil War.* Urbana, Ill.: University of Illinois Press.

Hennessy, John J. (1993) *Return to Bull Run: The Campaign and Battle of Second Manassas.* New York: Simon and Schuster.

Hess, Earl J. (1988) *Liberty, Virtue and Progress: Northerners and their War for the Union.* New York: New York University Press.

Hess, Earl J. (1997) *The Union Soldier in Battle: Enduring the Ordeal of Combat.* Lawrence, Kan.: University Press of Kansas.

Linderman, Gerald F. (1987) *Embattled Courage: The Experience of Combat in the American Civil War.* New York: Free Press.

McPherson, James M. (1997) *For Cause and Comrades: Why Men Fought the Civil War.* New York: Oxford University Press.

Mitchell, Reid (1995) *The Vacant Chair: The Northern Soldier Leaves Home.* New York: Oxford University Press.

Nevins, Allan (1971) *Ordeal of the Union.* Volume 8: *The War for the Union: The Organized War to Victory, 1864–1865.* New York: Charles Scribner's Sons.

O'Reilly, Francis Augustin (2002) *The Fredericksburg Campaign: Winter War on the Rappahannock.* Baton Rouge, La.: Louisiana State University Press.

Peterson, Merrill D. (1994) *Lincoln in American Memory.* New York: Oxford.

Pickett, LaSalle Corbell (1908) "My Soldier," *McClure's Magazine.*

Potter, David M. (1960) "Jefferson Davis and the Political Factors in Confederate Defeat," in David Donald (ed.) *Why the North Won the Civil War.* Baton Rouge, La.: Louisiana State University Press.

Powell, William H. (1892) "Ulysses S. Grant," in *War Papers and Reminiscences 1861–1865 Reard Before the Commandery of the State of Missouri, Military Order of the Loyal Legion of the United States,* vol. 1, St Louis, Miss.: Becktold & Co.

Rhea, Gordon C. (1994) *The Battle of the Wilderness, May 5 and 6, 1864.* Baton Rouge, La.: Louisiana State University Press.

Rhea, Gordon C. (1997) *The Battles for Spotsylvania Court House and the Road to Yellow Tavern, May 7–12, 1864.* Baton Rouge, La.: Louisiana State University Press.

Rhea, Gordon C. (2000) *To the North Anna River: Grant and Lee, May 13–25, 1864.* Baton Rouge, La.: Louisiana State University Press.

Rhea, Gordon C. (2002) *Cold Harbor: Grant and Lee, May 26–June 3, 1864.* Baton Rouge, La.: Louisiana State University Press.

Royster, Charles (1991) *The Destructive War: William Tecumseh Sherman, Stonewall Jackson, and the Americans.* New York: Alfred A. Knopf.

Sheridan, Philip H. (1888) *The Personal Memoirs of P.H. Sheridan, General United States Army,* two vols. New York: Charles H. Webster.

Steele, Matthew Forney (1909) *American Campaigns,* two vols. Washington, DC: Byron S. Adams.

Weigley, Russell F. (1973) *The American Way of War: A History of United States Military Strategy and Policy.* New York: Macmillan.

Weigley, Russell F. (2000) *A Great Civil War: A Military and Political History, 1861–1865.* Bloomington, Ind.: Indiana University Press.

Williams, T. Harry (1952) *Lincoln and his Generals.* New York: Alfred A. Knopf.

Williams, T. Harry (1960) "The Military Leadership of North and South," in David Donald (ed.) *Why the North Won the Civil War.* Baton Rouge, La.: Louisiana State University Press.

CHAPTER THIRTEEN

Civil War Military Campaigns: The Confederacy

STEVEN WOODWORTH

Possible starting places for reading about the history of Confederate military campaigns are classic studies of the entire Civil War by Bruce Catton and Shelby Foote. Catton's (1961–5) work is known collectively as the *Centennial History of the Civil War*. Its three volumes are entitled *The Coming Fury, Terrible Swift Sword*, and *Never Call Retreat*. Catton's prose is unsurpassed among Civil War books in its lyric beauty. His account is both informative and evocative. Foote's (1958–74) three-volume work, *The Civil War: A Narrative*, is more than twice as long, much more detailed, and also superbly written. Unlike Catton, Foote did not use footnotes. The current standard one-volume account of the Civil War is James M. McPherson's (1988) *Battle Cry of Freedom*.

The military problem facing the Confederate high command was dictated by the South's war aims, culture, and politics. That the Confederacy's war aims were fundamentally aggressive is often overlooked because, as James M. McPherson (1996) points out in his excellent essay "The War of Southern Aggression," the aggressive phase of Confederate operations was so quickly and easily completed. Between December 20, 1860, and April 12, 1861, Confederate forces – mostly insurgent state militias – seized control of almost every federal fort, post, arsenal, customs house, and other installation in seven southern states, taking control of a vast expanse of territory and effectively dismembering the United States. This first and most successful Confederate military campaign was completely unopposed, quiet, and bloodless up until its very end. The only two federal outposts remaining by the time of Abraham Lincoln's inauguration, March 4, 1861, were Fort Pickens, outside the harbor of Pensacola, Florida, and Fort Sumter, inside the harbor of Charleston, South Carolina. When on April 12, 1861, Confederate forces moved to complete their catalog of seizures by taking Fort Sumter, the Union garrison's steadfast refusal to surrender necessitated the use of military force and a noisy bombardment. Even then success came within 36 hours and again without bloodshed, but the North finally gathered its resolve to resist further encroachments and to attempt to win back what had been lost to the opening Confederate onslaught.

Despite that resolve, Confederate success continued during the next several weeks, not now because the North lacked the will to resist but because it lacked effective means. Confederate forces seized most of the federal installations in four more southern states, necessitating the withdrawal of US forces from the Gosport Navy Yard in Norfolk, Virginia, and the Harpers Ferry arsenal in the western part of that state, and flaunting the new Confederate banner in Alexandria, Virginia, on the banks of the Potomac within sight of the unfinished dome of the United States Capitol. While the North was still struggling to raise its armies and prepare for war, the South had secured almost all of its goals. All that remained for southern leaders to accomplish was, first, to seize the isolated Union coastal strongholds of Fort Pickens in Florida and Fort Monroe in Virginia, second, to seize vital installations in and take control of the wavering border slave states of Maryland, Kentucky, and Missouri, and third, to hold on to what had already been won against any possible northern attempts to retake it.

Since mid-February, Confederate military efforts had been, for the most part, centrally controlled by Jefferson Davis, a West Point-trained former US Army officer, Congressman, secretary of war, and, most recently, Senator from Mississippi. His Mexican War exploits at the head of a regiment of Mississippi volunteers had made him one of the South's foremost military heroes, and the same February 1861 convention that organized the Confederacy selected Davis as its president. Until the end of May, Davis directed operations from the temporary Confederate capital at Montgomery, Alabama. As the aggressive phase of southern operations came to a close, the Confederate government shifted its seat from Montgomery to Richmond, Virginia, largely so that Davis, the commander-in-chief, would be near the most likely scene of fighting when Union forces finally moved to recover what southerners had so quickly and easily seized almost before the first shots were fired.

Southerners were correct in anticipating action in Virginia. This was true for several reasons. The growing strength produced by the North's frenzied mobilization meant that further Confederate gains would be difficult or impossible. Taking the coastal forts and adding Maryland to the Confederacy would have to wait. Action in Missouri would be limited mostly to guerrilla warfare because the South did not have sufficient force available to conquer it. Kentucky was teetering precariously between the two contending sides, its population divided and uncertain. In that condition it had declared its neutrality. Such an unrealistic policy could not last, but neither side dared violate that neutrality and risk driving Kentucky into the arms of the other. The state became thus a buffer between North and South, stretching from the Mississippi to the Appalachians. In short, southern forces could not advance any further at that time, and the only practical avenue for a northern advance was in Virginia. Since the North carried the onus of having to retake what it had lost at the outset, reason dictated that such an advance would shortly occur.

To combat it, Davis established two small field armies in Virginia, both under the command of former US Army officers now in Confederate service. One, under the command of General Joseph E. Johnston, he placed at Harpers Ferry. The other, under Brigadier General P. G. T. Beauregard, he posted at Manassas Junction. Located just 35 miles from Washington, DC, Manassas was a key railroad connection for communications with the Shenandoah Valley. Harpers Ferry, at the lower, or northern, end of the Shenandoah Valley, lay at the junction of the Shenandoah and Potomac rivers, and though indefensible from close up, was nevertheless a highly strategic location.

Both Johnston and Beauregard soon found their forces menaced from a distance by larger US forces, Beauregard's by the army of Union General Irvin McDowell and Johnston's by a northern force under Robert Patterson. Each general reacted in the way that became characteristic of him during the war. Johnston began to bombard Richmond with complaints that he was outnumbered and pleas for orders to retreat – anything that would get him further away from the enemy without having to take public responsibility for retreating. Davis finally obliged him with orders to withdraw from Harpers Ferry, and Johnston lost no time in retreating up the valley (southward) to the vicinity of Winchester at what seemed like a safe distance from the notably unaggressive Patterson.

As T. Harry Williams (1955) explains, Beauregard, by contrast, was full of far-fetched schemes for dramatically winning the war in a fortnight. He fantasized that Johnston might sneak away from Patterson and join him, Beauregard, to deal with McDowell. For this purpose Beauregard imagined that Johnston would bring far more troops than Johnston had ever actually had. Once the combined Confederate forces had crushed McDowell, they would capture Washington, take such vast quantities of Union supplies, wagons, and horses that they could ignore logistics for the remainder of the campaign, and then turn and finish off Patterson. At least half a dozen different points in Beauregard's plan required absolute impossibilities, but that never seemed to faze the flamboyant Creole. He sent a staff officer down to Richmond to press it on Davis, but the president had too firm a grasp on reality to fall for Beauregard's pipe-dreaming. Combining Johnston's and Beauregard's forces at whichever point was threatened was obviously a good idea, but it would have to wait until the Federals revealed their intentions.

That occurred in mid-July when McDowell's army marched from the vicinity of Washington toward Beauregard's position at Manassas Junction. Davis immediately ordered Johnston to join Beauregard and insisted that the move be carried out despite Johnston's expressions of misgiving and Beauregard's frantic dispatches to the effect that it was too late and all was lost.

Johnston's troops did indeed arrive in time, so that when McDowell attacked Beauregard's position, on the south bank of a stream called Bull Run, the Confederates actually had more troops available in the Manassas area than the attacking Federals. Nonetheless, Beauregard and Johnston barely staved off disaster in the July 21 battle. As Williams (1955) explains, Beauregard made plans for an attack on the Union left. Before he could execute them, McDowell skillfully attacked the Confederate left. The Union offensive came close to succeeding, but was finally stopped by the hard fighting of Confederate troops, including a brigade of Virginians under the command of Thomas J. Jackson, who this day won the nickname "Stonewall." The Union retreat became hasty and disorderly, creating a great Confederate victory out of what had been, up until its later stages, a very near-run thing.

Davis arrived on the battlefield as the fighting was ending, and that evening he urged his two generals to follow up the victory with aggressive pursuit. Neither general was eager to take responsibility for such a movement, and Davis issued the order himself before succumbing to doubts and countermanding it. In fact, as Ethan S. Rafuse makes clear in *A Single Grand Victory* (2002), little more could have been accomplished. The Confederate army was badly disorganized and in no condition for further action. Heavy rain began falling during the night after the battle, rendering army movements all but impossible.

Although the southern public rejoiced at the great victory, it was sobered in coming weeks to realize that the battle had not ended the war but only begun it. During those same weeks of late summer and early fall, as I described in *Davis and Lee at War* (Woodworth 1995), the Confederate high command, led by Beauregard, began bickering over the credit for victory and the blame for the inconclusive character for the battle that southerners would come to call Manassas (First Manassas after another battle was fought there the following summer). Beginning in September, Johnston waged his own feud with Jefferson Davis over his rank relative to the Confederacy's other four full generals. Meanwhile, the real war went on, but without much action. Johnston and Beauregard moved their combined force northward until their advanced pickets could see the unfinished dome of the US Capitol in Washington. By late fall, however, it was apparent that the Confederacy would not be able to marshal sufficient forces in Virginia to enable its army there to take the offensive, so as winter came on, the Confederate army fell back to the vicinity of Centreville, near the old Bull Run battlefield. Union forces in Virginia also remained idle that fall.

The next major military campaigns occurred west of the Appalachians. Because of Kentucky neutrality, western action in the summer of 1861 was focused on Missouri, another sharply divided border slave state. There, as ably described by William Garrett Piston and Richard W. Hatcher (2000), Confederate forces on August 10 won a minor victory at Wilson's Creek, near Springfield, in the southwestern part of the state, and subsequently ranged northward into the Missouri Valley. Most of the fighting in Missouri, however, was and would continue to be of the guerrilla variety.

The overall western situation changed drastically in September. As I explain elsewhere (Woodworth 1992), Confederate Major General Leonidas Polk, commanding the defenses of the Mississippi Valley in Tennessee and Arkansas, decided on his own authority and without the approval of Richmond that he needed to violate Kentucky neutrality in order to seize a strong defensive position on bluffs overlooking the Mississippi River at Columbus, Kentucky. Polk, until recently an Episcopal bishop, had been appointed directly from civilian life by his old crony Jefferson Davis. Davis at first countermanded Polk's Kentucky incursion but allowed himself to be talked into acquiescence. Predictably, the move alienated many wavering Kentuckians, so that four-fifths of Bluegrass State residents who served in the war did so in blue uniforms. Even more disastrously, the end of Kentucky neutrality opened the long, vulnerable, and unprepared northern border of Tennessee to Union advance.

Davis responded to the new situation by giving overall command of Confederate forces west of the Appalachians to his friend, former colonel of the Second US Cavalry, Albert Sidney Johnston, now the top-ranking Confederate field commander. Johnston made the best he could of a difficult situation. He kept Polk at Columbus and moved his own small field army forward to Bowling Green, in south-central Kentucky. Between these two forces flowed the Tennessee and Cumberland rivers, vulnerable potential highways of Union advance guarded only by two inadequate forts, Henry on the Tennessee and Donelson on the Cumberland, both just south of the Tennessee line. There was no time to start fortifications in new locations, so Johnston directed Polk to strengthen the existing forts. At the east end of Johnston's thin line was a small force in eastern Kentucky under Brigadier General Felix K. Zollicoffer, lately a Nashville newspaper editor. Davis had made Zollicoffer a general to please Tennessee Whigs who had been hesitant about secession, and he had sent him to east Tennessee to suppress unionists there. With the end of Kentucky neutrality, Johnston ordered Zollicoffer into that state to anchor his right flank.

Johnston's numerical weakness left him little to do but keep up a bold front and hope he would not be attacked. Shortly after the turn of the year, that hope failed. A Union column advanced against Zollicoffer, and he advanced to meet it. On January 19, 1862, the forces clashed at Mill Springs, Kentucky, where Zollicoffer was killed and his army routed. Only supply problems, muddy roads, and wet winter weather kept the Federals from following up by taking east Tennessee.

Less than a month later disaster struck again in even more serious form. In early February Union land and naval forces under Brigadier General Ulysses S. Grant and Flag Officer Andrew H. Foote advanced up the Tennessee River, threatening Fort Henry and thus the back door to Polk's stronghold at Columbus. Only then did Johnston discover that Polk had disobeyed his orders and failed to strengthen the inadequate fort at all. On February 6, after a pitifully ineffective defense, the fort surrendered, opening the Tennessee River to Union incursion all the way to its head of navigation in northern Alabama.

Most of Fort Henry's Confederate garrison escaped before the surrender and joined the garrison of Fort Donelson, a dozen miles away on the Cumberland River. That fort was Grant's next target. If it fell, Union gunboats could range up the Cumberland River all the way to Nashville, cutting off Johnston's Bowling Green force unless it could get south first. To help the fort buy time and assure that the garrison could successfully cut its way out when the Union gunboats could be staved off no longer, Johnston sent additional reinforcements, bolstering the garrison to some 20,000 men.

At first all went well. As ably recounted in Benjamin Franklin Cooling's *Forts Henry and Donelson* (1987), Fort Donelson's artillery beat off a gunboat attack, inflicting severe damage. Judging that enough time had been won, the fort's three top generals, Brigadier Generals John B. Floyd, Gideon J. Pillow, and Simon B. Buckner, in that order of rank, decided the time had come for their breakout. On February 15 their attack surprised Grant's encircling force and thrust it out of the way. With the escape route clear, Pillow and Floyd, two incompetent generals appointed for political reasons, agreed to march their army back into the fort, despite Buckner's objections, and prepare to march away the next morning. They were amazed when Grant immediately encircled them again and even counterattacked, seizing positions that made the further defense of the fort problematic. In council that night, the three Confederate generals decided that the fort and its garrison must be surrendered, but Floyd and Pillow determined to turn the command over to Buckner and try to make their own personal escapes (which both succeeded in doing), leaving most of their soldiers to face captivity.

The loss of the Tennessee and Cumberland rivers and 15,000 irreplaceable troops was a devastating blow to Confederate fortunes west of the Appalachians. Johnston ordered Polk to withdraw from the now hopelessly turned stronghold at Columbus and fall back to join the rest of Johnston's forces concentrating at the vital rail junction town of Corinth, in northeastern Mississippi. There they were met by reinforcements ordered by Jefferson Davis in hopes of helping Johnston to recover from the debacles at the forts. These included Braxton Bragg and a force he had commanded since before the outbreak of hostilities, watching the inactive Federals at Fort Pickens, on the Florida coast. Johnston also summoned a Confederate force in Arkansas under Earl Van Dorn to join him at Corinth but could not wait for Van Dorn's arrival before taking action.

A pause in Union operations gave Johnston the opportunity for a counterstroke. Grant's Union army encamped on the west bank of the Tennessee River at Pittsburg Landing, Tennessee, about 20 miles from Corinth, while waiting for another Union army under Don Carlos Buell to march down from Nashville and join it. For Johnston, the obvious course was to attempt to destroy Grant before Buell arrived. With the latter drawing near, Johnston, on April 2, 1862, could wait no longer and put his army in motion. Muddy roads and an inexperienced army kept him from actually engaging Grant until the morning of Sunday, April 6.

The ensuing battle became known as Shiloh, after a small Methodist meeting house in the midst of it. The most comprehensive history of the battle is Larry J. Daniel's *Shiloh* (1997). Johnston, who held a small numerical advantage, slowly drove the Federals back toward the river. The fighting was ferocious and casualties high. By 2.30 p.m., Johnston himself had become one of them. Wounded in the leg while leading a successful charge on a Union position, he bled to death. Beauregard, recently transferred to the west and serving as Johnston's second-in-command, succeeded to the command and in a controversial decision ordered the attack halted shortly before sundown. As Grady McWhiney (1983) ably argues, there might have been one more chance of driving Grant into the river before Buell arrived in significant numbers. Beauregard did not put it to the test.

By the morning of April 7, Buell's troops were in Grant's lines and the Federals counterattacked. In a day-long battle Beauregard's army fell back across the ground over which it had driven Grant's men the day before. In late afternoon Beauregard disengaged and put his battered force on the road back to Corinth. There he waited for the new Union commander, Henry W. Halleck, to make a move. Halleck's movement was as slow and as inexorable as a glacier. Having combined the Union armies of Grant, Buell, and John Pope to a total force of over 100,000 men, Halleck took six weeks to advance from Pittsburg Landing to Corinth. Beauregard, though reinforced now by Van Dorn, was far too weak to oppose Halleck's advance directly, and he made no attempt to take the initiative from him by turning movements or other operations. During the night of May 29–30 Beauregard evacuated Corinth and fell back to Tupelo, Mississippi, 50 miles further south. Thereafter an extended lull ensued, and Beauregard went on sick leave, being replaced by Braxton Bragg.

In the east, both Davis and his top eastern general, Joseph E. Johnston, had become convinced by March 1862 that the army needed to fall back from its positions around Centreville, Virginia, to the line of the Rappahannock River. This would afford a more defensible position and it would also place the Confederacy's main Virginia army closer to Richmond, in case the Yankees tried a water-borne turning movement via Chesapeake Bay against the eastern approaches to the Confederate capital. Beyond that agreement, however, Johnston and Davis differed vastly in their ideas. Davis wanted Johnston to prepare for a possible retreat to the Rappahannock by sending his sick and excess baggage and supplies to the rear. Johnston, on the other hand, wanted to get away from Centreville as fast as he could. On March 9, 1862, without informing Davis and before the president real-ized what was happening, Johnston hastened his army to the rear, burning vast amounts of supplies and baggage that he thought might retard his flight.

Johnston's haste was unnecessary, but the wisdom of relocating the army closer to Richmond became apparent when later that month the Union army of the Potomac, now commanded by Major General George B. McClellan, began landing at Fort Monroe, on the shores of Chesapeake Bay east of Richmond. As soon as McClellan's movement and its danger became apparent in Richmond, Davis ordered Johnston and the bulk of his army to confront McClellan as he began to advance up the peninsula between the James and York rivers toward the Confederate capital.

While Johnston was passing through Richmond on his way to the peninsula he met with Davis and his advisors, including the Secretary of War, George W. Randolph, and recently appointed Confederate General-in-Chief Robert E. Lee. Johnston, true to form, counseled retreat, advising that the army withdraw to the very outskirts of Richmond and there make a great attempt to defeat McClellan. Lee and Randolph on the other hand wanted to fight for every inch of the peninsula, holding on to valuable assets like Norfolk's Gosport Navy Yard and gaining time to make the large concentration of troops that all agreed would be needed. Davis sided with Lee and Randolph, ordering Johnston to take his army to the peninsula and hold as much ground as he could as long as he could.

Johnston went, and his army confronted McClellan's at Yorktown, scene of the Revolutionary War battle. The Peninsula Campaign that followed is recounted in Stephen Sears' *To the Gates of Richmond* (1996). McClellan's own slowness delayed the Union advance more than anything Johnston did, for the latter was determined to retreat, without fighting, whenever McClellan should advance in earnest. Thus Johnston planned to force his own scheme on the Richmond authorities, notwith-standing his orders to the contrary. When McClellan had siege batteries ready to bombard Johnston's Yorktown lines, the Confederate general hastily retreated, once again abandoning much valuable material. McClellan pursued, slowly, and the pattern was repeated until by May 31, 1862, the Union army was indeed on the outskirts of the Confederate capital. Under heavy pressure from Davis, Johnston finally initiated a battle on that day, attempting to crush the left wing of the Union army. The battle (which Confederates called Seven Pines) was very poorly coor-dinated on the southern side and produced no significant results except that Johnston was wounded and put out of action. Davis replaced him with Lee, who began preparing a major offensive against McClellan.

While Johnston was falling back before McClellan that spring, a smaller Confed-erate force in Virginia's Shenandoah Valley had won spectacular success under the command of Major General Thomas J. "Stonewall" Jackson. As ably recounted by Robert G. Tanner (1996), Jackson was charged with the task of keeping Union forces in the Shenandoah area from detaching troops to reinforce McClellan. On March 23, 1862, he attacked a superior Union force at Kernstown. Soundly de-feated, Jackson nevertheless accomplished his purpose by persuading Union com-manders not to detach troops from the area. Then, reinforced by another division under Major General Richard S. Ewell, Jackson, on April 29, 1862, launched a fast-moving campaign that dazzled the nation and led to the diversion of even more Union troops from McClellan's army. In a little over a month Jackson's troops marched some 400 miles and fought and won five battles. The three small Union armies defeated by Jackson had a combined troop strength far greater than his own, but so skillful was his generalship that his force outnumbered the enemy on each of the battlefields of what became known as the Valley Campaign.

Back in the Virginia tidewater region, Lee prepared to launch his own great offensive against McClellan. For that purpose he summoned Jackson to bring his force east from the Shenandoah and fall on McClellan's vulnerable right flank and the supply line that it protected. With the addition of Jackson's force, Lee's numbers would almost equal McClellan's. The campaign that followed marked the emergence of Robert E. Lee as a great field commander. Lee has been the subject of many books. Some of the most famous are by Douglas Southall Freeman, a four-volume study entitled *R. E. Lee: A Biography* (1934–6), and a three-volume study of command in Lee's army of northern Virginia entitled *Lee's Lieutenants* (1943–4). Freeman's books are detailed and well written, in many ways masterpieces of history. However, he tended to be rather adulatory toward Lee. A more modern and balanced view of Lee is to be found in Emory Thomas's *Robert E. Lee* (1994).

When on June 26, Lee began his attack, the result was dismal. At Mechanicsville, an eastern suburb of Richmond on the north bank of the Chickahominy River, Lee's forces suffered a bloody repulse while Jackson failed to get into the flanking position Lee had intended for him. Still the threat alone was enough to prompt McClellan to cast loose of his old supply line (the one Lee was trying to cut) and to retreat southeastward toward Harrison's Landing on the James River, where he could be supplied by Union shipping. The conflict over the next five days became one in which Lee strove to cut off and destroy McClellan's retreating army. Poor staff work and other mistakes on the Confederate side – along with very tough fighting by Union soldiers – combined to prevent Lee from achieving his goal. The week of battles culminated in an ill-advised Confederate attack at Malvern Hill. Union artillery mowed down thousands of southern troops in one of Lee's worst days of the war. Overall, the Seven Days' Battles, as they came to be called, had seen bloodshed on a scale previously unimagined in the nation's history, and Lee's army had suffered higher casualties than McClellan's. Nonetheless, Richmond was saved and the Union army "driven" many miles away. As Gary W. Gallagher (1997) points out in *The Confederate War*, southern morale soared.

The two armies watched each other for the next several weeks on the peninsula. Then Richmond was threatened from the north by another Union army under the command of Major General John Pope. Lee dispatched Jackson to "suppress" (Lee's word) Pope. Jackson checked Pope's advance at the battle of Cedar Mountain, August 9, 1862. Perceiving that Union authorities were rapidly shifting troops from McClellan's army to Pope's, Lee moved aggressively to destroy Pope before the transfer could be completed. As on the eve of the Seven Days' Battles, Jefferson Davis expressed reservations about Lee's propensity to gamble, but acquiesced in the general's plan out of personal confidence in him. Leaving only a small force to cover Richmond on the east, Lee hurried to join Jackson. With the combined Confederate force he attempted to trap Pope along the Rappahannock, but the latter proved too wily. Then Lee sent Jackson on a turning movement deep in the Union rear. When Pope turned to face this new threat and attacked Jackson near the old Manassas battlefield, Lee moved up on the flank of the hapless Union general's army and dealt it a crushing defeat in the Second Battle of Manassas, August 28–30, 1862.

"The present seems to be the most propitious time since the commencement of the war," Lee wrote to Davis three days later, "for the Confederate Army to enter Maryland" (US War Department 1881–1901). His army was worn, bloodied, and tired, he admitted, and there was "much risk." Still, he assured the president, "I do not consider success impossible." For a gamble of this magnitude, Davis preferred to join Lee in person, but when he expressed that intention in dispatches, Lee fired back several missives urging him not to come (for reasons of safety) and even dispatched a staff officer to meet Davis and persuade him to turn back. The latter precaution was unnecessary, as the president took Lee's advice and stayed in Richmond. This would be Lee's campaign.

Lee's army marched north and crossed the Potomac northwest of Washington. Then Lee turned northwest and passed through Frederick, Maryland, and over South Mountain, an extension of the Blue Ridge north of the Potomac. Things did not, however, develop as Lee had hoped. The people of western Maryland were Union-loyal and not, as the Confederates had imagined, incipient rebels awaiting only the arrival of a southern army to rise up and throw off Lincoln's government.

Of more immediate consequence, the Union garrison at Harpers Ferry, about 10,000 men, stayed where it was. Lee had expected that when his army reached a position west of South Mountain and north of the Potomac, the Harpers Ferry garrison would evacuate rather than face possible capture. Instead, the bluecoats stayed put, and by doing so, kept Lee from implementing his plan to establish a supply line through the Shenandoah Valley. His bluff called, Lee moved to surround and capture the stubborn Yankees. Doing so would take time and would mean dangerously dividing his army in enemy country, but Lee had heard that McClellan was back in command of Union forces in Washington, substituting for the disgraced Pope, and Lee was confident that McClellan would move as slowly in Maryland as he had on the Virginia peninsula. In this too, Lee was disappointed, as political pressure forced McClellan to move with unwonted speed. Worse still, when on September 13 the Union army of the Potomac camped at Frederick, one day behind Lee's men, Union troops found a copy of Lee's entire plan for capturing Harpers Ferry, and McClellan had complete information as to where he could find and destroy the scattered pieces of Lee's army.

Fortunately for Lee, McClellan, even under political pressure and with all the information he needed to beat Lee in detail, was still McClellan, and he moved slowly enough to give Lee time to recover. In a further piece of Confederate good fortune, the Union commander at Harpers Ferry surrendered almost the moment Lee's forces appeared in the neighborhood, giving additional help to Lee's efforts to reunite his forces before facing McClellan. By September 16 Lee's army was beginning to come together, and he turned at bay on the west bank of Antietam Creek near the town of Sharpsburg, Maryland. Lee's audacity was at its height, and many historians since have criticized him for offering battle with his back to the Potomac and in front of him an army that outnumbered him more than two to one. Lee, however, hoped that the Federals would exhaust themselves in attacks, as at Second Manassas, and then in imitation of his successful tactics at that battle he would launch a devastating counterattack.

McClellan did attack on September 17. The resulting battle is best described in Sears's *Landscape Turned Red* (1983). True to form McClellan launched his attack in piecemeal fashion, getting scarcely 60 percent of his troops into the fight. Still, the exhaustion of Lee's army and the fierce determination of the Union foot soldiers nearly finished him that day. First on Lee's left, then in the center, and finally on the left, Confederate troops came within a hair's breadth of utter defeat. In the last case, only the timely arrival of Lee's last remaining troops, Major General A. P. Hill's division, hurrying up from Harpers Ferry, saved the day. By nightfall the Civil War had seen its bloodiest day – a battle the Confederates called Sharpsburg and the Federals Antietam. One-third of Lee's men were down. Had McClellan coordinated his attacks or thrown in even half his reserves, it is hard to imagine how Lee could have escaped complete annihilation.

Yet the following morning, Lee and his army were still there, having passed up the opportunity of making off under cover of darkness. Not only was Lee daring McClellan to renew his assault, but also he was looking for ways to go over to the offensive himself. Neither occurred. McClellan's nerve and Lee's army were both spent. During the night of September 18–19, Lee withdrew across the Potomac, still hoping to find a way to turn McClellan and get back into Maryland. Within a few days, however, Lee had realized that his army could do no more and pulled back to the south. McClellan did not pursue, and a long pause ensued in the eastern theater.

Meanwhile, action had flared again in the west. In mid-summer the main Confederate army in the west, commanded by General Braxton Bragg, was encamped at Tupelo, Mississippi, facing a much larger Union army 50 miles north at Corinth. A small Confederate force under Major General Edmund Kirby Smith held east Tennessee against dual Union threats, one from a small column advancing southward from Cumberland Gap, on the Tennessee–Kentucky line, and the other an army moving eastward across northern Alabama from the Union base at Corinth. In response to Smith's pleas for help, Bragg arranged to shift the bulk of his army to Chattanooga, thus securing that key gateway to east Tennessee before joining Kirby Smith in turning the Union army in northern Alabama. Bragg's infantry moved by rail via Mobile (the most extensive and innovative strategic military use of rail transport to that date), while his artillery and supply trains crossed northern Alabama at a safe distance from the Union army. The operation began on July 21.

The movement held great promise, but several factors marred it from the start. First, to occupy the Union forces remaining in Mississippi, Bragg left a divided command structure, one small army under Major General Sterling Price confronting Corinth, another under Major General Earl Van Dorn guarding Vicksburg. Second, Davis did not allow Bragg to purge his army of incompetent senior officers, forcing him instead to keep as commanders of corps and divisions men who were both unfit and all but impossible to work with, chief among them the wretched Leonidas Polk. Finally, Davis declined to place Kirby Smith under Bragg's command. Though the latter was superior in rank, he could not command Smith until the two forces actually combined in the same place, something Smith was careful to avoid. Thus the divided command structure in Mississippi was echoed in Tennessee and, shortly, in Kentucky as well.

It was to Kentucky that Bragg's and Kirby Smith's forces were bound, turning (and thus forcing the retreat of) the Union army under Major General Don Carlos

Buell in northern Alabama. As Bragg thrust into middle Tennessee and Buell fell back toward Nashville, Bragg wished to fight Buell with his and Smith's combined forces, but Smith refused, kept clear of Bragg's army and thus his command, and veered northward into Kentucky, contrary to Bragg's wishes. Bragg had to follow him into the state, keeping his own army between Buell's Federals and the head-strong Kirby Smith's smaller force. Bragg succeeded in reaching a position at Munfordville, Kentucky, between Buell and the Union base at Louisville but then found himself in a strange predicament. Though he was on Buell's supply line, Buell was also on his. The Union general had a larger stock of supplies on hand and could therefore out-wait Bragg. Kirby Smith steadfastly refused to cooperate, and without him Bragg dared not take the offensive against Buell. Reluctantly, Bragg withdrew to the east, toward Kentucky's Bluegrass region, where Kirby Smith was ensconced.

With that, the momentum of the campaign shifted. Though Kirby Smith could no longer avoid coming under Bragg's command, even their united forces were by this time insufficient to deal with Buell, now once again in contact with his Louisville base and resupplied as well as massively reinforced. Worst of all, contrary to Confederate hopes, Kentuckians did not rise en masse to throw off their supposed Yankee oppressors. The Confederates brought 20,000 extra rifles to Kentucky in order to arm new recruits, but few recruits came forward and the rifles stayed in their crates. As a last desperate expedient, Bragg hoped to install a pro-Confederate governor in the state capital at Frankfort and then use him to invoke the Confederacy's conscription law to force Kentuckians into the rebel ranks. This too failed as Buell advanced before the scheme could be fully implemented. Bragg tried to meet the Union advance but was hamstrung by the repeated disobedience of his generals, particularly Polk. Fighting finally flared up near Perryville, Kentucky, south of Lexington. In a confused battle on October 8, 1862, the Confederates won some local successes, but not enough to offset the Union advantage in numbers. Bragg at last realized that he had no choice but to retreat out of Kentucky. Buell did not pursue.

Meanwhile, back in Mississippi, the two officers Bragg had left in that state, Sterling Price and Earl Van Dorn, squabbled and failed to cooperate until it was too late for them to achieve significant success or to prevent reinforcements departing from their front to bolster the Union army Bragg had to face in Kentucky. Finally, as Bragg's unfortunate campaign was nearing its culmination, Van Dorn and Price combined their forces, and the former, as senior, took command. On October 2 and 3, 1862, Van Dorn led the combined force in a bloody and disastrous attack on the Union garrison at Corinth, Mississippi. Thereafter, his battered army narrowly escaped Union pursuit and withdrew into the interior of Mississippi.

As I discuss in *Jefferson Davis and His Generals* (Woodworth 1990), Jefferson Davis made adjustments to the Confederate command system in the fall of 1862. No change was needed in Virginia, where Lee had all but worked miracles in shifting the scene of fighting from the Chickahominy to the Potomac and making fools of two Union generals. The west was a different case. Davis quickly dispatched John C. Pemberton from his previous assignment commanding idle South Carolina forts to take overall command of Price and Van Dorn's forces in Mississippi. In November, Joseph E. Johnston reported back for duty, having recovered from the wounds he received at Seven Pines. Davis assigned him to a theater command extending from the Appalachians to the Mississippi and comprising the armies of

Bragg, now based in Murfreesboro, Tennessee, 33 miles southeast of Nashville, and Pemberton in Mississippi, guarding the northern approaches to Vicksburg and Jackson. Johnston immediately objected to the assignment. He wanted Lee's job in Virginia, and he complained that it was vain to try to supervise army commanders and that in any case Bragg and Pemberton were too far apart to work together. Rather, Johnston argued, Pemberton should be combined with the trans-Mississippi forces now commanded by Theophilus Holmes. Davis insisted, however, and Johnston had little choice but to go through the motions of obedience.

The Federals quickly put the new command arrangement to the test. Later in that same month of November 1862, a Union column under Ulysses S. Grant advanced overland toward Jackson, Mississippi. Shortly thereafter another column under William T. Sherman, Grant's subordinate, moved down the Mississippi by steamboat to attack Vicksburg. Davis urged Johnston to reinforce Pemberton with troops from Bragg's army. Johnston said there was no time and urged that troops be taken from Holmes. Davis wrote to Holmes for troops, but Holmes, though not seriously threatened, refused to send any. Davis did nothing to compel him and finally decided to make a personal inspection tour of the west. Passing through Murfreesboro, Davis, over the protests of Bragg and Johnston, ordered one-quarter of Bragg's infantry, 10,000 men, to set out at once for Pemberton.

In the event Pemberton did not need them, and, as Johnston had predicted, they would have been too late to have influenced the outcome in Mississippi. Grant's army had to retreat when the formerly hapless Van Dorn, now leading Pemberton cavalry, got behind it and cut its supply lines. Sherman's force reached Vicksburg, but due to local geography could approach the river bluff town only by a single, narrow, and absolutely impregnable avenue. The bluecoats suffered a bloody repulse on December 29, 1862.

If Pemberton did not need the extra 10,000 men, Bragg certainly missed them. No sooner had they departed than news of their move appeared in the newspapers and found its way to the new Union commander in Nashville (Buell's replacement), Major General William S. Rosecrans, who learned of it and advanced to attack Bragg. By the evening of December 30, the two armies faced each other just north of Murfreesboro. As explained by James Lee McDonough in *Stones River* (1980), each general's plan for the morrow featured an attack on the other's right flank. On the morning of December 31, however, Bragg's men were afoot earlier and struck Rosecrans a stunning blow that folded the right wing of his army back like the blade of a jackknife about to close. There, however, his success ended, for he lacked reserves to make his success complete. Things might have been different if he had had those extra 10,000 men Davis had taken from him, but they were long gone on the road to Mississippi. The Union line stiffened and held. The next day, January 1, 1863, the two armies eyed each other warily. The day after that, Union forces occupied an important hill on the Confederate right, and Bragg tried but failed to retake it. That night, January 2, 1863, Bragg's generals insistently urged him to retreat, and he finally acquiesced, falling back another 44 miles southeast to Tullahoma, Tennessee.

While the December campaigns developed in Mississippi and Tennessee, the Virginia armies finally stirred again. Major General Ambrose Burnside, who had replaced the lethargic McClellan, attempted to turn Lee's new position south of the Rappahannock by going around his right via the town of Fredericksburg. Burnside moved too slowly, and Lee got into position to block him on the high ground south of town. The resulting battle is discussed in Gallagher's *The Fredericksburg Campaign* (1995). On December 13, 1862, Burnside launched his army on a series of foolish attacks that gave Lee an easy victory with only 5,309 casualties to Burnside's 12,653. The armies faced each other the following day, and the next night Burnside withdrew.

Winter brought an end to most active campaigning. Out along the Mississippi, Grant established his army with a secure base on the west bank of the river just above Vicksburg, determined to take the town and trying one means after another of gaining an advantageous approach to it. In Virginia, Lee and Jackson contemplated a campaign deep into Pennsylvania, studying maps and waiting for spring to restore roads and draft animals to suitable conditions.

Grant struck first. He marched his army down the west bank while a cooperating naval squadron ran the Vicksburg batteries. Then with naval support Grant crossed to the east bank below Vicksburg. In a daring campaign Grant made skillful use of terrain, the rapid marching of his troops, and a clever diversionary cavalry raid to completely out-general John C. Pemberton. Davis dispatched Johnston to Mississippi to take personal command there, but Johnston was equally outclassed by Grant, who seized and neutralized Jackson, Mississippi, before turning and defeating Pemberton at the battle of Champion's Hill and then driving toward Vicksburg from the rear, trapping Pemberton and some 30,000 Confederate troops. Pemberton and his army might have escaped the trap save that he interpreted a telegram from Davis as an order to hold Vicksburg at all costs. Throughout the six weeks that followed, Davis hastened reinforcements to Johnston and tried to persuade him to take some action to lift the siege or at least save the garrison. All was to no avail. Johnston did nothing, and Pemberton surrendered Vicksburg and its garrison on July 4, 1863. The subsidiary Confederate Mississippi River stronghold at Port Hudson, Louisiana, fell five days later. The Confederacy had lost irreplaceable manpower and its last hold on the Mississippi River.

Meanwhile back east, Lee's contemplated offensive had to wait when the Army of the Potomac, now commanded by Joseph Hooker, attacked first. The battle of Chancellorsville, May 1–4, 1863, is dealt with by Ernest B. Furgurson in *Chancellorsville 1863* (1992). There Lee and Jackson combined for their most brilliant piece of tactical wizardry, sending a thoroughly whipped Hooker back across the Rapidan River with 17,287 casualties. Lee had also suffered serious losses – 12,764 killed, wounded, and missing – including Stonewall Jackson himself, mortally wounded in America's most famous friendly-fire incident. This incident is analyzed by Robert K. Krick in *The Smoothbore Volley that Doomed the Confederacy* (2002).

Before the month was out, however, Lee gained Davis' permission to launch his long-contemplated northern offensive. The classic study of the campaign that followed is Edwin B. Coddington's *The Gettysburg Campaign* (1968). On June 3 Lee's army began pulling out of its camps south of the Rapidan and Rappahannock rivers and marching westward on the first leg of its journey. Over the next four weeks Lee's troops marched over the Blue Ridge, then up the west side of that range and across the Potomac into Maryland and then Pennsylvania. As the army of northern Virginia swung northeastward up the Cumberland Valley, it seriously threatened the Pennsylvania capital at Harrisburg and sparked consternation in

Philadelphia and Baltimore. Hooker's army of the Potomac pursued Lee, but the Confederate general did not realize how close the enemy was until a scout brought him word on June 28. The reason for his ignorance was that normally reliable cavalry leader J. E. B. Stuart had made an ill-advised attempt to ride his cavalry all the way around the army of the Potomac and in so doing had effectively ridden himself right out of the campaign. Without a supply of good information from Stuart, Lee was handicapped.

Learning on June 28 of the proximity of northern forces, Lee ordered his army to concentrate at Cashtown, Pennsylvania, just east of South Mountain. Three days later, July 1, Major General Henry Heth, on a foray to plunder shoes, collided with elements of the army of the Potomac at Gettysburg, 8 miles east of Cashtown. Lee's other units, already approaching the area, converged quickly on Gettysburg and soundly defeated two of the army of the Potomac's seven corps. The next day the rest of the army of the Potomac, now commanded by George G. Meade, came up and joined the remnants of the first day's fight on high ground south of town. Lee determined to attack them. Striving for a repetition of his victory at Chancellorsville, Lee dispatched a strong flanking column under James Longstreet to roll up the Union left. Amid some of the most intense fighting of the war, the effort failed. Still seeking the elusive decisive victory, Lee struck at the Union center on July 3, in an attack spearheaded by his only remaining fresh division, that of George E. Pickett. It was a bloody failure. The next day, July 4, while Pemberton was surrendering to Grant 1,000 miles to the southwest, the defeated Lee began his retreat.

Yet these two debacles at opposite ends of the Confederacy did not complete the summer's catalog of southern woes. The three subsequent campaigns in Tennessee – Tullahoma, Chickamauga, and Chattanooga – are discussed in my *Six Armies in Tennessee* (Woodworth 1998). Just over halfway from Gettysburg to Vicksburg, and almost on a direct line between them, lay Tullahoma, Tennessee, where Braxton Bragg's Army of Tennessee had wintered after the defeat at Murfreesboro. After a six-month hiatus, the Union army of the Cumberland, still commanded by Rosecrans, advanced against Bragg. Rosecrans' campaign was skillful and well coordinated. Bragg and his top generals, Leonidas Polk and William J. Hardee, were scarcely on speaking terms and incapable of making a coordinated response. The result was that in nine days, concluding July 4, 1863, Rosecrans maneuvered Bragg almost completely out of Tennessee. Bragg retreated to Chattanooga, near the Georgia line, and Rosecrans paused just north of the Cumberland Mountains, preparing his next advance.

This was one defeat that Confederate authorities believed they could retrieve, and so Davis directed the transfer of Longstreet and two divisions from Lee and substantial forces from Johnston in Mississippi to reinforce Bragg and help win back the summer's losses in Tennessee. They arrived just in time to help meet Rosecrans' next advance but not before the skillful Union general had forced Bragg out of Chattanooga and all the way back to La Fayette, Georgia, 28 miles to the south. Reinforced, Bragg turned at bay and nearly caught Rosecrans' army spread out in headlong pursuit. Only the repeated disobedience of Bragg's subordinates allowed Rosecrans to escape and reunite his forces. Bragg then attempted to cut Rosecrans off from Chattanooga, and the result was the battle of Chickamauga, September

18–20, 1863. The Confederates failed to secure a position between Rosecrans and Chattanooga, but a midday assault on the last day of the battle succeeded in crushing Rosecrans' center and right, sending him into Chattanooga in full retreat.

Bragg took most of the high ground around Chattanooga, commanding the viable supply routes into the town, but he continued to struggle with his fractious subordinates. When Union command at Chattanooga passed to Ulysses S. Grant, the Confederate position began to deteriorate rapidly. Grant pushed aside Confederate forces and opened a supply line. More bickering in the Confederate high command prevented Bragg from closing it. Bragg then made a bid to clear the Federals out of east Tennessee, paving the way for turning Grant by moving the army of Tennessee through that region. This too failed, as Longstreet, who was tasked with the job, proved slow and ineffective. While Longstreet dithered in front of Knoxville, Grant, heavily reinforced, completed his preparations and attacked Bragg at Chattanooga. The Battle of Chattanooga, November 23–25, 1863, was a resounding defeat for Bragg, culminating in the rout of his troops at Missionary Ridge. The army of Tennessee fell back to Dalton, Georgia, and Bragg was relieved from command at his own request. Longstreet's detachment returned to Lee via east Tennessee – which remained securely in Union hands.

The remainder of 1863 saw inconsequential maneuvering in Mississippi and Virginia. In the spring of 1864 Grant became overall Union commander and the North entertained high hopes of an end-the-war offensive. Yet Confederate morale was also high due to several minor successes that nevertheless loomed large at the time. Confederate troops defeated small Union expeditions at Olustee, Florida, on February 20, and Mansfield, Louisiana, on April 8. The Confederacy's two main forces awaited the advances of Grant and his lieutenants – Lee's army of northern Virginia defended Richmond, and the army of Tennessee, now commanded by Joseph E. Johnston, covered Atlanta.

Those advances, both in Virginia and Georgia, began on May 4, 1864. In Virginia, Meade's army of the Potomac, accompanied and directed by Grant, crossed the Rapidan that day and ran into Lee's army the next. The resulting Battle of the Wilderness was fought in the same dense thickets in which the Battle of Chancellorsville had been fought almost exactly a year before. The best account of the battle is by Gordon C. Rhea (1994). The outcome was similar in some ways – high casualties for both sides and even a Confederate friendly-fire incident that left Longstreet badly, but not mortally, wounded. It differed in that, unlike Hooker the year before, Grant was anything but cowed and continued his advance. Henceforth in Virginia, battles would no longer make a pretense of being decisive encounters but were merely incidents along Grant's road to Richmond. Though Confederate authorities quickly made good Lee's heavy losses in manpower, the Confederate general found that he could bleed Grant's army but not stop it. By June 18 the armies in Virginia had fought the bloody Battles of Spotsylvania and Cold Harbor and the initial assaults at Petersburg, and Grant had settled down for a joint siege of Richmond and its vital transportation link, Petersburg. These operations are ably handled by Gordon C. Rhea (1997, 2000, 2002). A shorter but highly insightful treatment of the campaign is to be found in Mark Grimsley's *And Keep Moving On* (2002).

The campaign in Georgia has been the topic of three recent outstanding books: Albert Castel's *Decision in the West* (1992); Richard M. McMurry's *Atlanta 1864*

(2000); and Stephen Davis' *Atlanta Will Fall* (2000). As these works explain, the fighting in Georgia was different from that in Virginia, largely because neither commander there was as pugnacious as Grant and Lee. With the exception of the doomed June 27 assault on Kennesaw Mountain, Sherman maneuvered instead of attacking. Johnston responded to Sherman's skillful maneuvers by retreating rather than fighting to hold ground. Constant intense skirmishing made the campaign like "a big Indian war" in Sherman's words, but that "war" was moving steadily closer to Atlanta and at the same time uncovering valuable Confederate industrial assets in northern Alabama. By July 17 when Davis replaced Johnston with General John B. Hood, the Confederate army had retreated all the way to the outskirts of Atlanta. With no more room to retreat, Hood had no choice but to give battle in response to every new turning maneuver by Sherman. The battles of Peachtree Creek (July 20), Atlanta (July 22), and Ezra Church (July 28) followed in quick succession. Tactical defeats that bled Hood's army badly, they nevertheless forced Sherman to proceed cautiously in his final movements against Atlanta, delaying the city's fall by a month or more. When in late August Sherman moved against Hood's railroad lifeline at Jonesboro, southwest of Atlanta, Hood had to respond once more. This time his effort was not sufficient, and on September 1 he was forced to evacuate the city. The resultant boost to Union morale helped insure Lincoln's reelection and extinguish whatever small chance of Confederate victory still remained by that time.

Back in Virginia that summer, pinned to the Richmond and Petersburg defenses, Lee tried to wrest the initiative from Grant by detaching Jubal A. Early's Second Corps to operate in the Shenandoah Valley and threaten Washington. The campaign that followed is ably covered in Cooling's *Jubal Early's Raid on Washington 1864* (1989) and Gary W. Gallagher's *Struggle for the Shenandoah* (1991). At first Early enjoyed success, defeating small Union forces and marching to the outskirts of Washington before Union reinforcements blocked him. Grant responded to the situation by placing the hard-driving Major General Philip H. Sheridan in command of all of the Union forces opposing Early. Sheridan waged a successful campaign that not only dealt Early repeated defeats but also substantially neutralized the Shenandoah Valley as a base of Confederate operations. In a final effort, Early attacked Sheridan's army at Cedar Creek, October 19, 1864, but after initial Confederate success the tide turned and the battle became the culminating defeat that ended Confederate hopes in the Shenandoah Valley. Back at Richmond and Petersburg, the siege ground on.

In Georgia, Hood, with nothing else to do, moved to threaten Sherman's supply line between Atlanta and Chattanooga. This led to several weeks of maneuvering in north Georgia with little tangible result. Frustrated, Sherman devised his plan for a march from Atlanta to Savannah and the Atlantic Ocean. Ironically, Hood also decided his best strategy was to penetrate far behind the enemy's lines. That November and December, while Sherman marched across Georgia, demonstrating the Confederacy's helplessness, Hood took his army through northern Alabama into Middle Tennessee. The story of this last desperate Confederate campaign in the West is ably told by Wiley Sword in *Embrace an Angry Wind* (1992). Hoping to trap a smaller Union force under Major General John Schofield at Spring Hill, Tennessee, Hood narrowly missed his purpose and followed up with a foolhardy frontal assault on Schofield at Franklin, Tennessee. This debacle cost his army 6,252 casualties or about one-quarter of its remaining strength. Among the dead were six generals, including the army's best, Major General Patrick R. Cleburne. Union casualties were scarcely one-third of Hood's. Schofield fell back to join a larger Union force under George H. Thomas at heavily fortified Nashville. Hood could think of nothing better to do but follow and camp outside a city he had no hope of taking. In the December 15–16 Battle of Nashville, Thomas attacked and effectively destroyed Hood's army as a coherent fighting force. Some of its remnants later made their way to North Carolina to serve there once again under the command of Joseph E. Johnston.

The reason for Johnston's recall was that after taking Savannah and pausing for several weeks of rest along the coast, Sherman turned north and marched through South Carolina, forcing the evacuation of Charleston and taking Columbia, which subsequently burned under circumstances that remain the subject of dispute. As Sherman moved into North Carolina the Confederacy had to face the threat that he and Grant would crush Lee between them, ending the war by removing the South's last remaining major army. On February 6 the Confederate Congress gave Lee command of all Confederate armies, and Lee subsequently assigned Johnston to duty in North Carolina with a ragtag force trying (vainly) to stop Sherman. In fact they could scarcely slow him down.

Yet the end came even faster than Sherman's swift-marching veterans. At the Battle of Five Forks, April 1, 1865, Grant succeeded in breaking Lee's vital right flank west of Petersburg. Before dawn the next day, Grant launched an assault all along the line, crushing Lee's front. Under duress his army retreated through Richmond and then westward with Grant in hot pursuit. The end came seven days later and 90 miles to the west when some of Grant's units managed to work their way around in front of Lee, trapping him at Appomattox Court House, Virginia. There Lee surrendered on April 9, 1865. Nine days later Johnston surrendered to Sherman at Durham Station, North Carolina. With that, though other surrenders followed piecemeal over the next few weeks, the war, for all practical purposes, was over.

BIBLIOGRAPHY

Castel, Albert (1992) *Decision in the West: The Atlanta Campaign of 1864*. Lawrence, Kan.: University Press of Kansas.

Catton, Bruce (1955) *This Hallowed Ground: The Story of the Union Side of the Civil War*. New York: Doubleday.

Catton, Bruce (1958) *America Goes to War*. Middletown, Conn.: Wesleyan University Press.

Catton, Bruce (1961–5) *Centennial History of the Civil War*, three vols. Garden City, NY: Doubleday.

Coddington, Edwin B. (1968) *The Gettysburg Campaign: A Study in Command*. New York: Charles Scribner's Sons.

Cooling, Benjamin Franklin (1987) *Forts Henry and Donelson: The Key to the Confederate Heartland*. Knoxville, Tenn.: University of Tennessee Press.

Cooling, Benjamin Franklin (1989) *Jubal Early's Raid on Washington 1864*. Baltimore, Md.: Nautical and Aviation Publishing Company of America.

Daniel, Larry J. (1997) *Shiloh: The Battle that Changed the Civil War*. New York: Simon and Schuster.

Davis, Stephen (2000) *Atlanta Will Fall: Sherman, Joe Johnston, and the Yankee Heavy Battalions*. Wilmington, Del.: Scholarly Resources.

Foote, Shelby (1958–74) *The Civil War: A Narrative*, three vols. New York: Random House.

Freeman, Douglas Southall (1934–6) *R. E. Lee: A Biography*, four vols. New York: Charles Scribner's Sons.

Freeman, Douglas Southall (1943–4) *Lee's Lieutenants: A Study in Command*, three vols. New York: Charles Scribner's Sons.

Furgurson, Ernest B. (1992) *Chancellorsville 1863: The Souls of the Brave*. New York: Alfred A. Knopf.

Gallagher, Gary W. (1991) *Struggle for the Shenandoah: Essays on the 1864 Valley Campaign*. Kent, Ohio: Kent State University Press.

Gallagher, Gary W. (ed.) (1995) *The Fredericksburg Campaign: Decision on the Rappahannock*. Chapel Hill, NC: University of North Carolina Press.

Gallagher, Gary W. (1997) *The Confederate War*. Cambridge, Mass.: Harvard University Press.

Grimsley, Mark (2002) *And Keep Moving On: The Virginia Campaign, May–June 1864*. Lincoln, Nebr.: University of Nebraska Press.

Krick, Robert K. (2002) *The Smoothbore Volley that Doomed the Confederacy: The Death of Stonewall Jackson and Other Chapters on the Army of Northern Virginia*. Baton Rouge, La.: Louisiana State University Press.

McDonough, James Lee (1980) *Stones River: Bloody Winter in Tennessee*. Knoxville, Tenn.: University of Tennessee Press.

McMurry, Richard M. (2000) *Atlanta 1864: Last Chance for the Confederacy*. Lincoln, Nebr.: University of Nebraska Press.

McPherson, James M. (1988) *Battle Cry of Freedom: The Civil War Era*. New York: Oxford University Press.

McPherson, James M. (1996) "The War of Southern Aggression," in McPherson, *Drawn with the Sword: Reflections on the American Civil War*. New York: Oxford University Press.

McWhiney, Grady (1983) "General Beauregard's 'Complete Victory' at Shiloh: An Interpretation," *Journal of Southern History* 49: 421–34.

Piston, William Garrett and Hatcher, Richard W., III (2000) *Wilson's Creek: The Second Battle of the Civil War and the Men Who Fought It*. Chapel Hill, NC: University of North Carolina Press.

Rafuse, Ethan S. (2002) *A Single Grand Victory: The First Bull Run Campaign*. Wilmington, Del.: Scholarly Resources.

Rhea, Gordon C. (1994) *The Battle of the Wilderness, May 5 and 6, 1864*. Baton Rouge, La.: Louisiana State University Press.

Rhea, Gordon C. (1997) *The Battles for Spotsylvania Court House and the Road to Yellow Tavern, May 7–12, 1864*. Baton Rouge, La.: Louisiana State University Press.

Rhea, Gordon C. (2000) *To the North Anna River: Grant and Lee, May 13–25, 1864*. Baton Rouge, La.: Louisiana State University Press.

Rhea, Gordon C. (2002) *Cold Harbor: Grant and Lee, May 26–June 3, 1864*. Baton Rouge, La.: Louisiana State University Press.

Sears, Stephen W. (1983) *Landscape Turned Red: The Battle of Antietam*. New Haven, Conn.: Ticknor and Fields.

Sears, Stephen W. (1996) *To the Gates of Richmond: The Peninsula Campaign*. New York: Ticknor and Fields.

Sword, Wiley (1992) *Embrace an Angry Wind: The Confederacy's Last Hurrah: Spring Hill, Franklin, and Nashville*. New York: HarperCollins.

Tanner, Robert G. (1996) *Stonewall in the Valley: Thomas J. "Stonewall" Jackson's Shenandoah Valley Campaign, Spring 1862*. Mechanicsville, Pa.: Stackpole.

Thomas, Emory M. (1994) *Robert E. Lee: A Biography*. New York: Norton.

US War Department (1881–1901) *The War of the Rebellion: Official Records of the Union and Confederate Armies*, series 1, vol. 19, pt. 2. Washington, DC: Government Printing Office.

Williams, T. Harry (1955) *P. G. T. Beauregard: Napoleon in Gray*. Baton Rouge, La.: Louisiana State University Press.

Woodworth, Steven E. (1990) *Jefferson Davis and his Generals: The Failure of Confederate Command in the West*. Lawrence, Kan.: University Press of Kansas.

Woodworth, Steven E. (1992) "'The Indeterminate Quantities': Jefferson Davis, Leonidas Polk, and the End of Kentucky Neutrality, September 1861," *Civil War History* 38: 289–97.

Woodworth, Steven E. (1995) *Davis and Lee at War*. Lawrence, Kan.: University Press of Kansas.

Woodworth, Steven E. (1998) *Six Armies in Tennessee: The Chickamauga and Chattanooga Campaigns*. Lincoln, Nebr.: University of Nebraska Press.

CHAPTER FOURTEEN

The Confederate Home Front

MARY DeCREDICO

"Future years will never know the seething hell and the black infernal background of countless minor scenes and interiors, (not the official surface-courteousness of the Generals, not the few great battles) of the Secession War; and it's best they should not – the real war will never get in the books." So wrote poet Walt Whitman in 1882–3, in his work, *Specimen Days*, and for years, he was correct. As soon as the last shots were fired, the participants, and later, historians began to analyze the military phases of the conflict. Hundreds of volumes devoted to battles, campaigns, and leadership appeared over the years. Scholars also turned to the political side of the contest and weighed in on the constitutionality of secession and the role of the respective governments in the conflict. The war behind the lines, the "real war," was seldom mentioned. It was as if the armies and their leaders operated in a vacuum.

Beginning in the 1920s and 1930s, several monographs appeared that dealt with specific elements of the southern home front. Indeed, Ella Lonn and Georgia Lee Tatum wrote on topics that scholars had not been addressed previously. Lonn (1933, 1940) looked at foreigners in the Confederacy and analyzed the impact that salt (or the lack thereof) had on the people behind the lines. Meanwhile, Tatum (1934) examined disloyalty in the Civil War South and tried to determine how disaffection and the emergence of peace societies may have undermined the Confederacy's war effort. These two historians tackled difficult issues and suggested to other scholars that non-military topics could produce interesting results that furthered our understanding of southerners at war. Their work would set the standard for future generations of scholars.

Perhaps it is no coincidence that Charles W. Ramsdell (1972 [1944]) turned to the Confederate home front when he delivered a series of lectures under the auspices of the Walter Lynwood Fleming Lecture Series at Louisiana State University in 1943. At that time, the United States was engulfed in another titanic struggle, though this conflict was thousands of miles away. The title of his lectures, published posthumously, was *Behind the Lines in the Southern Confederacy*. It marked a renewed attempt to portray the people of the South, those not at the front lines, at war.

Ramsdell's slim volume is divided into three chapters. In each, he explored a facet of the Confederate home front. For Ramsdell, ongoing problems with Confederate finances, most notably the tendency of the government to print money without adequate specie backing and to rely on numerous bond issues, caused serious problems that particularly affected the yeomen and poor whites of the country. Continued hardship forced most southerners to abandon their deeply held notions of limited government and prompted them to embrace state activism (Ramsdell 1972 [1944]: 40–1). That activism accelerated as the war reached its midpoint in 1863. Confronted with Federal invasions and ongoing privations, southerners within the Confederate states allowed, indeed demanded, "an unprecedented extension of political authority and control which not only would never have been tolerated before the war but which ran counter to the whole political philosophy of the southern people" (Ramsdell 1972 [1944]: 61).

Sadly for those who suffered in the cities and on the farms of the southern home front, these activities were not enough. Spiraling inflation, continued shortages, and the government's policies of impressment and the tax-in-kind heightened the suffering and led to the general demoralization of the southern people. By 1864, war weariness was everywhere, and the "whole social order moved to collapse" (Ramsdell 1972 [1944]: 113). For Ramsdell, the complete failure to manage the war financially doomed the Confederacy to defeat (Ramsdell 1972 [1944]: 85).

Ramsdell's pithy work touched upon some crucial elements relating to life "behind the lines." He identified the chronic money problems that ultimately crippled the Confederacy and led to the utter destitution of its people. By focusing on the people and the sacrifices they made and tribulations they endured, Ramsdell forced us to acknowledge the tempo of every day life away from the "fog" of battle.

Interestingly, Bell I. Wiley followed Professor Ramsdell in delivering the Fleming Lectures in 1944, and he, too, addressed the theme of the home front. *The Plain People of the Confederacy* looked at three elements: the "common soldiers," "the folk at home," and "the colored folk" (Wiley 1944). The picture Wiley painted was of struggle, hardship, and privation, themes Ramsdell had addressed in his series of lectures. For Wiley, as Ramsdell, the heavy sacrifices demanded of the plain folk ultimately caused an internal collapse that in some ways predated the surrender at Appomattox.

Ramsdell's and Wiley's books focused on specific parts of the home front. But embedded in their works was the notion that the home front played a significant role in how and why the South lost the war. Whether it was shortages, financial problems, the overwhelming sense of war weariness, or a combination of all three, the common folk's despair ultimately produced Confederate defeat. Recently, scholars have begun to address that element of the home front experience, the decline of popular support for the war, and the resulting scholarship has illuminated our understanding enormously.

Paul D. Escott is one of the first historians to turn to the people on the home front to assess the Confederate collapse. In *After Secession*, Escott (1978) advances the argument that "the primary cause of waning loyalty was the failure of the Davis administration to respond to the problems of the common people, who were the backbone of the Confederacy" (Escott 1978: x). As Ramsdell and Wiley had argued almost 35 years earlier, Escott finds that administration policies fell disproportionately hard on the yeomanry and poor whites. Slowly, but seemingly inexorably, the plain folk became disillusioned with the "rich man's war and poor man's fight."

They began leaving the army to tend to the problems their families suffered behind the lines. The more exacting the Richmond government became, the less the majority of whites supported the administration. Indeed, the situation grew so dire that many decided something had to be done. The famous Richmond Bread Riot of April 1863, along with similar riots in other southern cities, indicated that all was not well within the Confederacy (Escott 1978: 112–28).

Interestingly, the more Davis tried to enact measures that enabled the South to fight a total war, the more the yeomanry turned to their states for succor. Escott compares the policies of Georgia Governor Joseph E. Brown and the Confederate president, and concludes that the Georgian's genuine concern, coupled with concrete relief measures, served to shore up support and loyalty to the state while diminishing allegiance to the Confederacy. Davis may have realized this too late. After the war, he confessed the South was defeated by a "theory": state's rights. Nowhere was this more apparent than in Georgia during the war.

Again echoing earlier works, Escott ends his monograph with "An Assessment of Jefferson Davis as Leader." It is not a favorable portrait. For Escott, Davis's major flaw was his lack of understanding and empathy for the common people. Indeed, he "ignored their problems and often made them worse by new policies which demanded further sacrifice" (Escott 1978: 269).

Recent biographers of the Confederate president have treated him more kindly and have, in a sense, revised earlier assessments. William C. Davis, in *Jefferson Davis: The Man and his Hour* (1991), asserts that certain "character traits" were "exaggerated" (Davis 1991: 689–90). Still, in offering an exhaustive and even-handed study of the Confederate South's first and only chief executive, he states categorically that "for all Davis's flaws as an executive, without the performance of his civil functions as president, the Confederacy would not have lasted as long as it did" (Davis 1991: 704). In a similar vein, William J. Cooper Jr's prize-winning biography, *Jefferson Davis, American* (2000), also challenges Escott's rather critical judgment of the Confederate president. According to Cooper, Davis had more than his share of supporters, even in such contentious states as Georgia and North Carolina. Revising earlier treatments, Cooper concludes that Davis remained a popular and effective leader among all classes of Confederate society to the very end. Indeed, he terms anti-Davis opposition as "localized and largely ineffectual" (Cooper 2000: 477ff., 553). It may be that future treatments of Davis' relations with the yeomen will also highlight the Confederate president's success in keeping the vast majority of southerners loyal to the cause even when all seemed lost.

The impact of Davis' policies on the yeomen, planters, and poor whites within the Confederacy has remained a popular and fruitful area of research. Beginning in the late 1970s and continuing into the 1990s, numerous scholars identified specific Confederate communities to investigate the impact of war on those social classes. Works by Stephen V. Ash (1988), Wayne K. Durrill (1990), James L. Roark (1977), and Daniel E. Sutherland (1995) in particular have informed our knowledge of life away from the battle lines. Interestingly, each historian identifies specific examples of internal collapse in the various communities they study. Their conclusions seem to mirror ideas that Escott, Wiley, and Ramsdell advanced: defeat at home anticipated the surrender at Appomattox.

Ash's *Middle Tennessee Society Transformed, 1860–1870* (1988) traces the experience of people, "blacks and whites, aristocrats and plain folks, townspeople and villagers and farmers," living in the Confederate heartland (Ash 1988: xi). His work has two major themes: that middle Tennessee was a "'third South,'" an area of prosperous farms, and that it was a "dual society divided by race" (Ash 1988: xi). How that society, which was defined by racial boundaries, would react to secession, war, defeat, and Reconstruction forms the basis of his book.

Middle Tennessee initially greeted the sectional crisis with confidence, but that slowly turned to fear as whites in the region suspected slaves and free blacks might take advantage of the unsettled state of affairs to rebel. But even as they increased their vigilance, middle Tennesseans remained committed to the Union, notwithstanding the actions of the deep South. Only Fort Sumter and President Abraham Lincoln's call for 75,000 ninety-day volunteers changed their minds. Faced with the reality of war, residents of the region mobilized. Confidence and optimism quickly gave way to fear as Union forces moved into the middle Tennessee heartland on land and via the Tennessee and Cumberland rivers. The fall of Nashville in February 1862, shattered the sense of invincibility some residents had. Union occupation of this agricultural center brought tremendous changes to the people of middle Tennessee and their institutions (Ash 1988: 73–95).

For the slaves of the region, the presence of Federal troops brought nothing but joy. Although the Union high command did not desire to tamper with the institution of slavery, the army's need for laborers forced changes. Moreover, the slaves' desire to exercise their freedom as the white agricultural world crumbled created a different labor environment as well. In the end, Ash concludes, "The death of slavery in the heartland can be concisely . . . explained thus: rural chaos permitted it, the Union army encouraged it, and the slaves desired and perpetuated it" (Ash 1988: 111).

Soon, however, the newly freed slaves discovered the Union army was not the agent of change and relief they expected. Sadly for those people of color, liberation meant increased hardship and privation. Physical abuse also took its toll, as many freedmen and freedwomen encountered vicious soldiers who beat them and raped them at will. Continued uncertainty, genuine hardship, and disorder would last well into the postwar period (Ash 1988: 132–42).

White society in middle Tennessee was similarly affected. Not long after Union troops occupied middle Tennessee, guerrillas emerged as a dangerous threat. Local members of the white community, these guerrillas did everything they could to lash out at the enemy: they harassed southern unionists and attacked any Federal target they could. What made the guerrillas especially effective was their knowledge of and support in the community. As Ash points out, these were not "footloose partisans," but rather "men (and boys) of the rural communities, known to their families and neighbors, harbored and supported by them, and committed to safeguarding their world." Though the Union occupiers believed the guerrillas represented "anarchy," Ash contends the contrary was true: "An extension of rural society, the guerrillas of the occupied heartland became the surrogate instruments of communal integrity and discipline when the customary instruments faltered or disappeared under the stress of war" (Ash 1988: 148). In response, the Federals abandoned whatever "soft" policy they had followed in favor of force to quell the guerrillas and the people who supported them (Ash 1988: 153). By 1864, middle Tennessee's white society had disintegrated. Bandits joined guerrillas, crime skyrocketed, and Union retaliation continued. General John B. Hood's ill-fated invasion of the region was the final blow. Demoralization and the sense of impending defeat enveloped those at home (Ash 1988: 168–72).

It is here that Ash sees a great difference between Confederates in middle Tennessee and the rest of the South. Elsewhere, though "challenged or altered," the southern white social structure stayed basically intact. This was not the case in the Confederate heartland: "by 1864 [white society] virtually ceased to exist as an entity, its fragments drifting chaotically after the bonds of hierarchy, community, and ideology had been snapped" (Ash 1988: 172). In short, whites in middle Tennessee faced a harrowing future with few benchmarks to guide them.

Although white society came apart after the Union army's triumph, the fragmentation did not last long. Ash states plainly that the aristocracy of the Tennessee heartland was "prostrate" by the surrender at Appomattox, but he adds that with the advent of Reconstruction, "the aristocracy regained its commanding position in white society." Three reasons accounted for the planters' resurgence: there was little change in the composition of the aristocratic classes, the "economic foundation of upper-class ascendancy" endured even defeat and occupation, and the yeomanry "continued to sanction the traditional class structure" (Ash 1988: 227, 230–2).

Ash expands upon many of the themes in *Middle Tennessee Society Transformed* in his more recent monograph, *When the Yankees Came* (1995). Again, Ash is interested in looking at the impact of the war on all those who lived behind the lines. Indeed, this is the first comprehensive study of southerners who lived under Union occupation.

Ash addresses three themes in his book: how Federal policies evolved during the occupation, how different regions within the occupied South had varying experiences with the occupiers, and how the experiences of occupation often led to internal battles between friend and foe. Ash's depiction of the varying geographical locales within the South is most effective as he sets the scene prior to the Federal invasion. The region was quite diverse, both topographically and socially. The "rural culture" bound all southerners together, as did notions of hierarchy. But as Ash clearly demonstrates, the existence of unionists within the Confederate South indicated that all were not united wholly behind the Confederate standard (Ash 1995: ix–x, 2–4, 11).

The shock of invasion stunned southerners and led many, especially in the cities and towns, to flee the hated Yankees. The majority, however, stayed behind, though they trembled at the thought of the enemy in their midst. So many horrible stereotypes of the northern foe had been bandied about that the reality of generally well-behaved troops allayed many fears. The Union high command's embrace of a "'rosewater' policy of lenience and suasion" was designed to bring the erring rebels back into the Union fold (Ash 1995: 29).

Ash chronicles how southerners in the "garrisoned towns," the "Confederate frontier," and "no-man's-land" reacted to the rosewater policy. Confident that the southern armies would eventually push back the Federals, many Confederates remained outspoken in their defiance of Federal control. But the appearance of guerrilla bands forced a change in Union policy. Their activities led the Federal armies to wage war against the civilians who harbored the guerrillas (Ash 1995: 38–61).

Ash's analysis of the towns, the so-called frontier and southern no-man's-land, depicts a Confederacy fighting enemies within and without. As the Federal armies endeavored to destroy the southern aristocracy and as the slave system disintegrated, southerners saw their families and local institutions "battered." Mirroring what he found in middle Tennessee, Ash sees the occupied South's internal collapse giving rise to a new group, bandits. But the bandits moved in smaller groups and were further differentiated from guerrillas because of the brutal nature of their attacks. Concentrated in no-man's-land, which was not under constant Federal control, the bandits exploited the "unpacified" nature of the land by operating at will. At the end, war-weary Confederates teamed up with the Union army to try and wipe out the bandit threat. Continued hardship and the "apparent endlessness of the war" convinced most Confederates peace was worth any price (Ash 1995: 99, 205–10, 215, 217).

The picture Ash paints in *When the Yankees Came* is one of upheaval, uncertainty, danger, and collapse. It is yet another sobering account of how Confederate society, this time in the occupied regions, was often not so much behind the lines as within them.

Durrill also finds "conflict and chaos" in another region of the southern home front. Washington County, North Carolina, on Albemarle Sound, is the focus of *War of Another Kind* (1990). This area, with its white population of almost 3,200 divided between planters, yeomen and poor whites, and its slave population comprising more than half of that number, became, over the course of the war, another community at war with itself (Durrill 1990: 3–6, 10).

North Carolina, like Tennessee, was lukewarm initially to secession. Planters in Washington County, however, had a very real interest in boosting secession to protect their property from possible Federal invasion. They succeeded in getting the yeomen to join them in support of secession, but they knew the future of that alliance might be strained. Those strains became apparent early, when Federal forces captured Hatteras Inlet in the summer of 1861 (Durrill 1990: 38–44).

According to Durrill, the fall of Hatteras prompted many unionist yeomen to assert their control over the local militia. The planters, however, responded with brute force which led the yeomen to form an alliance with local tradesmen and poorer whites. This new coalition approximated nothing less than the haves versus the have-nots, and the latter vowed to destroy the planters by appealing to the Federal soldiers for support (Durrill 1990: 44, 66–7).

Durrill's analysis of Washington County dovetails neatly with Ash's observations of middle Tennessee and the occupied South as a whole. Beginning in 1863, frustrated secessionists banded together into guerrilla bands, determined to fight back against local unionists. The outcome was a series of bloody skirmishes that pitted secessionists and unionists against each other and the Federal troops. These battles succeeded in dividing the yeomanry from their laborer allies, and led to the arrival of veteran Confederate units from General Robert E. Lee's Army of Northern Virginia. Ostensibly deployed to scour the area for much needed supplies, the Confederate commander, D. H. Hill, a native North Carolinian, used the army's presence to "re-establish planter rule throughout eastern North Carolina" (Durrill 1990: 174). Federal countermeasures served only to force the planters to flee into the interior with their slaves, which effectively ended Hill's attempt to solidify planter rule.

The emergence of a peace movement in North Carolina prompted Davis to send more Confederate troops into Washington County in an attempt to scotch the Heroes of America and other, like-minded organizations. Confederate forces under General Robert Hoke launched a series of assaults against the Union troops stationed in Plymouth. The goal was to defeat the Yankees and thus cause the peace movement to dissolve. Hoke succeeded in his mission: the Federal commander was compelled to surrender. But the Confederate victory intensified suffering in the area, as Federal and Confederate troops, as well as local landless whites, used the planters' evacuation to loot and pillage their properties (Durrill 1990: 176–84). According to Durrill, the Battle of Plymouth served to destroy the planters' dreams of reestablishing their dominance in eastern North Carolina.

The tensions within Washington County were not unique, but they do underscore the latent stresses between planters and plain folk. Roark's *Masters without Slaves* (1977) addresses this class of southerners and how they staked everything on their way of life. Examining large and small planters throughout the Confederate South, Roark finds that regardless of landholding and slaveholding size, planters demonstrated a "cohesiveness and unanimity on fundamental principles": slavery was the cornerstone of their civilization. Though many planters resisted secession, "few were willing to fight against the Confederacy." Indeed, the Civil War became, quite simply, the "War for Southern Security," a conflict to safeguard the planters' property and their place in society (Roark 1977: ix, x, 8, 32).

As the war developed, however, many planters reassessed their commitment to the Confederate cause. According to Roark, a rift developed between the planters and the Confederate government because of "the difference between their ultimate goals." Davis and his lieutenants were dedicated to independence at any cost, and this alarmed the planters. As Roark argues convincingly, "To found an independent nation and lose the plantations would be no victory at all," for the planters were convinced that slavery and plantations were inseparable (Roark 1977: 54, 104). As a result, the ruling class reacted strongly to Davis' proposal to arm the slaves and to offer them freedom upon southern independence. Most echoed the words of the *Charleston Mercury*: "We want no Confederate Government without our institutions," and that included slavery (Roark 1977: 102).

Defeat and emancipation presented planters with new worries. Convinced that without slavery the region would be engulfed by a race war, planters struggled to maintain the status quo antebellum in the wake of massive upheaval. They also confronted a seemingly unsolvable dilemma: how to continue staple crop agriculture without forced labor. Their solution was to create "effective alternatives to slavery." That was the reality that would play out in the Reconstruction era (Roark 1977: 106–8).

One community that seemed to lack planter influence was nonetheless deeply affected by its Confederate experience. Sutherland's *Seasons of War* (1995) analyzes the impact of war on Culpeper County, Virginia, a community located almost in the middle of the state, midway between the Federal capital and Charlottesville. Using the changing of the seasons as a metaphor, Sutherland finds that the hopes of "spring" (1861) were eventually lost in the grim years of "winter" (1864–5):

> What emerges is a portrait of a people initially keen to wage war but increasingly plagued by self-doubt, weariness and fear. The people of Culpeper gradually turned away from rebellion, not so much because they lost faith in their cause, but because they became intimidated by the destructive power and demoralizing forces of the war. (Sutherland 1995: vii)

Culpeper County, Virginia, occupied a central place in the commonwealth. With its prosperous farms and thriving commercial economy, the county seemed more akin to central Pennsylvania than Georgia or Mississippi. Sutherland finds Culpeper a "contented, peaceful place" (Sutherland 1995: 5–9, 27). That peacefulness would be shattered with the election of Lincoln and the secession of the southern states.

According to Sutherland, whites in Culpeper embraced secession and fell out in support of locals who joined the Confederate army. Preparations for war further bolstered the county's economy and led many residents to have renewed confidence in the southern cause. Culpeper's slave population of about 6,600 (which represented more than half of the county's total) remained "inscrutable," an observation many whites throughout the South made that spring (Sutherland 1995: 5, 30–8, 47–8, 54–5).

The battle at Manassas in July 1861, crushed the hopes of many in Culpeper. Local men fought in that engagement and died. But more sobering still was the arrival of the wounded to the county. Residents who had cheered their neighbors as they marched off to fight were now confronted with the overwhelming reality of war: death and dying. Even as the men and women of the community struggled to adapt to these new conditions, they would be presented with additional challenges.

Sutherland chronicles the efforts of Culpeper citizens to pursue normal lives while their home state was under attack. Using the present tense to "recreate the confusion and chaos of war," he describes how fiercely loyal Confederates became troubled and victimized by shortages, a slow down in the local economy, and the ever-present threat of invasion (Sutherland 1995: vii, 89–111). That threat became a reality when Union forces assigned to General John Pope's Army of Virginia occupied Culpeper in July 1862. Pope's decision to wage war against citizens who supported the Confederate cause prompted outrage among the residents of Culpeper. Union pillaging of their community was ended only when General Robert E. Lee's army arrived in Culpeper.

The story of Culpeper is the story of a community on the front lines. Whites and blacks followed the fortunes of the war by observing which army occupied their land at what time. Battles raged so close that in many ways, there was no home front; all were engulfed in war. Civilians could only watch and try to maintain some normality. But, Sutherland notes, by the winter of 1864, people in Culpeper could see only "uncertainty" about the future. The "utter devastation of the countryside" and the onset of campaigns with a new, relentless Federal commander boded ill for the people. When General Ulysses S. Grant began his onslaught against Lee's army in the spring, all that was left in Culpeper were old men, children, and women. Once a prosperous community, Culpeper became, as so many other southern communities, a ravaged shell of its former self. According to Sutherland, Culpeper's people weathered the "seasons of war" until the very end, when war weariness simply overwhelmed them (Sutherland 1995: 349–64, 382).

In each of these studies, the authors stress that often the most vocal and outspoken defenders of the Confederate cause, and concomitantly, the most defiant in resisting the Yankees, were southern women. Bell Wiley (1944) and Mary Elizabeth Massey (1966) first touched upon southern women and their role in the war effort. Their works remained the standard for close to 50 years. Happily, one of the recent trends in home front historiography has been a renewed examination of this segment of the Confederate population. What has emerged is a consensus that women may have been belles, but they were far from the helpless, weak, and fragile creatures nineteenth- and, often, twenty-first-century observers thought them to be.

George C. Rable's *Civil Wars* (1989) made the first major contribution to this topic. Acknowledging that southern women had been given "short shrift" among Civil War scholars, Rable endeavored to produce a monograph that combined original research with a synthesis of pertinent secondary works. Of especial interest to Rable is how issues of race, class, and gender (what has become the holy trinity of sorts among southern historians), not to mention patriarchy, factored into women's reactions to the stresses of war. Though Rable makes clear he has limited his study to the "women of the ruling race," he hastens to add that he included women "from varying economic classes." Still, his sources are biased toward those women who had the time, energy, and ability to record their thoughts (Rable 1989: ix, 15).

Rable's book is organized both chronologically and topically. Not surprisingly, he begins with an examination of women's roles in the antebellum south. He asserts that southern women continually supported a society that kept them in a subordinate status. Yet women's domestic roles contained "ambiguities and contradictions" that were not lost on them. Further complicating these roles were class differences (Rable 1989: 2–6).

The onset of war created new challenges to women and their prescribed roles within southern society. Women were expected to exhort their menfolk to the battlefield, maintain a confident, optimistic air, and bear whatever trials came their way. Yet as the tide of war turned against the Confederacy in 1862, women's commitment to these ideals was strained. Concern for loved ones serving at the front, government policies of conscription, impressment, and the tax-in-kind, and the ever present threat of Federal invasion placed tremendous burdens on Confederate women. The yeomen and poor white families were especially hard hit, as their principal breadwinners were drawn away to the army. Gradually, these women came to see that the burdens of war were not being borne equally, which further fueled disillusionment (Rable 1989: 50–5, 74–8, 83–92).

By 1863, hardships affected virtually every class of southern women. As those privations multiplied, "faith in the Confederate cause declined, and calls for continued patriotic sacrifice were met with laughter, cynicism, anger, or disbelief." Rable contends that this phenomenon, the basic collapse of the domestic economy, has been overlooked by historians: other scholars, he argues, neglect to examine the Confederacy's fiscal problems in relation to popular support for the cause behind the lines (Rable 1989: 97–102). This is an interesting, if not curious assertion, given the reality that Ramsdell (1972 [1944]) and Escott (1978) made similar observations in their works on the southern home front and the collapse of the Confederacy at least ten years before Rable wrote his book.

As women of all classes struggled to make ends meet in a society overwhelmed by war, major changes in gender roles took place. With their husbands, fathers, brothers, and sons at the front, women had no choice but to tend to the fields, oversee the slaves, seek employment in government agencies – anything to keep their families intact. As women embraced new responsibilities – and Rable chronicles everything from factory jobs to hospital nursing – they became less dependent upon the advice of the men in their lives. But Rable maintains no permanent transformation took place: "Most Southerners saw the changes in sex roles between 1861 and 1865 as an aberration, an experiment launched out of necessity that would not soon be repeated" (Rable 1989: 112–35). One must wonder, however, if those gender roles did, indeed, remain unaltered. With a high percentage of men killed and missing in action, not to mention suffering from major wounds that may have necessitated amputation, it appears any return to prewar norms was well-nigh impossible. For better or worse, many southern women had no choice after the war but to continue in the role of breadwinner. And many would remain in what had been untraditional or unconventional positions.

The advent of total war, as evidenced by Sherman's march through Georgia and the Carolinas, brought the conflict literally to the South's front doorsteps. Many women greeted the advance of "Lucifer's Legions" with despair and terror. Some sought to flee the juggernaut; others tried to make the best of the situation. The net result was nothing less than psychological trauma. "Society became atomized," notes Rable, "as more and more people simply looked after their own interests" (Rable 1989: 156–66, 168ff.). The final collapse left women bewildered and uprooted, uncertain if God really was in control (Rable 1989: 216).

Many of the themes Rable (1989) raises in *Civil Wars* are also addressed in Drew Gilpin Faust's *Mothers of Invention* (1996). Faust, like Rable, contends that most scholarship on the Confederacy tends to ignore southern women. Because of that, she endeavors to prove "that not only did leaders of Confederate opinion and government talk about the proper place of white women in both the new nation and the war to secure its independence; they executed plans and passed legislation that had direct effects on women's lives. Whether or not Confederate leaders recognized these implications," Faust asserts, "Confederate women certainly did" (Faust 1996: xiii).

Faust finds that secession and war forced southern women, who occupied "separate spheres" from their male relations, into new roles. Suddenly confronted with the reality that "war seemed to belong to the men," southern women struggled to find a place in society. Various attempts to redefine their position led to different results: the establishment of benevolent associations, the staging of theatrical tableaux, and the like. In virtually every instance, however, these contributions remained in the decidedly feminine, traditional sphere. But as they expanded their efforts, southern women discovered they were moving into areas that were, by antebellum standards, quite "unconventional" (Faust 1996: 10–12, 20–9).

Like Rable, Faust sees conscription and the overall loss of the menfolk necessitating major changes on the southern home front. Given the dominance of agriculture, the absence of able-bodied male hands hit hard, especially among the middle-class and poor whites. But even women of the elite found themselves forced to manage in order to provide for their families. Rising prices, shortages, and the constant threat of invasion and occupation caused more than a little stress. For Faust, the most significant change was manifested in the major realignment in the social structure: the absence of men created a vacuum in the patriarchy, the very element that defined women's roles in southern society (Faust 1996: 30, 32–3, 51ff.).

The loss of their husbands, the quest to find a new place within the war, the unsettled nature of the home front – all these elements created tension, uneasiness, and often a sense of uselessness. Being women in a world at war was a trying experience, contends Faust. The reality that many women had to go to work to support their families caused further difficulties. "However imperative for both individual and national survival," Faust argues, "women's transition to paid public employment was not easy – either personally or ideologically – for it controverted deep-seated assumptions about female dependence and about the appropriateness of a separate and necessarily domestic sphere" (Faust 1996: 82).

Some of the work women did fell within the domestic sphere: teaching and nursing, for example, were jobs women performed at home and on the plantation on a regular basis. But other positions, serving as government clerks or even factory workers, lay well outside traditional duties. In all these venues, women came across members of other social classes which merely added to the tension and strains of the time. Indeed, elite women became even more jealous of their need to be socially superior in an economy disrupted by war (Faust 1996: 88–109, 111).

The women on the Confederate home front also discovered that the absence of loved ones awakened new feelings of love, desire, and for unmarried women, fears of spinsterhood. Understandably, women worried about their husbands at the battle front, for news of military engagements brought heightened fears of death or wounding. They also wondered about the morality of the camps, and if their marriage vows would be held sacred during lengthy periods of separation. Furloughs elicited joy tempered by worry, for invariably the respite home resulted in the prospect of pregnancy, a dreaded event for many women, particularly during a time of war. For those who bewailed the lack of young, eligible bachelors, deepened female relationships became the norm, some with homosexual connotations. Finally, women adapted to the change in relationship roles by writing. Be it letters, journals or novels, women faced the war and its horrors with pen and ink. In the process, they "nurtured new female self-consciousness" (Faust 1996: 114–23, 126–9, 139, 142, 161ff.).

As the war dragged on and Federal armies began yet more offensives on the shrinking Confederacy, many women came face to face with the threat of conquest and occupation. Long terrified of the evils the dreaded Yankees would visit upon them, women found increasingly that the cost of supporting the war effort was too high: battlefield losses, chronic shortages, spiraling inflation, and serious poverty caused many women to seek self-preservation over further sacrifice. As other scholars have observed, women, once the Confederacy's staunchest patriots and supporters, began writing to their husbands begging them to come home to defend them and help them make ends meet. That truly marked the end.

One Confederate woman wrote poignantly after the war, "we shall never be the same." For Faust (1996), such words are prophetic. Women of the elite witnessed first-hand the end of their world of leisure and prosperity. Yeomen and poor white women were left in even worse straits. Yet Faust concludes that despite four years of wrenching changes, southern women continued to yearn for the traditional ways. They would use those "years of crisis . . . as the bases for inventing new selves erected firmly upon the elitist assumptions of the old" (Faust 1996: 248, 251, 254).

Both Faust and Rable focus on women of all social classes and often mention their attempts to keep their families together during trying circumstances. Faust and Rable also discuss how separation challenged the bonds of marriage, and why the happy prospect of furloughs home also created very real concerns about unwanted pregnancy, with its complications and potential for death (not to mention the added strain on shrinking family budgets). The children of both northerners and southerners, and how they reacted to the horrors of war, is traced in James Marten's book, *The Children's Civil War* (1998).

According to Marten (1998), Americans are transfixed by the idea of children and war. He traces current events as well as popular books and movies to demonstrate how we have dealt with the concept of war coming to our children. But Marten is the first scholar to look at America's children during the period 1861–5. He argues that the total experience of the war – the loss of loved ones, the threat of invasion, the hardships of war – "politicized children in the North and South and guided them to integrate the war into their everyday lives and to contribute in a myriad of ways to their countries war efforts." Using manuscript collections, diaries, newspapers, and children's books and periodicals of the era, Marten contends "the war affected, in striking ways, how they viewed the world, their country, their communities, and themselves" (Marten 1998: 3).

For children, the most wrenching element of the war was the loss of fathers who went off to fight. Fathers attempted to keep the parental bond strong, corresponding with their children and promising them they would return home quickly. Mothers also helped ease the anxiety associated with separation by talking to their children about their fathers and how much they missed them. Fathers also saw a need to dispense advice and guidance to their sons and daughters. Eventually, fathers would share with their children the experiences in battle and the horrors they witnessed. Marten concludes these children learned a great deal "about the men they called father and through their examples learned the nature of sacrifice and the profound costs of patriotism" (Marten 1998: 99).

Southern children experienced a very different war from their northern counterparts. Galloping inflation, food, fuel and clothing shortages, and the arrival of Federal troops all affected the material condition of southern families. This was most poignantly observed over the Christmas holidays in 1863 and 1864, when children discovered the bounty of past years was gone. Mothers tried to soften the blow, telling their children Santa Claus, too, was a victim of the Yankee blockade. At other times, southern women, worried and anxious about their husbands and brothers away at the front, unwittingly neglected their sons' and daughters' very real needs. This was often the case among families forced to become refugees (Marten 1998: 113, 120–5).

The "other" southern children, slave children, also had unique and dangerous trials during wartime. According to Marten, the "most basic experience" for slave children was "hunger." Slave subsistence had always been at the level of a bare minimum, and wartime privations only made that worse. Planters saw their income decline and their crops impressed or seized. Often barely able to support themselves, they were forced to pass their poverty and destitution on to their slaves. Masters continued to try to control their slaves, but they faced new obstacles. In an effort to clamp down on slave runaways, white planters increased the ever-fearsome slave patrols. They also embarked upon a propaganda campaign to convince slaves that the Union armies would unleash a reign of terror once they arrived (Marten 1998: 125–7, 136–7).

Many slave children had to confront the reality of separation from their parents. As their fathers ran away to join the advancing Union armies, black children, their mothers, and other siblings also left the master's house and sought refuge in Federal contraband camps that popped up throughout the southern countryside. The camps were universally miserable, and those who experienced them often discovered freedom brought overcrowding, appalling living conditions, and disease. Northern white teachers who journeyed to the camps soon discovered there were serious cultural differences between the races. Nonetheless, black children did receive an education of sorts. Still, not all southern black–northern white contact was cordial. Black children "remembered their liberators as bullies and bandits who left pillaged plantations and hungry slaves in their wakes. They seemed little different from the marauding bands of Confederates" (Marten 1998: 138).

Marten contends that children's activities during the war and their awareness that a great struggle was unfolding around them led to heightened politicization. He finds that although separated by race and region, all children "were united in their responses to the crisis." Popular literature, be it magazines, children's books, or textbooks, "offered children examples of how they could honorably and usefully support their country." Accordingly, all children came to realize there was an "enemy" that needed to be stopped (Marten 1998: 148–9).

To be sure, parents had a major influence on their children and how they reacted to and supported the war. Hearing their parents' conversations, reading political speeches, learning the results of battles – all these elements factored into how children in both sections responded to the war. Pressures upon the southern family structure, however, often led to different reactions. Some children became violent and joined gangs that preyed on innocent civilians; others took on added responsibilities, including paying jobs, in order to ease the hardships felt at home. In the process, children North and South, white and black, became further politicized, which "inspir[ed] ardent patriotism that could either lead to a life-long devotion to the Union, or in the case of Confederate children, make them permanently suspicious of the government of the United States" (Marten 1998: 150, 167–74, 186).

Marten concludes his monograph with an analysis of Civil War children as adults. Perhaps not surprisingly, he discovers adult experiences and perceptions often depended upon one's race and place of birth. For the former slaves, peace brought poverty and renewed fears of violence as southern whites lashed back at emancipation with Black Codes and the Ku Klux Klan; for southern whites, the war was a "turning point," one which required them to explain what their war experiences meant. All the children who lived through the war would be forever changed by it (Marten 1998: 188, 190, 195ff., 219–21).

Marten's (1988) discussion of black children and the perils they faced is unique in the literature. Scholars studying slaves during the war have been stymied because of the dearth of primary source materials. Fortunately, Ira Berlin and the other scholars affiliated with the Freedmen and Southern Society Project have gathered and published a host of documents that chronicle the rise and fall of chattel slavery in the South (Berlin et al. 1982–93). Coupled with recent monographs by Clarence L. Mohr (2001 [1986]) and Ervin L. Jordan, Jr (1995), our understanding of the role people of color played behind the lines is being expanded and enlightened.

Clarence Mohr's *On the Threshold of Freedom* (1986) tells the complex story of whites and blacks and how they adapted to the demands of war. According to Mohr, slavery in Georgia occupied a "dynamic nexus," in which change was constant. The secession of Georgia and the taking up of arms would cause the dynamics to be altered even more.

Mohr sets the context for his book by surveying white Georgians' attitudes towards their bondmen from 1859 to 1861. John Brown's raid on Harpers Ferry had been every white southerner's worst nightmare come true. Although Georgia's master class continued to argue their slaves possessed "innate docility," they feared that docility masked a potential Nat Turner. Accordingly, as political passions heightened and the fire-eaters became more bellicose, white southerners clamped down on slaves and free blacks. Vigilance committees, increased legal restrictions (which actually threatened to enslave free blacks), and lynchings became the methods used to combat any slave plots, real or imaginary (Mohr 1986: 3–4, 6–11, 21–30, 47–55).

The Federal conquest of Port Royal in 1861 and the Union navy's successful assault against Fort Pulaski at the mouth of the Savannah River in 1862 led many Georgia planters to flee into the interior of the state. Fully aware of the opportunity this presented, slaves in the region began to flock to the conquering forces. Many of the bondmen sought actively to serve in the Union army. According to Mohr, such a reaction was predictable: Georgia blacks "shared a hatred of bondage and a desire to strike out directly at the slave system" (Mohr 1986: 69–77). Still, relations between the slaves and the white Union troops were not without problems. Officers noticed the former slaves possessed "ambivalent" attitudes toward their masters. Moreover, many blacks feared the continued invasion of Federal forces would cause them real privations – the loss of a home, the destruction of what few possessions they had, and separation from family members. The bondmen also greeted their liberators with trepidation. How would they be treated? As Mohr points out, Sherman's legions swept through the state in 1864, but the commander and most of his men were "reluctant liberators" to say the very least. In short, the arrival of the Union army was a mixed blessing (Mohr 1986: 77, 89–94).

In other ways, the flight of the planter class and the slaves' decision to run away or stay and reclaim part of their master's land produced dramatic and lasting changes. Suddenly, the old verities of the plantation were no longer valid and the power of the master was no longer limitless. The planters may have retained their rights legally and theoretically, but the slaves knew "the foundations of the old regime were crumbling" (Mohr 1986: 100, 113, 119).

Those planters who did not leave faced mounting problems as Confederate military fortunes waxed and waned on distant and not so distant battlefields. Confederate economic policies hit the countryside hard. As economic hardships deepened, masters often had no choice but to lessen their role as paternal caretaker. Slaves watched helplessly as food and clothing allowances dwindled and disappeared entirely. Added to the mix was the master class's very real fear of slave revolts, not to mention deep-seated concerns that the lack of white men would encourage slaves to perpetrate crimes against white women and white property. All the while, the slaves, though outwardly still deferent to their white masters, were testing the slave system and were "laying claim to a larger share of the prerogatives that would accompany legal freedom" (Mohr 1986: 210–11, 220, 222, 232).

Mohr shifts his focus from the countryside to the city when he turns to the role Georgia's bondmen played in the state's war effort. With a vast array of tables to complement his written text, Mohr shows effectively that black labor on coastal defenses, in nitre production, in war materiel manufacturing, at the hospitals and in the Ordnance and Quartermaster Bureaus, proved essential to the Confederacy's mobilization and its waging of war. In the process, however, black family ties were strained. Indeed, though planters tried to keep slave families together, slave hiring practices militated against it. Mohr observes, "Except for the refugee experience, no wartime phenomenon posed a greater threat to slave domestic ties than did military and industrial employment" (Mohr 1986: 120–48, 160, 172).

Planters found economic benefits to hiring out their bondmen, yet unwittingly they helped unleash an urban-industrial revolution that "knew no color line," and that served to destroy what remained of the "rural localism" which defined the antebellum south. The more slaves were hired out, the larger and more integrated the slaves' urban milieu became. Moreover, continued separation from their masters further undermined the slave system. As Mohr observes, urban bondmen "felt the easing of institutional restraints as the structure of urban bondage slowly crumbled under the stress of a war environment" (Mohr 1986: 200, 203, 207).

According to Mohr, the final sign that war had totally "undermine[d]" the institution of slavery appeared once Davis and the Congress began considering arming the slaves and freeing them after southern independence was achieved. As Mohr and other historians have noted, the "debate over arming the slaves involved a search for Southern identity and a quest for national purpose." Would the Confederacy arm and free their bondmen in return for independence? The decision came too late for us to ever know. Still, the reality that southerners in general and Georgians in particular discussed this issue shows how far the South had departed from its antebellum ways.

Of course freeing the slaves to achieve independence also raised the issue of what race relations would be in postwar Georgia. Mohr concludes his monograph by echoing an observation Allan Nevins made almost 50 years before Mohr wrote his book. Those southerners who favored manumission in return for Confederate freedom assumed they would have " 'the right to deal with the problems of slavery and race adjustment in their own time and on their own terms' " (Mohr 1986: 236, 275, 292). In a sense, then, postwar race relations would approximate the status quo antebellum.

Mohr argues that the activities of Georgia's bondmen, as contracted military laborers and as field hands left to provide for their absentee owners, pushed the slaves toward their freedom. Ira Berlin, Barbara J. Fields, Steven F. Miller, Joseph P. Reidy, and Leslie S. Rowland of the Freedom History Project emphasize this as well in the essays that accompany the massive collection of primary documents they have published as *Freedom: A Documentary History of Emancipation, 1861–1867* (Berlin et al. 1982–93). Those scholars maintain slaves were very aware of what transpired around them. Indeed, they claim, "The war provided the occasion for slaves to seize freedom," but add, "the character of slave society," "the course of the war itself," and "the policies of the Union and Confederate governments" created a complex evolution to the slaves' emancipation.

Berlin and his colleagues, via the primary sources and their interpretive essays, discuss how slavery was ultimately extinguished. The activities of the slaves, coupled with the "genesis" of free labor and the enlistment of slaves in the Union army, worked to make "the Confederacy's cornerstone . . . its tombstone." Throughout, it is evident the slaves were active and willing participants in attaining their freedom (Berlin et al. 1992: xiv, 4, 70).

The importance, perhaps even primacy of the slaves' role in undermining the peculiar institution that Berlin and Mohr stress, not to mention the complexity of the entire process, may also be seen in points Jordan raises in *Black Confederates and Afro-Yankees in Civil War Virginia* (1995).

Jordan's title captures the reader's attention instantly, and he moves quickly to define who composed those groups of blacks. "*Afro-Virginians*," according to Jordan, consisted of slaves and free blacks who, one way or another, found themselves in the Old Dominion. "*Afro-Confederates* were pro-Southern blacks who privately or publicly supported and allied themselves with the Confederacy; *Afro-Yankees* were Southern blacks who supported the Union" (Jordan 1995: xii).

In many ways, Jordan's book is unique in the literature on the southern home front. Using southern newspapers, memoirs, the *Official Records of the War of Rebellion*, and a multitude of manuscript collections, he is the first historian to attempt a comprehensive portrait of slaves and free blacks within a Confederate state. Jordan's conclusions, however, mirror those of other scholars who have found both irony and complexity in the black response to civil war.

Perhaps not surprisingly, Jordan (1995) begins his volume by surveying slavery in antebellum Virginia. With a slave population of over half a million, the Old Dominion ranked as the largest slave state in the South. Virginia's bondmen toiled in factories and worked in the fields. War and secession would see this pattern change very little.

Yet, the advent of war did lead a number of Virginia's slaves to run away. According to Jordan, the bondmen saw the war ushering in a "millennium of freedom." Slaveholders, who had long convinced themselves that their slaves were contented, were stunned at the turn of events. But even as they ran to freedom, Virginia's slaves encountered racism. Jordan notes that "Although the Civil War evolved into an apocalyptic contest of slavery versus freedom, blacks were generally held in low opinion by Confederates and Yankees" (Jordan 1995: 70, 136, 153).

The most provocative parts of Jordan's book deal with those slaves who stayed loyal to the Confederacy. This seeming paradox, remaining true to the system that stripped them of all civil liberties and which treated them as chattel, is, according to Jordan, one of the real "riddles" of the war. He maintains that blacks enlisted in the fight and supported the Confederate government because they hoped to better their status in the postwar world. Jordan refers to Confederate efforts to recruit and train Confederate States Colored Troops as the South's "Great White Hope." "In the span of less than four years," Jordan writes, "Confederate slaves evolved from a hereditary labor force into armed indigenous allies." Nonetheless, whites in Virginia tried to convince themselves, "They were not giving up slavery in arming their slaves." Although most historians have treated the South's efforts at arming the slaves in 1865 as a gesture that was too little, too late, Jordan disagrees. He notes that numbers alone indicate they could have made a major difference in the outcome of the conflict. Moreover, he believes southern slaves "suffered hostile fire and attacked Union troops, white men supposedly fighting to free them." The brave black soldiers who fought for the Confederacy, Jordan concludes, have been too long ignored, and should be recognized for their sacrifices (Jordan 1995: 216, 229, 232–44, 246–51).

To be sure, many Virginia slaves who left the farms and plantations journeyed to Federal lines and enlisted, once it was created, in the US Colored Troops (USCT). These Afro-Virginians saw that by fighting for the Union, they could help destroy the system of slavery. The USCT faced more than southern bullets; they knew that if captured they would be executed, for the Confederacy believed the enlistment of black troops was tantamount to unleashing a race war.

Despite the many contributions Virginia slaves made to both sides, the advent of peace and the attainment of freedom brought new problems. Jordan concludes his monograph by noting that white racism and "animosity" toward the freedmen, coupled with their very precarious status – the freedmen were poor and propertyless – made blacks aware they "faced ambiguous futures." Still, Jordan argues those freedmen "were determined to exercise their hard-won rights" (Jordan 1995: 264–76, 287, 307).

The work of Berlin et al. (1992), Jordan (1995), and Mohr (2001 [1986]) on the treatment of southern slaves and free blacks during the Confederate era foreshadows the problems that southerners, both white and black, faced in Reconstruction. Freedom and peace did not include an end to racism and the quick establishment of equality. That would take a second reconstruction almost one hundred years later.

The scholarship on the Confederate home front continues to flourish. Historians are finally beginning to delve into the urban experience. Monographs on Atlanta and other Georgia cities such as Augusta, as well as Richmond, Montgomery, Mobile, and Nashville, have helped to correct the stereotype of a totally agrarian region. Further, these urban histories portray dynamic wartime economies which enabled the Confederacy to field and supply its armies longer than anyone thought possible before 1861. We need a more detailed analysis of the urban Confederacy and its people at war to further inform our knowledge of the home front in the cities.

Within those cities, historians are also looking at people who stayed loyal to the United States, often at great risk. Southern Unionism first attracted Tatum's imagination back in 1934, but now other scholars see similar phenomena in Richmond, Atlanta, and elsewhere in the south. Too, historians are beginning to look at how some southern unionists created fifth-column movements, such as the Heroes of America, in an effort to bring the Confederate states back into the Union. Fuller treatments of these activities and the impact they had on the ultimate Confederate defeat are needed, for they indicate still further how diverse, if not divided, the Confederacy was.

We are finally gaining a clearer picture of what life was like for wealthy planters and southern ladies; for yeoman farmers and poor whites; for factory workers and slaves. We are coming to appreciate that life in the cities was often vastly different from life in the countryside; and we are seeing that where one lived often determined allegiance to the Confederate nation. Yet we really do not have a synthesis of this vast topic, a study that ties the variegated elements of the Confederate home front together. Perhaps now is the time for a scholar to write a history of the southern Confederacy from behind the lines. That project may be the vehicle through which we can better understand the sacrifices and hardships those 9 million people endured for four long years.

BIBLIOGRAPHY

Ash, Stephen V. (1988) *Middle Tennessee Society Transformed, 1860–1870: War and Peace in the Upper South.* Baton Rouge, La.: Louisiana State University Press.

Ash, Stephen V. (1995) *When the Yankees Came: Conflict and Chaos in the Occupied South.* Chapel Hill, NC: University of North Carolina Press.

Berlin, Ira et al. (eds.) (1982–93) *Freedom: A Documentary History of Emancipation, 1861–1867,* four vols. New York: Cambridge University Press.

Berlin, Ira, Fields, Barbara J., Miller, Steven F., Reidy, Joseph P., and Rowland, Leslie S. (1992) *Slaves No More: Three Essays on Emancipation and the Civil War.* New York: Cambridge University Press.

Cooper, William J., Jr (2000) *Jefferson Davis, American.* New York: Alfred A. Knopf.

Davis, William C. (1991) *Jefferson Davis: The Man and his Hour, a Biography.* New York: HarperCollins.

Durrill, Wayne K. (1990) *War of Another Kind: A Southern Community in the Great Rebellion.* New York: Oxford University Press.

Escott, Paul D. (1978) *After Secession: Jefferson Davis and the Failure of Confederate Nationalism.* Baton Rouge, La.: Louisiana State University Press.

Faust, Drew Gilpin (1996) *Mothers of Invention: Women of the Slaveholding South in the American Civil War.* Chapel Hill, NC: University of North Carolina Press.

Jordan, Ervin L., Jr (1995) *Black Confederates and Afro-Yankees in Civil War Virginia.* Charlottesville, Va.: University of Virginia Press.

Lonn, Ella (1933) *Salt as a Factor in the Confederacy.* New York: Neale.

Lonn, Ella (1940) *Foreigners in the Confederacy.* Chapel Hill, NC: University of North Carolina Press.

Marten, James (1998) *The Children's Civil War.* Chapel Hill, NC: University of North Carolina Press.

Massey, Mary Elizabeth (1966) *Bonnet Brigades: American Women in the Civil War.* New York: Alfred A. Knopf.

Mohr, Clarence L. (2001 [1986]) *On the Threshold of Freedom: Masters and Slaves in Civil War Georgia.* Baton Rouge, La.: Louisiana State University Press.

Rable, George C. (1989) *Civil Wars: Women and the Crisis of Southern Nationalism.* Urbana, Ill.: University of Illinois Press.

Ramsdell, Charles W. (1972 [1944]) *Behind the Lines in the Southern Confederacy.* Baton Rouge, La.: Louisiana State University Press.

Roark, James L. (1977) *Masters without Slaves: Southern Planters in the Civil War and Reconstruction.* New York: Norton.

Sutherland, Daniel E. (1995) *Seasons of War: The Ordeal of a Confederate Community, 1861–1865.* New York: Free Press.

Tatum, Georgia Lee (1934) *Disloyalty in the Confederacy.* Chapel Hill, NC: University of North Carolina Press.

Wiley, Bell I. (1944) *The Plain People of the Confederacy.* Baton Rouge, La.: Louisiana State University Press.

SUGGESTED FURTHER READING

Bergeron, Arthur W., Jr (1991) *Confederate Mobile.* Jackson, Miss.: University Press of Mississippi.

Clinton, Catherine (1995) *Tara Revisited: Women, War, and the Plantation Legend*. New York: Abbeville Press.

DeCredico, Mary A. (1990) *Patriotism for Profit: Georgia's Urban Entrepreneurs and the Confederate War Effort*. Chapel Hill, NC: University of North Carolina Press.

Degler, Carl (1982 [1974]) *The Other South: Southern Dissenters in the Nineteenth Century*. Boston, Mass.: Northeastern University Press.

Doyle, Don H. (2001) *Faulkner's County: The Historical Roots of Yoknapatawpha*. Chapel Hill, NC: University of North Carolina Press.

Dyer, Thomas G. (1999) *Secret Yankees: The Union Circle in Confederate Atlanta*. Baltimore, Md.: Johns Hopkins University Press.

Harris, J. William (1985) *Plain Folk and Gentry in a Slave Society: White Liberty and Black Slavery in Augusta's Hinterland*. Middletown, Conn.: Wesleyan University Press.

Klingberg, Frank (1955) *The Southern Claims Commission*. Berkeley, Calif.: University of California Press.

Massey, Mary Elizabeth (1952) *Ersatz in the Confederacy*. Columbia, SC: University of South Carolina Press.

Rogers, William Warren, Jr (1999) *Confederate Home Front: Montgomery during the Civil War*. Tuscaloosa, Ala.: University of Alabama Press.

Thomas, Emory M. (1998 [1971]) *The Confederate State of Richmond: A Biography of the Capital*. Baton Rouge, La.: Louisiana State University Press.

Tripp, Steven Elliott (1997) *Yankee Town, Southern City: Race and Class Relations in Civil War Lynchburg*. New York: New York University Press.

Whites, LeeAnn (1995) *The Civil War as a Crisis in Gender: Augusta, Georgia, 1860–1890*. Athens, Ga.: University of Georgia Press.

CHAPTER FIFTEEN

Emancipation

JOSEPH P. REIDY

Since the early 1960s, scholarship on slave emancipation in the Civil War era has undergone an interpretive sea-change. As of 1963, the centennial of Abraham Lincoln's Emancipation Proclamation, most scholars viewed emancipation within the context of the Civil War and Reconstruction and through the lens of public policy. From such a perspective, President Lincoln and his Republican colleagues in Congress were the architects of emancipation. A growing body of scholarship over the prior three decades had challenged the influential views of William Archibald Dunning and his students, who had viewed emancipation as at best an unfortunate experiment in political equality and at worst a sinister plot to promote racial amalgamation. The revisionist scholars depicted the destruction of slavery as a positive good and credited both slave resistance and abolitionist agitation as important contributing factors. Yet in 1963 most historians viewed Lincoln as the proximate cause of emancipation even if not necessarily as the Great Emancipator.

Political and intellectual currents moved in new directions. The Civil Rights Movement, for instance, provided daily evidence that a mass movement of ordinary citizens might promote social change as profoundly as the actions of elected officials did. Much of the revisionist scholarship published between the mid-1950s and the late 1960s reflected this insight while retaining an ultimate interest in federal policy and its enforcement. At the same time, historians and other students of human society in Europe and the Americas began developing new analytical techniques and theoretical frameworks for interpreting how politically and socially subordinate groups affect the historical process. Although one variant of this approach soon came to be known loosely as the New Social History, its advocates spanned a wide spectrum of political ideologies and research methodologies. What they shared was a commitment to democratize the concept of historical agency, freeing it from its traditional representation as the monopoly of political elites. To one extent or another, all the historians whose work came to be labeled "revisionist" shared a similar interpretive purpose.

In reexamining the Civil War and Reconstruction periods, revisionists necessarily cast a fresh eye on emancipation. Many drew inspiration from W. E. B. DuBois' monumental *Black Reconstruction in America* (1935), which set the modern agenda for understanding the place of emancipation in the Civil War and Reconstruction. In his scathing review of the "Propaganda of History" (Chapter 17), DuBois blasted the Dunning School. Far from a foolhardy attempt to let ignorant former slaves legislate, DuBois argued, Reconstruction represented a legitimate attempt to establish representative government in the southern states based on the full participation of all adult men, regardless of their ancestry or former condition. He carefully chronicled the freedpeople's aspirations of freedom, their support for the Union during the Civil War, their enthusiasm for education, and their dogged pursuit of justice. Freely acknowledging his debt to John R. Lynch, Carter G. Woodson, and Alrutheus A. Taylor, and others whose works combated the popular stereotypes, DuBois also employed quasi-Marxist interpretive tools – referring, for instance, to enslaved African Americans as a "black proletariat" (1935: 381) who conducted a "general strike" (Chapter 4) against the Confederacy during the Civil War – which he had first encountered during his student days in Berlin and which had achieved popularity in the United States during the Great Depression. And although it relied more on secondary scholarship than on primary sources, *Black Reconstruction* succeeded grandly in identifying the destruction of slavery, the development of a system of compensated labor in the South, and the incorporation of the freedpeople into the body politic of the region and the nation as the central drama of the Civil War era.

The scholarship of the 1960s employed the principles of racial equality and political democracy against the racist interpretations of the Dunning School. Four monographs and a biography serve to illustrate: John Hope Franklin's *The Emancipation Proclamation* (1963), Willie Lee Rose's *Rehearsal for Reconstruction* (1964), James M. McPherson's *The Struggle for Equality* (1964), Joel Williamson's *After Slavery* (1965), William S. McFeely's *Yankee Stepfather* (1968). Though different in focus and style, each of these works advanced a new understanding of slave emancipation and its role in Reconstruction. Each also drew inspiration from the emerging body of scholarship contesting the Plantation School's racist interpretations of antebellum slavery as a benign social institution. Indeed, Kenneth M. Stampp, whose *Peculiar Institution* (1956) was the landmark revisionist study of slavery, also published *The Era of Reconstruction* (1965). Similarly, John Hope Franklin wrote authoritatively about the antebellum as well as the wartime and postbellum periods.

Commemorating the centennial of the Emancipation Proclamation, Franklin (1963) provided a brief narrative account of the origins and consequences of one of the key documents in the nation's history. Like DuBois, Franklin appreciated the art of policy-making as more than the work of an individual. Accordingly, he examined the roles of Congress and assorted military leaders in experimenting with emancipationist measures during the first year of the war. Notwithstanding this perception on the policy-making process as a whole, Franklin gives special credit to Lincoln. Although the president's public pronouncements against slavery before the war clearly indicated his personal animosity to slavery, broadly constitutional as well as narrowly political reasons at first kept him wedded to a policy of compensated emancipation coupled with colonization. After announcing his policy of emancipation, however, Lincoln abandoned that position, and in time came to hope "that the Proclamation would provide the basis for a new attitude and policy for Negroes." Although Lincoln did not live to witness, much less guide, such a transformation, Franklin maintained that the proclamation changed "the course of the war" (Franklin 1963: 152).

Although their works concentrated largely on the formulation of public policy, both DuBois (1935) and Franklin (1963) emphasized the interaction between policy-makers and the persons most affected by the policies. In addition to chronicling the ways in which such prominent leaders as Frederick Douglass attempted to influence the president's thinking regarding emancipation, Franklin illustrated how African Americans expanded the concept of emancipation beyond the narrowly confined wording of the proclamation. Specifically, he cited the joyous celebrations that the black communities at Norfolk, Virginia, and Port Royal, South Carolina, conducted on January 1, 1863, despite the fact that both of those areas had been exempted from the proclamation. By emphasizing the active part that the enslaved population played in the struggle for freedom, he anticipated a major emphasis of the next generation of historical scholarship.

The other revisionist authors of the 1960s did the same, though each somewhat differently. In a study characterized by its stunningly beautiful prose no less than by its interpretive acuity, Rose's *Rehearsal for Reconstruction* (1964) examined the interactions between the freedpeople of coastal South Carolina and the assortment of evangelical missionaries, government officials, and entrepreneurs that descended from the North following the Union's occupation of Port Royal in November 1861. This "rehearsal" for Reconstruction afforded Rose a rich canvas on which to sketch how those whom war and fate had cast together contended with the challenges posed by emancipation. In one characteristic passage, Rose mimicked the freedwomen who both chided the missionaries and forgave their faults, branding their often contradictory "assessments of Negro character" as "a tribute to the myriad forms of human personality and a witness to missionary confusion" (Rose 1964: 166).

James M. McPherson's *The Struggle for Equality* (1965) followed the abolitionist crusade for freedom and equal rights from the start of the Civil War through the ratification of the Fifteenth Amendment in 1870. Starting from the premise that the movement did not cease its activity in 1861, McPherson traced the movement's ongoing attempts to influence federal policy regarding emancipation and its consequences. Though far from unanimous in their views, the abolitionists pressured political leaders and undertook campaigns of public awareness surrounding the plight of the freedpeople and the need for decisive government action to enlarge the scope of freedom. Yet for all their radical rhetoric about freedom and equality, the abolitionists could not entirely escape the political culture in which they functioned and the logic of their own professed convictions. Nowhere was this clearer than in their contradictory pronouncements regarding black suffrage. While some advocated open and equal access to the ballot on the part of all adult men regardless of color or previous condition, others believed that the evils of slavery ill-equipped freedmen for the vote. Even William Lloyd Garrison himself equivocated, for practical no less than philosophical reasons. On the grounds that the ballot was a "conventional" rather than a natural right and that states enjoyed the prerogative to grant such rights, he saw no relevant historical precedent for such action and little hope that the states would grant suffrage to the freedmen. At the end of the decade abolitionists had much to celebrate, but they nonetheless regretted that "[t]he North's conversion to emancipation and equal rights" rested on "expediency" rather than "conviction" (McPherson 1965: 294, 430). When political circumstances changed, so did the commitment to the cause; Jim Crow, disfranchisement, and lynching ensued.

William S. McFeely's (1968) biography of Oliver Otis Howard, *Yankee Stepfather*, both advanced the revisionist reinterpretation of Reconstruction and contributed to a deeper understanding of emancipation. Renowned Civil War general, commissioner of the Freedmen's Bureau, and third president of the university that bears his name, Howard played a significant role in translating the legal mandate of emancipation into practical operation. McFeely's treatment explored the tension between Howard's strong sense of Christian stewardship and the political controversies that attend public service, particularly in an agency designed to provide social welfare. Howard's encounter with President Andrew Johnson over the restoration of confiscated land to its antebellum owners illustrates the point. In a particularly dramatic episode that occurred on the Sea Islands of South Carolina in October 1865, Howard himself delivered to the freedpeople the hard news that they must relinquish the land. On the one hand Howard shrank before the enormity of his task; but on the other hand, "hoping to make a lie a truth by saying it as if it were a moral commitment," he "tried to make the Edisto Islanders believe that President Johnson cared about them" (McFreely 1968: 144). In the final analysis, the bureau relieved destitution among white and black refugees, promoted the development of compensated labor in the plantation economy, and otherwise mediated social relations between former masters and former slaves in the war-torn South, all under Howard's direction. Despite the limitations of the agency no less than of its commissioner, McFeely found much to admire in what they accomplished.

Joel Williamson's *After Slavery* (1965) occupies a curious place among the revisionist works of the 1960s. Acknowledging an intellectual camaraderie with the new scholarship, Williamson acknowledged no debt to DuBois (1935). Similarly, he drew greater insight from his lifetime of observing the sights of his native South and listening to the stories of its people than he did from contemporary events. Hence, although the book anticipated the post-revisionist scholarship of the 1970s and 1980s in some ways it also reflected formative experiences in the pre-Civil Rights era. In Williamson's view, for instance, black politicians responded to opportunities that outsiders made available to them; and even the freedpeople's "attitudes . . . toward native whites were largely reponses to attitudes manifested by whites themselves" (Williamson 1965: 252).

Notwithstanding those limitations, *After Slavery* explored facets of emancipation that transcended any single state and that have preoccupied subsequent scholars of the subject. Williamson (1965) established clearly that rural freedpeople aspired to economic independence through land-ownership, failing which they rented land, found supervisory employment, or worked for wages. Like their urban (and frequently freeborn) counterparts, the rural folk desired to enjoy citizenship rights without discrimination and took active part in public affairs during Reconstruction. They organized churches, schools, and other similar civic organizations and associations for the collective improvement. In short, they defied the stereotypes of political buffoons and lazy dependants that had been the hallmark of hostile interpretations from Reconstruction to the mid-twentieth century. Instead, Williamson viewed the freedpeople as a poor working class of people, struggling against the legacy of slavery and the active resistance of their former owners to their economic, social, and political progress. Every later work of revisionist and post-revisionist scholarship has done the same.

Although the revisionist scholarship of the 1960s employed the principles of racial equality and political democracy against the racist interpretations of the Dunning School, for the most part it stopped short of articulating a new conception of the historical dynamic in the way that the post-revisionists of the 1970s and 1980s did. The New Social History cast a long shadow across the post-revisionist intellectual landscape. A host of new studies examined the role of African Americans in affecting the circumstances of their own lives and the larger course of national events. Related developments in other subdisciplines of the field of history (such as economic history) provided a major impetus behind investigations into the evolution of the southern plantation system from one based on slavery to one based on tenancy and sharecropping. By the 1980s, the influence of the women's rights movement on historical interpretation was evident in the level of interest being paid to the effect of emancipation on gender relations, a trend that continues to the present.

Three books that appeared during the 1970s transcended the limitations of revisionist scholarship while building upon its notable achievements. The first, Louis S. Gerteis' *From Contraband to Freedman* (1973), examined revisionist assumptions about abolition – how it came about, what motivated its proponents, and what lasting changes resulted – and found them wanting. Rather than extolling emancipation as the culmination of an idealistic struggle, Gerteis insisted that military exigency loomed above not only the Emancipation Proclamation but also every policy that federal officials formulated regarding the freedpeople during the war. Far from considering federal policy as monolithic, Gerteis carefully charted the differences from one military theater to another and in all theaters over the course of the war. The book made three major points. First, the federal government's wartime policies toward persons escaping slavery – "contrabands" in the vernacular of the time – were anything but systematically developed or consistently applied. Instead, they were a hodgepodge of steps often initiated as temporary expedients to address particular circumstances at a given place and time. Second, the policy-makers were often at odds with each other regarding the best course of action to take. Governmental officials from the War and Treasury departments rarely saw eye to eye, and the labor policies of neither agency coincided with "the humanitarian concerns of the Northern missionaries" (Gerteis 1973: 183). Third, the policies developed during the war, for all their positive local effects in terms of relieving destitution and establishing models of compensated labor, had limited applicability to the postwar world. In the first place, federal policy did not extend beyond the reach of federal arms, which in practical terms exempted the vast interior of the Confederacy. In human terms, Gerteis estimated that of the 4 million persons held as slaves in 1861, roughly 1 million resided in Union-occupied territory at the end of the war. Of that number, not quite one-quarter lived and labored under the direct supervision of federal authorities. By this estimate, approximately 3 million persons were still being held as slaves when the war ended. The vast majority of the former Confederate states and their people, white and black, knew little if anything of the federal government's experiments and the fate of the emancipated slaves in the months and years after the war. And even after the war, congressional efforts to monitor the transition from slavery to freedom fell far short of the mark. "The Freedmen's Bureau," Gerteis aptly concludes, simply "lacked the means to affect the lives and labor of Southern blacks" (Gerteis 1973: 193, 191).

The second notable work of post-revisionist scholarship was Thomas Holt's *Black over White* (1977), which offered liberating insights into the dynamics of African American politics in South Carolina during Reconstruction. It bore on the larger theme of emancipation in the sense that from the 1870s through the 1940s most hostile interpreters of Reconstruction used South Carolina to demonstrate the folly of "Negro rule." Because persons of African descent constituted a numerical majority of the population, and because (for a time, at least) African American men held a majority of the seats in the state house of representatives, they influenced public policy in a way unique among all the states. Holt focused particularly on the role that persons of African descent who were free before the Civil War played in this process.

Holt's (1977) work was notable in other ways as well. As the integrationist emphasis of the Civil Rights Movement retreated before the nationalist emphasis of the Black Power movement, scholarship subtly reflected the nationalist position that emphasized the essential unity among people of African descent. Bucking that tide, Holt (1977: 163) insisted that the formerly free and the formerly enslaved did not necessarily share the same goals and aspirations; indeed, he flatly asserted the presence of divisions "along lines of prewar status and color." When the prewar advantages of wealth and education that free persons often enjoyed were added into the mix, little wonder that their interests often diverged from those of the freedpeople. In sum, Holt's analysis succeeded in demonstrating that persons of African descent did not have a single stake in the outcome of emancipation, nor could they be lumped together as a homogeneous group.

The third important work in this trio of early post-revisionist scholarship was Herbert Gutman's (1976) monumental study, *The Black Family in Slavery and Freedom*, which surveyed the African American experience in North America from colonial times into the twentieth century. Gutman pursued two major interpretive goals. The first was to refute the thesis of Daniel Patrick Moynihan suggesting that the social problems associated with the late twentieth-century cities derived from the absence of a viable family structure during slavery. Armed with a narrative strategy and interpretive insights that drew upon recent trends in anthropology no less than history, Gutman (1976: 465) insisted that despite the harsh and confining character of slavery, its victims retained the capacity "to adapt and sustain the vital familial and kin associations and beliefs that served as the underpinning of a developing Afro-American culture." The second interpretive goal was to contest Eugene D. Genovese's (1974) influential interpretation of slavery, which, in Gutman's view, concentrated unduly on the late antebellum era and neglected to account appropriately for change over time. By marshaling evidence that spanned the late eighteenth to the early twentieth centuries, Gutman posited a view of black institutional life that remained true to underlying ideals while responding to new challenges. Most significantly, the adaptive "kin networks" provided a foundation for "developing Afro-American communities, which prepared slaves to deal with legal freedom" (Gutman 1976: 3).

Gutman's study had special relevance for the emerging study of emancipation for two major reasons. First, he drew attention to the marriage registers in the manuscript records of the Freedmen's Bureau. These records demonstrated clearly that enslaved African Americans had strong family ties that spanned generations. Contrary to popular misconceptions, slaves' marriages served the range of social and emotional purposes that the institution did for free persons (excepting, of course, the custodial role over accumulated property that constitutes so central a part of modern bourgeois family relations). Gutman's study also suggested that the desire of freedpeople to preserve the integrity of prewar family units – by reuniting those fragmented by the interstate slave trade, for instance – affected the shape of postbellum labor relations. Strong family units provided a modicum of institutional protection to family members. Parents could send their children to school, and extended kin could take in orphaned relatives thereby shielding them from lengthy apprenticeships. In the end, Gutman's work identified the preservation and affirmation of a strong yet flexible family structure as a central feature of the African American experience in North America. The era of emancipation provides the interpretive window for understanding the central relationship of the family to other African American social institutions.

The work of two economic historians, Roger L. Ransom and Richard Sutch, entitled *One Kind of Freedom* (1977) opened a range of new interpretive possibilities and, like Gutman's (1976) work, brought the impact of scholarship on the slave era to a deeper understanding of emancipation in the Civil War era. Reflecting the transformation in economic analysis resulting from the development of econometric techniques, Ransom and Sutch (1977) were able for the first time to quantify a number of economic and social relationships of longstanding interest to historians of the post-emancipation South. Chief among these was the evolution of sharecropping in the cotton-growing region and the transformation of agricultural credit from a system based on large cotton factors to a decentralized one whose key players were local merchants and cotton ginners and traders. Though not as wealthy or well placed as their antebellum counterparts, the postbellum creditors of the cotton economy succeeded in establishing local territorial monopolies with profound influence over labor and land-ownership patterns within their respective bailiwicks.

Despite their sweeping conceptual framework, Ransom and Sutch (1977) paid close attention to detail. From credit rating reports on local merchants, for instance, they extracted rich anecdotal evidence on conditions throughout the cotton region. And from their sympathetic reading of other contemporary sources, they argued that freedpeople played a major part in the reorganization of postbellum agriculture, despite their lack of property, political power, and social influence. The two authors attributed much of this success to the freedpeople's desire to command their families' labor, chiefly by withdrawing women "from dawn to dusk labor in the fields . . . so that they might better care for their children and the household" (Ransom and Sutch 1977: 55). This insight enabled them to theorize the magnitude of the reduction in social labor performed in raising the region's cotton crop, while at the same time opening intriguing insights into the dynamic of freedpeople's households. Like Gutman's (1976) work on the African American family, *One Kind of Freedom* helped establish a baseline from which other scholars could explore how emancipation affected relations between men and women, parents and children, and freedpeople and their employers.

Several notable studies – Jonathan Wiener's *Social Origins of the New South* (1978), Gavin Wright's *Old South, New South* (1986), and Gerald David Jaynes' *Branches Without Roots* (1986) – contested the portrait that *One Kind of Freedom* painted.

Wiener's (1978) argument rested on three pillars. Although Wiener took special aim at C. Vann Woodward's famous contention in *Origins of the New South* (1951) that the post-Civil War planter elite represented a new social class, oriented toward the business interests of the New South rather than toward the slaveholding past of the Old South, he also disputed the claim of Ransom and Sutch (1977) regarding the economic power that derived from the hypothesized ability of each cross-roads merchant to establish a "territorial monopoly" (Wiener 1978: 127). Marshaling evidence from Alabama, Wiener contended that the planter elite, with direct ties to the antebellum slaveholding plantation system, dominated the black-belt politically as well as economically after the Civil War. Lacking comparable political and economic power, the merchants were overmatched. Those who chose not to subordinate their interests to those of the landed elite contented themselves with furnishing white yeoman farmers with supplies outside the plantation belt.

In related journal articles, Wiener (1975, 1976, 1979) characterized sharecropping as a distinct mode of production. In this view, which the economist Jay Mandle (1978) was advocating at the same time, emancipation destroyed slavery but did not result in the abolition of coerced labor: sharecroppers were not slaves, but neither were they free laborers comparable to those in other sectors of the national economy. The term sharecropping mode of production also provided a framework for understanding the broader political economy of the post-Civil War South. Planters wielded such a conservative political and social influence over the region precisely because they enjoyed a unique level of command over their labor force. Harold Woodman (1995) weighed into this debate recognizing the revolutionary transformation that emancipation wrought but drawing much different theoretical conclusions from those of Wiener (1978) and Mandle (1978, 1992).

From a perspective more attuned to mainstream economic interest in markets than in modes of production, Gavin Wright (1986) and Gerald David Jaynes (1986) offered competing interpretations of the impact of the Civil War and slave emancipation on the southern economy, both of which appeared in 1986. Whereas Wiener (1978) emphasized the continuity between antebellum and postbellum planter classes based on the political influence that control over the land conveyed, Wright's *Old South, New South* stressed the profound differences between the two. In Wright's (1986) deft phrasing, antebellum "labor lords" gave way to postbellum "landlords." Viewing the evolution of markets, particularly in labor, as the key to understanding broader patterns of development, Wright did not deny the advantages that planters enjoyed due to the South's position as "a low-wage region in a high-wage country." Wiener (1978) attributed these advantages to the planters' calculated use of political power, but for Wright the key to the puzzle lay in the ability of freedpeople no less than landowning planters to "adapt" to evolving "market categories" (Wright 1986: 49, 76, 103).

For his part, Jaynes (1986) did not offer a sweeping framework for understanding the postbellum labor system so much as a careful inventory of labor arrangements that arose from the ashes of slavery. Although essentially an economic history of the evolution of labor markets in emancipated labor, *Branches without Roots* also employed the technique of thick description that anthropologists had earlier popularized and that Gutman's (1976) *The Black Family in Slavery and Freedom* evidenced. Like other post-revisionist scholars, Jaynes credited the formerly enslaved with creative input into this process. Although the freedpeople lacked sufficient economic resources to influence the regional economy, they enjoyed strength in numbers and a common determination to enjoy the fruits of freedom.

The technique of thick description that Jaynes (1986) employed to such telling effect was the foundation on which one of the landmark studies of the post-revisionist era stood: Leon F. Litwack's Pulitzer Prize-winning *Been in the Storm So Long* (1979). Litwack did not focus narrowly on the transformation of labor relations or of African American families or of the southern body politic, although he offered insightful commentary on all those topics. The strength of the work derived from its stunning breadth and its emphasis on the fundamental uncertainty, indeed serendipity, of the emancipation process. Anecdotes of personal encounters – between former masters and former slaves, African American soldiers and their Confederate counterparts, freedmen and freedwomen, Klansmen and their victims – drove Litwack's narrative. With graceful and moving prose, his analysis ranged across the complex terrain between two poles: the bitter resentment that most white southerners harbored and the daunting struggle that freedpeople waged for freedom, dignity, and equality. In the face of challenge, black southerners' accomplishments were remarkable even if the results often fell short of the original goal. The struggle itself constituted "an epic chapter in the history of the American people" (Litwack 1979: xiv).

The 1980s witnessed the full flowering of interpretations that placed the aspirations and activities of African American people at the center of the emancipation process. To be sure, scholars continued to produce superb work in the traditional mold wherein governmental leaders catalyzed the process. For obvious reasons, President Lincoln figured largely in this scholarship. LaWanda Cox's (1981) *Lincoln and Black Freedom*, for instance, depicted Lincoln as a staunch opponent of black liberty despite his oft-cited ambiguity on the matter of black equality. Cox argued convincingly that Lincoln did not march far ahead of general public opinion on matters of racial policy. Cox claimed that the Emancipation Proclamation was a significant document that could not be dismissed as either a heartless excuse for a declaration of equality or a cynical ruse that freed no slaves immediately. Instead, the document provided a blueprint for the future conduct of the Civil War that committed the Union's armed forces to freeing slaves. Even more significantly, she insisted, Lincoln took firm steps to overcome the legal limitations on what he clearly understood to be a policy articulated under presidential authority in time of war that might be susceptible to reversal upon the return of peace. His lobbying of Louisiana unionists on behalf of limited black suffrage in 1864 and his support for the Thirteenth Amendment in 1865 illustrate this awareness. In these and other examples, Cox (1981: 178) found clear evidence that though "a man of his age," Lincoln did not simply pay lip-service to the principle of emancipation; instead, he took great pains to insure that freedom would not be undone after the war.

Notwithstanding such traditional studies as Cox's, the outpouring of work on the freedpeople's role in emancipation marked a profound turning point in the historiography of the 1980s. The works published by the Freedmen and Southern Society Project at the University of Maryland under the direction of Ira Berlin have had a marked influence on this transformation. *The Black Military Experience* (Berlin et al. 1982) examined the mobilization of African American soldiers, their contribution to the Union's military victory, and the pivotal role they played in undermining slavery in the Union's slave states no less than in the Confederacy. Subsequently, *The Destruction of Slavery* (Berlin et al. 1985) and *The Wartime Genesis of Free Labor* (Berlin et al. 1990, 1993) sketched the processes whereby slavery ended and various experiments in compensated labor emerged during the war. These works were notable in two important respects. First, they employed a combination of interpretive narrative and annotated documents to build their arguments. Second, while emphasizing both the complexity and the contingency of the social processes they described, they took special pains to chronicle the ways that actions by African Americans affected the outcome of events. Neither the origins of emancipation "nor its mainspring could be found in the seats of executive and legislative authority from which the great documents issued," *The Destruction of Slavery* affirms. "Instead, they reside in the humble quarters of slaves, who were convinced in April 1861 of what would not be fully affirmed until December 1865, and whose actions consistently undermined every settlement short of universal abolition" (Berlin et al. 1985: 55).

Eric Foner stands as another major architect of this shift in understanding the freedpeople's central role in constructing new economic, social, and political relationships to take the place of slavery. Foner's (1983) *Nothing but Freedom* cast emancipation in the wartime United States in an international context that both reflected the significant body of comparative work on the history of slavery produced during the preceding generation and anticipated even greater interest in comparative emancipation during the last two decades of the twentieth century. Foner's chief preoccupations were the common challenges that freedpeople in all post-slavery societies shared in relationship to labor and citizenship. Whether they sought access to land and other productive resources with which to support themselves or struggled with employers (often former masters) over the terms and conditions of compensation for labor, Foner found no post-slavery society in which the issues were settled quickly and amicably. Instead, the end of slavery ushered in complex transitions to new routines of labor and methods of compensation. Given the political auspices under which emancipation occurred, freedpeople frequently found themselves interacting with a hostile state apparatus, whose actions often "redefine[d] class and property relations and enhance[d] labor discipline" to the disadvantage of the emancipated workers (Foner 1983: 60). Although in some cases select freedmen assumed all the rights of citizenship, including the suffrage, in others that possibility was foreclosed. But even in societies where the limitations loomed larger than the opportunities, freedpeople engaged any and every institutional structure to achieve their aspirations of freedom. The book's final chapter on a famous strike by rice-plantation workers in South Carolina illustrates the multiple levels of this struggle.

Foner's (1988) masterpiece, *Reconstruction*, retreated from the international back to the national scene. Among its many virtues, the book situates emancipation squarely at the center of the Reconstruction process. Northern and southern political strategists contested much more than the terms whereby the former Confederate states would rejoin the Union and the role that federal military officials, including those of the Freedmen's Bureau, would play in the process. Ultimately the stakes included reconstructing the social fabric of a region whose framework of economic and social relationships had stood on the foundation of slavery. Foner paid special attention to the evolution of new economic and political relations that rested on the principles of compensated labor and black male suffrage.

Although freedpeople lacked the wealth and other productive resources that their former owners possessed, their ability to work gave them leverage in the struggle over the labor arrangements to replace slavery. Like Berlin and his colleagues, Foner (1988) found considerable variation in these arrangements, from plantation to plantation within the same neighborhood, from state to state, and from one crop region to another. Despite these variations, two characteristics stood out. First, these arrangements fluctuated widely during the early postwar period before settling into more discernible patterns. The example of the cotton-growing region illustrates. Whereas gang labor under the direction of overseers survived for several years following the war, particularly in areas where large plantations had dominated the antebellum landscape, family-based labor arrangements emerged within the first few postwar years. From those beginnings, fully articulated systems of tenancy and sharecropping later emerged. To be sure, freedpeople used the political process, and particularly their newfound right of suffrage to help influence the evolution of these labor arrangements, yet all parties also found themselves beholden to larger political and economic forces. Most notable among these was the onset of an international depression following the Panic of 1873. Although historians frequently associate the prolonged period of depressed trade, which in fact persisted through the rest of the nineteenth century, with the emergence of the Populist Movement in the 1880s and 1890s, they have rarely appreciated the effects of falling commodity prices on southern agriculture during the infancy of the system of free labor. In the circumstances, producers on the ground had to scramble in the face of shifting national and world commodity markets. Though typically possessing only limited productive resources of their own, freedpeople nonetheless found ways to influence the emancipation process, through individual and collective action.

In treating the early days of African American citizenship, Foner (1988) emphasized the dynamic interaction between grassroots developments in local communities and the actions of governmental officials at local, state, and national levels. In the process, the formerly enslaved found themselves struggling to exercise the rights of citizenship (including the suffrage itself) as well as contesting government actions through the electoral process. As the larger history of Reconstruction attests, they had mixed success. Although only 16 African American officeholders won seats in Congress during Reconstruction and another 18 held executive-level offices in the states, "the fact that well over 600 blacks served as legislators – the large majority, except in Louisiana and Virginia, former slaves – represented a stunning departure in American politics" (Foner 1988: 355). Both during and after congressional Reconstruction, hundreds of African Americans held elected positions at the county or municipal level, where, like their counterparts in the legislative and executive branches of government, they performed creditably even as they stretched the traditional boundaries of representative government in new directions.

Foner's (1988) analysis of the political dimensions of emancipation complements Thomas Holt's (1977) in accounting for the variety within the broad patterns of experience. Like other commentators on the African American contribution to the political history of Reconstruction in the southern states, they stressed the freedpeople's passionate desire to exercise the prerogatives of citizenship, in the interest both of holding government accountable to all its citizens and of effecting social change. Once Holt (1977) gave scholarly legitimacy to examining the fault lines within

African American communities, no scholar has ignored the internal differences and strains that complicated the quest for political unity.

The monographic works on emancipation published during the 1980s and 1990s fell into two broad categories: local studies of particular regions or states, and topically focused studies of particular aspects of emancipation. Julie Saville's *The Work of Reconstruction* (1994) stands as the premier example of the former. By carefully rereading well-known sources, Saville drew fresh insights into the evolution of compensated labor in South Carolina during and after the Civil War. Whereas earlier scholars had attempted to discern a clearly defined developmental line from slavery to wage labor in gangs under overseers, to tenancy and sharecropping, Saville both blurred the distinctions among those categories and notes the retrogressive as well as progressive possibilities in each. In an insight whose implications reach far beyond South Carolina, Saville argued that even in the best of circumstances in which freedpeople had access to land, the demands of subsistence required that the land include a mixture of tillable acreage, pasture, and woodland. The lack of such access, either direct or negotiable, threatened access to the vital subsistence re-sources of "fuel, fertilizer, pasturage, herbs, and game" and left freedpeople subject to the arbitrary whims of a landowner or employer (Saville 1994: 42). To be sure, most freedpeople in South Carolina and throughout the South found themselves beholden to an employer, yet Saville's analysis helps better to explain the internal struggle in which freedpeople (and other similarly situated producers who lacked full access to productive resources) engaged. Their choices were not narrowly centered on the polar extremes of compensated labor for a landowner and subsistence-oriented landownership. Indeed, it was often only through the avenue of compensated labor that freedpeople were able to negotiate access to the mixture of land types from which subsistence could be derived. Moreover, even those who managed to gain title to small parcels of land could not very well abstain from transactions within commodity and labor markets. In short, Saville's study exposed the subtlety and independent mindedness with which freedpeople negotiated the collapse of slavery.

Other notable studies illustrate the profound influence that the women's move-ment and gender theory have had on understanding emancipation. Leslie Schwalm's *A Hard Fight for We* (1997) catalogues the many ways in which the freedwomen of South Carolina's coastal lowcountry carved their own path into the post-slavery era. In a nutshell, she aimed to counter the notion, which the recent historiography had not succeeded in expelling, "that freedwomen were observers of, not participants in, the interrelated struggles to define freedom and free labor in the postbellum South" (Schwalm 1997: 7). The particular burdens that women had borne under slavery cast a distinctive stamp on their dealings with former masters after the Civil War. Yet freedwomen also asserted themselves in new ways within their own communities, in their relationships with men and in their roles in the social institutions that formed the backbone of their communities. At once a story peculiar to the distinct cultural and historical environment of coastal South Carolina, *A Hard Fight for We* also offers provocative insights into the experience of African American women through-out the reconstructed South.

The works by Peter W. Bardaglio (1995), Laura F. Edwards (1997), and Amy Dru Stanley (1998) examined legal and political aspects of emancipation through the prism of gender theory. Bardaglio's *Reconstructing the Household* treated the ways in which "southern elites developed new public policies in the late nineteenth century that reshaped relations not only between former masters and slaves, but also between husbands and wives, and parents and children" (1995: 131). "The pressure of wartime, defeat, and the collapse of slavery," he concluded, "compelled southern governing elites to abandon the household as the primary means of social control, and to turn to the state as the chief vehicle for maintaining social order." In the aggregate, Bardaglio traced the evolution of a system of "state paternalism," which was ideologically inconceivable and politically impossible in the slave era yet the order of the day in one southern state after the other during the postwar years (Bardaglio 1995: 131–2, xvi, 148). Although affecting the entire spectrum of domestic relations, this process of reconstruction would have remained unattempted much less unaccomplished without the collapse of slavery, the foundation of the antebellum southern family.

In *Gendered Strife and Confusion*, Edwards examined postbellum southern women's struggles against antebellum conventions and their various institutional expressions that associated "blackness and femininity with dependence" (1997: 72). Edwards' insights into the transformation in gender relations after the Civil War neatly complemented Bardaglio's. For Edwards, three factors accounted for the change. First, emancipation shattered the ideal image of the southern household in which persons held as slaves were beholden to the master or mistress who presided over the larger household. Freed from that relationship of abject dependency enabled – indeed required – freedpeople to negotiate new domestic relationships, which evolved from the kinship networks that the enslaved had maintained before emancipation but which assumed new significance after freedom. Second, the appearance of a federal bureaucracy flushed not only with military victory but also with legislative mandates to adjudicate contested domestic relationships enabled women to bypass the traditional avenues of redress. As Edwards demonstrated, the records of just one agency, the Freedmen's Bureau, chronicle the extent to which women no less then men approached federal officials to resolve their grievances. In addition to the successful interventions into domestic disputes that resulted, these encounters also produced a cumulative sense of confidence that "the Freedmen's Bureau and then, particularly after Republicans took control, the local courts" might serve as "potential allies" (Edwards 1997: 63). Third, Edwards illustrated how women encroached upon public space to air domestic matters. Although not all of these actions achieved the desired results, they nonetheless dramatically affected the evolution of gender relations during the postwar period. To be sure, although women still suffered under the lingering effects of patriarchal laws and domestic practices, they nonetheless began identifying venues and techniques for challenging the status quo antebellum. Women of African descent only recently freed from slavery contributed to these developments no less than their freeborn counterparts of European descent did.

Amy Dru Stanley's *From Bondage to Contract* (1998) peered deeply into the legal struggles over emancipation to find the implicit assumptions that lay beneath the formal wording of the law. She discovered a widespread, though hardly uncontested, assumption that contract law provided guidelines for negotiating virtually every human relationship. In the aftermath of emancipation, the principles and practices of contract law served to define "the nature of freedom that was established by abolition." Yet affirming total contractual sovereignty of the individual free adult proved difficult to achieve in the face of the intertwined histories of domestic relations and labor relations. Following the Civil War, "the abolitionist view of wage labor" achieved ascendancy: "No longer was the laborer human property, a commodity possessed by a slave master," she observed; "rather, the self-owning hireling brought labor – something abstracted from self – into the free market to sell as a commodity in exchange for a wage" (Stanley 1998: 4, 75). As laborers began questioning the extent to which such relationships embodied their best notions of freedom, public officials in the North no less than in the South contended with assorted renegades from the growing orthodoxy of contract freedom, often lumping them together under the pejorative label of "vagrants."

The principles of contract law also permeated domestic relations in the postwar years, although the notion of equal partnership in marriage warred against traditional conceptions of the institution as "a legal relation of personal dominion and dependence" favoring the husband. Stanley deftly showed the contradiction inherent in too strict an adherence to the virtues of the contract in analyzing the campaigns against prostitutes. By the logic of contract freedom, these women were independent proprietors. Yet, by standing "outside the matrix of the legitimate contracts of labor and marriage," prostitutes also "evoked the nightmare of freedom" that had haunted proslavery apologists and that perplexed the postbellum apologists for the unalloyed virtues of contractual relations (Stanley 1998: 181, 218). In the North no less than the South, the conservators of public morality viewed the women as fugitives from productive labor no less than social pariahs. Denying the legitimacy of this particular variety of independent proprietorship and market exchange, civic authorities also aimed to subject its practitioners to the discipline of labor law. Through this extreme example, Stanley demonstrated the contradictions embedded within the notion that contract law might serve as a cure for the dissolution of domestic law and labor law following emancipation.

A rich harvest of insights has emerged from the body of works produced over the past generation that has examined emancipation in comparative geographical or chronological perspective. In a real sense, this scholarship built on the comparative studies of slavery in the Americas over the prior generation. During the age of democratic revolutions, as the pioneering works of David Brion Davis – including *The Problem of Slavery in the Age of Revolution* (1975) and *Slavery and Human Progress* (1984) – demonstrate, the wholesale use of terms linking personal freedom with natural human rights set the defenders of slavery on the defensive. For if freedom was the natural state of humans, how could the enslavement of humans be justified? Resolving the contradiction posed no great problem for those willing to cast the victims as subhuman. But for persons unwilling to take that step, including, of course, the enslaved themselves, the ideological battle between slavery and freedom was joined.

Like that of Davis, the work of scholars such as Orlando Patterson, whose remarkable survey titled *Freedom* appeared in 1991, and whose sweep ranges from the ancient Mediterranean through medieval Europe, has helped establish a comparative international context for understanding slave emancipation in the United States. Between the 1780s, when the northern states of the United States began abolishing slavery, and 1865, when the Thirteenth Amendment to the US constitution was ratified and slavery was banned throughout the land, all of the European nations with colonial possessions in the Americas except for Spain and Portugal had abolished slavery. The Russian empire, which by many measures was the most reactionary regime in Europe, abolished serfdom in 1865. Systems of bound labor throughout Europe and the Americas appeared in full retreat before economic and political pressures favoring reform. In the quarter-century after the American Civil War, slavery collapsed in its two last American strongholds, Cuba and Brazil.

Although some observers may have perceived in the relatively rapid demise of slavery the outline of an age of emancipation, such a perspective misses the individual circumstances that characterized each emancipation and that, among other things, left the ultimate outcome of events uncertain to the historical actors at every step of the way. Because emancipation did not constitute a single defining act but, rather, a protracted and hotly contested process, achievements often appeared more as the shifting sands of the seashore than as granite monuments rising above the plain. In most cases, war provided the critical stimulus for change but often in the unpredictable ways that characterize armed contests. Individual battles and campaigns might determine whether pro- or antislavery forces might emerge victorious, to be sure, but even those outcomes at times reflected the mobilization of bound laborers, often as much by accident as by design. War also disrupted the structures of authority upon which systems of bound labor relied even far away from active military operations and well before the forces of emancipation emerged victorious.

Only in the case of Haiti did wholesale social revolution accompany emancipation. Elsewhere, despite claims by contemporaries that their societies had been turned upside down, the abolition of bound labor did not demolish hierarchical social structures and the unequal distribution of wealth and power. Regardless of the spatial and temporal setting, a wide array of political actors on stages ranging from the local to the international vied to influence the emancipation process. Not surprisingly, they addressed a range of issues that no number of relevant historical precedents could have made less perplexing or less contentious to resolve. In every instance except Haiti, the liberated laborers found themselves constrained by disabilities that hampered their integration into the civic life of the nations that boasted having liberating them. Everywhere they enjoyed comparatively few fruits of their labor and contended with grinding poverty. After more than a century (and in some instances more than two), the descendants of bound laborers still seek the benefits that emancipation promised. *Beyond Slavery*, a collection of essays by Frederick Cooper, Thomas Holt, and Rebecca J. Scott (2000), aims to elevate the understanding of post-emanciption societies to new theoretical heights.

For the policy-makers of the national government at the end of the Civil War, the lessons of these earlier emancipations cut in several directions, none of which proved particularly serviceable to the circumstances they faced. In the northern states of the United States, the so-called First Emancipation resulted from mixed motives and extended over a generation. Even more fascinating for present purposes is the way in which in New England, revolutionary-era emancipationists grappled with the political, religious, and ethical dilemmas associated with slavery in their midst and decided they could live without it. Yet, as the work of Joanne Pope Melish (1998) contends, nineteenth-century New Englanders found the region's slaveholding past incompatible with contemporary political and ideological needs – specifically relating to the future of slavery in the southern states – so they selectively excised from their collective memory the unwanted features of their past. Ironically, emancipation also achieved a kind of "erasure" of African Americans from the mental and physical landscape of New England (Melish 1998: 188). Melish's work throws into stark relief the mixed motives animating political actors. As they maneuvered to secure their political future, they constructed accounts of the past to suit their current purposes.

A considerable (and, indeed, growing) body of literature has emerged since the early 1990s addressing these increasingly complex interpretive issues. As historians move beyond a simple reconstruction of the events and social dynamics involved in the assorted transformations that abolition wrought on slave societies, they have developed a fuller recognition that the narratives constructed to explain these processes themselves have a history for which the tools and techniques of traditional historiography prove inadequate. Far from an abstract exercise, much less a progressive accumulation of objective knowledge, the act of reconstructing and interpreting the emancipation process has contributed to the ongoing formulation of public policy regarding the lingering aftereffects of slavery.

Although emancipation studies has to the present time reflected only a minimal influence of interdisciplinary research, and that chiefly by social scientists rather than biomedical scientists, that picture may also be changing. The ongoing revolution in the life sciences both reflected by and to some extent also fueled by the human genome project has given rise to a range of biomedical questions (focusing on specific immunogenetic characteristics and not simply the random distribution of genetic traits in a population) that must of necessity be addressed by historians and the spectrum of social scientists. The collaborative scholarly work on the African Burial Ground Project in New York City paints an outline of such possibilities.

That said, traditionally trained economic, political, and social historians can also take heart in knowing that the rich documentary record of the Civil War era continues to yield fresh insights. Michael Vorenberg's fine book on the Thirteenth Amendment, *Final Freedom* (2001), makes this point. In contrast to the law of slavery, which was specific in its details, even if contradictory and changeable over time, the law of emancipation was deliberately vague. The Thirteenth Amendment to the US constitution, passed by Congress in March 1865 and ratified by the requisite number of states in December 1865, prohibited slavery but said nothing about the state of freedom that the absence of slavery implied. Supporters of the Amendment (including President Lincoln himself) viewed it as a means of insuring that wartime emancipation measures would not be reversed. Yet, as Vorenberg (2001) demonstrates, the precise wording of the Amendment also reflected the repudiation of radical Republican efforts to guarantee equal citizenship to the formerly enslaved. Only after several former Confederate states enacted "Black Codes" that granted limited rights while severely curtailing others did Congress legislate the Civil Rights Act 1866, the first significant step toward national citizenship. When the radical Republicans gained firm control over the federal government in 1868, they soon established reconstructed governments in the former Confederate states and proposed the Fourteenth Amendment (establishing national citizenship with express protections of citizens' privileges and immunities, including the enjoyment of due process of law and equal protection under the law) and the Fifteenth Amendment (prohibiting denial of the vote based on race, color or previous condition of servitude) to the US constitution.

In conclusion, the study of emancipation is as vibrant today as it was half a century ago, when the post-World War II revisionists began identifying the discrete interpretive challenges and opportunities inherent in the topic. Post-revisionists breathed fresh life into the field in viewing the freedpeople as important contributors to the emancipation process. While those possibilities have still not been fully exhausted, recent trends point in new directions, not the least significant of which involve interdisciplinary work and the role of collective memory in larger historical processes. Given the ubiquity of slavery in the historical record and current debates over its reappearance in various locales across the world during the late twentieth century, the study of emancipation will enjoy ongoing contemporary relevance well into the future.

BIBLIOGRAPHY

Bardaglio, Peter W. (1995) *Reconstructing the Household: Families, Sex, and the Law in the Nineteenth-Century South.* Chapel Hill, NC: University of North Carolina Press.

Berlin, Ira, Reidy, Joseph P., and Rowland, Leslie S. (eds.) (1982) *The Black Military Experience.* Cambridge: Cambridge University Press.

Berlin, Ira, Fields, Barbara J., Glymph, Thavolia, Reidy, Joseph P., and Rowland, Leslie S. (1985) *Freedom: A Documentary History of Emancipation, 1861–1867.* Volume 1: *The Destruction of Slavery.* Cambridge: Cambridge University Press.

Berlin, Ira, Glymph, Thavolia, Miller, Steven F., Reidy, Joseph P., Rowland, Leslie S., and Saville, Julie (1990) *Freedom: A Documentary History of Emancipation, 1861–1867.* Volume 3: *The Wartime Genesis of Free Labor: The Lower South.* Cambridge: Cambridge University Press.

Berlin, Ira, Miller, Steven F., Reidy, Joseph P., and Rowland, Leslie S. (1993) *Freedom: A Documentary History of Emancipation, 1861–1867.* Volume 2: *The Wartime Genesis of Free Labor: The Upper South.* Cambridge: Cambridge University Press.

Cooper, Frederick, Holt, Thomas C., and Scott, Rebecca J. (2000) *Beyond Slavery: Explorations of Race, Labor, and Citizenship in Postemancipation Societies.* Chapel Hill, NC: University of North Carolina Press.

Cox, LaWanda (1981) *Lincoln and Black Freedom: A Study in Presidential Leadership.* Columbia, SC: University of South Carolina Press.

Davis, David Brion (1975) *The Problem of Slavery in the Age of Revolution, 1770–1823.* New York: Oxford University Press.

Davis, David Brion (1984) *Slavery and Human Progress.* New York: Oxford University Press.

DuBois, W. E. B. (1935) *Black Reconstruction: An Essay toward a History of the Part which Black Folk Played in the Attempt to Reconstruct Democracy 1860–1880.* New York: Harcourt Brace.

Edwards, Laura F. (1997) *Gendered Strife and Confusion: The Political Culture of Reconstruction.* Urbana, Ill.: University of Illinois Press.

Foner, Eric (1983) *Nothing but Freedom: Emancipation and its Legacy.* Baton Rouge, La.: Louisiana State University Press.

Foner, Eric (1988) *Reconstruction: America's Unfinished Revolution, 1863–1877.* New York: Harper and Row.

Franklin, John Hope (1963) *The Emancipation Proclamation.* Garden City, NY: Doubleday.

Genovese, Eugene D. (1974) *Roll, Jordan, Roll: The World the Slaves Made.* New York: Pantheon.

Gerteis, Louis G. (1973) *From Contraband to Freedman: Federal Policy toward Southern Blacks, 1861–1865*. Westport, Conn.: Greenwood Press.

Gutman, Herbert G. (1976) *The Black Family in Slavery and Freedom, 1750–1925*. New York: Pantheon.

Holt, Thomas (1977) *Black over White: Negro Political Leadership in South Carolina during Reconstruction*. Urbana, Ill.: University of Illinois Press.

Jaynes, Gerald David (1986) *Branches without Roots: The Genesis of the Black Working Class in the American South, 1862–1882*. New York: Oxford University Press.

Litwack, Leon F. (1979) *Been in the Storm So Long: The Aftermath of Slavery*. New York: Alfred A. Knopf.

McFeely, William S. (1968) *Yankee Stepfather: General O. O. Howard and the Freedmen*. New Haven, Conn.: Yale University Press.

McPherson, James M. (1965) *The Struggle for Equality: The Abolitionists during the Civil War and Reconstruction*. Princeton, NJ: Princeton University Press.

Mandle, Jay R. (1978) *The Roots of Black Poverty: The Southern Plantation Economy after the Civil War*. Durham, NC: Duke University Press.

Mandle, Jay R. (1992) *Not Slave, Not Free: The African American Economic Experience since the Civil War*. Durham, NC: Duke University Press.

Melish, Joanne Pope (1998) *Disowning Slavery: Gradual Emancipation and "Race" in New England, 1780–1860*. Ithaca, NY: Cornell University Press.

Patterson, Orlando (1991) *Freedom*. Volume 1: *Freedom in the Making of the Modern World*. New York: Basic Books.

Ransom, Roger L. and Sutch, Richard (1977) *One Kind of Freedom: The Economic Consequences of Emancipation*. Cambridge: Cambridge University Press.

Rose, Willie Lee (1964) *Rehearsal for Reconstruction: The Port Royal Experiment*. Indianapolis, Ind.: Bobbs-Merrill.

Saville, Julie (1994) *The Work of Reconstruction: From Slave to Wage Laborer in South Carolina, 1860–1870*. New York: Cambridge University Press.

Schlesinger, Arthur M., Jr (1949) "The Causes of the Civil War: A Note on Historical Sentimentalism," *Partisan Review* 16: 968–81.

Schwalm, Leslie A. (1997) *A Hard Fight for We: Women's Transition from Slavery to Freedom in South Carolina*. Urbana, Ill.: University of Illinois Press.

Stampp, Kenneth M. (1956) *Peculiar Institution: Slavery in the Antebellum South*. New York: Knopf.

Stampp, Kenneth M. (1965) *The Era of Reconstruction, 1865–1877*. New York: Alfred A. Knopf.

Stanley, Amy Dru (1998) *From Bondage to Contract: Wage Labor, Marriage, and the Market in the Age of Slave Emancipation*. New York: Cambridge University Press.

Vorenberg, Michael (2001) *Final Freedom: The Civil War, the Abolition of Slavery, and the Thirteenth Amendment*. Cambridge: Cambridge University Press.

Wiener, Jonathan M. (1975) "Planter-Merchant Conflict in Reconstruction Alabama," *Past and Present* 68 (Aug.): 73–94.

Wiener, Jonathan M. (1976) "Planter Persistence and Social Change: Alabama, 1850–1870," *Journal of Interdisciplinary History* 7 (Aut.): 235–60.

Wiener, Jonathan M. (1978) *Social Origins of the New South: Alabama, 1860–1885*. Baton Rouge, La.: Louisiana State University Press.

Wiener, Jonathan M. (1979) "Class Structure and Economic Development in the American South, 1865–1955," *American Historical Review* 84: 970–1006.

Williamson, Joel (1965) *After Slavery: The Negro in South Carolina during Reconstruction, 1861–1877*. Chapel Hill, NC: University of North Carolina Press.

Woodman, Harold D. (1995) *New South – New Law: The Legal Foundations of Credit and Labor Relations in the Postbellum Agricultural South.* Baton Rouge, La.: Louisiana State University Press.

Woodward, C. Vann (1951) *Origins of the New South, 1877–1913.* Baton Rouge, La.: Louisiana State University Press.

Wright, Gavin (1986) *Old South, New South: Revolutions in the Southern Economy since the Civil War.* New York: Basic Books.

PART III

Reconstruction and the New Nation

CHAPTER SIXTEEN

Defining Reconstruction

O. VERNON BURTON, DAVID HERR, AND MATTHEW CHENEY

In 1965, near the conclusion of the nation's Civil War centennial observation, C. Vann Woodward remarked, "No one has so far called for a commemoration of Reconstruction" (Woodward 1965: 54). After 40 years, still no one has called for that commemoration. Moreover, after more than a century of scholarly consideration, Reconstruction not only fails to be commemorated, but also fails to be understood.

Early Reconstruction studies developed three primary emphases: judging the period as a success or failure, addressing political change, and studying elite persistence. More recently, emancipation studies stressing the experience of former slaves have enhanced our understanding of the period dramatically. Responding to the presence of Eric Foner's (1988) masterwork during the intervening years, historians have increasingly offered varied analyses that mostly share a narrowing of scope. That is not to say that these more narrowly focused efforts have not been helpful; rather it suggests the need for a new paradigm of study. The importance of a new focus becomes evident when one examines how Reconstruction shaped the "new" postbellum nation. The very identity of modern America first emerged during Reconstruction.

Reconstruction scholarship gives little consideration to the importance of when Reconstruction actually "ended." Whereas the Civil War has a distinct beginning and end, determining the period of Reconstruction proves more complicated. Traditionally defined as spanning the years 1865 to 1877, the standard pedagogical and historiographical convention defines Reconstruction as an era marked on one side by the collapse of the Confederacy and on the other by the withdrawal of federal troops from the South. Traditional political analysis suggests that Reconstruction fundamentally centered on the return of the rebellious states to the Union. This process could be considered to have begun as early as 1862, when Lincoln appointed provisional military governors for Louisiana, Tennessee, and North Carolina. This action encompassed amnesty, new state constitutions, and representation in the US Congress. In turn, the state-level political evolution of the Reconstruction era saw conservative whites ultimately in political control of every southern state by 1877. This political perspective suggests the hostile resumption of power by the white elite defined the end of Reconstruction, making the end of Reconstruction vary according to the political history of each state.

Beginning in the 1960s, social historians stressed the importance of understanding how power flowed along lines of gender, class, and race. The end of Reconstruction, when viewed through this lens, still tended to follow the lines of political change. As Republicans lost control of state governments, most former slaves once again found themselves removed from positions of influence. These historians also wanted to understand the economic consequences of the era. Such efforts more frequently found connections to the early twentieth century, and they included studies of the New South. National market forces, elite persistence, and the rise of Jim Crow suggested Reconstruction did not end, so much as it was transformed by, elite southerners' economic choices.

Complicated as it is to define the beginning and end of Reconstruction, the problem represents a larger one of conventional periodization. We have separated Reconstruction from the Civil War when, historically, they are conjoined. Rather, it is better to view the mid-nineteenth century as the Civil War era. Certainly in the South, Reconstruction in many areas embodied a continuation of the Civil War – indeed, a truly communal civil war. Unfortunately, the use of this periodization hinders the teaching of this subject. The discipline of United States history, as divided between two semesters, too often neglects Reconstruction in the first half of the survey and begins after Reconstruction in the second half. This deficiency lends itself to a general misunderstanding of Reconstruction in the public eye. A survey of more than 700 historians by a major textbook publisher indicated that over two-thirds of departments have not considered changing the division (McGraw-Hill online survey spring 2003, http://www.mheducation.com/college.html). Whereas the history profession has moved beyond the interpretations of early twentieth-century white historians, the public has not yet made this transition.

To better conceptualize the era of Reconstruction, one must consider it in a process that does not fit within firm chronological boundaries. The Civil War was about slavery, and the place of African Americans within American society. During Reconstruction, the victors, including African Americans, and the "losers," conservative white southerners, negotiated the terms of the peace. Race relations changed dramatically during the war itself, as African Americans departed for the Union lines to free themselves. After the war, communities adjusted to the new economic realities of emancipation. Therefore, understanding the new dynamics of race is of primary importance in understanding Reconstruction.

Scholars who explore the "end" of Reconstruction through changing meanings of race suggest it was a process vitally dependent on local circumstances that often ranged beyond the conventional chronological framework. This perspective raises the question of whether Reconstruction can be defined as a singular success or failure. It also emphasizes former slaves' crucial role in the process without excluding a broader view of the interracial environment. When examining the end of Reconstruction through this lens, it appears that the era fundamentally consisted of a reordering of race relations in the South after emancipation, and this social process has neither a clear beginning nor end. However, even this proposition is not entirely adequate. Important works fall outside the primary focus of race relations. Moreover, the recent fragmentation of Reconstruction studies demonstrates a strong interest in the field, but no one problem focuses the varied interests of current scholars.

Two historiographical festschrifts for southern history reflect historians' interests in the Civil War and Reconstruction during the second half of the twentieth century. Link and Patrick's (1965) *Writing Southern History* offered four chapters on the Civil War era, three on the war itself, and one on Reconstruction. Link and Patrick also included two other separate essays, "The 'New South'" (Gaston 1965) and "Southern Negroes Since Reconstruction: Dissolving the Static Image" (Tindall 1965). Two decades later, after the Civil Rights Movement and an emergent national concern with race relations, Boles and Nolen's *Interpreting Southern History* (1987) provided a single chapter that incorporated both the war and Reconstruction, as well as two separate chapters on Reconstruction, "From Emancipation to Segregation: National Policy and Southern Blacks" and "Economic Reconstruction and the Rise of the New South, 1865–1900." In 1965, scholars emphasized the importance of the Civil War and the politics of the era more than that of Reconstruction. The 1987 festschrift reflected the ascendancy of social history, an increased interest in the lives of ordinary people, and the importance of the Reconstruction period.

The more recent Blackwell Companions to American History illustrate the profession's concerns with race, class, and gender. In *A Companion to the American South*, John Boles (2002) adheres to a traditional chronological organization, as is evident by the five essays that appear in the section on "Civil War and Reconstruction": "Sectionalism and the Secession Crisis," "The Civil War: Military and Political Aspects along with Social, Religious, Gender, and Slave Perspectives," "Emancipation and its Consequences," "Political Reconstruction, 1865–1877," and "Economic Consequences of the Civil War and Reconstruction." The broad perspective of nineteenth-century American studies suggests that contemporary historians fill the standard chronology with a multitude of concerns. Consider *A Companion to 19th-Century America*, edited by William L. Barney (2001). He includes only one chapter on Civil War and Reconstruction, and dates that era from 1861 to 1877. Other topics within his work discuss ramifications of this period on foreign relations, the economy and class formations, race, gender, and ethnicity. These various historiographical works also suggest how interest in the Civil War and Reconstruction has evolved over time.

Regardless of one's approach, however, there are certain works that span the spectrum of Reconstruction studies. Historians no longer accept the Dunning (1898) myth of "Black Reconstruction," whereby venal "carpetbaggers," viciously ignorant former slaves, and low-white-trash "scalawags" ruled the South and made a mockery of honest government and democracy during "the tragic era." In the nadir of race relations in America, the historical profession largely ignored the dissenting views of African American scholars such as Taylor (1924, 1926, 1941) and DuBois (1935). However, beginning with Simkins and Woody (1932) and other revisionists (Wharton 1947; Tindall 1952), new interpretations began to hold sway. Since Rose (1964) and Williamson (1965), scholars began to emphasize the positive achievements of Reconstruction's radical Republican governments, especially constitutional reform and public education. Historians also balanced the prevalence of corruption in the South against levels in the North, the Grant administration, and the Great Gilded

Age Barbecue of private greed at public expense. Mark Twain's sobriquet of a "Gilded Age" for the last third of the nineteenth-century United States applied more to the North than the South. Historians have continued to view Reconstruction as a tragic chapter in American history, due to the failure to achieve lasting equality for African Americans. These interpretations, however, have not reached the conventional wisdom of the public.

An early work on Reconstruction that still has some bearing on the field is John Hope Franklin's *From Slavery to Freedom* (1967), which helped institute the revisionist studies of the 1970s and 1980s. Vernon Burton's (1978, 1982, 1985) studies of race in Reconstruction in Edgefield County, South Carolina, the political dimensions of tenantry's development and community during the war and Reconstruction, benefited from Franklin's interpretation. Dan Carter (1985) and John Boles (2002) also credit Franklin for their new awareness of the history of Reconstruction. Before emancipation studies viewed many of the old arguments in light of the former slaves' perspective, a group of scholars honored this great pioneer of revisionist scholarship. The resulting collection of essays (Anderson and Moss 1991) suggested possible new directions for Reconstruction scholarship. It is instructive to sample briefly how these scholars reconsidered the ending of the Reconstruction era.

A few of the essays represent efforts to break new ground in the traditional political approach. Michael Les Benedict (1991), for example, argued that radical Reconstruction ended because radical reformers passed from the scene or abandoned their positions. After dismissing racism as a possible factor for the mindset change, Benedict (1991) discusses the intellectual changes in the country after the Civil War. He argued that Republicans focused on issues of liberty and federalism – embracing notions like *laissez-faire* capitalism – and made support for radical Reconstruction policies untenable. According to Benedict, former radical reformers like *Chicago Tribune* editor Horace White, businessman Edward Atkinson, and academic Charles W. Eliot so drastically changed their minds that they became openly hostile to radical Reconstruction efforts, though only a few years earlier they had been in full support. Benedict also argues that much radical reformer strength lay in their prominent and strong stances taken on the war. Without the support of Union troops, those who sought the most radical of reforms lost influence in the South. Subsequently, the passage of the Fifteenth Amendment decreased the force of their arguments as many people turned to issues of economics (Benedict 1991: 53–78). The author uses the traditional date of 1877 as the end of Reconstruction.

The historiography of Reconstruction has gone back and forth between these two approaches: race and social Reconstruction, and congressional and political Reconstruction. Both approaches include political, social, economic, and legal aspects, as well as the public and private. As one former Confederate woman observed in late 1865, "Political reconstruction might be unavoidable now, but social reconstruction we hold in our hands & might prevent" (Faust 1996: 248). One explanation for this dichotomy is the remarkable influence of a single historian. Though not specifically about Reconstruction, C. Vann Woodward's classic, *Origins of the New South, 1877–1913* (1951a), contended that the South's twentieth-century poverty and racism grew from postwar recovery efforts by a new industrial class. Woodward argued that accumulation of land by this new elite separated most middling families from the land they worked and made crops the primary commodity from which they obtained credit. Crop-liens placed the merchant in control and their interest in cash crop production indicated that cotton was the only crop with credit value. This one-crop, absentee-owner system was inefficient and ultimately counterproductive. The South failed to rebuild its economy from the Civil War and declined as the rest of the nation grew through industrialization. Woodward himself wrote later that "the fruits of reconciliation meant a colonial status for the Southern economy" (1986: 65).

The new elite's accumulation and control of capital destroyed the once independent southern farmer, leaving them a dependent landless poor who found themselves threatened further by freedmen trying to emerge from slavery with little aid. The prospect of direct competition between the social mudsill class and the bottom rail generated fear and animosity. Separation by choice and then by law was a way to maintain white dominance without losing black labor. Woodward contended the new white power structure brought northern values, particularly the idolatry of money. The old planter elite grabbed the coattails of the new elite, taking the South into a period where government supported development of states' infrastructure and the old independent states' right mentality faded. This Woodward thesis holds no clear-cut "end" of Reconstruction.

Economic historians first chipped away at the Woodward (1951a) thesis in the early 1970s, arguing that market forces and the destruction of the war created the postwar economy, not elite exploitation of resources. The primary evidence was the similar growth rates of the North and South. The crop-lien, sharecropping, and tenancy system were, they argued, a reasonable response that garnered the most gain for all the parties in their particular context. The concepts of persistence and continuity dominated the historical debate. Jonathan Wiener (1978) provided strong evidence of persistence by identifying the old elite's ability to hold onto their land. Their survival did not insure unity, and Wiener found that, while most of the old elite became obstructionists to modernization, the number of large landholders who listed their occupation as other than "planter" increased dramatically in one sample. Wiener's class-based analysis ends Reconstruction in the late 1880s as industrialization and planter persistence translated into a new form of consistent labor oppression. Gavin Wright (1978) argued that the most significant change during Reconstruction involved human relations and the decline of independent farmers. These massive and sudden transitions overshadowed elite persistence. Within this persistence debate, social historians questioned the existence of a new elite. Quantitative studies of states including North Carolina, Mississippi, and Alabama suggested that a new elite did not run the New South. The antebellum planter families survived the war, maintained their economic dominance, and strove to impose a social system similar to their fallen slave society. Studies of political leadership demonstrate little change in political outlook (Wiener 1978; Billings 1979; Greenberg 1985). These studies define the end of Reconstruction as having occurred later than the traditional date of 1877, some extending into the 1950s, as they follow elite families' survival and prosperity.

Nevertheless, little doubt remains that the economy changed, and while it might be an exaggeration to suggest that these changes fully underlay US economic development in the Gilded Age, they certainly served a facilitating role. The southern economy was not revolutionized; rather it was devastated. This devastation may have had a retarding effect on the North as compared to the anticipated course of US economic development projected from before the war. The significance of labor and economic studies cannot be ignored. In 1860, nearly 4 million African Americans were held in slavery. Those not held in bondage existed in political, social, and economic subservience. In 1870, they were all free, politically equal, and owed no compensation to their former masters. In 1860 there had never been black elected officials; in the 1870s African Americans held elective office at almost every level of government. For that brief interlude, the bottom rail truly was on top. This was revolution – sudden and transforming. The concept of Civil War as a Republican capitalist revolution proved the foundation of the "Second American Revolution" school of thought. With southerners gone from Congress at the very outset of the conflict, the federal government passed a variety of measures that transformed American government and economics. Decades after it was first proposed, the so-called American system came into being: tariffs, banks, and internal improvements, as well as new planks on westward expansion, education, taxation, and immigration. These measures contributed to making a very different America, and the effects of that transformation, which mostly took place during the Reconstruction period, remain with us to the present day.

James McPherson (1991) portrays the period as a successful revolution. McPherson argues that the Civil War era did more to shape and change institutions and government than did the American Revolution. He concentrates on the inner revolution in the spirit of the freedmen. Political equality, economic opportunity, and the respect of society could be, and were, taken away, but the knowledge of freedom and its potential could not be removed. This was not at all new to McPherson. Charles and Mary Beard (1933) originated the modern debate by arguing that the Civil War had been America's Second Revolution because it shifted the national balance of power from southern planters to northern capitalists. The means for this power shift came from the various Morrill Tariffs, Internal Revenue Acts, Legal Tender Act, Public Land Grant College Act, Pacific Railroad Acts, Immigration Act, Homestead Act, and National Bank Act. These pieces of legislation, largely passed between 1861 and 1864, eroded the power of the states and paved the way for future economic development.

More recent scholars have continued this trend, but with an awareness that these economic benefits were not attained as the result of a conscious plan of any unified business community. Thus, as opposed to the Beards, modern scholars do not consider this a revolutionary or counter-revolutionary plan because there was no conspiracy on the part of the capitalist class. The opportunity simply arose because southern legislators had withdrawn from Congress where they had blocked that sort of legislation. Robert Sharkey (1959) follows the Beards and points to the heterogeneity of capitalist interests. Richard Bensel (1990), tracing the foundations of the modern American state to this transformational period, notes the various ways in which the creation of a new class of finance capitalist actually undermined radical Republicans in Reconstruction. Using a broader canvas, John Ashworth (1995) prefaces his argument that the turn to capitalism was in fact a bourgeois revolution through the Freedmen's Bureau Act 1864, the various Reconstruction Acts, Force Acts and Civil Rights Acts, and the Fourteenth Amendment. He determines, however, that equality was not achieved and that, while gains were made, Reconstruction failed to achieve a lasting revolution.

Another scholar in this school of thought is Heather Cox Richardson (1997), who provides a nuts-and-bolts account of the various legislative measures. She points to the ways in which the antebellum Republican ideology undermined its own vision by failing to provide for the regulation of capital or the nurturing of labor. Richardson chooses labor as her organizing theme in *The Death of Reconstruction* (2001). Without discounting racism, actually without even considering it, Richardson argues that northerners turned on African Americans when they decided they were disaffected laborers. By the end of the war, Richardson finds that many Republicans had overcome initial racial attitudes because of reports from the frontlines that the freed slaves had proven themselves to be valiant soldiers and industrious workers. These whites thought that black Americans could become worthy citizens if unshackled from legal inequality. They believed African Americans would find their place in the rebuilt South as self-standing farmers and artisans (Richardson 2001). Richardson also argues, however, that Republican enthusiasm turned to distress when African American voters, while loyal to the party, expressed radical political sentiments that paralleled the class-conscious demands of the northern white working class. The Republican free-labor ideology provided the political support for the eradication of slavery and *de jure* black male civil rights. All but the most radical politicians, however, blanched at the insistence of freedmen that the state intervene to correct economic inequalities that survived the end of slavery (Richardson 2001: 64, 68).

Richardson stimulates debate over the perception of "corruption" in the Reconstruction South by illustrating that many of Reconstruction's political enemies saw the extension of government involvement into economic relations such as wages and working conditions as proof of malfeasance. This skepticism was nourished by press reports from the South, which alleged that African Americans were attempting to exact revenge on former masters through the machinery of the state. Republican newspapers also noted with disapproval that southern blacks seemed more inclined to better their social standing through legislation than work. Increasingly, newspapers began to equate the demands of freedmen with the equally revolutionary positions of organized labor, most especially labor's call for an eight-hour workday. They characterized these demands as "socialistic" and unworthy of serious consideration in political discourse. One of the more original insights of the book is that many white elites feared the rise of socialist ideology among African American and white workers during the 1880s (Richardson 2001: 206, 211).

Richardson argues that under the weight of negative press, northern whites abandoned their previous hopes that African Americans could assume the responsibility of citizenship. Therefore, Congress gradually acceded to voter demands that it return power in the South to whites who claimed that they could "redeem" the institutions of state government (Richardson 2001: 195, 213).

At least a portion of Richardson's interpretation resonates with David Montgomery's (1967) comprehensive work. Befitting the radical perspective of wageworkers and socialists brought forth in his book, Montgomery's thesis challenges much of the historiography about the end of Reconstruction. He argues that the failure of the radical wing of the Republican party to enact a far-reaching social and legislative agenda stemmed from its conflict with northern organized labor, which offered a rival plan for social and economic reform. In short, labor representatives demanded that the federal government undertake a reconstruction of northern society to free workers from the condition of "wage slavery" to capitalist employers (Montgomery 1967: ix). Overall, the richness of Montgomery's book may have dissuaded other historians from tackling some or all of his arguments. Montgomery makes almost no link between labor politics in the North and resistance to Reconstruction in the South.

Richardson's (2001) ideas tie together class and race as factors in the decline of federal intervention in the postwar South. Her thesis that organized labor and black Reconstruction politics ran afoul of free-labor ideology is creative, and it shows the need for more attention to the changing definitions of free labor through the 1870s and 1880s (Perman 2001: 252–8). Richardson (2001) dates the end of Reconstruction in 1901 with Theodore Roosevelt and the solidification of the middle class and its identification with the American ideal.

Another scholar to look at labor law and Reconstruction is James D. Schmidt (1999). Schmidt uses legal, social, and labor history to argue that the northern system of labor, when it came south after the Civil War, became the molding force behind the change from a bondage labor system to a free labor system in the South. Through three relevant examples – the Wartime Reconstruction Act, the adoption of the Thirteenth Amendment, and the Freedmen's Bureau – Schmidt argues that the northern notion of using governmental coercion to create a system of free labor through vagrancy laws and enforcement of labor contracts was adopted quickly by southerners looking for a way to control and exploit the newly emancipated black laboring class, but that other aspects of the northern system of labor – such as the right to quit – were downplayed because social mobility and freedom for blacks were not desired by southern property owners.

If labor and economics have been important to Reconstruction studies, the political analyses have been the foundation of the entire enterprise. When Warren Ellem reviewed the scholarship from the mid-1980s, he agreed with David Donald's (1965) statement that Reconstruction historiography needed "a new pattern for the whole" (Ellem 1987: 53). Scholars had built their work refining or refuting Woodward, and there was no clear pattern to the body of scholarship. According to Ellem, historians at best underscored the centrality of race in southern politics. The end of the era, however, was not of particular interest to these scholars. According to Ellem's (1987) review of Carter (1985), Carter argued that the rejoinder to the Reconstruction Acts by whites was personal and "not the product of any group consensus" (Carter 1985: 247). If the reaction was not organized, the prerogative of race elicited a uniform response. Carter believed the white power structure could not escape the limits of its racial bigotry. Also according to Ellem (1987), Rable (1984) contended that white political leaders refused to acknowledge any change in their claim to power and radical Reconstruction forced them to confront the disjunction between their feelings of entitlement and the new political landscape. The distance between the two fostered a counter-revolutionary outlook. Rable, however, did not address how this posture might have engendered uncontrolled violence from other disaffected whites. The white leadership denied involvement, and complicit or not, it became obvious that violence would restore control to the antebellum leaders.

Michael Perman (1984) was among these historians, but his efforts did focus on the political end of the era. While Rable argued that Democrats saw violence as a legitimate means of restoring white supremacy, Perman argued more narrowly that violence was one of many means to achieve victory over Republicans. The fulcrum for change, however, was not violence but internal disagreements within both parties as they tried to secure their position. Perman centered his argument on the Democrats changing their party platform after the election of Grant, signaling a general acceptance of congressional Reconstruction. The ensuing battle was a series of internal party fights between "competitive" and "expressive" political practice. This framework from Austin Ranney's *Curing the Mischiefs of Faction* (1975) defines competitive behavior as political activity focused on acquiring the widest constituency through messages of inclusiveness. The swing vote is the target. Expressive politics caters to the core of the party by stressing principles.

Democrats recognized rejecting the major tenets of congressional Reconstruction – the amendments and black suffrage – was consolidating the black vote in the Republican party and pushing it toward a more consistently radical position. The Democrats' efforts to find a moderate position failed, as did the Republicans'. Expressive factions rose to power in the parties, and congressional Reconstruction moved from a potential watershed to the political equivalent of street brawls.

Historians engaged in the politics of Reconstruction had considered 1877 and the inauguration of Rutherford B. Hayes the conventional ending. Yet scholars debate the conventional wisdom of the "Compromise of 1877" around another book, C. Vann Woodward's *Reunion and Reaction* (1951b). In the aftermath of the 1876 election, almost every Democrat agreed that Samuel Tilden had won the presidency. He had won the popular vote, had already secured all but one of the electoral votes he needed to be formally elected as the president, and the 15 undecided votes were from states with significant Democratic majorities. To the southern white Democrats, this represented the end of Reconstruction. Tilden would remove the Federal troops from the South and restore to the elite white Democrats local control and patronage power.

And yet, when Rutherford B. Hayes was selected by the Electoral Commission and sworn in as the nineteenth president, there was not the violent resistance that the white South had shown a generation earlier over another election of a Republican and what they felt to be the destruction of the constitutional process. Woodward argued that the South's refusal to challenge the installation of Rutherford Hayes as president was the result of a secret deal that southern Democratic politicians struck with Hayes. Among other things promised by Hayes for the support of southerners in Congress was an agreement to withdraw all federal troops from the South and to end federally directed Reconstruction policies. Moreover, Hayes would admit that the South should solve its race problems and that the federal government had no role interfering. Woodward contended that the southern Democrats were willing to support a Republican president because of the relative similarities between southern Democrats and northern Republicans. Unlike the northern Democrats, many of the southern Democrats were former Whigs with a very strong pro-business focus, and unlike the southern Republicans who were often preoccupied with racial matters, the northern Republicans made big business and infrastructural improvement their top priority.

Many scholars – most notably Allan Peskin (1973), Keith Polakoff (1973), William Gillette (1979), Michael Les Benedict (1980), and George Rable (1989) – disagreed with Woodward's interpretation. Generally, they all deny a secret deal between southern Democrats and Hayes and argue that the reason why Hayes ended up as president was the result of overwhelming Republican control of the army, the presidency, the Supreme Court, and the Senate. They argue the Republicans did not negotiate because there was simply no need – the Republicans had control of the government and public opinion and as a result were able to install Hayes as president.

Responding to these criticisms, Woodward (1986) initially points to the complexity of the problem of determining what actually happened during the "Compromise of 1877." Taking the title of "historian-detective," Woodward admitted that the historical process of investigation is not free of errors and acknowledged that some of the criticism leveled at his work is valid and well taken. He also argued that Congress frequently neglected parts of most major nineteenth-century compromises – he had in mind the 1850 compromise – and that if one accepts the idea of the Compromise of 1877, it is remarkable because it had more parts fully realized and lasted longer than all the other major nineteenth-century compromises put together (Woodward 1986: 53).

Woodward (1986) also responded to Michael Les Benedict who argued, from a legalistic and quantitative perspective, that the Republican efforts to negotiate with the southern Democrats were not the most important factor in installing Hayes into office and that other factors led to only a calm Democratic resistance to Hayes' installment. Conceding that much of what Benedict says is accurate, Woodward explained that he did not try to specify the determining factor in the seating of Hayes. All he claimed, he reiterated, was the primacy of home rule in the minds of the white southern Democrats.

Woodward's final comments in *Thinking Back: The Perils of Writing History* (1986) best represent his thoughts about his arguments in *Reunion and Reaction* (1951b). He claimed he "would not write such a book in the same way now. To concede that economic interpretations have sometimes been overstressed, however, is not to concede that economic motive is unimportant, much less absent" (Woodward 1986: 56). In the end, Woodward believed that his "inside picture" of the aftermath of the election of 1876 "might incidentally have provided revealing insights on America in the Gilded Age – as well on the sort of forces shaping the New South." Interesting as the debate over the Compromise of 1877 is, it does not at all offer an explanation of the larger question of why or even when Reconstruction ended.

Eric Foner's (1988) *Reconstruction: America's Unfinished Revolution, 1863–1877* provided a great synthesis on Reconstruction, incorporating relevant literature up to that time. Like many scholars since, Foner was greatly influenced by the Freedom Project, directed by Ira Berlin et al. (1982–93), and its emphasis on the role of African Americans at the time. With Foner (1988), the focus of scholars shifted to emancipation and its consequences more than to the politics of the era. Foner begins the Reconstruction period during the Civil War itself, with the Emancipation Proclamation 1863.

Foner's (1988) study acknowledges African Americans as the central figures and actors. His synthesis incorporates 80 years of historiography of Reconstruction in which the African American was not always central, and in which cost (social, economic, and political upheaval) was not always adjudged worth the outcome (transitory black freedom). For Foner, while Reconstruction was a failure and would take a century or more to fully mature, the era was still one in which African Americans made considerable gains that were to last them through the following years of trial. In particular he stresses education and institutional stability in religion and the family.

Within the complex story of Reconstruction, Foner (1988) outlines four broad themes: the remaking of southern society; the interactions of freedmen, antebellum free blacks, Republican unionists, poor whites, white planters, merchants, and yeomen in the New South; the extension of agrarian commercialism even to previously self-sufficient farmers; and the interconnection of race and class, a matter especially complicated because former slaves constituted an agrarian black laboring class at the same time as a white ethnic industrial laboring class developed elsewhere. Foner places Reconstruction in a national context; he shows how the Civil War and Reconstruction affected the development of the powerful nation-state and how, in turn, a more activist federal government affected the evolution of Reconstruction. He carefully relates changes in the North's economy and class structure to the eventual undermining of Reconstruction, and he shows reciprocity of northern and southern Reconstructions. Placing Reconstruction in a comparative framework, Foner emphasizes that enfranchisement itself was a revolutionary step for a nation. While Foner is sensitive to the dynamics of race, especially in the South, it is class, especially in the North, that becomes the driving force of his analysis. Since Foner's work, the consensus view has been his: "Perhaps the remarkable thing about Reconstruction was not that it failed, but that it was attempted at all and survived as long as it did" (Foner 1988: 603). Foner places the end of Reconstruction in 1877 with the withdrawal of Federal troops.

After the master accomplishment of Foner's study, it is only natural that Michael Perman (1989) should ask in his review of Foner's *Reconstruction*, "What is left to be done?" Foner's work was a watershed for the revisionists. Such a work may still be sending the next generation of scholars into the dense underbrush rather than wrestling with dominant challenges. Woodward, however, returned the focus to race when, in 1989, he wrote that nineteenth-century southerners were "fatefully stuck with a perverse mystique of squatter sovereignty," the primary tenet of which was white supremacy at all costs (Woodward 1989: 200). In the most recent Reconstruction historiography, scholars have supported this idea while finding it did not always create the cultural hegemony white racists desired.

When scholars consider race as a significant factor, the transition between Reconstruction and the New South proves important. The overwhelming spread of violence demands consideration. As early as Dunning (1898) and the "Tragic Era" interpretation so important to unreconstructed white southerners, race and the end of the era have been linked. Dunning emphasized the futility of trying to change the South or any deep-seated social attitudes such as those regarding race relations. He and his students argued Reconstruction was destined to fail since military occupation and black political power only induced hostility in those whom it was intended to change. The alternative would have been gradual amelioration of racial understanding for blacks and whites through economic and educational improvement. McKitrick (1960) makes this argument, albeit in a much more sophisticated fashion, in his biography of Andrew Johnson. Based as it is on Union troop occupation in the South, Reconstruction according to this school of thought ended in 1877.

Scholars who look into the violence of the period also find that political interests complicated the relationship between race and violence. Perman (1991) argued that Reconstruction was ended by a coordinated effort to resist and remove northern Reconstruction policies. Perman rejects the notion that violence alone brought the end of Reconstruction; instead, heavy and consistent political pressure from the white Democrats worked in concert with violent groups such as the Klan. These Democrats adopted a policy of winning elections peacefully if possible and with violence if necessary.

Ellem (1996) found support for this school of thought in his own examination of Adelbert Ames, the Union officer and Reconstruction governor of Mississippi. Ames died in 1933 and in his later years reflected about his Reconstruction experience. He consistently argued that white southerners refused to accept the tenets of congressional Reconstruction and northerners misjudged the depth of this enmity. Poor whites' hostility toward freed people also amazed Ames. He claimed they were the dupes of the elite who used caste and race as a means to support their own insatiable greed (Ellem 1996: 120).

In his study of the most studied of Reconstruction states, South Carolina, Richard Zuczek (1996) sees Reconstruction as a continuation of the Civil War, with widespread terrorism and mayhem. He concludes that Reconstruction was hopeless, it "did not fail; it was defeated." Zuczek's *State of Rebellion* (2001) is one of the few relatively recent political examinations and reflects the now substantial body of social examinations where race is central. Ample evidence points to white South Carolina's unrelenting militancy and social conservatism. Whites resisted defeat by quickly reinstating a white supremacist society through legislation and private action. After the Reconstruction Acts, white elites resorted to fraud and terrorism to reclaim their power. They had the eager cooperation of middling whites, who often committed the unlawful deeds. Zuczek (1996) acknowledges nothing about this is new but claims that examinations of South Carolina have been too narrow and do not offer a context for the entire state.

The logic of white racist resistance was not simply predicated on a quest for undeserved power but came from an uncontrollable desire to resist any context where an African American was other than servile. Zuczek (1996) points out that black troops threatened whites, who argued the troops would create unrest among former slaves. Local whites attacked and murdered black soldiers. As early as 1865 whites organized local militias to terrorize African Americans. Whites rejected each effort by the federal government to mitigate the end of slavery with reconciliation as loudly as they did the Reconstruction Acts. The elections of 1868 and 1870 marked failed attempts to reclaim political control but succeeded in opening the floodgates to extralegal actions against Republicans. Three years of terrorist practice made 1871 Democratic victories a foregone conclusion, thus implying 1871 as the end of Reconstruction in South Carolina. Zuczek's political focus precludes consideration that the fall of the Republicans was only part of the process whereby whites were reordering race relations. While his work offers a more complete consideration of the state, he misses the opportunity to consider where the line between Reconstruction South Carolina and its New South incarnation lies.

Zuczek (1996) is not alone in teasing new information from older ideas and approaches. Other historians have inserted racial analysis through the earlier notion that the fundamental problem with Reconstruction was a national lack of commitment to the arduous task set before the country. This view, first presented by Franklin (1961) and Stampp (1965), argued that the Republican party in Congress gave up its attempt to force on the South a new balance of political power. When it did, northern Republicans, in effect, decided that their political and economic interests were better served through cooperating with the southern land owning elite, thus leaving to that native white establishment the control of race relations.

LaWanda Cox (1958) argued early that the major flaw of Reconstruction strategy was the federal government not providing the freedpeople with land. South Carolina was the one state to set up an agency to help former slaves acquire land (Bleser 1969). Ransom and Sutch (1977), in the most careful econometric study of Reconstruction, agree that failure to provide land to former slaves left them vulnerable to a very flawed southern capitalistic marketplace. Both black and white sharecroppers were victims of the wealthier white landowners and the general store merchant who demanded tenants grow cotton, charged them high interest rates for supplies, and obtained first lien on crops. Most African Americans refused to work as gang labor, and the tenant system resulted as a compromise whereby family units provided the requisite labor on their own schedule (Burton 1978, 1982, 1998).

An interpretation by an African American scholar (Holt 1977) suggests that class differences between the conservative, lighter-skinned, property-owning free blacks and the darker-skinned, formerly enslaved landless laboring class hastened the failure of the Reconstruction experiment. This more intricate examination of class has also, oddly enough, de-emphasized the impact of white racism. Holt's insightful distinctions of caste and class among African Americans found a very receptive ear among some southern whites.

One consideration of the older elite persistence argument, which falls short in its racial analysis, is from Carl H. Moneyhon (1994), who rigorously traced the changes that occurred in Arkansas because of the war and has found "Persistence in the Midst of Ruin." Throughout the book, with his focus on economic development, Moneyhon shows that the plantation elite controlled the state before, during, and after the war, and well into the twentieth century. He explains the grim reality behind reestablishment of white control. A student of John Hope Franklin's, Moneyhon uses Arkansas as a case study, challenging C. Vann Woodward's (1951a) assertion of leadership by a new class. He demonstrates that despite the vast social, political, and economic change, the antebellum elite held on to power in the postwar period.

Unsurprisingly, Moneyhon (1994) contends it was the average white family that was most damaged by the Civil War. Lack of currency and loss of land and equipment exacerbated their recovery. These problems pushed status tensions to the fore after the war, but the old elite nevertheless managed to regain power, first under pres-idential Reconstruction and then through political machination. Moneyhon skillfully employs census and tax roll data to prove the high rate of persistency among the elite. The missing piece of Moneyhon's picture is why common whites consented and even helped restore the old elite while in the midst of class strife. Strangely, he does not examine the role of race as a bridge across status differences. He does, however, support Woodward's (1951a) idea that poverty and racism were born anew, with new dynamics during Reconstruction. New circumstances generated a different social order controlled by the same elite.

While these efforts have sharpened the edges of older ideas, they mostly continue to miss the mark when applying racial analysis and addressing the transition out of Reconstruction. Most progress has been made when scholars recognize not only the significance of race, but also the importance of place. J. William Harris (2001) offers perhaps the best of these efforts when his primary interest is the New South era, not Reconstruction. Often the fulcrum for racial control, economic dominance worked differently in different parts of the South. Harris contrasts southern regions, illuminating the vital context of place. At one point he examines the plantation journal of Frances Butler Leigh, the Reconstruction era descendant of the prewar Manigault slave empire along the Georgia and South Carolina coasts. He describes it as a lesson book for "the new school of free labor" (Harris 2001: 11). The rich coastal region offered former slaves a bounty of game animals, seafood, and space away from whites. While plantation wages were important, they were not necessary. Leigh misunderstood the freedpeople's insistence on continuing the task system of labor until he tried importing English laborers for the work. This experiment was so unsuccessful that it cast the work ethics of former slaves in a different light. Fundamental misunderstandings abounded in the uncertain postwar South. The coastal rice empire would decline in the Reconstruction period because white planters could not effectively exploit their laborers and maintain the complex infrastructure rice agriculture demanded.

Harris (2001) also looked at the Piedmont cotton country, and while most African American families were sharecroppers, they strove for independence in their daily affairs. Land-ownership was an arduous challenge, but mobility allowed croppers to seek better terms. The economic prospects for Piedmont families were better than for coastal blacks because the land was more productive. Harris uses census data to prove that even on shares, a Piedmont family would likely earn more money. In what may seem a paradoxical argument, Harris also demonstrates life was significantly more difficult in the Piedmont. Blacks lived in closer proximity to whites who had obtained control of most land before 1890. There was little available land, the pressure to grow cotton only was strong, and African American farmers had to give up much of their financial control when they became tenants or sharecroppers. Unlike coastal blacks, Piedmont African Americans had only their mobility as a bargaining tool and had little choice about working under some form of white control. The price of more earning potential was greater oppression.

Again stressing the importance of place, Harris (2001) also examined Reconstruction and the New South in the Mississippi Delta. Although African American farms were smaller in the Delta than in the Piedmont, they were more productive. Total farm production was triple that of the average black Piedmont farmer. Settling the Delta presented physical challenges, but also allowed room for independent African Americans to compete successfully. As a frontier region there was social room. Exceptions were those counties settled in the antebellum period. There, the process of land concentration was mature and most African Americans were landless laborers or tenants. Harris' examination draws a strong correlation among autonomous space, land ownership, and productivity.

Marginal coastal farmland would never produce significant income, but natural resources provided independence. Their African American neighbors frustrated white residents on the Georgia and South Carolina coast, but they did not threaten their world. Where black families engaged the commercial market, whites perceived them as a social and economic threat. The choices people made, however, were not built solely around race.

Harris (2001) finds intense change throughout the late nineteenth and early twentieth centuries, emerging from many sources. The transformation of the landscape, the movement of labor and capital, the boll weevil, world war, family mobility, the Depression and the New Deal, all contributed to southern life. African American competition in the marketplace first generated the harsh realities of Jim Crow. The rise of social segregation and white supremacy simultaneously ushered the decline of the systems segregation sought to uphold. Plantation agriculture faded, a black middle class emerged in southern cities, wage labor and service industry employment gave African Americans a small claim in local economies.

Harris (2001) insists that place is vital to understanding the end of Reconstruction, identifying the dynamics of race within the context of a place. Even within one state, for example Mississippi, Reconstruction had no abrupt end; rather white control spread from the older, more settled counties into the new parts of the Delta as whites forced back into their control forces that were slipping from their grasp. Harris emphasizes autonomous space for blacks, land-ownership, and land productivity as measures for judging the end of Reconstruction. More important, Harris remarks that, "In each generation, blacks had resisted white supremacy in whatever ways made sense" (Harris 2001: 329). In this type of detailed analysis, no clear-cut ending date is possible.

Another scholar for whom place is a primary consideration is John C. Rodrigue (2001), who examined freedom in Louisiana's sugar cane region – the southeast part of the state. Like rice plantations, the exigencies of sugar cultivation granted former slaves considerable advantage in the new labor system. Rodrigue argues former slaves negotiated from a position of strength. Knowledge and skill contributed to the former slaves' position. It also encouraged them to accept work routines similar to slavery and to maintain wage labor rather than accept sharecropping or land-ownership.

Sugar parishes before the war had a sex ratio favoring male slaves and while some planters sought to achieve a better balance, labor concerns dominated their choices and limited the growth of slave families. Perhaps most interesting to the persistency debate is Rodrigue's argument the sugar plantations were essentially wiped out by the war. From more than 1,000 in 1861, only a little more than 200 were operating in 1864. Reconstruction in this part of the South required new arrangements if anything of the previous agricultural system was to persist. After the war, planters and former slaves tried different labor arrangements. In an unusual combination of practical and cultural needs both sides would agree to wage labor. Tenancy and sharecropping posed cultural threats to whites and gave up too much control from the perspective of the African American laborer. Wage labor offered control and guaranteed more income. Ultimately Rodrigue contends African American workers understood it as the first step along the road to property holding.

The sugar market was depressed after the war, so being a sugar planter came with problems beyond new labor relations. Planters, new or old, needed wealth, a new ideology to address labor, and luck. Improved mill efficiency helped offset continuing labor problems. Modernization was crucial and encouraged consolidation in the industry. On the other side, African American political power was unable to gain full advantage and dramatically help laborers, but it did not allow the advantage to fall to the planters either.

Labor mobility was a powerful tool in negotiating employment. A mobile labor market constantly annoyed planters because labor competition forced wages to remain competitive, preserved the labor market, and required planters to pay most of the wages on a monthly basis. After the 1870s, planters sought illegal means to control labor and the decline of radical Reconstruction provided the opportunity for them. After Louisiana's "Redemption," however, the sugar parishes remained Republican until the 1890s. State intervention broke up sugar strikes in 1874 and 1880, signaling the advantage planters eventually gained through the return of white Democratic rule. Rodrigue's epilogue is a depressing recounting of the 1887 Thibodaux Massacre. Sugar workers pressed to maintain their wages and struck during a crucial part of the season. The issue became that of African Americans not staying in their place, and whites, sensing a challenge to white supremacy, drove the situation to a violent resolution.

Rodrigue's (2001) scholarship suggests how difficult it is to argue for a distinct end to Reconstruction when analyzing race relations and helps illuminate the real sense of possibility African Americans recognized and worked to claim. It was not at all clear they would lose the long-term goal of economic independence. Even within a centralized plantation system, the former slaves emphasized personal autonomy and collective self-determination. An important part of their ability to maintain a bargaining position was gaining suffrage. Even when Reconstruction ended, it did not remove their relatively good position. The state became the coercive force and gave white planters the advantage. Even with this oppressive end to relatively free labor, the nature of race relations continued to develop in a complex fashion that was building on the new relations required after slavery.

If one draws the conclusion that Rodrigue's (2001) focus on Louisiana sugar parishes reflects an exceptional case, Julie Saville's (1994) earlier study of emancipation in South Carolina deflates such a notion. Saville contends that with emancipation, South Carolina former slaves claimed ownership of property and product created under slavery. Coastal slaves, under the protection of Union troops, established family tracts and sought land-ownership. Although autonomy and freedom to participate in a market economy were short-lived, the effort was significant, particularly considering the circumstances.

The Sherman reserve area, a place controlled by white planters, offered the ability to labor under less than favorable conditions. Whites sought to keep the environment as close to slavery as possible and, to make matters worse, local African Americans found themselves being undercut by war refugees from Georgia who agreed to work for less. The depression of wages left little room for alternatives to cash crop production. Saville reveals the insecurity of the reserve worsened conditions. In 1865, Confederate marauders raided plantations and attacked former slaves. When Federal troops restored order, they also imposed labor contracts. During 1866 and 1867, coastal rice workers on the Sea Islands and around the Savannah River resisted the restoration of white control. Unfortunately, they did not enjoy support from freed people in Charleston. Sea Island workers tried to possess land in general accordance with federal policy while Savannah workers seized land and made an explicit stand against federal policy. Neither approach proved sustainable.

New concepts of labor and social behavior competed with other concerns. Saville contends the former slaves of the lower Piedmont placed a premium on reclaiming family members. Movement and kinship association was more important than land. Whites resisted reorganizing family units through kinship, which Saville argues was a direct challenge to a master's authority. For example, families could defend against corporal punishment through group retaliation. On the other side, planters sought to control their labor by whatever means. Labor contracts varied widely. Some planters hired day laborers as strikebreakers. Coastal rice plantations declined amidst the tumult.

Agricultural wage labor, which white people called free labor, became a matter of politics when the Reconstruction Act 1867 extended suffrage to black males. South Carolina experienced a wave of African Americans ritualizing military drills and marching in the late 1860s as a means to express their newly won rights. Saville (1994) argues this was the earliest example of former slaves gaining a sense of collective power. Whites strenuously tried to control the instant African American constituency while black war veterans and northerners tried to educate former slaves to protect their rights. Because whites were willing to use dishonesty, coercion, and terrorism, newly politicized African Americans could not simply expect the right of suffrage to solve their problems. They resorted to clandestine action, as they had in slavery. Saville points out this behavior was indispensable for their political survival, but also encouraged harsh retaliation. Much as Rodrigue (2001) argues his case for Louisiana, Saville (1994) contends South Carolina's Reconstruction did not so much end as degenerate into an increasingly narrow fight over the nature of race and labor relations. There was not a moment of black capitulation, instead African Americans resisted where they could and succeeded in maintaining autonomous spaces even as they lost the ability to avoid poverty and economic independence.

These studies' focus on race neither excludes the economic and political issues, nor gives them the prominence they have enjoyed in other efforts. Following their example does mean, however, the old marker of 1877 and the withdrawal of troops no longer signifies Reconstruction's end. Reconstruction represented a Civil War between most southern whites and African American Republicans with some white allies, and scholars have looked at the wrong places and neglected the challenge of rethinking the period's end to judge the success or failure of Reconstruction. Instead of studying only Congress or a state legislature, scholars looking at the local level have found that some locales confirm great success for African Americans as the people experimented with interracial democracy and responsive government. These studies have often been of particular communities (Kenzer 1987; Bryant 1996), regions or sections of a state (Morgan 1992; Reidy 1992; Saville 1994), and specific studies, especially of African American women (Hunter 1997; Schwalm 1997). All of the studies generally unfold backward and forward from emancipation to understand what sort of free-labor system replaced African American slavery. While these studies of Reconstruction have chronologically looked to earlier beginnings, few considered an emphasis on the ending date.

Again, the tragedy is that too many whites preferred racial discrimination, low taxes, and few governmental services, and southern whites unwilling to share citizenship, let alone political power, with African Americans relied on violence. Thus, it was the very success of former slaves in politics, accompanied by economic gains and some social mobility, that led conservative whites to end the experiment in interracial democracy with illegal, violent tactics (Burton 1978, 1985, 1998).

The rise of social history afforded more attention to gender as well as race and these efforts have contributed important nuances to our grasp of Reconstruction. Although more problematic, some scholars suggest an incipient gender revolution, beginning with the fight to include women in the provisions of the Fourteenth Amendment and continuing through the gendered relations of postbellum North and South. Scott (1970) refers to the Civil War with the metaphor of a tidal wave, threatening patriarchy in the South. DuBois (1978) points to the unsuccessful crusade of northern suffragists to include gender equality in the Fourteenth Amendment and argues that the passage of that amendment freed women from the cause of abolitionism and catalyzed them to act for suffrage. Both Scott and DuBois credit the war as a definite watershed in American women's history and as an opportunity for revolutionary change. Contrary to Scott (1970), both Rable (1989) and Faust (1996) argue that, in the South, the changes wrought by the war lasted only until soldiers returned home. Others, such as Hoffert (1995), remind us that the ideological and organizational thrust of the women's movement preceded the outbreak of war, downplaying any discontinuity. Still, revolutionary potential existed, and the gains and lessons of the war sustained and motivated the movement in subsequent years.

According to Glenda Gilmore (1996), the idea of racially differentiated masculinity was at the center of repression campaigns throughout the South as the nation retreated from the promise of the First Reconstruction. Laura Edwards in *Gendered Strife and Confusion* (1997) examines the household as the site where social and political relations are created. In her analysis, Reconstruction was a time when all facets of southern life, gender ideals, social rituals, and political beliefs were reconfigured. African Americans attempted to live up to white expectations of independence, and white men and women had to remake definitions of a free man in a way that African Americans could not achieve. Thus, Reconstruction is a time of the contestation and emergence of new identities, a process without a distinct ending. Edwards does not specify a date for the end of Reconstruction; however, it can be inferred that Reconstruction in the South ended when Jim Crow and white supremacy severely limited changes to political and gender identities and roles. Thus, the return of politics to white domination, and the winning of the white man as the "best" man in the South, results in, as Laura Edwards (1997) points out, changes in everything. At the same time, nothing changed because it returned to pre-Civil War social and political structures that Reconstruction ended.

LeeAnn Whites (1995) examines shifts in gendered concepts and construction in Augusta, Georgia, from antebellum slavery through 1890. For Whites, the Civil War's loss emasculated white southern men, a loss of manhood not only on the battlefield but also on the home front as they failed to protect their women and country. After the war, then, as in antebellum times, women agreed to "reconstruct" white manhood and womanhood during Reconstruction. Whites (1995) agrees with Laura Edwards (1997) that "everything had changed, and nothing had changed." Despite transformations in men's and women's roles, the New South continued to look much as the Old South had, with a social system based on white supremacy and white male domination. These reconstructions of masculinity and femininity led to white men regaining their position in society over black males. Thus, for Whites, Reconstruction ends with the rehabilitation of the old hierarchy of race and gender.

If Reconstruction is, as Laura Edwards (1997) and LeeAnn Whites (1995) paint it, a time of contestation, a refashioning of identity, albeit one that is refashioned from antebellum nostalgia for control over black bodies, then Reconstruction ends when this contestation ends. In this case, we are back to *The Strange Career of Jim Crow* (Woodward 1966), and 1896 is the end of Reconstruction. Nevertheless, how one arrives is much different than Woodward or his critics posited.

One last point regarding gender studies during the Civil War era needs to be covered. Before the war, white southerners saw themselves as the masculine counterpoint to the effeminate Yankee. Northern victory reversed this relationship, and the North became the masculine counterpart to the South as handmaiden. Silber (1993), Whites (1995), and Laura Edwards (1997) all address this theme to a degree, and taken together they provide another instance of a bottom rung reversing positions, only this time with gendered regionalism instead of race. Feminist scholars find that much of intellectual discussion uses gender to portray the relationship of North and South. "Furthermore, national as well as regional discursive needs to expand or contain, inflate or diminish, sentimentalize or denigrate the region, in short to represent the South as Other, have used gender as a tool" (Jones and Donaldson 1997: 3–4).

Finally, one should not say that the recent variety of topics within Reconstruction studies has not been useful, even when their focus has been particularly narrow. These tributaries maintain their importance as they flow into the main current. One such tributary is religious Reconstruction. According to Daniel Stowell (1998), religion is a significant aspect of cultural and social Reconstruction. Certainly the church as an institution was a key to optimism for the African American community during Reconstruction. Gaines M. Foster (2002) agrees on the importance of religion as he looks at moral Reconstruction, Christian lobbyists, and the legislation of morality. Foster's work is an analysis of the postbellum attempt by Christian lobbyists to use the power of the federal government to legislate morality and religion. Beginning with the end of slavery and the moral victory it represented, Foster (2002) traces the Christian moralist movement's initial attempts to regulate sexuality, promote religious observance of the Sabbath, outlaw the state lottery, and finally prohibit the sale and consumption of alcohol. Reconstruction, to Foster, represents much more than the political reconstitution of the institutions of power in the South. Reconstruction is the overarching desire to rework society after the chaos of the Civil War and ground society on the moral principles of Christianity. Foster assigns a date of 1920 to the end of Reconstruction, but the goal of a moral Reconstruction is never-ending.

Each state, North and South, had its own story on Reconstruction, when it began, when it ended, if it ended. Barbara Fields (1985) argues there was no Reconstruction in Maryland. And the people of Kentucky would include themselves in that category. Georgia's political and military occupation lasted only two years. Certainly the recent scholarship has proven various communities in states had different experiences with the meaning and timing of Reconstruction. The implications of all this variance, political, social, economic, legal, are still under investigation.

Dates may be fuzzy, but the essence of Reconstruction remains. It was a time when many had great hope for the country's better nature. Historians addressing the politics of the period have proven that in a sense, Reconstruction attempted two revolutions, and while one succeeded, the other failed. Emancipation was a successful and lasting revolution, brought about by the convictions of abolitionists, the courage of leading Republicans, and the actions of individual slaves. From Fort Monroe in May 1861 through the Confiscation Acts 1861 and 1862, the Emancipation Proclamation and the Thirteenth Amendment, emancipation was a successful revolution based on limited goals. Reconstruction, on the other hand, had far more wide-ranging goals, which it failed to achieve over the long haul. The Freedmen's Bureau Act 1864, the various Reconstruction Acts, Force Acts, Civil Rights Acts, and the Fourteenth Amendment failed to produce equality, but they did produce change that lasted longer than the Compromise of 1877.

The contention over race and gender roles in the New South is perhaps never over. If whites had "won" with segregation, if the system had been stable, then there would have little need for the spectacle of lynchings and other public forms of whites creating and exhibiting their own culture and using fear to maintain a system of domination. So perhaps Reconstruction does not end until the 1930s when the fallout of the Great Migration forced a restructuring of race in the South. Eric Anderson has stated: "The more deeply scholars study the Reconstruction era, the more apparent it becomes that Reconstruction was a long-term process, extending in many respects well beyond 1877 and beginning before 1865" (Anderson and Moss 1991: 227). Perhaps Reconstruction does not completely end until the Civil Rights Movement. Or maybe that end is actually a renewal. If Reconstruction means African American resistance to racism, it is still going on today.

BIBLIOGRAPHY

Anderson, Eric and Moss, Alfred A., Jr (eds.) (1991) *The Facts of Reconstruction: Essays in Honor of John Hope Franklin*. Baton Rouge, La.: Louisiana State University Press.

Ashworth, John (1995) *Slavery, Capitalism and Politics in the Antebellum Republic*. Volume 1: *Commerce and Compromise, 1820–1850*. Cambridge: Cambridge University Press.

Barney, William L. (ed.) (2001) *A Companion to 19th-Century America*. Malden, Mass.: Blackwell.

Beard, Charles A. and Beard, Mary R. (1933) *The Rise of American Civilization*, two vols. New York: Macmillan.

Benedict, Michael Les (1980) "Southern Democrats in the Crisis of 1876–77: A Reconsideration of Reunion and Reaction," *Journal of Southern History* 46: 489–524.

Benedict, Michael Les (1991) "Reform Republicans and the Retreat from Reconstruction," in Eric Anderson and Alfred A. Moss Jr (eds.) *The Facts of Reconstruction: Essays in Honor of John Hope Franklin*. Baton Rouge, La.: Louisiana State University Press.

Bensel, Richard F. (1990) *Yankee Leviathan: The Origins of Central State Authority in America, 1859–1877*. Cambridge: Cambridge University Press.

Berlin, Ira et al. (eds.) (1982–93) *Freedom: A Documentary History of Emancipation, 1861–1867*, four vols. New York: Cambridge University Press.

Billings, Dwight B. (1979) *Planters and the Making of a "New South": Class, Politics, and Development in North Carolina, 1865–1900*. Chapel Hill, NC: University of North Carolina Press.

Bleser, Carol (1969) *The Promised Land: The History of the South Carolina Land Commission, 1869–1890*. Columbia, SC: University of South Carolina Press.

Boles, John B. (2002) *A Companion to the American South*. Malden, Mass.: Blackwell.

Boles, John B. and Nolen, Evelyn Thomas (eds.) (1987) *Interpreting Southern History: Historiographical Essays in Honor of Sanford W. Higginbotham*. Baton Rouge, La.: Louisiana State University Press.

Bryant, Jonathan M. (1996) *How Curious a Land: Conflict and Change in Greene County, Georgia, 1850–1885*. Chapel Hill, NC: University of North Carolina Press.

Burton, Orville Vernon (1978) "Race and Reconstruction: Edgefield County, South Carolina," *Journal of Social History* 12: 31–56.

Burton, Orville Vernon (1982) "The Development of Tenantry and the Post-Bellum Afro-American Social Structure in Edgefield County, South Carolina," in E. LeRoy Ladurie and J. Goy (eds.) *Présentations paysannes, dîmes, rente foncière et mouvement de la production agricole a l'époque préindustrielle: Actes du Colloque préparatoire (30 juin et 2 juillet 1977) au VIIe Congrès international d'Histoire économique Section A3*. Edimbourg 13–19 août 1978, Vol. 2: 762–78. Paris: Editions de l'Ecole des Hautes Etudes en Sciences Sociales.

Burton, Orville Vernon (1985) *In my Father's House are Many Mansions: Family and Community in Edgefield, South Carolina 1848–1889*. Chapel Hill, NC: University of North Carolina Press.

Burton, Orville Vernon (1998) "African American Status and Identity in a Postbellum Community: An Analysis of the Manuscript Census Returns," *Agricultural History* 72: 213–40.

Carter, Dan T. (1985) *When the War was Over: The Failure of Self-Reconstruction in the South, 1865–1867*. Baton Rouge, La.: Louisiana State University Press.

Cox, LaWanda (1958) "The Promise of Land for the Freedmen," *Mississippi Valley Historical Review* 45: 413–40.

Donald, David M. (ed.) (1960) *Why the North Won the Civil War*. Baton Rouge, La.: Louisiana State University Press.

Donald, David M. (1965) *The Politics of Reconstruction, 1863–1867*. Baton Rouge, La.: Louisiana State University Press.

DuBois, Ellen (1978) *Feminism and Suffrage: The Emergence of an Independent Women's Movement in America, 1848–1869*. Ithaca, NY: Cornell University Press.

DuBois, W. E. B. (1935) *Black Reconstruction: An Essay toward a History of the Part which Black Folk Played in the Attempt to Reconstruct Democracy 1860–1880*. New York: Harcourt Brace.

Dunning, William A. (1898) *Essays on the Civil War and Reconstruction and Related Topics*. New York: Macmillan.

Edwards, Laura F. (1997) *Gendered Strife and Confusion: The Political Culture of Reconstruction*. Urbana, Ill.: University of Illinois Press.

Ellem, Warren A. (1996) "Doing God's Service: Adelbret Ames and Reconstruction in Mississippi," in Bruce Clayton and John Salmond (eds.) *Varieties of Southern History: New Essays on a Region and its People*. Westport, Conn.: Greenwood.

Ellem, Warren A. (1987) "The Politics of Reconstruction," *Australasian Journal of American Studies* 6 (July).

Faust, Drew Gilpin (1996) *Mothers of Invention: Women of the Slaveholding South in the American Civil War*. Chapel Hill, NC: University of North Carolina Press.

Fields, Barbara Jeanne (1985) *Slavery and Freedom on the Middle Ground: Maryland during the Nineteenth Century*. New Haven, Conn.: Yale University Press.

Foner, Eric (1988) *Reconstruction: America's Unfinished Revolution, 1863–1877*. New York: Harper and Row.

Foster, Gaines M. (2002) *Moral Reconstruction: Christian Lobbyists and the Federal Legislation of Morality, 1865–1920*. Chapel Hill, NC: University of North Carolina Press.

Franklin, John Hope (1961) *Reconstruction: After the Civil War*. Chicago: University of Chicago Press.

Franklin, John Hope (1967) *From Slavery to Freedom: A History of American Negroes*, 3rd edn. New York: Knopf.

Gaston, Paul (1965) "The New South," in Arthur S. Link and Rembert W. Patrick (eds.) *Writing Southern History*. Baton Rouge, La.: Louisiana State University Press.

Gillette, William (1979) *Retreat from Reconstruction, 1869–1879*. Baton Rouge, La.: Louisiana State University Press.

Gilmore, Glenda E. (1996) *Gender and Jim Crow: Women and the Politics of White Supremacy in North Carolina, 1896–1920*. Chapel Hill, NC: University of North Carolina Press.

Greenberg, Kenneth S. (1985) *Masters and Statesmen: The Political Culture of American Slavery*. Baltimore, Md.: Johns Hopkins University Press.

Harris, J. William (2001) *Deep Souths: Delta, Piedmont, and Sea Island Society in the Age of Segregation*. Baltimore, Md.: Johns Hopkins University Press.

Hoffert, Sylvia D. (1995) *When Hens Crow: The Women's Rights Movement in Antebellum America*. Bloomington, Ind.: Indiana University Press.

Holt, Thomas (1977) *Black over White: Negro Political Leadership in South Carolina during Reconstruction*. Urbana, Ill.: University of Illinois Press.

Hunter, Tera W. (1997) *To 'Joy my Freedom: Southern Black Women's Lives and Labors after the Civil War*. Cambridge, Mass.: Harvard University Press.

Jones, Ann Goodwyn and Donaldson, Susan V. (eds.) (1997) *Haunted Bodies: Gender and Southern Texts*. Charlottesville, Va.: University of Virginia Press.

Kenzer, Robert C. (1987) *Kinship and Neighborhood in a Southern Community: Orange County, North Carolina, 1849–1881*. Knoxville, Tenn.: University of Tennessee Press.

Link, Arthur S. and Patrick, Rembert W. (1965) *Writing Southern History: Essays in Historiography in Honor of Fletcher M. Green*. Baton Rouge, La.: Louisiana State University Press.

McKitrick, Eric (1960) *Andrew Johnson and Reconstruction*, Chicago: University of Chicago Press.

McPherson, James M. (1991) "Abraham Lincoln and the Second American Revolution," in *Abraham Lincoln and the Second American Revolution*. New York: Oxford University Press.

Moneyhon, Carl H. (1994) *The Impact of the Civil War and Reconstruction on Arkansas: Persistence in the Midst of Ruin*. Baton Rouge, La.: Louisiana State University Press.

Montgomery, David (1967) *Beyond Equality: Labor and the Radical Republicans, 1862–1872*. New York: Alfred A. Knopf.

Morgan, Lynda J. (1992) *Emancipation in Virginia's Tobacco Belt, 1850–1870*. Athens, Ga.: University of Georgia Press.

Perman, Michael (1973) *Reunion without Compromise: The South and Reconstruction, 1865–1868*. New York: Cambridge University Press.

Perman, Michael (1984) *The Road to Redemption: Southern Politics, 1869–1879*. Chapel Hill, NC: University of North Carolina Press.

Perman, Michael (1989) "Eric Foner's Reconstruction: A Finished Revolution," *Reviews in American History* 17: 73–8.

Perman, Michael (1991) "Counter Reconstruction: The Role of Violence in Southern Redemption," in Eric Anderson and Alfred A. Moss, Jr (eds.) *The Facts of Reconstruction*. Baton Rouge, La.: Louisiana State University Press.

Perman, Michael (2001) *Struggle for Mastery: Disfranchisement in the South, 1888–1908*. Chapel Hill, NC: University of North Carolina Press.

Peskin, Allan (1973) "Was there a Compromise of 1877?," *Journal of American History* 60: 63–75.

Polakoff, Keith Ian (1973) *The Politics of Inertia: The Election of 1876 and the End of Reconstruction*. Baton Rouge, La.: Louisiana State University Press.

Rable, George C. (1984) *But There Was No Peace: The Role of Violence in the Politics of Reconstruction*. Athens, Ga.: University of Georgia Press.

Rable, George C. (1989) *Civil Wars: Women and the Crisis of Southern Nationalism*. Urbana, Ill.: University of Illinois Press.

Ranney, Austin (1975) *Curing the Mischief of Faction: Party Reform in America*. Berkeley, Calif.: University of California Press.

Ransom, Roger L. and Sutch, Richard (1977) *One Kind of Freedom: The Economic Consequences of Emancipation*. Cambridge: Cambridge University Press.

Reidy, Joseph P. (1992) *From Slavery to Agrarian Capitalism in the Cotton Plantation South: Central Georgia, 1800–1880*. Chapel Hill, NC: University of North Carolina Press.

Richardson, Heather Cox (1997) *The Greatest Nation on Earth: Republican Economic Policies during the Civil War*. Cambridge, Mass.: Harvard University Press.

Richardson, Heather Cox (2001) *The Death of Reconstruction: Race, Labor, and Politics in the post-Civil War North*. Cambridge, Mass.: Harvard University Press.

Rodrigue, John C. (2001) *Reconstruction in the Cane Fields: From Slavery to Free Labor in Louisiana's Sugar Parishes, 1862–1880*. Baton Rouge, La.: Louisiana State University Press.

Rose, Willie Lee (1964) *Rehearsal for Reconstruction: The Port Royal Experiment*. Indianapolis, Ind.: Bobbs-Merrill.

Saville, Julie (1994) *The Work of Reconstruction: From Slave to Wage Laborer in South Carolina, 1860–1870*. New York: Cambridge University Press.

Schmidt, James D. (1999) *Free to Work: Labor Law, Emancipation, and Reconstruction, 1815–1880* [Studies in the Legal History of the South]. Athens, Ga.: University of Georgia Press.

Schwalm, Leslie A. (1997) *A Hard Fight for We: Women's Transition from Slavery to Freedom in South Carolina*. Urbana, Ill.: University of Illinois Press.

Scott, Ann Firor (1970) *The Southern Lady: From Pedestal to Politics, 1830–1930*. Chicago: University of Chicago Press.

Sharkey, Robert P. (1959) *Money, Class and Party: An Economic Study of Civil War and Reconstruction*. Baltimore, Md.: Johns Hopkins University Press.

Silber, Nina (1993) *The Romance of Reunion: Northerners and the South, 1865–1900*. Chapel Hill, NC: University of North Carolina Press.

Simkins, Francis B. and Woody, Robert H. (1932) *South Carolina during Reconstruction*. Chapel Hill, NC: University of North Carolina Press.

Stampp, Kenneth M. (1965) *The Era of Reconstruction, 1865–1877*. New York: Alfred A. Knopf.

Stowell, Daniel (1998) *Rebuilding Zion: The Religious Reconstruction of the South, 1863–1877*. New York: Oxford University Press.

Taylor, Alrutheus A. (1924) *The Negro in South Carolina during the Reconstruction*. Washington, DC: Association for the Study of Negro Life and History.

Taylor, Alrutheus A. (1926) *The Negro in the Reconstruction of Virginia*. Washington, DC: Association for the Study of Negro Life and History.

Taylor, Alrutheus A. (1941) *The Negro in Tennessee, 1865–1880*. Washington, DC: Associated Publishers.

Tindall, George Brown (1952) *South Carolina Negroes, 1877–1900*. Columbia, SC: University of South Carolina Press.

Tindall, George Brown (1965) "Southern Negroes Since Reconstruction: Dissolving the Static Image," in Arthur S. Link and Rembert W. Patrick (eds.) *Writing Southern History*. Baton Rouge, La.: Louisiana State University Press.

Wharton, Vernon Lane (1947) *The Negro in Mississippi, 1865–1900*. Chapel Hill, NC: University of North Carolina Press.

Whites, LeeAnn (1995) *The Civil War as a Crisis in Gender: Augusta, Georgia, 1860–1890*. Athens, Ga.: University of Georgia Press.

Wiener, Jonathan M. (1978) *Social Origins of the New South: Alabama, 1860–1885*. Baton Rouge, La.: Louisiana State University Press.

Williamson, Joel (1965) *After Slavery: The Negro in South Carolina during Reconstruction, 1861–1877*. Chapel Hill, NC: University of North Carolina Press.

Woodward, C. Vann (1951a) *Origins of the New South, 1877–1913*. Baton Rouge, La.: Louisiana State University Press.

Woodward, C. Vann (1951b) *Reunion and Reaction: The Compromise of 1877 and the End of Reconstruction*. Boston, Mass.: Little, Brown.

Woodward, C. Vann (1965) "An Expert," *New York Times Book Review* Christmas issue, Section 7, December 5.

Woodward, C. Vann (1966) *The Strange Career of Jim Crow*. New York: Oxford University Press.

Woodward, C. Vann (1986) *Thinking Back: The Perils of Writing History*. Baton Rouge, La.: Louisiana State University Press.

Woodward, C. Vann (1989) *The Future of the Past*. New York: Oxford University Press.

Wright, Gavin (1978) *The Political Economy of the Cotton South: Households, Markets, and Wealth in the Nineteenth Century*. New York: Norton.

Zuczek, Richard (1996) *State of Rebellion: Reconstruction in South Carolina*. Columbia, SC: University of South Carolina Press.

SUGGESTED FURTHER READING

Belz, Herman (1998) *Abraham Lincoln, Constitutionalism, and Equal Rights in the Civil War Era*. New York: Fordham University Press.

Clinton, Catherine and Silber, Nina (eds.) (1992) *Divided Houses: Gender and the Civil War*. New York: Oxford University Press.

Durrill, Wayne K. (1990) *War of Another Kind: A Southern Community in the Great Rebellion*. New York: Oxford University Press.

Ginzberg, Lori (1990) *Women and the Work of Benevolence: Morality, Politics, and Class in the Nineteenth Century United States*. New Haven, Conn.: Yale University Press.

Litwack, Leon F. (1979) *Been in the Storm So Long: The Aftermath of Slavery*. New York: Alfred A. Knopf.

McPherson, James M. (1982) *Ordeal by Fire: The Civil War and Reconstruction*. New York: Oxford University Press.

McPherson, James M. (1997) *For Cause and Comrades: Why Men Fought in the Civil War*. New York: Oxford University Press.

Mohr, Clarence L. (2001 [1986]) *On the Threshold of Freedom: Masters and Slaves in Civil War Georgia*. Baton Rouge, La.: Louisiana State University Press.

Perman, Michael (1973) *Reunion without Compromise: The South and Reconstruction, 1865–1868*. New York: Cambridge University Press.

CHAPTER SEVENTEEN

The Politics of Reconstruction

Michael Perman

The Reconstruction period in American history was concerned, above all, with politics. The problem that defines the era was how to reorganize the politics of the former Confederate states in such a way as to enable them, without undermining the gains achieved by the Union victory on the battlefield, to return to Congress and become reincorporated into the political life of the nation. Indeed, the period is named after the Reconstruction Act 1867, the groundbreaking piece of legislation that established a new political order in the southern states and provided for their readmission into Congress. The period ends in 1877 when the federal government reached a fateful political decision to terminate its decade-long involvement in the South, after trying to sustain the state governments set up under the provisions of the Reconstruction Act. So political considerations permeated and shaped the era of Reconstruction.

In the 1950s or 1960s, a collection of essays examining the historical writing on Reconstruction would have been primarily political in content and scope. But, in the meantime, other aspects of its history have been explored as part of the revision and reinterpretation of the period since the 1950s. Of these, the most important development has been the investigation by historians of the social history of the South during Reconstruction. They have examined the systems of labor and race relations that emerged in the aftermath of emancipation, the experiences of the freedpeople themselves as they tried to gain control over their lives, and the struggles of ordinary men and women – especially women – with the economic and social turmoil of the postwar era.

The introduction of these previously excluded facets of Reconstruction has resulted in two developments. First, the earlier emphasis on the failure of Reconstruction has given way to a recognition that social processes were at work that enabled individuals and groups to register gains and effect improvements during the era. Second, the political arena has been reduced to just one of many elements in the region's life. Nevertheless, the prospects for social change and individual progress were very much dependent upon and bound up with the fate of the political regimes set up in the former Confederacy under Reconstruction. The political system still held the key to the duration and impact of the Reconstruction experiment that affected most aspects of the South's existence.

An appropriate starting point for a survey of the major books on the politics of Reconstruction is the debate over 1866 as the "critical year" in the period's political history. In 1930, Howard K. Beale published an innovative and provocative treatment of the contest between President Andrew Johnson and the Republican majority in Congress. In contrast to Beale's (1930) emphasis on Washington, most of the writing on Reconstruction in the first 30 years of the century had focused on the South, mainly through a series of studies of Reconstruction in individual states. Written by a generation of southern-born but northern-trained historians, these books created what has been called the Dunning School after William A. Dunning, the Columbia University professor who supervised most of them as dissertations. But this group of historians is more accurately styled the "New South school" because of their regional mindset. In their state studies and other writings, they showed how the South had been mistreated, even wronged, by a Reconstruction policy that was ill informed and "vindictive." And this line of interpretation was dominant until the 1960s when a very different, almost antithetical, approach superseded it. These earlier historians did not know too much about the Republican Congressmen who designed the Reconstruction policies and what precisely they intended. Beale, who was by no means a neo-Confederate but a young northerner with progressive leanings, nevertheless shared their view about the tone of postwar policy. And he was puzzled as to why "a Northern people, not normally vindictive, [should] have adopted toward the defeated South a policy which their grandchildren generally condemn as both harsh and unwise" (Beale 1930: vii). Had President Andrew Johnson prevailed in his contest with Congress, a less demanding set of terms would have resulted. Beale clearly sympathized with Johnson's policy of "leniency," observing that it "would have been approved overwhelmingly" in the North if a referendum had been taken in December 1865 (Beale 1930: 50). The president's approach demanded reasonable evidence of repentance and concession from the South, while reassuring it that there would be limits to the federal government's demands, one of which was "Universal suffrage, [which] Johnson, a Southerner who knew the negro, could not favor" (Beale 1930: 47).

Unlike those of his opponents in Congress, the president's predispositions appeared quite understandable to Beale. Although neither was "tolerant" of each other's position, "the Radicals," in Beale's view, "were avowedly extremists who used extreme methods to educate people to extreme ends" (Beale 1930: 112). Except for a small group of conservative Republicans who supported Johnson, Beale believed that the party was dominated by the radicals who proceeded to battle with the president in preparation for the showdown in the congressional elections of 1866. In this contest, the radicals presented the Fourteenth Amendment as their alternative proposal to the president's "restoration" policy that Congress had rejected in December 1865.

While Beale's (1930) criticism of the Republicans for being extreme and hostile to the South did not depart much from the prevalent view ever since the New South school had set the tone, his interpretation of the motives and agenda of the radicals was quite novel, though thoroughly disparaging. Beale attacked the radicals for practicing political deception. Coining the memorable phrase, "Claptrap and Issues," as the title of his short but pivotal Chapter 5, he depicted them as a well-organized faction determined to gain control of their party as well as of national politics.

Although they claimed that their objective was to "keep the South out," their primary goal was actually to advance their economic agenda for promoting the industrial and commercial interests of the northeast. So tariff, banking, and monetary policies were the real issues and, under the guise of punishing the rebels, the radicals managed to forge a northern coalition to prevent the West and South from forming an alliance in opposition. Thus, the election of 1866 was critical because it determined the outcome of the battle over southern policy and also ensured the hegemony of the radicals and their allies, the northeastern economic interests who came to dominate the Age of Big Business.

Three decades later, Beale's interpretation of this critical moment was challenged by LaWanda and John Cox in their *Politics, Principle, and Prejudice* (1963). Rejecting Beale's (1930) assertion that the Republicans were motivated primarily by economic interests, they argued instead that principle played a major role in their approach to the South, essentially a commitment to delay southern readmission until the former slaves had been guaranteed "basic civil rights" (Cox and Cox 1963: 207). On this issue, the radical faction of the party took a more advanced position, arguing for suffrage for the freedmen and a long delay before readmitting the South. But neither they nor the Republican party in general were united on economic matters. Rather than the simplistic distinction between rhetoric and interests propounded by Beale, the Coxes treated politics with rather more sophistication, acknowledging that politicians are rarely either opportunistic or principled, but in fact have to be both if they are to be effective. Accordingly, they took questions of political maneuver and tactics seriously, even paying considerable attention to disputes over patronage and the influence it gave to those who controlled it. Just as patronage and party infighting were important to the more principled radicals and their party colleagues, so too Andrew Johnson, on closer examination, seemed very much aware of, and concerned about, jobs and influence. Indeed, he was an experienced, skillful, and ambitious politician who was no passive victim of radical deception and plots. Moreover, he too had principles that he could not easily abandon, for example an unwavering belief in a limited role for government and a strong dislike of blacks.

Besides reassessing the protagonists and offering a perceptive and more realistic understanding of how politics actually works, the Coxes' treatment of the critical contest of 1866 introduced a quite new and surprising story line. Rather like Beale's (1930) insight about the radicals' supposed "hidden agenda," LaWanda and John Cox (1963) produced their own political subtext by suggesting that, beneath the public and verbal contest for control over Reconstruction policy, a deeper, institutional dynamic was at work, namely "a party realignment."

After the Civil War, the political situation was very fluid. A real possibility existed that a party of the center, a party that was national and moderate, might emerge, thereby pushing to the margins the sectional and contentious Republicans and Democrats. As agents in this maneuver, there were two possible candidates. The War Democrats led by the Blair family of Maryland (Montgomery had been Lincoln's postmaster-general) and moderate to conservative Republicans headed by William H. Seward, the secretary of state. At the center of this struggle was the president, whose lenient southern policy and supposed opposition to extremists in both parties could become the catalyst for the realignment. Savvy politician that he was, Johnson was quite aware of this substructural dimension of the party political scene in 1866 and he embarked actively on an initiative aimed at forming a National Union party. To this end, he called a convention – symbolically it was to be held in Philadelphia – to lead off the movement in preparation for the fall election. This subtext to the Johnson–radical contest was, in fact, a very real aspect of the struggle in the critical year. However, the movement soon foundered, mainly because the political forces pushing for it were just not strong enough, but also because Johnson and his advisors miscalculated. Instead of distancing himself from the radicals alone, he picked a fight with the Republican party as a whole when he opposed the Freedmen's Bureau and Civil Rights bills in the spring. These represented a consensual stance within the party, not a radical, factional one. Thus, by denouncing these measures, he made war on the party itself, leaving as his option only an uneasy alliance with the pro-southern Democratic party. That the realignment collapsed does not, however, diminish its importance as a central feature and concern of "the critical year," a year considerably more complicated politically than previously imagined.

The emerging reassessment of national politics was consolidated in the early 1960s by two other books that covered a broader canvass and were probably more influential than *Politics, Principle, and Prejudice*. In 1960, Eric L. McKitrick thoroughly revised the reputation and image of Andrew Johnson. The target of McKitrick's brilliant study was the group of historians that included Beale – though none was as stimulating or original as he – who published positive, even eulogistic, biographies of Johnson around 1930, namely Claude Bowers (1929), Lloyd P. Stryker (1929), George F. Milton (1930), and Robert W. Winston (1928), all of them journalists actually, not academic historians. Whereas the Coxes had acknowledged Johnson's political intuition and experience, McKitrick saw only ineptitude and obtuseness as he "threw away his own power both as president and as party leader" (1960: 14).

When he assumed the presidency after Lincoln's assassination, Johnson was in a strong position, McKitrick argues, since the former Confederates were expecting the worst and were ready to accept anything less, while the Republicans in Congress were anticipating that Johnson would take a fine line. But the new president embarked on a conciliatory policy and, when he encountered resistance from the South, proceeded to yield even further. As a result, he lost control and encouraged the southerners to believe that recalcitrance paid off. Then, in 1866, instead of trying to reassure the Republicans, he decided to oppose them on every single aspect of southern policy. In the process, he took on the entire party, not just its radical faction, a serious mistake as the Coxes also noted.

Unlike the Coxes, however, McKitrick did not consider Johnson an adept politician. Instead, he was an "outsider," "a lone wolf," for whom "Politics . . . was essentially a matter of principles that had to be defended rather than of a party organization that had to win elections" (McKitrick 1960: 88). And those principles, consisting mainly of a Jacksonian belief in the virtue of minimal government, and therefore strict constitutional construction, hardened as the Tennessean encountered opposition. Simultaneously, his feeling that he was an outsider fighting a lone battle to protect the constitution grew into a fantasy that he was a victim of persecution. In speeches on his disastrous "Swing around the Circle" to the Midwest in the summer of 1866, he began to liken his troubles to Christ's crucifixion, a development that not only dishonored the office but revealed an instability in Johnson that

McKitrick thought contributed to his failure to act rationally and with political discernment. This psychological dimension, McKitrick believed, also applied to the impeachment imbroglio. The attempt to remove Johnson from office so late in his term made little political sense for the Republicans, so McKitrick concluded that the only conceivable way of explaining it was as "a long-needed psychological blow-off," some sort of catharsis in a situation of great national danger that had become increasingly irrational (McKitrick 1960: 507).

A few years after the appearance of *Andrew Johnson and Reconstruction*, William R. Brock's *An American Crisis* focused on the other end of Pennsylvania Avenue with an examination of Congress and Reconstruction. While McKitrick's assessment of Johnson reversed Beale's by arguing that the seventeenth president was politically incompetent, and maybe emotionally too, Brock's (1963) interpretation of the Republicans who controlled Congress also countered Beale's stance decisively by claiming that they were motivated, not by economic interests, but by ideological imperatives – and by ideology, he meant "a coherent view of what America ought to be" (Brock 1963: 248). In broad terms, their worldview was very similar to the "free-labor ideology" that Eric Foner analyzed later with great precision in his *Free Soil, Free Labor, Free Men* (1970). As Brock saw it, ideology was the force driving the Republicans on Reconstruction. Most of them had been shaped intellectually and politically by the struggle in the 1840s and 1850s to contain the South's political influence. And they came from small towns in otherwise rural areas of the North which were experiencing rapid economic development, a result that was attributable to individual "energy and enterprise" (Brock 1963: 245). The felicitous outcome of these remarkable changes that they witnessed, even participated in, was economic progress, accompanied by individual social mobility. By contrast, southern society was stratified and stagnant, the very opposite of what America should be. The Republicans' ideology included both economic concerns and moral principles as crucial ingredients of a developing, prospering society. "Moral and material progress were intertwined" therefore, in contrast to Beale's assertion that the Republicans' economic interests and political principles were incompatible (Brock 1963: 242). Besides eliding the distinction between interests and ideals in the Republicans' motivation, Brock's treatment of the factions within the party blurred differences in similar fashion. Although the "radicals" seemed to be the creators and proponents of this ideology, the party also included a group whom Brock referred to as "moderates." But it is unclear why they pursued a different course on the Reconstruction measures and whether they had a different ideological position from the radicals. At all events, Brock, like McKitrick, asserted that the moderates, not the radicals, had greater influence over the shape that the Republicans' Reconstruction policy assumed, whether during the "First Congressional Reconstruction" when their proposals consisted of the Civil Rights Act and the Fourteenth Amendment or in the "Second" when it was the Reconstruction Act.

The element missing so far from the historical writing on the dispute over Reconstruction policy between 1865 and 1868 comprises its intended victims, the former Confederates in the South. In 1973, ten years after Brock's volume, my own *Reunion without Compromise* provided the remedy. Its subtitle, *The South and Reconstruction*, paralleled McKitrick's (1960) *Andrew Johnson and Reconstruction* and Brock's (1963) *Congress and Reconstruction*. Despite the focus on the South in the publications of the New South school, little attention had been paid to the attitudes and calculations of the region's leaders while the president and Congress were deciding their fate. This omission was surprising, since the South's state of mind and expectations would shape how it responded to proposals from Washington. Indeed, the reaction of the region's leadership, after Johnson's policy had run into trouble, seems to have been quite puzzling. Rather than cooperating and helping the president, an approach that McKitrick had suggested Johnson should have pursued in his dealings with the Republicans, the South became more defiant and recalcitrant. This behavior further weakened the president's position and actually provided the justification for Congress to impose tougher terms, which in fact it did. So was the South failing to consult its best interests and acting self-destructively?

From the start, Perman (1973) contended, the South's leaders conceived of northern terms for readmission as a matter of negotiation. With Washington seeking their assent to the proposed terms, the South's only weapon seemed to be its ability to withhold consent. As leading southerners saw the political situation, compliance ran the risk of the South's simply being taken for granted or of justifying even harsher terms. By contrast, noncompliance, it was believed, gave the South some influence over events in Washington and control over its own political affairs. When they demurred over some of his requirements in 1865, Johnson backed down. If they now rejected the Fourteenth Amendment, the Republicans would have to decide what to do next, and disputes and divisions would arise among them. In fact, southern resistance was likely to force the Republicans to adopt ever more radical policies that would provoke a reaction against them on the part of Johnson's supporters and the Democrats. Counting on the North's desire for an end to sectional wrangling as well as its attachment to localism and state rights and its deep-seated racial antipathy, the South calculated that noncompliance would cause northerners to reassess and reject the Republicans' policies, leading to their electoral defeat and the anticipated realignment of the nation's political parties. In the meantime, the South's political leaders would remain in office and the region would be spared the upset and interference of Reconstruction.

Even when the game seemed to be up after the Reconstruction Act was passed in March 1867, the southern leadership still attempted to delay its implementation or even undermine its objectives. Indeed, whenever they were asked to give their consent, as was the case in all of the plans formally proposed by the president or Congress, the southern response, so Perman (1973) found, was always to withhold it. If the course of the former Confederates and their allies was ultimately self-defeating, there was method to their madness. Quite consciously, they calculated that noncompliance and "masterly inactivity" gave them short-term security, while the long-term risks seemed worth the gamble. The South may have been defeated but it was not going to act that way.

In the late 1960s and early 1970s, the new interest in Andrew Johnson's opponents, the previously overlooked Republicans, generated several other interpretive studies. Two of the more influential of them also employed the innovative methods of statistical analysis that were beginning to generate interest among historians. The first was David Donald's *The Politics of Reconstruction, 1863–1867* (1965), published just two years after Brock's study. Originally presented at the Walter L. Fleming

Lectures in Southern History at Louisiana State University (interestingly, Fleming was one of the most prominent of the "New South school"), their avowed purpose was to provoke and challenge. Despite the sudden surge in new books on Reconstruction, Donald felt that Reconstruction was in an "unpromising state" (Donald 1965: xiii). His reasons for jumping to this conclusion were that no new archival sources were being used, while the questions about motivation and significance that dominated the discussion involved value judgments that, by their very nature, were inconclusive. So Donald (1965) took a startlingly different tack. First, he noted that, in the mid-1860s, the Democrats and Republicans were so closely balanced that Republicans had to appeal to Democrats if they wanted to win nationally or in individual states; this required them to adopt platforms and policies that were moderate and centrist. Second, the moderate and radical factions within the Republican party could not be differentiated on ideological grounds since there was broad consensus within the party on the issues. Instead, their differing voting records were explained by their relative electoral security, moderates coming from competitive districts and radicals from safe ones.

Third, Donald analyzed the voting process involved in the passage of the Reconstruction Act in the House and discovered that no one faction was responsible for the bill's final form. Rather, all groups participating in the debates and votes, including even the Democrats, played a role in fashioning what Donald regarded simply as a compromise measure that a majority of the participants could agree upon. Likening the legislative process to a pendulum, he argued that it finally settled at dead center after swinging back and forth while amendments were introduced and votes taken. The measure in its final form was therefore neither radical nor moderate, and it was "determined less by abstract ideas than by the degree of strength and security each [member] felt in his home district" (Donald 1965: 81–2).

Donald's attempt to reduce the outcome of a matter of such enormous significance as the Reconstruction Act 1867 to a merely mechanical operation was bound to be provocative, while it also revealed the problems involved in trying to differentiate the two Republican factions on ideological grounds, as Brock had tried to do. A more persuasive interpretation was proposed 10 years later in Michael Les Benedict's *A Compromise of Principle* (1974). Benedict used traditional sources like personal correspondence and speeches and then confirmed and elaborated them with statistical analysis. Instead of roll-call analysis, he employed Guttman scaling, a method initially used by psychologists to analyze attitudes, which he used to assess the intensity of reactions to particular legislative proposals. By this means, Benedict was able to separate out three groups within the party whose votes revealed a pattern of consistency: conservatives, centrists and radicals, with the remaining Congressmen difficult to categorize. The centrists had no clear position but clustered as a small swing group. The radicals and the conservatives (the latter corresponding to the moderates in previous studies) were more distinctive and larger. Nevertheless, the notion that the radicals were ever a majority was dismissed by Benedict. Although naturally most numerous in the House, they fell far short of a majority, and in the Senate, there were just 11 of them. Despite all their efforts to mobilize support, the radicals failed to seize control of any of the major pieces of legislation when Congress was fighting the president over Reconstruction policy. The Civil Rights Act and the Fourteenth Amendment were not radical measures; neither was the

Reconstruction Act, the most important measure that is generally considered the embodiment of radicalism.

While Benedict (1974) managed to identify the factions and their members – something that none of his predecessors had attempted – he was also able to account for their differences in ways that contrasted with Beale, Brock, and Donald. Neither programmatic ideology nor economic interests separated the radicals from other Republicans, Benedict concluded. Instead, Republicans were all pretty much agreed on their approach to Reconstruction since they shared the same antislavery heritage and all of them wanted Reconstruction to cement the Union firmly, with the southern loyalists receiving protection and the former slaves legally guaranteed equal rights and justice. Where the groups differed was in their approach – either vigorous and urgent or conciliatory and cautious. These differing stances derived from an individual Republican's political temperament and policy preferences. In contrast to this stance, which Benedict categorized as "legislative," a Republican might take a position for "political" reasons. This "political" stance was primarily strategic and organizational and was influenced by an individual's position within the party apparatus of his state. If his main rival was a radical supported by the radical faction, he might find it wise to associate himself with the conservatives in his state.

Benedict's (1974) statistical method as well as his explanation for a Republican's factional identification was quite different from Donald's (1965). Also different was Benedict's depiction of how Reconstruction legislation was formulated. Rather than a swinging pendulum, the process seemed to be one in which a radical initiative was amended until it became conservative. The case of the Reconstruction Act 1867 illustrated this. The debate began with Thaddeus Stevens' initial proposal in the form of a military bill intended to keep the South out indefinitely until it was deemed sufficiently reconstructed to be ready for readmission. In effect, Reconstruction was to occur before readmission. But his plan was continually amended until it provided a mechanism for the speedy readmission of the South, with the governments set up under Johnson's plan remaining in office while the plan of Reconstruction went into operation. Rather than a prerequisite for readmission as Stevens had intended, the act in its final form (with black suffrage and new state governments and constitutions as its requirements) made Reconstruction part of the readmission procedure. As a consequence, "Radicals, dissatisfied with the Reconstruction acts when enacted, grew more so as years passed by," Benedict wrote. "They blamed Reconstruction's failure on this untoward haste to end it before it had barely begun" (Benedict 1974: 243). Historians have experienced considerable difficulty in trying to explain and categorize the Republican party at its moment of greatest influence and danger in the Civil War era. This puzzle has two aspects. The first stems from the controversy swirling around the radicals. Those historians who were unsympathetic to their policies have labeled them as extremists, vindictive, and punitive or else as hypocritical, partisan, and opportunistic. By contrast, those who share their hopes and frustrations have considered them idealistic, ideological, foresighted. So, a cool, disinterested approach has been hard to develop. The second relates to the radicals' influence within the party. Reconstruction policy eventually included features that were radical for the time: black suffrage, military governments, proscription of former Confederates, and so on. Consequently, it has seemed obtuse to suggest that the policy was not radical and that the radicals were not responsible.

Yet, in fact, the Radicals were not in control of the party but were constantly trying to pull it in a more forceful and radical direction only to fail repeatedly. And they failed because they just did not have the support and votes and because the party operated under the compulsion to produce two-thirds majorities for its legislation so as to protect it from the anticipated presidential veto. While historians now concur that Andrew Johnson was not nearly as incompetent as McKitrick (1960) believed him to be, they are also agreed that what has been called "Radical Reconstruction" was not what the radicals really wanted. Johnson, the Democrats, and the southern governing class may have thought it was radical – it was certainly far too extreme for them. But congressional Republicans knew the radicals' aims had been thwarted. Reconstruction was, in many respects, radical but not sufficiently so for the radical wing of the Republican party at the time. In that case, perhaps "Radical Reconstruction" is a misnomer.

If Reconstruction is understood to cover the period 1865–77, then two-thirds of it occurred while Ulysses S. Grant was serving two terms as president, from 1869 to 1877. Yet most of the attention has been focused on the tumultuous policy-making contest at the national level under Johnson. And this is strange because the reorganization and reconstruction of the South that the Republicans had struggled for four years to achieve marked the beginning of an experiment that offered great hope for new directions in the relations between the sections and the races as well as for the emergence of a "New South." Furthermore, the Republicans now controlled the White House and both Houses of Congress. No longer having to defend themselves against presidential vetoes, the Republicans could move ahead, feeling secure and powerful.

Yet the exact opposite happened. The situation in the South began to unravel and collapse. As a result, the Grant years became preoccupied with saving Reconstruction, rather than strengthening and consolidating it. William Gillette's (1979) study was the first to examine how the Republican-controlled legislative and executive branches handled Reconstruction after 1868. The book's title, *Retreat from Reconstruction*, captured both the direction of national policy and the tone and mood of the author's treatment of it. "Reconstruction, which had once stirred up such great hopes and such fear, was virtually over almost as soon as it had begun," he lamented (Gillette 1979: 363).

The Republicans who were single-minded and determined in 1867 were "soon unable and finally unwilling to carry out reconstruction" (Gillette 1979: 369). For one thing, the president, a popular general who had succeeded as a soldier because of his grasp of strategy, failed to develop a firm and coherent policy toward the South in peacetime. Initially, he acted vigorously when problems arose in Virginia, Georgia, North Carolina, Alabama, and Texas, with the result that the Reconstruction governments in those states were sustained. His approach was to handle each case differently because of differing circumstances. But the upshot was neither a clear policy nor a successful outcome since all five had fallen into the Democrats' hands by 1874. And this pattern persisted because he responded, or failed to respond, without a coherent or decisive formula. "Had Grant provided an effective policy, clear direction, and strong leadership, he might have achieved a great deal," Gillette concluded, appearing to cast the bulk of the blame for the retreat from Reconstruction at the president's door (Gillette 1979: 185).

Of course, Grant was not the only Republican with responsibility for Reconstruction. But the record of the Republicans in Congress seemed only marginally better. Admittedly, further legislation was enacted to strengthen and sustain Reconstruction, such as the enforcement legislation of 1870–1, the Civil Rights Act 1875 and numerous other laws dealing with problems in specific states. Yet, Gillette argued, the Republicans seemed to have had "second thoughts" after 1868 and "indecision and division" replaced their earlier determination and ability to close ranks (Gillette 1979: 370). Lest the Republicans as a group be blamed for failure to follow through on their own policy initiative, the author acknowledged that they had labored under severe constraints such as a poorly managed and under-financed federal administrative apparatus, a constitutional system designed to curb action by the federal authorities, and a deep-seated racism in the North as well as the South (Gillette 1979: 363–9). Furthermore, the resistance that had been unleashed by the Democrats in the South was immense, probably far worse than the Republicans had imagined, and the northern Democrats gave it their unstinting support. Meanwhile, the Republican party had to prevail in national elections in which the South was now participating and, by 1872, it was becoming apparent that the struggle to save the southern governments was jeopardizing the party's base in the North. After losing the 1874 congressional elections, partly because of an economic depression the year before, the party switched priority, deciding to abandon the losing battle in the South to try to save the North. After 1874, the retreat from Reconstruction "turned into a rout" (Gillette 1979: 368). But the bill of indictments and catalog of complaints that Gillette presented were so long and so seemingly inexorable that it is hard to imagine any possible outcome than dismal failure.

While the record of northern Republicans was one of disappointment and failure, their opponents in the South were experiencing something quite different. My own study of the South in the Grant years, *The Road to Redemption* (Perman 1984), was not intended to show how the Democrats succeeded in overthrowing Reconstruction. Instead, my emphasis was on process, rather than outcome. What was the political system of the South like now that there were two competitive parties in existence there for the first time in almost two decades? And how did the two major parties deal with each other at a moment so unpropitious for the normal interaction of political parties in a representative democracy? Despite the obvious contrast between the newly created party of Reconstruction and its Democratic foe, I argued that the first four years witnessed an attempt by both parties to move to the political center and control the region electorally. Not only did the Republicans need desperately to be accepted as legitimate by their opponents and the electorate at large, but they also had to command broad support and respect so as to enable them to govern effectively. In control of state government throughout the South after 1868, the Republicans opted, for the most part, to follow a cautious and responsible course. Similarly, their opponents had to establish their reputation and support. Led by anti-secessionists and former Whigs rather than by the secession-tainted ex-Democrats, the party, often calling itself "Conservative," endorsed the three Reconstruction amendments (at the national level, this was called the "New Departure") and tried to allay the suspicions of Congress and of the newly enfranchised African Americans whom they hoped to win over, or at least reassure. This drive to the center by both parties marked a phase that I called "the politics of convergence." Although the ascendant element in both parties embarked on this electoral strategy, each of them was opposed vehemently by its intra-party rival, the radical and die-hard faction which was insisting that this strategy was a betrayal of principles and party identity.

These dissidents soon forced their respective parties to change direction and emphasize their distinctiveness, not their similarities. The national political campaign of 1872 when Horace Greeley ran at the head of a coalition of Liberal Republicans and Democrats had been the culmination and model for "the politics of convergence." But its abject electoral failure and the confusion it sowed about the identity of each party prepared the way for a return to rigid partisanship. In the South, the radicals in the Republican party and the former secessionists and the orthodox among the Democrats took over and inaugurated the second phase of Reconstruction in the South. This introduced "the politics of divergence" (Perman 1984), in which the differences between the parties now assumed political salience. With most of the more conciliatory southern whites (usually referred to as "scalawags") leaving the party, the Republicans became increasingly identified with their voting base of African Americans. Accordingly, the Democratic party, which had already gained control of many of the state governments by 1873, sensed the opportunity to attack the remaining bastions of Republican control by stressing white supremacy, and also advocating a curb on government activism and the taxes and expenditures that ensued. Violence against the Republicans' mainly black voters added lethal power to the Democrats' assault.

Once they won control and the federal commitment to sustain the Reconstruction governments was brought to an end in 1877, as Perman (1984) argued, the new Democratic regimes proceeded to enact legislation to reduce taxation, cut funding, repudiate public debts, and enable planters to regain control over their labor force. The Democratic party that now took control of the South was heavily influenced by the old guard, while race had regained its centrality in the party's identity. As Reconstruction collapsed, the extremists in the Democratic party rose to power.

The struggle to reconstruct the South had ended. Perhaps, as many contemporaries and subsequent historians have concluded, the task was simply too great and the disappointing outcome predictable. But others have wondered whether a more satisfying, even successful, result was possible. After all, the North had managed to defeat the Confederacy on the battlefield. Why was it unable to consolidate this hard-won achievement by mobilizing its resources to win the peace? In the 1980s, two historians investigated this puzzling discrepancy by examining how the Republicans went about building their party in the South, a task that their hard-won victory over Johnson had made possible. Richard H. Abbott's *The Republican Party and the South, 1855–1877* (1986) examined the attitudes and expectations of the northern Republicans about creating a branch of their party in the South as well as the actions they took to develop an electoral base and party organization there after 1867. In *The South Returns to Congress*, Terry L. Seip (1983) concentrated on a different aspect of this relationship. The reception of their fellow Republicans from the South by northern Congressmen, especially the Republicans, was Seip's focus, and so he examined how southern Republicans were treated in the North, rather than in their own region.

Both of these inquiries into the nature and extent of the northerners' relations with and encouragement of their southern counterparts revealed the surprising paucity of resources and respect given them. According to Abbott, northern Republicans' interest in creating a southern base was quite limited. Despite their hopes of making the Republican party a national political organization once the war was over, they supplied very little funding to sustain the newspapers and the managers and workers so necessary to establish party organization and infrastructure. They also offered minimal help in election campaigns through providing speakers or publications. And they seemed to be oblivious when southern Republicans made specific requests for intervention in their states. Moreover, northerners expressed little confidence in a party reliant on the votes of blacks and they frequently confided in private as well as public that they regarded their southern colleagues "as liabilities, rather than assets" (Abbott 1986: x). Yet a viable southern party was crucial for keeping the former Confederates out of power, for protecting the freedmen, and for providing the national party with votes in presidential and congressional elections.

Corroboration for this remarkable unconcern was provided by Seip's (1983) examination of how northern Republican Congressmen treated the 251 representatives and senators sent to Washington from the Reconstruction South. Half of these were Republicans, 16 of them African Americans, and they dominated the southern delegation during the three Congresses from 1868 to 1874. These inexperienced Congressmen who represented the besieged southern Republican party might have expected understanding and encouragement from their northern equivalents. But, to their chagrin, so Seip reports, "Northern congressmen, especially the Republicans, tended to view their colleagues from the ex-Confederate states as Southerners first and only secondarily as fellow party members" (Seip 1983: 111).

Prejudices against the South, and later against the Republican-controlled governments there, colored their thinking and precluded empathy and collaboration. As a result, southern Republicans received little help in obtaining committee assignments and ended up with less than their due. On the matter that concerned them most, the economic reconstruction of their region, they encountered similar treatment. Had the region's Republicans been able to show that they and the national party could deliver economic benefits, their party's reputation would have been boosted significantly. But on fiscal matters such as tariff adjustment and reduction of the cotton and tobacco taxes; on monetary questions such as a fairer distribution of national bank notes, an increase in the volume of greenbacks in circulation and the remonetization of silver; and on appropriations and subsidies for internal improvements, the South's Republicans invariably encountered opposition (Seip 1983: 277). Northeastern Republicans in particular could be counted on to resist southern entreaties for more flexible monetary and fiscal policies. But, on appropriations, northern Republicans as a group were unwilling to give away anything to the South. Although its need for levee building and repair, harbor and river improvement, and railroad development was considerable, the "disloyal South" was not to receive benefits at the expense of the party's more deserving and loyal northern constituents. Indeed, as time passed and the southern governments became increasingly shaky and therefore, it was claimed, unworthy of continued support, the incentive to give funds to the South became less and less compelling.

This extraordinary disdain and lack of concern for their fellow Republicans' predicament in the inhospitable climate of the Reconstruction South is hard to fathom. The creation of a viable Republican party was surely central to the national party's plans for the postwar South and the nation. Yet, almost as soon as the party was placed in power in the South, the means to sustain it were withheld. Some insight into this paradoxical behavior can perhaps be derived from the contradictions embedded in the federal plan for reconstructing the South. In its final form, the Reconstruction Act 1867 created a procedure for the immediate readmission of the southern states, a process that superseded the Radicals' objective of delay and con- tinued federal supervision. This seemingly more acceptable and more realistic scheme was, in practice, a formula for ending federal tutelage and involvement in the South. Once they had elected new, and Republican-controlled, governments, the southern states were to be self-governing, and their future was theirs to determine. Only if problems arose later might the federal government take further action. Even then, its intervention was constrained by the dual sovereignty of the federal system. The Reconstruction Act 1867 therefore provided a mechanism for federal withdrawal and local self-government. Yet Congress's plan assumed that, with the establishment of Republican governments in the South, the experiment of Reconstruction had just begun. And its success would depend on the ability of these governments not just to survive but to introduce change. On this dilemma, this paradox, rested the fate of the readmitted and reorganized, but not yet reconstructed, South. This perhaps explains the ambivalence of the northern Republicans after 1868: they were caught between both ending and continuing federal involvement in southern Reconstruc- tion, a dilemma they could not resolve.

The historical writing on Reconstruction was built on a foundation established by the New South school's studies of individual southern states. Since the late 1970s, historians of the South during Reconstruction have continued to publish state stud- ies, but permeated by a very different set of assumptions and attitudes. No matter how well written and conceived, these kinds of books are, by their nature, variations on a theme – a Mississippi version of the same general story already recounted for Georgia. But two state studies in particular have introduced generalizations or taken approaches that have wider implications.

In his examination of Reconstruction in Louisiana, *Crucible of Reconstruction* (1984), Ted Tunnell rose above the localism of most state studies. The Republican- controlled government that took office in Louisiana in 1868, with Henry C. Warmoth, a Union soldier from Illinois, as governor, had been elected under the Reconstruc- tion Act 1867. Thus, it was a creature of the federal government and so lacked legitimacy. Added to this disability was its reliance on the votes of African Americans, even though many were mulattoes from New Orleans who had been free for years.

Naturally, the Republicans' lack of legitimacy made it very difficult for them to govern because they could command neither respect nor obedience. This problem confronted every Reconstruction government put into power in 1868 and 1869. In Tunnell's (1984) view, they were faced with one of two possible courses. "The policy of force" required, first, that police and military organizations be created capable of compelling obedience and, second, that an electoral apparatus be formed to keep the election machinery and the counting of votes in the hands of the government so as to prevent intimidation and fraud by the Republicans' opponents. The other approach, "the policy of peace," required the government to conciliate and reassure the Democrats by giving them favors, such as access to patronage, funding for their favored projects, removal of their political disabilities, and assurance that the influence of African Americans would be curbed. The two strategies were incompatible, of course. But Warmoth's administration, and every other Republican government in the South, pursued both of them simultaneously or in sequence, knowing that reliance on one or the other was too risky. In Tunnell's opinion, these "contradictions of power" lay at the heart of Republican governance in the Reconstruction South. And, because they were structural, they burdened southern Republicans with a fundamental yet virtually insoluble dilemma.

Louisiana's government stayed Republican until 1877. One of the other states to hold out that long was South Carolina, and a primary reason for Republicanism's longevity there was the size of the black electorate, a feature it shared with Louisiana. In the Palmetto State, the influence of African Americans extended even further, for over half of the 487 men elected to state and federal office between 1867 and 1876 were black. The emergence of many black officials in one state provided the opportunity to examine, not just who these men were and what they did, but how they functioned within the political system. In *Black over White* (1977), Thomas Holt looked at the recruitment of black candidates in South Carolina as well as their voting behavior and influence once elected. His investigation revealed that African Americans who went into Republican party politics had learned their skills and gained prominence, not through white organizations like the Freedmen's Bureau or the missionary societies, but through their own institutions such as the churches or the colored regiments in the US Army. And these abilities that were obtained independently from whites proved effective later in the state assembly when black representatives mobilized as a group to use committees and caucuses to increase their legislative and party influence. Between 1872 and 1876, black Republicans controlled the speakership and headed the pivotal Ways and Means committee in the House, while chairing 16 of the 24 committees in the Senate. As a result, African Americans began to obtain control over both houses and also over the party.

Nevertheless, the Republican party proved unable to maintain discipline and conserve its strength, constantly succumbing to factionalism and allowing dissatisfied groups to bolt and form coalitions with the opposition Democrats who used this dissidence to undermine the party. Despite the Democrats' eager exploitation of any crack in Republican unity, Holt (1977) tended to consider this lack of cohesion and discipline a Republican problem, rather than a difference in strategic priorities endemic in "the contradictions of power" the Republicans faced. Interestingly, he suggested that part of this division could be traced to the existence within the African American group of a significant distinction between those he referred to as the "blacks" and the "browns." The free-born and lighter-skinned browns had class interests, he claimed, at odds with the black freedmen who had less public experience and less education and whose constituency consisted mainly of farm laborers. Although the "browns" sometimes ended up voting alongside the "blacks," the divergences between them exacerbated the factional splits since the former often favored fusion with the Democrats. Whatever the extent and significance of these intra-racial divisions, there is no doubting that South Carolina's African American Republicans were actors in the political arena and were not as inexperienced and passive as they had once been depicted. If blacks as a group were less influential in most of the other southern States, it was probably because they lacked the critical mass and opportunities existing in South Carolina.

Even more critical of the southern Republicans than Holt was Mark W. Summers. In *Railroads, Reconstruction, and the Gospel of Prosperity* (1984), his region-wide study of how the party, once in power, handled the issue of state aid to railroads, Summers handed down an indictment as severe as any that the New South school had produced. "With many conspicuous exceptions, Republicans had ruled badly, and they admitted it," he charged, adding that "Republicans could not even invest themselves with the look of legitimacy" (Summers 1984: 295). This was a far cry from Tunnell's (1984) explaining the Republicans' defeat as an outcome of the structural dilemma they faced or Holt's (1977) placing the responsibility on the Republicans' inability to overcome factional divisions. As Summers saw it, the Republicans had squandered the one real opportunity to erase the taint of illegitimacy that surrounded their party. For the provision of state aid to railroads made it possible for the new governments to foster economic development and thereby generate prosperity. And prosperity meant, not just profits for the railroads, but revenue for the state, infrastructure for its economy, and growth for the areas where the railroads were built. Furthermore, success in this initiative would demonstrate that Republican governments were supportive of business interests and the economy and not unduly preoccupied with the needs of their own primary constituents, the disadvantaged blacks and whites who needed public services.

But the prosperous new South that beckoned was never reached. Instead, the Republicans extended aid in the form of state endorsement of the roads' bonds, with far too little discrimination and virtually no collateral, to operators who were unreliable and often unsavory. And when the railroads failed, the state was left holding their debts and responsible for paying them off. The irresponsibility of the Republicans' generous but unwise policy was compounded by the favoritism and bribery that now came to light as well as by the enormous indebtedness that burdened the states with nothing much to show for it. Rather than producing prosperity and success, the railroad aid programs, embarked on so hopefully by all the state governments, provided their enemies with proof that the Republicans were incompetent, corrupt, and gullible. Success in this economic initiative might have helped dispel the Republicans' burden of illegitimacy. But failure simply confirmed it and, in Summers' view, doomed an experiment that was shaky to begin with. The propaganda was certainly hyperbolic and the outcome catastrophic, but whether the Republicans could have managed the situation any better is debatable. They were, after all, inexperienced and beleaguered and looking for a quick success to dispel voters' doubts. Railroads offered an "open sesame" the party could not pass up, but the risks were considerable.

There are three approaches that historians can take in attempting to explain why the Reconstruction governments fell, and so quickly. The first is the role of the Republican-controlled federal government, the arena investigated by Gillette (1979), Seip (1983), and Abbott (1986). Then there is the performance of the southern Republicans themselves in bringing about the collapse of Reconstruction. In differing ways, this is the subject matter of the studies by Holt (1977), Summers (1984), and Tunnell (1984). Finally, there is the part played by the resistance in the South. This perspective can be explored through Perman's *Road to Redemption* (1984) and by two books on the role of violence in destabilizing the Reconstruction governments (Trelease 1971; Rable 1984). Allen W. Trelease's *White Terror* (1971)

presented an almost encyclopedic examination of the origins, organization, and operations of the Ku Klux Klan in the Reconstruction South. Quite unsympathetic to the
Klan, unlike the several accounts published prior to his, Trelease's study revealed that,
in the areas where it operated, the secret organization created a reign of terror that
was directed primarily at blacks whom they "whipped, shot, hanged, robbed, raped,
and otherwise outraged" (Trelease 1971: xi). The overall objective was to restrain
and subordinate the former slaves and thus restore white supremacy. But, after 1867
when the Reconstruction governments were being formed, Klan activity became
more specific as it focused its operations on preventing the Republicans from being
elected and then destabilizing and undermining them once they took office.

As destabilization became the goal, the areas in which the organization was most
active were those counties where the Republicans' electoral margins were slim.
Usually they were located in the Piedmont, or foothills, in the upcountry section of
each state where "the two parties or the two races were nearly equal, or where there
was a white majority large enough to intimidate the freedmen" (Trelease 1971: 64).
But this generalization did not apply universally because, as Trelease himself noted,
the Klan was also active in some counties with black majorities, and even some
predominantly white ones. Even though intimidation and suppression of blacks
without any overt political purpose was often engaged in, the violence was nevertheless aimed at weakening Republican authority. And, in this respect, the Klan was
extremely effective, especially in Georgia, North Carolina, and Alabama. But it was
not so decisive, Trelease acknowledged, that it could be "credited with overthrowing Republican control" (Trelease 1971: 419). Still, the Klan held numerous communities and counties in their thrall and it could count on the support and protection
of men of status and influence. Almost certainly, its night-riding would have continued, had not the federal government intervened in 1871–2 to arrest and try some of
the leaders, mainly in South Carolina, a move acquiesced to by the southern Democrats who feared the Klan's tactics might hurt their chances in the 1872 elections.

While Trelease concentrated on the Klan alone, George C. Rable's *But There Was
No Peace* (1984) surveyed violence in the South throughout the entire period and
in its various manifestations. In Rable's view, violence was not just a feature of
southern life during the turbulent Reconstruction era. Rather, it was an indispensable weapon in the resistance of southern whites against Reconstruction. As a way
of repressing black assertiveness, it was never far from the surface of white thoughts
and emotions, even before Reconstruction began. But when the fear of black insurrection, "the specter of Saint Domingue," as Rable described it, was compounded
by a widespread determination to resist what they despised as the meddling and
tyranny of Yankee outsiders, this combination made violence central to the campaign to restore white supremacy and overthrow Reconstruction.

The violence initiated by whites after the war can be divided, so Rable argues, into
three phases. In the first, it took the form of race riots that broke out in Memphis
and New Orleans in 1866. In the next phase beginning in 1868, the Klan was the
primary instrumentality as a "counter-revolution" against Reconstruction began to
take hold. Rable assessed the impact of the Klan in terms similar to Trelease,
dismissing it as "the instrument of redemption" for the southern states (Rable 1984:
101). Its subsequent decline he attributed to its failure "to achieve its central
objective – the overthrowing of Republican state governments in the South" (Rable

1984: 101). Moreover, since the Klan was decentralized in its structure and episodic in its operation, it did not have the means to accomplish such a major task.

In the third and final phase, between 1874 and 1876, the counter-revolution reached its culmination as the Democrats mobilized their state party organizations to coordinate intimidation and violence during the election campaigns. In Alabama in 1874, in Mississippi in 1875, and in South Carolina in 1876, the party organized strident white supremacy campaigns and used violence to intimidate targeted Republican voters and their party candidates. This official and centralized violence was quite different from the methods of the Klan and it was more effective, sweeping away the last remaining Republican governments in those states with significant black populations. Violence was, therefore, a crucial ingredient in the overthrow of Reconstruction, so Rable claimed. And its central importance is not diminished by its more indirect and less decisive impact prior to the showdown of 1874–6, or even by its effectiveness only at the local level in Louisiana during these latter years.

For the first half of the twentieth century, amateur and professional historians who wrote about Reconstruction regarded the Republicans' attempt to reconstruct the South as mistaken and unnecessarily harsh, and therefore it deserved to fail. In the second half when a very different approach became dominant, called the Revisionist school, the idea of reconstructing the South was viewed far more favorably. Revisionists assumed that federal involvement in the former Confederacy was necessary, not only to protect the Union's wartime sympathizers and the 4 million African Americans who had been freed from slavery, but also to rearrange the political order there and bring about significant changes in the political system, and possibly even more.

But, as the preceding discussion has revealed, the difficulties and obstacles in the way of achieving such an outcome were immense. Despite their sympathy for the Reconstruction experiment, the Revisionists' scholarship has demonstrated that few possibilities existed for a Reconstruction policy capable of changing the South's political attitudes and structures. They have found that the Republicans' plans for the South were not shaped by the party's radical wing but by its moderates, and therefore it was less far-reaching than it might have been. Nevertheless, noncompliance and obstruction on the part of the South's governing class were evident from the outset and became even stronger once the new governments were formed in 1868, intensifying thereafter into overt resistance laced with a strong dose of force and violence. Worsening the situation further, the northern Republicans seemed to be ambivalent about their party allies in the South and uncertain whether to strengthen, or even support, them. Finally, the newly created Republican party in the South, although admittedly under enormous pressure, did not act as shrewdly or as effectively as it might have done, and in the process lost the small amount of leverage available to it. Regrettably, Revisionist writing on the politics of Reconstruction confirms the suspicion that the problem was, in all likelihood, intractable. The Reconstruction episode was, therefore, not a failure. Rather, it was a tragedy.

BIBLIOGRAPHY

Abbott, Richard H. (1986) *The Republican Party and the South, 1855–1877.* Chapel Hill, NC: University of North Carolina Press.

Beale, Howard K. (1930) *The Critical Year: A Study of Andrew Johnson and Reconstruction.* New York: Harcourt Brace.

Benedict, Michael Les (1974a) *A Compromise of Principle: Congressional Republicans and Reconstruction, 1863–1869.* New York: Norton.

Bowers, Claude G. (1929) *The Tragic Era: The Revolution after Lincoln.* Boston, Mass.: Houghton Mifflin.

Brock, William R. (1963) *An American Crisis: Congress and Reconstruction, 1865–1867.* New York: Macmillan.

Cox, LaWanda and Cox, John (1963) *Politics, Principle, and Prejudice, 1865–1866, Dilemma of Reconstruction America.* New York: Free Press.

Donald, David M. (1965) *The Politics of Reconstruction, 1863–1867.* Baton Rouge, La.: Louisiana State University Press.

Dunning, William A. (1907) *Reconstruction, Political and Economic, 1865–1877.* New York: Harper and Bros.

Foner, Eric (1970) *Free Soil, Free Labor, Free Men: The Ideology of the Republican Party before the Civil War.* New York: Oxford University Press.

Gillette, William (1979) *Retreat from Reconstruction, 1869–1879.* Baton Rouge, La.: Louisiana State University Press.

Holt, Thomas (1977) *Black over White: Negro Political Leadership in South Carolina during Reconstruction.* Urbana, Ill.: University of Illinois Press.

McKitrick, Eric L. (1960) *Andrew Johnson and Reconstruction.* Chicago: University of Chicago Press.

Milton, George F. (1930) *The Age of Hate: Andrew Johnson and the Radicals.* New York: Howard-McCann.

Perman, Michael (1973) *Reunion without Compromise: The South and Reconstruction, 1865–1868.* New York: Cambridge University Press.

Perman, Michael (1984) *The Road to Redemption: Southern Politics, 1869–1879.* Chapel Hill, NC: University of North Carolina Press.

Rable, George C. (1984) *But There Was No Peace: The Role of Violence in the Politics of Reconstruction.* Athens, Ga.: University of Georgia Press.

Seip, Terry L. (1983) *The South Returns to Congress: Men, Economic Measures, and Intersectional Relationships, 1868–1879.* Baton Rouge, La.: Louisiana State University Press.

Stryker, Lloyd P. (1929) *Andrew Johnson: A Study in Courage.* New York: Macmillan.

Summers, Mark W. (1984) *Railroads, Reconstruction, and the Gospel of Prosperity: Aid under the Radical Republicans, 1865–1877.* Princeton, NJ: Princeton University Press.

Trelease, Allen W. (1971) *White Terror: The Ku Klux Klan Conspiracy and Southern Reconstruction.* New York: Harper and Row.

Tunnell, Ted (1984) *Crucible of Reconstruction: War, Rebellion and Race in Louisiana, 1862–1877.* Baton Rouge, La.: Louisiana State University Press.

Winston, Robert W. (1928) *Andrew Johnson, Plebeian and Patriot,* New York: Holt and Sons.

SUGGESTED FURTHER READING

Benedict, Michael Les (1974) "Preserving the Constitution: The Conservative Basis of Radical Reconstruction," *Journal of American History* 61: 65–90.

Carter, Dan T. (1985) *When the War was Over: The Failure of Self-Reconstruction in the South, 1865–1867.* Baton Rouge, La.: Louisiana State University Press.

Current, Richard N. (1988) *Those Terrible Carpetbaggers: A Reinterpretation.* New York: Oxford University Press.

Fitzgerald, Michael W. (1989) *The Union League Movement in the Deep South: Politics and Agricultural Change during Reconstruction.* Baton Rouge, La.: Louisiana State University Press.

Harris, William C. (1997) *With Charity for All: Lincoln and the Restoration of the Union.* Lexington, Ky.: University Press of Kentucky.

Mohr, James C. (ed.) (1976) *Radical Republicans in the North: State Politics during Reconstruction.* Baltimore, Md.: Johns Hopkins University Press.

Moneyhon, Carl H. (1980) *Republicanism in Reconstruction Texas.* Austin, Tex.: University of Texas Press.

Montgomery, David (1967) *Beyond Equality: Labor and the Radical Republicans, 1862–1872.* New York: Alfred A. Knopf.

Powell, Lawrence N. (1982) "Carpetbaggers and the Problem of Republican Rule in the South," in J. Morgan Kousser and James M. McPherson (eds.) *Region, Race, and Reconstruction: Essays in Honor of C. Vann Woodward.* New York: Oxford University Press.

Rabinowitz, Howard N. (ed.) (1982) *Southern Black Leaders of the Reconstruction Era.* Urbana, Ill.: University of Illinois Press.

Richardson, Heather Cox (2001) *The Death of Reconstruction: Race, Labor and Politics in the Post-Civil War North, 1865–1901.* Cambridge, Mass.: Harvard University Press.

Schweniger, Loren (1978) *James Rapier and Reconstruction.* Chicago: University of Chicago Press.

Simpson, Brooks D. (1998) *The Reconstruction Presidents.* Lawrence, Kan.: University Press of Kansas.

Summers, Mark W. (1993) *The Era of Good Stealings.* New York: Oxford University Press.

Taylor, Joe Gray (1974) *Louisiana Reconstructed, 1863–1877.* Baton Rouge, La.: Louisiana State University Press.

Thornton, J. Mills (1982) "Fiscal Policy and the Failure of Reconstruction in the Lower South," in J. Morgan Kousser and James M. McPherson (eds.) *Region, Race, and Reconstruction: Essays in Honor of C. Vann Woodward.* New York: Oxford University Press.

Trefousse, Hans L. (1997) *Thaddeus Stevens: Nineteenth-Century Egalitarian.* Chapel Hill, NC: University of North Carolina Press.

Vorenberg, Michael (2001) *Final Freedom: The Civil War, the Abolition of Slavery, and the Thirteenth Amendment.* New York: Cambridge University Press.

Wang, Xi (1997) *The Trial of Democracy: Black Suffrage and Northern Republicans.* Athens, Ga.: University of Georgia Press.

Williams, Lou Falkner (1996) *The Great South Carolina Ku Klux Klan Trials.* Athens, Ga.: University of Georgia Press.

Zuczek, Richard (1996) *State of Rebellion: Reconstruction in South Carolina.* Columbia, SC: University of South Carolina Press.

CHAPTER EIGHTEEN

The Economics of Reconstruction

PETER A. COCLANIS AND SCOTT MARLER

What Bernard Weisberger (1959: 427) once called the "dark and bloody ground of Reconstruction historiography" continues to present a treacherous field for historians writing in the twenty-first century. Although the issues and events surrounding Reconstruction still provoke intense debate today, matters are certainly less ideologically charged than when Weisberger wrote nearly half a century ago, at the onset of the "Second Reconstruction" being ushered in by the direct action Civil Rights Movement. Interestingly enough, basic terms of debate over the economic history of Reconstruction have changed only slightly during the intervening decades, and consequently most issues remained contested.

Let us also state that significant difficulties intrude when considering the economic history of Reconstruction. Foremost among these is the fact that economic change often proceeds at a slow pace inherently more amenable to analysis over longer time frames than the 15 years traditionally defined as the Reconstruction era, 1863–77. A closely related problem is that Reconstruction is a period defined by reference to a quintessentially political agenda; hence, its beginning and end points are ill suited to a full consideration of many economic issues. Yet another obstacle to the holistic consideration of the Reconstruction-era economy is the uneven nature of development in the various regions of the United States – the North, the West, and, of course, the South (the region ostensibly being "reconstructed"). These difficulties are further compounded by the complex relationship between agriculture and industry in national economic development during the late nineteenth century (Ferleger 1990), as well as by the emergence of a recognizable "national market" in this period (Carlton 2003). While acknowledging these problems, for the purposes of this chapter, we will try to work around them by reviewing some of the most important historiography from the standpoint of the divergent historical methods that have been employed to grapple with economic change during the period. We hope also to take advantage of the ebbing ideological passions surrounding Reconstruction to suggest a potential way around impasses.

For the most part, economic history necessarily focuses on developments in the aggregate and often deals with structural considerations whose existence, while partly "socially constructed" and given meaning by human experience, also maintains very real causative force and momentum independently of it. It is not that economic historians believe that human volition doesn't matter, only that the scope of human action is relatively narrowly circumscribed. Since the 1970s, such structure-based studies have largely fallen out of fashion among mainstream historians in favor of histories "from the bottom up," which focus on recovering narratives of individual agency. At the risk of some oversimplification, we will deal with two opposing "structuralist" approaches to economic history that have been historiographically important to studies of Reconstruction, as well as to American history more generally.

First, for many years, mainstream historians were attracted to methodologies that can be lumped under the awkwardly named rubric "political economy." Often relying on various forms of class analysis, historians employing the political economy approach described the distribution of and access to power among competing interest groups, and how economic structures are necessarily shaped and manipulated according to (unequal) political resources. Second, and by contrast, contemporary specialists in the thriving but balkanized subdiscipline of economic history tend to be trained in the assumption, methods, models, and mathematics of neoclassical economics. Such historians, often housed in economics departments, usually move questions regarding political power into the deep background if they consider them at all. For them, the market serves as a methodological playing field on which a "general equilibrium" or an "efficient competitive balance" is naturally achieved. Unfortunately, these economic historians usually tend to be uninspired storytellers. Moreover, too many economic historians exacerbate matters by seeing their task less as one of accessibly *narrating* the past than of finding clever ways of *modeling* it, most often in arcane quantitative terms (see, for example, Williamson 1974b).

These two sides first engaged in heated battles over Reconstruction era economic issues back in the 1950s, and though they have tended simply to ignore and talk past one another since roughly the mid-1970s, we still find their ongoing stalemate disturbing, particularly since theoretical advances have been made in the interim that suggest a possible synthesis. From our own perspectives, and with appropriate caveats, it strikes us that, to a very workable degree, a historicizing and contextualizing political economy focus can be combined with the procedural rigor of contemporary economic theory through the vehicle of the "new institutional economics." For this "school" of economics, whose intellectual roots can be found in early twentieth-century American pragmatism, institutions refer to the wider formal and informal systems that shape and restrict behavior and decision-making – the law, for example, is a key "institution" in this sense. Making such a definition one's analytical linchpin is but a short leap from political economy's focus on the distribution and shape of power relationships (Foldvary 1996). But the "new institutional" school has also been increasingly influential among economic historians because of its emphasis on fluctuating, "path-dependent" issues like contractualism, transaction costs, and property rights (Davis and North 1971). Thus, by insisting on the influence of structural and other "exogenous" factors, relative attention to contingency and unanticipated consequences in social settings and apparent lack of faith in the behavioral underpinnings of neoclassicism (particularly the necessary assumption of rationality among actors in a free-market setting), the new institutional economics (NIE) looks a lot like the sort of multicausal form of inductive inquiry that most historians in fields other than economic history have traditionally associated with their craft. If we do not purport to share everything with practitioners of NIE – many new institutionalists are more politically conservative than are we – we do share a belief that institutions matter a great deal and perforce must be featured prominently in any realistic model of change in economic history. With this in mind, then, we hope that our discussion might show the hints of synthesis that have appeared in recent years and demonstrate how the new institutional economics, broadly conceived, can help to bring the two old "sides" together in a profitable way.

Since the word *revolution* gets bandied about quite a bit by the period's historians of whatever stripe, we will start with perhaps the most infamous example: Charles and Mary Beard's (1927) characterization of the Civil War as a "Second American Revolution." Although the Beards wrote just prior to the New Deal era, these controversies occurred for the most part a full generation later, when a group of new economic historians, who led the "cliometric revolution" during the 1960s, made it one of their first tasks to shred the Beards' thesis, along with its echo in the work by Charles Beard's student Louis M. Hacker (1940). However, the cliometricians properly regarded themselves as *counter*-revolutionaries, for they led an assault against a "Beard–Hacker thesis" that had stealthily emerged on the dominant economic interpretation of the war and its aftermath.

The Beards presented an interpretation of the Civil War and Reconstruction grounded in the tradition of critical, and vaguely socialist, political economy. In the Beards' view, the Civil War had been "at bottom . . . a social war, ending in the unquestioned establishment of a new power in the government, making vast changes in the arrangement of classes, in the accumulation and distribution of wealth, in the course of industrial development, and in the Constitution inherited from the Fathers." In essence, the Beards saw the war as a successful bourgeois revolution, a "social cataclysm in which the capitalists, laborers, and farmers of the North and West drove from power in the national government the planting aristocracy of the South" (Beard and Beard 1927, vol. 2: 53–4). To the Beards' explicit chagrin, however, the state apparatus in industrial America had quickly fallen under the control of one part of the victorious Union coalition – the northeastern industrial and financial elite, which then employed this apparatus to further its own class interests. For the Beards, then, the economic history of Reconstruction and the late nineteenth century was simply the continuation and consolidation of gains first won under wartime conditions by a new industrial bourgeoisie.

In retrospect, it is easy to understand why the Beards would become "the much-maligned strawmen" of the cliometric assault (Williamson 1974a: 644). The Beards intended *The Rise of American Civilization* as a popular (even populist) narrative history for a mass audience; indeed, it was a national bestseller and a Book-of-the-Month Club selection. But its exhortatory style – while fine in a muckraker like their friend Matthew Josephson – proves grating coming from an esteemed academic couple, even to those sympathetic to its broad outlines. *The Rise of American Civilization* did not pretend to approximate the relative scholarly rigor of Beard's earlier controversial monograph, *An Economic Interpretation of the Constitution of the United States* (1913), with no source notes to provide a safety net of verifiability. The two-thirds of the chapter devoted to the "Second American Revolution" is a rather pedestrian recounting of the events of the war itself, military and narrowly political, and mostly centered on the Lincoln administration. To be blunt, then, *The Rise of American Civilization* now comes across as a fairly poor performance by academic standards.

The Beards were obviously carried away by their dramatic rhetoric in emphasizing the war's causative role in promoting American industrial growth, and furthermore, when they did hazard to make something approximating a "factual" statement, they were often simply wrong. One revealing example is their vague insistence that "the economic structure of machine industry towered high above agriculture" immediately after the war (1927: 105); basic census data that were readily available to the Beards clearly show that the aggregate value of US manufactures failed to surpass that of farm products for decades after the war, that is to say, until *circa* 1890. Ultimately, the wider thesis about the "Second American Revolution" does not stand or fall according to such mistaken arguments. One can distill the general drift of the Beards' position using the broad frame of the new institutional economics, thereby seeing the Union victory as the original source of several overlapping structural and institutional changes that buttressed ongoing economic transformations increasingly apparent during Reconstruction and the so-called Gilded Age.

There may still be sufficient grounds for disputing this view; certainly, there is room for a great deal more verifiable empirical specification than the Beards (or Hacker) provided. Moreover, it must be admitted that the Beards' thesis, as they presented it, was rife with logical inconsistencies. For example, one of the major points of the revisionist attack on the Beardian view – that the American economy's "take-off" into self-sustaining growth predicated on industrialization had occurred during the antebellum period (roughly by the 1840s, according to Walt Rostow 1956) – is contained, albeit in a typically generalized and unsubstantiated form, in the Beards' work itself. "The main economic results thus far noted," the Beards declared, "would have been attained had there been no armed conflict, for the census returns with rhythmic beats were recording the tale of the fates" (1927: 115). Similarly, and more emphatically, they had written earlier in the chapter that "[i]n fact the real revolution – the silent shift of social and material power – had occurred before secession and civil war" (1927: 55). Thus, *either* the war – the "revolution" – caused the economic transformations of the late nineteenth century, *or* they were bound to happen regardless.

Matters were, of course, rather more complicated, and revisionist economic historians, beginning in the late 1950s, set themselves to showing exactly how and why this was so. But we would be extremely remiss if we did not first pause briefly to acknowledge some of the trailblazing empirical work in economic history produced during the immediate post-World War II years on which these revisionists would rely in their attacks on the Beard–Hacker thesis. Three works in particular were to serve as ûr-texts of the cliometric revolution: the Bureau of the Census's *Historical Statistics of the United States, from Colonial Times to 1957* (1960); Volume 24 of the National Bureau of Economic Research's (NBER) *Trends in the Nineteenth-Century Economy* (1960); and a modestly named set published under the auspices of the American Philosophical Society, *Population Redistribution and Economic Growth, 1870–1950* (Kuznets and Thomas 1957–64). Remarkably, the data sets in these works (compiled, remember, in the days of slide rules, mainframes, and punch cards) have yet to be superseded; despite a half-century's worth of prodigious technological advances, they are still mostly valid and remain in service today. At the time, however, these works laid the foundation for no less than a paradigmatic shift in American economic history, one that moved away from the qualitative, even literary, practices of the Beard–Hacker generation toward the quantitative, social-scientific historical methods of nascent cliometrics.

Beginning in the late 1950s, a group of revisionist economic historians would employ these data sets (which, in fairness, had been unavailable to the Beards or Hacker) to prove that the Civil War years had served to interrupt or even, in Thomas C. Cochran's stronger titular phrase, to "retard" American industrial growth (Cochran 1962). Less enraptured with theories of social change that emphasized revolutions, radical disjunctures, and turning points, scholars such as Cochran and Stanley L. Engerman (1966) preferred to study Civil War era developments in the context of the performance of the American economy over the course of the whole nineteenth century, rather than to focus solely on the war years, the decade of the 1860s, or even the entire postbellum period. Brandishing their new statistical bibles, they demonstrated that national economic growth during the 1860s was actually the worst of any decade between 1839 and 1899 for which data series exist. According to the revisionists, growth rates for total commodity output in the United States, as well as for manufacturing output specifically, were higher for the decades between 1840 and 1859 than they were from 1860 to 1869, or between 1870 and 1899, for that matter.

Such shibboleth-toppling arguments would soon prove to be the cliometricians' stock-in-trade, yet to a large degree these statistically based arguments provide an example of why quantitative history would soon provoke a great deal of hostility among mainstream historians. In this instance, the revisionist emphasis on lower growth rates after the war strongly implied that American manufacturing did not enjoy any great surge or advantage in the late nineteenth century. This interpretation flew in the face of the Beard–Hacker thesis and contradicted less ideological historiographical wisdom about the period – a consensus based on overwhelming evidence, "anecdotal" as well as statistical, from the late nineteenth century. For that matter, even cliometric pioneer Robert E. Gallman had noted in the opening sentence of his seminal lead contribution to the aforementioned NBER Volume 24 that "[b]etween 1839 and 1899 the US economy expanded at an extraordinarily high rate and in the process, changed from a predominantly agricultural to a predominantly industrial economy" (NBER 1960: 13).

There proves to be a simple mathematical explanation for the "lower growth rates" argument, one completely apart from the question of the war's effects. As one of the cliometric foundation texts had sensibly pointed out, "[A] common characteristic of growth phenomena [is that] at some point [an] increase in the size of the base begins to be attended by a decrease in the rate of change" (Kuznets and Thomas 1957–64, vol. 3: 217). To give a hypothetical example: if there were one factory in Maine in 1840, and five in 1850, the state's growth rate in manufacturing for that decade would have been a staggering 400 percent – yet in real terms, not all that impressive. Now say there were 20 factories in 1860, 60 in 1870, and 120 in 1880. Based on these figures, one could indeed argue with a straight face (as did the revisionists) that growth rates expressed on a percentage basis were steadily "declining" over time. However, such a use of statistical data obviously elides the very significant economic transformations underway.

Such facts helped prompt some economic historians, such as Stephen Salsbury (1962), to strongly demur from the revisionist line. Salsbury conceded the profound economic disruptions of the war, yet he pointed out that a far more apt basis for comparing economic growth before and after the war was the 1866–75 decade, during which "the most important indicators . . . evidence[d] a substantial boom with growth rates much above those of the Civil War era" (Salsbury 1962: 165). Later, even some cliometricians began to find other bases from which to offer support to the Beard–Hacker position, even concerning the short-term effects of the war. For example, Stephen DeCanio and Joel Mokyr (1977) constructed a model that made a case for the efficacy of the "wage-lag" hypothesis, which held that wartime inflation prompted a redistribution of resources that favored capital over labor. John A. James (1981) and Jeffrey G. Williamson (1974a) published separate studies on the economic impact of Civil War financing, especially debt repayment policies, that also come to mind in this regard. Williamson showed that, beginning during Reconstruction, the wartime bond issues steadily retired by the federal government had the effect of redistributing income toward the capital goods sector, especially benefiting producer goods vital to heavy industry (i.e., building materials, fabricated metals); he also showed the parallel support that new, steep protectionist tariffs offered the same domestic sector.

Clearly, the revisionists were right to believe that the pinched and narrow timeframe employed by the Beards and Hacker had led them to succumb to the *post hoc* fallacy, that is, to argue as though mere temporal succession implied a causal relationship. But the revisionists proved intent on conflating a minor and obviously weak aspect of the Beardian argument into a stand-in for the inadequacy of the whole. For some reason, the revisionists focused their assault on an argument just barely articulated by the Beards. "[T]he feverish stimulus of war," the Beards (1927: 105) had written, had made the "revolution" a *fait accompli* by 1865. One has to skip about considerably to find this argument in the Beards' volume, but scattered here and there are its three basic components. First, federal "contractors" in the North enjoyed increased concentrations of capital (pp. 92–3) – that is, wartime profiteering. Second, "tens of thousands" of capitalists made windfall profits from "the rising prices of manufactured goods" (p. 105) – that is, inflationary gains by producers. Finally – least articulated of all by the Beards yet perhaps most attacked by the revisionists – was the ostensible contention that the Civil War had itself propelled a shift to factory-style, mechanized industry.

Since this was the subject of so much revisionist brouhaha, the argument, strawman though it is, is worth elaborating. Like most wars (especially the great world wars of the twentieth century) the Civil War had induced an increased demand for weapons, ammunition, uniforms, provisions, and supplies. This demand was so great as to create a supply bottleneck, which was itself exacerbated by the (civilian) labor shortage brought on by the war. To satisfy strong demand in a market characterized by relatively scarce (and possibly inferior) manpower, American manufacturers were forced to mechanize to a greater degree than they might have otherwise, and in so doing, they found that greater mechanization – measured in terms of capital invested in manufacturing enterprises – not only allowed them to solve the bottleneck but also to enhance productivity. Thus pleased with gains in output and efficiency, after the war this new breed of industrial capitalist quickly accelerated the mechanization effort, thereby ushering in America's own "industrial revolution."

The revisionists, led by Cochran (1962) and Engerman (1966), concentrated their considerable intellectual firepower on battering down the notion of a war-induced manufacturing surge. (This despite the ironic fact that the wartime mechanization argument had once been made in convincing detail by Cochran in *The Age of Enterprise* (Cochran and Miller 1961 [1942]: 111–16.) Cochran and Engerman pointed out, for example, that any "positive" war-induced tendency toward mechanization was necessarily dwarfed by the economic disruptions caused by four years of bloodshed and misallocated resources. They also suggested that, analytically speaking, Beard (and Hacker too) had failed to understand that the need for war materiel at best constituted a shift along the existing demand schedule – a *relative* shift, from butter to guns, as it were. Finally, the revisionists challenged the notion that wartime inflation had resulted in a massive reallocation of resources in favor of entrepreneurs and industrialists, who used their windfalls to promote the manufacturing sector. Any redistribution of economic resources, they argued, whether caused by wartime inflation or a putative "wage lag," was minor.

Wartime profiteering, inflation, and mechanization – one is hard-pressed to find these arguments made in much detail by the Beards (and only slightly more so by Hacker). More recently, some scholars have attempted to tease out what is at best implicit in the Beardian line: a view of Reconstruction's programmatic national concomitants that first began to be established during the southern absence from the federal government during the war. Any shortlist of such pro-manufacturing federal activism during and after the war would include, at a minimum: the National Banking Act 1863; the stiff manufacturing tariffs in place between the 1860s and the passage of the Underwood Tariff in 1913; generous subsidies (particularly land grants) to private railroad companies in the postbellum era; state promotion of overseas recruitment of labor; federal aid to education (through land-grant universities) and funding for applied research in science and engineering; and the repeated use of federal military power to put down labor actions of one sort or another. Such legislation is indicative of a decided shift in American political economy after the war toward greater governmental activism in favor of business at the federal level. To be sure, the revisionists were correct to point out that such activism had sometimes been undertaken on behalf of business interests throughout the antebellum period (though the attitude of regnant Jacksonian democracy was most often one of antipathy toward business interests). It is also true, however, that the *federal* government's role in the economy was much greater during and after the Civil War than prior to it, and that after secession its role was not merely pro-business generally, but pro-manufacturing specifically.

Revisionists, however, were on the right track in trying to broaden the temporal framework for understanding American industrialization, because the war years, or even the 15 years of Reconstruction as traditionally defined, are indeed inadequate for a full understanding of this evolving postbellum economic framework. Rather than focusing solely on strictly political actions, we recommend that economic historians view them in the context of other institutional developments. They might profit from insights provided by recent historians of law, technology, and business, as well as from work about the late nineteenth-century American political economy by historical sociologists such as Richard F. Bensel (1990), Stephen Skowronek (1992), and William G. Roy (1997).

The gradual evolution of American law in the postwar period shows the somewhat Janus-faced attitude of triumphant federalism, for even as there was evidence of a new federal activism on behalf of industry, at the same time "the most central tenet of late nineteenth-century legal orthodoxy [was] its commitment to a neutral, non-redistributive state" (Horwitz 1992: 16). Skowronek (1992) has shown how the emergence of a "national administrative state" was actually delayed by party factionalism and the spoils system until the late 1890s – roughly the same time that postbellum *laissez-faire* legal doctrines inhibiting the growth of a regulatory state gradually began to be replaced upon the advent of Progressivism. Still, a juridical tilt toward the promotion of commercial interests, particularly in manufacturing, first became apparent during the Reconstruction years. The Beards (1927) and Hacker (1940) had famously emphasized the legislative machinations arrogating civil rights to "persons" rather than "citizens" in the Fourteenth Amendment (1868), which thereby opened the door for private corporations to enjoy constitutional protections understood to have been crafted primarily to protect the freedpeople of the South. But why attribute to conspiracy what can be understood from the standpoint of sheer institutional momentum? In fact, in its first real opportunity to review the meaning of the "equal protection" clause, the complicated *Slaughterhouse* cases of 1873, the Supreme Court opted to reject a broad interpretation that would have favored corporate access to the Fourteenth Amendment's privileges (Ross 2003). Yet Justice Stephen Field's famous dissent in *Slaughterhouse* would prove the wave of the not-too-distant future: by 1886, in its *Santa Clara* decision, the Court would peremptorily and unequivocally hold corporations to be persons, with all the rights and privileges pertaining thereto.

This change of heart proved consistent with other Reconstruction era changes in legal attitudes toward property. As outlined by Morton Horwitz (1992), these included the 1870s shift in the law of eminent domain from a "physicalist" to a "market-based" definition of property (p. 146); the 1871 *Pumpelly* decision, which laid the groundwork for a growing consensus that "any interference with the future income stream of an owner constitutes a taking of property" (p. 148); and two leading cases from 1872–3 that marked the onset of increasingly frantic efforts to reject strict liability principles in tort law (p. 13). Similarly, in contract law, a tendency from the 1850s to standardize commercial transactions and to gear the law toward emergent business organizational forms accelerated rapidly during Reconstruction (p. 54).

Besides these gradual institutional changes in property law, another area in which Reconstruction historiography is still decidedly underdeveloped – and clearly relevant to the vague Beardian notion of wartime mechanization – is technological change. Factory-style production processes continued to improve rapidly after the war, especially benefiting from the development of the capital goods sector of the economy. Refrigeration processes in meatpacking pioneered in this period by Gustavus Swift, for example, helped create a hugely important symbiotic relationship between the livestock and railway industries (Chandler 1977), a symbiosis necessary to sustain increasingly dense urban concentrations on the upper East Coast in the late nineteenth century. Even more important, the rail and communications networks first became truly national in scope during Reconstruction, and only because the territorial squabbles of the antebellum period had finally been settled by military fiat.

Telegraphy continued to develop, but in an increasingly privatized corporate form underwritten and consolidated by Morgan interests. A harbinger of the corporate future in this regard was the famous rivalry between Thomas Edison and Alexander Graham Bell to develop the telephone, which culminated during Reconstruction in laboratory settings that were themselves prototypes of invention-as-production process (Noble 1977). While Bell won the race to perfect the actual device, the system that emerged and bore Bell's name actually owed more to Edison's business acumen, especially the finance capital he was able to tap from New York City. This would also be the case from the late 1870s forward with the incandescent light bulb that Edison "invented" and the electric-power-generation industry necessary to make it a practical reality. As the litigation-happy Edison proved, however, the institutional matrix of patent law in which such technological change unfolded remained backward for decades, and significant improvements to it, while discussed, were delayed until the early twentieth century.

Edison's example also illustrates the importance of specifying the particular trajectories and interrelationships that developed between different sectors of the American business community. Hacker (1940), for example, had attempted to describe a movement from an economy dominated by "merchant capitalists" toward one in which manufacturing and finance became increasingly strong and independent – a thesis that would be unconsciously buttressed by work in business history beginning in the late 1960s. In some respects, Alfred D. Chandler Jr's classic description of the synergistic development of mass distribution and mass production from the 1860s forward as an "organizational revolution" nonetheless is demonstrative of precisely such ongoing institutional change in American business during this period (Chandler 1977: 235). However, Chandler was certainly no fan of the Beard–Hacker thesis. As he had put it earlier: "The War may have accelerated and refined, but it did not start or create, new patterns of economic and institutional change" (Chandler 1965: 137). Nevertheless, despite Chandler's insistence that "the widespread adoption of the factory . . . came in the 1850s and not in the 1860s" (Chandler 1965: 148), subsequent scholarship seemed to revise this belief considerably. For example, in their all-too-often neglected study of nineteenth-century "merchants and manufacturers," work by Chandler's own students, Glenn Porter and Harold C. Livesay (1971), closely examined business records and other statistical data to show that antebellum manufacturers tended to be small-scale firms (with the largest exceptions being in textile production) which were only sporadically profitable. The most important reason for these manufacturers' dreary profit picture was their limited access to capital. Partly because banks considered them poor credit risks, and partly due to the predominance of proprietary organizational forms that were unable to take advantage of public funds through the sale of securities, most prewar manufacturers remained dependent on the firms that distributed their products – mainly wholesale merchants – for financing. But the war resulted in "sustained, high-volume demand, rising prices, and shorter terms of payment" for many manufacturers, all of which helped them "break the vicious cycle of deficit financing" by predatory merchant capitalists (Porter and Livesay 1971: 118). "At the end of the war there were firms (often the largest producers) in virtually every manufacturing field" that were, for the first time, "debt-free and able to use retained earnings to meet most of their own capital requirements" (Porter and Livesay 1971: 118). In this sense, then, the war inadvertently allowed manufacturers the chance to become significantly independent of the old mercantile class and to blossom, for the first time, into a full-scale "bourgeoisie." Echoing Louis Hacker's (1940) emphasis on American merchant capital's increasing obsolescence after the Civil War, Sven Beckert (2001) relates this transformation in compelling detail in a study of the commercial class in mid-nineteenth-century New York City.

By the same token, merchants increasingly saw their function restricted to distribution and soon found themselves irrelevant as provisioners of capital. Still, although manufacturing indeed gained momentum in the postbellum decades, most firms outside of rail and communications were still traditional, entrepreneurial, unincorporated, community-based, and often family-controlled businesses (Scranton 1997). Some studies have suggested that the most important institutional changes that occurred in American business during the Civil War and Reconstruction were in the financial sector. Lance Davis (1965) was among the first to stress that, despite the gradual, regionally uneven evolution of a national capital market through the Progressive era, institutional changes wrought during and after the Civil War resulted in the emergence of increasingly sophisticated financial mechanisms for marshalling and deploying investment that were essential to large-scale industry. But in a sociological study – one that is unfortunately not very well versed in the earlier controversies surrounding the Beard–Hacker thesis – William G. Roy (1997) adds another welcome level of specificity to views of institutional change in the American political economy during and after Reconstruction. Roy convincingly showed that manufacturing remained largely a stranger to the corporate form of organization until the turn of the century. What was in place "by 1880," he writes, was "the basic institutional structure of corporate capitalism" (Roy 1997: 117): a stock exchange newly capable of handling transactions in volume and on margin; stable brokerage houses; and a new class of investment bankers – pioneered by Jay Cooke, but soon led by J. P. Morgan – who were skilled at tapping sources of capital not only domestically but from overseas, especially from Europe.

These factors laid the foundation necessary for the full-scale industrialization of the American economy from Reconstruction forward, and this is so regardless of whether these developments were "caused" by the Civil War, were mere unintended consequences of exigencies attendant on it, or were unrelated to the war altogether. Looking at the economic effects of the Civil War in this manner helps finesse the ostensible paradox raised by Patrick K. O'Brien (1988) in his historiographical review of the subject. "It is difficult to discern the economic interest of the North in armed conflict," O'Brien opined; but here Eric Hobsbawm's astute observation that the Civil War effectively transformed the South from "a virtual semi-colony of the British" into a state of effective economic dependence on the industrializing North (Hobsbawm 1974: 154) applies. Regardless of whether the North gained any direct advantage from freeing the slaves, the effects of emancipation are paramount, of course, when considering the economic consequences of the war for the South – the declared object of what Eric Foner (1988) called Reconstruction's "unfinished revolution," to which we now turn our attention.

The Beards actually said very little about the South, except to focus on the overthrow of the so-called slave power in the federal government as a precondition for full industrialization, yet what they did say implied a viewpoint decidedly odd for ostensible "progressives." As Thomas J. Pressly pointed out long ago, the Beards' incessant grousing about the course of the northern-dominated postbellum political economy implied an almost "pro-Confederate" stance on their part (Pressly 1962 [1954]: 242). For example, in one of their few references to emancipation, they called it the "greatest act of sequestration" in history – a dubious proposition in its own right, and one that led W. E. B. Du Bois to strongly condemn the Beards' approach as morally obtuse (Du Bois 1992 [1935]: 714–15). It would be left to a later generation of left-leaning political economists, especially Barrington Moore (1966), to try not only to buttress the Beard–Hacker thesis of the Civil War as a "bourgeois revolution," but also to acknowledge the coercive nature of the Old South regime and similar aspects of it that carried over into the New. Moore's sprawling world-comparative study, one of the few classics of "New Left" historiography, would inspire later attempts by a few "new social historians" of the 1970s – especially Jonathan D. Wiener (1978) and Dwight B. Billings Jr (1979) – to describe the slow pace of postwar southern industrialization as having followed a "Prussian Road," that is, a modernization process directed from above by reactionary, vestigial planter–elites.

Still, the Beard–Hacker thesis and its offshoots ultimately did not set the agenda for studies of the Reconstruction era southern economy as they had for studies of the nation more broadly. In that respect, one book looms large in contemporary historiography as the single most important work of economic history devoted exclusively to Reconstruction in the South: Roger Ransom and Richard Sutch's *One Kind of Freedom* (1977). Originally published at the tail end of a decade's worth of scholarly debate over cliometrics, the two economists did not pretend to offer a study of Reconstruction in all its aspects, but rather of the "economic consequences of emancipation" in the South – in particular, in "the cotton South." The central argument of *One Kind of Freedom* is beholden to the new institutional economics in ways that are vital – but frequently misunderstood. Ransom and Sutch's thesis, admirably and straightforwardly stated up front in their book, shows the unmistakable influence of the new institutionalism (indeed, both studied under Douglass C. North, a founder of the school and, more recently, a Nobel laureate in economics). They seek to show how the prevalence of poverty in the postbellum South and the lack of reasonable progress in alleviating it was "the consequence of flawed institutions erected in the wake of the Confederate defeat" (Ransom and Sutch 1977: 2). For them, "flawed institutions" are not merely organizations, groups, or even classes, although all of these can potentially be subsumed under the book's analytical rubric. Instead, institutions are the wider formal and informal systems that shape and restrict behavior and decision-making; most important among which, for Ransom and Sutch, was the development of the system of sharecropping, the primary means of cotton production in the postbellum South.

In *One Kind of Freedom* Ransom and Sutch begin by attacking what they call "the myth of the prostrate South," a view that maintains that the devastation of the war accounts for the failure of the southern economy to match or surpass that of the rapidly industrializing North. The authors argued that southern losses from the war, whether physical or otherwise, tended to be overstated by historians. In terms of the former slave population, newly freed, they dismiss the Beardian argument that emancipation was an "act of sequestration" that had, at one stroke of a pen, abolished an enormous amount of the South's capital stock with no compensation to its former owners. Emancipation, Ransom and Sutch insist, did not represent "a loss to the South, but a transfer of ownership of 'capitalized labor' from the slaveholders to the ex-slaves themselves" (1977: 52).

Matters were not so simple, according to Gavin Wright (1986) and others (Goldin and Lewis 1975; Margo 1995). For Wright (1986), emancipation forced postwar planters to endure a momentous shift in the basis of their wealth, one that transformed them from "laborlords" into "landlords." This was partly due to the elimination of their slaveholdings, which had served not only as a labor force but also as collateral for credit in the southern financial system (Kilbourne 1990). Wright also concedes, however, that the forced alteration of southern elite investment portfolios – from slaves to land – profoundly altered planters' class character. Bypassing such questions entirely, Ransom and Sutch make the "transfer of ownership of 'capitalized labor'" (noteworthy in itself as a stance redolent of the new institutionalist focus on evolving property rights) central to their attempt to explain why the South failed to duplicate the experience of other economies recovering from wars. In part, they explain continued regional impoverishment by reference to racism and the slowdown in the growth rate of the world market for cotton; but perhaps the most important aspect of their argument concerning the "demise of the plantation," its fragmentation into the small, family-sized parcels associated with sharecropping and tenancy, and subsequent regional economic underdevelopment, concerned the decreased labor inputs into the system that accompanied emancipation. While rightly distancing themselves from former slaveholders' complaints that the freedpeople were "lazy," Ransom and Sutch argued that such lamentations, properly understood, reflected the withdrawal of many freedwomen and children from prolonged work in the fields; increasing urban migration by former slaves; and freedpeople's understandable reticence to put in the crushing hours associated with toil under plantation slavery – all of which amounted to a substantial "withdrawal of black labor" from the regional workforce (Ransom and Sutch 1977: 44). Translated into the language of the economist as a net loss in productivity hours available, the post-emancipation shrinkage of the regional labor force of necessity helped limit the prospects for a rapid southern economic recovery, according to Ransom and Sutch. Furthermore, the loss of economies of scale in production helped impel a search for enhancing profits elsewhere in the system, such as in marketing the crop, which may ironically have had deleterious developmental consequences as well.

Due to planters' unsuccessful efforts during early Reconstruction to revive the plantation system as gang-based wage labor, and partly because of the federal government's failure to support land redistribution in favor of the freedpeople ("forty acres and a mule"), Ransom and Sutch present the emergence of forms of agricultural tenancy by the early 1870s as a logical outcome of circumstances – but with an important dissenting caveat from the emergent neoclassical conventional wisdom. (An early volume of collected criticisms of *One Kind of Freedom*, mainly from neoclassical perspectives, is Walton and Shepherd 1981.) According to Ransom and Sutch, the form that such arrangements took – sharecropping, in particular – was not an "understandable market response," as Joseph Reid (1973) would have it, nor did it represent the most equitable distribution of profit and risk between landlord and tenant (Higgs 1977). Displaying a far greater sensitivity to contextual factors, such as racism, than such neoclassical explanations, Ransom and Sutch insist that "flawed institutions" distorted the operation of a free market in the postbellum South, and in this sense, southern sharecropping developed as an inherently inequitable system that inhibited rational decision-making by hampering efficiency and misallocating resources.

In the final chapters of *One Kind of Freedom*, Ransom and Sutch trace the institutional basis of sharecropping's "flaws" to the weakness of the postbellum South's financial system. After describing the desperate situation in the specie-starved region, along with the failure of southern banking to either resuscitate or develop mechanisms to provide the seasonal credit so fundamental to an agricultural economy, Ransom and Sutch turn their attention to the furnishing merchant in the postbellum South. Merchants took advantage of such ongoing technological advances as the improving regional rail and communications network (sponsored under northern capitalist auspices) to extend staple-crop production – and thus, market relationships – deeper into the southern hinterlands than before the war, facilitating the entry of the formerly self-sufficient white yeomanry into the "vortex of the cotton economy" (Hahn 1983: 135). But more importantly, furnishing merchants stepped into the South's financial breach by developing a decentralized ramshackle credit system based on advances to petty producers through the crop-lien system.

Ransom and Sutch's characterization of the postbellum furnishing merchant and his exorbitant interest rates tends to leave the not entirely correct impression that avaricious storekeepers presided over an enormous "pawn-shop economy" (see Coclanis 2000), with the cycle of indebtedness they fostered also serving as a "lock-in" mechanism that prevented small farmers, owners and renters alike, from reallocating production away from cotton toward either other, more profitable staple crops or greater self-sufficiency in foodstuffs. Ransom and Sutch also situated the institutional victory of the postbellum furnishing merchant in an abstract geo-economic context, famously arguing that the spatial dispersal of country stores in a region hampered by poor transportation resulted in effective "territorial monopolies." This analysis inadvertently proved congruent with Wiener's (1978) discussion of planter–merchant conflict in postwar Alabama, but both have been called into question by Louis M. Kyriakoudes (2002), who showed that successful merchants actually tended to "cluster" in the many small-town entrepôts springing up throughout the region. Overall, it is high time for a sustained monographic focus to supplant Ransom and Sutch's (1977) rather two-dimensional villainization of the postbellum merchant (Coclanis 2000), as well as to revisit themes in older works such as Thomas D. Clark's (1944) and even Harold D. Woodman's (1968) classic study of cotton marketing in the nineteenth-century South. One of this chapter's authors has provided a discussion of such merchants in Louisiana as part of a wider ongoing study (Marler 2001).

Ransom and Sutch's characterizations of tenant-farming and sharecropping, and the associated institutional framework, should be seen as distinct from those mainstream neoclassicists who see southern sharecropping as an "understandable market response"; indeed, to properly situate *One Kind of Freedom* on a historiographical continuum requires that we understand the new institutional economics' often-revisionist relationship to neoclassical orthodoxy regarding market economies. It is not exactly the case, as Wiener (1979) argued in his important article on southern "class structure and economic development," that Ransom and Sutch "[start] from neoclassical market theory." Wiener ultimately characterized the conclusions of *One Kind of Freedom* as "occupying a middle ground," but why this should be the case seemed to elude him – precisely because he, like others, misconstrued the significance and distinctiveness of the school of economic thought from which Ransom and Sutch drew their initial assumptions and methods. In fact, one of the probable reasons for the persistent regard in which *One Kind of Freedom* is held is due to the "middle ground" it occupies between true neoclassicists (like Robert Higgs, Joseph Reid, and Stephen DeCanio) and neo-Marxists (like Wiener and Woodman). The institutional approach employed by Ransom and Sutch allowed them to maintain a great deal of the methodological rigor of mathematically inclined economics, yet its built-in emphasis on historical context and development left room for the acknowledgement and incorporation of "exogenous" factors – like racism, political power, and even class structure – that neoclassical economists often underestimate or ignore, in large part, we suspect, because such factors are so resistant to quantification.

From the standpoint of critics like Wiener and Woodman, however, Ransom and Sutch do not go far enough in their critique to merit full distinction from the neoclassicists. This is not merely because Ransom and Sutch failed to speak the patois of class analysis, but because neo-Marxists reject the very notion of the normative "free market" so central to neoclassical theory, and hence eschew interpretations which rest on alleged flaws in free market operations. Ransom and Sutch emphasized the perversions of free-market mechanisms, such as merchants' territorial monopolies, but did not highlight qualitative injustices of the system they analyzed. For Ransom and Sutch, sharecropping and its associated institutional framework led to widespread debt peonage. But Woodman maintained that "beneath [the] sharp differences" between Ransom and Sutch and neoclassicists like Higgs "lies their common acceptance of bourgeois institutions" (Woodman 1987: 269), and for him, the crop-lien laws derived their greatest significance as the juridical corollary of an emergent free-labor system for the reconstructed South.

Woodman (1987), who is certainly no apologist for either southern elites or regional injustice, takes issue with characterizations of southern sharecropping as a form of tenancy, insisting that half the crop was not paid *by* the farmer to the landowner after the fall harvest as *rent*; instead, he examines post-Civil War laws and statutes state by state to argue that southern legislatures and courts increasingly maintained that a half-portion of the crop was paid *to* farmer-employees as a *wage*. This question of whether croppers were tenants or employees is an important one – by no means is it merely "half-empty/half-full" semantic hairsplitting – yet the distinction has been insufficiently appreciated. Ransom and Sutch's characterization of croppers as tenants is commensurate with the "peonage" interpretation advanced by "new social historians" like Wiener, Pete Daniel (1972), and others during the 1970s; it implies a view of the New South as an atavistic society that would be long encumbered by the cultural, political, and economic vestiges of the centuries-long racially based slave mode of production. Woodman's examination of the bourgeoisification of southern lien laws after emancipation, by contrast, serves as the fundamental premise for a wider analysis of the post-Civil War South, in which he emphasizes the radical break with the antebellum socioeconomic order represented by emancipation.

The significance of these differences has been obscured to some degree by the slow unfolding of Woodman's logic over the course of his long career, and in this respect, a more contentious article by Barbara J. Fields (1983) is better at highlighting the potentially deep divisions over postbellum southern economic development that exist within the political economy approach itself. Still, the drift of mainstream scholarship by historians since the early 1980s has clearly been in Woodman's direction (Marler 2004; cf. Harris 1997). Rather than emphasizing debt peonage or even neo-paternalism, the current "conventional wisdom" (Rodrigue 2002) is to regard the emergent economic and social structure of the New South as what one of its adherents ambitiously calls "a keyhole through which to observe processes shaping much of the Atlantic world during the nineteenth century" (Reidy 1992: 242) – that is, merely a moderately peculiar exploitative mode of production among the many possible on the world-capitalist developmental arc of the nineteenth century. And the "croppers-as-wage-workers" view provides what Woodman calls the "evolving bourgeois society" of the post-Civil War South with what it logically (or dialectically) seems to call for – a "rural proletariat." Nor has there been any shortage of candidates to serve as the region's ostensible bourgeois vanguard. For some historians, southern merchants became a "cohesive bourgeoisie" (Ford 1984: 317); others align merchants alongside other professionals, such as lawyers and an expanding class of would-be manufacturers, on an urban-based bourgeois continuum (Carlton 1982; Doyle 1990); and finally, some maintain that Reconstruction-era southern planters "transformed themselves into an agrarian bourgeoisie, comparable . . . to the northern industrial bourgeoisie" (Reidy 1992: 247).

It remains to be seen whether the spatially dispersed, household-based farm units of New South sharecropping can be said to form much of a "proletariat" (Marler 2004), but with the epic struggle between industrialism and agrarianism now transformed into a class struggle between a *nouveau* southern bourgeoisie and a rural proletariat, we thus begin to glimpse the outlines of a resurgent, more sophisticated Beardianism applied to the postwar South. (Woodman's (2001b) explicit attempt to rehabilitate the Beardian aspects of Woodward's (1951) classic *Origins of the New South* is worth perusing in this regard.) But here it also becomes necessary to flesh out the implications of Ransom and Sutch's (1977) arguments, because although they have consistently referred to croppers as tenants rather than employees, they have never made their basis for doing so satisfyingly explicit, unlike Woodman and others. Certainly, their understanding of croppers as tenants is more in keeping with studies of sharecropping elsewhere in the world, which usually view croppers as little better than a peasantry (see Byres 1983; Lichtenstein 1998). Interestingly, Marx himself did not regard sharecropping as part of a fully developed capitalist agriculture, but rather as a transitional mode of production with prominent feudal remnants (Mann 1994). But since Ransom and Sutch work from within a social-scientific tradition that circumvents rather than directly addresses such questions regarding the political economy, they tend to elide the fundamental differences between their views and other interpretations.

Gerald D. Jaynes offers one way around this apparent impasse in his *Branches without Roots* (1986). He calls attention to the similarities between southern sharecropping and the "putting-out" system of home manufactures during the prolonged European transition to industrial capitalism. The reliance on dispersed household units of production, the relative inattention to the internal dynamics by which commodities are produced, the largely absentee nature of capital in the production process – these are all redolent of a slow process that has been called "protoindustrialization." Although such historical analogies are by their very nature provisional and inexact, from what we know of southern sharecropping and the other steps along the complicated agricultural ladder that would develop from Reconstruction forward, protoindustrialization may offer a more accurate portrait of the New South than interpretations that blame an incipient, rather monolithic, "bourgeois" capitalism for regional economic woes. One path worth investigating in this regard is a comparison of the prominent role conservative forms of merchant capital have historically played in domestic-based forms of production under protoindustrializing regimes, both internally (the actual processes of financing – in the South, a role assumed mainly by the furnishing merchant) and externally (merchants' role as an urban comprador class facilitating extraregional investments, which may help add nuance to C. Vann Woodward's (1951) famous thesis of a "colonial economy" in the New South – a task also undertaken in several essays by Carlton and Coclanis 2003).

Clearly, however, such disputes over the fundamental nature of southern sharecropping – and, by implication, the entire postbellum South – are of profound importance, and they deserve closer evaluation even by non-economic historians, many of whom often adopt aspects of the "New [Capitalist] South" interpretation without careful consideration of the assumptions on which they apparently rest. Some recent works are more or less explicitly indebted to Woodman's neo-Beardian interpretive framework for understanding the Reconstructed South: for example, see studies by Barbara J. Fields (1985), Joseph P. Reidy (1992), and the collection edited by Thavolia Glymph and John J. Kushma (1985). Yet other scholarship that rests mainly on other interpretive frameworks for its guiding themes and premises often seems content to accept Woodman's version of a bourgeois New South as well – as does Edward Ayers' influential anti-narrative *The Promise of a New South* (1992), Laura F. Edwards' insightful *Gendered Strife and Confusion* (1997), and Amy Dru Stanley's *From Bondage to Contract* (1998). Even self-proclaimed "new institutionalist" economic historians Lee J. Alston and Joseph P. Ferrie, in a recent work that insightfully explains the persistence and significance of paternalism in postbellum southern economic relationships, accept Woodman's definition of cropping as wage labor with little explanation (Alston and Ferrie 1999: 15). By contrast, Jay Mandle (1992) has offered a neo-Marxist view of mutant "market paternalism" in the post-emancipation South that runs counter to Woodman's views. Ultimately, and particularly in light of the misplaced criticisms of *One Kind of Freedom* as neoclassically derived, it is ironic that the notion of an inexorable impulse in the post-emancipation South toward deeply imbricated capitalist social relations – whether sublimated as structural forces, directed by the agency of self-interested elites, or both – actually seems more redolent of the neoclassical sense of free-market development and primacy than does Ransom and Sutch's insistence on the primacy of "flawed institutions" in causing and prolonging the stagnation of the southern agricultural economy after the war.

Nevertheless, there are some shortcomings, in our view, to the arguments in *One Kind of Freedom*. For example, Ransom and Sutch pay little attention to demographic factors, such as urbanization and patterns of internal migration. Health and nutritional data, which have been analyzed to good effect in recent years in the burgeoning field of anthropometric history, could have enriched Ransom and Sutch's conclusions concerning the freedpeople's stature and status (Coclanis 2000). Greater attention to categories such as class and gender might have made the "cotton South" appear as less the two-dimensional world understandably mistaken as merely a perverse version of neoclassical economics' free-market paradigm. Indeed, Ransom (1989) aligned himself more explicitly with the political economy approach in a later solo-authored work, and more recent studies by Susan Archer Mann (1994), Terence J. Byres (1996), Alex Lichtenstein (1998), and Ronald E. Seavoy (1998) call into question Woodman's sophisticated rationale for considering sharecropping blacks to be a "rural proletariat." Lichtenstein explicitly asks a question raised by Sidney Mintz about the antebellum slave population in a postwar context: Would it be more apt – as was customary among the pioneering Chapel Hill sociologists of the 1930s – to regard rural southern freedpeople as a class more akin to a peasantry than to a free labor force? In terms of gender, the works by Laura Edwards (1997) and Amy Dru Stanley (1998) provide highly suggestive discussions of women's role in southern Reconstruction; however, the economic implications of their arguments – for example, vis-à-vis the revamping and extension of decentralized, household-based production units – merit further study.

Similarly, Ransom and Sutch's (1977) economic analysis would have been thickened by greater attention to regional political developments. J. Mills Thornton's (1980) neglected essay about increases in southern state taxation during Reconstruction offers important data whose effects call for in-depth investigation similar to that provided by Michael L. Lanza (1990) on the Southern Homestead Act 1866. Peter Wallenstein's (1987: 2) broad study of the "distributive mechanism" of public policy in nineteenth-century Georgia discusses post-emancipation changes in state government spending, and in a related vein, but more specifically focused on the Reconstruction era, Mark W. Summers (1984) links the provision of state financial aid to railroad development with the Republican party's failure to firmly establish itself in the South. All of these works point the way toward a reconsideration of institutional change in the Reconstruction era political economy.

Finally, and perhaps most important, *One Kind of Freedom* lacks a comparative dimension that would have made its conclusions regarding the cotton South more convincing. Ransom and Sutch allude to this shortcoming in their second edition (2001) when they agree that they took insufficient account of the differences with the burgeoning of cotton production in former yeoman regions like those famously examined in Georgia by Steven Hahn (1982). This holds true internally to the black-belt as well: for example, differential growth patterns between, say, the lower Atlantic seaboard (where absentee landlordism increased steadily) and the burgeoning Mississippi Delta (home to the centralized business plantation) are short-shrifted by Ransom and Sutch (1977). Recently, scholars such as J. William Harris (2001) and Charles S. Aiken (1998) have begun to describe and evaluate such differences, as has Robert Tracy McKenzie (1994) in his valuable economic study of subregional varia-tions in Tennessee agriculture during Reconstruction.

There are other comparative dimensions neglected by Ransom and Sutch that are now beginning to receive attention. The role of race and class in other types of southern agricultural production provides important contrasts to the cotton experience. For example, John C. Rodrigue (2001) has examined the development of a wage labor system (as opposed to tenancy) in the capital-intensive sugar industry of southern Louisiana after the war (see also Heitmann 1986); tobacco and rice production deserve similar treatments. Extraregional comparisons are a powerful tool for understanding southern economic development as well. Surprisingly few recent scholars have followed the lead long ago established by historians such as Douglas Dowd (1956) and Morton J. Rothstein (1966) in comparing the trajectories of midwestern and southern agriculture, although aspects of William Cronon's (1991) work on the former region are highly suggestive in this regard. More to scholars' liking of late have been comparative studies that are international in scope: Italy (Halpern and Dal Lago 2002), South Africa (Cell 1982; Ochiltree 1998), Russia (Kolchin 1987), and the Caribbean (McGlynn and Drescher 1992; Scott 1994) have all provided counterpoints to the experience of the nineteenth-century American South. However, these studies frequently employ political rather than economic premises as their starting points of investigation; and furthermore, the recent enthusiasm of historians for situating their subjects within overarching "Atlantic world" or "transnational" contexts should not necessarily trump other understandings based on local specificities and variations that are often only tenuously related to such global considerations.

In fairness to *One Kind of Freedom*, however, no one book can be all things, and what Ransom and Sutch do within a new institutionalist framework for the postbellum South has no real counterpoint as yet in the historiography on the northern, midwestern, or national economies. Although the outlines of such an approach to institutional change in the post-Civil War decades are partly visible in the simple, powerful truths rooted out by the Beards (1927) long ago, unfortunately they opted to present their insights muddied by late Progressive era rhetoric as well as squeezed nearly dry of discernible empirical content. With his emphasis on the decline of merchant capital, Louis Hacker's subsequent and more explicit Marxist approach (though interestingly he would become an outspoken conservative over the course of his later career) was better developed than the Beards'; but still missing was sufficient empirical specificity or sensitivity to the nuanced, gradual nature of economic change. Revisionists scored heavily against Beard and Hacker, and indeed, many still have yet to change their minds much in the intervening decades. For example, although Stanley L. Engerman no longer finds it necessary to mention the long-vanquished Beard by name, this great economic historian has asserted in a co-authored essay that "the political shifts of the Civil War era [are] no longer seen as necessary for an expansion in the manufacturing sector" (Engerman and Sokoloff 2000: 379).

Perhaps – but we still think it difficult to argue convincingly against the fact that the economic climate and its various associated mechanisms established under wartime political conditions were further institutionalized during Reconstruction and the decades thereafter. Perhaps lingering ideological entropy might be lessened if we simply reoriented the questions regarding the postwar economy away from cause-and-effect toward an acknowledgement and delineation of the profound changes that indisputably occurred. Even so, we agree with William G. Roy that "theretofore unthinkably radical changes adopted for the crisis situation were only partially rescinded afterward and became institutionalized into taken-for-granted practices" (Roy 1997: 129). In a similar vein, the various aspects of the Chandlerian "organizational revolution" that unfolded between 1840 and 1880 are rarely considered separately from the economic effects of the war in most of the historiography we have discussed, and they probably should be (Carlton and Coclanis 2003). Politico-military events, even ones as cataclysmic as the Civil War, should not necessarily be considered demarcation points for explaining all that occurs before and after them. For example, Steven Hahn (2003) has narrated the history of African Americans across the chasm of the Civil War, just as he previously fruitfully reconsidered the experience of the South's white yeomanry from 1850 to 1890. The same could be done with Reconstruction, whose supposed "end" in 1877 (with the final withdrawal of Federal troops from the South) effectively serves as a misplaced historiographical *cordon sanitaire*. In fact, as J. Morgan Kousser (2000) has pointed out, there are good reasons for viewing Reconstruction in the South as a period that continues through the consolidation of Jim Crow in the 1890s, and a similar viewpoint could be adopted to good effect with regard to post-1877 economic changes, both regionally and nationally. From such a flexible, unorthodox, and somewhat less dramatic temporal perspective – and here we are also willing to lend unintended consequences at least as much credence as the Beards did elite conspiratology – the interminable debates over whether the Civil War "caused" or "retarded" subsequent economic development begin to seem as ineffectual and pointless as were the tired old debates in southern history over "continuity or change."

While the new institutional economics is most assuredly a diverse school of thought, we neither underestimate its breadth nor intend to present it herein as a panacea for the lengthy historiographical impasse over the Reconstruction economy. Obviously, there will never be any single, ready-made theory that one can simply plug into events to explain them. But an important advantage of the new institutional economics as a theory of economic development is its methodological insistence on the importance of process and context, which often present inconvenient variables excluded by definition from economists' elaborate models ("ceteris paribus," as they say) and thereby forgotten. Nonetheless, the new institutional economics' working assumption of a broadly conceived, interwoven, and shifting institutional playing field for economic behavior remains helpfully distinct not only from the neoclassical insistence on the primary importance of the rules of an ahistorical, abstract free market, but also from a "vulgar" Marxist view that considers institutions to be merely superstructural to the mode of production. It is perhaps suggestive that the two authors of this chapter – one of whom was trained in the methods and techniques of cliometrics, the other more disposed toward analytical frameworks emphasizing the political economy; yet both of whom are eager to find ways to acknowledge and incorporate "other" approaches – have found the new institutional economics to offer a welcome basis for common ground, as well as some necessary correctives for the indisputable excesses of the respective "schools" from which each emerged.

It is from this shared and hopeful perspective, therefore, that we echo a shrewd lament that Gavin Wright made regarding postbellum economic history in the early 1980s. " '[C]lass' and 'market'," he wrote, "should not be viewed as incompatible opposites" (Wright 1982: 164). Indeed, it would be preferable to find a standpoint that can accommodate the fruitful insights – and empirical data supporting them – that each approach has generated over the years. While the potential of the new institutional economics to dissolve or mediate the longstanding mutual exclusivity of approaches emphasizing political economy or the free market has yet to be fully proven – or even adequately explored – we encourage others, historians and economists alike, to consider it as a possible tool for clearing a negotiable path through the tangled thickets of Reconstruction historiography in future studies of late nineteenth-century economic change in the United States.

BIBLIOGRAPHY

Aiken, Charles S. (1998) *The Cotton Plantation South since the Civil War*. Baltimore, Md.: Johns Hopkins University Press.

Alston, Lee J. and Ferrie, Joseph P. (1999) *Southern Paternalism and the American Welfare State: Economics, Politics, and Institutions in the South, 1865–1965*. New York: Cambridge University Press.

Andreano, Ralph (ed.) (1962) *The Economic Impact of the American Civil War*. Cambridge, Mass.: Schenkman.

Ayers, Edward L. (1992) *The Promise of the New South: Life after Reconstruction*. New York: Oxford University Press.

Beard, Charles A. (1913) *An Economic Interpretation of the Constitution of the United States*. New York: Macmillan.

Beard, Charles A. and Beard, Mary R. (1927) *The Rise of American Civilization*, two vols. New York: Macmillan.

Beckert, Sven (2001) *The Monied Metropolis: New York City and the Consolidation of the American Bourgeoisie, 1850–1896*. New York: Cambridge University Press.

Bensel, Richard F. (1990) *Yankee Leviathan: The Origins of Central State Authority in America, 1859–1877*. Cambridge: Cambridge University Press.

Billings, Dwight B. (1979) *Planters and the Making of a "New South": Class, Politics, and Development in North Carolina, 1865–1900*. Chapel Hill, NC: University of North Carolina Press.

Bureau of the Census (1960 [1957]) *Historical Statistics of the United States, from Colonial Times to 1957*. Washington, DC: US Government Printing Office.

Byres, Terence J. (ed.) (1983) *Sharecropping and Sharecroppers*. London: Frank Cass.

Byres, Terence J. (1996) *Capitalism from Above and Capitalism from Below: An Essay in Comparative Political Economy*. New York: St. Martin's Press.

Carlton, David L. (1982) *Mill and Town in South Carolina, 1880–1920*. Baton Rouge, La.: Louisiana State University Press.

Carlton, David L. (2003) "The Revolution from Above: The National Market and the Beginnings of Industrialization in North Carolina," in David L. Carlton and Peter A. Coclanis (eds.) *The South, the Nation, and the World: Perspectives on Southern Economic Development*. Charlottesville, Va.: University of Virginia Press.

Carlton, David L. and Coclanis, Peter A. (2003) *The South, the Nation, and the World: Perspectives on Southern Economic Development*. Charlottesville, Va.: University of Virginia Press.

Cell, John W. (1982) *The Highest Stage of White Supremacy: The Origins of Segregation in South Africa and the American South*. New York: Cambridge University Press.

Chandler, Alfred D., Jr (1965) "The Organization of Manufacturing and Transportation," in David T. Gilchrist and W. David Lewis (eds.) *Economic Change in the Civil War Era*. Greenville, Del.: Eleutherian Mills-Hagley Foundation.

Chandler, Alfred D., Jr (1977) *The Visible Hand: The Managerial Revolution in American Business.* Cambridge, Mass.: Belknap Press.

Clark, Thomas D. (1944) *Pills, Petticoats, and Plows: The Southern Country Store.* Indianapolis, Ind.: Bobbs-Merrill.

Cochran, Thomas C. (1962) "Did the Civil War Retard Industrialization?," in Ralph Andreano (ed.) *The Economic Impact of the American Civil War.* Cambridge, Mass.: Schenkman.

Cochran, Thomas C. and Miller, William (1961 [1942]) *The Age of Enterprise: A Social History of Industrial America.* New York: Harper and Row.

Coclanis, Peter A. (2000) "In Retrospect: Ransom and Sutch's One Kind of Freedom," *Reviews in American History* 28: 478–89.

Cronon, William (1991) *Nature's Metropolis: Chicago and the Great West.* New York: Norton.

Daniel, Pete (1972) *The Shadow of Slavery: Peonage in the South, 1901–1969.* Urbana, Ill.: University of Illinois Press.

Davis, Lance E. (1965) "The Investment Market, 1870–1914," *Journal of Economic History* 25: 355–99.

Davis, Lance E. and North, Douglass C. (1971) *Institutional Change and American Economic Growth.* New York: Cambridge University Press.

DeCanio, Stephen, and Mokyr, Joel (1977) "Inflation and the Wage Lag during the American Civil War," *Explorations in Economic History* 14: 311–36.

Dowd, Douglas F. (1956) "A Comparative Analysis of Economic Development in the American West and South," *Journal of Economic History* 16: 558–74.

Doyle, Don H. (1990) *New Men, New Cities, New South: Atlanta, Nashville, Charleston, Mobile, 1860–1910.* Chapel Hill, NC: University of North Carolina Press.

DuBois, W. E. B. (1992 [1935]) *Black Reconstruction in America, 1860–1880.* New York: Free Press.

Edwards, Laura F. (1997) *Gendered Strife and Confusion: The Political Culture of Reconstruction.* Urbana, Ill.: University of Illinois Press.

Engerman, Stanley L. (1966) "The Economic Impact of the Civil War," *Explorations in Economic History* 3: 176–99.

Engerman, Stanley L. and Sokoloff, Kenneth L. (2000) "Technology and Industrialization, 1790–1915," in Engerman and Robert E. Gallman (eds.) *The Cambridge Economic History of the United States.* Volume 2: *The Nineteenth Century.* New York: Cambridge University Press.

Ferleger, Lou (ed.) (1990) *Agriculture and National Development: Views on the Nineteenth Century.* Ames, Iowa: Iowa State University Press.

Fields, Barbara Jeanne (1983) "The Nineteenth-Century American South: History and Theory," *Plantation Society in the Americas* 2: 7–27.

Fields, Barbara Jeanne (1985) *Slavery and Freedom on the Middle Ground: Maryland during the Nineteenth Century.* New Haven, Conn.: Yale University Press.

Foldvary, Fred E. (ed.) (1996) *Beyond Neoclassical Economics: Heterodox Approaches to Economic Theory.* Brookfield, Vt.: Edward Elgar.

Foner, Eric (1988) *Reconstruction: America's Unfinished Revolution, 1863–1877.* New York: Harper and Row.

Ford, Lacy K., Jr (1984) "Rednecks and Merchants: Economic Development and Social Tensions in the South Carolina Upcountry, 1865–1900," *Journal of American History* 71: 294–318.

Gilchrist, David T. and Lewis, W. David (eds.) (1965) *Economic Change in the Civil War Era.* Greenville, Del.: Eleutherian Mills-Hagley Foundation.

Glymph, Thavolia and Kushma, John J. (eds.) (1985) *Essays on the Postbellum Southern Economy.* College Station, Tex.: Texas A & M University Press.

Goldin, Claudia Dale and Lewis, Frank (1975) "The Economic Costs of the American Civil War: Estimates and Implications," *Journal of Economic History* 35: 299–326.

Hacker, Louis M. (1940) *The Triumph of American Capitalism*. New York: Columbia University Press.

Hahn, Steven (1983) *The Roots of Southern Populism: Yeomen Farmers and the Transformation of the Georgia Upcountry, 1850–1890*. New York: Oxford University Press.

Hahn, Steven (2003) *A Nation under our Feet: Black Political Struggles in the Rural South from Slavery to the Great Migration*. Cambridge, Mass.: Harvard University Press.

Halpern, Rick and Dal Lago, Enrico (eds.) (2002) *The American South and the Italian Mezzogiorno*. Basingstoke: Palgrave.

Harris, J. William (1997) "The Question of Peonage in the History of the New South," in Samuel C. Hyde Jr (ed.) *Plain Folk of the South Revisited*. Baton Rouge, La.: Louisiana State University Press.

Harris, J. William (2001) *Deep Souths: Delta, Piedmont, and Sea Island Society in the Age of Segregation*. Baltimore, Md.: Johns Hopkins University Press.

Heitmann, John A. (1986) *The Modernization of the Louisiana Sugar Industry, 1830–1910*. Baton Rouge, La.: Louisiana State University Press.

Higgs, Robert (1977) *Competition and Coercion: Blacks in the American Economy, 1865–1914*. New York: Cambridge University Press.

Hobsbawm, Eric J. (1974) *The Age of Capital, 1848–1875*. New York: Charles Scribner's Sons.

Horwitz, Morton J. (1992) *The Transformation of American Law, 1870–1960*. New York: Oxford University Press.

James, John A. (1981) "Financial Underdevelopment in the Postbellum South," *Journal of Interdisciplinary History* 11: 443–54.

Jaynes, Gerald David (1986) *Branches without Roots: The Genesis of the Black Working Class in the American South, 1862–1882*. New York: Oxford University Press.

Kilbourne, Richard H., Jr (1990) *Debt, Investment, Slaves: Credit Relations in East Feliciana Parish, Louisiana, 1825–1885*. Tuscaloosa, Ala.: University of Alabama Press.

Kolchin, Peter (1987) *Unfree Labor: American Slavery and Russian Serfdom*. Cambridge, Mass.: Harvard University Press.

Kousser, J. Morgan (2000) "Reconstruction," in Paul S. Boyer (ed.) *The Oxford Companion to United States History*. New York: Oxford University Press.

Kuznets, Simon and Thomas, Dorothy Swaine (eds.) (1957–64) *Population Redistribution and Economic Growth, 1870–1950*, three vols. Philadelphia, Pa.: American Philosophical Society.

Kyriakoudes, Louis M. (2002) "Lower-Order Urbanization and Territorial Monopoly in the Southern Furnishing Trade: Alabama, 1871–1890," *Social Science History* 26: 179–98.

Lanza, Michael L. (1990) *Agrarianism and Reconstruction Politics: The Southern Homestead Act*. Baton Rouge, La.: Louisiana State University Press.

Lichtenstein, Alex (1998) "Proletarians or Peasants? Sharecroppers and the Politics of Protest in the Rural South, 1880–1940," *Plantation Society in the Americas* 5: 297–331.

McGlynn, Frank and Drescher, Seymour (eds.) (1992) *The Meaning of Freedom: Economics, Politics, and Culture after Slavery*. Pittsburgh, Pa.: University of Pittsburgh Press.

McKenzie, Robert Tracy (1994) *One South or Many? Plantation Belt and Upcountry in Civil-War Era Tennessee*. New York: Cambridge University Press.

Mandle, Jay R. (1978) *The Roots of Black Poverty: The Southern Plantation Economy after the Civil War*. Durham, NC: Duke University Press.

Mandle, Jay R. (1992) *Not Slave, Not Free: The African American Economic Experience since the Civil War*. Durham, NC: Duke University Press.

Mann, Susan Archer (1994) *Agrarian Capitalism in Theory and Practice*. Chapel Hill, NC: University of North Carolina Press.

Margo, Robert A. (1995) "The South as an Economic Problem: Fact or Fiction?," in Larry J. Griffin and Don H. Doyle (eds.) *The South as an American Problem*. Athens, Ga.: University of Georgia Press.

Marler, Scott P. (2001) "Merchants in the Transition to a New South: Central Louisiana, 1840–1880," *Louisiana History* 42: 165–92.

Marler, Scott P. (2004) "Fables of the Reconstruction: Reconstruction of the Fables," *Journal of the Historical Society* 4: 113–37.

Moore, Barrington, Jr (1966) *Social Origins of Dictatorship and Democracy: Lord and Peasant in the Making of the Modern World*. Boston, Mass.: Beacon Press.

National Bureau of Economic Research (NBER) (1960) *Trends in the Nineteenth-Century Economy* [Studies in Income and Wealth, Volume 24]. Princeton, NJ: Princeton University Press.

Noble, David F. (1977) *America by Design: Science, Technology, and the Rise of Corporate Capitalism*. New York: Alfred A. Knopf.

O'Brien, Patrick K. (1988) *The Economic Effects of the American Civil War*. London: Macmillan.

Ochiltree, Ian D. (1998) "'A Just and Self-Respecting System?' Black Independence, Sharecropping, and Paternalistic Relations in the American South and South Africa," *Agricultural History* 72: 352–80.

Porter, Glenn and Livesay, Harold C. (1971) *Merchants and Manufacturers: Studies in the Changing Structure of Nineteenth-Century Marketing*. Baltimore, Md.: Johns Hopkins University Press.

Pressly, Thomas J. (1962 [1954]) *Americans Interpret their Civil War*, rev. edn. New York: Free Press.

Ransom, Roger L. (1989) *Conflict and Compromise: The Political Economy of Slavery, Emancipation, and the American Civil War*. New York: Cambridge University Press.

Ransom, Roger L. and Sutch, Richard (1977) *One Kind of Freedom: The Economic Consequences of Emancipation*. Cambridge: Cambridge University Press.

Ransom, Roger L. and Sutch, Richard (2001) *One Kind of Freedom: The Economic Consequences of Emancipation*, 2nd edn. New York: Cambridge University Press.

Reid, Joseph (1973) "Sharecropping as an Understandable Market Response: The Post-Bellum South," *Journal of Economic History* 33: 106–30.

Reidy, Joseph P. (1992) *From Slavery to Agrarian Capitalism in the Cotton Plantation South: Central Georgia, 1800–1880*. Chapel Hill, NC: University of North Carolina Press.

Rodrigue, John C. (2001) *Reconstruction in the Cane Fields: From Slavery to Free Labor in Louisiana's Sugar Parishes, 1862–1880*. Baton Rouge, La.: Louisiana State University Press.

Rodrigue, John C. (2002) "More Souths?," *Reviews in American History* 30: 66–71.

Ross, Michael A. (2003) *Justice of Shattered Dreams: Samuel Freeman Miller and the Supreme Court during the Civil War Era*. Baton Rouge, La.: Louisiana State University Press.

Rostow, W. W. (1956) "The Take-off into Sustained Growth," *Economic Journal* 66: 25–48.

Rothstein, Morton (1966) "Antebellum Wheat and Cotton Exports: A Contrast in Marketing Organization and Economic Development," *Agricultural History* 40: 91–100.

Roy, William G. (1997) *Socializing Capital: The Rise of the Large Industrial Corporation in America*. Princeton, NJ: Princeton University Press.

Salsbury, Stephen (1962) "The Effect of the Civil War on American Industrial Development," in Ralph Andreano (ed.) *The Economic Impact of the American Civil War*. Cambridge, Mass.: Schenkman.

Scott, Rebecca J. (1994) "Defining the Boundaries of Freedom in the World of Cane: Cuba, Brazil, and Louisiana after Emancipation," *American Historical Review* 99: 70–102.

Scranton, Philip (1997) *Endless Novelty: Specialty Production and American Industrialization, 1865–1925*. Princeton, NJ: Princeton University Press.

Seavoy, Ronald E. (1998) *The American Peasantry: Southern Agricultural Labor and its Legacy, 1850–1995*. Westport, Conn.: Greenwood Press.

Skowronek, Stephen (1992) *Building a New American State: The Expansion of National Administrative Capacities, 1877–1920*. New York: Cambridge University Press.

Stanley, Amy Dru (1998) *From Bondage to Contract: Wage Labor, Marriage, and the Market in the Age of Slave Emancipation*. New York: Cambridge University Press.

Summers, Mark W. (1984) *Railroads, Reconstruction, and the Gospel of Prosperity: Aid under the Radical Republicans, 1865–1877*. Princeton, NJ: Princeton University Press.

Thornton, J. Mills, III (1980) "Fiscal Policy and the Failure of Radical Reconstruction in the Lower South," in J. Morgan Kousser and James M. McPherson (eds.) *Region, Race, and Reconstruction: Essays in Honor of C. Vann Woodward*. New York: Oxford University Press.

Wallenstein, Peter (1987) *From Slave South to New South: Public Policy in Nineteenth-Century Georgia*. Chapel Hill, NC: University of North Carolina Press.

Walton, Gary M. and Shepherd, James F. (eds.) (1981) *Market Institutions and Economic Change in the New South, 1865–1900*. New York: Academic Press.

Weisberger, Bernard (1959) "The Dark and Bloody Ground of Reconstruction Historiography," *Journal of Southern History* 25: 427–47.

Wiener, Jonathan M. (1978) *Social Origins of the New South: Alabama, 1860–1885*. Baton Rouge, La.: Louisiana State University Press.

Wiener, Jonathan M. (1979) "Class Structure and Economic Development in the American South, 1865–1955," *American Historical Review* 84: 970–1006.

Williamson, Jeffrey G. (1974a) "Watersheds and Turning Points: Conjectures on the Long-Term Impact of Civil War Financing," *Journal of Economic History* 34: 636–61.

Williamson, Jeffrey G. (1974b) *Late Nineteenth-Century American Development: A General Equilibrium History*. New York: Cambridge University Press.

Woodman, Harold D. (1968) *King Cotton and his Retainers: Financing and Marketing the Cotton Crop of the South, 1800–1925*. Lexington, Ky.: University Press of Kentucky.

Woodman, Harold D. (1987) "Economic Reconstruction and the Rise of the New South, 1865–1900," in John B. Boles and Evelyn Thomas Nolen (eds.) *Interpreting Southern History: Essays in Honor of Sanford W. Higginbotham*. Baton Rouge, La.: Louisiana State University Press.

Woodman, Harold D. (1995) *New South – New Law: The Legal Foundations of Credit and Labor Relations in the Postbellum Agricultural South*. Baton Rouge, La.: Louisiana State University Press.

Woodman, Harold D. (2001b) "The Political Economy of the New South: Retrospects and Prospects," *Journal of Southern History* 67: 789–810.

Woodward, C. Vann (1951) *Origins of the New South, 1877–1913*. Baton Rouge, La.: Louisiana State University Press.

Wright, Gavin (1982) "The Strange Career of the New Southern Economic History," *Reviews in American History* 10: 164–80.

Wright, Gavin (1986) *Old South, New South: Revolutions in the Southern Economy since the Civil War*. New York: Basic Books.

CHAPTER NINETEEN

Southern Labor and Reconstruction

R. TRACY McKENZIE

As black and white southerners took stock of their situation in the spring of 1865, one thing was abundantly clear to almost all of them: slavery was dead. After four years of civil war and an incalculable cost in blood and treasure, the combined efforts of Union soldiers and defiant slaves had laid to rest the South's "peculiar institution." What this would mean in the long run, practically and concretely, was far from clear, however. Uncertainty, even a measure of bewilderment, was nearly universal. This was entirely understandable. Over the course of nearly 250 years, slavery had become inextricably intertwined with the fabric of everyday life all the way from Maryland to Texas. It was the central pillar of the region's economy, social structure, and race relations. And yet in less than four years – a blink of an eye, historically speaking – it had been dealt a mortal blow from without and within. The history of labor and Reconstruction in the South is the story of a struggle among former slaves, former masters, and (for a brief period) representatives of the federal government to shape the social and economic meanings of emancipation. For both white and black southerners, the stakes could not have been higher.

As late as the 1960s, historians seemed largely uninterested in this potentially revolutionary moment. The field of postbellum southern agriculture – the most obvious context for an assessment of this post-emancipation drama – was still largely undeveloped. In 1965, for example, a comprehensive survey of published scholarship on southern history revealed almost no interest in questions such as the expansion of sharecropping, a phenomenon at the heart of the reorganization of southern labor during Reconstruction. Beginning in the 1970s, however, a number of developments in the academy dovetailed to promote a remarkable upsurge in scholarly interest in this long-neglected field. First, there was the rise of the "new social history" that had begun during the previous decade. Advocates of this approach borrowed heavily from other social sciences and focused on the experiences of common folk rather than elites, striving to write history "from the bottom up," as they put it. Overlapping this trend was the emergence of African American history as a distinct field within the discipline. In the 1960s most of the work in this area had concentrated on the study of antebellum slavery, but by the 1970s specialists had begun to broaden their gaze to include the labor arrangements that replaced it.

Finally, there was the spectacular (and controversial) emergence of cliometrics, an approach to the past that combines the explicit use of economic theory with highly sophisticated statistical techniques. Sharing the opinion that W. E. B. DuBois (1935: 721) had expressed decades earlier, cliometricians viewed Reconstruction as "primarily an economic development," and they recognized that many of the most pressing questions concerning the southern countryside after Appomattox – those involving land and labor, poverty and wealth, mobility and productivity – were eminently susceptible to quantification. The cumulative result of these three trends has been an outpouring of scholarly work since the late 1970s on almost every imaginable facet of the reorganization of southern labor after slavery's demise. Although this extensive literature has been often quite contentious, historians agree about enough that we can speak of a widely accepted "standard scenario," a basic understanding of the contours of labor reorganization during Reconstruction that frames most ongoing research in the field. It is worthwhile to summarize this common ground before turning to major issues of contention.

Slavery's demise began well before Union victory was secured on the field of battle, as numerous studies attest. Among the earliest and most eloquent works to drive home this point was James L. Roark's *Masters without Slaves* (1977), and Leon F. Litwack's Pulitzer Prize-winning *Been in the Storm So Long* (1979). Roark (1977) showed that, even before the invasion of Union armies, the exigencies of war undermined masters' control over their slaves in countless ways. The "Twenty-Negro Law" notwithstanding, the war drew thousands of slaveowners and overseers into the Confederate army and navy, leaving many plantations and farms without a significant white male presence. Confederate state governments discouraged the production of cotton, interfering significantly with labor routines, while Confederate army units committed the cardinal sin of impressing slave laborers for a variety of military needs. The result, as Roark explained, was that plantation discipline gradually but inexorably disintegrated, with the result that "slavery eroded, plantation by plantation, often slave by slave, like slabs of earth slipping into a Southern stream" (Roark 1977: 77).

The penetration of the South by invading Union armies simply exacerbated an already unstable situation. The arrival of Federal troops regularly prompted slaves to run away, and by the spring of 1862 (well before the Emancipation Proclamation), the US Articles of War had been amended to prohibit any Union military personnel from assisting in the return of black fugitives. By making their way to Union lines in prodigious numbers (some 25,000 runaway slaves flocked to the army of William T. Sherman during his famous "March to the Sea"), thousands of southern blacks played an especially active role in their own liberation. Even when slaves remained with their owners, as Litwack observed, with "the appearance of the first Yankee soldier . . . nearly every master and mistress sensed that the old loyalties and mutual dependencies were about to become irrelevant" (Litwack 1979: 116). Most troubling of all from the perspective of white slaveowners, the Lincoln government began to recruit southern slaves for service in the Union army. The black soldier was a powerful symbol of the radical social changes wrought by the war. Whether these changes would be permanent was another question.

In the end, there was no single day of jubilee across the South, and the timing and circumstances by which individual bondmen realized their freedom varied extensively across the region. This much is clear, however: by the summer of 1865 slavery was extinct throughout the former Confederacy, and 3.5 million former slaves and over 300,000 former masters were poised on the threshold of a new and foreign world. Their goals for the future were fundamentally irreconcilable. By and large, former slaveowners – and landowning whites generally – recoiled from the idea of a free labor system in which they would negotiate as equals with black employees. A tiny percentage fled the country for Mexico or Brazil, lands where slavery, or some approximate facsimile, was still legal. Larger numbers hoped to attract to the South reliable alternatives to black labor, looking to the North or outside of the United States for European immigrants or Chinese "coolies" who might constitute a submissive and docile labor force. Most eventually dismissed these hopes as unrealistic and accepted the necessity of dependence on the former slaves, but this pragmatic majority generally determined to maximize their control over black workers by creating a labor system as closely akin to slavery as possible. For their part, the former slaves sought to reunite with loved ones, regulate their familial affairs without interference, and gain access to education and – above all – to land. Their larger goal was crystal clear: to confirm the reality of their new freedom by maximizing their independence from their former masters.

Both groups were eventually forced to settle for something considerably short of their original objectives. Both had hoped to enlist the power of government in accomplishing their aims, and both, during Reconstruction at least, were disappointed. During the early phase of "self-Reconstruction," white landowners hoped that the federal government would mind its own business while sympathetic southern state governments acted to forestall the development of a free labor market in southern agriculture. Beginning in the fall of 1865, Democratic majorities in southern state legislatures passed a series of "Black Codes" that typically criminalized vagrancy, established an "apprentice" system for black youth without "adequate" parental support, and forbade employers to "entice" workers already under contract. In some instances they even prohibited blacks from renting land and imposed exorbitant taxes on freedmen who engaged in skilled occupations. The goal was transparent: to limit the economic "opportunities" of former slaves to agricultural labor on farms and plantations owned by whites. The great majority of freepersons were to be made to sign agricultural contracts and forced to honor them upon pain of severe criminal penalties. As Dan T. Carter noted trenchantly, southern whites were ready to accept the demise of legal slavery and to submit to the supremacy of the federal government, "but they were unwilling to accept the legal equality of freedmen or even . . . to feign such acceptance" (Carter 1985: 231).

The federal government did not mind its own business, however, much to the chagrin of southern whites. Representatives of the Freedmen's Bureau, a temporary agency created by Congress in March 1865 to facilitate the freepersons' transition from slavery to free labor, acted aggressively to suspend the most discriminatory provisions of the Black Codes. The codes were effectively nullified the following spring when Congress passed the Civil Rights Act 1866, a measure that defined the former slaves as US citizens entitled to enjoy "full and equal benefit of all laws and proceedings for the security of person and property as is enjoyed by white citizens." A smoothly functioning free labor market did not immediately emerge, but the Republican majority in Congress had made clear that it would not allow southern white landowners simply to legislate it out of existence.

For their part, the former slaves looked to the federal government to confiscate the lands of disloyal former masters and distribute them among the black laborers whose ancestors had worked those lands for generations. There was support for land redistribution among the most radical Republicans in Congress, but the majority viewed such a proposal as far too extreme, and the possibility of such a policy effectively evaporated with Andrew Johnson's May 1865 amnesty proclamation. In one of his first major acts as president, Johnson offered full restoration of property, with the exception of slaves, to almost all ex-Confederates willing to swear an oath of loyalty to the United States. Thus the freedmen's dream of being immediately established as an independent black yeomanry was essentially stillborn, handicapped not only by the president's initiative but also by the widespread conviction among Republican policy-makers that indiscriminate redistribution would "demoralize" former slaves who needed to learn the benefits of industry and thrift.

In sum, the freepersons were to be given "nothing but freedom," to quote the title of a famous study of emancipation's aftermath by Eric Foner (1983). Whites would continue to monopolize the cultivable land, as well as almost every other resource essential to the prosperity of agricultural producers: work animals and other livestock, farm implements, seed, fertilizer, and access to credit. With proportionally few exceptions, the freedmen's economic assets consisted of strong backs and the freedom to move about from employer to employer. The importance of the latter should not be underestimated, though. By moving about freely in search of the best working environment (however defined), the former slaves forced landholders to compete for black labor. In so doing, they introduced the marketplace, at least partially, into black–white relations.

Although historians have long acknowledged that the former slaves moved about extensively in the immediate aftermath of emancipation, several studies in the 1970s and early 1980s insisted that the freedmen were rather rapidly immobilized by the coercive tactics of white landowners and merchants. Increasingly, however, historians have come to reject that view. Without minimizing the extent of repression and intimidation in the postbellum South, scholars writing from a broad range of ideological perspectives now agree that, although black migration *from* the South was proportionally slight until at least World War I, black mobility *within* the South was quite extensive. The most systematic investigation of the question is William Cohen's *At Freedom's Edge* (1991). In this careful study Cohen contended that white elites failed miserably in their efforts to control black labor during Reconstruction and maintained that southern blacks moved about "with considerable freedom" throughout the half century after the Civil War (Cohen 1991: xv). His conclusions reaffirmed the earlier speculation of social historian Jay Mandle (1978) that the absence of job opportunities in the North and West – rather than extensive peonage – explained the minimal exodus of blacks from the South after emancipation. Cohen's findings similarly reinforced economic historian Gavin Wright's assertion that the most crucial feature of the southern economy after the Civil War "was not poor performance or failure but isolation" (Wright 1986: 64). There was definitely a functioning labor market in the postbellum South, Wright had argued, but it was essentially separated from larger national and international labor flows until World War II. Within the South, the comparatively limited extent of industrialization, combined with the prevalence of discriminatory hiring practices in mills and factories, meant that the former slaves had relatively few non-farm job possibilities.

Within the agricultural sector, however, the freedmen were "mobile and market responsive" (Mandle 1978: 27).

Across the southern countryside, therefore, former masters in need of labor squared off against former slaves in need of land, but with the conspicuous ability to move when and where they pleased. A minority of freedmen sought to make a new life in urban areas. Contemporary sources repeatedly attest that the newly freed slaves flocked to towns and cities in the early months of their freedom, but they also suggest that a large proportion returned to the countryside soon thereafter. The South's urban sector was small to begin with, and after 1865 many of the skilled occupations in the cities were closed to blacks, even though both slaves and free blacks had frequently labored in skilled crafts prior to the war. Those who stayed were relegated almost entirely to unskilled, low-wage positions as draymen, warehouse and dock workers, porters, cooks, and laundresses, to name the most common. The cities generally afforded superior protection from harassment and abuse and made possible a tighter and more cohesive black community. More than 90 percent of the region's white and black population lived in the countryside, however, and it was there, of necessity, that most of the freedpeople looked for their economic livelihoods.

Scholars have universally agreed that in 1865 and 1866 white landowners did their best to impose a gang-labor wage system on the freedmen who sought to earn their livings on the land. Under this system, black laborers would work in large groups under the close and constant supervision of white superintendents, receiving typically either a fixed cash wage or a specific share of the crop ("share wages") as compensation. In these early years most labor agreements were formalized by written contracts approved by agents of the Freedmen's Bureau. The Bureau's standardized contracts called for a fixed monthly wage, causing historians formerly to assume that fixed-wage labor wholly predominated in the immediate aftermath of emancipation. More recent research has proven otherwise, however (Schlomowitz 1979; Jaynes 1986), and it is now undeniable that numerous southern landowners resorted to share wages from the beginning. Although the scarcity of cash and credit in the early postwar era surely encouraged this, many employers likely preferred share wages because the method allowed them to postpone paying their hands until after the harvest, a tactic that discouraged freedmen from leaving in the middle of the crop year to accept a better offer. Indeed, even employers who could pay in cash often contractually stipulated that a significant proportion of the monthly wage (frequently one-half) be withheld until the close of the year.

Convinced that the former slaves would never be reliable workers without compulsion, white landowners preferred the gang-labor wage system because of the control over labor that it facilitated. According to most scholars, the freedmen generally disliked it for much the same reason. The predominant view is that the former slaves resented the imposition of gang labor as a carryover from slavery and sought out employers who offered less centralized arrangements. Disastrous crop years in 1865 and 1866 put white landowners in a weak position to resist the opposition of the freedmen, and by 1867 (if not sooner) white landowners had begun to experiment with a variety of other labor arrangements designed to attract a sufficiently large, stable, and productive labor force. The key to all of these alternatives, as rural sociologist Edward Royce observed in *The Origins of Southern Sharecropping* (1993), lay less in the method of payment than in the decentralization of production. Notwithstanding some exceptions, what the former slaves seemed to desire above all was greater freedom from the close daily supervision of whites, which meant that landowners who wanted to attract the best laborers needed to find a way to provide that without suffering devastating losses in productivity. Although the precise timing is in dispute, there is no question that this trend toward decentralization led steadily toward a family-based labor system. Traditionally, the consensus among scholars was that the process was quite rapid. Many asserted that it was no longer than five years, and almost all agreed that it was complete by 1880, the first year that the federal agricultural census recorded systematic information on farm tenancy. The 1880 census showed that more than one-third of southern farmers had become tenants and indicated that the average size of southern farms had declined by more than one-half. There was a glaring problem with the agricultural census, however – it did not record information about farm laborers, only farm operators. Quite recently, a number of scholars have undertaken painstaking analyses of the federal population manuscript censuses and concluded that the shift from wage labor to family-based arrangements among the freedmen was much more gradual than scholars previously believed. Indeed, it is almost certainly the case that a majority of black households in the South were headed by wage laborers as late as 1880, and family-based arrangements did not become predominant until near the end of the century (McKenzie 1994, 1995; Burton 1998; Irwin and O'Brien 1998).

Even so, it is still undeniable that the process began almost immediately, and although wage laborers were still extremely important to the rural economy, all across the South landowners increasingly subdivided their farms and plantations into small plots to be worked by individual families under far less daily supervision than the wage system typically afforded. Technically, black families who labored in this fashion could fall into one of three categories. One group consisted of *fixed-rent tenants* who rented a plot from the landowner in return for a fixed amount of cash or a specified quantity of farm products. In a similar category were *share tenants*, families who rented land for a share of the output. Theoretically, at least, both groups provided their own work stock, seed, and implements, and both were legally vested in the crop that they produced; they legally owned the crop and paid their landlord from its proceeds. A third group consisted of *sharecroppers*, an arrangement that included features of both tenancy and wage labor. Sharecroppers often brought nothing to the arrangement but their labor power, meaning that it was necessary for the landlord to provide all the other requisites for production. In contrast to fixed-rent tenants and share tenants, sharecroppers came to be viewed legally as wage laborers in almost all southern states. Either legislative acts or judicial decisions stipulated that sharecroppers – unlike tenants – did not have legal ownership rights in their crops prior to harvest and sale (Woodman 1995). Although they resembled tenants in that they were responsible for working specific plots, they were akin to wage laborers in that they *received* a portion of the crop they produced as wages from the landowner. Precise legal distinctions notwithstanding, in practice the line between share tenancy and sharecropping was often blurred, and the sharecropping arrangement, including related variations thereof, grew steadily in importance throughout the latter third of the nineteenth century.

These are the basic contours of the post-emancipation reorganization of southern agriculture, as the process is currently understood by most scholars. The "standard scenario" is well defined enough to provide a framework for most ongoing research on the topic, and yet sufficiently vague to accommodate extensive disagreement on a broad range of related issues. It encompasses vital questions of race, class, mentality, and the functioning of the free market, so it is perhaps not surprising that the relevant scholarship has been ideologically charged and frequently polemical.

Although something of an oversimplification, the scholars who have investigated the postbellum reorganization of southern labor can be conveniently divided between those who interpret the process in terms of market forces and those who believe that conflict between classes was more central. The former approach has been espoused predominantly – although not exclusively – by economists and economic historians, most of whom have also employed sophisticated statistical analysis, thereby earning the label "econometricians." From the mid-1970s to the mid-1980s, in particular, economists and economic historians seemed to pay special attention to the Reconstruction era, and they are responsible for much of the most stimulating and ambitious scholarship pertaining to the postbellum reorganization of southern labor. In the span of a single decade, they churned out a multitude of specialized journal articles as well as four sweeping interpretive overviews that dealt either wholly or significantly with the early postbellum period. Although they disagreed over numerous questions, the econometricians who investigated the postbellum South shared a number of unifying assumptions and methodological approaches. Most obvious, they offered analyses grounded explicitly in neoclassical economic theory and presented arguments based primarily, if not exclusively, on quantitative evidence. They assumed that, in the absence of serious imperfections, free-market competition produced socially beneficial results. Finally, they understood the reorganization of southern agriculture after emancipation as primarily the outcome of a market process in which individual decision-makers pursued their short-term self-interest in economically rational ways. Here the similarities ended.

By far the most important single work from this theoretical perspective was the monumental *One Kind of Freedom* (1977) by Roger L. Ransom and Richard Sutch. Based on a massive data sample drawn from the manuscript agricultural and population schedules of the 1880 census, *One Kind of Freedom* was stunning in both the breadth of its scope and the precision of its analysis. More than any other single study the book transformed the field of postbellum southern economic history and shaped the ongoing investigation of southern agricultural labor.

The authors sought above all to explain the "agonizingly slow" pace of black economic progress after emancipation (Ransom and Sutch 1977: 8). They granted that emancipation itself had been an economic boon to the freedmen. The former slaves had ceased to work like slaves when given the choice. Women and children in particular had decreased their labor participation dramatically, with the result that the amount of hours worked per capita among southern blacks dropped between 28 and 37 percent between 1859 and 1879. During the same period, according to their estimates, blacks' average material incomes increased by 29 percent. This growth in tangible income, combined with the estimated value of released labor time, meant that the slaves' "relative welfare" had increased by between 80 and 105 percent relative to slavery in less than two decades.

The freedmen's record of economic advancement thereafter was abysmal, however, because "flawed economic institutions" that emerged during Reconstruction –

specifically sharecropping and the crop-lien system – "effectively prevented blacks from progressing beyond the first step taken with emancipation" (Ransom and Sutch 1977: 2, 12). As Ransom and Sutch described it, sharecropping was a compromise that gave black laborers a modicum of independence from whites (although not as much as they had hoped for) and white landowners a modicum of control over blacks (albeit less than they desired). Sharecropping produced short-run returns to landlords that were comparable to what they might have received with centralized gang labor, but the arrangement encouraged both parties to focus on immediate returns and eschew long-term soil conservation and improvement practices. Such present-mindedness was further exacerbated by the tradition of contracting for only a year at a time, a practice which definitely discouraged croppers from expending energy on long-term improvements.

Even more detrimental to the freedmen's economic progress, Ransom and Sutch (1977) argued, was their reliance on credit secured by crop liens granted to rural storekeepers. Credit had always been indispensable to southern farmers, but in the aftermath of the Civil War, they contended, crossroads merchants developed a territorial monopoly that allowed them to charge exorbitant interest rates to the former slaves. These merchants, who were thinking in terms of exploiting powerless customers more than of abusing freedmen *per se*, demanded that their clients grow cotton as collateral for the supplies that they furnished. The result, the authors maintained, was that freedmen found themselves in perpetual debt to rural merchants and effectively "locked in" to the economically irrational "overproduction" of cotton during a time of falling prices (Ransom and Sutch 1977: 162). Despite these significant deterrents, Ransom and Sutch maintained, the freedmen still should have saved enough money over time to acquire significant amounts of land. That the freedmen remained largely landless they attributed to whites' racist determination to prevent the former slaves from gaining the degree of independence that land-ownership made possible.

One Kind of Freedom sparked a lively debate that proved, if nothing else, that economists could disagree as passionately among themselves as they did with historians. Even before its publication, a number of econometricians had been constructing a view of the postbellum southern economy that contradicted that of Ransom and Sutch in numerous crucial respects. Their far more positive view was best represented by the work of Robert Higgs, whose book *Competition and Coercion* (1977) was published in the same year as *One Kind of Freedom*. As the book's title was intended to suggest, Higgs interpreted the economic history of the freedmen "as an interplay of two systems of behavior: a competitive economic system and a coercive racial system" (Higgs 1977: 13). While acknowledging the presence of extensive racism among southern whites, he argued that such racism was primarily manifested in non-market social and political contexts. In the economic sphere, on the other hand, the free interplay of competitive forces made discrimination costly and minimized its incidence. Higgs maintained that the expansion of sharecropping during Reconstruction was not simply the outcome of a racist compromise; rather, it made good sense from an economic point of view. In a cash-poor economy, the arrangement was a creative means of bringing together land and labor. Because of their flexibility, share agreements were "easily altered to suit the varying demands of landlords and tenants" (Higgs 1977: 47), and they also distributed risk more evenly than either cash wages or fixed-rent tenancy, an important feature at a time when agricultural conditions were volatile. Thus blacks as well as whites benefited from the expansion of sharecropping and tenancy. For the freedmen specifically, the development meant not only greater independence from white supervision but also markedly higher incomes.

Higgs acknowledged that rural merchants frequently charged extremely high interest rates, but he denied that they typically wielded true monopoly power over freedmen and attributed high interest rates to the scarcity of credit and the high risks involved in renting to impoverished, highly mobile agricultural producers. While conceding that the average black household "remained desperately poor" by modern standards, he calculated that real per capita income among southern blacks rose 2.7 percent annually between the end of the Civil War and the close of the nineteenth century, a rate well above the national average of 2 percent. (Critics noted that the absolute difference between average black and white incomes continued to grow substantially.) Black land accumulation was neither rapid nor extensive, Higgs admitted, but this reflected the overwhelming poverty of the recently freed slaves more than active racial discrimination in the land market. Indeed, Higgs concluded, "considering the circumstances surrounding their enslavement and emancipation, one might well marvel that the freedmen did so well" (Higgs 1977: 117, 61).

After sufficient time to digest its most controversial assertions, numerous other scholars responded directly to *One Kind of Freedom*. Within a year a scholarly symposium was held at Duke University to provide a forum for critical assessment, and econometricians used the opportunity to contest the book's arguments concerning the origins of sharecropping, the extent of the alleged territorial monopoly enjoyed by country storekeepers, and the importance of racism as a deterrent to black economic progress. Numerous economists continued to modify or refine the book's chief assertions, but only Gavin Wright and Gerald D. Jaynes joined Higgs in offering comprehensive, book-length interpretations.

Gavin Wright acknowledged that the highly personalized credit arrangements that emerged after the war constituted an important source of economic localism that contributed to the isolation of southern labor markets. But in the concluding chapter of *The Political Economy of the Cotton South* (1978), which focused primarily on the antebellum southern economy, and more fully in *Old South, New South* (1986), Wright fashioned an argument that de-emphasized the importance of land tenure and credit mechanisms as causes of black poverty and pointed instead to the changing international demand for cotton, the black-belt's chief staple. Like Ransom and Sutch (1977) and Higgs (1977), Wright maintained that the reorganization of southern labor after the Civil War resulted from a market process, which to an economist implied "that the outcome represented a balance of forces" (Wright 1986: 85). Wright concluded that sharecropping represented a balance between the freedmen's quest for independence and white landowners' desire to control labor. Although these competing desires might have been accommodated by means of a variety of land and labor arrangements, sharecropping offered an additional advantage in that it mitigated the effects of the severe shortage of credit that plagued the postbellum economy.

Wright agreed with Ransom and Sutch that after the war small farmers on the whole increased their production of cotton during a time of falling prices for the

fiber – regularly sacrificing household self-sufficiency in the process – but he disagreed with their assertion that small farmers shifted their resources toward cotton
because they were "locked in" to such a crop choice by merchants who forced them
to do so. On the contrary, Wright argued that both the merchant and the farmer
favored an emphasis on cotton. Because cotton was more predictably marketable
than food crops, merchants viewed cotton as the most reliable collateral for the
supplies that they furnished on credit. Sharecroppers and tenants of both races now
also had a rational incentive to concentrate on the production of cotton relative to
foodstuffs. In the aftermath of emancipation, the South's former masters had evolved
"from laborlords to landlords" (Wright 1986: 17) – a point central to Wright's
analysis – causing them to focus for the first time on maximizing the return to land
rather than the return to labor. They accomplished the former by keeping the plots
of sharecroppers and tenants as small as possible, effectively forcing them to farm
their acreage intensively simply to eke out a living for their families. Because the cash
value of cotton per acre significantly exceeded that for any other crop they might
grow, farmers on such small plots recognized that an emphasis on cotton constituted their best chance of earning sufficient revenue to free them from having to
borrow from the merchant for the next year. They thus concentrated on cotton, a
gamble that might have paid off before the Civil War, but one that was a poor risk
afterwards because of a sharp decline in the world demand for the staple, which had
grown by 5 percent annually before 1860 but by only 1.3 percent per year during
the three decades after 1865. Concerning the freedmen specifically, Wright argued
that despite the prevalence of racial discrimination blacks' low incomes had "much
more to do with their place in the low-wage Southern economy than with overt
forms of oppression and coercion." Probably the single most important cause of
black–white income differentials after emancipation was the federal government's
failure to distribute land among the former slaves. Echoing Higgs, Wright concluded that, all things considered, the former slaves made "remarkable progress" in
accumulating wealth, but "it was not easy to translate this wealth into land ownership unless they were acceptable to the white community." For the freedmen, the
prospects for upward mobility within postbellum agriculture were real, but they
were largely limited to freedmen who "knew their place" (Wright 1986: 12, 101).

A fourth broad overview by an economist emerged during the same year as *Old
South, New South*, but Gerald D. Jaynes' *Branches without Roots* (1986) differed in
crucial respects from the three previously mentioned. Although an economist at
Yale, Jaynes also held an appointment in African American Studies there, and his
research methods revealed an immersion in non-quantitative sources usually slighted
in the econometric literature. Drawing extensively from records of the Freedmen's
Bureau between 1865 and 1868, Jaynes offered compelling evidence that the severe
shortage of cash in the South after the Civil War had forced white landowners to
turn to some form of share system literally from the beginning. The freedmen, as a
result, had the realistic alternative of either share wages (working in gangs or in
squads) or sharecropping (working as families), and chose the latter as preferable.
Their first choice he argued in contradiction to the consensus position, was actually
fixed-cash wages paid at regular intervals, a system that allowed greater movement
during the crop year and was less susceptible to fraudulent manipulation by employers.
Like Ransom and Sutch (1977), Jaynes found the crop-lien system to be a prime

factor in the freedmen's persistent poverty, and he went much further than they in arguing for the prevalence of debt peonage, although he offered no systematic evidence to suggest that black mobility was seriously restricted. Focusing on crop-lien laws passed widely across the former Confederacy near the end of Reconstruction, Jaynes concluded that "no government which allows its laboring population to mortgage its labor by enforcing debt peonage can claim to have free labor" (Jaynes 1986: 314).

With a few exceptions, econometricians have turned their attention away from the Reconstruction era South since the mid-1980s. In 1999, economists and historians gathered a second time for a symposium on *One Kind of Freedom* – this time to reassess the study's persistent salience more than two decades after its publication – but the bibliography of the papers that emerged from the meeting included extremely few citations to recent work by economists (Coclanis 2000; Woodman 2001; Wright 2001). Ransom and Sutch (2001) acknowledged as much in their own published retrospective, admitting that "we have long felt some disappointment that our contribution did not stimulate much cumulative research by economic historians on the period immediately following emancipation." They attributed this to a bad case of "analytic *interruptus*," the penchant of scholars obsessed with innovation and originality to forsake a half-studied topic in order to reap the benefits of investigating other "under-studied" subjects (Ransom and Sutch 2001: 36).

Historians are probably inclined to the same disease, but in this case they have exhibited admirable perseverance, if for no other reason than their desire to rebut the econometricians. Most of the historians writing about the postbellum reorganization of southern labor have been social historians. Although, like the economists, they have typically accepted the basic contours of the "standard scenario" of post-emancipation labor reorganization, differences of ideological orientation and disciplinary method have led them to strikingly different conclusions.

To begin with the most obvious, in contrast to the predominant view among econometricians, social historians have been almost universally predisposed to interpret major historical developments as the outcome of the conflict between social groups rather than the decisions of individually oriented producers. The difference has been manifested most strikingly in the analyses of several historians who employed a Marxist framework. These scholars approached emancipation in the American South as part of a larger global trend toward the ascendancy of capitalist social relations. Within a year of the publication of *One Kind of Freedom*, two influential Marxist studies set forth such an interpretation and concluded that the prewar planter class had successfully preserved their control over labor and, as a result, postponed the triumph of liberal capitalism within the region. In *The Roots of Black Poverty* (1978), Jay R. Mandle attributed the persistent poverty of the former slaves to the survival of a low-wage plantation system after the Civil War. Events during the Reconstruction era demonstrated, in Mandle's view, that the preservation of slavery was not essential to the preservation of the plantation system. Two factors were critical to its survival after emancipation: the failure of the federal government to distribute land among the freedmen, and the severely restricted employment opportunities for blacks in either southern or northern industry, due primarily to discriminatory hiring practices. The result was that, although the former slaves could move freely among agricultural employers, the lack of competitive alternatives meant that blacks in the Cotton South were effectively confined to some form of plantation labor, sharecropping being the most common.

The Roots of Black Poverty was a sweeping interpretive essay built on a thin empirical foundation. In the same year Jonathan M. Wiener published his provocative monograph *Social Origins of the New South* (1978), a close analysis of five counties in the Alabama black-belt, from which he generalized broadly. Reconstruction, Wiener asserted unequivocally, "was the culmination of a bourgeois revolution, a life-or-death struggle over the nature and extent of the nation's transition to modern society" (Wiener 1978: 3). Drawing on evidence from the federal manuscript censuses from before and after the war, Wiener concluded that Alabama's planter class preserved its social position, effectively repelling challenges from rural merchants and Birmingham industrialists and insuring that the South followed a road of economic modernization that would perpetuate their class hegemony. The new social relations of production that evolved in the process were the result of class conflict, not guided by the "invisible hand" of the free market. The shift toward sharecropping "represented a substantial defeat" for the planters, Wiener asserted, because they vastly preferred the gang-labor system; it was not a victory for the freedmen, however, because the arrangement "was established as a repressive system of labor allocation and control" and evolved into a form of "bound" labor. The crop-lien system was instrumental in this regard, Wiener contended without the benefit of systematic evidence, in that it severely limited workers' movement "and came close to abolishing the free market in agricultural labor." Overall, the decentralized trend away from the gang system toward sharecropping "was a move away from a mature capitalist organization of agriculture" (Wiener 1978: 69, 108, 70).

More commonly, historians writing from a Marxist perspective have viewed emancipation as the precipitating factor in the South's transition from a precapitalist to a capitalist society, while granting that the system that developed there was a peculiar form of capitalism. (The characterization of the antebellum South as precapitalist has been hotly debated, but most social historians investigating the effects of emancipation have defined capitalism in such a way that it requires a free-labor system, which makes the identification of the Old South as precapitalist a truism.) Like Mandle (1978) and Wiener (1978), they stress that class conflict was at the heart of the evolution of the labor system in the southern countryside, and they find it most fruitful to conceive of the Reconstruction era as the historical moment during which former masters became employers and former slaves became wage laborers. Barbara J. Fields (1985), Joseph P. Reidy (1992), and Julie Saville (1994) each made this argument explicitly in focused studies of particular southern regions. Concentrating on Maryland, Georgia, and South Carolina respectively, each maintained that the freedmen rapidly developed into a rural proletariat of landless workers who sold their labor as a commodity in the marketplace.

Whether Marxist or non-Marxist in their approach, social historians have been almost universal in rejecting econometricians' common portrayal of white and black southerners as guided by a bourgeois preoccupation with the rational pursuit of economic self-interest. Almost all have maintained that slavery imbued slaves with a preindustrial mentality inconsistent with free-labor ideology, and most have further contended that large numbers of masters as well as nonslaveholding whites were similarly affected. The consensus is that emancipation necessitated a difficult process of ideological adaptation for both races, but the timing and extent of this adaptation has been a subject of disagreement. At one extreme is the view that the freedmen stubbornly resisted bourgeois values throughout the postbellum period. In *Slavery and Freedom on the Middle Ground* (1985), Fields was openly contemptuous of economists' assumption that the major actors in the postbellum countryside all belonged to the "species *homo economicus.*" Slavery was a poor training ground for the development of capitalist social relations, she argued forcefully, and neither race "automatically assumed the habits of thought and conduct appropriate to a system of labor disciplined by the marketplace." Even if freedmen did appear to seek out employment opportunities that offered the greatest material return, they typically did so, Fields maintained, not to maximize their income – as the "pet fiction of the political economists" would suggest – but rather to shorten the amount of time they would have to work for others (Fields 1985: 165, 157, 163). In her study of the transition to freedom in South Carolina, *The Work of Reconstruction* (1994), Saville offered a similar assessment of the former slaves' mentality. The freedpeople of South Carolina were engaged in a "dual struggle" after emancipation, Saville posited, striving to resist both the attempted domination of their former masters and the "discipline of an abstract market" that the Freedmen's Bureau hoped to impose. In sum, they found the northern brand of free labor as objectionable as southern slavery, and according to Saville, in resisting both they "were fashioning a corporate identity advanced in comparison with other American agricultural workers of the time" (Saville 1994: 150). As Saville described them, South Carolina's former slaves were in the vanguard of nineteenth-century agrarian radicalism. Jeffrey R. Kerr-Ritchie (1999) echoed this assessment in his study of the transition from slavery to freedom in the tobacco-producing regions of Virginia. The freedpeople's "emancipatory aspirations" were incompatible with the bourgeois vision of free-market competition espoused by the Freedmen's Bureau in Virginia, according to Kerr-Ritchie. Whereas Bureau agents tended to view free labor "as only the freedom to labor as opposed to labor's freedom," the former slaves "insist[ed] on reconstructing emancipation in their own image" (Kerr-Ritchie 1999: 84, 91).

In contrast, a number of historians have described the process of ideological adaptation to the marketplace as relatively rapid and pervasive. Three studies of Louisiana exemplify this perspective. In his study of the rich cotton plantations of the Natchez District, Michael Wayne (1983) intimated that "the road to the New South plantation ran through the marketplace." Although "neither the gentry nor the former slaves evidenced much of what might be termed a market consciousness" immediately after the Civil War, the freedmen rather quickly learned how to take advantage of a severe labor shortage to exact significant concessions from the planters, who almost in spite of themselves began to abandon paternalism in favor of market incentives (Wayne 1983: 149, 200). In another study of the same area, Ronald L. F. Davis (1982) found that the freedmen effectively wielded considerable economic power during Reconstruction, although their goals were not necessarily strictly economic. Davis averred that the former slaves in the Natchez District resisted a gang-labor wage system for two reasons: a determination to distance themselves from white supervision, and the desire to reap more of the benefits of the high price of cotton during the early postbellum years. However complex the freedmen's motives, their former masters were literally powerless to resist them and "had no choice in the matter." It was the freedmen who imposed sharecropping on white landowners – rather than the other way around – for "planters literally were dragged kicking and screaming into the system" (Davis 1982: 190). In his study of Louisiana's sugar parishes, John C. Rodrigue (2001) has maintained that freedmen working in the cane fields understood that the unique demands of harvesting and processing sugar cane made a large, centralized labor force imperative, and they were apparently quite willing to forgo the greater independence of sharecropping or tenancy in exchange for the unusually high wages that experienced sugar workers could command. Historians investigating other sections of the postbellum South have reached similar conclusions. Numerous scholars would now assert that, whatever their ultimate objectives, the freedpeople quickly learned to use their market power to their benefit, whether in securing higher compensation, increasing familial autonomy, or securing access to education.

The common thread in all these studies is an emphasis on the ability of the freedmen, in the face of enormous obstacles, to play an active role in defining the shape of freedom. Whereas the former slaves all too often seemed little more than "exogenous variables" in the major econometric studies, a hallmark of historians' analyses since the early 1980s has been the stress on black "agency." To cite the most obvious example, by the mid-1980s the view that the freedmen were primarily responsible for the rise of sharecropping had become an unassailable dogma. Historians have emphasized black agency in other respects, as well. In a meticulous survey of black property-ownership, Loren Schweninger (1990) documented statistically the impressive extent of land acquisition among former slaves. By 1900 fully one-quarter of black farm operators owned their own farms. More effectively than Schweninger's statistical overview, case studies such as Sharon Ann Holt's *Making Freedom Pay* (2000) illustrate the heroic efforts of the freedmen to acquire land and the immense personal significance that they attached to their success. Focusing on "the story of how freed people made a freedom for themselves," she placed great emphasis on the former slaves' household production – the production of foodstuffs and homemade clothing, in particular (Holt 2000: xv). Such production yielded valuable income without attracting the attention of potentially hostile whites, she maintained, while at the same time assisting the freedpeople in promoting vital community institutions such as churches and schools.

Two other themes in various studies dovetail with the current emphasis on black agency. Since the early 1990s, scholars have closely scrutinized the interrelationship between freedpeople's political activism and their struggle to exercise control over their working lives. Rather than relegating politics to a separate realm of "non-market" activities, they have insisted that the reorganization of agricultural labor after emancipation was inseparable from the political context that framed it. The line between marketplace and polling place was blurred. Freedpeople sought political power in part to protect themselves from economic exploitation; white landlords and employers used their control over labor as a weapon in elections. According to Saville (1994), local political mobilization was an important part of the efforts of South Carolina blacks "to construct from the wrecked remains of slavery a life and labor worthy of free people." The former slaves formed Republican clubs and "loyal leagues" not merely to further a political party but to give expression to a burgeoning social movement bent on redefining the relations between labor and capital.

"Electoral politics was a component of, not an alternative to social struggles", Saville concluded (1994: 7, 183). Coming at the same interrelationship from a different angle, a study of the Union League in Alabama and Mississippi (Fitzgerald 1989) argued that the political agenda of that short-lived organization was inseparable from the freedpeople's pursuit of social and economic independence. Other historians have called attention to a probable correlation between labor forms and the effectiveness of black political mobilization. In his study of a black-belt county in Georgia, Jonathan M. Bryant (1996) repeated the common emphasis on black agency – "landowners may not have liked the new system of sharecropping and tenancy, but they were forced to accept it by their laborers" – but he further noted the irony that this "victory" may have had adverse political consequences for the freedmen. The defining feature of the shift toward sharecropping was decentralization, which meant, among many things, that the freedmen became less concentrated spatially. This trend, according to Bryant, undermined "the physical and psychological unity" of local black communities (Bryant 1996: 152, 153). Building on this insight, John Rodrigue (2001) argued that the impressive and enduring political mobilization of freedmen in the Louisiana sugar parishes had much to do with the survival of the gang system there throughout Reconstruction and beyond. While the sharecropping system scattered workers and impeded collective political efforts in much of the Cotton South, in the cane fields the "centralized plantation regimen provided a solid foundation for black grassroots activity" (Rodrigue 2001: 78).

The stress on black agency is also evident in historians' increasing attention to the role played by freed*women* in the reorganization of southern labor. Well into the 1980s, scholars typically retold the story of the transition from slavery to freedom as if black women had not been involved. Ransom and Sutch (1977) had pinpointed the widespread withdrawal of black women from field labor as a crucial contributor to declining agricultural output after emancipation, but they had done nothing to explore women's underlying motives. Indeed, black women are essentially invisible in *One Kind of Freedom*. Jacqueline Jones (1985) was the first historian to investigate the behavior of freedwomen after emancipation in any depth. In *Labor of Love, Labor of Sorrow* (1985), she followed the efforts of freedwomen to gain control over their productive and reproductive lives and to further the interests of themselves and their families. "Only at home," Jones concluded, could black women "exercise considerable control over their own lives and those of their husbands and children and impose a semblance of order on the physical world" (Jones 1985: 58). Focusing specifically on the lowcountry of South Carolina, Leslie A. Schwalm (1997) vividly portrayed the active part that freedwomen played in resisting planters' efforts to reimpose control over black labor during the early years of Reconstruction. When long-absent planters returned to reclaim their plantations at the war's end, black women were often at the forefront of efforts by angry freedpeople to repulse their former masters and protect the property they deemed as rightfully theirs. Anticipating the emphasis of Sharon Ann Holt (2000), she stressed the crucial economic contribution of women's household production. In a similar vein, Tera Hunter (1997) documented the determination of black female domestic servants to redraw the boundaries of obligation within the white households that employed them. Black cooks, laundresses, and nurses used their willingness to leave abusive employers to procure higher wages and a less demanding workload. Finally, studies of South

Carolina, Georgia, Virginia, and Louisiana each attest to freedwomen's crucial role in furthering black political activism, taking note of their highly visible presence at political rallies as well as at polling places on election day, where they helped to insure that the men in their communities cast their ballots with the best interests of the freedpeople in mind (Saville 1994; Bryant 1996; Kerr-Ritchie 1999; Rodrigue 2001).

The prevailing emphasis on black agency in recent scholarship serves to highlight a glaring weakness in the work of both economists and historians on postbellum southern labor. The majority of tenants in the Reconstruction South were white, not black. While knowledge of the behavior and mentality of the former slaves has increased significantly over the last generation, and scholars have long paid considerable attention to the experience of white planters, they still know comparatively little about the largest population group in the southern countryside – middling and poor whites who had not been slaveowners before the war. Unlike wealthy planters, white yeomen did not typically leave behind extensive diaries or detailed plantation accounts that reveal their role in the reorganization of rural labor; unlike the former slaves, no government agency such as the Freedmen's Bureau recorded copious observations about their behavior and experiences. As a result, much of the evidence about the economic experience of middling whites during Reconstruction is statistical in nature, primarily information drawn from the federal agricultural censuses for 1860 and 1880. These demonstrate beyond doubt that white producers on small farms on the periphery of the cotton belt shifted heavily away from food production toward cotton after the Civil War. Predictably, large numbers ceased to be able to feed their own families without purchasing foodstuffs. How and why this occurred, however, as well as what the trend reveals about the mentality of rural yeomen, are controversial questions. Census statistics also make clear that the tenancy rate among whites increased sharply between the Civil War and the end of the nineteenth century, prompting numerous historians to speculate that white smallholders frequently "fell" into tenancy in the decades after emancipation. There are other feasible explanations for this statistical trend, however, and the underlying cause of the pattern is still very much in question.

Unquestionably, the single most influential book to treat the postwar fate of non-elite whites has been Steven Hahn's *The Roots of Southern Populism* (1983). Hahn's study centered on two counties in Georgia's Upper Piedmont, an area on the northern fringe of the cotton belt prior to the Civil War. Upcountry yeomen, according to Hahn, focused on self-sufficiency and household reproduction rather than wealth accumulation *per se*, and "kinship rather than the marketplace mediated most productive relations." White farmers produced most of what they consumed, and to the extent that they produced a surplus for commercial exchange, "the market served their interests rather than dominated their lives." All this changed, Hahn contended, as a result of the cruel devastation visited upon the region during the war. Invariably plagued by mounting debts, small farmers grew more and more cotton, a strategy made more viable by the growing availability of commercial fertilizers and improved railroad connections with the upcountry. The result was tragic, for with the loss of self-sufficiency white producers rapidly found themselves at the mercy of the rural merchants who extended them credit while reducing them to "a position tantamount to debt peonage." One result was the transformation of agricultural tenancy, which before the war had been a rung on an agricultural ladder to farm ownership and independence, but which after the war became more commonly a "path of proletarianization." A second consequence was an all too frequent descent of antebellum landholders into the ranks of the landless, "as the auction block increasingly became the resort for the hopelessly indebted" (Hahn 1983: 29, 39, 162, 186, 197). Echoing the argument of a provocative essay by Forrest McDonald and Grady McWhiney (1980), Hahn maintained that the plight of the yeomen was further exacerbated in the 1880s by a series of local fencing laws that effectively ended the open range for livestock grazing and cemented their economic subservience.

At the present time, Hahn's study remains the most detailed treatment by a historian of the place of middling whites in the postbellum reorganization of agriculture, and his conclusions are widely accepted in textbook treatments of the period. And yet critics – mostly economic historians – noted immediately that the evidence Hahn presented was consistent with an entirely different set of conclusions. Econometrician David F. Weiman (1983) contested Hahn's central assertions concerning the mentality of upcountry petty producers. Weiman observed that the shift toward cotton production in the Georgia Piedmont had not occurred until after 1870, about the time that the greater development of railroads and marketing centers in the region made such a commercial orientation feasible. Whereas Hahn argued that the minimal production of cotton in the upcountry before the Civil War reflected a pre-bourgeois mentality, Weiman maintained that it resulted from the area's geographical isolation from major markets. The mentality of the upcountry's "petty commodity producers" had always combined a "bourgeois ethic of private accumulation with traditional communal and family values," but they had been "confined" to the periphery of the cotton economy before the Civil War by the lack of an adequate transportation and marketing network (Weiman 1983: 442). More recently, historian J. William Harris (1994) employed a longitudinal analysis that traced individual Piedmont farm operators across time. Harris found that relatively few producers significantly modified their relative emphasis on cotton and foodstuffs between 1860 and 1880, suggesting the likely possibility that the sharp rise in cotton production in the Georgia upcountry did not occur because formerly self-sufficient farmers shifted markedly toward cotton, but rather reflected the crop choices of "new" farm operators, that is of owners and tenants who had first entered the ranks of farm operators after the Civil War.

Longitudinal analysis can similarly yield light on the contention that large numbers of farm-owners lost their farms and fell into tenancy after the Civil War. Basing his argument on rising tenancy rates, Hahn had concluded that "the Upcountry was fast becoming a territory of the dispossessed" (Hahn 1983: 168). Gavin Wright (1986), however, speculated that dispossession was less to blame for the increase in white tenancy than a decline in opportunities for young farmers to acquire land. I tested this hypothesis by tracing individual farmers from eight Tennessee counties across the 1850s, 1860s, and 1870s. In these sample counties (which spanned from the Appalachian Mountains to the Mississippi River), farm-owners did lose their farms with slightly greater frequency after 1860, as Hahn's argument would suggest, but landless farmers also found it more difficult to acquire farms, a finding consistent with Wright's hypothesis. Both trends contributed to an increase in the tenancy rate among white farmers. I also discovered a changing pattern of in- and out-migration in west Tennessee's plantation counties. No longer required to compete against slave labor, landless whites from other regions moved in greater numbers to the cotton belt after emancipation, whereas white tenants and laborers already living there were less likely to move away. This new pattern also had the effect of increasing the tenancy rate, although ironically the trend resulted from a more positive perception of economic opportunity in the area. Finally, I found that the single greatest cause of increasing white tenancy resulted from a development that neither Hahn nor Wright anticipated, namely a dramatic shift among landless whites from wage labor to tenancy. Historians have traditionally assumed that white farm laborers were rare in the antebellum South (not counting the landless sons of small landowners who were living and working at home). Tennessee Civil War veterans interviewed in their old age often referred to its importance in the prewar era, however. In Tennessee, at least, emancipation seems to have created significant opportunities for white farm laborers to become tenants. Given that former masters widely viewed free black labor as inherently unreliable, white farm laborers may have been able to exercise a degree of leverage in the labor market that they had not enjoyed before the Civil War. Whatever the reason, they moved into tenancy in far greater numbers than did former slaves, at least until after 1880 (McKenzie 1994, 1995). Scholars have not searched for such a shift in other regions of the postbellum South, although if present, such a trend could do much to explain not only the increase in white tenancy after 1865 but also the apparent reorientation of white producers in upcountry areas toward production for the market.

The period since the late 1970s has yielded a rich scholarly literature on the reorganization of southern labor during Reconstruction. With very little to build on, given the minimal interest in the topic prior to the 1970s, scholars have explored the process with energy and insight and have forged a much fuller understanding of the crucial aftermath of slavery in the southern countryside. They are still far from agreeing on numerous fundamental questions, however. What did the evolution of new labor arrangements reveal about class and racial dynamics and the realities of power in the postbellum South? How did the process reflect the ideological values or mentality of both former slaves and former masters? What did the reorganization of southern agriculture mean for poor and middling whites who had never owned slaves? The field remains dynamic and constructively contentious, and after a quarter-century of intensive investigation very few important questions can be considered as resolved.

BIBLIOGRAPHY

Bryant, Jonathan M. (1996) *How Curious a Land: Conflict and Change in Greene County, Georgia, 1850–1885*. Chapel Hill, NC: University of North Carolina Press.

Burton, Orville Vernon (1998) "African American Status and Identity in a Postbellum Community: An Analysis of the Manuscript Census Returns," *Agricultural History* 72: 213–40.

Carter, Dan T. (1985) *When the War was Over: The Failure of Self-Reconstruction in the South, 1865–1867*. Baton Rouge, La.: Louisiana State University Press.

Coclanis, Peter A. (2000) "In Retrospect: Ransom and Sutch's One Kind of Freedom," *Reviews in American History* 28: 478–89.

Cohen, William (1991) *At Freedom's Edge: Black Mobility and the Southern Quest for Racial Control, 1861–1915*. Baton Rouge, La.: Louisiana State University Press.

Davis, Ronald L. F. (1982) *Good and Faithful Labor: From Slavery to Sharecropping in the Natchez District, 1860–1890*. Westport, Conn.: Greenwood.

DuBois, W. E. B. (1935) *Black Reconstruction: An Essay toward a History of the Part which Black Folk Played in the Attempt to Reconstruct Democracy 1860–1880*. New York: Harcourt Brace.

Fields, Barbara Jeanne (1985) *Slavery and Freedom on the Middle Ground: Maryland during the Nineteenth Century*. New Haven, Conn.: Yale University Press.

Fitzgerald, Michael W. (1989) *The Union League Movement in the Deep South: Politics and Agricultural Change during Reconstruction*. Baton Rouge, La.: Louisiana State University Press.

Foner, Eric (1983) *Nothing but Freedom: Emancipation and its Legacy*. Baton Rouge, La.: Louisiana State University Press.

Hahn, Steven (1983) *The Roots of Southern Populism: Yeomen Farmers and the Transformation of the Georgia Upcountry, 1850–1890*. New York: Oxford University Press.

Harris, J. William (1994) "Crop Choices in the Piedmont before and after the Civil War," *Journal of Economic History* 54: 526–42.

Higgs, Robert (1977) *Competition and Coercion: Blacks in the American Economy, 1865–1914*. New York: Cambridge University Press.

Holt, Sharon Ann (2000) *Making Freedom Pay: North Carolina Freed People Working for Themselves, 1865–1900*. Athens, Ga.: University of Georgia Press.

Hunter, Tera W. (1997) *To 'Joy my Freedom: Southern Black Women's Lives and Labors after the Civil War*. Cambridge, Mass.: Harvard University Press.

Irwin, James R. and O'Brien, Anthony Patrick (1998) "Where Have All the Sharecroppers Gone? Black Occupations in Postbellum Mississippi," *Agricultural History* 72: 280–97.

Jaynes, Gerald David (1986) *Branches without Roots: The Genesis of the Black Working Class in the American South, 1862–1882*. New York: Oxford University Press.

Jones, Jacqueline (1985) *Labor of Love, Labor of Sorrow: Black Women, Work, and the Family from Slavery to the Present*. New York: Basic Books.

Kerr-Ritchie, Jeffrey R. (1999) *Freed People in the Tobacco South: Virginia, 1860–1900*. Chapel Hill, NC: University of North Carolina Press.

Litwack, Leon F. (1979) *Been in the Storm So Long: The Aftermath of Slavery*. New York: Alfred A. Knopf.

McDonald, Forrest and McWhiney, Grady (1980) "The South from Self-Sufficiency to Peonage: An Interpretation," *American Historical Review* 85: 1095–118.

McKenzie, Robert Tracy (1994) *One South or Many? Plantation Belt and Upcountry in Civil-War Era Tennessee*. New York: Cambridge University Press.

McKenzie, Robert Tracy (1995) "Rediscovering the 'Farmless' Farm Population: The Nineteenth-Century Census and the Postbellum Reorganization of Agriculture in the US South, 1860–1900," *Histoire Sociale* 28: 501–20.

Mandle, Jay R. (1978) *The Roots of Black Poverty: The Southern Plantation Economy after the Civil War*. Durham, NC: Duke University Press.

Ransom, Roger L. and Sutch, Richard (1977) *One Kind of Freedom: The Economic Consequences of Emancipation*. Cambridge: Cambridge University Press.

Ransom, Roger L. and Sutch, Richard (2001) "*One Kind of Freedom*: Reconsidered (and Turbo Charged)," *Explorations in Economic History* 38: 6–39.

Reidy, Joseph P. (1992) *From Slavery to Agrarian Capitalism in the Cotton Plantation South: Central Georgia, 1800–1880*. Chapel Hill, NC: University of North Carolina Press.

Roark, James L. (1977) *Masters without Slaves: Southern Planters in the Civil War and Reconstruction*. New York: Norton.

Rodrigue, John C. (2001) *Reconstruction in the Cane Fields: From Slavery to Free Labor in Louisiana's Sugar Parishes, 1862–1880*. Baton Rouge, La.: Louisiana State University Press.

Royce, Edward (1993) *The Origins of Southern Sharecropping*. Philadelphia, Pa.: Temple University Press.

Saville, Julie (1994) *The Work of Reconstruction: From Slave to Wage Laborer in South Carolina, 1860–1870*. New York: Cambridge University Press.

Schlomowitz, Ralph (1979) "The Transition from Slave to Freedman: Labor Arrangements in Southern Agriculture," unpublished PhD dissertation, University of Chicago.

Schwalm, Leslie A. (1997) *A Hard Fight for We: Women's Transition from Slavery to Freedom in South Carolina*. Urbana, Ill.: University of Illinois Press.

Schweninger, Loren (1990) *Black Property Owners in the South, 1790–1915*. Urbana, Ill.: University of Illinois Press.

Wayne, Michael (1983) *The Reshaping of Plantation Society: The Natchez District, 1860–1880*. Baton Rouge, La.: Louisiana State University Press.

Weiman, David F. (1983) "Petty Commodity Production in the Cotton South: Upcountry Farmers in the Georgia Cotton Economy, 1840–1880," unpublished PhD dissertation, Stanford University.

Wiener, Jonathan M. (1978) *Social Origins of the New South: Alabama, 1860–1885*. Baton Rouge, La.: Louisiana State University Press.

Woodman, Harold D. (1995) *New South – New Law: The Legal Foundations of Credit and Labor Relations in the Postbellum Agricultural South*. Baton Rouge, La.: Louisiana State University Press.

Woodman, Harold D. (2001) "*One Kind of Freedom* after 20 Years," *Explorations in Economic History* 38: 48–57.

Wright, Gavin (1978) *The Political Economy of the Cotton South: Households, Markets, and Wealth in the Nineteenth Century*. New York: Norton.

Wright, Gavin (1986) *Old South, New South: Revolutions in the Southern Economy since the Civil War*. New York: Basic Books.

Wright, Gavin (2001) "Reflections on *One Kind of Freedom* and the Southern Economy," *Explorations in Economic History* 38: 40–7.

CHAPTER TWENTY

Northern Women during the Age of Emancipation

NINA SILBER

Historians, by and large, thrive on watersheds. So, it should not be surprising that they, and their readers, have shown a voracious appetite for the drama of the Civil War. The wartime and postwar years clearly marked a turning point for, among other things, the permanence of the national union, America's dependence on racial slavery, and the political and economic fortunes of the American South. The Reconstruction period, dating from wartime policies on slave liberation through the official pronouncements and reorganizations of the postwar years, was indeed an "age of emancipation" for the 4 million black men and women who had been the south's enslaved labor force. Whether this was, likewise, an "age of emancipation," or even a significant turning point, for the women of the northern states is a question that is not nearly so clear cut.

There were, of course, some obvious readjustments which wartime circumstances imposed. With hundreds of thousands of men departing for southern battlefields, women throughout the North stepped in to assume expanded breadwinning roles. Because most northerners, including most northern soldiers, were employed in agricultural pursuits, some of the keenest burdens were felt by women on farms. "Women," observed Civil War relief worker Mary Livermore, "were in the field everywhere, driving the reapers, binding and shocking, and loading grain, until then an unusual sight" (Livermore 1888: 146). Women's contributions to farm life had always been essential but their work, prior to this, had been more invisible: milking, washing, gardening, and cooking (Paludan 1988: 157). Now, they spent their time in the direct production of marketable commodities, and so their work seemed ever more vital to sustaining American agriculture.

Women on farms, as well as in cities, learned to juggle family finances, negotiate monetary transactions with neighbors, handle mortgage and other payments, and figure out how to make ends meet. Few found it easy to manage on the scant wages earned – and then forwarded to them – by their men in the military. In some states and cities, wives and mothers could draw upon public relief funds established for the benefit of soldiers' families (Gallman 1994: 83). Many women did extra sewing in order to bring in more income. Some sought work in factories where wartime circumstances expanded employment opportunities for both men and women.

During the war years, women held about one-third of all manufacturing jobs, up from one-quarter in 1860, a modest but significant gain. The new jobs, however, were generally in traditional female occupations such as shoemaking and textiles, occupations where wages had always been low and where unscrupulous wartime contractors often depressed the wage levels even lower (Gallman 1994: 105). In fact, the increased competition from so many sewing women seeking work in these years gradually reduced the amount of work, and the wages, for female seamstresses (Sigerman 2000b: 281).

Still, there were a few new economic doors that opened for women in the wartime years. Perhaps most noteworthy, in this regard, was civil service work. Hundreds of women got jobs in the Treasury Department and the Post Office, thus creating a new venue for female employment that would continue, and increase, in the postwar period. Much of this was due to wartime changes in fiscal policy that created a demand for an expanded office staff (Massey 1966: 132–3). Women's entry into government work was hardly smooth; rumors often spread regarding the alleged promiscuity of the "government girls." In 1864, in fact, scandal rocked the US Treasury Department when one New York Congressman, apparently intent on discrediting a Treasury Department official, maliciously asserted that this branch of government had become "a house for orgies and bacchanals" (Massey 1966: 137). A long-drawn-out investigation ensued, only to prove the charges unfounded, while also damaging the careers of several female employees.

Despite the allegations, evidence does suggest that northern society, more so than the South, offered greater employment opportunities to women in the wartime and postwar years. In part this was due, no doubt, to the North's greater reliance on industry. But the employment discrepancy also spoke to northerners' greater tolerance for women in public roles. Northern women, for example, could be found more often on the lecture platform, even speaking on subjects that were intensely controversial and highly partisan. The young Philadelphian Anna Dickinson became one of the most famous, and well-paid, lecturers of the period, speaking throughout the North on how the war had been and should be fought. She seldom shied away from biting political commentary and even stumped for Republican candidates in Connecticut and New Hampshire in the spring of 1863. Although Dickinson was critical of the Republican reluctance to pursue slave emancipation, many nonetheless believe that she swung the tide for the Republican party in those electoral campaigns. Having established her reputation in the Civil War years, Dickinson continued her career as a political orator during Reconstruction.

For other northern women who, like Dickinson, had been dedicated abolitionists, war and Reconstruction opened up unique opportunities for aiding the former slaves. As parts of the Confederacy came under Union occupation, a whole new field of labor became available for women: as teachers and missionaries to southern blacks. The teachers were mostly young white women, although some African American women came as well. They generally made less than male teachers, but many women nonetheless committed themselves to difficult circumstances in strange surroundings. Northern women endured abuse and hostility – from both male co-workers and local southern whites – but persevered in teaching their students basic literacy skills, as well as lessons in punctuality, attire, and housekeeping. When the war ended, some of the wartime teachers remained at their posts while new ones remained South to take part in the Reconstruction experiment. By 1869, some 9,000 educators had worked as teachers for the former slaves (Sigerman 2000b: 301), and were scorned by local whites as "Yankee schoolmarms."

Like northern society more generally, women in the North were divided in their political loyalties and their views of the war effort. With the war placing a new premium on displaying one's viewpoints, northern women found many opportunities to make their views heard. Women in New York and other northern cities rioted against the draft laws and decried the inequities of wartime conscription. Women in border regions were, on occasion, pressed into taking loyalty oaths to prove their patriotic allegiance. Seamstresses in Philadelphia and Cincinnati sent public petitions to President Lincoln proclaiming their loyalty to the Union but challenging the unscrupulous subcontracting system which had depressed their incomes (Paludan 1988: 183; Gallman 1994: 106).

Unionist women from the middle and upper classes also wrote and spoke on behalf of the war effort, while those who were less inclined to public pronouncements offered various skills and services to aid the soldiers. Several thousand tried their hand at nursing before the war ended. Some worked under the auspices of the US Army Bureau established for female nurses by the antebellum reformer Dorothea Dix. Anxious to discourage youthful romantics, and concerned, too, to have her nurses taken seriously, Dix recruited only women who were older and "plain in appearance" (Massey 1966: 46–7). Others – including some, no doubt, who were loath to meet Dix's standards – worked as nurses through private relief agencies like the United States Sanitary Commission and the United States Christian Commission. Again, northern women seemed to face fewer obstacles than their southern sisters in gaining acceptance in this not-yet-feminized profession, even to the point of working in dangerous southern outposts near where the battles raged. Working independently of the commissions and Dorothea Dix, Clara Barton nursed the wounded right on the battlefields in Maryland and Virginia. The example set by Barton and others during the war helped pave the way for expanded training and job opportunities for women nurses in the postwar years.

Far more numerous than the few thousand who became nurses, though, were the tens of thousands of northern women who became part of a highly organized home front relief operation. Filling in the gaps where government did not yet reach, women in small towns and larger cities formed a vast network of "ladies' aid" societies throughout the North in which they sewed and knit for absent soldiers, rolled bandages for army hospitals, and packed countless boxes with food and supplies for the men in camp. Women in these ubiquitous relief societies gave one another emotional support and encouragement, and became educated in the ways of organization-building and political leadership. In the later years of the war, they became especially adept at fundraising, organizing a series of Sanitary Fairs that occurred in cities throughout the North. Selling everything from food to war relics to handmade pincushions, the women behind these Sanitary Fairs ultimately raised $4.4 million for the Union war effort (Gallman 1994: 171).

Yet, while significant changes occurred, historians must exercise some caution before judging this "an age of emancipation" for northern women. Women, perhaps, assumed more visible roles in agriculture but significant farming responsibilities were by no means new for most rural northern females. Women, too, occupied a greater number of manufacturing jobs, but they did not generally move into wholly new occupations. Even more, many lost their new positions once the war had ended. After 1865, women again held the same percentage of manufacturing jobs which they occupied before the war began (Gallman 1994: 107). In addition, the soldier relief efforts – vast as they were – were not completely new venues for many Yankee ladies. Middle- and upper-class northern women had already committed themselves to the work of voluntary benevolence, long before the first soldiers' aid societies came into existence. Indeed, the whole field of benevolent work – including charitable endeavors, abolitionism, and missionary activity – had long been sanctioned as a distinctly feminine, and thus morally uplifting, enterprise.

And then, there were countless northern families who experienced the war only indirectly. Seldom caught in the war's destructive path, rarely targeted by an occupying enemy, northern women generally did not withstand the dramatic turbulence which the war brought to southern females. Even more, many northern men, more than in the South, never even left home, thereby allowing traditional familial relationships to remain intact. Of the roughly 4.5 million northern men eligible for military service, fewer than one-half saw active service (compared to about three-quarters of eligible southern men). Numerous women kept up their usual routines and activities and only occasionally commented on the war as a distant, albeit noteworthy, series of events.

Finally, consider, too, that the war appears more as a gap than as an instigator for the women's rights movement: 13 years before the war began, northern women had gathered at Seneca Falls to express their own "Declaration of Sentiments," urging lawmakers to recognize and ameliorate women's subordinate status in public life, including their lack of the vote. During the war, women's rights activists organized the Women's Loyal National League in which they worked to secure a constitutional amendment (the Thirteenth) to abolish slavery; they consciously downplayed their own demands for suffrage and political rights. When the war ended, women, in some respects, seemed further than ever from realizing the demands first put forward at Seneca Falls. With most male abolitionists no longer willing to support female suffrage and most Republicans emphasizing suffrage for black men, the women's rights movement emerged from the war disheartened and disorganized. Female political activists ultimately split between those who agreed with the emphasis on black male suffrage and those who insisted on voting rights for women. Given this disorganization, along with the federal government's explicit directive to protect the voting rights of "male" citizens, some might even maintain that women's political rights took a step backward in this extended and complicated "age of emancipation."

Not surprisingly, the scholarly literature on women in the wartime and postwar North has reflected this ambiguous historical record, with historians offering varied assessments of how full or how empty they see this cup of northern women's "emancipation." Few have found evidence for a thorough dismantling of Victorian boundaries or domesticated barriers. Most maintain that the notion of separate spheres – with women assumed to be more suited to private domesticity – survived the war largely intact. Not that the separate spheres ideology held true for all women, as many working-class and black women could hardly be said to be sheltered within the confines of Victorian domesticity. But these exceptions predated the onset of sectional hostilities. The Civil War saw no permanent movement of women into the workforce, or of women into the public sphere, or of masses of women in a pro-suffrage direction.

However, a careful consideration of the literature on northern women in the Civil War and Reconstruction eras does suggest that Victorian boundaries and barriers, if not broken, were bent and reshaped in noteworthy ways. In the course of the sectional conflict, many northern women began to develop new attitudes about themselves and their relationships to homes and families. Even more, many developed new ideas about their civic and political obligations to the nation and the government; perhaps even more significantly, lawmakers and Union officials developed new attitudes about women's accountability to the nation and the government. Finally, we need to realize that as the war exerted subtle changes on northern women's lives, northern women themselves exerted subtle changes on the war. Active and willing participation as nurses, as teachers of freed slaves, and as wartime fundraisers probably made Union women's contributions to their cause more significant than that of their southern sisters for the Confederacy. While, as one scholar argues, southern women may share some responsibility for the Confederate loss, northern women no doubt hastened the Union triumph.

Some of the first acknowledgements of Yankee women's contribution to that Union triumph appeared soon after the war had ended. By 1867, two volumes on the Civil War work of Yankee women had appeared – Frank Moore's *Women of the War* (1866) and Linus P. Brockett and Mary C. Vaughan's *Woman's Work in the Civil War* (1867). Neither work suggested anything revolutionary or transformative about the war's effect on northern women; the goal of these books, in fact, was to do precisely the opposite. Both works took extreme care to present women's warwork in a typically Victorian context. As such, they provide evidence of just how strong the separate spheres ideology remained at the war's conclusion. In celebrating women's patriotic devotion to the Union effort through vignettes of a few dozen women, both books stressed women's selflessness, patience, and high moral character. Women who may have trespassed beyond the domestic sphere in their wartime work were applauded for returning to the home in the Reconstruction years. Few stories were told of women's newly acquired professional skills or political abilities. In the work of Moore (1866) and Brockett and Vaughan (1867), northern women had been heroic and patriotic, yet appropriately demure and reserved in the era of the Civil War.

Historical writings for the next one hundred years did little to alter the image presented in these postwar Victorian renderings. But, by the time of the Civil War's centennial, scholars returned to the subject of women and the war, armed with a new appreciation for female activism and the stifling repercussions of nineteenth-century Victorianism. In this new crop of literature, one of the most significant contributions was Mary Massey's *Bonnet Brigades* (1966). Massey's work, in fact, remains a classic in the field, a standard and exhaustive survey of the work of women, from all walks of life and from all parts of the country, in the years during and immediately after the war. Well-known heroines of the war – Clara Barton, Harriet Beecher Stowe, Louisa May Alcott – parade through the pages of Massey's book, as do countless lesser-known figures. In part, Massey – like many other pioneers in the field of women's history – simply wished to document, and demonstrate, women's vital and constant presence on the Civil War scene. She also assumed that women's emancipation could be measured in terms of even incremental steps taken into the masculine sphere. In this regard, she showed less interest in the typical woman of the period who stayed home and coped with wartime emergencies, and more in those who made a visible mark in public life. While she scrutinized women of both the North and the South, her interest in women's public wartime work generally led her to give more focused attention to females who lived north of the Mason–Dixon line.

Massey gave particular emphasis to increased economic opportunities made possible by the military conflict, including in her discussions the activities of working-class and black women. Here, her message was not that women broke down occupational barriers, but that they made significant inroads into male arenas like government service. She concluded:

> The economic emancipation of women was the most important single factor in her social, intellectual, and political advancement, and the war did more in four years to change her economic status than had been accomplished in any preceding generation. (Massey 1966: 340)

Massey focused on other gains as well, including the small political achievements that women registered in the wartime and postwar years. Despite the setback in the demands for women's suffrage, Massey contended that, in indirect ways, women demonstrated their awareness of and facility for political debate: by gathering petitions for an amendment to end slavery; by writing political tracts on the war; by protesting their subordinate economic status. "Instead of talking about their rights," Massey argued, women "were usurping them under the cloak of patriotism" (Massey 1966: 174).

Because the economic gains were not dramatic, because the campaign for female suffrage was derailed by the postwar demands for black male suffrage, and because there was little public acknowledgement of women's wartime contributions, Massey's women emerged from the war with a decidedly pessimistic outlook about the future. Many were worn out from their long years of toil; others were profoundly discouraged by their lack of progress. The movement for female emancipation appeared to many to be at a dead end. Still, Massey found cause for optimism. The Civil War, she wrote, provided a "springboard from which [women] leaped beyond the circumscribed 'woman's sphere' in that heretofore reserved for men" (Massey 1966: 367). Ultimately, it is hard not to question the basis for Massey's optimism, considered in light of the evidence presented. Northern women were perhaps underpaid and unacknowledged at the war's conclusion but not, at least when much of Massey's evidence is evaluated, "emancipated."

For the next 25 years, scholars churned out volumes on the Civil War and Reconstruction, but with little analysis offered of women's involvement in those efforts. The war remained insulated in a masculine world of soldiering, weaponry, and male camaraderie; at the same time, the one-time villains of the Reconstruction era – the radical Republicans – received new respect in the revisionist tide that swept the historical profession in the 1960s and 1970s. But a new wave of women's historians was beginning to make their own assault on the era of sectional conflict, albeit from a different perspective. Interested in more self-conscious expressions of feminism and the more explicit demands of women's rights activists, these scholars found evidence of women's intellectual liberation in nineteenth-century America. In the work and ideas of leading nineteenth-century suffragists, such as Elizabeth Cady Stanton and Susan B. Anthony, feminist historians saw the roots of some of the political gains achieved by women in the twentieth century. To understand the accomplishments of Stanton and Anthony, these historians inevitably found themselves returning to the Civil War era.

In that era, the women's rights movement underwent a profound transformation, from its formal launch at the 1848 Seneca Falls convention to its ultimate split in the Reconstruction era, between those who supported the constitutional amendments that gave political rights to black men and those who insisted on a renewed campaign for women's right to vote. Some of this terrain was first surveyed by Eleanor Flexner (1959) in her *Century of Struggle*. Two decades later Ellen DuBois (1978) looked more specifically at the years bracketing the Civil War to understand the shifts in the women's suffrage movement. Her goal, she explained in *Feminism and Suffrage*, was not to trace the struggle for winning the vote, but to understand how the movement for the vote advanced the ideas of feminism and liberation among the women of the United States. The vote, she explained, was less important than the movement that women created to attain it. Much of that movement's history was closely bound up with the broader struggles of the Age of Emancipation.

DuBois's (1978) book is not about women and the Civil War. The war itself, in fact, demands only a few paragraphs of DuBois's attention. But DuBois does recognize how closely linked the women's movement was with the causes and struggles of the Civil War and Reconstruction eras, most notably the struggle to end slavery and the campaign to advance black equality. Indeed, as she explains, the campaign for women's rights first took shape amidst the abolitionist uprising of the antebellum era. Northern women responded to the abolitionists' calls for human equality, they learned to organize and agitate for human advancement, and they even came to reject various forms of male leadership in developing their own arguments about the immorality of racial slavery. In the antebellum and wartime years, though, the women's rights campaign took a back-seat to racial emancipation; leading female activists themselves made the cause of ending slavery paramount. But, when the war ended, and the abolitionists now found themselves in a new and more influential relationship with the Republican party, they showed little or no interest in placing the demands for women's rights, especially suffrage, back on the political agenda. The turbulence of the Reconstruction era put renewed attention on the power of suffrage, but most abolitionists and Republicans argued that the suffrage fight must be waged first for the former slaves whose votes were needed to offset the possible resurgence of the Democratic party as a national contender. Only much later, they explained, would it be time for women's right to vote. "Abolitionists' commitment to women's rights," DuBois explained, "was a casualty of their new political strategy and relationship to the Republican party" (DuBois 1978: 59). The defeat became apparent when abolitionists endorsed the language of the Fourteenth Amendment, including the first use of the word "male" in the US constitution. Radical Republicans, so recently celebrated in revisionist Reconstruction writings, took on a far less heroic stature in DuBois's telling of their opportunistic abandonment of female suffrage.

Feminist leaders responded to Republican indifference by attempting various arguments and varied political alliances to bring women's suffrage to the forefront. They broadened the political demands of the Reconstruction era by calling for universal adulthood suffrage. They also, DuBois (1978) found, called special (albeit superficial) attention to the demands of black women, who were seemingly ignored by Republicans' insistence that this was "the Negro's hour." Eventually, though, they sought a more dramatic break with the Republican party; in 1867, Elizabeth Cady Stanton and Susan B. Anthony joined with racists in the Democratic party to push a women's suffrage plank in the Kansas state elections. Most notably, women were beginning to make their own campaign and their own organization central to the work of women's suffrage, without trying to link that work with some other movement. They did seek out allies for their campaign – including Democrats and labor leaders. But ultimately, by the time of the Fifteenth Amendment (which formally granted black men the right to vote), a significant group of women's rights reformers had decided "to shift feminist political demands from the edges of other reform movements to an organized body of women themselves" (DuBois 1978: 164). This shift culminated in the formation of Stanton and Anthony's National Woman Suffrage Association. "The creation of this independent women's movement was the greatest achievement of feminists in the postwar period," wrote DuBois, "and its significance continued to be felt well after Reconstruction and the reform pretensions of the Republican party had passed into history" (DuBois 1978: 164).

But if postwar feminists emerged with greater independence, they also emerged with a more explicit racism. While DuBois recognized this fact, she failed to fully reckon with its ramifications in her enthusiasm for the feminist triumph. Postbellum feminists learned, in particular, to score points for elite white women's demands by denigrating immigrants and people of color. Their attempted alliance with the labor movement, moreover, showed their lack of support for the needs of working women. The "emancipation" of the women's rights movement was thus dramatically offset by the racism and elitisim which now became part and parcel of that movement's historical legacy.

In any event, DuBois made clear a point that many nineteenth-century Americans implicitly understood – that northern women's quest for emancipation had, perhaps inevitably, become linked to the central issues of slavery and racial emancipation which shaped the Civil War era. The links between those two struggles could often be felt through personal actions. The prominent abolitionist and former slave, Frederick Douglass, frequently gave his support to the movement for women's suffrage; prominent feminists had learned their first political lessons in the antebellum abolitionist campaign. As Jacqueline Jones (1980) explained in her *Soldiers of Light and Love*, middle-class northern women pursued a course of liberating themselves from the restrictions of Victorianism when they assumed their own significant parts in the Reconstruction experiment as the teachers of freed slaves.

Like DuBois's *Feminism and Suffrage*, Jacqueline Jones's book is less interested in the specific actions of women during the Civil War, and more interested in the postwar possibilities which wartime politics created for northern women. But, unlike DuBois, Jones looked more critically at the racial, and sometimes racist, thinking which northern women learned to espouse after the war. Jones considered the work of female teachers – primarily those attached to the American Missionary Association

– who went to Georgia in the Reconstruction period. Intrigued by the conflict between northern white values of individualistic uplift and the former slaves' "ethos of mutuality" (Jones 1980: 9), Jones's book provides evidence for some of the ideological ambiguities of the postwar era and some of the "failures" which historians had begun to detect in radical Reconstruction efforts. Northern female teachers, she found, were often insensitive to the particular concerns and dilemmas of former slaves, both male and female. While critical of the government's lack of a humanitarian agenda, the teachers – according to Jones – nonetheless advanced the inequities of the government program. By railing against idleness and by promoting education over civil rights, northern female teachers helped position the freed slaves as second-class citizens. Like DuBois' *Feminism and Suffrage*, *Soldiers of Light and Love* represented a post-revisionist trend which turned a more critical spotlight on radical Reconstruction; Jones' book, however, argued that women as well as men bore some responsibility for the failures of the Reconstruction experiment.

Still, Jones (1980) argued that northern women's educational work in the South did, in some ways, allow them to push at the boundaries of woman's sphere. She noted, for example, the increased sense of professionalism many women gained from their experience and the willingness of some to challenge what seemed to be meddling interference from male officials. She observed, too, how many relished the opportunity to test their own limits for physical and mental endurance. Yet, she also found that female teachers fell back on familiar refrains regarding feminine self-sacrifice and moral uplift which they could use to their own advantage. "The teachers' struggle to assert themselves within the female-missionary-teacher sphere of moral reform," Jones argued, "reveals the strength, as well as flexibility, of role designations based on sex in early Victorian America" (Jones 1980: 8).

Historian Wendy Venet (1991), like DuBois (1978) and Jones (1980), has also pondered some of the personal links between the movements for slave and female emancipation, but she has searched for evidence of feminist strides not in postwar organizing or teaching, but in wartime lecturing and petitioning. In *Neither Ballots nor Bullets* (1991), Venet examines abolitionist women's activities during the Civil War years, looking at lecturers like Anna Dickinson and writers like Harriet Beecher Stowe. She also provides yet another view of Stanton and Anthony. Here they appear as active wartime organiziers who, even as they gathered a record-breaking number of signatures on antislavery petitions, never – Venet maintains – lost sight of women's suffrage. Thus, in Venet's argument, the war provided the momentum and the opportunities which allowed these women to come into their own. "The petitioning, public speaking, and political organizing that Northern women performed during the war," Venet writes, "helped to gain new acceptance for women in the public sphere after the war" (Venet 1991: 161). Women's work in decrying slave oppression and upholding the Union, Venet finds, gave their postwar political campaigns a greater legitimacy.

Women, then, could not vote when the Civil War ended, but their work in this era seems to have advanced the cause of women's emancipation considerably. They built an independent suffrage movement; they honed their political and lecturing skills; they won greater public appreciation for their wartime efforts. Yet perhaps a more revealing indication of women's emancipation might be gained not by evaluating women's public speaking, organizing or professional skills, but by assessing the very idea of emancipation in the Civil War era. Recent historians have shifted the analysis in this direction, finding that most nineteenth-century Americans had an exceedingly limited idea of what they meant by emancipation. In *From Bondage to Contract* (1998), Amy Stanley argues that lawmakers and federal officials increasingly counterposed the freedom of contract to the bondage of slavery. Emancipation, they claimed, would allow slaves the right to enter freely into contracts, to freely sell their labor in exchange for wages. Yet, the celebration of the contract could, and often did, blind the eyes of lawmakers to the inequalities that were inscribed. This was true not only of the wage contract, but also of the marital contract. Freedom, in other words, would at last be achieved – at least in the eyes of many northerners – when the lives of former slaves would be shaped no longer by the tyranny of the lash but by the possibilities of contractual relationships.

As part of this new elevation of contracts, the Reconstruction period saw a new appreciation of the marriage institution. Northern teachers and Union officials urged former slaves to marry, often in extended ceremonies that wed dozens of couples at the same time. Former abolitionists and northern Republicans likewise put a special emphasis on the sanctity of the freedpeople's household, seeing this as a clear counterpoint to the abused home life of slaves. Even more, they argued that the inviolability of the marriage contract would be sustained by the opportunities of the wage contract, that a freedman's right to earn his income would allow him to protect and maintain his wife and his children. In short, northerners reasserted and defended the inequalities of the marital contract, because it shielded American women, both black and white, from the abuses of slavery and from the turbulence of the commercial market. The marriage contract, and the sacred home life it encouraged, was, Stanley (1998: 143) explains, "proof of the wage contract's moral and economic legitimacy, marking a crucial difference between the commodity relations of freedom and slavery."

Yet, as Stanley (1998) makes clear, when it came to individual cases of black women who worked for wages, northerners remained untroubled by this seeming rebuke to their contract theory. They might disparage black women for their failure to adhere to Victorian domestic standards, yet simultaneously urge them to seek employment outside their homes. But, as Stanley (1988) argues, a process of gradual emancipation for married women, generally white, did occur in a few northern states, in the 20 years or so after Appomattox. State legislatures began freeing some women from some of the inequalities of the marital contract when they allowed working women to control their own wages. In this way, the notion of emancipation as a free and unfettered contract was slowly extended to some women who earned an income outside the home.

Stanley's (1998) analysis of freedom and contract allows us to reread the wartime and postwar struggles over women's rights in a new light. First, and perhaps most significantly, Stanley's focus on the limited meanings of emancipation provides a way to evaluate not only elite women's liberation, but also emancipation for women across class and race lines. Her work sheds light on the decidedly mixed accomplishments that black women, middle-class white women, and working-class women experienced in this period. Stanley also forces us to reexamine some of the specific arguments advanced in the earlier historical literature. Thus, where DuBois' (1978) analysis paints the radical Republicans as political opportunists who anxiously distanced themselves from women's rights demands, Stanley's argument suggests how much radicals were imprisoned by the limitations of their own emancipation theories. Whether applied to former slaves, or to women, the notion of contract made freedom a by-product of market relationships. This meant that even as the war itself was beginning to challenge aspects of women's subordination, the emancipation arguments worked to maintain women in unequal marriage bonds. Furthermore, by taking another look at Jacqueline Jones' (1980) conclusions, we see how northern women themselves, especially those who worked with the former slaves, could become the unwitting accomplices of their own subordination. Like the abolitionists who celebrated the inviolability of the marital contract, northern female teachers in the South also upheld the sanctity of the domestic sphere and the propriety of traditional Victorian relationships, even as they challenged some of that Victorianism for themselves. Thus, northern women who lived and worked on southern plantations might indulge in new and unchaperoned relationships with strange men while insisting that the freedpeople uphold a strict code of sexual propriety. Likewise, female teachers challenged the sanctity of their own domestic spheres when they moved to the South, but they romanticized a male-breadwinner model of domestic life for the former slaves. Victorianism, in other words, may well have received ideological sustenance from white northerners' postwar considerations of race. And Yankee women, as much as men, helped enshrine that Victorian sensibility.

While one strain of women's history has been absorbed by women's explicit struggles for emancipation, especially in the context of antislavery work and women's suffrage campaigns, another strain has begun, more recently, to reexamine the Civil War itself as a moment of shifting gender boundaries for both women and men. Along these lines, a few scholars had already focused their attention on one of the more carefully documented aspects of northern women's Civil War experience – nursing. Indeed, nurses were recognized during the war itself, and in the immediate aftermath, as shining examples of feminine sacrifice. Nineteenth-century Americans knew of the heroic contributions made by women such as Clara Barton, Mary Ann Bickerdyke, and Mary Livermore. These were precisely the kinds of women who had been honored and enshrined in the Victorian literature of the postwar period. The challenge for twentieth-century historians was to reexamine those "angels of mercy" without the dewy-eyed sentimentalism which had given them their heavenly cast since the 1860s.

One of the first to do so was Ann Douglas Wood (1972), whose path-breaking essay argued that northern female nurses – women like Clara Barton and Louisa May Alcott – used the guise of domesticity and maternalism to advance their professional claims in the medical field. Women nurses, said Wood, did not abandon the language of Victorianism. In fact, they used it – frequently and skillfully – to challenge men's monopolization of medical knowledge and professional authority. Women thus became adept at highlighting their feminine intuition, their maternal nurturing, and their self-sacrificing attitudes in establishing their right to be nurses and even to overrule male decisions. Wood noted, in particular, how nursing women took aim at government red tape and bureaucracy, decrying a tendency to standardize and routinize medical care to the point that individual and personal needs were overlooked. Yet, as she suggested, these women endowed their own "anti-institutional unprofessionalism with the forces of a profession – money, publicity, and organized labor" (Wood 1972: 210). Female nurses, said Wood, changed their own attitudes about work and professionalism, moving from a position of "feminine self-abnegation" to one of "competitive involvement" (Wood 1972: 201). They were thus apparently prepared to shed the sentimentalism of the antebellum era in favor of the business and professionalism of the postbellum world.

Elizabeth Leonard (1994) expands on Wood's (1972) initial examination of women nurses in a larger study of northern women's involvement in Civil War relief efforts. In *Yankee Women* (1994), Leonard provides an in-depth study of three northern women's Civil War experiences in order to consider if, and how, women managed to shift the boundaries of the separate spheres ideology. Her women were white, middle class, and deeply involved in various aspects of soldier relief work and were, in this regard, perhaps in the best position to affect the predominant gender ideology. Indeed, the women who followed more traditional routes in aiding the soldiers – in this case, nurse Sophronia Bucklin and relief worker Annie Wittenmyer – seemed to have a more significant impact on Victorian boundaries than Leonard's unconventional woman, the physician Mary Walker. Both Bucklin and Wittenmyer found ways to challenge male officials, claiming a more intimate awareness of soldiers' needs. Both also took considerable pride in their wartime accomplishments and felt less compelled to live by the more traditional domestic standards prescribed for nineteenth-century women. Most notably, both demonstrated the possibilities for women's professionalism by finding new arenas in which to establish their authority and efficiency. Wittenmyer, in particular, who pioneered the establishment of "diet kitchens" for sick and wounded soldiers, showed how women could become "leaders and administrators of work they initiated on their own, in ways they themselves devised, and with vigor, determination, and efficiency that caught off guard men who considered themselves the masters of such endeavors" (Leonard 1994: 103). In contrast, Mary Walker's Civil War career was a story of repeated frustrations. In attempting to enter the male field of doctoring, often wearing her own form of male attire, Mary Walker received little recognition and considerable scorn from the masculine establishment. Walker's failures, combined with the renewed emphasis on domesticity sounded in postwar Victorian tributes to the self-sacrificing women of the Civil War epoch, and point to what Leonard (1994: 201) sees as the "remarkable rigidity" in the gender system of the nineteenth century.

Other historians concur with many of Leonard's arguments about the ambiguous nature of women's advancement in this era. Both Lori Ginzberg (1990) and Jeannie Attie (1998) have tackled the question of women's benevolent work in home front relief efforts. In *Women and the Work of Benevolence* (1990), Ginzberg detects a notable change in the nature and style of reform work. Antebellum reformers, she argues, conflated femininity and morality, thus giving women an influential position in benevolent work. So powerful, in fact, was the Victorian faith in feminine goodness, it could even mute class distinctions. Working-class women who aspired to the prescribed model of female morality could, in effect, achieve a sort of middle-class status. The era of the sectional conflict, especially the onset of political hostilities in the 1850s, began to transform the movement for reform and women's place in that movement. Gradually, as political work and electoral strategies assumed greater importance, less significance was attached to women's morality. Indeed, by the time of the Civil War, both male and female reformers placed a higher premium on male standards of professionalism, efficiency, and scientific rationalism.

Few institutions, argues Ginzberg, reveal the shift as clearly as the United States Sanitary Commission (USSC), the largest relief organization of the Civil War. Spearheaded by a new type of nationalizing and rationalizing male reformer, the USSC sought to channel the massive outpouring of female benevolence that materialized in the hundreds of ladies' aid societies that sprang up everywhere throughout the North. In the context of the USSC's efforts to systematize this sentimental deluge, a new generation of women reformers learned to repudiate the older style of female benevolence. Even more, they often downgraded their own individual efforts in favor of work that had a more political or official focus. While the earlier model of moral benevolence did not completely disappear, it now "took place more than ever in settings that were defined by government action" (Ginzberg 1990: 177). By the time the war had ended, both male and female reformers placed significantly less stock in the power of "virtuous femininity" and more in government directives. At the same time, philanthropy became a more explicitly class-based endeavor, resting on a new set of elitist standards that demanded order, productivity, and efficiency. These would be the standards that would shape reform efforts in the Reconstruction years and beyond.

Jeannie Attie provides an even more in-depth view of the Sanitary Commission, and the men and women who shaped it. She is, however, less convinced than Ginzberg that the women who were involved in the USSC fully repudiated the power of female benevolence. At the heart of Attie's *Patriotic Toil* (1998) is her analysis of how the war, and northern wartime relief efforts, exposed the tensions and falsehoods behind what she calls the nineteenth-century "gender compromise" (Attie 1998: 11–13). That compromise, she explains, refused to recognize the economic value of women's domestic work, or to acknowledge a formal political status for women, but did grant women moral authority over their sphere and over society more generally. Yet, in the course of the war, Sanitary Commission women became less content with this arrangement. They added up their economic contributions to the relief efforts, and demanded accountability from the USSC for that work. Attie also shows how the centralizing nationalism of the Sanitary Commission men came increasingly into conflict with local women's determination to control their own charitable offerings. Rumors of Commission corruption made women even more suspicious of the USSC bureaucracy. Thus, says Attie, Union women held ever more firmly to the principle that "charity begins at home," promoting the autonomy of their local aid societies. For Attie, the war did not end the era of middle-class women's benevolent influence; instead, it ignited a conflict between the new standards of professionalism and women's desire for local autonomy, a conflict that would be carried over into women's postwar benevolent work.

In December 1862, the female author of the most famous novel of the Civil War era met President Abraham Lincoln. According to legend, Lincoln exclaimed, upon meeting Harriet Beecher Stowe, "So this is the little lady who made this big war." Lincoln's reference was, of course, to Stowe's authorship of *Uncle Tom's Cabin*, a book that did indeed seize hold of the public imagination as few other works of fiction have done. While many doubt the veracity of this Lincoln story, the tale does attest to one widely perceived phenomenon: the power of women's writing in the age of emancipation. Indeed, some of the most avidly read literature in these years came from the pens of northern female authors, women such as Stowe, Louisa May Alcott, Elizabeth Phelps, and Mary Abigail Dodge. Already well established in literary circles, northern women left an indelible mark on the literary offerings of the period. Recent scholars have begun to consider how Civil War literature, what historian Alice Fahs (2001) calls "the imagined Civil War," affected the established gender ideologies of the period. Much of that literature, as Fahs (2001) and Lyde Sizer (2000) show, not only was authored by women, but also gave women prominent parts to play. An examination of wartime and postwar literary offerings, these authors argue, can show how women, and American readers more generally, began to carve a new place for women's influence in national life.

Recounting the outpouring of Civil War fiction in which female characters played prominent parts, Alice Fahs suggests in her book *The Imagined Civil War* (2001) that the American reading public embraced the notion of a "feminized war." Numerous short stories and poems not only called attention to women's great suffering and sacrifices, but also legitimized women's wartime problems as issues of national import and concern. When women were called upon, in story after story, to give their consent to a son or lover who wished to enlist for the war effort, they became vital participants in the national drama. Or, when the sensational literature portrayed heroic young women as wartime spies or even as combatants, it allowed women to step outside the private domestic sphere and occupy a new position, albeit a subordinate one, in national life. Significantly, Fahs finds that these gendered literary trends were much more pronounced in northern than in southern wartime writing. Female characters in northern fiction, much more than their southern literary counterparts, suggested acceptance for a more expansive and engaged involvement on the part of women in Civil War America.

Yet, as Fahs (2001) indicates, those expansive possibilities disappeared in the postwar years. The fictional and historical accounts that considered the Civil War increasingly narrowed their focus to military and political events. A new emphasis was placed on reconciliation, and more specifically on male bonding, across sectional lines. Thus, where the war itself created a more inclusive literary culture, which drew on the heroic efforts of women and blacks and even children, the postwar period created a much more narrow literary culture that seemed "to include only white men and Southern white women" (Fahs 2001: 316).

Like Fahs, Lyde Sizer also sees evidence, in Civil War literature, of expanding roles for northern women. In considering the wartime and postwar writings of nine prominent female authors, she detects an overwhelming desire among these writers to give women a vital and active place in the national polity. Sizer argues in *The Political Work of Northern Women Writers and the Civil War, 1850–1872* (2000) that, in the beginning of the war, northern women writers constructed a "rhetoric of unity" in which they pledged themselves to a unified national cause that stood above differences based on class or race or politics (Sizer 2000: 75–107). Female authors – such as Stowe and Alcott – believed that women should use their influence to bind up class and social divisions. Sizer also suggests that women writers adopted an increasingly political tone in the course of the war, expressing more explicitly partisan views as the conflict wore on, and moving in a more explicitly pro-suffrage direction by war's end. In recognizing their own place in this national enterprise, northern female authors felt more acutely, and with greater resentment, the limitations which American society imposed upon them. In fact, says Sizer, the war did not significantly transform northern women, doing little to alter their real political or economic positions. It did, however, give the impression of transformation because it showed women, and women authors in particular, "a personal and cultural vision of possibility" as it drew them into the center of the nation's political struggles (Sizer 2000: 4).

Yet, when all is said and done, perhaps this impression of a transformation was itself evidence of a real turning point for northern women. Women not only began to imagine a new relationship with the nation-state, but also began to forge one as well. The influx of women into government positions was certainly one sign of this, as was women's heightened sense of responsibility, when they served both as teachers and as nurses, for federal wartime efforts. More generally, this work spoke to a new type of political accountability which both women and the federal government began to acknowledge: that women had their own political identities, apart from their relationships with men. The Civil War, in other words, advanced the process by which women became politically accountable citizens whose relationship to the nation-state was not wholly mediated by their familial connections. Women themselves spoke to this change as they became more explicitly political and partisan in their writings and in their attitudes. Their ideas could be heard in the sharp partisan speeches of lecturers like Anna Dickinson, in the petitions of oppressed female seamstresses, and in the countless letters which thousands of more "ordinary" women addressed to President Lincoln and other representatives of the federal government. Still, this field of inquiry – especially the question of how the multitude of these more "ordinary" women coped with the political adjustments and other dislocations of wartime – remains largely unexplored. While scholars since the late 1970s have certainly helped to open up the questions and have begun to offer some intriguing answers, questions of gender, politics, and northern women's identities in this age of emancipation still await further scrutiny.

BIBLIOGRAPHY

Attie, Jeannie (1998) *Patriotic Toil: Northern Women and the Civil War*. Ithaca, NY: Cornell University Press.

Brockett, Linus P. and Vaughan, Mary, C. (1867) *Woman's Work in the Civil War: A Record of Heroism, Patriotism and Patience*. Philadelphia, Pa.: Zeigler, McCurdy.

DuBois, Ellen (1978) *Feminism and Suffrage: The Emergence of an Independent Women's Movement in America, 1848–1869*. Ithaca, NY: Cornell University Press.

Fahs, Alice (2001) *The Imagined Civil War: Popular Literature of the North and South, 1861–1865*. Chapel Hill, NC: University of North Carolina Press.

Flexner, Eleanor (1959) *Century of Struggle: The Woman's Rights Movement in the United States*. Cambridge: Cambridge University Press.

Gallman, J. Matthew (1994) *The North Fights the Civil War: The Home Front*. Chicago: University of Chicago Press.

Ginzberg, Lori (1990) *Women and the Work of Benevolence: Morality, Politics, and Class in the Nineteenth Century United States*. New Haven, Conn.: Yale University Press.

Jones, Jacqueline (1980) *Soldiers of Light and Love: Northern Teachers and Georgia Blacks, 1865–1873*. Chapel Hill, NC: University of North Carolina Press.

Leonard, Elizabeth (1994) *Yankee Women: Gender Battles in the Civil War.* New York: Norton.

Livermore, Mary (1888) *My Story of the War.* Hartford, Conn.: A. D. Worthington.

Massey, Mary Elizabeth (1966) *Bonnet Brigades: American Women in the Civil War.* New York: Alfred A. Knopf.

Moore, Frank (1866) *Women of the War: Their Heroism and Self-Sacrifice.* Hartford, Conn.: Scranton.

Paludan, Phillip Shaw (1988) *A People's Contest: The Union and Civil War, 1861–1865.* New York: Charles Scribner's Sons.

Sigerman, Harriet (2000a) "An Unfinished Battle: 1848–1865," in Nancy Cott (ed.) *No Small Courage: A History of Women in the United States.* New York: Oxford University Press.

Sigerman, Harriet (2000b) "Laborers for Liberty: 1865–1890," in Nancy Cott (ed.) *No Small Courage: A History of Women in the United States.* New York: Oxford University Press.

Sizer, Lyde (2000) *The Political Work of Northern Women Writers and the Civil War, 1850–1872.* Chapel Hill, NC: University of North Carolina Press.

Stanley, Amy Dru (1988) "Conjugal Bonds and Wage Labor: Rights of Contract in the Age of Emancipation," *Journal of American History* 75: 471–500.

Stanley, Amy Dru (1998) *From Bondage to Contract: Wage Labor, Marriage, and the Market in the Age of Slave Emancipation.* New York: Cambridge University Press.

Venet, Wendy (1991) *Neither Ballots nor Bullets: Women Abolitionists and the Civil War.* Charlottesville, Va.: University of Virginia Press.

Wood, Ann Douglas (1972) "The War within a War: Women Nurses in the Union Army," *Civil War History* 18: 197–212.

SUGGESTED FURTHER READING

Baker, Paula (1984) "The Domestication of Politics: Women and American Political Society, 1780–1920," *American Historical Review* 89: 620–47.

Brown, Thomas (1998) *Dorothea Dix: New England Reformer.* Cambridge, Mass.: Harvard University Press.

Clifford, Deborah Pickman (1979) *Mine Eyes Have Seen the Glory: A Biography of Julia Ward Howe.* Boston, Mass.: Little, Brown.

Clinton, Catherine (1984) *The Other Civil War: American Women in the Nineteenth Century.* New York: Hill and Wang.

Clinton, Catherine and Silber, Nina (eds.) (1992) *Divided Houses: Gender and the Civil War.* New York: Oxford University Press.

Coryell, Janet L. (1990) *Neither Heroine nor Fool: Anna Ella Carroll of Maryland.* Kent, Ohio: Kent State University Press.

Cott, Nancy (1998) "Marriage and Women's Citizenship in the United States, 1830–1934," *American Historical Review* 103: 1440–74.

Dannett, Sylvia (1959) *Noble Women of the North.* New York: Yoseloff.

Diffley, Kathleen (1992) *Where my Heart is Turning Ever: Civil War Stories and Constitutional Reform, 1861–1876.* Athens, Ga.: University of Georgia Press.

DuBois, Ellen (1987) "Outgrowing the Compact of the Fathers: Equal Rights, Woman Suffrage, and the United States Constitution," *Journal of American History* 74: 836–62.

Endres, Kathleen (1984) "The Women's Press in the Civil War: A Portrait of Patriotism, Propaganda and Prodding," *Civil War History* 30: 31–53.

Fahs, Alice (1999) "The Feminized Civil War: Gender, Northern Popular Literature, and the Memory of the War, 1861–1900," *Journal of American History* 85: 1461–94.

Faust, Drew Gilpin (1998) "'Ours as Well as That of the Men': Women and Gender in the Civil War," in William Cooper and James McPherson (eds.) *Writing the Civil War: The Quest to Understand*. Columbia, SC: University of South Carolina Press.

Fox-Genovese, Elizabeth (1998) "Days of Judgement, Days of Wrath: The Civil War and the Religious Imagination of Women Writers," in Randall M. Miller, Harry S. Stout, and Charles Reagan Wilson (eds.) *Religion and the American Civil War*. New York: Oxford University Press.

Giesberg, Judith Ann (2000) *Civil War Sisterhood: The US Sanitary Commission and Women's Politics in Transition*. Boston, Mass.: Northeastern University Press.

Gollaher, David (1995) *Voice for the Mad: The Life of Dorothea Dix*. New York: Free Press.

Hedrick, Joan (1994) *Harriet Beecher Stowe: A Life*. New York: Oxford University Press.

Jeffrey, Julie Roy (1998) *The Great, Silent Arm of Abolitionism: Ordinary Women in the Abolitionist Movement*. Chapel Hill, NC: University of North Carolina Press.

Kerber, Linda (1998) *No Constitutional Right to be Ladies: Women and the Obligations of Citizenship*. New York: Hill and Wang.

Oates, Stephen (1995) *A Woman of Valor: Clara Barton and the Civil War*. New York: Free Press.

Painter, Nell (1996) *Sojourner Truth, a Life, a Symbol*. New York: Norton.

Rose, Anne (1992) *Victorian America and the Civil War*. New York: Cambridge University Press.

Schultz, Jane (1992) "The Inhospitable Hospital: Gender and Professionalism in Civil War Medicine," *Signs* 17: 363–92.

Schultz, Jane (1995) "'Are We Not All Soldiers?': Northern Women in the Civil War Hospital Service," *Prospects* 20: 38–56.

Young, Agatha (1959) *Women and the Crisis: Women of the North in the Civil War*. New York: McDowell Obelensky.

Young, Elizabeth (1999) *Disarming the Nation: Women's Writing and the American Civil War*. Chicago: University of Chicago Press.

CHAPTER TWENTY-ONE

Southern Women during the Age of Emancipation

JEANNIE WHAYNE

America's "age of emancipation" radically altered the lives of southerners – black and white, male and female. As the old slave regime crumbled in the face of a challenge almost unprecedented in world history, black southerners strove to define the meaning of freedom, and white southerners struggled to contain the changes that threatened to overwhelm them. The eradication of slavery by presidential edict and the actions of slaves themselves dramatically illustrated the impotence of the South's patriarchal system and forced the reordering of not only political and economic arrangements but also racial and gender relationships. With slavery repudiated, some other means had to be devised to organize social relations, and new systems of class and racial superiority had to be worked out. Elite whites were ultimately able to reassert their political and economic control and reestablish racial supremacy, but not without challenge from below. Gender played a key role in the struggle to reorder society, given the crucial roles that sex, family, and the household played in defining work, legal rights, and political representation.

The circumstances of white women placed them in a better, if more ambiguous, position than black women. While elite and middle-class women faced challenges that set them apart from their contemporaries in the North, poor white women found themselves marginalized even more than they had been in antebellum years. African American women, who had the most to gain by the demise of slavery, clung to their own concepts of family and community in order to endure the demands placed upon them in a world turned upside down. They adapted strategies of resistance from the past, from their period of enslavement, in their efforts to insist on a definition of freedom that was of their own making.

Emancipation, Reconstruction, and gender have all been the subjects of innovative scholarship since the mid-1970s. Some of the new works on women's history have focused specifically on white women, others on black women, and a few have attempted to analyze the experiences of both. Other studies have utilized gender as a category of analysis and have focused less on the experiences of women than on the way that notions of gender influenced the unfolding of southern history after the war. Given the centrality of "family" in the lives of women, black and white, all of the new works have touched on family history, a subject about which there is a rich historiography that is separate, to some extent, from women's historiography. Aside from these broad categories of analysis, a number of important questions have surfaced in the various studies, and two questions in particular are omnipresent: "was the Civil War a watershed" for white women and "did emancipation really mean anything" for black women? Some historians address these questions directly, others indirectly, but they are inescapably a part of every important book written on the subject of women's history covering this period. In addressing these questions, historians are also making arguments about the nature of antebellum society, although, to be sure, sometimes these arguments are more implicit than explicit.

Historians' understandings of the impact of the "age of emancipation" on women have inevitably been shaped by contemporary concerns. Many of the issues facing women in the middle of the nineteenth century continue to confront women at the beginning of the twenty-first century, and many women's historians are very much aware of the implications of their findings. Those who focus on African American women's history are especially sensitive to the way their findings might be interpreted. Perhaps no debate in African American history has been as fraught with controversy as that over the nature of the black family, a controversy that has political implications for all twenty-first-century Americans, male and female. Jacqueline Jones (1985), in *Labor of Love, Labor of Sorrow*, writes from a presentist perspective and is quite consciously responding to certain assertions made in the second half of the twentieth century about the nature of the black family. These assertions attempt to explain a perceived crisis in the black community as black males experienced high rates of unemployment and black females assumed the breadwinner role and became the heads of their own households, households plagued by poverty. Echoing Herbert Gutman's (1976) *The Black Family in Slavery and Freedom*, she rejects the notion, posited in the famous Moynihan (1967) report, that the black family was destroyed by the brutal and repressive slave system and, instead, argues that black women nurtured and sustained the black family before and after emancipation. Fully aware of the political implications of Moynihan's assertions and equally cognizant of the possible political ramifications of her own argument, Jones (1985) suggests that the "nuclear" black family, strengthened by the devotion of black women, served as a fortress against a capitalist system bent on exploiting black labor. It was true in the Old South, where "racial and patriarchal ideologies [were] wedded to the pursuit of profit," and it was even more true in the postbellum period when freedmen and freedwomen entered the labor market and found themselves seriously disadvantaged by poverty and racial discrimination. Jones develops this argument in the second half of her book, which covers the period 1915 to the present and focuses on the northern urban experience of African Americans. She concludes that it is the failure of the capitalist system to provide sufficient employment that accounts for the poverty of many African Americans, not something inherently deficient about the black family.

The first half of Jones' book is devoted to an analysis of rural blacks in the South from the antebellum period until 1915, and she argues that the determination of slave women to maintain their families in the face of the demands of owners and overseers was a political act, an effort to fashion some control over the fate of their children. As Jones (1985: 12) puts it, "slave women's unfulfilled dreams for their children helped to inspire resistance against 'the ruling race' and its attempts to subordinate the integrity of black family life to its own economic and political interests." Sharecropping black women in the postbellum period continued in this struggle to sustain the family and construct it as a bulwark against white oppression despite the concerted efforts of plantation owners to exploit the labor of black men, women, and children in the interest of maximizing their profits. In the face of the power of white planters, black women sought to focus their energies within the family and to assume a sexual division of labor that kept them insulated from the workplace. In other words, Jones would agree with the findings of many historians of emancipation who argue that black women withdrew from field labor as soon as they could, as soon as emancipation made this possible. This led to the white perception that free black families performed less work than slave families, but as Jones puts it, black women preferred to devote their energies to their households in a "labor of love," rather than to engage in a "labor of sorrow" outside the home. Jones also assumes that the black female accepted the traditional subordinate role that white women were subject to within the family and, in fact, preferred to be relegated to domestic chores within the home as opposed to field labor as it represented an enhancement of their status. Ironically, even as white women began to struggle to free themselves of their domestic prisons and assume public roles, black women, according to Jones, withdrew into the sanctuary of the home. It was a home, moreover, free of gender conflict between black men and women; thus Jones views exploitation of black females as occurring only outside the family relationship, principally in the workplace.

Women's historians writing a decade later would take issue with much of what Jones had to say. Two of the key points of contention revolved around the place of black women in the labor force and the nature of the black family. Julie Saville, in *The Work of Reconstruction* (1994), emphasizes the importance of the black family and community to freedpeople and black women's role in sustaining it even as they struggled, along with their men, to negotiate the contentious post-emancipation economic arrangements with planters. In fact, for Saville, the freedpeople's dedication to a family dynamic that emphasized equality among family members put them on a collision course not simply with Freedmen's Bureau officials and with missionaries who promulgated a subordinate role for women but also with planters who found the black family model distinctly problematic. Freedwomen, like freedmen, held out hope for land-ownership as an alternative to laboring on restored plantations, and once this hope was vanquished, women supported the efforts of their enfranchised men to politicize their struggle to control their daily work routine through the military clubs they formed and through their association with the Republican party. This was not simply a struggle against planters – whether southern or northern-born – it was a struggle against a capitalist system bent on turning freedpeople into a rural proletariat. While Jones (1985) argues that black women acted within the nuclear family to struggle against the power of the capitalist system, Saville (1994) sees the distinctive (and non-nuclear) black family structure as a crucial element in the war they waged against those who sought to dominate them.

Although it is certainly arguable that South Carolina represents a special case because a heavy black majority existed there, allowing for a more powerful black community to emerge, Saville's sophisticated analysis persuasively challenges Jones.

Jones' approach was much more far-ranging. She traced the black family from the antebellum period into the twentieth century, from South to North, and while such a broad synthesis is useful, it runs the risk of generalizing too much and obscuring differences within regions. Another study that focuses on South Carolina and, at the same time, takes on Jones, is that produced by Leslie A. Schwalm in *A Hard Fight for We* (1997). She draws on Saville's (1994) work and challenges Jones (1985) directly, arguing that there was no sharp division between labor within the home and labor outside the home, and that the women of the South Carolina rice country did not withdraw from field labor after emancipation. Again, South Carolina may be unique, particularly when the female withdrawal from field labor is considered, and, in any case, some have argued that even in the cotton South, withdrawal from field labor occurred in the early years of emancipation. Nevertheless, *A Hard Fight for We* establishes, as does Saville, the value of more narrowly focused studies. While drawing on Saville, Schwalm (1997) elaborates on certain antebellum precedents. Her analysis depends upon a certain interpretation of how, during the antebellum period, black women were involved in both kinds of labor and both were of intrinsic value to the plantation enterprise and to the black family and community. In looking after the welfare of the slave community, slave women were helping planters maintain their investment and contributing to the efficient functioning of the plantation enterprise. While black women's dedication to the black family and community helped sustain the plantation system, it also kept the slave family and community intact. This linkage of interests during the antebellum period, according to Schwalm, does not survive emancipation.

Like Saville and in contradiction to Jones, Schwalm disputes the notion that the black family mirrored the white nuclear family. Both before and after slavery, it included an extended kinship network which by its very nature created community. She joins a long list of historians – Eugene Genovese (1974), Herbert Gutman (1976), and John Blassingame (1976), to name but a few – in her exploration of the role of the black family and community, but one of her unique contributions is her appreciation of the way in which mechanisms of resistance in the antebellum period survived emancipation and, in the case of the black women of the South Carolina rice region, were adapted to deal with new circumstances. In fact, an important element in the tacit negotiation between the interests of planters and those of slaves were the subtle, and sometimes not so subtle, acts of resistance that enabled black women to sustain their families and communities even as they served the interests of planters. Schwalm (1997) argues that these mechanisms were adapted after the war as the free-labor system evolved, but during the war more overt and confrontational forms of resistance were employed. For example, before the war, slaves frequently but quietly appropriated articles, particularly food, that belonged to the master. This was tolerated as long as it did not get out of hand. As the war unfolded, the rice country quickly fell to Union troops and planters abandoned plantations, losing control over their slaves. Slave women began to defiantly appropriate the property of their mistresses. For example, according to Schwalm (1997: 130), a slave woman named Peggy was described by her outraged master as having taken "my wife's Large & handsome Mahogany Bedstead & Mattrass & arranged it in her own Negro House on which she slept for some time." But even more dramatic confrontations occurred. One slave woman actually directed the burning of her master's house during the war, almost certainly deriving much satisfaction from the destruction of an edifice that represented the power of the planter. Although the actions of these women might be attributed to exacting vengeance for wrongs suffered during their enslavement, the hardships endured by slaves/freedpeople during the war also help explain their determination to either appropriate or destroy planter symbols of power and authority. Indeed, the adoption of direct confrontation is hardly surprising given Schwalm's account of what happened to black women in the South Carolina rice country as the Civil War progressed. It is a harrowing tale of brutality, disease, and starvation. The close proximity of Union troops provided opportunities for violence against and sexual exploitation of black women, something that Confederate troops, given the opportunity, were also guilty of. Meanwhile, many black women lost what little they accumulated during the antebellum period to marauding soldiers of both armies. But, given the centrality of the family and community in the lives of slaves, the most significant blow was the disruption of the slave community as black men enlisted in the Union army or were conscripted to work on fortifications. Another important element of Schwalm's (1997) argument involves her contention that slave women's pivotal place in the rice fields in the antebellum period positioned them to play a significant role in the economic negotiation between planters and freedpeople in the postbellum era. Black women, according to Schwalm, were the ones who led the demand that land be redistributed to them, land they considered their own by virtue of their years of labor. There is a considerable historiography on the question of freedmen's expectations concerning land redistribution, and Schwalm's contribution is her appreciation of the role of black women in the confrontation between planters and freedpeople.

As Schwalm (1997) demonstrates, freedwomen were successful in forcing work arrangements that allowed them to continue nurturing their families in the traditional manner. According to Schwalm, when land redistribution did not occur, black women engaged in a series of confrontations with former owners and with Freedmen's Bureau officials who were together attempting to force upon the freedmen and freedwomen their own conception of a free-labor system: contractual wage labor. Black women routinely challenged unacceptable terms in labor contracts, much to the chagrin of white officials. A crucial element in black women's activism in this regard is Schwalm's contention, in another departure from Jones (1985), that freedwomen in the rice country did not voluntarily remove themselves from the rice fields. Schwalm admits, however, that what took place in the South Carolina rice fields was distinct from what was taking place elsewhere in the South. Nevertheless, the fact that black women continued to labor there put them in a position to force the adoption of the work-rent system which gave them more time for their families and for themselves, thus providing the opportunity to continue nurturing and sustaining the black family and community, and thereby continuing the connection between work and family. Schwalm might have observed that a similar dynamic plays a role (later, to be sure) in the development of a sharecropper system based on family labor in cotton areas.

Finally, unlike Jones, Schwalm acknowledges that tension arose within the African American household as the freedmen and freedwomen struggled to reconstitute and reshape their families in the face of unprecedented pressures from the agents of the federal government. The US Army, Freedman's Bureau officials, and various missionaries attempted to "educate" African Americans about the efficacies of the bourgeois family structure and particularly the subordination of women to men. But African American women were accustomed to contributing to the family and community in a manner inconsistent with the relegation of women to a subordinate role within the household and, in fact, the realities of their postwar work experiences also made their subordination particularly inappropriate. In this struggle within their own families and with the white power structure, African American women were engaged in nothing less than an effort to define the meaning of freedom.

Tera Hunter, in *To 'Joy my Freedom* (1997), shifts the focus to the experiences of black domestic workers in postwar Atlanta and provides a rich analysis of their efforts to control their own lives and to define the meaning of freedom. Her assumptions about the nature of the antebellum black female sensibility is reminiscent of Schwalm's. The slave woman was family- and community-focused and the family was not nuclear, as Jones (1985) would have it. In the postbellum period freedwomen struggled to reconstitute their households and communities, and they were determined to do so despite the efforts of planters who, often acting in concert with Freedmen's Bureau agents, appropriated the labor of orphaned black children. When extended family members (aunts and uncles, for example) petitioned to have these children released from apprenticeships into their care, they were speaking of the centrality of the extended kin network and their determination to maintain it.

Hunter's (1997) primary focus, however, is on what happens in Atlanta as domestic laborers, especially washerwomen, fashion a life that maximizes their freedom from white supervision. The typical domestic housekeeper refused to live in, choosing instead to live apart from white domination. Hunter finds them exercising a variety of strategies to demonstrate their independence, such as not showing up when the white mistress scheduled a dinner party requiring extra work. Meanwhile, black laundresses refused to perform their services on white premises and, instead, took laundry home where they could enjoy the presence of their families and other women. For laundresses an opportunity arose in 1881 when the World's Fair was about to take place. Recognizing how important their tasks were to the daily lives of white Atlanta, they organized a laundry strike and won concessions. Even as they struggled with white women in their work lives, poor black women were indulging a sense of freedom and independence in their leisure hours, going to bars and honkytonks, dressing flamboyantly, dancing provocatively, and otherwise offending the sensibilities of both the white and black middle-class world. Hunter characterizes these activities as acts of resistance and argues that poor black women were defining their own sense of freedom both in their workplace struggles and in their nightlife excursions.

Another way of looking at how African American women fashioned their own definition of freedom comes from Amy Dru Stanley (1998), who focuses not simply on the South but on nineteenth-century America. She puts the emancipation experience at center stage and finds that black women indeed found themselves in a new kind of struggle. Stanley's *From Bondage to Contract* (1998) was published the year after Schwalm's *A Hard Fight For We* (1997). Stanley is interested in elucidating the importance of the idea of "contract" and how it related to the post-Civil War debates over the meaning of freedom. These debates took place throughout America, but had special relevance for African Americans in the South, both male and female.

The federal government, acting first through the US Army and then through the Freedmen's Bureau, sought to educate freedmen about the primacy of contract and encouraged African American men to enter contractual arrangements with those running plantations. At the same time, men and women both were "educated" in the importance of the marriage contract, and, as both Schwalm and Saville argue, the interpretation provided to them was one that stressed the dependence of the female upon the male. This interpretation of the proper role for women was being touted to African American freedmen and freedwomen even as something different was taking place elsewhere in the nation. As more and more northern women entered the workforce, new laws were adopted that challenged husbandly prerogatives. Under the laws of coverture, wives were not entitled to own property independently of their husbands, but states began to fashion laws giving working-women some rights to their wages. Nevertheless, the law and custom both contrived to privilege male authority and undermined full contractual freedom for married women. Thus, while southern freedwomen were being introduced and "educated" in the necessity to submit to their husbands, northern working-class women were struggling to break free of similar restraints.

Laura Edwards, in *Gendered Strife and Confusion* (1997), contributes to this discussion of freedwomen's struggle to define freedom in the postwar South, but turns the question of freedwomen's subordination to their black husbands upside down. Privileging gender analysis over women's history, Edwards draws her evidence from a perusal of records from the tobacco-producing area of North Carolina's border with Virginia between the end of the war and 1887. She accepts Jones' (1985) argument that black women withdrew from field labor, but argues that black women in tobacco country embraced the opportunity to remove themselves from the fields and accepted subordination to their husbands in part because they believed it would empower their husbands, and thus their entire families, given the traditional construction of the household in the South. In other words, by adopting the antebellum white model of marriage and family and elevating the black male to undisputed household head, freedmen and freedwomen were engaging in a political act that they hoped, vainly it turned out, would provide them with enough ammunition to maneuver the minefield of race relations in the postbellum South.

Underlying Edwards' (1997) analysis is an intriguing conception of how antebellum southern society was organized and how it refashioned itself in the absence of slavery. The twin pillars of southern society in the antebellum period were marriage and slavery. All dependants, including women, children, and slaves, were contained within the household structure with a male head of household ruling supreme. Edwards is echoing Stephanie McCurry's *Masters of Small Worlds* (1995), a study of South Carolina slaveholders and yeoman farmers. According to McCurry the conception of the propertied male household head ruling his own small world linked him to the planters in a manner that submerged their profound economic differences. Antebellum proslavery theorists, aided by evangelical preachers, linked the institutions of marriage and slavery, arguing that both were ordained by God. While marriage organized relations between males and females, slavery organized relationships between blacks and whites. In marriage, women were properly subordinate to men just as in slavery blacks were properly subordinate to whites. At the apex of both, however, was the white male head of household ruling all the dependants within his household: women, children, and slaves. According to McCurry, this fostered the development of a peculiarly southern variant of republicanism.

Laura Edwards (1997) takes this analysis beyond the antebellum period and finds that elite whites proved adept at refashioning both ideology and reality to maintain their primacy. The attempt by African American men to claim the political, legal, and social power commensurate with their new status as heads of households of their own was undermined by their continuing economic dependence and the strident racism that confronted them in the postwar period. It turned out that they were ill positioned to assume the role they attempted to embrace, for in the antebellum period, even white men without property found themselves on ambiguous ground as only propertied men could claim standing in society. This remained true for them and equally true for black men in the post-Civil War period, but both white and black men, nevertheless, pressed their assertions of authority over their own dependants and households. They clung to the traditional prerogatives of the male head of household even as these prerogatives eroded in the postwar period.

Elite whites themselves faced something of a challenge, and the necessity, to reconfigure the definition of social status in the absence of the possession of slaves. As Edwards (1997: 20) puts it, "their solution, which incorporated central tenets of liberal ideology and northern consumer culture, centered on the ability to construct and display a certain kind of domestic household." It was a household that was fitted with items of comfort and luxury afforded by the labor of successful and "industrious men of strong moral fiber" who could retreat to its environs assured of the devotion of their wives who themselves were "paragons of domestic virtue." They positioned themselves as "the best men" and it was a position based on the accumulation of material possessions. Poor whites and blacks, however, could not hope to construct such households, and, as Edwards would have it, they did not wish to. For them, "social ties and mutual responsibilities, not physical structures and material possessions, constituted households" (Edwards 1997: 20).

Central to Edwards' provocative analysis is the notion that despite the inherently private dimension to the household, there existed an equally important public dimension to it, and it was here, in the public sphere, that the clash between elite whites and the poor of both races occurred: at the ballot box and in the courtroom. In the post-Civil War period, poor whites and blacks, who were themselves divided by racial differences that became even more manifest as racism became institutionalized, asserted their rights as household heads, using the antebellum patriarchal model as their blueprint, in the public sphere. Even as elite whites remained determined to maintain their class and racial privileges, poor whites and blacks "rejected the idea that race or class positioned them as dependents and insisted on the power of household heads to represent and protect their family members." But the elite had constructed a new ideology, the ideology of the "best men," and African Americans and poor whites would find themselves increasingly marginalized politically as the notion of the "best men" evolved to the point where it became clear that white elite males alone were to be "trusted with the responsibilities of public life" (Edwards 1997: 21, 22). The disfranchisement of poor black and white men was the ultimate result of this clash. And what of poor white and black women? They would find their efforts to use their rights as dependants seriously undermined in the postwar period. In a fascinating analysis of the attempts of black and poor white women to pursue legal remedies in cases of rape, Edwards finds that courts increasingly came to dismiss their claims and those of their male "protectors" on the basis of their marginality in society.

Victoria Bynum, in *Unruly Women* (1992), also focuses on women who lived on the margins of southern society, but her subjects are poor black and white women who operated outside the traditional household structure entirely. They were white women who eschewed, in one fashion or another, male authority and discovered the limits of their ability to negotiate a legal system bent on the subordination of women within such a structure; or, in the alternative, they were free black women who could not avail themselves of the protection of their own male household head. Bynum concentrates on three groups of "unruly" women: those who sued for divorce; those who challenged the social and sexual mores of southern society; and, finally, those who acted out during the Civil War in unprecedented ways. She selected three rural counties in the North Carolina Piedmont for her study where, she argues, the region's distinctive egalitarian republicanism and its non-slaveholding yeomanry created its own interpretation of the "cult of true womanhood" which emphasized the hard-working farm wife who was obedient to her husband. This was the accepted social norm for women and those who challenged it faced a court system that determined to manage them. It was determined to do so in the antebellum period and continued to exercise this authority during and after the war. In other words, women were supposed to be regulated within the household structure and those who were not were subject to state control. Laws against fornication, interracial sex, and bastardy were designed to circumscribe their behavior and were scrupulously enforced. Nevertheless, the Civil War marked a crucial moment. It brought devastation and starvation, and the unruliness of Bynum's poor white women shifted to food riots and stealing. Meanwhile, Bynum's black women found themselves in a particularly vulnerable position during the war, for they were likely to fall victim to abuse from angry planters and Confederates who recognized slavery as a cause of the war and from Union troops and runaway slaves who understood that slave women had no legal protections and thus were fair game. In her epilogue, which covers the immediate postwar period, Bynum finds a continuation of the antebellum restrictions on poor black and white women and the tendency of courts to step in and assume patriarchal authority over women who violated the accepted social norm and traditional gender constraints.

While marginal white women confronted courts determined to punish them for behavior deemed inappropriate or threatening to the social order, middle-class and elite women also engaged in their own peculiar struggle. Elite white women, as Laura Edwards (1997) suggests, embraced the household as their domain but reshaped what defined it in the post-Civil War period and, in the meantime, played a role in insuring the ascendancy of their race and class. Poor black women and poor white women (with the exception of Bynum's marginal women) attempted to use the traditional definition of the household, but this did not serve them well in the postwar environment. One thing that complicates the historiographical debate over the status of white women in the postbellum period is that historians writing about white women, like those writing about black women, have differed in their interpretation of the antebellum period and the strictures white women endured. Consequently, they have evaluated the impact of the Civil War in different ways.

By its title alone, *Southern Lady: From Pedestal to Politics* (1970), by Anne Firor Scott, reveals both its orientation and its trajectory. However, *Southern Lady* challenged the view that the plantation mistress was happily ensconced on a pedestal, a dependent and submissive wife whose reward for slavish obedience to her husband was a life of ease and comfort afforded by the work of enslaved blacks. In fact, Scott argues, the pedestal upon which she was placed was itself an illusion, and there was considerable distance between the ideal of the lady and the reality of her everyday experience. Supervising and running an antebellum plantation household was hard work, bearing children was often difficult, dangerous, and deadly. The plantation mistress struggled to fulfill the obligations imposed by a patriarchal system wherein she was responsible for the health and welfare of her own close kin and that of the extended family of slaves and dependants on the plantation. For Scott, these women were not unaware of the contradictions between the reality and the ideal but for the sake of the patriarchal system they lived within, they attempted, often valiantly, to live up to the ideal. Many hated slavery, according to Scott, particularly the sexual exploitation of black females by white masters, but they largely suppressed these feelings until the Civil War liberated them from the responsibility for their extended family of black slaves. The deaths of husbands together with the economic dislocation caused by the loss of the war and the loss of slave property led women to employment outside the home, expanding their horizons and freeing them from their domestic prisons. By the end of the nineteenth century, they were founding women's clubs and temperance societies which provided them with the experience necessary to prepare them to play crucial roles in the Progressive Era reforms of the early twentieth century. For Scott (1970), then, white elite women were themselves emancipated from the necessity of attempting to conform to the myth of the virtuous and innocent plantation mistress and freed to embrace opportunities made available in the postwar period.

Jean Friedman's *The Enclosed Garden* (1985) focused not simply on plantation mistresses but also on white farm women and black female slaves in six rural North Carolina and Georgia congregations. She analyzes the letters, diaries, and even the dreams of these women and concludes, like Scott (1970), that women were more than a little ambivalent about their status in the antebellum South. Friedman (1985) disputes, however, Scott's notion that the Civil War freed them from the dependence that was so much a part of their antebellum lives. "Influenced by the studies of Nancy Scott, Carroll Smith-Rosenberg, and Barbara Berg, who found that modernization and its attendant sexual segregation prompted [northern] women to form independent women's networks that ultimately challenged the patriarchy," Friedman (1985: ix) was motivated to investigate the failure of women's associations to develop in the preindustrial South until late in the nineteenth century. She finds that a rural kinship network existed in the South, a kinship network which was not sexually segregated and thus inhibited the development of women's associations. This rural-based kinship network was carried into the few urban areas existing in the South, Friedman explains, and so southern urban women were not any more likely to form female associations than were their rural counterparts. Whereas Scott (1970) explains the eventual emergence of women's associations to develop in the South as coming out of the war experience which freed white women from patriarchal authority, Friedman finds the war experience did nothing to free women from antebellum constraints. The Civil War challenged women but both the kinship structure and the southern social structure remained intact and survived into the post-Civil War period precisely because of the trauma of the war. When women fled before the Union army, they fled with kin and to kin. Although sometimes living so close with kin created strains, these strains did not disrupt the function of the kinship system. The survival of the kinship system made southern women less eager to adapt to new roles. So, in other words, their dependence on the traditional kinship relationship inhibited development of independent women's networks.

Another important element of Friedman's analysis of the antebellum inhibitions on the development of women's associations involves the role that evangelical religion played in constraining the development of women's associations. These were women whose lives were circumscribed not simply by the domination of their husbands alone but by a patriarchy buttressed by evangelical ministers who did not hesitate to discipline women who showed any signs of activism or nascent feminism. The design was to force such women to refocus their energies on their families and communities, to confine themselves within their kinship and religious networks alone. Beth Barton Schweiger (2000) in *The Gospel Working Up*, suggests that Friedman (1985) goes too far in assuming the unanimity of evangelical ministers in the antebellum period, arguing instead that some of them did encourage women to play active roles within the church bureaucracy. However, although women raised money for the church, they were required to turn it over to men. Schweiger argues that this changes in the postbellum period when ministers began to encourage greater activity among women with regard to church matters, and women proved particularly adept at raising funds and were allowed to disperse those funds themselves. Schweiger thus challenges Friedman on at least two points. Not only does Schweiger find women forming associations in the antebellum period, she sees their activism extending into, and expanding in, the postwar period. But for Friedman, writing 15 years earlier than Schweiger, the ability of churchmen and planters in the antebellum period to thwart women's activism contributed to the failure of a separate women's culture to develop in the antebellum South. By making this argument, Friedman is directly challenging the argument made by some historians that there was something inherent in the slave system which inhibited the development of female associations in the South, something that was taking place in the North where slavery was not a factor. Thus, for Friedman, the destruction of slavery alone would not free women of their "enclosure" and, in fact, the antebellum model survived.

According to Friedman (1985), black women, too, were restricted in the antebellum period, but not in the same way as white women. Instead, their status as slaves, which severely limited their mobility, acted as a check to the development of a cohesive collective network of black women. Nevertheless, the different structure of the black family gave black women greater opportunity to express themselves and their desires within their families, positioning them to assume leadership roles. The turmoil and upheaval of the war, however, caused both black and white women to focus more than ever on the maintenance and sustenance of their families and, at the same time, drew these women closer to their religious values and, simultaneously, their kinship networks. Women's activism was, therefore, doubly delayed, first by the antebellum patriarchal-evangelical-kinship system that circumscribed them or, for slave women, their lack of mobility, and then by the war which forced both black and white women ever inward. Their first efforts at organizing would come through their churches as they worked to rebuild them in the aftermath of the war. Their success there led to the development of permanent missionary societies, and it was this work that led to the development of a collective identity. From that followed an interest in larger social issues, and by the end of the century, women were becoming active in both suffrage and temperance organizations.

Drew Gilpin Faust, in *Mothers of Invention* (1996), turns the lens back to plantation mistresses and, like Friedman (1985), finds that their experience during the Civil War delayed the development of women's associations after the war. Although, like Scott (1970), she recognizes that plantation mistresses experienced a growing sense of autonomy during the war and that they carried this new identity into the postwar period. She believes they resented many of the new roles the war forced them to assume and were eager to reestablish the antebellum hierarchy and their privileged position within it. In fact, according to Faust, they quite consciously sought a return to their traditional subordinate roles after the war and, for Faust, this accounts for the delay in the emergence of a movement for women's rights in the South. Nevertheless, women's harsh experiences during the war essentially undermined their faith in their men, and thus when they did become active in the suffrage movement in the late nineteenth century, it was because they understood that male control of the political system alone would not protect women and children.

Not only does Faust (1996) differ from Scott (1970) in the way she interprets women's reactions to the "opportunities" presented by the wartime experience, she views the antebellum plantation mistress very differently. Unlike Scott's strong, resilient, knowledgeable women who understood every aspect of the plantation household, Faust's plantation mistresses were essentially ignorant of even the most basic fundamentals of how their households worked. They felt helpless and were sometimes overcome by a sense of uselessness. They had agreed to a tacit quid pro quo with their men. In return for protection, they obeyed their husbands without question. Given this understanding of antebellum plantation mistresses' mentality, it is no surprise that Faust would find that the Civil War was an overwhelming experience for them and that they were eager to return to their prewar subordinate status. It was, after all, a privileged position which insulated them from the harsher realities of life.

George C. Rable's *Civil Wars: Women and the Crisis of Southern Nationalism* (1989) provides a fascinating and graphic account of the many hardships confronting white women during the war, hardships that necessitated behavior that was uncharacteristic for southern women. Like Friedman's "enclosed" women and Faust's "mothers," however, Rable finds that nothing that happened during the Civil War permanently altered the power of the patriarchy. Rable's region-wide focus attempts to evaluate the experiences of white women, rich and poor, slaveholding and nonslaveholding. He suggests, not that challenges to male authority were not forthcoming, but that, in the end, the political order dominated by white males reasserted itself and women, for the most part, agreed to return to their subordinate status. Rable finds that the "activism" of women during the war was only in response to hardships that were difficult to bear and were manifestations of self-sacrifice rather than self-assertion. Not only were elite women forced to run plantations in the face of invading armies and increasingly unruly slaves, but also poor women were reduced to a state of impoverishment that left them no choice, in their view, but to stage demonstrations characterized as "riots" demanding food. Class tensions began to surface, something that Rable views as unique to the war period, as poor women demanded that elite women share precious resources. As conditions became increasingly desperate and elite women faced financial ruin, they began to petition Confederate authorities, chastising them for corruption and pleading for the release of their men from service. Despite this uncharacteristic behavior, they were never truly comfortable with the roles they were forced to assume, and as the costs of the war mounted, they became increasingly disenchanted and began to withdraw their support for the war itself. This last assertion places Rable (1989) in direct conflict with Bell Wiley (1975), whose *Confederate Women* explored the role that southern women played in sustaining the war effort. Nevertheless, Wiley, like Rable, concludes that despite the remarkable performance of southern women in supporting the war and sustaining the home front, the power of the patriarchy reasserted itself in the postwar period and women returned to their subordinate roles.

Like Scott (1970) and others writing about southern plantation women, Rable's (1989) analysis of the impact of the war years on them is influenced by his understanding of the status of women in the antebellum period. Although he finds that women were often ambivalent about the roles assigned to them in the antebellum period, rigid sex roles prevailed and women largely abided by them. Rable acknowledges the fact that in the late antebellum period, reforms in divorce and property law developed and an expansion of educational opportunities surfaced, but he argues that few women truly benefited from them. The South was ruled by an unrelenting patriarchy, but one that allowed elite women certain privileges and protections. Thus despite the upheaval of the war, which forced them into the public sphere in unprecedented ways, they were eager to return to the confinement of traditional sex roles once their men returned to take up the reins of power and authority. Thus the war did not create an opportunity for women to throw off the strictures of the patriarchy and, in fact, Rable finds them becoming its most stalwart champions in the postwar period. Rather than turning their anger and disappointment toward their men, who had taken them into the conflagration and then lost the war, they focused their fury on northerners and on the freedmen. For the latter, in fact, they reserved a special bitterness. In their view, their former slaves had betrayed them and were undeserving of any special favors and particularly undeserving of any expansion of their civil rights. For Rable, then, southern white women returned to their traditional roles and thus the war proved to be no watershed.

Suzanne Lebsock, in *Free Women of Petersburg* (1984), turned the focus to women – both white and free black – in the city of Petersburg, Virginia, and argued that the Civil War caused the deterioration of certain privileges women had won in the antebellum period. One important aspect of Lebsock's (1984) inquiry was her attempt to explore whether the situation for women in the South was improving or declining in the antebellum period, and in analyzing this question she searches for the existence of a "woman's culture," something Friedman (1985) takes great pains to address in *The Enclosed Garden* (published a year later). Unlike Friedman, Lebsock finds such a culture, but she notes the failure of organized feminism to surface. Also unlike Friedman, she discovers that the economic situation for women (in Petersburg) was improving as women enjoyed greater autonomy and some came to hold independent possession of property. These improvements did not survive the Civil War, however. The war was much too great a disaster, creating significant economic losses for businesswomen, for example, and returning them to economic vulnerability. Despite a heightened sense of self-esteem that accompanied their extraordinary efforts to support the Confederacy, Petersburg's white women suffered disillusionment and shared with all southerners the impoverishment of the postwar era. She suggests that defeated and physically weakened or maimed Confederate veterans suffered psychological damage because their male authority was wounded, and that since "losers are not inclined to be generous" their contributions to the improvement in women's status before the war slowed or ceased altogether (Lebsock 1984: 284).

Lebsock's conclusions follow logically from her emphasis on economics and on her understanding of the experiences of her subjects in the antebellum period. Unlike Friedman (1985), who sees even urban women enduring a life circumscribed by a restrictive kinship network and by the combined power and authority of both evangelical religion and the southern patriarchy, and unlike Rable (1989) who finds that women did not benefit from certain reforms in the antebellum period, Lebsock (1984) argues that the women of Petersburg enjoyed an expansion of opportunities, largely, it turns out, because their men hoped to insulate them from the uncertainties of the capitalist system they were operating within and thus provided them with some economic independence by awarding them independent possession of property. The women of Petersburg took advantage of these opportunities and, in the meantime, created what Lebsock calls a distinctive women's culture, one based on "personalism." This worked two ways. On the one hand, they were much more likely to behave emotionally toward their slaves (in either a negative or a positive manner), and they would often make special provisions in their wills for their female children. Recognizing the constraints that women operated within, they both passed on their good fortune in their wills to their own daughters and, to some extent, made special provisions for their slaves. Their sense of vulnerability, moreover, sometimes led them to aid their less fortunate sisters within Petersburg, women who were not of their own family or class but made manifest the unfortunate status that all women too often suffered within. Nevertheless, the war reconfirmed the subordination of all women and eroded the economic opportunities that had previously existed for some. In an examination of the wills filed between 1861 and 1870, Lebsock finds that despite the fact that more men than ever appointed their wives executors of their wills, fewer women inherited property in fee simple and there was a decline in the proportion of wills written by women.

Free black women in Petersburg, whose status in the antebellum period was at once more vulnerable than that of white women and much better than that of enslaved women, urban or rural, also enjoyed some autonomy and independence. While emancipation brought them decided gains – the freedom of relatives, the right to at least an elementary education – the impoverishment of the South and the strident racism that surfaced in the postwar period proved disastrous. Lebsock does not carry this analysis as far as she might, perhaps because her attention is diverted by the concentration on economic standing of black women in an urban setting. Nevertheless, her findings are, at least in their nascent state, consistent with what

Saville (1994) and Schwalm (1997) suggest about the difficulties confronting rural black women during Reconstruction.

LeeAnn Whites (1995) also focuses on the urban experience of women – the women of Augusta, Georgia – and while their experiences were somewhat similar to those of Lebsock's women of Petersburg, Whites draws some very different conclusions. They certainly bear little resemblance to Rable's southern women. Whites finds, for example, in *The Civil War as a Crisis in Gender* (1995), evidence of patriotism among white elite women at the end of the war, challenging Rable's notion that women helped to bring about the collapse of the Confederacy by withdrawing their support for it. In an analysis that borrows something from both Friedman (1985) and Lebsock (1984), without sounding quite like either, Whites sees "same-sex female kin networks" strengthened by the wartime experience. Also unlike both Friedman and Lebsock, Whites argues that traditional gender roles, both male and female, were fundamentally challenged by the wartime experience facing Augusta and were forever altered by it. As the needs of the war machine dictated greater production of textiles and armaments, the most important economic activity shifted away from the production and marketing of cotton. Whites argues that social power shifted to those producing textiles and armaments and those supplying "the domestic and subsistence labors of household dependents." No longer producing and marketing cotton or, in fact, playing much of any kind of economic role in the way that a male head of household had in the antebellum period, men, as Whites puts it, "came increasingly to resemble their women, whose worthiness had always been vested in their bodies and their potential to produce offspring, or even their slaves, whose bodies were expected to produce staple crops and more bodies to work those crops in the future" (Whites 1995: 12). Men now laid their "bodies" on the line in battle.

There was a check to the enhancement of power that women experienced, however. Augusta endured the onslaught of armies, the flight of desperate white refugees to its environs, and the presence of thousands of freedpeople who threatened the established order. As the war became increasingly hopeless and conditions worsened, merchants raised their prices for basic necessities, and the city struggled in vain to protect the needy. The responsibility for providing for the wives and children of Confederate soldiers and, eventually, for the soldiers' widows and orphans, simply overwhelmed Augusta's ability to cope. Elite women began to exercise greater independence and authority, as it became necessary for them to assume new public roles, but came to fear social leveling when white working-class women sought to assume some of the same new privileges, particularly when they found employment within Augusta's growing armament and textile industries. No longer so dependent on the antebellum elite, working-class women threatened to disrupt the social order. Already shaken by the economic chaos that accompanied the war, elite women welcomed a return to their subordinate positions, but this did not mean that gender roles had not been fundamentally reshaped.

At the heart of Whites' (1995) gendered analysis is an appreciation that the war was fought to protect white men's prerogatives, especially their domination of the dependants within their households, including, of course, their women. Whites' appreciation of the status of women in the antebellum period is more implicit than explicit, but she assumes a relative passivity on their part. The hardships and turmoil of the war created space for women to refashion their respective roles. As it became clear that the Confederacy depended, to a large extent, on the labor of working-class women in the armament and textile factories and on the ability of elite women to maintain the social hierarchy, women began to redefine the meaning of the war. No longer was it a war about male privilege and authority. It was now about the defense of hearth and home. This process of redefining the war continued into the postwar experience, at which point women also "rehabilitated the tattered honor" of their men, creating the Ladies Memorial Association, which was dedicated to celebrating Confederate men. Significantly, men came to accept this female perspective, and by the end of the nineteenth century white southerners of both genders had obscured the significance of slavery and states' rights in bringing about secession and war. But then came the creation of the Confederate Survivors' Association, which essentially took over the memorialization of the war, pushing women out at the same time that it retained the female definition of what the war was about: the protection of women and children. This development was accompanied by a massive expansion of industrial development which depended on a largely female workforce and directly challenged southern manhood. However, southern men were ultimately able to reassert their position as protectors, albeit of a very different sort. These two developments – the Confederate Survivors' Association and industrial development – enabled white men to reaffirm their manhood. Thus, while women played a crucial role in creating the cult of the Lost Cause, it was a cult that came to be dedicated in part to gender domination.

All of the above authors writing about white women considered the restraints or opportunities existing in the antebellum period and suggested how they influenced women's experience during and after the Civil War. Some of them touched on how changes occurring in the law in the antebellum South affected the lives and labors of women. George Rable (1989), for example, acknowledged that certain reforms occurred in the antebellum period, but argued that they actually benefited few women. Peter Bardaglio (1995) takes issue with this point of view in *Reconstructing the Household*, which broadens the focus to family history, and in so doing, enters a contentious debate. On the one hand are those historians who view the powerful patriarchy as the dominant characteristic of the southern family. Certainly Scott (1970), Friedman (1985), and Faust (1996) assume the existence of the patriarchal system, although their understandings of how it worked differ in some respects. Scott, significantly, departs from Friedman and Faust in outlining how women successfully maneuvered within the patriarchal system and how the Civil War freed them even more from its constraints. Another view of the antebellum southern family de-emphasizes the influence of the patriarchy and stresses a more egalitarian spirit existing within the family. Many historians regard this phenomenon as occurring only in the North, arguing that the existence of slavery and the power of the patriarchy inhibited the development of the "republican family" in the South. Michael Grossberg (1985), in a path-breaking book on family law in Victorian America, defined the republican family as one that was bound together by affection and "a new domestic egalitarianism." It was a "middle class creation" which "dominated household ideology and practice in an increasingly bourgeois nation" (Grossberg 1985: 6, 9). Bardaglio (1995) finds something of this republican family emerging in the South in the nineteenth century, even before the Civil War threatened the patriarchy and emancipation freed the slaves. Still, Bardaglio seeks a middle ground between the two opposing views. He finds the republican family growing in the South, especially in the last decade before the Civil War, even as the patriarchy remained a potent force.

Significantly, Bardaglio traces important changes in the law which worked to the advantage of women, but at the same time he recognizes that courts demonstrated some reluctance to challenge the rights of men even when the new interpretations gave them the legal authority to do so. Nevertheless, reforms in property law made it easier for women to own property independently of their husbands. Women found it easier to secure divorces from abusive husbands or from those who failed to support or abandoned them, and the courts awarded women legal standing in cases involving guardianship and even in child custody disputes. Women began to enjoy the benefits of these changes in the 1850s even as the patriarchy remained an inhibiting factor. The Civil War presented a monumental challenge to the patriarchy's ability to contain the changes evolving in the law, and the postwar period saw what Bardaglio characterizes as the emergence of state paternalism. While the antebellum courts had been reluctant to limit patriarchal power, the post-Civil War courts moved more forthrightly in that direction, particularly in cases involving incest and rape. At the same time, however, the courts upheld one aspect of the old southern patriarchy and that was its continued domination of African Americans. Although the black family was recognized as legitimate, African American men were singled out for special treatment and racial distinctions generally were codified and enforced.

The fact that the state courts assumed greater authority and, in some cases, even challenged white male prerogatives, suggests that Civil War and emancipation had clearly shaken the southern patriarchy. But as the various historians writing on the topic of women and gender in the age of emancipation have established, the southern elite was by no means vanquished. That they yielded some power and authority to other forces is beyond question. That they transformed themselves in order to adapt to the new world that confronted them in the wake of war and emancipation is clearly evident. There is much disagreement, however, over the degree of freedom that black women were able to fashion in this period and over the extent to which the Civil War interrupted or forestalled meaningful change for white women. Some of the disagreement can be explained by the focus of the given historian. Those who attempted to fashion a region-wide perspective on the extraordinarily varied South offered the possibility of understanding the whole of the experience, but if they attempted to impose an analytical structure or model in their approach, their studies suffered from the necessity of eliminating the apparent aberrations, the bits that failed to fit the larger general pattern. But perhaps this is unfair. Only by sacrificing analysis in favor of a catalog of experiences could they hope to provide a mosaic where all voices are heard, all the realities of the everyday lives of southern women are revealed. Most of those writing on the experience of southern women in the age of emancipation have chosen to focus more narrowly, on a specific area for example, and their decisions to do so have influenced their findings. One point of view might be corroborated by a discrete study on a city and another shaped by findings gleaned from a focus on a few rural counties in one state. Thus, because of the differences in perspective, because of factors like race, class, and geography, no one study can capture it all in a manner that is intellectually satisfying, but a review of the many important works that have been generated in the last 30 years can together provide a window into the larger world of southern women in America's "age of emancipation."

BIBLIOGRAPHY

Bardaglio, Peter W. (1995) *Reconstructing the Household: Families, Sex, and the Law in the Nineteenth-Century South.* Chapel Hill, NC: University of North Carolina Press.

Blassingame, John W. (1976) *The Slave Community: Plantation Life in the Antebellum South,* rev. edn. New York: Oxford University Press.

Bynum, Victoria E. (1992) *Unruly Women: The Politics of Social and Sexual Control in the Old South.* Chapel Hill, NC: University of North Carolina Press.

Edwards, Laura F. (1997) *Gendered Strife and Confusion: The Political Culture of Reconstruction.* Urbana, Ill.: University of Illinois Press.

Faust, Drew Gilpin (1996) *Mothers of Invention: Women of the Slaveholding South in the American Civil War.* Chapel Hill, NC: University of North Carolina Press.

Friedman, Jean F. (1985) *The Enclosed Garden: Women and Community in the Evangelical South, 1830–1900.* Chapel Hill, NC: University of North Carolina Press.

Genovese, Eugene D. (1974) *Roll, Jordan, Roll: The World the Slaves Made.* New York: Pantheon.

Grossberg, Michael (1985) *Governing the Hearth: Law and the Family in Nineteenth Century America.* Chapel Hill, NC: University of North Carolina Press.

Gutman, Herbert G. (1976) *The Black Family in Slavery and Freedom, 1750–1925.* New York: Pantheon.

Hunter, Tera W. (1997) *To 'Joy my Freedom: Southern Black Women's Lives and Labors after the Civil War.* Cambridge, Mass.: Harvard University Press.

Jones, Jacqueline (1985) *Labor of Love, Labor of Sorrow: Black Women, Work, and the Family from Slavery to the Present.* New York: Basic Books.

Lebsock, Suzanne (1984) *The Free Women of Petersburg: Status and Culture in a Southern Town, 1784–1860.* New York: Norton.

McCurry, Stephanie (1995) *Masters of Small Worlds: Yeoman Households, Gender Relations, and the Political Culture of the Antebellum South Carolina Low Country.* New York: Oxford University Press.

Moynihan, Daniel P. (1981) "The Negro Family: The Case for National Action," in Lee Rainwater and Elisabeth Muhlenfeld, *Mary Boykin Chestnut: A Biography.* Baton Rouge, La.: Louisiana State University Press.

Rable, George C. (1989) *Civil Wars: Women and the Crisis of Southern Nationalism.* Urbana, Ill.: University of Illinois Press.

Saville, Julie (1994) *The Work of Reconstruction: From Slave to Wage Laborer in South Carolina, 1860–1870.* New York: Cambridge University Press.

Schwalm, Leslie A. (1997) *A Hard Fight for We: Women's Transition from Slavery to Freedom in South Carolina.* Urbana, Ill.: University of Illinois Press.

Schweiger, Beth Barton (2000) *The Gospel Working Up: Progress and the Pulpit in Nineteenth-Century Virginia.* Oxford: Oxford University Press.

Scott, Ann Firor (1970) *The Southern Lady: From Pedestal to Politics, 1830–1930.* Chicago: University of Chicago Press.

Stanley, Amy Dru (1998) *From Bondage to Contract: Wage Labor, Marriage, and the Market in the Age of Slave Emancipation.* New York: Cambridge University Press.

Whites, LeeAnn (1995) *The Civil War as a Crisis in Gender: Augusta, Georgia, 1860–1890.*
   Athens, Ga.: University of Georgia Press.
Wiley, Bell I. (1975) *Confederate Women.* Westport, Conn.: Greenwood Press.

SUGGESTED FURTHER READING

Alexander, Adele Logan (1991) *Ambiguous Lives: Free Women of Color in Rural Georgia,
   1789–1879.* Fayetteville, Ark.: University of Arkansas Press.
Bercaw, Nancy (ed.) (2000) *Gender and the Southern Body Politic.* Jackson, Miss.: University
   Press of Mississippi.
Blair, Karen J. (1980) *The Clubwoman as Feminist: True Womanhood Redefined, 1868–1914.*
   New York: Holmes and Meier.
Boles, John B. and Nolen, Evelyn Thomas (eds.) (1987) *Interpreting Southern History: Historio-
   graphical Essays in Honor of Sanford W. Higginbotham.* Baton Rouge, La.: Louisiana State
   University Press.
Bordin, Ruth (1981) *Women and Temperance: The Quest for Power and Liberty, 1873–1900.*
   Philadelphia, Pa.: Temple University Press.
Burton, Orville Vernon (1982) *In my Father's House are Many Mansions: Family and Com-
   munity in Edgefield, South Carolina.* Chapel Hill, NC: University of North Carolina Press.
Cashin, Joan E. (1991) *A Family Venture: Men and Women on the Southern Frontier.* New
   York: Oxford University Press.
Censer, Jane Turner (1984) *North Carolina Planters and their Children, 1800–1860.* Baton
   Rouge, La.: Louisiana State University Press.
Deutsch, Sarah (1987) *No Separate Refuge: Culture, Class, and Gender on an Anglo-Hispanic
   Frontier in the American Southwest, 1880–1940.* New York: Oxford University Press.
DuBois, Ellen Carol (1978) *Feminism and Suffrage: The Emergence of an Independent
   Women's Movement in America, 1848–1869.* Ithaca, NY: Cornell University Press.
Gilmore, Glenda Elizabeth (1996) *Women and the Politics of White Supremacy in North
   Carolina, 1896–1920.* Chapel Hill, NC: University of North Carolina Press.
Higginbotham, Evelyn Brooks (1993) *Righteous Discontent: The Women's Movement in the
   Black Baptist Church, 1880–1920.* Cambridge, Mass.: Harvard University Press.
Hine, Darlene Clark (1989) *Black Women in White: Racial Conflict and Cooperation in the
   Nursing Profession, 1890–1950.* Bloomington, Ind.: Indiana University Press.
Jeffrey, Julie Roy (1979) *Frontier Women: The Trans-Mississippi West, 1840–1880.* New York:
   Hill and Wang.
Kraditor, Aileen S. (ed.) (1968) *Up from the Pedestal: Selected Writings in the History of
   American Feminism.* Chicago: Quadrangle.
McDowell, John Patrick (1982) *The Social Gospel in the South: The Woman's Home Mission
   Movement in the Methodist Episcopal Church, South, 1886–1939.* Baton Rouge, La.: Louisi-
   ana State University Press.
McMillen, Sally (2001) *To Raise up the South: Sunday Schools in Black and White Churches,
   1865–1915.* Baton Rouge, La.: Louisiana State University Press.
Neverdon-Morton, Cynthia (1989) *Afro-American Women of the South and the Advancement
   of the Race, 1895–1925.* Knoxville, Tenn.: University of Tennessee Press.
Ownby, Ted (1990) *Subduing Satan: Religion, Recreation, and Manhood in the Rural South,
   1865–1920.* Chapel Hill, NC: University of North Carolina Press.
Pascoe, Peggy (1990) *Relations of Rescue: The Search for Female Moral Authority in the
   American West, 1874–1939.* New York: Oxford University Press.
Sterling, Dorothy (1984) *We Are your Sisters: Black Women in the Nineteenth Century South.*
   New York: Norton.

Stevenson, Brenda E. (1996) *Life in Black and White: Family and Community in the Slave South*. New York: Oxford University Press.

Thomas, Mary Martha (ed.) (1995) *Stepping Out of the Shadows: Alabama Women, 1819–1990*. Tuscaloosa, Ala.: University of Alabama Press.

Wedell, Marsha (1991) *Elite Women and the Reform Impulse in Memphis, 1875–1915*. Knoxville, Tenn.: University of Tennessee Press.

Weiner, Marli F. (1998) *Mistresses and Slaves: Plantation Women in South Carolina, 1830–80*. Urbana, Ill.: University of Illinois Press.

Wood, Peter (1974) *Black Majority: Negroes in Colonial South Carolina from 1670 through the Stono Rebellion*. New York: Norton.

Woodward, C. Vann and Muhlenfeld, Elisabeth (eds.) (1984) *The Private Mary Chestnut: The Unpublished Civil War Diary*. New York: Oxford University Press.

CHAPTER TWENTY-TWO

The Legacy of Confederate Defeat

GAINES M. FOSTER

In 1998, 133 years after Appomattox, journalist Tony Horwitz toured the South and wrote what he termed *Dispatches from the Unfinished Civil War* (1998). That few thought his title peculiar suggests that the legacy of the Civil War for the white South has been persistent and powerful. Yet no consensus has emerged on its nature. Almost four decades earlier, in an extended meditation on *The Legacy of the Civil*, poet Robert Penn Warren (1964: 15) observed that at the "moment" of its death at Appomattox "the Confederacy entered upon its immortality." Later in the book, Warren (1964: 54) described what he called the "Great Alibi", white southerners' tendency to escape reality and responsibility by blaming their region's problems on the war. At about the same time as Warren wrote, his friend and the region's distinguished historian C. Vann Woodward (1960) offered a very different interpretation of the impact of defeat, one embraced by many southern intellectuals. He contended that the poverty, frustration, and failure that followed the war created among white southerners a distinctive sense of guilt and an appreciation for the ironies of history. More recently, other scholars and observers of the South have implicitly denied altogether the importance of defeat and instead proclaimed the South victorious in the Civil War. A scholarly book entitled *Why the South Lost the Civil War* (Beringer et al. 1986) included a chapter on "State Rights, White Supremacy, Honor, and Southern Victory," and a *New York Times* headline for David Brian Davis' (2001) analysis of the nation's memory of slavery proclaimed "The Enduring Legacy of the South's Civil War Victory."

Evaluating claims of victory or exploring the legacy of defeat requires careful distinctions, particularly between the impacts of the war and emancipation. The two were linked, of course, but whether the South's postwar problems grew out of the slave system, and would have developed whether its demise came through war or by other means, makes a difference. Distinguishing the inevitable results of defeat from the effects resulting from decisions reached by the white South in its aftermath is also important. The war has long been blamed for the postwar southern social order – economic underdevelopment, rigid racial segregation, and intense loyalty to the Democratic party and states' rights. Since 1960 that social order has passed;

as it has, historians have located the legacy of the war less often in the structure of southern society than in its culture.

For almost a century after the Civil War, the South seemed a land apart and left behind in an increasingly industrialized national economy. White supremacy and Democratic control were established, and a new plantation system, this one based on sharecropping and tenantry, settled over much of the region. A few whites attained great wealth, but per capita income in the region remained at best half of the national average. In the 1890s, some southern orators nevertheless praised the South's recovery from defeat, but few talked of winning the war and many embraced the "Great Alibi." Decades later, in 1941, W. J. Cash still referred to the South in the postwar period as the "Frontier the Yankee Made" (Cash 1991 [1941]: 103). Nothing has been as central to the "Great Alibi" as the contention that the South's postwar poverty and economic underdevelopment resulted from the destruction of the war and the refusal of the Yankees to aid the prostrate South. The white South's sense of grievance thrived on stories of stolen silver, ruined lands, and impoverished families, and Hollywood later made Scarlett O'Hara's clawing for food in a devastated landscape a national symbol of the postwar South's plight. The destruction was certainly real. The South experienced a frightful loss of life: 18 percent of young, southern white males died in the war. It had several cities reduced to rubble, 9,000 miles of railroads destroyed, one-third of its hogs killed, and land values fell to half of their previous levels. Between two and three billion dollars of capital invested in slaves disappeared at the moment of emancipation. Yet economists and historians have not agreed on the importance of such devastation.

Gavin Wright (1978) concludes that the loss of hogs undermined traditional patterns of self-sufficiency; Steven Hahn (1983) similarly contends that, in upcountry Georgia, their loss and other destruction brought by the war forced yeoman farmers into the market and, ultimately, into debt and poverty. Looking at the whole of the southern economy, economists Claudia D. Goldin and Frank D. Lewis (1975) attribute the region's persistent poverty to the costs of the war, but Peter Temin (1976) challenges their findings, judging those costs to be much lower than they did. Roger L. Ransom and Richard Sutch (1977), too, dismiss "The Myth of the Prostrate South"; much of the region's "transportation and manufacturing sectors," they claim, experienced "a rapid regeneration" (Ransom and Sutch 1977: 41) and the drop in land prices resulted primarily from the withdrawal of black labor following emancipation. Whatever wartime damage the southern economy experienced, they conclude, had been restored by the late 1870s.

At the very least, though, the South struggled from what Elizabeth Sanders (1999: 112) calls its "anomalous position" in the nation's economy that resulted from "a complex of economic and political factors emanating from the effects of the Civil War." Some southern partisans and a few scholars place much of the blame on the federal government, either for what it did or for what it failed to do. It should have, some contend, done more to rebuild the southern economy. Both William Parker (1980) and Gerald D. Jaynes (1986) argue that only massive federal intervention could have produced any other economic outcome. "The roots of black and white southern poverty lie in this failure to construct a 'Marshall Plan' for the recognition of the cotton economy on the basis of free labor," writes Jaynes (1986: 15). Others blame policies the federal government did develop, such as the Union pension system in which large transfer payments went predominantly to areas other than the South. Although the pension system may only have played a small role, a lack of capital and the high price of credit were certainly among the region's most debilitating economic problems. The loss of slave capital and the wartime destruction of southern banks, exacerbated by the fact that the national banking system had been established while the South was out of the Union, surely contributed to shortages of credit and capital. Perhaps the most important factor of all, as Jaynes shows, was the "lowered . . . credit-worthiness of planters" when their "wealth collateral" decreased because of the loss of their slaves and the "transfer of labor supply decisions to the laborer," which undermined "the landlord's control of the production process *and* increased the real cost of labor services" (Jaynes 1986: 31, emphasis in original).

Such problems, though, inhered in the adjustment to emancipation more than they resulted from the Yankee army's destructiveness or the war itself. Even the South's "anomalous position" in the national economy after the Civil War owed much to its commitment to slavery before it. "Because of slavery," writes Gavin Wright (1986), "the North and the South developed as separate economies, each with its own dynamic logic." Compared to the American North, Wright continues, "the incentives of slave property tended to disperse population across the land, reduce investments in transportation and in cities, and limit the exploration of southern natural resources" (Wright 1986: 11). Most important, slavery contributed, along with postwar immigration flows, to what became crucial after the war, a separate labor market in the South from that of the industrializing North, a separation that helped depress wages in the South for almost a century after emancipation. With little migration out of the region and few towns to attract labor from the farm, the "rural population" was, according to Gilbert C. Fite (1984: xii), too large "in relation to the developed land resources." In other words, the land simply could not support so many people, which in a macabre way undermines at least the argument that Civil War deaths played a significant role in southern underdevelopment. All of these trends, however, were exacerbated by the steady fall in the price of cotton in the international market, an economic development that had little if anything to do with the war, but much to do with the South's persistent poverty. Indeed, Wright (1978: 158) convincingly argues, "cotton's loss of status and leverage in world affairs would have occurred without the war, and the South's own position would have followed cotton in decline." The New South, in short, would have been poor even in the absence of war and emancipation.

Many leaders in the upcountry towns and cities realized that defeat and the end of slavery necessitated a change in southern life and that industrialization promised an escape from the poverty of the cotton economy. These New South prophets achieved much, but not enough. The absence of capital and credit contributed to their failure, but so too did the South's place in a nationalizing economy, another heritage of slavery. The region's "industrialists," David L. Carlton (1990: 447) argues, "had to grapple with the structural disabilities bequeathed the region by its plantation past," among them "thin and poorly articulated internal markets for manufactured goods." Moreover, Carlton explains, the region's entrepreneurs had to make their way in an already developed national economy, within which it was very difficult to compete in most existing industries.

The South's postwar economic woes, however, were not solely the legacy of slavery or the result of vast, impersonal economic forces. The postwar agricultural order owed much to the determination of white landowners to maintain as much control over their laborers as they could. The planters, many small merchants, and their political allies in the Democratic regimes that took power at the end of Reconstruction shaped the law, as Harold D. Woodman (1995) describes, in ways that limited the possibilities for advancement for many white and black southerners. Decisions by the same Democratic governments to restrict spending on education and thereby to do very little to develop the human capital of the South similarly hindered progress in the region. In both instances, economics and race became intertwined – whites strove to control labor and neglected education in part because they sought to prevent black advancement and preserve white supremacy.

Scholarship on the underdevelopment of the New South economy thus provides only meager support for the "Great Alibi" because the South's persistent poverty owed relatively little to the destruction of the war or to the vindictiveness of the Yankees. It resulted far more from the legacy of slavery and the context of a developing national and international economy, exacerbated by the decisions made by white southerners after the war. Credit shortages plagued the West, too, and it had experienced neither defeat nor emancipation. The South's problems even more closely resembled those that followed the end of slavery elsewhere in the western hemisphere, where emancipation came without a war. Historians have contrasted the forms that free labor took in various areas, but the central reality may be the similar economic stagnation that befell each. If anything, the South eventually became the most prosperous of them. The South is more often and rightly compared with the North, though, and if blame is to be rendered for its relative underdevelopment, its total commitment to the institution of slavery, far more than the war that ended it, should be held responsible.

Most post-emancipation societies also experienced difficulties in creating a biracial social order because their white populations were determined to preserve white supremacy. Whites in the American South certainly held fast to such a commitment, and some of the scholars who contend that the South won the Civil War point to southern battles for white supremacy during Reconstruction. George C. Rable (1984: 188), in a study of the role of white violence during Reconstruction, maintains that the "Confederacy never surrendered beyond the mere laying down of arms." Richard Zuczek (1996) agrees. The disputes between 1865 and 1877, he writes, were "a continuation of the struggle of 1861–1865, albeit carried on by different means." Changes occurred after Appomattox, Zuczek admits, but the white South Carolinians he studied reestablished their supremacy and in "a small way . . . achieved their independence and regained some of what had been lost through secession" (Zuczek 1996: ix–x, 210). Although Rable and Zuczek have a point, they have to dismiss as a small factor the obvious one, that the South was not an independent slaveholding republic, and they ignore the real changes that survived Reconstruction. While the post-Civil War plantation system rested on white control, African Americans still had more freedom and greater mobility, as William Cohen (1991) has shown, than under slavery. Even the compensation they received for their labor, Ransom and Sutch (1977) demonstrate, rose in the cotton South. John C. Rodrigue (2001) reports a similar trend in Louisiana's sugar cane fields; in a study of a tobacco-producing county, Sharon Ann Holt (2000) details how the freedpeople succeeded in creating "households" that allowed them to shape their lives. By 1900, therefore, African Americans had advanced in many areas: life-expectancy, literacy, land-ownership. African American political participation did not increase, but at least it continued after the end of Reconstruction. A burst of segregation legislation, dis-franchisement schemes, and savage white violence in the 1890s brought that progress and participation to an end and imposed a rigid racial order. At that point, most historians would agree, white supremacy had been firmly established. Perhaps for no aspect of the New South does the argument for a southern "victory" in the Civil War make more sense. The South did insure white supremacy, which the Confeder-ates had sought, but certainly not in the form they had desired. To treat Jim Crow as a renewal of slavery, moreover, diminishes the harsh realities of the Old South and demeans the importance of freedom. Turn-of-the-century developments are best interpreted as a restoration not of the prewar but of the pre-Reconstruction order.

Nor is the twentieth-century racial order accurately portrayed as a long-delayed victory for Confederate determination over Yankee equalitarianism. The imposition of the new racial order followed, not forced, a loss of northern interest in southern race relations, what C. Vann Woodward (1974: 69) described as a "relaxation of the opposition" when "Northern liberal opinion in the press, the courts, and the gov-ernment" ceased to care about enforcing African American rights. Xi Wang (1997) carefully traces the process through which the Republican party and the federal government abandoned African Americans. He identifies many contributing factors, most of them unrelated to southerners' action but instead reflective of northerners' own racism and reservations about a powerful federal government. Wang also notes that the northern retreat was never complete; Congress refused to repeal the Fif-teenth Amendment, as many in the South advocated. Wang stresses the long-term importance of that failure for the civil rights revolution of the 1960s, but other scholars have noted its importance in the intervening years. In the early twentieth century, Benno C. Schmidt (1986) argues, the Supreme Court relied on the Fourteenth and Fifteenth Amendments to limit certain forms of segregation. Racist whites found ways around these amendments, of course, but their continued exist-ence, as George M. Fredrickson (1981: 197) observes, meant "legalized discrimina-tion remained a localized exception rather than a national norm" and helped distinguish the subsequent history of race relations in the South from those in South Africa. Of course, few blacks in the early twentieth-century South took much conso-lation from that fact.

In explaining the period of white racial hysteria and repression at the turn of the century, the legacy of slavery seems a likely source. But, as the editors of a collection of essays, *Jumpin' Jim Crow*, aptly put it, "Jim Crow was not the logical and inevitable culmination of civil war and emancipation" (Dailey et al. 2000: 4). Like the evolution of the southern agricultural system, with which it was intricately related, the new system of white supremacy resulted from conscious decisions by white southerners. Historians have offered myriad explanations of why they reached those decisions, not the least important of which was their fear of African American progress since emancipation. Other scholars offer more complex explanations. John W. Cell (1982) credits the tensions and change that came with modernization; Joel Williamson (1984) points to the depression of the 1890s that left white males unable to provide for "their" women and anxious to prove their manhood by "protecting" them from an imagined black beast rapist. Several other scholars, some with essays in *Jumpin' Jim Crow*, build on that insight to link the triumph of white supremacy to an attempt to reestablish manhood, independence, and male domination of the household. None of their explanations makes the legacy of the Civil War central to the racist hysteria at the turn of the century.

Two historians, though, do. David H. Donald (1981) attributes the origins of the new racial order to the "generation of defeat." "Cherishing a bitter sense of defeat and betrayal" and inured "to suffering and bloodshed," southerners who had fought the war, Donald writes, "had no qualms about using terrorism, as well as economic pressure and political chicanery, to suppress the Negro vote." They devised laws and institutions to make "sure" that the next generation of white southerners, "who had not themselves had a baptism of fire, who had not experienced the traumas of defeat and betrayal," would maintain white supremacy (Donald 1981: 17). Building on Donald's interpretation, Bertram Wyatt-Brown (2001: 256) argues that the "sense of unrelenting humiliation" brought by defeat "was bound to be turned into anger, racial hatred, and revenge, despite the economic and moral costs." Honor, he concludes, was to be redeemed in blood, most often the blood of lynched African Americans. Although the savage sadistic frenzies of ritualistic lynchings almost cry out for some sort of psychological interpretation, a very prosaic but deadly determination to maintain social and economic control over a hated, but rising, race may be explanation enough. Blaming lynching and Jim Crow on the humiliation that Appomattox brought echoes the long southern refrain of the "Great Alibi," even though its proponents among scholars do not mean to do so. To attribute it simply to the South still fighting the Civil War rightly acknowledges the role that white supremacy played in the creation of the Confederacy but ignores the fact that the South could conceivably, although this was not likely, have abandoned racial supremacy when it abandoned independence. Stressing a continued Civil War also ignores the fact that white supremacy has been a national, not just a southern, phenomenon and may actually serve to dignify rather than expose the racial motives at work.

Similar issues in discussing the legacy of the war arise when analyzing a third central characteristic of the New South – solid support for the Democratic party and an ideology of states' rights. "The war," writes Lawrence Goodwyn (1978: 3), "not political ideas," dominated postwar politics. Symbols of the Confederacy and evocations of the Lost Cause, and in the North the Bloody Shirt, certainly played a role in post-Reconstruction politics. The Bourbons, as many have labeled the Democrats who controlled southern politics in this era, in the words of historian William J. Cooper Jr (1991),

> formed, out of the chaos of military devastation and Reconstruction, an image of a South united by bloodshed in a noble battle for independence. They paid tribute – lip service by some, conviction in others – to glories of what had existed before the war and to the nobility of the war. . . . The holiness of the Democratic party and the white race together with reverence for the Confederacy and the conviction of the horror of Reconstruction have, with the Protestant faith, formed the basic creed of the white Southerners. (Cooper 1991: 15)

The Bourbons' evocation of a Confederate heritage may have been less successful than historians have thought; much recent scholarship demonstrates that the post-Reconstruction South witnessed considerable political dissent and that the Bourbons had to employ fraud and intimidation to retain power. They not only wrapped themselves in the mantle of the Confederacy, but also employed it to cloak their own misdeeds and justify their own political and economic self-interest. Even then, the solid Democratic South emerged only after disfranchisement, as two very different studies – one by J. Morgan Kousser (1974), the other by Michael Perman (2001) – conclude. A systematic reduction in black and poor white voters who might well have supported an opposing party allowed the Democrats to achieve dominance. They then retained white loyalties during the 1920s and 1930s in large measure because, as a majority in a minority party, as David M. Potter (1972) so aptly puts it, Democrats in Washington could protect the South from hostile federal action.

Potter (1972) even claims southern Democrats achieved John C. Calhoun's ante-bellum goal of allowing a southern veto of sorts on national legislation. Southerners in Washington used their position within the Democratic party primarily to protect the region from federal intervention in race relations. Finding a consistent, coherent ideology of states' rights within the politics of the New South, which along with the one-party system some have seen as a legacy of the war, proves very difficult. Elizabeth Sanders (1999) convincingly demonstrates that southern farmers, in large part because of their status on the periphery of a nationalizing economy, joined with their counterparts in the West and urban workers to secure a major expansion of the American state and national power during the Progressive era. Later in the twentieth century, especially during the New Deal of the 1930s, as Jordan A. Schwarz (1994) shows, some southerners embraced a role for the national government in economic development; others advocated what Chester M. Morgan (1985) calls "redneck liberalism," a willingness to support federal aid for the poor and needy. Southern conservatives persisted, but in the face of such political diversity and the South's contribution to the Progressive era and New Deal expansion of federal power, singling out "a" southern political ideology that championed states' rights and limited government, especially one that may have resulted from the heritage of the Civil War, proves difficult. Only when the federal government threatened to intervene in southern race relations did cries of "states' rights" drown out all other voices. In politics as in race relations and economics, evocations of the Civil War and its endur-ing legacy obscure what was actually the result of conscious, contemporary decisions by white southerners determined to maintain white supremacy and by their leaders happy to benefit from a very unequal postwar political and economic order.

Thus the one-party system, like the other two fundamental characteristics of the New South, the one-crop rural economy and a system of rigid racial repression, was not the direct result of the Civil War. Rather, the poverty and structure of southern society resulted in large measure from how white southerners chose to act in the environment created by the demise of slavery. As Robert Penn Warren (1964) perceived, the primary function of the "alibi" – of blaming conditions on the war, defeat, and the Yankees – was to allow white southerners to ignore their own responsibility for slavery, the problems that slavery created, and the costs of main-taining white supremacy in its wake. The Great Alibi thereby led white southerners away from the very confrontation with failure and guilt that Woodward proclaimed the legacy of defeat.

In the years since 1960, the need to invoke the Great Alibi has decreased as the South has changed. At the beginning of the twenty-first century, most white southerners vote Republican, legal segregation has been outlawed, and the one-crop economy and widespread poverty have given way, at least in many areas of the region, to suburban growth, increasing prosperity, and a dynamic diversified economy. In so far as segregation has ended, its demise resulted primarily from the determination of African Americans in the Civil Rights Movement and from the intervention of the federal government. As Bruce J. Schulman (1991) and others demonstrate, the South's post-World War II economic transformation also owed much to the assistance programs of the New Deal and the military spending of World War II and the Cold War. The success of this federal "Marshall Plan" for the South vindicated one tenet of the Great Alibi, the need for federal aid, but it did not follow any southern success in convincing the Yankees that they had wronged Dixie. Rather it arose out of reigning liberal political ideologies and occurred because some southerners saw the potential for a governmental role in economic development. Powerful members of Congress from the South also helped locate military bases in the region, which had an ideal climate for them.

As the need for the Great Alibi declined, historians of the South did not lose interest in the legacy of the Civil War. Since the early 1960s, though, they have become less likely to trace its impact on the structure of the southern society than to explore its influence on its culture. They have defined "culture" broadly, but the impact of the war on four aspects has garnered the most scholarly attention and yielded the most interesting insights: literature, religion, gender relations, and the memory of the Civil War, or the Lost Cause as it is known.

Although some scholars, for example Sarah Gardner (1999), have studied the treatment of the war in the novels and poems of the late nineteenth- or early twentieth-century South, most discussions of how the Civil War shaped southern literature rest on the novels and poems of the Southern Renaissance of the 1920s and 1930s. Woodward (1960: 35) attributed much of its authors' insight to a "consciousness of the past in the present." Stories of the war abound, and Confederate monuments haunt it, but as historians Richard H. King (1980) and Daniel Joseph Singal (1982) demonstrate, the historical consciousness of the writers of the Renaissance emerged not from a continuing spell cast by the war but rather from the writers' confrontation with the modern world and its intellectual life. In the Civil War writers found a story out of which they could create a symbol or idea that could be manipulated for their own ends. Singal (1982: 8) locates those ends in modernism, an intellectual perspective that plumbed "the nether regions of the psyche," perceived "the universe as turbulent and unpredictable" as opposed to "an orderly place governed by natural law," and embraced a world of uncertainty and conflict. The modernist tradition, rather than white southern culture or the legacy of the Civil War, may well have been the source of C. Vann Woodward's perspective on the burden of southern history. Although historians have clung to Woodward's (1960) portrayal of white southerners ennobled by defeat, they and, more surprisingly, literary scholars have spent less effort in exploring the legacy of the war in literature than they once did – perhaps wisely so. Literary works may well not be the best source in which to analyze its influence.

Many historians have instead focused on southern religious life. In his classic, *Southern Churches in Crisis*, Samuel S. Hill Jr (1966) barely mentioned the Civil War, but in a second overview of southern Protestantism 14 years later, he stressed that the region's distinctive faith grew out of a sense of " 'inferiority, antagonism, and insulation' " (1980: 91) that he implied owed much to the Civil War. That same year, Charles Reagan Wilson (1980) explored the link between southern Protestantism and the Lost Cause, concluding that the churches played a central role in sustaining what Wilson terms a "civil religion" rooted in a myth of "Crusading Christian Confederates." The Confederacy, in the stories told by preachers and others after the war, became a "religious-moral crusade" (Wilson 1980: 43) against the heathen Yankees. During the war, they preached, southern soldiers imbued with Protestant virtues fought for sexual purity and other moral values; their achievement then came not through military victory but a triumph of character after the war. The memory of the war thereby contributed to what Wilson calls a sacralization of southern society.

Paul Harvey (1997) offers a similar interpretation in his study of southern Baptists in the New South era. He, too, finds that white southern ministers "preserved the sense of the sacred in white southern history originally learned in the Confederate camps." After the war, "ministers preached a Lost Cause theology" in which the "sacrifice of brave Confederate soldiers . . . cleansed the South of its sin, while the cultural determination of whites . . . ensured the return of a righteous order. Once preached in the idiom – the language of the white evangelical South – this view hardened into an orthodoxy that pervaded southern historical interpretation for a century to come" (Harvey 1997: 11). Confident in the justness of their society, Harvey goes on to explain, white Baptists in the South clung to an intense conservative orthodoxy, which emphasized preventing personal sin and preserving the social order from the various forces of modernization. Meanwhile, he also shows, the newly independent black Baptists played a more overtly political role during Reconstruction and after it continued to struggle for the uplift of the race. As a result, Harvey (1997: 13) concludes, the "religious culture of blacks and whites in the South provided the moral and spiritual force both for the Civil Rights movement and for the dogged resistance to it." Although far from explaining away the racism of the white South, such interpretations as Harvey's and Wilson's once more made the legacy of the Civil War central not just to southern Protestantism but, through it, to southern culture.

In *A Consuming Fire*, Eugene D. Genovese (1998) offers a seemingly similar but ultimately very different argument. Like Wilson, Genovese writes of how traumatic defeat was for the white southerners who believed God had guided their battle to establish a slaveholding republic. Faced with defeat, some questioned God's existence, but most chafed under his judgment and believed that it came not because they held slaves but because they had not treated "their slaves in accordance with scriptural injunctions" (Genovese 1998: 67) but Genovese never quite embraces Woodward's guilt thesis. Defeat, Genovese (1998: 120) then argues, "opened the floodgates to the absorption of the South into the mainstream of transatlantic capitalism" and "into the mainstream of theological and ecclesiastical liberalism." He goes on to blame the New South's racism and defense of segregation not on the persistence of conservative orthodoxy, as Harvey (1997) does, but on its abandonment. The white South's embrace of liberalism led to its capitulation to scientific racism and secularism, on which southerners rested their defense of segregation. Genovese, a scholarly defender of the Old South's intellectual life, comes close to offering a version of the

Great Alibi; the racism of the New South, which Genovese condemns, was the legacy not of the Old South's values, but the ways that defeat and the Yankees brought.

In both Harvey's and Genovese's view, however, the legacy of war remains import-ant, either in sustaining an orthodoxy stained by racism or in destroying one free from it. The importance of the legacy of the war in southern religion seems obvious, especially because, just as a separate labor market persisted in the New South, a separate religious "market" did as well. The major southern denominations – the Southern Baptist Convention, the Methodist Episcopal Church, South, and the Presbyterian Church in the United States – remained "independent" long after the Confederacy succumbed. Not until the 1930s did the Methodists and in the 1980s did the Presbyterians achieve reunion with their denominational counterparts in the North. The Baptists remain independent, although the Convention now seems to be more of a national church. But did church reunion take so long because of lingering bitterness from the war or for other reasons? Wilson and Harvey make a strong case for the role of defeat in encouraging a tendency toward theological orthodoxy among white southerners, and religious conservatism complicated reun-ion. But so, too, did the problem of race and the white South's determination to preserve segregation in church and society, a point made by Ernest Trice Thompson (1965), a distinguished historian of the southern Presbyterian Church and a veteran in its battles over church union. Distinguishing the roles of theological rigidity and the legacy of the war in southern opposition to Church reunion, especially if they are intertwined, proves difficult; weighing the importance of both against fears of racial change in the present is even harder. Determining the legacy of the Civil War, though, may require such judgments.

At about the same time as historians began to explore the legacy of defeat in southern Protestantism, they began to examine the war's impact on gender rela-tions. In *The Southern Lady*, Anne Firor Scott (1970) argued that with men off at war, the plantation mistresses of the Confederacy took on many new responsibilities that changed their lives and those of white southern women who followed them. In the wake of the war, women threw off the "patriarchy" of the Old South. Since Scott's pioneering work, two major studies of southern women during the Civil War have challenged at least part of Scott's argument. George C. Rable (1989), in *Civil Wars*, concludes that the war changed the lives of southern women, but that after the war, gender relations returned to a prewar pattern of subservience to males. In *Mothers of Invention*, Drew Gilpin Faust (1996) reaches a similar conclusion, although often expressing far more ambivalence about it. The war, Faust writes, "dealt a significant blow to the logic of Christian – and, by implication – female submission . . . A new sense of God's distance and disengagement combined with a distrust of the men on whom they had so long relied to impel Con-federate women toward a new independence in the postwar world" (Faust 1996: 195). Yet when peace and the perils of Reconstruction came, Faust concludes, the demands of preserving class and racial superiority necessitated a return to gender subordination. In the face of black emancipation, in other words, southern women believed they had to accept male authority and protection.

Other scholars consider whether the war changed the roles of men and women. In discussing the implications of defeat for both sexes, Gaines M. Foster (1987) rejects the idea that the war overturned male dominance but explores how it did undermine many veterans' sense of their own manliness. Other historians have done far more to trace the implications of the war for gender relations. In perhaps the most sustained examination of the issue, LeeAnn Whites (1995) maintains that the Civil War was "A Crisis in Gender." Like Faust, Whites explores how the war brought a new sense of independence and an expanded public role for women in Augusta, Georgia, but also how "class and race divisions among women" there "served to blunt this transformation of gender relations." After the war, southern white women "acquired a new kind of public voice and a public cultural power" by "celebrating the reconstruction of white southern manhood." In the end Whites, too, finds that "the transformation of Confederate gender relations . . . initially set in motion by the war was closed off" by the 1890s as the Confederate veterans' own celebration and the beginnings of industrialization in Augusta allowed men "to continue to 'protect'" women (Whites 1995: 13–14). Faust and Whites both suggest that racial and economic fears after the war proved more important than its direct legacy in shaping gender roles.

In a study of Reconstruction in North Carolina, Laura F. Edwards (1997) similarly links a postwar crisis in gender to defeat and the end of slavery yet reaches a different conclusion about the outcome. She shows how even though male dominance and traditional spheres persisted, definitions of manhood and womanhood changed, in part becoming more like those in the North. Virtuous manhood came to include economic success and "self-control, proper manners, and devotion to home, family, and God"; the ideal of womanhood remained domestic, but easily accommodated "hard work or even waged work and reform activity" (Edwards 1997: 126, 142). Like Edwards, Stephen Kantrowitz (2000) contends that gender identities proved central to public and political life after the war, but stresses continuity rather than change, by arguing that white males reestablished "mastery" over their households. Elite males, in Kantrowitz's view, thereby laid the basis for white supremacy as well. Peter W. Bardaglio (1995), however, questions whether the reconstruction of the household after the Civil War was so total. Though a distinctive southern legal tradition remained, he writes, in "the regulation of domestic and sexual relations, as in the North, a household-centered patriarchy had yielded for the most part to an emergent state paternalism" (Bardaglio 1995: 227). No real consensus, to say the least, has emerged on the war's impact on gender relations; more work will surely be done.

The discussion of postwar gender relations has already become intertwined with that of historical memory. Like Whites (1995), several scholars have explored the role women played in the development of the Lost Cause. In a close reading of the novels of Mary McClelland and Julia Magruderir, Jane Turner Censer (1999) finds that in the 1880s they challenged the celebration of the war and offered an alternative view of southern masculinity. The novelists proved unusual, however. Historian Fitzhugh Brundage (2000) makes a strong case that women were central to the glorification of the Confederacy and does not find in the Lost Cause so radical a challenge to gender ideals. Brundage (2000), plus Anastatia Sims (1997), in an earlier study of women's groups in North Carolina, do contend that historical activities allowed women to expand their presence in the public sphere but, Sims adds, without abandoning their femininity. Sims (1997) and Rebecca Montgomery

(2000) also show how some white women of the New South employed the memory of women's wartime efforts to support their own efforts to enhance the public role and authority of women. In contrast, Marjorie Spruill Wheeler (1993), in her study of *New Women of the New South*, describes southern women as hostages to the Lost Cause and concludes that it hindered the South's adoption of woman suffrage. The arguments of Sims, Montgomery, and Wheeler are by no means irreconcilable, and they provide a splendid example of what students of historical memory term its constructed and contested nature. They nevertheless do raise questions crucial to an understanding of the legacy of the Civil War, and to the function of historical memory for that matter. If the memory of the war can serve two such disparate, indeed almost opposite, functions, is the legacy of the war as important as contemporary attitudes toward women? Is the Lost Cause only a vehicle for women who want women's rights to assert their independence and for men who want to continue to hinder their advancement rather than a source or cause of the attitudes of either? Answering such questions will do much to explain the true legacy of the war.

As with the effect of the war on gender roles, historians are far from reaching a consensus on the definition of the Lost Cause, the dominant white southern memory of the war. Almost all of the ever-increasing number of scholars who have analyzed the white South's response to defeat have agreed on its immediate impact. After Appomattox, most find, white southerners tended to be devastated but determined to interpret defeat in such a way as to justify their actions, their godliness, and their honor. Interpretations of the long-term function of the resulting celebration of the Lost Cause differ, however. At least four major variations have been offered. In *The Southern Tradition at Bay* (written in 1943 but not published until 25 years later), and which can be seen as one of the first scholarly studies of the Lost Cause or one of the last manifestos of the southern agrarian movement, Richard M. Weaver (1968) offers an impressive survey of postbellum southern writings on the war in which he discovers values that he associates with the Old South. Rooted in agrarian ways, he argues, southern thought was characterized by skepticism toward science and technology, a deep spirituality, and a hierarchical vision of society – in other words, a worldview in stark contrast to that which Weaver felt dominated modern society. Not unlike Genovese, whose work he influenced, Weaver laments that the New South all too quickly abandoned such a worldview, although, he adds, modern Americans could still "learn something of how to live" from the writers of the Lost Cause (Weaver 1968: 396). More recently, one of Genovese's students, Mark G. Malvasi (1997), finds similar tendencies in the writings of the leading Agrarians, John Crowe Ransom, Allen Tate, and Donald Davidson. They did not "revel in the defeat of the South or celebrate the lost cause," Malvasi concludes, but rather "renewed the attack of antebellum southern thinkers on the destructive power of capitalism and on the perils of unfettered individualism" (Malvasi 1997: 8, 9).

A second approach to the Lost Cause, perhaps the most widely accepted, originated with Charles Wilson's book *Baptized in Blood* (1980), which proved as important to the study of the Lost Cause as it did to scholarship on southern Protestantism. Wilson emphasizes that the Lost Cause promised southerners "that God was working from a plan, a design, which man was unable to understand," a plan that would allow the ultimate triumph of southern principles. The Lost Cause also functioned, and here Wilson sounds a bit like Weaver, as a "jeremiad" against the developing New South, one in which adherents "contrasted the materialism of the New South with the spirituality of the Confederacy" (Wilson 1980: 73, 79). At the same time, the Lost Cause "promoted" an image of "virtue and holiness and thus helped maintain the cohesiveness of Southern society." Yet Wilson, not unlike Woodward, also finds in the southern past an experience of "[d]efeat, poverty, guilt, disillusionment, isolation, dread of the future" that "resulted in . . . a distinctly existential outlook among Lost Cause devotees" (Wilson 1980: 15, 8). In *God and General Longstreet*, Thomas L. Connelly and Barbara L. Bellows (1982) perceive a similar sense of alienation in the Lost Cause. It developed, they argue, in the cult of Robert E. Lee but persisted in the lyrics of country music, when Elvis Presley replaced Lee as its central icon. "Country music may say little directly about the Civil War," Bellows and Connelly (1982: 146) admit, "but it is grounded squarely in . . . southern defeat"; its "core . . . is continual striving amid perpetual disappointment – that is the heart of the Lost Cause." Wilson (1980) and Connelly and Bellows (1982) agree that defeat in the Civil War fostered a very distinctive southern culture, an interpretation like Woodward's (1960) in that the resulting white southern sensibility is at odds with the reigning American myths of innocence and success.

In *Ghosts of the Confederacy*, Foster (1987) offers a third and very different interpretation of the nature and function of the memory of the war. He agrees with other scholars on the war's devastating cultural impact and the South's initial theological response to defeat, but he finds that the rituals of the Lost Cause, especially in the 1890s, helped heal the resulting scars of defeat, restore the manhood and honor of the veterans, and foster a sense of triumph and vindication in the South. At the same time, the emerging memory of the war allowed reconciliation with the North, by ignoring the war's issues such as slavery, and contributed to an unquestioning patriotism and militarism. It also served to ease the region's transition to a New South that accepted commercial values. At the same time, the celebration of the Lost Cause supported a deferential social order, in which the lower class deferred to the leadership of their "betters" and white women and African Americans remained subservient to white males. The memory of the war therefore helped shape southern society, but the white South "gained little wisdom and developed no special perspective from contemplating defeat" (Foster 1987: 196). In a more recent series of articles, Fred A. Bailey (1991, 1992, 1994, 1995) even more strongly argues that the Lost Cause served the purposes of the southern white elite.

Neither Bailey, nor Foster, nor Wilson ignores the role of racism in the Lost Cause, but still other scholars render it more central to the white South's celebration of the Confederacy. One early study, Rollin G. Osterweis' *The Myth of the Lost Cause* (1973), did, although its discussion of the continuing influence of romanticism often overwhelmed that of white supremacy. Two important articles by Catherine W. Bishir (1993, 2000) do a better job of showing the centrality of race to the Lost Cause. In one, a study of Raleigh, North Carolina, Bishir (2000) shows how the memorialization of the Confederacy challenged African Americans' attempt to define the memory of the war. In the other, she analyzes how leading North Carolinians shaped the physical environment of their state, its monuments and architecture, to help preserve elite and white power. Grace Elizabeth Hale (1998) also posits a close relationship between white supremacy and the Lost Cause in *Making Whiteness: The Culture of Segregation*. The white South's view of its past, she argues, linked "white southern glory" in the Old South and Civil War with "Reconstruction horror." It locked "the plantation garden firmly away in an Old South destroyed by Yankee 'aggression' and black 'betrayal' during Reconstruction" (Hale 1998: 49). For whites, the resulting historical narrative justified white supremacy and became part of a sense of whiteness that persisted into the twentieth century. Joan Marie Johnson (2000: 562) makes a similar case for the important role women's clubs made in using the Lost Cause to construct "a southern identity based on racial identity." David Goldfield (2002) also stresses how white supremacy lay at the heart of the South's memory of the war, a meaning he sees created when the white South fused history and religion, much as Wilson (1980) and Harvey (1997) suggest.

In the twentieth century, many outside the South accepted the validity of the Lost Cause view of history. At the beginning of the century, as Connelly and Bellows (1982), Nina Silber (1993), David W. Blight (2001), and others contend, the nation ratified much of the white South's celebration of itself in the Lost Cause. With a few exceptions, white northerners granted the Confederate soldiers nobility of purpose and heroic status as warriors, even as both sides agreed not to discuss, at least not too often, the issues of the war. As Stuart McConnell (1992) shows, however, northern veterans in the Grand Army of the Republic continued to celebrate their preservation of the Union even as they ceased to say much about their role in emancipating the slaves and relegated African American veterans to separate camps (or chapters). In other words, most Union veterans ignored what Blight (2001) terms the emancipationist legacy of the Civil War. Blight also writes of reconciliation on "Southern terms," of how southerners had lost the war "but were winning the hearts of millions," and of how the Lost Cause now "marched to a victory song" (Blight 2001: 272, 276, 278). For him and others, the North's denial of the role of slavery in the war constitutes a southern victory in the battle over its memory, another way in which the South has been construed "to win the Civil War." If so, as with the imposition of the new racial order at the turn of the century (and the two developments were related), the Confederates "won" not by storming Yankee barricades but by overrunning a field all but deserted by white northerners who had even earlier retreated from what support for full equality for African Americans they had managed to muster during Reconstruction. Nevertheless, the nation's embrace of the plantation legend and a proslavery historiography seemed total. Although some northerners, as Warren (1964: 54) put it, still claimed for the North a "Treasury of Virtue" for having rid the republic of slavery, only a few whites and many African Americans continued to proclaim the emancipationist legacy of the war.

Most existing studies of northern and southern memories of the war focus on the years before 1920, when Wilson (1980) and others claim interest in the Lost Cause dwindled. Connelly and Bellows (1982) take their account into the 1970s and argue that it remained a powerful force, but few other historians have examined very closely what happened to the Lost Cause after 1920. Many have noted the segregationists' use of Confederate symbols, primarily the flying of the flag and the playing of a dirge-like version of "Dixie," during the Civil Rights era. Yet, surprisingly, little systematic work on the role of the memory of the Civil War during the civil rights era has appeared, although Andrew M. Manis' (1987) book on the conflict between white and black civil religions and John M. Coski's (1996, 2000) articles on the use of the Confederate flag explore aspects of it. The segregationists' use of Confederate symbols and evocations of a "southern way of life" certainly provided validation for the interpretations of the Lost Cause offered by Hale (1998) and Bishir (1993, 2000) and to a lesser extent those of Wilson (1980) and Harvey (1997). More studies of the issue will soon appear.

With the victory of the Civil Rights Movement – the destruction of the South's repressive racial order based on rigid legal segregation and disfranchisement – the white South in the 1970s seemed freed at last from the heritage of slavery and perhaps even the memory of the war. For some, the Confederate flag became the "Dukes' flag," something painted on the top of a souped-up car called the "General Lee" and driven in the television show *The Dukes of Hazzard* by two cartoon-like good ol' boys who continually frustrated neither Yankees nor blacks but a corrupt old southern sheriff. Like the illusion that the South was freed from the legacy of slavery, such an innocent fate for Confederate symbolism proved short-lived. As early as the mid-1970s, even as John Egerton (1974) chronicled the way in which the South had changed, he also wrote of the *Southernization of America*. By the 1990s, a virtual journalistic genre revived the idea that the South was, at long last, dominating national cultural and political developments, in its own way a version of the South-won-the war argument. In 1996, Peter Applebome, who had covered the South for the *New York Times*, published *Dixie Rising* which purported to show *How the South is Shaping American Values, Politics, and Culture*. Egerton, Applebome, and others like them refer to the growing national popularity of such "southern" cultural forms as country music, stock car racing, or the musings of professional good ol' boy Lewis Grizzard. They also attribute to southern influence the nation's growing commitment to conservative politics, traditional religion, and a subtle but powerful form of racism. They would have done well, however, to take more seriously Howard Zinn's (1964) *The Southern Mystique*, written in the midst of the civil rights battles in the 1960s, that found conservative religion and racism in the South to be only exaggerated forms of America's values.

Applebome (1996: 14) also argued that the South "at the end of the twentieth century, amazingly is still fighting most of its oldest battles." Two years later, Tony Horwitz's (1998) *Confederates in the Attic*, an exploration of contemporary southern attitudes about the war, reached a similar conclusion. He and Applebome agreed that the Confederacy was once more on the march primarily because of the rise of a new conservative political movement within the region, widespread participation in Civil War reenactments, and a raging battle over the Confederate flag. Historian David Goldfield (2002) pointed to the same phenomena when he concluded that the South was *Still Fighting the Civil War*, but he put much more emphasis on resurgent racism. At first glance, and maybe even at second or third, such phenomena reaffirm the conclusion of Warren and others who believed the Confederacy achieved immortality at Appomattox.

After a hard look, though, things may appear a little different; too much can easily be made of the more extreme forms of contemporary Confederate loyalty. Two decades earlier, sociologist John Shelton Reed (1983) found in his public opinion surveys that only 10 percent of southerners expressed any interest in secession and, although more, still not that many had much interest in Confederate history. Reed's (2001) more recent poll, conducted in 1994, found that only 22 percent of southerners knew that they had an ancestor who fought in the war – a figure that went up only to 28 percent in the deep South and to 30 percent for people over 45 years of age; 45 percent of southerners agreed with the assertion that the Civil War was not important, and 39 percent agreed that they wanted to put the past behind them. When Reed's pollsters asked northerners, the result on the question of the war's importance was virtually identical and a good bit less (28 percent) on the merits of putting the past behind them. Even Horwitz makes clear that he had to search for the Confederate loyalists he interviewed and that many of the folks he encountered during that quest thought the Confederates among them a bit crazy. He also observes that in "rereading the diary of my time in Mississippi, I was struck by how rarely I'd noted anything to do with the Civil War" (Horwitz 1998: 190) and acknowledges how trivial and commercialized some persisting symbols of the Lost Cause have become. Nevertheless, as his account, the persistence of groups such as the United Daughters of the Confederacy and the Sons of Confederate Veterans, and other evidence make clear, a small but very visible group of white southerners still remember the war.

A still smaller group of white southerners dream of renewing it. Among them, Applebome (1996) and Horwitz (1998) show, are such "neo-Confederate" groups as the Council of Conservative Citizens and the League of the South. Both defend the display of Confederate symbols, and the League openly avows secession, drawing on what they, and historians such as Weaver and Genovese, consider the southern political tradition. Their existence certainly seems to point to an enduring legacy not just for the Civil War but for the Confederacy itself. Such groups are exceedingly small. Even the Southern Poverty Law Center (2000), not given to underestimating the influence of groups it considers dangerous, places the membership of the Council at only 15,000 and that of the League at 9,000 people. Those numbers hardly suggest a movement that can be considered to speak for the South, although they do suggest that a small group of white southerners cherish a link to the Confederacy and its goals – and that they form part of a persistent tradition.

Applebome, however, makes a far more sweeping claim. The "spirit of the Lost Cause – the states' rights of Calhoun; the messianic religiosity of Stonewall Jackson; the paeans to tradition, history, faith, smaller government, and old-time values; the ubiquitous presence of race – tracks remarkably well with the ascendant conservative agenda of the 1990s." It is difficult, he adds, "to know these days where the Confederacy ends and the Republican party begins" (Applebome 1996: 120). So sweeping a statement raises questions similar to those raised by the differing uses of the Civil War in the battle over women's rights. Do neo-Confederates perpetuate a continuing tradition of Confederate values or do conservative southerners revive the memory of the war in support of their conservative agenda? In the final analysis, is modern southern conservatism similar to the conservatism of the West and other areas of the country, one rooted in the more recent history of the United States? A plausible case can be made either way, but given the intervening history of the South, such conservatism seems at best a dissenting tradition, in historical though not contemporary terms. Its sources are rooted in changes since World War II, not the Civil War. Genovese and others would no doubt disagree, and the continuing revival of interest in the Confederacy needs to be studied in a larger context, one which will allow its motives and its roots to be fully explored.

Similar issues arise in evaluating the origins and importance of the less overtly political forms of contemporary interest in the Confederacy – Civil War reenactments and the display of the Confederate battle flag. The emergence of modern society, geographer David Lowenthal (1998) argues, has given rise to "heritage crusades" in many areas of the world. The complexities and frustrations of modernity, he explains, lead many to seek both escape and identity in an imagined past. Beyond their identity as Americans – and national patriotism is far more prevalent in the region than the Confederate version – white southerners in the throes of a modernizing society have few distinctive historical traditions on which to draw other than those that grew out of the Civil War. A significant revival of interest in a Celtic or Scottish heritage has developed (Ray 1998), but one suspects it will never become widely popular. Not too many good ol' boys will embrace a movement that might require that they wear a skirt. Even the fascination with Civil War reenactments may owe as much to the pace of modernization as to the legacy of the war. The reenactors' attention to detail in uniforms and obsession with recreating wartime conditions provides substance to their fantasy escape from modernity into a more "realistic" past. Nor is reenacting unique to the South; northerners participate, as do people in other countries who reenact other wars. Stephen Cushman (1999) reports there are 40,000 Civil War reenactors in the United States, which sounds impressive but actually constitutes only 0.0015 percent of the population of the United States. Cushman also observes that, although reenactment is a means to remembering and honoring the Confederacy and its dead, it is also a form of entertainment, one that took 125 years to become popular. "Civil War reenactment surged in popularity only after the war could be forgotten and what had been traumatic for millions no longer was," (Cushman 1999: 56) he concludes.

The fight over Confederate symbolism – primarily the official display of the Confederate battle flag either over state capitals, in Alabama and South Carolina, or on state flags, in Georgia and Mississippi – has drawn more widespread public involvement than either the neo-Confederate or reenactor groups. White support for the display of the flag therefore provides the most convincing evidence of a persistent legacy of the Civil War, and it has attracted considerable journalistic and scholarly attention. *Confederate Symbols in the Contemporary South* presents a helpful set of essays on the issue. In its introduction, J. Michael Martinez and William D. Richardson (2000) portray the confrontation as one between "traditionalists" and "reconstructionists." They admit that some "traditionalist thought embraces the dark side of the Confederacy by deliberately espousing racist views," but maintain that others rest their defense of the flag in "the best qualities of Southern life – namely, an almost mystical faith in agrarianism, a fierce love of liberty, a mistrust of obdurate, centralized authority, and an unabashed appreciation of home and family." The "reconstructionists," in contrast, see Confederate symbols as "offensive reminders of the worst aspects of Southern culture: a degrading, paternalistic view of African Americans as racially inferior people and a belief that slavery was necessary to the economic and cultural interests of the antebellum South" (Martinez and Richardson 2000: 6–7). This description of southern tradition offers a strange blend of American values – love of liberty and family – and neo-Confederate tenets – faith in agrarianism and mistrust of central authority. Assertions of the importance of the latter echo the views of Weaver (1968) and others on the war's influence. The volume includes one essay that offers statistical evidence on behalf of the "reconstructionists'" charge that support for Confederate symbols reflects not a broad ideological view but persistent racism, a point that Horwitz (1998), too, acknowledges at the end of his exploration of the contemporary fight over Confederate symbols.

African Americans have long nurtured a very different memory of the Civil War, one that, as Bishir (2000), Johnson (2000), Blight (2001), and others demonstrate, emphasizes the role of slavery in the war and the war's emancipationist legacy. The battle over the Confederate flag began when, for the first time since Reconstruction, blacks acquired the political and social power to make an issue of symbols that had long insulted them. The contemporary debate over Confederate symbols is therefore more about the present and future than the past. Many whites resent the growing African American influence in and on southern life and seek in the debate over the flag a means to challenge it – or at the very least to register their displeasure with it. For the many motivated primarily by racial resentment, the celebration of the Confederacy itself becomes a Great Alibi. In so far as the debate does focus on the past, it does not offer much support for Woodward's (1960) portrait of a guilt-ridden, ennobled white culture. If more white southerners had come to terms with defeat in the way that Woodward had hoped they would, white southerners would be more cautious in their celebration of their "heritage" and African Americans would probably not need to demand that the flag come down. Even the attitudes of the substantial number of whites who oppose governmental display of the Confederate flag seem rooted not in the lessons of the 1860s but those of the 1960s. The moral authority of the Civil Rights Movement, not the legacy of defeat, helped convince some white southerners of the need to address the legacies of slavery and segregation. Rather, widespread support for the traditionalists' position reveals that the white South has succeeded, at least in its own mind, in denying that the Civil War was fought over slavery and that southern "heritage," a phrase that many of them attempt to contrast with hate, includes a substantial component of racism.

That does not mean that the white South has won the Civil War, as the *New York Times* headline in 2001 suggested. If it had, African Americans would not have the freedom or the power to denounce Confederate symbols and, along with their white allies, manage to achieve victory or force a compromise over the state's use of the flag in three of the four states where the contests have recently raged. Nor would the neo-Confederates and even the moderate traditionalists feel so embattled. To portray as the continuation of the Civil War, or even simply as its legacy, the very real, continuing struggles of the South and the nation to come to terms with the heritage of slavery, with the promise of an equal, biracial society that the end of the war brought, is to revive the "Great Alibi." It deflects responsibility from generations of white southerners who consciously worked to perpetuate white supremacy. Similarly, evocations of southern victory in the Civil War provide an alibi for the rest of white America as well. If the South "defeated" the North, white northerners did not simply embrace racism or lose interest in black rights but rather were forced by the South to abandon them. Blaming the South allows white northerners to deflect onto southerners their own measure of responsibility for slavery and its aftermath – and thereby preserve their "Treasury of Virtue."

To be sure, the Civil War was a, if not the, central event in the history of the South and the nation. It, and more importantly, the end of slavery that it brought, shaped the social realities in which the New South emerged. But several generations have acted within that context; they made decisions, built institutions, or failed to build others and thereby shaped not just the economy but race relations and cultural values in the region. In the process, the Bourbons who wanted to retain power, men who wanted to keep women from voting, segregationists determined to keep blacks subservient, and even Woodward, who hoped for a wiser South, evoked the memory of the war to support their own agendas. For historians to accept uncritically their claims of historical justifications as evidence of historical causation confuses heritage and history.

Historians still have much work to do and many questions to answer in determining the legacy of the Civil War. They need to evaluate carefully the relative influence of factors such as racism, gender bias, the growth of southern suburban prosperity, or other more recent social or political developments before they too readily explain contemporary developments with reference to the continuing influence of the Civil War. The Confederacy may have proved "immortal" less because of the pervasiveness and persistence of its influence than for the utility of its memory. To attribute to the legacy of the Civil War the problems that plagued the New South and plague the modern South is to make history inevitable rather than contingent and to allow the southern past to be used as a justification for present attitudes or policies. Groups and nations do it all the time, as Lowenthal's (1998) discussion of the heritage crusades documents. Historians should not cooperate. Too much emphasis on the legacy of the Civil War can easily obscure, if not excuse, the history that southerners and northerners, blacks and whites, have made since Appomattox.

BIBLIOGRAPHY

Applebome, P. (1996) *Dixie Rising: How the South is Shaping American Values, Politics, and Culture*. New York: Time Books.

Bailey, F. A. (1991) "The Textbooks of the 'Lost Cause': Censorship and the Creation of Southern State Histories," *Georgia Historical Quarterly* 75: 507–33.

Bailey, F. A. (1992) "Free Speech at the University of Florida: The Enoch Marvin Banks Case," *Florida Historical Quarterly* 71: 1–17.

Bailey, F. A. (1994) "Mildred Lewis Rutherford and the Patrician Cult of the Old South," *Georgia Historical Quarterly* 78: 509–35.

Bailey, F. A. (1995) "Free Speech and the Lost Cause in the Old Dominion," *Virginia Magazine of History and Biography* 103: 237–66.

Bardaglio, Peter W. (1995) *Reconstructing the Household: Families, Sex, and the Law in the Nineteenth-Century South*. Chapel Hill, NC: University of North Carolina Press.

Beringer, Richard E., Hattaway, Herman, Jones, Archer, and Still, William N., Jr (1986) *Why the South Lost the Civil War*. Athens, Ga.: University of Georgia Press.

Bishir, C. W. (1993) "Landmarks of Power: Building a Southern Past, 1885–1915," *Southern Cultures*, inaugural issue: 5–45.

Bishir, C. W. (2000) "'A Strong Force of Ladies': Women, Politics, and Confederate Memorial Associations in Nineteenth-Century Raleigh," *North Carolina Historical Review* 77: 455–91.

Blight, D. W. (2001) *Race and Reunion: The Civil War in American Memory*. Cambridge, Mass.: Belknap Press.

Brundage, W. F. (2000) "White Women and the Politics of Historical Memory in the New South, 1880–1920," in J. Dailey, G. E. Gilmore, and B. Simon (eds.) *Jumpin' Jim Crow: Southern Politics from Civil War to Civil Rights*. Princeton, NJ: Princeton University Press.

Carlton, David L. (1990) "The Revolution from Above: The National Market and the Beginnings of Industrialization in North Carolina," *Journal of American History* 77: 445–75.

Cash, W. J. (1991 [1941]) *The Mind of the South*. New York: Vintage.

Cell, John W. (1982) *The Highest Stage of White Supremacy: The Origins of Segregation in South Africa and the American South*. New York: Cambridge University Press.

Censer, Jane Turner (1999) "Reimagining the North-South Reunion: Southern Women Novelists and the Intersectional Romance, 1876–1900," *Southern Cultures* 5: 64–91.

Cohen, William (1991) *At Freedom's Edge: Black Mobility and the Southern White Quest for Racial Control, 1861–1915*. Baton Rouge, La.: Louisiana State University Press.

Connelly, T. L. and Bellows, B. L. (1982) *God and General Longstreet: The Lost Cause and the Southern Mind*. Baton Rouge, La.: Louisiana State University.

Cooper, William J., Jr (1991) *The Conservative Regime: South Carolina, 1877–1900*. Baton Rouge, La.: Louisiana State University Press.

Coski, J. M. (1996) "The Confederate Battle Flag in American History and Culture," *Southern Cultures* 2: 195–231.

Coski, J. M. (2000) "The Confederate Battle Flag in Historical Perspective," in J. M. Martinez, W. D. Richardson, and R. McNinch-Su (eds.) *Confederate Symbols in the Contemporary South*. Gainesville, Fla.: University Press of Florida.

Cushman, S. (1999) *Bloody Promenade: Reflections on a Civil War Battle*. Charlottesville, Va.: University of Virginia Press.

Dailey, J., Gilmore, G. E., and Simon, B. (eds.) (2000) *Jumpin' Jim Crow: Southern Politics from Civil War to Civil Rights*. Princeton, NJ: Princeton University Press.

Davis, David Brion (2001) "The Enduring Legacy of the South's Civil War Victory," *New York Times*, August 26, 4: 1.

Donald, David Herbert (1981) "A Generation of Defeat," in W. J. Fraser Jr and W. B. Moore Jr (eds.) *From the Old South to the New: Essays on the Transitional South*. Westport, Conn.: Greenwood Press.

Edwards, Laura F. (1997) *Gendered Strife and Confusion: The Political Culture of Reconstruction*. Urbana, Ill.: University of Illinois Press.

Egerton, J. (1974) *The Americanization of Dixie: The Southernization of America*. New York: Harper's Magazine Press.

Faust, Drew Gilpin (1996) *Mothers of Invention: Women of the Slaveholding South in the American Civil War*. Chapel Hill, NC: University of North Carolina Press.

Fite, G. C. (1984) *Cotton Fields No More: Southern Agriculture, 1865–1980*. Lexington, Ky.: University Press of Kentucky.

Foster, Gaines M. (1987) *Ghosts of the Confederacy: Defeat, the Lost Cause, and the Emergence of the New South*. New York: Oxford University Press.

Fredrickson, George M. (1981) *White Supremacy: A Comparative Study in American and South African History*. New York: Oxford University Press.

Gardner, S. E. (1999) "Every Man Has Got the Right to Get Killed? The Civil War Narratives of Mary Johnston and Carolina Gordon," *Southern Cultures* 5: 14–40.

Genovese, Eugene D. (1998) *A Consuming Fire: The Fall of the Confederacy in the Mind of the White Christian South*. Athens, Ga.: University of Georgia Press.

Goldfield, D. (2002) *Still Fighting the Civil War: The American South and Southern History*. Baton Rouge, La.: Louisiana State University Press.

Goldin, Claudia Dale and Lewis, Frank (1975) "The Economic Costs of the American Civil War: Estimates and Implications," *Journal of Economic History* 35: 299–326.

Goodwyn, Lawrence (1978) *The Populist Moment: A Short History of the Agrarian Revolt in America*. New York: Oxford University Press.

Hahn, Steven (1983) *The Roots of Southern Populism: Yeomen Farmers and the Transformation of the Georgia Upcountry, 1850–1890*. New York: Oxford University Press.

Hale, G. E. (1998) *Making Whiteness: The Culture of Segregation in the South, 1890–1940*. New York: Pantheon.

Harvey, P. (1997) *Redeeming the South: Religious Cultures and Racial Identities Among Southern Baptists, 1865–1925*. Chapel Hill, NC: University of North Carolina Press.

Hill, S. S., Jr (1966) *Southern Churches in Crisis*. New York: Holt Rinehart Winston.

Hill, S. S., Jr (1980) *The South and the North in American Religion*. Athens, Ga.: University of Georgia Press.

Holt, Sharon Ann (2000) *Making Freedom Pay: North Carolina Freed People Working for Themselves, 1865–1900*. Athens, Ga.: University of Georgia Press.

Horwitz, Tony (1998) *Confederates in the Attic: Dispatches from the Unfinished Civil War*. New York: Pantheon.

Jaynes, Gerald David (1986) *Branches without Roots: The Genesis of the Black Working Class in the American South, 1862–1882*. New York: Oxford University Press.

Johnson, J. M. (2000) "'Drill into us . . . the Rebel Tradition': The Contest over Southern Identity in Black and White Women's Clubs, South Carolina, 1898–1930," *Journal of Southern History* 66: 525–62.

Kantrowitz, S. (2000) *Ben Tillman and the Reconstruction of White Supremacy*. Chapel Hill, NC: University of North Carolina Press.

King, R. H. (1980) *A Southern Renaissance: The Cultural Awakening of the American South, 1930–1955*. New York: Oxford University Press.

Kousser, J. Morgan (1974) *The Shaping of Southern Politics: Suffrage Restriction and the Establishment of the One-Party South, 1880–1900*. New Haven, Conn.: Yale University Press.

Lowenthal, D. (1998) *The Heritage Crusade and the Spoils of History*. Cambridge: Cambridge University Press.

McConnell, Stuart (1992) *Glorious Contentment: The Grand Army of the Republic, 1865–1900*. Chapel Hill, NC: University of North Carolina Press.

Malvasi, M. G. (1997) *The Unregenerate South: The Agrarian Thought of John Crowe Ransom, Allen Tate, and Donald Davidson*. Baton Rouge, La.: Louisiana State University Press.

Manis, A. M. (1987) *Southern Civil Religions in Conflict: Black and White Baptists and Civil Rights, 1947–1957*. Athens, Ga.: University of Georgia Press.

Martinez, J. M., Richardson, W. D., and McNinch-Su, R. (eds.) (2000) *Confederate Symbols in the Contemporary South*. Gainesville, Fla.: University Press of Florida.

Montgomery, R. (2000) "Lost Cause Mythology in New South Reform: Gender, Class, Race, and the Politics of Patriotic Citizenship in Georgia, 1890–1925," in J. L Coryell et al. (eds.) *Negotiating Boundaries of Southern Womanhood: Dealing with the Powers that Be*. Columbia, Mo.: University of Missouri Press.

Morgan, C. M. (1985) *Redneck Liberal: Theodore G. Bilbo and the New Deal*. Baton Rouge, La.: Louisiana State University Press.

Osterweis, R. G. (1973) *The Myth of the Lost Cause, 1865–1900*. Hamden, Conn.: Archon.

Parker, William (1980) "The South in the National Economy, 1865–1970," *Southern Economic Journal* 46: 1019–48.

Perman, Michael (2001) *Struggle for Mastery: Disfranchisement in the South, 1888–1908*. Chapel Hill, NC: University of North Carolina Press.

Potter, David M. (1972) *The South and the Concurrent Majority*, ed. Don E. Fehrenbacher and C. N. Degler. Baton Rouge, La.: Louisiana State University Press.

Rable, George C. (1984) *But There Was No Peace: The Role of Violence in the Politics of Reconstruction*. Athens, Ga.: University of Georgia Press.

Rable, George C. (1989) *Civil Wars: Women and the Crisis of Southern Nationalism*. Urbana, Ill.: University of Illinois Press.

Ransom, Roger L. and Sutch, Richard (1977) *One Kind of Freedom: The Economic Consequences of Emancipation*. Cambridge: Cambridge University Press.

Ray, C. (1998) "Scottish Heritage Southern Style," *Southern Cultures* 4: 28–45.

Reed, J. S. (1983) *Southerners: The Social Psychology of Sectionalism*. Chapel Hill, NC: University of North Carolina Press.

Reed, J. S. (2001) "Lay my Burden of Southern History Down," *Southern Cultures* 7: 100–3.

Rodrigue, John C. (2001) *Reconstruction in the Cane Fields: From Slavery to Free Labor in Louisiana's Sugar Parishes, 1862–1880*. Baton Rouge, La.: Louisiana State University Press.

Sanders, Elizabeth (1999) *Roots of Reform: Farmers, Workers, and the American State, 1877–1917*. Chicago: University of Chicago Press.

Schmidt, B. C. (1986) *The Judiciary and Responsible Government, 1910–1921*, Vol. 9, Pt. 1 of *The Oliver Wendell Holmes Devise History of the Supreme Court of the United States*. New York: Macmillan.

Schulman, B. J. (1991) *From Cotton Belt to Sunbelt: Federal Policy, Economic Development, and the Transformation of the South, 1938–1980*. New York: Oxford University Press.

Schwarz, J. A. (1994) *The New Dealers: Power Politics in the Age of Roosevelt*. New York: Vintage.

Scott, Ann Firor (1970) *The Southern Lady: From Pedestal to Politics, 1830–1930*. Chicago: University of Chicago Press.

Silber, Nina (1993) *The Romance of Reunion: Northerners and the South, 1865–1900*. Chapel Hill, NC: University of North Carolina Press.

Sims, A. (1997) *The Power of Femininity in the New South: Women's Organizations and Politics in North Carolina, 1880–1930*. Columbia, SC: University of South Carolina Press.

Singal, D. J. (1982) *The War Within: From Victorian to Modernist Thought in the South, 1919–1945*. Chapel Hill, NC: University of North Carolina Press.

Southern Poverty Law Center (2000) *Intelligence Report* 99: 28–9.

Temin, P. (1976) "The Post-Bellum Recovery of the South and the Cost of the Civil War," *Journal of Economic History* 36: 898–907.

Thompson, E. T. (1965) "Presbyterians North and South: Efforts toward Reunion," *Journal of Presbyterian History* 43: 1–15.

Wang, Xi (1997) *The Trial of Democracy: Black Suffrage and Northern Republicans, 1860–1910*. Athens, Ga.: University of Georgia Press.

Warren, R. P. (1964) *The Legacy of the Civil War: Meditations on the Centennial*. New York: Vintage.

Weaver, R. M. (1968) *The Southern Tradition at Bay: A History of Postbellum Thought*, ed. G. Core and M. E. Bradford. New Rochelle, NY: Arlington House.

Wheeler, M. S. (1993) *New Women of the New South: The Leaders of the Woman Suffrage Movement in the Southern States*. New York: Oxford University Press.

Whites, LeeAnn (1995) *The Civil War as a Crisis in Gender: Augusta, Georgia, 1860–1890*. Athens, Ga.: University of Georgia Press.

Williamson, Joel (1984) *The Crucible of Race: Black-White Relations in the American South since Emancipation*. New York: Oxford University Press.

Wilson, C. R. (1980) *Baptized in Blood: The Religion of the Lost Cause, 1865–1920*. Athens, Ga.: University of Georgia Press.

Woodman, Harold D. (1995) *New South – New Law: The Legal Foundations of Credit and Labor Relations in the Postbellum Agricultural South*. Baton Rouge, La.: Louisiana State University Press.

Woodward, C. Vann (1960) *The Burden of Southern History*. New York: Vintage.

Woodward, C. Vann (1974) *The Strange Career of Jim Crow*, 3rd edn. New York: Oxford University Press.

Wright, Gavin (1978) *The Political Economy of the Cotton South: Households, Markets, and Wealth in the Nineteenth Century*. New York: Norton.

Wright, Gavin (1986) *Old South, New South: Revolutions in the Southern Economy since the Civil War*. New York: Basic Books.

Wyatt-Brown, Bertram (2001) *The Shaping of Southern Culture: Honor, Grace, and War, 1760s–1880s*. Chapel Hill, NC: University of North Carolina Press.

Zinn, H. (1964) *The Southern Mystique*. New York: Alfred A. Knopf.

Zuczek, Richard (1996) *State of Rebellion: Reconstruction in South Carolina*. Columbia, SC: University of South Carolina Press.

SUGGESTED FURTHER READING

Aaron, D. (1973) *The Unwritten War: American Writers and the Civil War*. New York: Alfred A. Knopf.

Arnold, R., Jr (2001) *Long Gray Lines: The Southern Military School Tradition, 1839–1915*. Chapel Hill, NC: University of North Carolina Press.

Bodnar, J. (1992) *Remaking America: Public Memory, Commemoration, and Patriotism in the Twentieth Century*. Princeton, NJ: Princeton University Press.

Brundage, W. F. (ed.) (2000) *Where These Memories Grow: History, Memory, and Southern Identity*. Chapel Hill, NC: University of North Carolina Press.

Buck, P. (1937) *The Road to Reunion, 1865–1900*. Boston, Mass.: Little, Brown.

Chadwick, B. (2001) *The Reel Civil War: Mythmaking in American Film*. New York: Alfred A. Knopf.

Clinton, C. (1995) *Tara Revisited: Women, War and the Plantation Legend*. New York: Abbeville Press.

Cullen, J. (1995) *The Civil War in Popular Culture: A Reusable Past*. Washington, DC: Smithsonian Institution Press.

Davies, W. E. (1955) *Patriotism on Parade: The Story of Veterans' and Hereditary Organizations in America, 1783–1900*. Cambridge, Mass.: Harvard University Press.

Davis, S. (1982) "Empty Eyes, Marble Hand: The Confederate Monument and the South," *Journal of Popular Culture* 16: 2–21.

Dean, E. T., Jr (1997) *Shook over Hell: Post-Traumatic Stress, Vietnam, and the Civil War*. Cambridge, Mass.: Harvard University Press.

Dorgan, H. (1972) "The Doctrine of Victorious Defeat in the Rhetoric of Confederate Veterans," *Southern Speech Journal* 38: 119–30.

Dorgan, H. (1979) "Rhetoric of the United Confederate Veterans: A Lost Cause – Mythology in the Making," in W. W. Braden (ed.) *Oratory in the New South*. Baton Rouge, La.: Louisiana State University Press.

Frost, D. R. (2000) *Thinking Confederates: Academia and the Idea of Progress in the New South*. Knoxville, Tenn.: University of Tennessee Press.

Gallagher, G. W. and Nolan, A. T. (eds.) (2000) *The Myth of the Lost Cause and Civil War History*. Bloomington, Ind.: Indiana University Press.

Gaston, P. M. (1970) *The New South Creed: A Study in Southern Mythmaking*. New York: Alfred A. Knopf.

Gulley, H. E. (1990) "Southern Nationalism on the Landscape: County Names in Former Confederate States," *Names* 38: 231–42.

Gulley, H. E. (1993) "Women and the Lost Cause: Preserving a Confederate Identity in the American Deep South," *Journal of Historical Geography* 19: 125–41.

Hattaway, H. (1971) "Clio's Southern Soldiers: The United Confederate Veterans and History," *Louisiana History* 12: 213–42.

Kammen, M. (1991) *Mystic Chords of Memory: The Transformation of Tradition in American Culture*. New York: Alfred A. Knopf.

Levinson, S. (1998) *Written in Stone: Public Monuments in Changing Societies*. Durham, NC: Duke University Press.

Neely, M. E., Jr, Holzer, H., and Boritt, G. S. (1987) *The Confederate Image: Prints of the Lost Cause*. Chapel Hill, NC: University of North Carolina Press.

O'Leary, C. E. (1999) *To Die For: The Paradox of American Patriotism*. Princeton, NJ: Princeton University Press.

Parrott, A. (1991) "'Love Makes Memory Eternal': The United Daughters of Confederacy in Richmond, Virginia, 1897–1920," in E. L. Ayers and J. C. Willis (eds.) *The Edge of the South: Life in Nineteenth-Century Virginia*. Charlottesville, Va.: University of Virginia Press, 219–38.

Piston, W. G. (1987) *Lee's Tarnished Lieutenant: James Longstreet and his Place in Southern History*. Athens, Ga.: University of Georgia Press.

Rosenburg, R. B. (1993) *Living Monuments: Confederate Soldiers' Homes in the New South*. Chapel Hill, NC: University of North Carolina Press.

Royster, C. (1991) *The Destructive War: William Tecumseh Sherman, Stonewall Jackson, and the Americans*. New York: Alfred A. Knopf.

Simpson, J. A. (1994) *S. A. Cunningham and the Confederate Heritage*. Athens, Ga.: University of Georgia Press.

Sutherland, D. E. (1988) *The Confederate Carpetbaggers*. Baton Rouge, La.: Louisiana State University Press.

White, W. W. (1962) *The Confederate Veteran, Confederate Centennial Studies*, no. 22. Tuscaloosa, Ala.: Confederate.

Wilson, C. R. (1995) "God's Project: The Southern Civil Religion, 1920–1980," in Wilson, *Judgment and Grace in Dixie: Southern Faiths from Faulkner to Elvis*. Athens, Ga.: University of Georgia Press.

Wilson, E. (1966) *Patriotic Gore: Studies in the Literature of the American Civil War*. New York: Oxford University Press.

Winberry, J. J. (1983) "'Lest We Forget': The Confederate Monument and the Southern Townscape," *Southeastern Geographer* 23: 107–21.

CHAPTER TWENTY-THREE

Reconstruction and the Nation

HEATHER RICHARDSON

Historians of Reconstruction have focused overwhelmingly on the South from 1865 to 1877, finding gripping drama as the devastated region rebuilt in the years between the Thirteenth Amendment and the "Compromise of 1877." Yet post-Civil War northerners saw Reconstruction not as a southern story alone, but as the reconstruction of a nation from the South, North, and West after the divisive war. Indeed, for contemporary northerners, 1877 was significant not as the end of southern Reconstruction, but as the year of the Great Railroad Strike, seeming to herald a new civil war between labor and capital. The North's struggle with questions of labor, capital, and government after the war profoundly affected both the postwar era and the ultimate shape of the nation. After the war, as northerners saw southern and northern events as parts of the same national story, they read southern events into their growing anxiety over the labor unrest that increasingly shaped northern life. Ultimately they abandoned issues of racial equality to focus on "the labor question" that convulsed the North from 1865 until the 1890s, when new state constitutions and new voter registration laws drastically curtailed working-class voting, North and South. The interaction of northern workers and those northerners who did not identify with a labor interest was an important part of the story of national reconstruction in the wake of the Civil War.

The Civil War had fundamentally reshaped the nation's labor systems. The emancipation of 4 million African Americans and the end of racial slavery in America made the most dramatic and profound change, but the war also transformed northern labor. Before the war most northerners adhered to a free-labor ideology that promised a nation of independent, economically self-sufficient farmers, artisans, and small businessmen. Every able-bodied man, they believed, had been endowed by God with the ability to support himself. Applying his labor to the natural resources around him – fields, forests, oceans, mines – an individual would add value to those valueless raw materials. He would then use the products of his labor, or sell them, to sustain himself and a family. Because a man could produce more than he could reasonably consume, a worker would gradually accumulate the fruits of his labor in the form of capital, which he would then use to hire other economic beginners. Every member of such a society shared the same economic interests, for as one man acquired capital he employed others, and so on in an upward spiral of economic success. By the time of the war there were already specialized groups of workers who considered themselves permanent members of a working class, but for most northerners, surrounded by great natural resources, and the farmers and small manufacturers who processed them, the free-labor vision seemed self-evident.

As the Union government struggled to supply, move, and maintain its massive Civil War army, it pushed the North's economy from one of subsistence agriculture and small businesses toward a new, national, corporate system that would quickly render the free-labor vision invalid. After 1865 the North was a bustling, booming region where companies and farmers increasingly operated in national and international, rather than local, markets. After a brief postwar recession, industry continued to grow dramatically, employing 5 million new and native-born Americans by 1880 and producing in that year over 1 million tons of steel, 4,295,000 tons of pig iron, and a wide range of other products. The new industries thrived on new railroad lines and new communications systems like the typewriter and the telephone, which permitted companies to serve large markets efficiently. As the decades passed, new technologies also provided scores of novel products; electric lighting illuminated cities; rotary presses made newspapers cheaper than ever by printing on both sides of the paper at once; refrigerated meats, canned foods, cigarettes, and ready-made clothing filled new chain stores. This vibrant new economy supported a growing middle class while it also produced new extremes of wealth and poverty and drew new immigrant workers to America.

As the economy changed, so did the lives of workers and their employers, challenging the idea that all Americans shared the same economic interests and that an individual's labor guaranteed him eventual prosperity. Since the beginning of the nineteenth century there had been a labor movement in America, whose adherents believed not in economic harmony, but in a European vision of class conflict as wealth polarized and the condition of workers declined. This vision of America won adherents as the distance between workers and employers grew. Immediately after the war, a postwar recession squeezed workers. The economic recovery coincided with dropping international grain prices and the pogroms that drove immigrants from Europe to new homes in America, where they generally worked as unskilled laborers. By 1880 immigrants poured into the country at the rate of 500,000 a year, filling burgeoning cities like Chicago, Philadelphia, and New York, all of which had over 1 million inhabitants by 1900. Increasingly, the growing body of northern workers ended up in the region's new factories, in unskilled or semiskilled positions where they earned between $1.25 and $1.50 for ten hours of work, that is, $2.30 to $2.80 an hour in present-day money. An unskilled laborer's yearly income averaged just under $500 a year – equivalent to $9,225 in the present-day economy – about $100 less than it took to survive. Low wages and frequent unemployment destroyed the chance of accumulating enough capital to move out of wage labor into the self-sufficiency that characterized the northern ideal.

While workers became increasingly locked into wage labor, the nation's new large industrial factories, corporate financing, and national markets were building fortunes for a lucky few. Based on a presumption that labor would always be scarce and valuable in America, free-labor ideology had never offered a way to force employers to pay subsistence wages or to prevent concentrations of capital; its adherents weakly suggested only that public pressure should bring back into line employers flying in the face of God's natural system of political economy. While public disapprobation might have forced a small-town antebellum shoemaker to pay his few employees well, it was poor protection for urban immigrant factory workers, who had no personal relationship with their employers and who rarely worked all year as the market and supply vagaries caused periodic layoffs. At the same time that it permitted below-subsistence wages, the new economy also allowed men like steel-making giant Andrew Carnegie and railroad magnate Daniel Drew to amass huge fortunes. The wealthy built ostentatious homes, wore Parisian clothes, and hosted expensive parties, infuriating those workers who put food on the table only by sending their children to work in the factories or in the streets, where they could make money picking rags, gathering coal, selling papers, or turning to crime.

As soon as the Civil War was over, northerners had to consider what their victory meant for the free-labor ideal for which they had fought. Was America truly a land of free labor in which all worked together for the increased production that would guarantee everyone prosperity? Or was it, like European countries, a land where different economic classes had to fight each other to guarantee their own share of the pie? In the years after Appomattox, northerners had to resolve the relationship between an increasing permanent laboring population and its increasingly wealthy employers. How could the states reconstruct themselves into a nation that offered individuals political freedom and economic opportunity while also protecting private property and increasing national production?

These questions were not idle, for the dramatic wartime growth of national, state, and local government threatened the ideal of a harmonious, naturally operating national economy and the free-labor theory on which it was based. The small, inactive antebellum national government had been transformed by 1865 into a dynamic and growing body directing an army of more than 1 million men, controlling a new national currency, collecting national taxes, and promoting economic development by offering free land to farmers and beneficial legislation to entrepreneurs. At the same time, growing state and local governments struggled to handle rapid urban development and to provide welfare for increasing numbers of unemployed or disabled citizens.

If members of an interest group organized enough votes to elect sympathetic representatives, they could use growing governments to confiscate wealth they had not earned. A harmonious economy would be destroyed as the government recognized different interests in society and acted in the interest of a certain group, rather than for the good of all. Rich business people threatened the system as they worked quietly for beneficial legislation, but even more frightening to most northerners was the visible increase in workers' agitation for higher wages and better conditions. Even more threatening was that government jobs at all levels, including that of unskilled laborers, were filled by patronage, enabling politicians to hold power by parceling out positions in the new bigger governments. This system both invited an exchange of votes for jobs, and created what amounted to a *de facto* redistribution of wealth, since government jobs went to the unemployed while propertied Americans contributed the bulk of taxes that paid their wages. The growing postwar government forced the North to confront the questions of political economy raised by the changing economy. For northerners after 1865, issues of Reconstruction included not only the South, but also labor, capital, and government.

Postwar Republicans and northern Democrats both argued that their Reconstruction policies were an attempt to preserve and nurture America's traditional free-labor system, but they disagreed about its salient elements. Republicans, who controlled the national government from 1860, when they placed Abraham Lincoln in the White House, until 1874, when Democrats won control of Congress, argued that they truly defended free labor by guaranteeing men of all races the right to "run the race of life" unimpeded. Initially, all but the most radical Republicans were convinced that the free-labor system guaranteed by the Thirteenth Amendment would enable the freedpeople to prosper as they rebuilt the South. When southern landowners gulled their workers and Black Codes circumscribing black freedom indicated that free labor would not spring into life spontaneously in the South, Republicans used the national government to push the relatively moderate terms of the Fourteenth Amendment for southern readmission to the Union, establishing that black men were citizens and that the states could not deprive "any person of life, liberty, or property, without due process of law; nor deny to any person within its jurisdiction the equal protection of the laws." Then, when southerners rejected the Fourteenth Amendment, even moderate northern Republicans agreed to use the national government to enforce free labor in the South, trying to trump local recalcitrance with federal power through the Military Reconstruction Acts 1867, which divided the South into military districts and called for federal oversight of new constitutional conventions. To protect freedmen's rights as free laborers, Republicans established that black men could vote for delegates to the constitutional conventions. By summer 1867, Republicans had enlisted the federal government to enforce southern free-labor, and they had turned to black voters to support that policy.

Northern Democrats, who constantly threatened Republican ascendancy despite their minority in the national government, embraced free-labor ideas, but emphasized the sanctity of the nation's limited government and the protection of white workers both from black competition and from a wealthy aristocracy that would impinge on their liberty. As they sought to reintegrate the South in the Union, Democrats not only harped on their commitment to a "white man's" government, but also maintained that the high taxes required by the large government necessary to administer the Republican free-labor vision were crushing the working-man. Out of practicality as well as principle, Democrats opposed all measures that advanced free-labor ideas by creating larger bodies to enforce them. They recognized that, under the nation's patronage system – the so-called "spoils system" – the growing army in the South and the growing bureaucracy of government employees would be largely Republican as politicians parceled out jobs to their supporters. Democrats castigated Republican legislation to protect African Americans as efforts to create a national Republican "empire," run by party faithfuls and catering to black voters who would keep the Republicans in power.

While both parties claimed to speak for the American worker, it was not clear how northern white laborers would fit into the postwar world. During this period, many, perhaps most, American workers, whether skilled or unskilled, believed that they could succeed on their own through hard work, and thus supported the Republican party. Other workers, unconvinced of the efficacy of free-labor principles, followed the Democrats, who deliberately capitalized on worker resentment of wealthy employers profiting from high tariffs that raised the cost of living. Democrats also exploited white working-men's hatred of the black freedmen whose protection cost tax dollars and who, the Democrats insisted, were given jobs on government projects by Republican politicians anxious to buy their votes. Unsure that free-labor principles still functioned, many workers also organized into unions after the war. The immediate postwar years saw a dramatic increase in national trade unions that worked to defend their members against organized capitalists and unskilled competition; by 1873 there were 26 national unions, led by molders, shoemakers, and railway workers, which boasted a membership of about 300,000 by 1872.

Many working-men thought that they must work to restore the balance of the national economy as well as agitate for better work conditions. They organized labor-reform organizations that operated alongside the older trade unions, agitating for what they believed was the resuscitation of the free-labor dream. Across the North, while members of various trade unions struck for higher wages and worked to influence government regulations, eight-hour leagues and working-men's unions agitated for fewer hours of work, temperance, or any reform that they believed would return the nation to a true free-labor system. In August 1866, the first national congress of the National Labor Union (NLU) met to try to join the myriad different organizations into a national movement. Deploring "wage-slavery," they called for an eight-hour day and a restoration of individual self-sufficiency. In the next five years, the NLU attracted half a million members.

In the immediate postwar years, southern white recalcitrance had forced Republicans to champion the South's black workers, but party members disagreed about northern labor interests. Some radical Republicans made the logical connection between free-labor ideas and the protection of the northern worker. In 1867, the rough, brash president *pro tem* of the Senate, Benjamin Franklin Wade – who had worked as a cattle drover and day laborer – called for a redistribution of wealth when he told a Kansas audience that the theme of postwar America was the struggle between labor and capital. Despite his powerful Senate position, Wade did not speak for the majority of his party. Conservative and even moderate Republicans looked askance at the workers rapidly organizing around them, perceiving such class organization as a threat to the idea of a harmonious economy and society. The *New York Times* (June 8, 1867: 4) warned that workers advocating an eight-hour workday were communists trying "to get the first wedge of their theory introduced into our industrial system by statutory enactment."

Early Republican nervousness about organized labor was exacerbated after 1867 by the activities of the very southern freedmen the Republicans had championed as free laborers. A tiny population of upwardly mobile southern African Americans embraced free-labor attitudes and advocated hard work and individual advancement for freedpeople, but the majority of former slaves, unskilled and impoverished, tended toward economic radicalism. Most former slaves, for whom the new labor–capital relationship was superimposed directly on the old slave–master relationship, saw the world as a struggle between the haves and the have-nots. They agitated for land confiscation, squatted on planters' lands, engaged in work stoppages or even strikes to win better wages, and advocated taxation to fund social welfare programs.

Occasionally black workers took to the streets to protest conditions; Richmond, especially, saw a number of strike-related riots in the postwar years. Black workers seemed to unfriendly northern observers to echo the demands of labor organizers in the North, and the idea that black men were the majority of voters in the southern states seemed to forebode a true workers' government there.

By the early 1870s both moderate Republicans and northern Democrats opposed the growing power of black men who appeared to believe in class conflict and government aid rather than individual enterprise. In 1870, the ratification of the Fifteenth Amendment establishing black suffrage appeared to whites to establish equality across the nation, giving black men the same right to protect their own interests as all other male Americans. But southern blacks continued to work for additional favorable state and federal legislation. Southern African Americans made northern headlines in the early 1870s with their political presence in the South, especially in South Carolina. There, black members of the legislature, popularly and incorrectly portrayed as ignorant fieldhands, were in the majority and were popularly accused of confiscating white property, "plundering the property-holders" through the taxation they imposed. At the same time, African Americans and their radical supporters like Charles Sumner agitated for a Civil Rights Act to protect southern African Americans from the crippling discrimination under which they suffered. Proposed bills were widely unpopular among northern Democrats and northern Republicans both, who argued that African Americans had been made legally equal to whites with the Fifteenth Amendment, and further legislation on their behalf gave them privileges that other Americans did not share.

The example of black workers in southern state governments and advocating the civil rights law made northerners nervous about northern workers, who were concertedly trying to elect sympathetic representatives as well as agitating for better wages. By the early 1870s, politicians feared that the northern laborers could swing an election, handing the power of the government to any demagogue who promised them redistributive legislation. Middle-class Americans had a fearsome example of such a labor-controlled government in Paris, where Communards had assumed control in March 1871 after the Franco-Prussian War. For three months, northerners watched the Paris Commune in horror, perceiving a world turned upside down as laborers attacked the world of their betters, confiscated property, burned homes and businesses, and killed politicians and priests. Many northerners believed that the Commune was a harbinger of a coming revolution in America. When Chicago's Great Fire broke out in October 1871, some blamed the conflagration on communists, and noted that the headquarters of the International Workingmen's Association had been relocated to New York in 1867 where it was led by a lieutenant of Karl Marx. Reformer Charles Loring Brace wrote: "in the judgment of one who has been familiar with our 'dangerous classes' for twenty years, there are just the same explosive social elements beneath the surface of New York as of Paris" (Brace in Fogelson 1989: 24).

Workers' political power was not imaginary. By 1870, National Labor Union leaders had concluded that workers must organize politically to achieve their ends, and, under their encouragement, labor parties had organized in states across the North. In 1871, NLU leaders worked to organize a national labor party, and in February 1872, launched the National Labor Reform party. *Scribner's Monthly* (2

May, 1871: 24) warned in italics that "*the interference of ignorant labor with politics is dangerous to society.*" Examples of working-men's political power were at hand: New York City's infamous Tweed Ring plundered the city and padded contracts for friends who employed Tweed's immigrant constituents, while Benjamin F. Butler – scornfully dubbed "Spoons" for thievery when his army occupied New Orleans – rallied workers in a coalition that almost ousted old-guard Republicans from power in Massachusetts.

From this political tension between labor interests and their opponents came the first history of Reconstruction, written by a participant who wrote both to celebrate the triumph of the Union and to influence readers to support the policies of his party. Massachusetts Senator Henry Wilson, famous throughout his career for his support of labor, published his comprehensive *History of the Rise and Fall of the Slave Power in America* between 1872 and 1877. Wilson tried to hold voters to the Republican standard, reminding them of the prewar Republican belief that a "Slave Power" deliberately threatened individual success by monopolizing land and using slaves to undercut free labor. Convinced that Democratic gains in the postwar years would restore to power old southern Democrats, with their aristocratic ideas and determination to control government for their own ends, Wilson recalled his readers to a commitment to free-labor, reminding them that individual opportunity was the cornerstone of America. Republicans were not trying to build their own empire, Wilson suggested, but were opposing the construction of a Democratic one.

Wilson's formulation of the postwar years did not convince the nation to hold tight to his standard, for in the minds of moderate Republicans and Democrats, the traditional Republican defense of free labor had become associated with the Republican southern Reconstruction governments, where, it seemed, disaffected black workers were controlling government and confiscating property through taxation. In 1872, a reform wing of the Republican party joined with prosperous northern Democrats nervous about their party's growing ties to labor to launch the Liberal Republican party. Their platform reconciled outstanding differences between those Republicans and Democrats who were increasingly nervous about an organized labor interest which wanted to control government for its own benefit. The Liberal Republicans called not only for free labor and the acceptance of the Reconstruction Amendments, but also for sectional reconciliation and smaller government free of corruption, which meant not only national civil service reform to purify northern government but also white reform governments in the South. The Liberal Republican presidential candidate, eccentric blusterer and former radical Republican Horace Greeley, could not possibly unseat President U.S. Grant, but the Liberal Republican platform had set a new agenda for the nation, replacing war issues with labor issues – notably laborers' corruption of government – and pulling together those northerners and southerners, Republicans and Democrats, who rejected an organized labor interest.

The Liberal Republicans had deliberately attacked workers who believed in a class conflict that needed to be mediated by government, and, indeed, by the 1870s, organized workers seemed to be a force to be reckoned with. Sometimes taking their cue from European radicalism, late nineteenth-century American workers often embraced a different ethic than prosperous free-labor Americans, believing in mutualism and advancing an alternative to the emerging corporate capitalism that threatened to kill its labor force. Urban workers especially seemed alien to those

Americans who believed in individualism. They swaggered in the streets and hung out in saloons, delighting in bare-knuckle boxing, wearing cheap and distinctive bright clothing, speaking slang or, often, a foreign language. Their cultural differences from the prosperous Americans who feared them highlighted their new relationship to the workplace. No longer were they individualists accumulating capital for their own success as they joined America's dominant culture; more and more often they engaged in collective action to force employers to grant higher wages and better working conditions. When the Panic of 1873 threw laborers out of work or lowered their pay, frustration – on both sides – rose. If a business was suffering, worried those opposed to a labor interest, why would a good worker put more pressure on it by demanding higher pay? Such demands could destroy the business completely, turning underpaid workers into unpaid vagrants. But such arguments insulted men whose families were starving.

The elections of the mid-1870s reflected the popular alignment against a labor interest that could dominate government for its own ends as the North accepted and even lauded the destruction of the Reconstruction governments in the South. In 1874 northern voters gave the House to Democrats as people worried about the corruption of government by black workers anxious for favorable legislation. Then, in 1876, many moderate northerners – Republicans as well as Democrats – approved as reformers in the South "redeemed" different states from the "corruption" under which they appeared to suffer, effectively removing from political power the poor black men who called for government jobs and taxation to fund social welfare programs. In 1876, the powerful idea of reform and the destruction of the Republican empire made Democrats threaten to take up arms in defense of free government when Republicans insisted on Rutherford B. Hayes' presidential victory despite the competing claims of Democrat Samuel Tilden. It took the distance of an electoral commission to guarantee Hayes' peaceful inauguration, and even then "Rutherfraud's" administration drew constant fire from Democrats determined to denounce the Republicans as empire-builders. In 1878, the Senate, too, became Democratic.

With the South apparently "redeemed" from the corruption of government by poor black workers as reform coalitions jockeyed for the votes of "the better classes" of African Americans, northern fears began to focus on the North. In 1877 there was plenty to focus on. In that year, the growing conflict ignited between organized workers and their employers; 20 percent wage cuts on the Baltimore and Ohio Railroad touched off a strike in West Virginia that rapidly spread across the country, becoming the first national strike. As it shut down the nation's railroads, the Great Railroad Strike left 100 dead and destroyed $10 million in property, and induced President Hayes to send federal troops to Martinsburg, West Virginia, and Pittsburgh, Pennsylvania, to restore order. Only a dozen years before, Americans had seen their comrades fall in rows at Gettysburg and Cold Harbor; they had recoiled from the realization they could walk from one end of a battlefield to the other on corpses. Now, it seemed to shaken Americans, a new civil war was upon them. This one was between labor and capital.

The same strike that terrified middle-class northerners heartened workers suffering in the new economy. In 1879, Terence V. Powderly took over the Knights of Labor, a decade-old labor-reform organization, and tried to build it into a union of all workers; by 1886 the Knights boasted nearly 750,000 members. Powderly showed the Knights roots in reform as he called for economic harmony and a world in which each man could succeed. At the same time, his program for achieving that harmony borrowed all the methods that were popularly associated with those agitators who believed in class conflict. He hoped to restore America's free-labor world by electing sympathetic politicians and working for piecemeal reforms like the eight-hour work-day, better wages, and government regulation of trusts. While Powderly opposed strikes in theory, seeing them as a desperate last measure to be avoided at all costs, local unions often took to the streets. At the same time, working-men continued to work for political influence, joining the Greenback Labor Party, which was organ-ized in 1878 to work for inflationary currency, shorter hours for labor, and checks on Chinese immigration to reduce job competition. In the congressional elections of 1880, the Greenback Labor Party polled over 1 million votes and put 14 of its candidates in Congress.

By the late 1870s workers demanded and won from the dominant political parties the dramatic concession of the Chinese Exclusion Act as Republican and Democratic politicians tried desperately to undercut workers' political power. California had been pinched by a serious recession when the 1869 completion of the transcontin-ental railroad connected the state to international markets just in time to make it vulnerable to the Panic of 1873. Unemployed white workers in California turned first against the employers who hired Chinese immigrants at low wages, then turned their wrath on the vulnerable Chinese, calling for their exclusion from America. Easterners were horrified by the mobs that attacked Chinese workers, and appalled when the anti-Chinese workers and their leader, Irish-American businessman Dennis Kearney, worked with a radical working-men's party to control San Francisco's government and gain a strong voice in the California constitutional convention of 1878–9. Eastern Republicans – and Democratic business people – opposed Chinese restriction not only out of free-labor principles, but also out of reluctance to threaten American access to a huge market by affronting the Chinese. Nonethe-less, horrified by the evident power of workers, national politicians swung onto the anti-Chinese bandwagon as the Chinese issue became a rallying cry for white work-ers. By 1882, the anti-Chinese movement had enough power to force members of both parties to vote in favor of the Chinese Restriction Act, which forbade Chinese immigration to America.

By the early 1880s, labor organization was entering a new phase, its leaders recognizing both that workers were wielding more and more power and that they had become a distinct and largely permanent group in America. In 1881, English immigrant Samuel Gompers organized craft unions across the nation; five years later this national group reorganized as the American Federation of Labor (AFL). The AFL represented about 150,000 – mostly skilled – laborers, and Gompers used the promise of labor votes to work with whatever party promised short-term gains: better wages, conditions, and benefits, fewer hours. By the turn of the century, almost one-third of all American skilled workers – over 1 million men – belonged to the AFL. It seemed that workers' power was growing; in the 20 years after 1880, 6.5 million workers engaged in over 23,000 strikes. And that power was terrifying for those who did not identify with a labor interest. An 1886 labor rally in Chicago's Haymarket Square turned into a riot that left seven police officers and four civilians dead, as well as 70 officers and numerous civilians wounded, when someone – popularly believed to be a labor agitator – threw a bomb at police.

In the 1880s, politicians-turned-historians tried to make sense of the growing conflict in America. In 1884, prominent Senator James G. Blaine published his classic history of the Civil War and Reconstruction era, *Twenty Years of Congress.* Recalling the immediate postwar policies of his party, he insisted that the Republican commitment to free labor and its consequent protection of southern black citizens was the correct course for the nation. Liberal Republican and former Indiana Senator George W. Julian (1884) took a different approach: his *Political Recollections, 1840–1872* worried that the corruption that seemed to characterize the ballooning Republican government as it tried to protect southern blacks threatened the very values Blaine hoped to protect. As a Democrat, Samuel S. Cox of Ohio built on Julian's concerns about Republican Reconstruction. Cox's (1888) *Three Decades of Federal Legislation: 1855–1885* chronicled the increasing Republican expansion of the national government and worried over the corruption such expansion necessarily entailed. All agreed only on their profound unease with the disaffected laborers who seemed to threaten the government.

By the 1880s, hostile observers worried that disaffected laborers would increase their power by joining together with angry western farmers who were also demanding an activist government. Farmers had organized as Grangers in the late 1860s, and in the 1870s called for government regulation of the railroads and grain storage companies they blamed for stealing their profits. In the late 1870s, southern and western farmers experimented with different cooperative organizations like the Southern Alliance – founded in 1875 in Texas – and the Farmers' Mutual Benefit Association to increase their bargaining power. In 1878, farmers joined workers in the Greenback Labor Party, worrying opponents about the power of special interests to control American government.

Prosperity slowed farmers' organization in the early 1880s, but as American farm products entered international markets in the mid-1880s falling prices rekindled western radicalism. The Southern Alliance grew to become the National Farmers' Alliance and Industrial Union, and in 1890 Alliance members met in Ocala, Florida, to demand regulation of railroads, free coinage of silver, an income tax, popular election of senators, and government loans for crops stockpiled until market prices rose. "It is no longer a government of the people, by the people, and for the people," Alliance speaker Mary Elizabeth Lease told voters during the 1890 campaign, "but a government of Wall Street, by Wall Street, and for Wall Street" (Lease quoted in Hicks 1961: 160). After the elections, 44 southern representatives backed by the Alliance went to Congress, three to the Senate, and four to state governors' mansions. Alliance-backed Democrats controlled eight state legislatures in the South. In the North, Alliance support helped Democrats oust Republicans, while farmers' parties controlled both houses of the Nebraska legislature and gave Kansas and South Dakota two senators and five congressmen.

By 1890, workers and farmers who did not believe in a harmonious free-labor world seemed bent on grasping political power to control the government, and northerners who did not identify with a labor or farming interest were increasingly anxious to rein them in. "[S]ocialism of an extreme and dangerous type" had "reversed . . . the essentials of American life," worried a writer for the popular

Century magazine (Sloan 1891). By 1892, these fears had taken immediate shape both in the West and the North. Heartened by their 1890 electoral successes, disaffected westerners had come together in 1892 to launch a national third party, the People's party, which joined together farmers and industrial laborers in a demand for a government that would respond to the people. Populists tried to attract wage-earners by adding to the Ocala demands a call for an eight-hour day and immigration restriction. Their 1892 platform also offered support to the Knights of Labor and demanded a ban on employers' use of armed Pinkerton guards in labor disputes. "We believe that the power of government – in other words, of the people – should be expanded . . . as rapidly and as far as . . . good sense . . . and . . . experience shall justify, to the end that oppression, injustice, and poverty shall eventually cease in the land," the Populists announced (Pollack 1967: 59–65).

Even as the Populists were writing their 1892 platform, a strike at Andrew Carnegie's ironworks in Homestead, Pennsylvania, made tangible for opponents the potential dangers of farmers and laborers in control of government. The ironworks had been organized by the Amalgamated Association of Iron and Steel Workers, one of the largest unions at the time, and by 1892 Carnegie's manager, H. C. Frick, was determined to break the union. He discharged union members and hired Pinkertons to protect the workers remaining in the plant. The ensuing clash between Pinkertons and strikers left 16 dead, and strikers joined with sympathetic townspeople to assume control of the town. For four months, newspapers covered the strike, most echoing the sentiments expressed by *Harper's Weekly* (July 16, 1892: 672): "A strong mob had been organized and armed, by determined leaders, for the purpose of interfering with property rights, and hindering the peaceful employment of labor."

In 1893 began a four-year depression that cemented popular fears of disaffected workers. By 1894, 2 million were unemployed, and as the numbers climbed, workers first demanded government aid, then, when demands were unavailing, they worked actively to get government support. In the spring of 1894, 500 men, women, and children attracted national attention as they followed Jacob Coxey from Massillon, Ohio, to Washington, DC, to ask for a road-building program to provide jobs. When it reached the White House, the "Tramps' March on Washington" was dispersed by 100 mounted police and Coxey was arrested for trespassing, but the seriousness of the workers' demand that government should respond to their needs had been made plain. In the summer, workers showed what they could do if government support was not forthcoming. A strike began at George Pullman's Palace Car Company in Pullman, Illinois, when the company laid off 3,000 of 5,800 employees and cut wages from 25 to 40 percent, then fired members of a grievance committee sent to negotiate with management. Pullman employees were members of the American Railway Union, led by the charismatic and radical Eugene V. Debs. Under his direction, union workers refused to handle Pullman cars, spreading the strike across the nation and paralyzing the country's transportation system.

The growing visibility of those who believed in class conflict rather than economic harmony created a powerful backlash in the 1890s. In 1894, Americans who feared a labor interest applauded when President Grover Cleveland sent several thousand special deputies to Illinois to crush the Pullman strike. In 1895, when one laborer in five was out of work, a government reflecting the popular dislike of organized economic interests declared its unwillingness to permit workers to cooperate for their own interests. The Supreme Court handed down *In re Debs*, which declared the forcible obstruction of interstate commerce illegal, thus practically outlawing strikes. The following year, Americans rejected presidential candidate William Jennings Bryan, who had been labeled an "anarchist" and a "revolutionist" promoting socialistic ideas. Endorsed by the Populists as well as the Democrats, his platform had condemned trusts, monopolies, and a high tariff that served business, and had attacked *In re Debs*. In 1897, a writer for the conservative magazine *Forum* explained the connection between Reconstruction and prevailing fears of the power of disaffected workers:

> Many of those persons who advocated the emancipation of the Southern slave, and who contended with the ballot and the sword for his freedom to choose his vocation and enter into competition with the white laborer, now abandon the ideal of competition and adopt that of socialism. They would argue that it is better, not only for the colored man, but for the white man, to give up individual adventure, and to accept such an organization of society as would determine the career of each member of it and apportion to him his share of the productions of the whole. A small percentage of the citizens of the United States hold this theory of socialism in the full application of its principle; but very many have adopted some parts of the scheme, perhaps without seeing the drift of the reform which they would introduce into the community. (Harris 1897: 186–99)

Beginning in 1890, new state constitutions in the North as well as in the South severely restricted the suffrage, effectively removing the threat that poor workers could capture the government and use it for their own interests. Beginning with Mississippi, southern states enacted property or education qualifications, which guaranteed that no poor men, or men deemed vulnerable to the blandishments of a labor organizer, would cast a vote. To longstanding education or property qualifications, northern states added new registration laws or the Australian ballot, a secret non-partisan ballot which, unlike traditional partisan ballots which could be distinguished by color and shape, could be used only by the literate. These efforts stifled the power of both black and white working-men to influence the government. A new state constitution in Louisiana in 1898 dropped black registered voters 90 percent and white registered voters 50 percent; new voting laws in Pittsburgh at the turn of the century dropped the number of registered voters there 50 percent as well.

Early twentieth-century studies of Reconstruction drew heavily from the racist anti-labor version of the era constructed in the 1890s, arguing that during Reconstruction power-hungry northern politicians and their carpetbagger allies had catered to ignorant freedmen, using government jobs and bribes to rally blacks behind their corrupt political machines. The year 1877, which had not previously been recognized as a significant date in Reconstruction history, became important as the year when the South threw out the grasping carpetbaggers and was restored to "home rule." The historians Charles and Mary Beard (1933) added to this argument the Progressives' conviction that grand political principles hid economic machinations, and presented a world in which avaricious northern businessmen used freedmen to help overthrow the southern plantation aristocracy and prostitute government to their own interests. Reconstruction amendments, then, were efforts made by northeastern business people and western farmers to dominate the burgeoning southern economy. The era, they claimed, marked the "Second American Revolution." The Beards' formulation of Reconstruction as an economic program catering to northern business dominated historiography as long as scholars, informed by the virulent racism of the early and mid-twentieth century, found in the "radical Republicans" economic avarice rather than an impulse for racial equality.

The most complete examination of the postwar North came from those historians anxious to revise the work done in the early twentieth century. They overturned the idea that Reconstruction was an economic revolution in which business carried all before it, crushing the South and labor alike under a Republican-fostered industrial juggernaut. Historians in this school emphasized the moderation of northern Republican Reconstruction and its place in a gradually developing American society. Beginning in the 1950s, revisionist historians logically turned first to examining the collusion of business people and radical Republicans found by the Beards. They explored the policies of the radical Republican faction in Congress and determined that, in fact, voting on racial policies did not correlate with voting on economic policies. David H. Donald (1956) threw open the question of the link between business people and radical Reconstruction in his *Lincoln Reconsidered*; he maintained that radicals shared no economic or social goals, agreeing only about what they opposed. Three years later, Stanley Coben (1959) supported Donald (1956), denying that the two groups worked together.

Book-length studies of the relationship between Republicans and business turned first to the controversial system of paper money established by Republicans during the war and confirmed during Reconstruction, a system charged with catering to business at the expense of labor. Wartime Republicans had established two major forms of paper money: "greenbacks" – printed in green ink on the back – were backed only by the government's ability to fund them; "national bank notes" were backed by private capital invested in government bonds. After the war, a Republican treasury gradually retired the highly inflationary and popular greenbacks in favor of the limited and more stable national bank notes, earning themselves the enmity of laborers, western farmers, and entrepreneurs whose accusations of business collusion had been adopted by historians. In *Money, Class, and Party* (1959), Robert P. Sharkey reexamined the creation of paper money. Exploring the varied economic interests of wartime and postwar financial groups, he concluded that radicals shared no economic interests. Donald student Irwin Unger's Pulitzer Prize-winning *The Greenback Era* (1964) went further and removed the money question from the realm of pure economics; he explored the powerful cultural and social influences that affected postwar financial attitudes.

Once historians had concluded that the nation's finances had not been deliberately manipulated by a collusion of business people and politicians, they turned to other issues to examine whether or not businessmen had dictated Reconstruction. Robert William Fogel's *The Union Pacific Railroad* (1960), for example, suggested that, contrary to accepted wisdom, Republicans had not backed the national railroad in a pork-barrel scheme. In fact, he argued, investment in railroad ventures was terribly risky and governmental encouragement of such investment was imperative to promote these financially unattractive projects. Similarly, Ari Hoogenboom's

Outlawing the Spoils (1961) attacked the idea that civil service reformers were capitalists attempting to secure their own political influence and make the parties serve industry, finding their motivation instead in a drive to recover status lost in the changing postwar world.

Finally, historians reexamined the very idea that the Civil War had dramatically changed the American government. A series of studies of antebellum state governments completed from the 1940s to the 1960s concluded that American governments had not, in fact, set a *laissez-faire* precedent overturned by the war. Louis Hartz's *Economic Policy and Democratic Thought* (1948) and Oscar and Mary Flug Handlin's *Commonwealth: A Study of the Role of Government in the American Economy* (1969) denied that the antebellum world was one of passive government. Turning to the postwar years, Morton Keller's *Affairs of State* (1977) argued that government changes barely outlasted the war, and that a limited government was back in place by the end of the century. Far from manipulating a growing government to crush the South and labor, it appeared, Republicans had neither manipulated the government in any organized way nor even increased its size.

If Republicans were not deliberately constructing government for the benefit of northeastern business, were they truly interested in establishing black free labor? While some revisionist historians like LaWanda and John Cox (1963) focused on the radicalism of those advocating black rights after the war, most revisionists downplayed the efforts of these few people and emphasized that northerners of the postwar years valued moderation. James McPherson's *The Struggle for Equality* (1965) charted the eclipse of those fighting for black rights, while George M. Fredrickson's *The Inner Civil War* (1965) revealed the deep ambivalence with which northerners approached black advancement. John G. Sproat focused directly on the reform wing of the Republican party to examine its radicalism in his *"The Best Men": Liberal Reformers in the Gilded Age* (1968), which emphasized reformers' moderation and their dislike of both black and white workers. In *A Compromise of Principle* and "Preserving the Constitution," Michael Les Benedict (1974a, 1974b) made the case that northerners' overweening concern during Reconstruction was the preservation of the constitution. Five years later, William Gillette's *Retreat from Reconstruction* (1979) proposed that Reconstruction was a moderate, not radical, project, and that initial efforts for black rights collapsed in the face of northern racism. Benedict's (1991) masterful "Reform Republicans and the Retreat from Reconstruction," in the festschrift to historian John Hope Franklin, *The Facts of Reconstruction* (Anderson and Moss 1991), elaborated a nuanced portrait of nineteenth-century American moderation.

Historians of this era reevaluated the Democrats, too, reintegrating them into a long tradition of moderation and downplaying their nineteenth-century racism. Robert Kelly's *The Transatlantic Persuasion* (1969) maintained that American Democrats were part of a moderate international movement opposed to privilege. Joel H. Silbey's *A Respectable Minority* (1977) and Jean Harvey Baker's *Affairs of Party* (1983) emphasized the continuity of the Democratic experience from the antebellum to the postwar years. Lawrence Grossman's *The Democratic Party and the Negro* (1976) proposed that northern Democrats were so anxious to take the middle ground during Reconstruction that they abandoned their previous opposition to black rights and worked to attract black voters, offering their support to reformers and racial moderates like Grover Cleveland. The postwar years, it seemed, were part of a moderate, ongoing American story.

If Reconstruction was not a radical departure from American practice, then, it could be seen as part of the continuum of American history. Viewing Reconstruction as simply another part of American development dovetailed with the work of Bernard Bailyn (1967), Gordon Wood (1969), and J. G. A. Pocock (1975), whose seminal studies of republicanism strongly influenced American history in the last three decades of the twentieth century. Their work challenged historians to see American history as part of a transatlantic movement that valued the republican values of civic virtue, political and economic independence, and political representation. Was a commitment to republicanism the continuing story of nineteenth-century American society?

Labor historians working in the days before the republican synthesis had focused on the institutional histories of organized labor and denied a unifying class-consciousness among American workers. Drawing from Terence V. Powderly's (1967 [1890]) *Thirty Years of Labor: 1859–1889*, John R. Commons (1921–35) argued in his *History of Labour in the United States* that American unions were conservative and "job-conscious" rather than politically radical. Labor historians of the mid-twentieth century built on the work of their predecessors, added the influence of studies of the European working class, and integrated republicanism into labor history. They focused on the world of the nineteenth-century workers themselves, exploring the day-to-day lives of the North's growing working class, and arguing that workers did, indeed, embrace a class-consciousness that differentiated them from their employers. Examining workers' political and social responses to industrial pressure, studies like Herbert Gutman's *Work, Culture, and Society in Industrializing America* (1976b), Nick Salvatore's *Eugene V. Debs, Citizen and Socialist* (1982), Leon Fink's *Workingmen's Democracy* (1983), and David Montgomery's *The Fall of the House of Labor* (1987) found a distinctive form of republicanism in working-class culture as they explored the radical political activism that affronted mainstream middle-class values.

Republicanism in the late nineteenth-century North created not consensus, it seemed, but division between workers and employers. David Montgomery (1967) began to apply the idea of a divided society to the narrative of Reconstruction, exploring the demise of the Republican commitment to free labor in *Beyond Equality*, where he argued that Republican support for free labor broke apart in the postwar years as the party split over the issue of white labor organization. Iver Bernstein (1990) explored the divisions in northern society in his study of the *New York City Draft Riots*. While its title made it better known to Civil War scholars than to students of the postwar years, the book's argument centered on Reconstruction, whose growing class and ethnic tensions, Bernstein (1990) suggested, began in the war era. Similarly, Grace Palladino's slim volume *Another Civil War* (1990) closely examined the developing conflict between workers and employers in the Pennsylvania coal fields and revealed that the state deliberately and systematically used the army against labor allegedly in defense of property rights, a pattern encouraged before the war, exacerbated during the war, and established by the postwar years. Montgomery student Karin Sawislak's *Smouldering City* (1995) took the story of a divided society into the early 1870s, examining the scapegoating of the Irish and the uneven rebuilding efforts in the wake of the Great Chicago Fire.

Uncomfortable with the traditional racism of white workers, labor historians advocating class-consciousness had avoided issues of race. In the early 1990s, Alexander Saxton's *The Rise and Fall of the White Republic* (1990) and David Roediger's *The Wages of Whiteness* (1991) went so far as to argue that nineteenth-century America was a "white republic" which constantly reconceived racism to serve the economic, psychological, and social needs of white people. Labor historians demurred, broadening their approach to labor history, including race relations, and suggesting that in fact black and white workers were not irrevocably estranged, but that they worked together – sometimes with remarkable success – at certain times. Initial studies focused on the South, but by the end of the twentieth century scholars had also begun to explore relations between working-class blacks and whites in the North, although few ventured into the Reconstruction era. Nick Salvatore's *We All Got History* (1996) showed northern society of 1826 to 1904 from the perspective of a northern black worker. Eric Arnesen's *Brotherhoods of Color* (2001) picked up the story in the twentieth century, exploring the critical importance of labor organization to the struggle for civil rights.

At the same time that workers found inspiration for class-consciousness in republican values, historians suggested, those who did not identify with a labor interest found in republicanism the grounds for resisting organized labor. Eric Foner's (1970) pathbreaking book *Free Soil, Free Labor, Free Men* put republican ideas at the heart of northern society. He analyzed the ideology of the Republican party from its formation until the outbreak of the Civil War and argued that antebellum northerners with a predisposition to republican values coalesced in the Republican party and fought the Civil War to defend their principles. Mark Walgren Summers and James L. Huston followed Foner's examination of Republican ideology into the postwar years. Summers' *Railroads, Reconstruction, and the Gospel of Prosperity* (1984) examined northern approaches to the postwar South and made the point that the idea of the New South, with its vision of factories and growing capital, was an attempt to pull the whole nation into a northern vision of prosperity. Huston's *Securing the Fruits of Labor* (1998) tied the republican ideas of the Republicans into a century-long story. Following the rise and fall of the free-labor ideal, he argued that the weakness of the postwar Republican vision was its lack of a solution to economic concentration.

Both labor and political historians used republicanism as a paradigm for understanding aspects of the postwar era, but few used it to write a broad history of the late nineteenth century. In part this was because the period continued to seem unmanageable, with its contrasts of wealth and poverty, progress and nostalgia, political struggle and presidential monotony, and in part it was because the long-standing 1877 watershed artificially divided issues of Reconstruction from those of industrialization. To make sense of the late nineteenth century as a whole requires broadening the investigation of alternative visions of nineteenth-century American society, recognizing the ideological importance of government activism, focusing on the connection between citizenship and free-labor ideals, and throwing out 1877 as the end of Reconstruction.

The Civil War determined that the United States were not, after all, divisible, that there was a permanent and unbreakable United States. But the war did not determine what that nation would be. After Appomattox, different groups of Americans

– farmers, suffragists, freedpeople, white southerners, business people, politicians, laborers, housewives – each tried to advance their own vision of national identity. From 1865 to the end of the century, groups jockeyed and tensions flared as the struggles between different interests were fought out in strikes, injunctions, and at the polls. The question of citizenship – who got to have a say in the direction of the growing government – became of vital importance.

Different groups of Americans advanced their own vision of the new nation, and almost all of those visions had some basis in republican ideas. Republicans championed free labor to create a prosperous world of small farmers and business people. Democrats wanted small government because they feared that the wealthy would inevitably align with big government and use it to guarantee their own ascendancy over individual farmers and laborers. Laborers themselves emphasized economic independence to enable them to rise. While these are the groups traditionally included in studies of Reconstruction, they did not hold the stage alone. Agrarian protesters worked to regulate business and insure the competition that would protect small farmers. Women focused on civic virtue and reform to create a just nation. War veterans advocated pensions to repay them for their sacrifices in saving the republic. And while Native Americans opposed the incursions of American society, western cowboys convinced easterners that individualism was part of the American dream.

Based in republican ideas, these visions conflicted only because of the growing power and size of the government. A free-labor society depended on a small government that treated all individuals equally; success or failure was the responsibility of an individual. If an interest group took control of the government and used it for its own benefit, the very foundation of free-labor society would crumble. Since participation in the government carried with it the power to destroy America's free-labor society, the late nineteenth century became a battleground over the question of suffrage. The questions of national identity and citizenship became intertwined, and of vital importance. Black suffrage, immigration, government corruption, women's suffrage, labor organization, and eventual disfranchisement of the working class, all involved the nature of American citizenship, the activism of the American government, and the eventual shape of the nation.

Rethinking the nineteenth century in terms of citizenship and national identity rather than class consciousness offers a new approach to issues of labor and capital in postwar America. American workers were never easy with each other as a class, hating different racial groups at times, dividing within racial groups at others. Similarly, prosperous Americans were not uniformly united against workers. While they turned venomously against strikers, they championed certain workers of all races who seemed to embrace individualist values. If Americans saw the world through a lens of political economy rather than one of economic class, these seemingly strange bedfellows make sense. Those who endorsed individualism and economic harmony – whatever the size of their bank accounts – feared those who advocated government intervention in a natural class conflict, for that intervention would destroy the free-labor world. A focus on citizenship and national identity makes sense of the seemingly cross-class alliances that kept impoverished strike-breakers defending their right to work and prosperous whites advocating the suffrage rights of a select group of individualistic black voters.

Framing national postwar issues as questions of citizenship and national identity also reintegrates into postwar history issues that have been artificially isolated from it in twentieth-century historiography. The problem of women's suffrage and government's developing role in protecting female labor was an absorbing one in the nineteenth century, but women's issues until recently have not found their way into studies of national Reconstruction. In 1997, two books sought to remedy this absence. Rebecca Edwards' *Angels in the Machinery* (1997) maintained that nineteenth-century questions of increasing state responsibility grew out of debates over the proper relationship between men and women. Patrick J. Kelly's *Creating a National Home* (1997) found the state engaging in a gendered welfare system as it provided a "home" for Civil War veterans.

As Kelly (1997) suggests, exploring citizenship also raises the question of the development of the American state in the late nineteenth century. Robin Einhorn's *Property Rules* (1991) explained the apparently heartless city government abuse of poor inhabitants in Chicago by establishing that, in the late nineteenth-century North, the ownership of property that was so important to free-labor theorists meant that the proprietor literally owned part of the polity, which was supposed to make decisions based on the good of the property owners. Thus, Einhorn (1991) pointed out, city governments permitted factories to dump industrial byproducts into districts heavily populated by transient laborers, who had no voice in the rules made by the propertied. Theda Skocpol's *Protecting Soldiers and Mothers* (1992), and Stuart McConnell's *Glorious Contentment* (1992), explored the pressures on the national government to become increasingly responsive to its citizens. Gaines Foster's *Moral Reconstruction* (2002) concluded that government had expanded selectively in the late nineteenth century. Foster examined the efforts of late nineteenth-century moral reformers to make the government police morality and concluded that, while they had some successes, a majority of Americans had shunned federal government involvement in, for example, the regulation of divorce.

The issues of citizenship and the responsibilities of the American government in the late nineteenth century were, of course, national issues, of tremendous concern to northerners and southerners both. Recognizing them as defining rubrics for studies of Reconstruction also dictates that historians make the logical step of expanding postwar historiography to include the West, for westerners were also concerned about issues of citizenship and government. Questions of citizenship and suffrage were volatile in the West where Native Americans, African Americans, Mexicans, and Chinese mingled with European immigrants and eastern emigrants to construct western communities. Elliott West (2003) wondered in his presidential address to the Western Historical Association "how we have allowed the South to dominate the story of race in America."

The West's relationship to the government is also critical to postwar development, not only because the government exercised more power in the West than in the East, but also because western agitation potently dovetailed with the demands of other interest groups for government activism. Scholars have reconstructed the Populists' alternative vision of government activism, but studies like Lawrence Goodwyn's *The Populist Moment* (1978) have not worked Populism into the context of Reconstruction. In *Roots of Reform* (1999) Elizabeth Sanders began the reintegration of farmers back into the story of Reconstruction, attributing to agrarian protests the direction of national government development in the late nineteenth century; more work remains to be done.

The question of what America would become after the Civil War was certainly not settled in 1877. Indeed, in that year the Great Railroad Strike indicated that the eventual nature of the American nation was more in doubt than ever. The direction of America was settled only by the disfranchisement of those who seemed to deny individualism in favor of class organization and government aid. By 1900, they had been effectively purged from the electorate. When supreme individualist Theodore Roosevelt assumed the presidency in 1901, he could use the government to address the inequities of corporate capitalism with confidence that America was a nation in which socialism could never destroy individualism.

BIBLIOGRAPHY

Anderson, Eric and Moss, Alfred A., Jr (eds.) (1991) *The Facts of Reconstruction: Essays in Honor of John Hope Franklin*. Baton Rouge, La.: Louisiana State University Press.

Arnesen, Eric (2001) *Brotherhoods of Color: Black Railroad Workers and the Struggle for Equality*. Cambridge, Mass.: Harvard University Press.

Bailyn, Bernard (1967) *The Ideological Origins of the American Revolution*. Cambridge, Mass.: Harvard University Press.

Baker, Jean Harvey (1983) *Affairs of Party: The Political Culture of Northern Democrats in the Mid-Nineteenth Century*. Ithaca, NY: Cornell University Press.

Beard, Charles A. and Beard, Mary R. (1933) *The Rise of American Civilization*, two vols. New York: Macmillan.

Benedict, Michael Les (1974a) *A Compromise of Principle: Congressional Republicans and Reconstruction, 1863–1869*. New York: Norton.

Benedict, Michael Les (1974b) "Preserving the Constitution: The Conservative Basis of Radical Reconstruction," *Journal of American History* 61: 65–90.

Benedict, Michael Les (1991) "Reform Republicans and the Retreat from Reconstruction," in Eric Anderson and Alfred A. Moss Jr (eds.) *The Facts of Reconstruction: Essays in Honor of John Hope Franklin*. Baton Rouge, La.: Louisiana State University Press.

Bernstein, Iver (1990) *The New York City Draft Riots: Their Significance for American Society and Politics in the Age of the Civil War*. New York: Oxford University Press.

Blaine, James G. (1884) *Twenty Years of Congress: From Lincoln to Garfield*, two vols. Norwich, Conn.: Henry Bill.

Coben, Stanley (1959) "Northeastern Business and Radical Reconstruction: A Reexamination," *Mississippi Valley Historical Review* 46: 69–90.

Commons, John R. (1921–35) *History of Labour in the United States*. New York: Macmillan.

Cox, LaWanda and Cox, John (1963) *Politics, Principle, and Prejudice, 1865–1866, Dilemma of Reconstruction America*. New York: Free Press.

Cox, Samuel S. (1888) *Three Decades of Federal Legislation: 1855–1885*. Providence, RI: J. A. and R. A. Reid.

Donald, David Herbert (1956) *Lincoln Reconsidered: Essays on the Civil War Era*. New York: Alfred A. Knopf.

Edwards, Rebecca (1997) *Angels in the Machinery: Gender in American Party Politics from the Civil War to the Progressive Era*. New York: Oxford University Press.

Einhorn, Robin L. (1991) *Property Rules: Political Economy in Chicago, 1833–1872*. Chicago: University of Chicago Press.

Fink, Leon (1983) *Workingmen's Democracy: The Knights of Labor and American Politics.* Urbana, Ill.: University of Illinois Press.

Fogel, Robert (1960) *The Union Pacific Railroad: A Case in Premature Enterprise.* Baltimore, Md.: Johns Hopkins University Press.

Fogelson, Robert M. (1989) *America's Armories: Architecture, Society and Public Order.* Cambridge, Mass.: Harvard University Press.

Foner, Eric (1970) *Free Soil, Free Labor, Free Men: The Ideology of the Republican Party before the Civil War.* New York: Oxford University Press.

Foster, Gaines M. (2002) *Moral Reconstruction: Christian Lobbyists and the Federal Legislation of Morality, 1865–1920.* Chapel Hill, NC: University of North Carolina Press.

Fredrickson, George M. (1965) *The Inner Civil War: Northern Intellectuals and the Crisis of the Union.* Urbana, Ill.: University of Illinois Press.

Gillette, William (1979) *Retreat from Reconstruction, 1869–1879.* Baton Rouge, La.: Louisiana State University Press.

Goodwyn, Lawrence (1978) *The Populist Moment: A Short History of the Agrarian Revolt in America.* New York: Oxford University Press.

Grossman, Lawrence (1976) *The Democratic Party and the Negro.* Urbana, Ill.: University of Illinois Press.

Gutman, Herbert G. (1976b) *Work, Culture, and Society in Industrializing America: Essays in American Working-Class History.* New York: Alfred A. Knopf.

Handlin, Oscar and Handlin, Mary Flug (1947) *Commonwealth: A Study of the Role of Government in the American Economy: Massachusetts, 1774–1861.* New York University Press.

Harris, W. T. (1897) "Statistics *versus* Socialism," *Forum* 24 (October): 186–99.

Hartz, Louis (1948) *Economic Policy and Democratic Thought in Pennsylvania, 1776–1860.* Cambridge, Mass.: Harvard University Press.

Hicks, John D. (1961) *The Populist Revolt.* Lincoln, Nebr.: University of Nebraska Press.

Hoogenboom, Ari (1961) *Outlawing the Spoils: A History of the Civil Service Reform Movement, 1865–1883.* Urbana, Ill.: University of Illinois Press.

Huston, James (1998) *Securing the Fruits of Labor: The American Concept of Wealth Distribution, 1765–1900.* Baton Rouge, La.: Louisiana State University Press.

Julian, George W. (1884) *Political Recollections, 1840–1872.* Chicago: Jansen McClurg.

Keller, Morton (1977) *Affairs of State: Public Life in Late Nineteenth Century America.* Cambridge: Cambridge University Press.

Kelly, Patrick J. (1997) *Creating a National Home: Building the Veterans' Welfare State, 1860–1900.* Cambridge: Cambridge University Press.

Kelly, Robert (1969) *The Transatlantic Persuasion: The Liberal-Democratic Mind in the Age of Gladstone.* New York: Alfred A. Knopf.

McConnell, Stuart (1992) *Glorious Contentment: The Grand Army of the Republic, 1865–1900.* Chapel Hill, NC: University of North Carolina Press.

McPherson, James M. (1965) *The Struggle for Equality: The Abolitionists during the Civil War and Reconstruction.* Princeton, NJ: Princeton University Press.

Montgomery, David (1967) *Beyond Equality: Labor and the Radical Republicans, 1862–1872.* New York: Alfred A. Knopf.

Montgomery, David (1987) *Fall of the House of Labor: The Workplace, the State, and Labor Activism, 1865–1925.* Cambridge: Cambridge University Press.

Palladino, Grace (1990) *Another Civil War: Labor, Capital and the State in the Anthracite Regions of Pennsylvania, 1840–1868.* Urbana, Ill.: University of Illinois Press.

Pocock, J. G. A. (1975) *The Machiavellian Moment: Florentine Political Thought and the Atlantic Republican Tradition.* Princeton, NJ: Princeton University Press.

Pollack, Norman (ed.) (1967) *The Populist Mind.* Indianapolis, Ind.: Bobbs-Merrill.

Powderly, Terence V. (1967 [1890]) *Thirty Years of Labor: 1859–1889.* New York: A. M. Kelley.

Richardson, Heather Cox (2001) *The Death of Reconstruction: Race, Labor, and Politics in the Post-Civil War North, 1865–1901.* Cambridge, Mass.: Harvard University Press.

Roediger, David (1991) *The Wages of Whiteness: Race and the Formation of the American Working Class.* London: Verso.

Salvatore, Nick (1982) *Eugene V. Debs: Citizen and Socialist.* Urbana, Ill.: University of Illinois Press.

Salvatore, Nick (1996) *We All Got History: The Memory Books of Amos Webber.* New York: Times Books.

Sanders, Elizabeth (1999) *Roots of Reform: Farmers, Workers, and the American State, 1877–1917.* Chicago: University of Chicago Press.

Sawislak, Karin (1995) *Smouldering City: Chicagoans and the Great Fire, 1871–1874.* Chicago: University of Chicago Press.

Saxton, Alexander (1990) *The Rise and Fall of the White Republic: Class Politics and Mass Culture in Nineteenth-Century America.* London: Verso.

Sharkey, Robert P. (1959) *Money, Class, and Party: An Economic Study of Civil War and Reconstruction.* Baltimore, Md.: Johns Hopkins University Press.

Silbey, Joel H. (1977) *A Respectable Minority: The Democratic Party in the Civil War Era, 1860–1868.* New York: Norton.

Skocpol, Theda (1992) *Protecting Soldiers and Mothers: The Political Origins of Social Policy in the United States.* Cambridge, Mass.: Belknap Press.

Sloan, William M. (1891) "Pensions and Socialism," *Century* 42 (June): 179–88.

Sproat, John G. (1968) *"The Best Men": Liberal Reformers in the Gilded Age.* New York: Oxford University Press.

Summers, Mark W. (1984) *Railroads, Reconstruction, and the Gospel of Prosperity: Aid under the Radical Republicans, 1865–1877.* Princeton, NJ: Princeton University Press.

Unger, Irwin (1964) *The Greenback Era: A Social and Political History of American Finance.* Princeton, NJ: Princeton University Press.

West, Elliott (2003) "Reconstructing Race," *Western Historical Quarterly* 34 (Spring).

Wilson, Henry (1872–7) *History of the Rise and Fall of the Slave Power in America,* three vols. Boston, Mass.: J. R. Osgood.

Wood, Gordon S. (1969) *The Creation of the American Republic, 1776–1787.* Chapel Hill, NC: University of North Carolina Press.

SUGGESTED FURTHER READING

Anbinder, Tyler (2001) *Five Points: The Nineteenth-Century New York City Neighborhood that Invented Tap Dance, Stole Elections, and Became the World's Most Notorious Slum.* New York: Free Press.

Foner, Eric (1988) *Reconstruction: America's Unfinished Revolution, 1863–1877.* New York: Harper and Row.

Keyssar, Alexander (2000) *The Right to Vote: The Contested History of Democracy in the United States.* New York: Basic Books.

Laurie, Bruce (1997) *Artisans into Workers: Labor in Nineteenth Century America.* Urbana, Ill.: University of Illinois Press.

Peiss, Kathy (1986) *Cheap Amusements: Working Women and Leisure in Turn-of-the-Century New York.* Philadelphia, Pa.: Temple University Press.

Wang, Xi (1997) *The Trial of Democracy: Black Suffrage and Northern Republicans, 1860–1910.* Athens, Ga.: University of Georgia Press.

Bibliography

Abbott, Richard H. (1986) *The Republican Party and the South, 1855–1877.* Chapel Hill, NC: University of North Carolina Press.

Abernathy, Thomas P. (1961) *The South in the New Nation, 1789–1819.* Baton Rouge, La.: Louisiana State University Press.

Abzug, Robert (1995) *Cosmos Crumbling: American Reform and the Religious Imagination.* New York: Oxford University Press.

Address of the Cameron and Lincoln Club of the City of Chicago, Il., to the People of the North West (1860) Chicago, Ill.: The Club.

Aiken, Charles S. (1998) *The Cotton Plantation South since the Civil War.* Baltimore, Md.: Johns Hopkins University Press.

Albion, Robert G. (1939) *The Rise of New York Port, 1815–1860.* New York: Charles Scribner's Sons.

Alexander, Adele Logan (1991) *Ambiguous Lives: Free Women of Color in Rural Georgia, 1789–1879.* Fayetteville, Ark.: University of Arkansas Press.

Alston, Lee J. and Ferrie, Joseph P. (1999) *Southern Paternalism and the American Welfare State: Economics, Politics, and Institutions in the South, 1865–1965.* New York: Cambridge University Press.

Ambler, Charles H. (ed.) (1918) "The Correspondence of Robert M. T. Hunter, 1826–1876." *Annual Report of the American Historical Association for the Year 1916,* 2 volumes. Washington: Government Printing Office.

Ammon, Harry (1971) *James Monroe: The Quest for National Identity.* New York: McGraw-Hill.

Anbinder, Tyler (1992) *Nativism and Slavery: The Northern Know Nothings and the Politics of the 1850s.* New York: Oxford University Press.

Anbinder, Tyler (2001) *Five Points: The Nineteenth-Century New York City Neighborhood that Invented Tap Dance, Stole Elections, and Became the World's Most Notorious Slum.* New York: Free Press.

Anderson, Benedict (1981) *Imagined Communities: Reflections on the Origins and Spread of Nationalism.* London: Verso.

Anderson, Dwight G. (1988) "Quest for Immortality: A Theory of Abraham Lincoln's Political Psychology," in Gabor S. Boritt (ed.) *The Historians' Lincoln: Pseudohistory, Psychohistory, and History.* Urbana, Ill.: University of Illinois Press.

Anderson, Eric and Moss, Alfred A., Jr (eds.) (1991) *The Facts of Reconstruction: Essays in Honor of John Hope Franklin.* Baton Rouge, La.: Louisiana State University Press.

Andreano, Ralph (ed.) (1962) *The Economic Impact of the American Civil War.* Cambridge, Mass.: Schenkman.

Applebome, P. (1996) *Dixie Rising: How the South is Shaping American Values, Politics, and Culture.* New York: Time Books.

Appleby, Joyce Oldham (2000) *Inheriting the Revolution: The First Generation of Americans.* Cambridge, Mass.: Belknap Press.

Arnesen, Eric (2001) *Brotherhoods of Color: Black Railroad Workers and the Struggle for Equality.* Cambridge, Mass.: Harvard University Press.

Ash, Stephen V. (1988) *Middle Tennessee Society Transformed, 1860–1870: War and Peace in the Upper South.* Baton Rouge, La.: Louisiana State University Press.

Ash, Stephen V. (1995) *When the Yankees Came: Conflict and Chaos in the Occupied South.* Chapel Hill, NC: University of North Carolina Press.

Ashworth, John (1995) *Slavery, Capitalism and Politics in the Antebellum Republic.* Volume 1: *Commerce and Compromise, 1820–1850.* Cambridge: Cambridge University Press.

Ashworth, John (1996) "Free Labor, Wage Labor, and the Slave Power: Republicanism and the Republican Party in the 1850s," in Melvin Stokes and Stephen Conway (eds.) *The Market Revolution in America: Social, Political and Religious Expressions, 1800–1880.* Charlottesville, Va.: University Press of Virginia.

Attie, Jeannie (1998) *Patriotic Toil: Northern Women and the Civil War.* Ithaca, NY: Cornell University Press.

Ayers, Edward L. (1992) *The Promise of the New South: Life after Reconstruction.* New York: Oxford University Press.

Bailey, F. A. (1991) "The Textbooks of the 'Lost Cause': Censorship and the Creation of Southern State Histories," *Georgia Historical Quarterly* 75: 507–33.

Bailey, F. A. (1992) "Free Speech at the University of Florida: The Enoch Marvin Banks Case," *Florida Historical Quarterly* 71: 1–17.

Bailey, F. A. (1994) "Mildred Lewis Rutherford and the Patrician Cult of the Old South," *Georgia Historical Quarterly* 78: 509–35.

Bailey, F. A. (1995) "Free Speech and the Lost Cause in the Old Dominion," *Virginia Magazine of History and Biography* 103: 237–66.

Bailyn, Bernard (1967) *The Ideological Origins of the American Revolution.* Cambridge, Mass.: Harvard University Press.

Baker, Jean Harvey (1983) *Affairs of Party: The Political Culture of Northern Democrats in the Mid-Nineteenth Century.* Ithaca, NY: Cornell University Press.

Baker, Jean Harvey (2001) "Abraham and Mary: A Marriage," in Gabor S. Boritt (ed.) *The Lincoln Enigma: The Changing Faces of an American Icon.* New York: Oxford University Press.

Baker, Paula (1984) "The Domestication of Politics: Women and American Political Society, 1780–1920," *American Historical Review* 89: 620–47.

Baptist, Edward E. (2002) *Creating an Old South: Middle Florida's Plantation Frontier before the Civil War.* Chapel Hill, NC: University of North Carolina Press.

Bardaglio, Peter W. (1995) *Reconstructing the Household: Families, Sex, and the Law in the Nineteenth-Century South.* Chapel Hill, NC: University of North Carolina Press.

Barnes, Gilbert Hobbs (1950 [1933]) *The Anti-Slavery Impulse, 1830–1844.* New York: Harcourt, Brace and World.

Barnes, Gilbert Hobbs (1965 [1934]) (ed.) *Letters of Theodore Dwight Weld, Angelina Grimke and Sarah Grimke, 1822–1844.* Gloucester, Mass.: P. Smith.

Barney, William L. (1972) *The Road to Secession: A New Perspective on the Old South.* New York: Praeger.

Barney, William L. (1974) *The Secessionist Impulse: Alabama and Mississippi in 1860.* Princeton, NJ: Princeton University Press.

Barney, William L. (ed.) (2001) *A Companion to 19th-Century America.* Malden, Mass.: Blackwell.

Bartlett, Irving H. (1993) *John C. Calhoun: A Biography.* New York: Norton.

Basler, Roy P. (ed.) (1953–5) *The Collected Works of Abraham Lincoln,* eight vols., plus index. New Brunswick, NJ: Rutgers University Press.

Beale, Howard K. (1930) *The Critical Year: A Study of Andrew Johnson and Reconstruction.* New York: Harcourt Brace.

Beard, Charles A. (1913) *An Economic Interpretation of the Constitution of the United States.* New York: Macmillan.

Beard, Charles A. and Beard, Mary R. (1927, 1933) *The Rise of American Civilization,* two vols. New York: Macmillan.

Beckert, Sven (2001) *The Monied Metropolis: New York City and the Consolidation of the American Bourgeoisie, 1850–1896.* New York: Cambridge University Press.

Belz, Herman (1998) *Abraham Lincoln, Constitutionalism, and Equal Rights in the Civil War Era.* New York: Fordham University Press.

Bender, Thomas (1992) *The Antislavery Debate: Capitalism and Abolitionism as a Problem in Historical Interpretation.* Berkeley, Calif.: University of California Press.

Benedict, Michael Les (1974a) *A Compromise of Principle: Congressional Republicans and Reconstruction, 1863–1869.* New York: Norton.

Benedict, Michael Les (1974b) "Preserving the Constitution: The Conservative Basis of Radical Reconstruction," *Journal of American History* 61: 65–90.

Benedict, Michael Les (1980) "Southern Democrats in the Crisis of 1876–77: A Reconsideration of Reunion and Reaction," *Journal of Southern History* 46: 489–524.

Benedict, Michael Les (1991) "Reform Republicans and the Retreat from Reconstruction," in Eric Anderson and Alfred A. Moss Jr (eds.) *The Facts of Reconstruction: Essays in Honor of John Hope Franklin.* Baton Rouge, La.: Louisiana State University Press.

Bensel, Richard F. (1990) *Yankee Leviathan: The Origins of Central State Authority in America, 1859–1877.* Cambridge: Cambridge University Press.

Benson, Lee (1955) *Merchants, Farmers, and Railroads; Railroad Regulation and New York Politics.* Cambridge, Mass.: Harvard University Press.

Benson, Lee (1961) *The Concept of Jacksonian Democracy: New York as a Test Case.* Princeton, NJ: Princeton University Press.

Bergeron, Paul (1976) "The Nullification Controversy Revisited," *Tennessee Historical Quarterly* 35: 263–75.

Beringer, Richard E., Hattaway, Herman, Jones, Archer, and Still, William N., Jr (1986) *Why the South Lost the Civil War.* Athens, Ga.: University of Georgia Press.

Berlin, Ira (1998) *Many Thousands Gone: The First Two Centuries of Slavery in North America.* New York: Oxford University Press.

Berlin, Ira and Morgan, Philip (eds.) (1993) *Cultivation and Culture: Labor and the Shaping of Slave Life in the Americas.* Charlottesville, Va.: University of Virginia Press.

Berlin, Ira and Rowland, Leslie (1992) *Families and Freedom: A Documentary History of African-American Kinship in the Civil War Era.* New York: New Press.

Berlin, Ira et al. (eds.) (1982–93) *Freedom: A Documentary History of Emancipation, 1861–1867,* four vols. New York: Cambridge University Press.

Berlin, Ira, Reidy, Joseph P., and Rowland, Leslie S. (eds.) (1982) *The Black Military Experience.* Cambridge: Cambridge University Press.

Berlin, Ira, Fields, Barbara J., Glymph, Thavolia, Reidy, Joseph P., and Rowland, Leslie S. (1985) *Freedom: A Documentary History of Emancipation, 1861–1867.* Volume 1: *The Destruction of Slavery.* Cambridge: Cambridge University Press.

Berlin, Ira, Glymph, Thavolia, Miller, Steven F., Reidy, Joseph P., Rowland, Leslie S., and Saville, Julie (1990) *Freedom: A Documentary History of Emancipation, 1861–1867.* Volume 3: *The Wartime Genesis of Free Labor: The Lower South.* Cambridge: Cambridge University Press.

Berlin, Ira, Fields, Barbara J., Miller, Steven F., Reidy, Joseph P., and Rowland, Leslie S. (1992) *Slaves No More: Three Essays on Emancipation and the Civil War*. New York: Cambridge University Press.

Berlin, Ira, Miller, Steven F., Reidy, Joseph P., and Rowland, Leslie S. (1993) *Freedom: A Documentary History of Emancipation, 1861–1867*. Volume 2: *The Wartime Genesis of Free Labor: The Upper South*. Cambridge: Cambridge University Press.

Bernhard, Virginia, Brandon, Betty, Fox-Genovese, Elizabeth, and Perdue, Theda (eds.) (1992) *Southern Women: Histories and Identities* [Southern Women Series]. Columbia, Mo.: University of Missouri Press.

Bernstein, Iver (1990) *The New York City Draft Riots: Their Significance for American Society and Politics in the Age of the Civil War*. New York: Oxford University Press.

Berwanger, Eugene H. (1967) *The Frontier against Slavery: Western Anti-Negro Prejudice and the Slavery Extension Controversy*. Urbana, Ill.: University of Illinois Press.

Bigelow, John, Jr (1890) *The Principles of Strategy Illustrated Mainly from American Campaigns*. New York: Lippincott.

Bigelow, John, Jr (1912) *The Battle of Chancellorsville: A Strategical and Tactical Study*. New Haven, Conn.: Yale University Press.

Billings, Dwight B. (1979) *Planters and the Making of a "New South": Class, Politics, and Development in North Carolina, 1865–1900*. Chapel Hill, NC: University of North Carolina Press.

Bishir, C. W. (1993) "Landmarks of Power: Building a Southern Past, 1885–1915," *Southern Cultures* 1: 5–45.

Bishir, C. W. (2000) "'A Strong Force of Ladies': Women, Politics, and Confederate Memorial Associations in Nineteenth-Century Raleigh," *North Carolina Historical Review* 77: 455–91.

Blaine, James G. (1884) *Twenty Years of Congress: From Lincoln to Garfield*, two vols. Norwich, Conn.: Henry Bill.

Blassingame, John W. (1976) *The Slave Community: Plantation Life in the Antebellum South*, rev. edn. New York: Oxford University Press.

Bleser, Carol (1969) *The Promised Land: The History of the South Carolina Land Commission, 1869–1890*. Columbia, SC: University of South Carolina Press.

Bleser, Carol (ed.) (1990) *In Joy and in Sorrow: Women, Family, and Marriage in the Victorian South*. New York: Oxford University Press.

Blewett, Mary (1988) *Men, Women, and Work: Class, Gender, and Protest in the New England Shoe Industry, 1780–1910*. Urbana, Ill.: University of Illinois Press.

Blight, D. W. (2001) *Race and Reunion: The Civil War in American Memory*. Cambridge, Mass.: Belknap Press.

Bloch, Ruth (1987) "The Gendered Meanings of Virtue in Revolutionary America," *Signs* 13: 37–58.

Boatwright, Eleanor Miot (1994 [1941]) *Status of Women in Georgia, 1783–1860*. Brooklyn, NY: Carlson.

Boles, John B. (1984) *Black Southerners*. Lexington, Ky.: University Press of Kentucky.

Boles, John B. (1995) *The South through Time: A History of an American Region*. Englewood Cliffs, NJ: Prentice-Hall.

Boles, John B. (2002) *A Companion to the American South*. Malden, Mass.: Blackwell.

Boles, John B. and Nolen, Evelyn Thomas (eds.) (1987) *Interpreting Southern History: Historiographical Essays in Honor of Sanford W. Higginbotham*. Baton Rouge, La.: Louisiana State University Press.

Bolton, Charles C. (1994) *Poor Whites of the Antebellum South: Tenants and Laborers in Central North Carolina and Northeast Mississippi*. Durham, NC: Duke University Press.

Bond, Bradley G. (1995) *Political Culture in the Nineteenth-Century South: Mississippi, 1830–1900*. Baton Rouge, La.: Louisiana State University Press.

Bond, Bradley G. (1997) "The Vernacular Architecture of the South: Log Buildings, Dog-Trot Houses, and English Barns," in Samuel C. Hyde Jr (ed.) *Plain Folk of the South Revisited*. Baton Rouge, La.: Louisiana State University Press.

Boorstin, Daniel J. (1965) *The Americans: The National Experience*. New York: Random House.

Boritt, Gabor S. (ed.) (1988) *The Historians' Lincoln: Pseudohistory, Psychohistory, and History*. Urbana, Ill.: University of Illinois Press.

Boritt, Gabor S. (1992) "War Opponent and War President," in Boritt (ed.) *Lincoln the War President: The Gettysburg Lectures*. New York: Oxford University Press.

Boritt, Gabor S. (2001) "Did He Dream of a Lily-White America? The Voyage to Linconia," in Boritt (ed.) *The Lincoln Enigma: The Changing Faces of an American Icon*. New York: Oxford University Press.

Boswell, Angela (2001) *Her Act and Deed: Women's Lives in a Rural Southern County, 1837–1873*. College Station, Tex.: Texas A & M University Press.

Bowers, Claude G. (1929) *The Tragic Era: The Revolution after Lincoln*. Boston, Mass.: Houghton Mifflin.

Bowman, Shearer Davis (1993) *Masters and Lords: Mid-Nineteenth Century US Planters and Prussian Junkers*. New York: Oxford University Press.

Boyd, Julian P. (1948) "Thomas Jefferson's Empire of Liberty," *Virginia Quarterly Review* 24: 549–50.

Boydston, Jeanne (1990) *Home and Work, Housework, Wages, and the Ideology of Labor in the Early Republic*. New York: Oxford University Press.

Boylan, Anne (2002) *The Origins of Women's Activism, New York and Boston, 1797–1840*. Chapel Hill, NC: University of North Carolina Press.

Breeden, James O. (ed.) (1980) *Advice Among Masters: The Ideal in Slave Management in the Old South*. Westport, Ct: Greenwood Press.

Brekkus, Catherine A. (1998) *Strangers and Pilgrims: Female Preaching in America, 1740–1845*. Chapel Hill, NC: University of North Carolina Press.

Brock, William R. (1963) *An American Crisis: Congress and Reconstruction, 1865–1867*. New York: Macmillan.

Brockett, Linus P. and Vaughan, Mary C. (1867) *Woman's Work in the Civil War: A Record of Heroism, Patriotism and Patience*. Philadelphia, Pa.: Zeigler, McCurdy.

Brown, Kathleen M. (1996) *Good Wives, Nasty Wenches, and Anxious Patriarchs: Gender, Race, and Power in Colonial Virginia*. Chapel Hill, NC: University of North Carolina Press.

Brown, Thomas (1998) *Dorothea Dix: New England Reformer*. Cambridge, Mass.: Harvard University Press.

Browne, Gary L. (1980) *Baltimore in the New Nation*. Chapel Hill, NC: University of North Carolina Press.

Bruce, Dickson D. (1982) *The Rhetoric of Conservatism: The Virginia Convention of 1829–30 and the Conservative Tradition in the South*. San Marino, Calif.: Huntington Library.

Brundage, W. F. (2000) "White Women and the Politics of Historical Memory in the New South, 1880–1920," in J. Dailey, G. E. Gilmore, and B. Simon (eds.) *Jumpin' Jim Crow: Southern Politics from Civil War to Civil Rights*. Princeton, NJ: Princeton University Press.

Bryant, Jonathan M. (1996) *How Curious a Land: Conflict and Change in Greene County, Georgia, 1850–1885*. Chapel Hill, NC: University of North Carolina Press.

Buenger, Walter L. (1984) *Secession and the Union in Texas*. Austin, Tex.: University of Texas Press.

Bureau of the Census (1960 [1957]) *Historical Statistics of the United States, from Colonial Times to 1957*. Washington, DC: US Government Printing Office.

Burlingame, Michael (1994) *The Inner World of Abraham Lincoln*. Urbana, Ill.: University of Illinois Press.

Burne, Alfred H. (1938) *Lee, Grant, and Sherman: A Study in Leadership in the 1864–65 Campaign*. New York: Charles Scribner's Sons.

Burton, Orville Vernon (1978) "Race and Reconstruction: Edgefield County, South Carolina," *Journal of Social History* 12: 31–56.

Burton, Orville Vernon (1982) "The Development of Tenantry and the Post-Bellum Afro-American Social Structure in Edgefield County, South Carolina," in E. LeRoy Ladurie and J. Goy (eds.) *Présentations paysannes, dîmes, rente foncière et mouvement de la production agricole à l'époque préindustrielle: Aétes du colloque préparatoire (30 juin et 2 juillet 1977) au VIIe Congrès international d'Histoire économique Section A3*. Edimbourg 13–19 août 1978, Vol. 2: 762–78. Paris: Editions de l'Ecole des Hautes Etudes en Sciences Sociales.

Burton, Orville Vernon (1985) *In My Father's House Are Many Mansions: Family and Community in Edgefield, South Carolina 1848–1889*. Chapel Hill, NC: University of North Carolina Press.

Burton, Orville Vernon (1998) "African American Status and Identity in a Postbellum Community: An Analysis of the Manuscript Census Returns," *Agricultural History* 72: 213–40.

Bynum, Victoria E. (1992) *Unruly Women: The Politics of Social and Sexual Control in the Old South*. Chapel Hill, NC: University of North Carolina Press.

Byres, Terence J. (ed.) (1983) *Sharecropping and Sharecroppers*. London: Frank Cass.

Byres, Terence J. (1996) *Capitalism from Above and Capitalism from Below: An Essay in Comparative Political Economy*. New York: St. Martin's Press.

Campbell, John (1993) "As 'A Kind of Freeman?': Slaves' Market-Related Activities in the South Carolina Upcountry," in Ira Berlin and Philip Morgan (eds.) *Cultivation and Culture: Labor and the Shaping of Slave Life in the Americas*. Charlottesville, Va.: University of Virginia Press.

Campbell, Randolph B. and Lowe, Richard G. (1977) *Wealth and Power in Antebellum Texas*. College Station, Tex.: Texas A & M University Press.

Carby, Hazel (1987) *Reconstructing Womanhood, The Emergence of the Afro-American Woman Novelist*. New York: Oxford University Press.

Carey, Anthony Gene (1997) *Parties, Slavery and the Union in Antebellum Georgia*. Athens, Ga.: University of Georgia Press.

Carlton, David L. (1982) *Mill and Town in South Carolina, 1880–1920*. Baton Rouge, La.: Louisiana State University Press.

Carlton, David L. (1990) "The Revolution from Above: The National Market and the Beginnings of Industrialization in North Carolina," *Journal of American History* 77: 445–75.

Carlton, David L. and Coclanis, Peter A. (2003) *The South, the Nation, and the World: Perspectives on Southern Economic Development*. Charlottesville, Va.: University of Virginia Press.

Carter, Dan T. (1985) *When the War Was Over: The Failure of Self-Reconstruction in the South, 1865–1867*. Baton Rouge, La.: Louisiana State University Press.

Carwardine, Richard J. (2003) *Lincoln* [Profiles in Power Series]. London: Pearson Education.

Cash, W. J. (1991 [1941]) *The Mind of the South*. New York: Vintage.

Cashin, Joan (1991) *A Family Venture: Men and Women on the Southern Frontier*. New York: Oxford University Press.

Castel, Albert (1992) *Decision in the West: The Atlanta Campaign of 1864*. Lawrence, Kan.: University Press of Kansas.

Catton, Bruce (1955) *This Hallowed Ground: The Story of the Union Side of the Civil War*. New York: Doubleday.

Catton, Bruce (1958) *America Goes to War*. Middletown, Conn.: Wesleyan University Press.

Catton, Bruce (1961–5) *Centennial History of the Civil War*, three vols. Garden City, NY: Doubleday.

Cecil-Fronsman, Bill (1992) *Common Whites: Class and Culture in Antebellum North Carolina*. Lexington, Ky.: University Press of Kentucky.

Cell, John W. (1982) *The Highest Stage of White Supremacy: The Origins of Segregation in South Africa and the American South*. New York: Cambridge University Press.

Censer, Jane Turner (1984) *North Carolina Planters and their Children, 1800–1860*. Baton Rouge, La.: Louisiana State University Press.

Censer, Jane Turner (1999) "Reimagining the North-South Reunion: Southern Women Novelists and the Intersectional Romance, 1876–1900," *Southern Cultures* 5: 64–91.

Chandler, Alfred D., Jr (1965) "The Organization of Manufacturing and Transportation," in David T. Gilchrist and W. David Lewis (eds.) *Economic Change in the Civil War Era*. Greenville, Del.: Eleutherian Mills-Hagley Foundation.

Chandler, Alfred D., Jr (1977) *The Visible Hand: The Managerial Revolution in American Business*. Cambridge, Mass.: Belknap Press.

Channing, Steven A. (1970) *The Crisis of Fear: Secession in South Carolina*. New York: Simon and Schuster.

Clarfield, Gerald H. (1980) *Timothy Pickering and the American Republic*. Pittsburgh, Pa.: University of Pittsburgh Press.

Clark, Christopher (1990) *The Roots of Rural Capitalism: Western Massachusetts, 1780–1860*. Ithaca, NY: Cornell University Press.

Clark, Elizabeth (1995) "'The Sacred Rights of the Weak': Pain, Sympathy, and the Culture of Individual Rights in Antebellum America," *Journal of American History* 82: 463–93.

Clark, Emil (2003) *Masterless Mistresses: The New Orleans Ursulines and the Development of a New World Society, 1727–1834*. Chapel Hill, NC: University of North Carolina Press.

Clark, Thomas D. (1944) *Pills, Petticoats, and Plows: The Southern Country Store*. Indianapolis, Ind.: Bobbs-Merrill.

Clifford, Deborah Pickman (1979) *Mine Eyes Have Seen the Glory: A Biography of Julia Ward Howe*. Boston, Mass.: Little, Brown.

Clinton, Catherine (1982) *The Plantation Mistress: Women's World in the Old South*. New York: Pantheon.

Clinton, Catherine (1984) *The Other Civil War: American Women in the Nineteenth Century*. New York: Hill and Wang.

Clinton, Catherine (ed.) (1994) *Half Sisters of History: Southern Women and the American Past*. Durham, NC: Duke University Press.

Clinton, Catherine and Gillespie, Michele (eds.) (1997) *The Devil's Lane: Sex and Race in the Early South*. New York: Oxford University Press.

Clinton, Catherine and Silber, Nina (eds.) (1992) *Divided Houses: Gender and the Civil War*. New York: Oxford University Press.

Coben, Stanley (1959) "Northeastern Business and Radical Reconstruction: A Reexamination," *Mississippi Valley Historical Review* 46: 69–90.

Cochran, Thomas C. (1961) "Did the Civil War Retard Industrialization?," *Mississippi Valley Historical Review* 48: 197–210.

Cochran, Thomas C. (1962) "Did the Civil War Retard Industrialization?," in Ralph Andreano (ed.) *The Economic Impact of the American Civil War*. Cambridge, Mass.: Schenkman.

Cochran, Thomas C. and Miller, William (1961 [1942]) *The Age of Enterprise: A Social History of Industrial America*. New York: Harper and Row.

Coclanis, Peter A. (2000) "In Retrospect: Ransom and Sutch's One Kind of Freedom," *Reviews in American History* 28: 478–89.

Coddington, Edwin B. (1968) *The Gettysburg Campaign: A Study in Command*. New York: Charles Scribner's Sons.

Cohen, William (1991) *At Freedom's Edge: Black Mobility and the Southern White Quest for Racial Control, 1861–1915*. Baton Rouge, La.: Louisiana State University Press.

Cole, Stephanie (2003) *Servants and Slaves: Domestic Service in Antebellum North/South Border Cities*. Urbana, Ill.: University of Illinois Press.

Coleman, Peter J. (1963) *The Transformation of Rhode Island, 1790–1860*. Providence, RI: Brown University Press.

Commons, John R. (1921–35) *History of Labour in the United States*. New York: Macmillan.

Congressional Globe (1850) 31st Congress, 1st Session, US Senate, Washington, DC.

Connelly, T. L. and Bellows, B. L. (1982) *God and General Longstreet: The Lost Cause and the Southern Mind*. Baton Rouge, La.: Louisiana State University.

Cooling, Benjamin Franklin (1987) *Forts Henry and Donelson: The Key to the Confederate Heartland*. Knoxville, Tenn.: University of Tennessee Press.

Cooling, Benjamin Franklin (1989) *Jubal Early's Raid on Washington 1864*. Baltimore, Md.: Nautical and Aviation Publishing Company of America.

Cooper, Frederick, Holt, Thomas C., and Scott, Rebecca J. (2000) *Beyond Slavery: Explorations of Race, Labor, and Citizenship in Postemancipation Societies*. Chapel Hill, NC: University of North Carolina Press.

Cooper, William J., Jr (1978) *The South and the Politics of Slavery, 1828–1856*. Baton Rouge, La.: Louisiana State University Press.

Cooper, William J., Jr (1983) *Liberty and Slavery: Southern Politics to 1860*. New York: Alfred A. Knopf.

Cooper, William J., Jr (1991) *The Conservative Regime: South Carolina, 1877–1900*. Baton Rouge, La.: Louisiana State University Press.

Cooper, William J., Jr (2000) *Jefferson Davis, American*. New York: Alfred A. Knopf.

Coryell, Janet L. (1990) *Neither Heroine nor Fool: Anna Ella Carroll of Maryland*. Kent, Ohio: Kent State University Press.

Coryell, Janet L., Swain, Martha H., Treadway, Sandra G., and Turner, Elizabeth H. (eds.) (1998) *Beyond Image and Convention: Explorations in Southern Women's History* [Southern Women Series]. Columbia, Mo.: University of Missouri Press.

Coryell, Janet L., Appleton, Thomas H., Jr, Sims, Anastatia, and Treadway, Sandra G. (eds.) (2000) *Negotiating Boundaries of Southern Womanhood: Dealing with the Powers That Be* [Southern Women Series]. Columbia, Mo.: University of Missouri Press.

Coski, J. M. (1996) "The Confederate Battle Flag in American History and Culture," *Southern Cultures* 2: 195–231.

Coski, J. M. (2000) "The Confederate Battle Flag in Historical Perspective," in J. M. Martinez, W. D. Richardson, and R. McNinch-Su (eds.) *Confederate Symbols in the Contemporary South*. Gainesville, Fla.: University Press of Florida.

Cott, Nancy (1977) *The Bonds of Womanhood, "Woman's Sphere" in New England, 1780–1835*. New Haven, Conn.: Yale University Press.

Cott, Nancy (1998) "Marriage and Women's Citizenship in the United States, 1830–1934," *American Historical Review* 103: 1440–74.

Cox, LaWanda (1958) "The Promise of Land for the Freedmen," *Mississippi Valley Historical Review* 45: 413–40.

Cox, LaWanda (1981) *Lincoln and Black Freedom: A Study in Presidential Leadership*. Columbia, SC: University of South Carolina Press.

Cox, LaWanda and Cox, John (1963) *Politics, Principle, and Prejudice, 1865–1866, Dilemma of Reconstruction America*. New York: Free Press.

Cox, Samuel S. (1888) *Three Decades of Federal Legislation: 1855–1885*. Providence, RI: J. A. and R. A. Reid.

Crandall, Andrew W. (1930) *The Early History of the Republican Party, 1854–1856*. Boston, Mass.: R. G. Badger.

Craven, Avery O. (1939) *The Repressible Conflict, 1830–1861*. Baton Rouge, La.: Louisiana State University Press.

Craven, Avery O. (1960 [1942]) *The Coming of the Civil War*. New York: Charles Scribner's Sons.

Crofts, Daniel W. (1989) *Reluctant Confederates: Upper South Unionists in the Secession Crisis*. Chapel Hill, NC: University of North Carolina Press.

Cronon, William (1991) *Nature's Metropolis: Chicago and the Great West*. New York: Norton.

Cross, Whitney R. (1950) *The Burned-over District: The Social and Intellectual History of Enthusiastic Religion in Western New York, 1800–1850*. Ithaca, NY: Cornell University Press.

Current, Richard N. (1960) "God and the Strongest Battalions," in David Donald (ed.) *Why the North Won the Civil War*. Baton Rouge, La.: Louisiana State University Press.

Current, Richard N. (1963) *Lincoln and the First Shot*. Philadelphia, Pa.: Lippincott.

Cushman, S. (1999) *Bloody Promenade: Reflections on a Civil War Battle*. Charlottesville, Va.: University of Virginia Press.

Dailey, J., Gilmore, G. E., and Simon, B. (eds.) (2000) *Jumpin' Jim Crow: Southern Politics from Civil War to Civil Rights*. Princeton, NJ: Princeton University Press.

Dangerfield, George (1952) *The Era of Good Feelings*. New York: Harcourt Brace.

Daniel, Larry J. (1997) *Shiloh: The Battle that Changed the Civil War*. New York: Simon and Schuster.

Daniel, Pete (1972) *The Shadow of Slavery: Peonage in the South, 1901–1969*. Urbana, Ill.: University of Illinois Press.

Dannett, Sylvia (1959) *Noble Women of the North*. New York: Yoseloff.

Davidson, Cathy (1986) *Revolution and the Word: The Rise of the Novel in America*. New York: Oxford University Press.

Davis, David Brion (1969) *The Slave Power Conspiracy and the Paranoid Style*. Baton Rouge, La.: Louisiana State University Press.

Davis, David Brion (1975) *The Problem of Slavery in the Age of Revolution, 1770–1823*. New York: Oxford University Press.

Davis, David Brion (1984) *Slavery and Human Progress*. New York: Oxford University Press.

Davis, David Brion (2001) "The Enduring Legacy of the South's Civil War Victory," *New York Times*, August 26, 4: 1.

Davis, Lance E. (1965) "The Investment Market, 1870–1914," *Journal of Economic History* 25: 355–99.

Davis, Lance E. and North, Douglass C. (1971) *Institutional Change and American Economic Growth*. New York: Cambridge University Press.

Davis, Ronald L. F. (1982) *Good and Faithful Labor: From Slavery to Sharecropping in the Natchez District, 1860–1890*. Westport, Conn.: Greenwood.

Davis, Stephen (2000) *Atlanta Will Fall: Sherman, Joe Johnston, and the Yankee Heavy Battalions*. Wilmington, Del.: Scholarly Resources.

Davis, William C. (1991) *Jefferson Davis: The Man and his Hour, a Biography*. New York: HarperCollins.

Davis, William C. (2000) *Lincoln's Men: How President Lincoln Became Father to an Army and a Nation*. New York: Free Press.

DeCanio, Stephen, and Mokyr, Joel (1977) "Inflation and the Wage Lag during the American Civil War," *Explorations in Economic History* 14: 311–36.

DeConde, Alexander (1966) *The Quasi-War: The Politics and Diplomacy of the Undeclared War with France, 1797–1801*. New York: Charles Scribner's Sons.

Delfino, Susanna and Gillespie, Michele (eds.) (2002) *Neither Lady nor Slave: Working Women of the Old South*. Chapel Hill, NC: University of North Carolina Press.

Deyle, Steven (1992) "The Irony of Liberty: Origins of the Domestic Slave Trade," *Journal of the Early Republic* 12 (1): 37–62.

Diffley, Kathleen (1992) *Where my Heart is Turning Ever: Civil War Stories and Constitutional Reform, 1861–1876*. Athens, Ga.: University of Georgia Press.

Dillon, Merton L. (1959) "The Failure of the Abolitionists," *Journal of Southern History* 25: 159–77.

Dirck, Brian R. (2001) *Lincoln and Davis: Imagining America*. Lawrence, Kan.: University Press of Kansas.

Donald, David Herbert (1956) *Lincoln Reconsidered: Essays on the Civil War Era*. New York: Alfred A. Knopf.

Donald, David Herbert (1981) "A Generation of Defeat," in W. J. Fraser Jr and W. B. Moore Jr (eds.) *From the Old South to the New: Essays on the Transitional South*. Westport, Conn.: Greenwood Press.

Donald, David Herbert (1995) *Lincoln*. New York: Simon and Schuster.

Donald, David M. (ed.) (1960a) *Why the North Won the Civil War*. Baton Rouge, La.: Louisiana State University Press.

Donald, David M. (1960) "Died of Democracy," in David Donald (ed.) *Why the North Won the Civil War*. Baton Rouge, La.: Louisiana State University Press.

Donald, David M. (1965) *The Politics of Reconstruction, 1863–1867*. Baton Rouge, La.: Louisiana State University Press.

Dorsey, Bruce (2002) *Reforming Men and Women: Gender in the Antebellum City*. Ithaca, NY: Cornell University Press.

Douglas, Ann (1977) *The Feminization of American Culture*. New York: Alfred A. Knopf.

Douglass, Frederick (1986 [1845]) *Narrative of the Life of Frederick Douglass: An American Slave, written by Himself*. New York: Penguin.

Dowd, Douglas F. (1956) "A Comparative Analysis of Economic Development in the American West and South," *Journal of Economic History* 16: 558–74.

Doyle, Don H. (1990) *New Men, New Cities, New South: Atlanta, Nashville, Charleston, Mobile, 1860–1910*. Chapel Hill, NC: University of North Carolina Press.

Drescher, Seymour (1977) *Econocide: British Slavery in the Era of Abolition*. Pittsburgh, Pa.: University of Pittsburgh Press.

Dublin, Thomas (1979) *Women at Work: The Transformation of Work and Community at Lowell, Massachusetts, 1826–1860*. New York: Columbia University Press.

DuBois, Ellen (1978) *Feminism and Suffrage: The Emergence of an Independent Women's Movement in America, 1848–1869*. Ithaca, NY: Cornell University Press.

DuBois, Ellen (1987) "Outgrowing the Compact of the Fathers: Equal Rights, Woman Suffrage, and the United States Constitution," *Journal of American History* 74: 836–62.

DuBois, W. E. B. (1935) *Black Reconstruction: An Essay toward a History of the Part which Black Folk Played in the Attempt to Reconstruct Democracy 1860–1880*. New York: Harcourt Brace.

DuBois, W. E. B. (1992 [1935]) *Black Reconstruction in America, 1860–1880*. New York: Free Press.

Dumond, Dwight L. (ed.) (1931) *Southern Editorials on Secession*. New York: Century Co. for the American Historical Association.

Dunning, William A. (1898) *Essays on the Civil War and Reconstruction and Related Topics*. New York: Macmillan.

Dunning, William A. (1907) *Reconstruction, Political and Economic, 1865–1877*. New York: Harper and Bros.

Durden, Robert F. (1965) "Ambiguities in the Antislavery Crusade of the Republican Party," in Martin B. Duberman (ed.) *The Antislavery Vanguard: New Essays on the Abolitionists*. Princeton, NJ: Princeton University Press.

Durrill, Wayne K. (1990) *War of Another Kind: A Southern Community in the Great Rebellion*. New York: Oxford University Press.

Edwards, Laura F. (1997) *Gendered Strife and Confusion: The Political Culture of Reconstruction*. Urbana, Ill.: University of Illinois Press.

Edwards, Laura F. (1999) "Law, Domestic Violence, and the Limits of Patriarchal Authority in the Antebellum South," *Journal of Southern History* 65: 733–70.

Edwards, Laura F. (2000) *Scarlett Doesn't Live Here Anymore: Southern Women in the Civil War Era*. Urbana, Ill.: University of Illinois Press.

Edwards, Rebecca (1997) *Angels in the Machinery: Gender in American Party Politics from the Civil War to the Progressive Era*. New York: Oxford University Press.

Egerton, Douglas R. (1997) "Averting a Crisis: The Proslavery Critique of the American Colonization Society," *Civil War History* 43: 142–56.

Egerton, Douglas R. (1999) *He Shall Go Out Free: The Lives of Denmark Vesey*. Madison, Wis.: Madison House.

Egerton, Douglas R. (2002) "The Empire of Liberty Reconsidered," in Peter Onuf and Jan Lewis (eds.) *The Revolution of 1800*. Charlottesville, Va.: University of Virginia Press.

Egerton, J. (1974) *The Americanization of Dixie: The Southernization of America*. New York: Harper's Magazine Press.

Einhorn, Robin L. (1991) *Property Rules: Political Economy in Chicago, 1833–1872*. Chicago: University of Chicago Press.

Elkins, Stanley (1959) *Slavery: A Problem in American Institutional and Intellectual Life*. Chicago, Ill.: University of Chicago Press.

Ellem, Warren A. (1987) "The Politics of Reconstruction," *Australasian Journal of American Studies* 6 (July).

Ellem, Warren A. (1996) "Doing God's Service: Adelbret Ames and Reconstruction in Mississippi," in Bruce Clayton and John Salmond (eds.) *Varieties of Southern History: New Essays on a Region and its People*. Westport, Conn.: Greenwood.

Ellis, Joseph J. (1998) *American Sphinx: The Character of Thomas Jefferson*. New York: Alfred A. Knopf.

Ellis, Richard E. (1987) *The Union at Risk: Jacksonian Democracy, States' Rights and the Nullification Crisis*. New York: Oxford University Press.

Eltis, David (1999) *The Rise of African Slaves in the Americas*. New York: Cambridge University Press.

Endres, Kathleen (1984) "The Women's Press in the Civil War: A Portrait of Patriotism, Propaganda and Prodding," *Civil War History* 30: 31–53.

Engerman, Stanley L. (1966) "The Economic Impact of the Civil War," *Explorations in Economic History* 3: 176–99.

Engerman, Stanley L. and Sokoloff, Kenneth L. (2000) "Technology and Industrialization, 1790–1915," in Engerman and Robert E. Gallman (eds.) *The Cambridge Economic History of the United States*. Volume 2: *The Nineteenth Century*. New York: Cambridge University Press.

Engs, Robert F. (1991) "The Great American Slave Rebellion," lecture delivered to the Civil War Institute at Gettysburg College, June 27.

Epstein, Barbara (1981) *The Politics of Domesticity: Women, Evangelism, and Temperance in Nineteenth-Century America*. Middletown, Conn.: Wesleyan University Press.

Escott, Paul D. (1978) *After Secession: Jefferson Davis and the Failure of Confederate Nationalism*. Baton Rouge, La.: Louisiana State University Press.

Essig, James D. (1982) *The Bonds of Wickedness: American Evangelicals Against Slavery, 1770–1808*. Philadelphia, Pa.: Temple University Press.

Fahs, Alice (1999) "The Feminized Civil War: Gender, Northern Popular Literature, and the Memory of the War, 1861–1900," *Journal of American History* 85: 1461–94.

Fahs, Alice (2001) *The Imagined Civil War: Popular Literature of the North and South, 1861–1865*. Chapel Hill, NC: University of North Carolina Press.

Farmer, James O. (1986) *The Metaphysical Confederacy: James Henley Thornwell and the Synthesis of Southern Values*. Macon, Ga: Mercer University Press.

Farnham, Christie Anne (1994) *The Education of the Southern Belle: Higher Education and Student Socialization in the Antebellum South.* New York: New York University Press.

Farnham, Christie Anne (ed.) (1997) *Women of the American South: A Multicultural Reader.* New York: New York University Press.

Faust, Drew Gilpin (1982) *James Henry Hammond: A Design for Mastery.* Baton Rouge, La.: Louisiana State University Press.

Faust, Drew Gilpin (1996) *Mothers of Invention: Women of the Slaveholding South in the American Civil War.* Chapel Hill, NC: University of North Carolina Press.

Faust, Drew Gilpin (1998) "'Ours as Well as That of the Men': Women and Gender in the Civil War," in William Cooper and James McPherson (eds.) *Writing the Civil War: The Quest to Understand.* Columbia, SC: University of South Carolina Press.

Fehrenbacher, Don E. (1978) *The Dred Scott Case: Its Significance in American Law and Politics.* New York: Oxford University Press.

Feller, Daniel (1995) *Jacksonian Promise.* Baltimore, Md.: Johns Hopkins University Press.

Ferleger, Lou (ed.) (1990) *Agriculture and National Development: Views on the Nineteenth Century.* Ames, Iowa: Iowa State University Press.

Fett, Sharla M. (2002) *Working Cures: Healing, Health, and Power on Southern Slave Plantations.* Chapel Hill, NC: University of North Carolina Press.

Fields, Barbara Jeanne (1983) "The Nineteenth-Century American South: History and Theory," *Plantation Society in the Americas* 2: 7–27.

Fields, Barbara Jeanne (1985) *Slavery and Freedom on the Middle Ground: Maryland during the Nineteenth Century.* New Haven, Conn.: Yale University Press.

Fink, Leon (1983) *Workingmen's Democracy: The Knights of Labor and American Politics.* Urbana, Ill.: University of Illinois Press.

Finkelman, Paul (1989) "Slavery and the Northwest Ordinance: A Study in Ambiguity," *Journal of the Early Republic* 6: 343–70.

Finkelman, Paul (1996) *Slavery and the Founders: Race and Liberty in the Age of Jefferson.* Armonk, NY: Sharpe.

Finkelman, Paul (ed.) (1997) *Slavery and the Law.* Madison, Wis.: Madison House.

Fischer, Kirsten (2002) *Suspect Relations: Sex, Race, and Resistance in Colonial North Carolina.* Ithaca, NY: Cornell University Press.

Fite, G. C. (1984) *Cotton Fields No More: Southern Agriculture, 1865–1980.* Lexington, Ky.: University Press of Kentucky.

Fitzgerald, Michael W. (1989) *The Union League Movement in the Deep South: Politics and Agricultural Change during Reconstruction.* Baton Rouge, La.: Louisiana State University Press.

Flexner, Eleanor (1959) *Century of Struggle: The Woman's Rights Movement in the United States.* Cambridge: Cambridge University Press.

Fogel, Robert (1960) *The Union Pacific Railroad: A Case in Premature Enterprise.* Baltimore, Md.: Johns Hopkins University Press.

Fogel, Robert and Engerman, Stanley (1974) *Time on the Cross: The Economics of American Negro Slavery.* Boston, Mass.: Little, Brown.

Fogelson, Robert M. (1989) *America's Armories: Architecture, Society and Public Order.* Cambridge, Mass.: Harvard University Press.

Foldvary, Fred E. (ed.) (1996) *Beyond Neoclassical Economics: Heterodox Approaches to Economic Theory.* Brookfield, Vt.: Edward Elgar.

Foner, Eric (1969) "The Wilmot Proviso Revisited," *Journal of American History* 56: 267–79.

Foner, Eric (1970) *Free Soil, Free Labor, Free Men: The Ideology of the Republican Party before the Civil War.* New York: Oxford University Press.

Foner, Eric (1983) *Nothing but Freedom: Emancipation and its Legacy.* Baton Rouge, La.: Louisiana State University Press.

Foner, Eric (1988) *Reconstruction: America's Unfinished Revolution, 1863–1877*. New York: Harper and Row.

Foner, Eric (1996) "Free Labor and Nineteenth-Century Political Ideology," in Melvin Stokes and Stephen Conway (eds.) *The Market Revolution in America: Social, Political and Religious Expressions, 1800–1880*. Charlottesville, Va.: University of Virginia Press.

Foote, Shelby (1958–74) *The Civil War: A Narrative*, three vols. New York: Random House.

Ford, Lacy K., Jr (1984) "Rednecks and Merchants: Economic Development and Social Tensions in the South Carolina Upcountry, 1865–1900," *Journal of American History* 71: 294–318.

Ford, Lacy K., Jr (1988) *Origins of Southern Radicalism: The South Carolina Upcountry, 1800–1860*. New York: Oxford University Press.

Forgie, George B. (1979) *Patricide in the House Divided: A Psychological Interpretation of Lincoln and his Age*. New York: Norton.

Formisano, Ronald P. (1971) *The Birth of Mass Political Parties: Michigan, 1827–1861*. Princeton, NJ: Princeton University Press.

Foster, Gaines M. (1987) *Ghosts of the Confederacy: Defeat, the Lost Cause, and the Emergence of the New South*. New York: Oxford University Press.

Foster, Gaines M. (2002) *Moral Reconstruction: Christian Lobbyists and the Federal Legislation of Morality, 1865–1920*. Chapel Hill, NC: University of North Carolina Press.

Fox-Genovese, Elizabeth (1988) *Within the Plantation Household: Black and White Women of the Old South*. Chapel Hill, NC: University of North Carolina Press.

Fox-Genovese, Elizabeth (1998) "Days of Judgement, Days of Wrath: The Civil War and the Religious Imagination of Women Writers," in Randall M. Miller, Harry S. Stout, and Charles Reagan Wilson (eds.) *Religion and the American Civil War*. New York: Oxford University Press.

Fox-Genovese, Elizabeth and Genovese, Eugene D. (1983) *Fruits of Merchant Capital: Slavery and Bourgeois Property in the Rise and Expansion of Capitalism*. New York: Oxford University Press.

Franklin, John Hope (1961) *Reconstruction: After the Civil War*. Chicago: University of Chicago Press.

Franklin, John Hope (1963) *The Emancipation Proclamation*. Garden City, NY: Doubleday.

Franklin, John Hope (1967) *From Slavery to Freedom: A History of American Negroes*, 3rd edn. New York: Knopf.

Fraser, Walter J., Saunders, R. Frank, Jr, and Wakelyn, Jon L. (eds.) (1985) *The Web of Southern Social Relations: Women, Family, and Education*. Athens, Ga.: University of Georgia Press.

Fredrickson, George M. (1965) *The Inner Civil War: Northern Intellectuals and the Crisis of the Union*. Urbana, Ill.: University of Illinois Press.

Fredrickson, George M. (1971) *The Black Image in the White Mind: The Debate on Afro-American Character and Destiny, 1817–1914*. New York: Harper and Row.

Fredrickson, George M. (1981) *White Supremacy: A Comparative Study in American and South African History*. New York: Oxford University Press.

Freehling, William W. (1965) *Prelude to Civil War: The Nullification Controversy in South Carolina, 1816–1836*. New York: Harper and Row.

Freehling, William W. (1990) *The Road to Disunion: Secessionists at Bay, 1776–1854*. New York: Oxford University Press.

Freehling, William W. (1994) *The Reintegration of American History: Slavery and the Civil War*. New York: Oxford University Press.

Freehling, William W. (2001) *The South vs. the South: How Anti-Confederate Southerners Shaped the Course of the Civil War*. New York: Oxford University Press.

Freeman, Douglas Southall (1934–6) *R. E. Lee: A Biography*, four vols. New York: Charles Scribner's Sons.

Freeman, Douglas Southall (1943–4) *Lee's Lieutenants: A Study in Command*, three vols. New York: Charles Scribner's Sons.

Frey, Sylvia (1993) *Water from the Rock: Black Resistance in the Revolutionary Age*. Princeton, NJ: Princeton University Press.

Freyer, Tony A. (1994) *Producers versus Capitalists: Constitutional Conflict in Antebellum America*. Charlottesville, Va.: University of Virginia Press.

Friedman, Jean F. (1985) *The Enclosed Garden: Women and Community in the Evangelical South, 1830–1900*. Chapel Hill, NC: University of North Carolina Press.

Friedman, Lawrence J. (1984) *Gregarious Saints: Self and Community in American Abolitionism*. New York: Cambridge University Press.

Fuller, J. F. C. (1929) *The Generalship of Ulysses S. Grant*. New York: Dodd Mead.

Furgurson, Ernest B. (1992) *Chancellorsville 1863: The Souls of the Brave*. New York: Alfred A. Knopf.

Gallagher, Gary W. (1991) *Struggle for the Shenandoah: Essays on the 1864 Valley Campaign*. Kent, Ohio: Kent State University Press.

Gallagher, Gary W. (ed.) (1995) *The Fredericksburg Campaign: Decision on the Rappahannock*. Chapel Hill, NC: University of North Carolina Press.

Gallagher, Gary W. (1997) *The Confederate War*. Cambridge, Mass.: Harvard University Press.

Gallman, J. Matthew (1994) *The North Fights the Civil War: The Home Front*. Chicago: University of Chicago Press.

Gardner, S. E. (1999) "Every Man Has Got the Right to Get Killed? The Civil War Narratives of Mary Johnston and Carolina Gordon," *Southern Cultures* 5: 14–40.

Gaspar, David Barry and Hine, Darlene Clark (eds.) (1996) *More than Chattel: Black Women and Slavery in the Americas*. Bloomington, Ind.: Indiana University Press.

Gaston, Paul (1965) "The New South," in Arthur S. Link and Rembert W. Patrick (eds.) *Writing Southern History*. Baton Rouge, La.: Louisiana State University Press.

Gellman, David N. (2000) "Race, the Public Sphere and Abolition in Late Eighteenth Century New York," *Journal of the Early Republic* 20: 607–36.

Genovese, Eugene D. (1965) *The Political Economy of Slavery: Studies in the Economy and Society of the Slave South*. New York: Pantheon.

Genovese, Eugene D. (1974) *Roll, Jordan, Roll: The World the Slaves Made*. New York: Pantheon.

Genovese, Eugene D. (1998) *A Consuming Fire: The Fall of the Confederacy in the Mind of the White Christian South*. Athens, Ga.: University of Georgia Press.

Gerteis, Louis G. (1973) *From Contraband to Freedman: Federal Policy toward Southern Blacks, 1861–1865*. Westport, Conn.: Greenwood Press.

Gienapp, William E. (1986) "The Republican Party and the Slave Power," in Robert H. Abzug and Stephen E. Maizlish (eds.) *New Perspectives on Race and Slavery in America*. Lexington, Ky.: University Press of Kentucky.

Gienapp, William E. (1987) *The Origins of the Republican Party, 1852–1856*. New York: Oxford University Press.

Gienapp, William E. (2002) *Abraham Lincoln and Civil War America: A Biography*. New York: Oxford University Press.

Giesberg, Judith Ann (2000) *Civil War Sisterhood: The US Sanitary Commission and Women's Politics in Transition*. Boston, Mass.: Northeastern University Press.

Gilchrist, David T. (ed.) (1967) *The Growth of the Seaport Cities, 1790–1825*. Charlottesville, Va.: University of Virginia Press.

Gilchrist, David T. and Lewis, W. David (eds.) (1965) *Economic Change in the Civil War Era*. Greenville, Del.: Eleutherian Mills-Hagley Foundation.

Gilje, Paul A. (1996) *Rioting in America*. Bloomington, Ind.: Indiana University Press.

Gilje, Paul A. (1997) *Wages of Independence: Capitalism in the Early American Republic.* Madison, Wis.: Madison House.

Gillespie, Michele and Clinton, Catherine (eds.) (1998) *Taking Off the White Gloves: Southern Women and Women's History* [Southern Women Series]. Columbia, Mo.: University of Missouri Press.

Gillette, William (1979) *Retreat from Reconstruction, 1869–1879.* Baton Rouge, La.: Louisiana State University Press.

Gilmore, Glenda E. (1996) *Gender and Jim Crow: Women and the Politics of White Supremacy in North Carolina, 1896–1920.* Chapel Hill, NC: University of North Carolina Press.

Ginzberg, Lori (1990) *Women and the Work of Benevolence: Morality, Politics, and Class in the Nineteenth Century United States.* New Haven, Conn.: Yale University Press.

Glickstein, Jonathan A. (1991) *Concepts of Free Labor in Antebellum America.* New Haven, Conn.: Yale University Press.

Glymph, Thavolia and Kushma, John J. (eds.) (1985) *Essays on the Postbellum Southern Economy.* College Station, Tex.: Texas A & M University Press.

Goldfield, D. (2002) *Still Fighting the Civil War: The American South and Southern History.* Baton Rouge, La.: Louisiana State University Press.

Goldin, Claudia Dale and Lewis, Frank (1975) "The Economic Costs of the American Civil War: Estimates and Implications," *Journal of Economic History* 35: 299–326.

Gollaher, David (1995) *Voice for the Mad: The Life of Dorothea Dix.* New York: Free Press.

Goodman, Paul (1998) *Of One Blood: Abolitionism and the Origins of Racial Equality.* Berkeley, Calif.: University of California Press.

Goodwyn, Lawrence (1978) *The Populist Moment: A Short History of the Agrarian Revolt in America.* New York: Oxford University Press.

Gould, Virginia Meacham (ed.) (1998) *Chained to the Rock of Adversity: To be Free, Black and Female in the Old South.* Athens, Ga.: University of Georgia Press.

Graebner, Norman (1960) "Northern Diplomacy and European Neutrality," in David Donald (ed.) *Why the North Won the Civil War.* Baton Rouge, La.: Louisiana State University Press.

Grant, Ulysses S. (1885–6) *The Personal Memoirs of Ulysses S. Grant,* two vols. New York: Charles H. Webster.

Greenberg, Kenneth S. (1985) *Masters and Statesmen: The Political Culture of American Slavery.* Baltimore, Md.: Johns Hopkins University Press.

Griffith, Paddy (1989) *Battle Tactics of the Civil War.* New Haven, Conn.: Yale University Press.

Grimke, Sarah Moore (1838) *Letters on the Equality of the Sexes, and the Condition of Women: Addressed to Mary S. Parker.* Boston, Mass.: I. Knapp.

Grimsley, Mark (1995) *The Hard Hand of War: Union Military Policy toward Southern Civilians, 1861–1865.* New York: Cambridge University Press.

Grimsley, Mark (2002) *And Keep Moving On: The Virginia Campaign, May–June 1864.* Lincoln, Nebr.: University of Nebraska Press.

Grossberg, Michael (1985) *Governing the Hearth: Law and the Family in Nineteenth Century America.* Chapel Hill, NC: University of North Carolina Press.

Grossman, Lawrence (1976) *The Democratic Party and the Negro.* Urbana, Ill.: University of Illinois Press.

Guelzo, Alan C. (1999) *Abraham Lincoln: Redeemer President.* Grand Rapids, Mich.: William B. Eerdmans.

Gunther, Gerald (2001) *Constitutional Law,* 3rd edn. New York: Foundations Press.

Gutman, Herbert G. (1976a) *The Black Family in Slavery and Freedom, 1750–1925.* New York: Pantheon.

Gutman, Herbert G. (1976b) *Work, Culture, and Society in Industrializing America: Essays in American Working-Class History.* New York: Alfred A. Knopf.

Hacker, Louis M. (1940) *The Triumph of American Capitalism*. New York: Columbia University Press.

Hagler, D. Harland (1980) "The Ideal Woman in the Antebellum South: Lady or Farmwife?," *Journal of Southern History* 46: 405–18.

Hahn, Steven (1983) *The Roots of Southern Populism: Yeomen Farmers and the Transformation of the Georgia Upcountry, 1850–1890*. New York: Oxford University Press.

Hahn, Steven (2003) *A Nation under Our Feet: Black Political Struggles in the Rural South from Slavery to the Great Migration*. Cambridge, Mass.: Harvard University Press.

Hale, G. E. (1998) *Making Whiteness: The Culture of Segregation in the South, 1890–1940*. New York: Pantheon.

Hall, Gwendolyn Midlo (1992) *Africans in Colonial Louisiana: The Development of Afro-Creole Culture in the Eighteenth-Century*. Baton Rouge, La.: Louisiana State University Press.

Hall, Jacquelyn Dowd and Scott, Ann Firor (1985) "Women in the South," in John B. Boles and Evelyn Thomas Nolen (eds.) *Interpreting Southern History: Historiographical Essays in Honor of Sanford W. Higginbotham*. Baton Rouge, La.: Louisiana State University Press.

Halpern, Rick, and Dal Lago, Enrico (eds.) (2002) *The American South and the Italian Mezzogiorno*. Basingstoke: Palgrave.

Halttunen, Karen (1982) *Confidence Men and Painted Women: A Study in Middle-Class Culture in America, 1830–1870*. New Haven, Conn.: Yale University Press.

Handlin, Oscar and Handlin, Mary Flug (1947) *Commonwealth: A Study of the Role of Government in the American Economy: Massachusetts, 1774–1861*. New York: New York University Press.

Hanger, Kimberly S. (1997) *Bounded Lives, Bounded Places: Free Black Society in Colonial New Orleans, 1769–1803*. Durham, NC: Duke University Press.

Harding, Vincent (1981) *There is a River: The Black Struggle for Freedom in America*. New York: Harcourt Brace.

Harris, J. William (1985) *Plain Folk and Gentry in a Slave Society: White Liberty and Black Slavery in Augusta's Hinterlands*. Middletown, Conn.: Wesleyan University Press.

Harris, J. William (1994) "Crop Choices in the Piedmont before and after the Civil War," *Journal of Economic History* 54: 526–42.

Harris, J. William (1997) "The Question of Peonage in the History of the New South," in Samuel C. Hyde Jr (ed.) *Plain Folk of the South Revisited*. Baton Rouge, La.: Louisiana State University Press.

Harris, J. William (2001) *Deep Souths: Delta, Piedmont, and Sea Island Society in the Age of Segregation*. Baltimore, Md.: Johns Hopkins University Press.

Harris, W. T. (1897) "Statistics *versus* Socialism," *Forum* 24 (October): 186–99.

Hartz, Louis (1948) *Economic Policy and Democratic Thought in Pennsylvania, 1776–1860*. Cambridge, Mass.: Harvard University Press.

Hartz, Louis (1955) *The Liberal Tradition in America*. New York: Harcourt Brace.

Harvey, P. (1997) *Redeeming the South: Religious Cultures and Racial Identities Among Southern Baptists, 1865–1925*. Chapel Hill, NC: University of North Carolina Press.

Hatcher, Richard and Piston, William Garrett (2000) *Wilson's Creek: The Second Battle of the Civil War and the Men Who Fought It*. Chapel Hill, NC: University of North Carolina Press.

Hattaway, Herman and Jones, Archer (1983) *How the North Won: A Military History of the Civil War*. Urbana, Ill.: University of Illinois Press.

Hawks, Joanne V. and Skemp, Sheila (eds.) (1983) *Sex, Race, and the Role of Women in the South*. Jackson, Miss.: University Press of Mississippi.

Hedrick, Joan (1994) *Harriet Beecher Stowe: A Life*. New York: Oxford University Press.

Heitmann, John A. (1986) *The Modernization of the Louisiana Sugar Industry, 1830–1910*. Baton Rouge, La.: Louisiana State University Press.

Hennessy, John J. (1993) *Return to Bull Run: The Campaign and Battle of Second Manassas.* New York: Simon and Schuster.

Henretta, James A. (1991) *The Origins of American Capitalism: Collected Essays.* Boston, Mass.: Northeastern University Press.

Hershberger, Mary (1999) "Mobilizing Women, Anticipating Abolition: The Struggle against Indian Removal in the 1830s," *Journal of American History* 86: 15–40.

Hess, Earl J. (1988) *Liberty, Virtue and Progress: Northerners and their War for the Union.* New York: New York University Press.

Hess, Earl J. (1997) *The Union Soldier in Battle: Enduring the Ordeal of Combat.* Lawrence, Kan.: University Press of Kansas.

Hewitt, Nancy (1984) *Women's Activism and Social Change: Rochester, New York, 1822–1872.* Ithaca, NY: Cornell University Press.

Heyrman, Christine Leigh (1984) *Commerce and Culture: The Maritime Communities of Colonial Massachusetts, 1690–1750.* New York: Norton.

Heyrman, Christine Leigh (1997) *Southern Cross: The Beginnings of the Bible Belt.* New York: Alfred A. Knopf.

Hicks, John D. (1961) *The Populist Revolt.* Lincoln, Nebr: University of Nebraska Press.

Higgs, Robert (1977) *Competition and Coercion: Blacks in the American Economy, 1865–1914.* New York: Cambridge University Press.

Hill, Sarah H. (1997) *Weaving New Worlds: Southeastern Cherokee Women and their Basketry.* Chapel Hill, NC: University of North Carolina Press.

Hill, S. S., Jr (1966) *Southern Churches in Crisis.* New York: Holt Rinehart Winston.

Hill, S. S., Jr (1980) *The South and the North in American Religion.* Athens, Ga.: University of Georgia Press.

Hine, Darlene Clark and Thompson, Kathleen (1988) *A Shining Thread of Hope: The History of Black Women in America.* New York: Broadway Books.

Hirschfeld, Fritz (1997) *George Washington and Slavery: A Documentary Portrayal.* Columbia, Mo.: University of Missouri Press.

Hobsbawm, Eric J. (1975) *The Age of Capital, 1848–1875.* New York: Charles Scribner's Sons.

Hodes, Martha (1997) *White Women, Black Men: Illicit Sex in the Nineteenth-Century South.* New Haven, Conn.: Yale University Press.

Hodges, Graham Russell (1997) *Slavery and Freedom in the Rural North: African Americans in Monmouth County, New Jersey, 1665–1865.* Madison, Wis.: Madison House.

Hodges, Graham Russell (1999) *Root and Branch: African Americans in New York and East Jersey, 1613–1863.* Chapel Hill, NC: University of North Carolina Press.

Hoffert, Sylvia D. (1995) *When Hens Crow: The Women's Rights Movement in Antebellum America.* Bloomington, Ind.: Indiana University Press.

Hofstadter, Richard (1948) *The American Political Tradition and the Men Who Made It.* New York: Vintage.

Holt, Michael F. (1969) *Forging a Majority: The Formation of the Republican Party in Pittsburgh, 1848–1860.* New Haven, Conn.: Yale University Press.

Holt, Michael F. (1978) *The Political Crisis of the 1850s.* New York: Wiley.

Holt, Michael F. (1986) "Abraham Lincoln and the Politics of Union," in John L. Thomas (ed.) *Abraham Lincoln and the American Political Tradition.* Amherst, Mass.: University of Massachusetts Press.

Holt, Michael F. (1999) *The Rise and Fall of the American Whig Party: Jacksonian Politics and the Onset of the Civil War.* New York: Oxford University Press.

Holt, Sharon Ann (2000) *Making Freedom Pay: North Carolina Freedpeople Working for Themselves, 1865–1900.* Athens, Ga.: University of Georgia Press.

Holt, Thomas (1977) *Black over White: Negro Political Leadership in South Carolina during Reconstruction.* Urbana, Ill.: University of Illinois Press.

Holton, Woody (1999) *Forced Founders: Indians, Debtors, Slaves and the Making of the Revolution in Virginia*. Chapel Hill, NC: University of North Carolina Press.

Hoogenboom, Ari (1961) *Outlawing the Spoils: A History of the Civil Service Reform Movement, 1865–1883*. Urbana, Ill.: University of Illinois Press.

Horton, James and Horton, Lois (1997) *In Hope of Liberty: Culture, Community and Protest among Northern Free Blacks, 1700–1860*. New York: Oxford University Press.

Horwitz, Morton J. (1977) *The Transformation of American Law, 1780–1860*. Cambridge, Mass.: Harvard University Press.

Horwitz, Morton J. (1992) *The Transformation of American Law, 1870–1960*. New York: Oxford University Press.

Horwitz, Tony (1998) *Confederates in the Attic: Dispatches from the Unfinished Civil War*. New York: Pantheon.

Howe, Daniel Walker (1979) *The Political Culture of the American Whigs*. Chicago: University of Chicago Press.

Hubbell, John Thomas (1969) "The Northern Democracy and the Crisis of Disunion, 1860–1861," unpublished PhD dissertation, University of Illinois.

Hudson, Larry E., Jr (1997) *"To Have and to Hold": Slave Work and Family Life in Antebellum South Carolina*. Athens, Ga.: University of Georgia Press.

Hundley, Daniel R. (1860) *Social Relations in our Southern States*. New York: H. B. Price.

Hunter, Louis C. (1949) *Steamboats on the Western Rivers*. Cambridge, Mass.: Harvard University Press.

Hunter, Louis C. (1979, 1985) *A History of Industrial Power in the United States, 1780–1930*, three vols. Volume 1: *Water Power in the Century of Steam*. Volume 2: *Steam Power*. Charlottesville, Va.: University of Virginia Press.

Hunter, Tera W. (1997) *To 'Joy my Freedom: Southern Black Women's Lives and Labors after the Civil War*. Cambridge, Mass.: Harvard University Press.

Hurst, James Willard (1956) *Law and the Conditions of Freedom in the Nineteenth-Century United States*. Madison, Wis.: University of Wisconsin Press.

Huston, James L. (1987) *The Panic of 1857 and the Coming of the Civil War*. Baton Rouge, La.: Louisiana State University Press.

Huston, James (1998) *Securing the Fruits of Labor: The American Concept of Wealth Distribution, 1765–1900*. Baton Rouge, La.: Louisiana State University Press.

Inscoe, John C. (1989) *Mountain Masters, Slavery, and the Sectional Crisis in Western North Carolina*. Knoxville, Tenn.: University of Tennessee Press.

Irwin, James R. and O'Brien, Anthony Patrick (1998) "Where Have All the Sharecroppers Gone? Black Occupations in Postbellum Mississippi," *Agricultural History* 72: 280–97.

Isenberg, Nancy (1998) *Sex and Citizenship in Antebellum America*. Chapel Hill, NC: University of North Carolina Press.

Jabour, Anya (1998) *Marriage in the Early Republic: Elizabeth and William Wirt and the Companionate Ideal*. Baltimore, Md.: Johns Hopkins University Press.

Jacobs, Harriet A. (1987) *Incidents in the Life of a Slave Girl, Written by Herself*, ed. L. Maria Child, new edn. ed. by Jean Fagan Yellin. Cambridge, Mass.: Harvard University Press.

James, John A. (1981) "Financial Underdevelopment in the Postbellum South." *Journal of Interdisciplinary History* 11: 443–54.

Jaynes, Gerald David (1986) *Branches without Roots: The Genesis of the Black Working Class in the American South, 1862–1882*. New York: Oxford University Press.

Jeffrey, Julie Roy (1998) *The Great, Silent Arm of Abolitionism: Ordinary Women in the Abolitionist Movement*. Chapel Hill, NC: University of North Carolina Press.

Jensen, Joan (1986) *Loosening the Bonds: Mid-Atlantic Farm Women, 1750–1850*. New Haven, Conn.: Yale University Press.

Jimerson, Randall C. (1988) *The Private Civil War: Popular Thought during the Sectional Conflict*. Baton Rouge, La.: Louisiana State University Press.

Johannsen, Robert W. (1991) *Lincoln, the South, and Slavery: The Political Dimension*. Baton Rouge, La.: Louisiana State University Press.

Johnson, J. M. (2000) "'Drill into us . . . the Rebel Tradition': The Contest over Southern Identity in Black and White Women's Clubs, South Carolina, 1898–1930," *Journal of Southern History* 66: 525–62.

Johnson, Michael P. (1977) *Toward a Patriarchal Republic: The Secession of Georgia*. Baton Rouge, La.: Louisiana State University Press.

Johnson, Paul E. (1978) *A Shopkeeper's Millennium: Society and Revivals in Rochester, New York, 1815–1837*. New York: Hill and Wang.

Johnson, Walter (1999) *Soul by Soul: Life Inside the Antebellum Slave Market*. Cambridge, Mass.: Harvard University Press.

Jones, Ann Goodwyn and Donaldson, Susan V. (eds.) (1997) *Haunted Bodies: Gender and Southern Texts*. Charlottesville, Va.: University of Virginia Press.

Jones, Jacqueline (1980) *Soldiers of Light and Love: Northern Teachers and Georgia Blacks, 1865–1873*. Chapel Hill, NC: University of North Carolina Press.

Jones, Jacqueline (1985) *Labor of Love, Labor of Sorrow: Black Women, Work, and the Family from Slavery to the Present*. New York: Basic Books.

Jones, Norrece T. (1989) *Born a Child of Freedom yet a Slave: Mechanisms of Control and Strategies of Resistance in Antebellum South Carolina*. Middletown, Conn.: Wesleyan University Press.

Jordan, Ervin L., Jr (1995) *Black Confederates and Afro-Yankees in Civil War Virginia*. Charlottesville, Va.: University of Virginia Press.

Jordan, Winthrop (1965) *White over Black: American Attitudes toward the Negro, 1550–1812*. Chapel Hill, NC: University of North Carolina Press.

Julian, George W. (1884) *Political Recollections, 1840–1872*. Chicago: Jansen McClurg.

Kaminski, John P. (ed.) (1995) *A Necessary Evil? Slavery and the Debate over the Constitution*. Madison, Wis.: Madison House.

Kantrowitz, S. (2000) *Ben Tillman and the Reconstruction of White Supremacy*. Chapel Hill, NC: University of North Carolina Press.

Kaplan, Amy (1988) *The Social Construction of American Realism*. Chicago, Ill.: University of Chicago Press.

Kaplan, Sidney (1989) *The Black Presence in the American Revolution*. Amherst, Mass.: University of Massachusetts Press.

Keller, Morton (1977) *Affairs of State: Public Life in Late Nineteenth Century America*. Cambridge: Cambridge University Press.

Kelley, Mary (1996) "Reading Women/Women Reading: The Making of Learned Women in Antebellum America," *Journal of American History* 83: 401–24.

Kelly, Catherine (1999) *In the New England Fashion: Reshaping Women's Lives in the Nineteenth Century*. Ithaca, NY: Cornell University Press.

Kelly, Patrick J. (1997) *Creating a National Home: Building the Veterans' Welfare State, 1860–1900*. Cambridge: Cambridge University Press.

Kelly, Robert (1969) *The Transatlantic Persuasion: The Liberal-Democratic Mind in the Age of Gladstone*. New York: Alfred A. Knopf.

Kenzer, Robert C. (1987) *Kinship and Neighborhood in a Southern Community: Orange County, North Carolina, 1849–1881*. Knoxville, Tenn.: University of Tennessee Press.

Kerber, Linda (1988) "Separate Spheres, Female Worlds, Woman's Place: The Rhetoric of Women's History," *Journal of American History* 75: 9–39.

Kerber, Linda (1998) *No Constitutional Right to be Ladies: Women and the Obligations of Citizenship*. New York: Hill and Wang.

Kerr-Ritchie, Jeffrey R. (1999) *Freed People in the Tobacco South: Virginia, 1860–1900*. Chapel Hill, NC: University of North Carolina Press.

Keyssar, Alexander (2000) *The Right to Vote: The Contested History of Democracy in the United States*. New York: Basic Books.

Kierner, Cynthia (1998) *Beyond the Household: Women's Place in the Early South, 1700–1835*. Ithaca, NY: Cornell University Press.

Kilbourne, Richard H., Jr (1990) *Debt, Investment, Slaves: Credit Relations in East Feliciana Parish, Louisiana, 1825–1885*. Tuscaloosa, Ala.: University of Alabama Press.

King, R. H. (1980) *A Southern Renaissance: The Cultural Awakening of the American South, 1930–1955*. New York: Oxford University Press.

King, Wilma (1995) *Stolen Childhood: Slave Youth in Nineteenth-Century America*. Bloomington, Ind.: Indiana University Press.

Klein, Maury (1997) *Days of Defiance: Sumter, Secession, and the Coming of the Civil War*. New York: Alfred A. Knopf.

Knoles, George Harmon (ed.) (1965) *The Crisis of the Union, 1860–1861*. Baton Rouge, La.: Louisiana State University Press.

Knupfer, Peter B. (1991) *The Union As It Is: Constitutional Unionism and Sectional Compromise, 1787–1861*. Chapel Hill, NC: University of North Carolina Press.

Kolchin, Peter (1987) *Unfree Labor: American Slavery and Russian Serfdom*. Cambridge, Mass.: Harvard University Press.

Kolchin, Peter (1993) *American Slavery, 1619–1877*. New York: Hill and Wang.

Kousser, J. Morgan (1974) *The Shaping of Southern Politics: Suffrage Restriction and the Establishment of the One-Party South, 1880–1900*. New Haven, Conn.: Yale University Press.

Kousser, J. Morgan (2000) "Reconstruction," in Paul S. Boyer (ed.) *The Oxford Companion to United States History*. New York: Oxford University Press.

Kraditor, Aileen (1967) *Means and Ends in American Abolitionism: Garrison and his Critics on Strategy and Tactics, 1834–1854*. New York: Random House.

Krick, Robert K. (2002) *The Smoothbore Volley that Doomed the Confederacy: The Death of Stonewall Jackson and Other Chapters on the Army of Northern Virginia*. Baton Rouge, La.: Louisiana State University Press.

Kulikoff, Alan (1992) *The Agrarian Origins of American Capitalism*. Charlottesville, Va.: University of Virginia Press.

Kutler, Stanley I. (1971) *Privilege and Creative Destruction: the Charles River Bridge Case*. New York: Norton.

Kuznets, Simon and Thomas, Dorothy Swaine (eds.) (1957–64) *Population Redistribution and Economic Growth, 1870–1950*, three vols. Philadelphia, Pa.: American Philosophical Society.

Kyriakoudes, Louis M. (2002) "Lower-Order Urbanization and Territorial Monopoly in the Southern Furnishing Trade: Alabama, 1871–1890," *Social Science History* 26: 179–98.

Landers, Jane (1999) *Black Society in Spanish Florida*. Urbana, Ill.: University of Illinois Press.

Lanza, Michael L. (1990) *Agrarianism and Reconstruction Politics: The Southern Homestead Act*. Baton Rouge, La.: Louisiana State University Press.

Larson, John Lauritz (2001a [1984]) *Bonds of Enterprise: John Murray Forbes and Western Development in America's Railway Age*. Iowa City, Iowa: University of Iowa Press.

Larson, John Lauritz (2001b) *Internal Improvement: National Public Works and the Promise of Popular Government in the Early United States*. Chapel Hill, NC: University of North Carolina Press.

Laurie, Bruce (1997) *Artisans into Workers: Labor in Nineteenth Century America*. Urbana, Ill.: University of Illinois Press.

Lawson, Melinda (2002) *Patriot Fires: Forging a New American Nationalism in the Civil War North*. Lawrence, Kan.: University Press of Kansas.

Lebsock, Suzanne (1984) *The Free Women of Petersburg: Status and Culture in a Southern Town, 1784–1860*. New York: Norton.

Leonard, Elizabeth (1994) *Yankee Women: Gender Battles in the Civil War*. New York: Norton.

Lerner, Gerda (1967) *The Grimke Sisters from South Carolina: Rebels against Slavery*. Boston, Mass.: Houghton Mifflin.

Leslie, Kent Anderson (1995) *Woman of Color, Daughter of Privilege: Amanda America Dickson, 1849–1893*. Athens, Ga.: University of Georgia Press.

Lewis, Jan (1983) *The Pursuit of Happiness: Family and Values in Jefferson's Virginia*. Cambridge: Cambridge University Press.

Lichtenstein, Alex (1998) "Proletarians or Peasants? Sharecroppers and the Politics of Protest in the Rural South, 1880–1940," *Plantation Society in the Americas* 5: 297–331.

Linden, Fabian (1946) "Economic Democracy in the Slave South: An Appraisal of Some Recent Views," *Journal of Negro History* 31: 140–90.

Linderman, Gerald F. (1987) *Embattled Courage: The Experience of Combat in the American Civil War*. New York: Free Press.

Lindstrom, Diane (1978) *Economic Development in the Philadelphia Region, 1810–1850*. New York: Columbia University Press.

Link, Arthur S. and Patrick, Rembert W. (1965) *Writing Southern History: Essays in Historiography in Honor of Fletcher M. Green*. Baton Rouge, La.: Louisiana State University Press.

Litwack, Leon F. (1979) *Been in the Storm So Long: The Aftermath of Slavery*. New York: Alfred A. Knopf.

Livermore, Mary (1888) *My Story of the War*. Hartford, Conn.: A. D. Worthington.

Lockley, Timothy James (2001) *Lines in the Sand: Race and Class in Lowcountry Georgia, 1750–1860*. Athens, Ga.: University of Georgia Press.

Lonn, Ella (1933) *Salt as a Factor in the Confederacy*. New York: Neale.

Lonn, Ella (1940) *Foreigners in the Confederacy*. Chapel Hill, NC: University of North Carolina Press.

Lott, Eric (1993) *Love and Theft: Blackfaced Minstrelsy and the American Working Class*. New York: Oxford University Press.

Lounsbury, Richard C. (ed.) (1996) *Louisa S. McCord: Poems, Drama, Biography, Letters*. Charlottesville, Va.: University of Virginia Press.

Lounsbury, Richard C. (ed.) (1997) *Louisa S. McCord: Selected Writings*. Charlottesville, Va.: University of Virginia Press.

Lowenthal, D. (1998) *The Heritage Crusade and the Spoils of History*. Cambridge: Cambridge University Press.

Lyerly, Cynthia Lynn (1998) *Methodism and the Southern Mind, 1770–1810*. New York: Oxford University Press.

Mabee, Carleton (1970) *The Non-Violent Abolitionists*. New York: Harper and Row.

McCardell, John (1979) *The Idea of a Southern Nation: Southern Nationalists and Southern Nationalism, 1830–1860*. New York: Norton.

McColley, Robert (1973) *Slavery and Jeffersonian Virginia*, 2nd edn. Urbana, Ill.: University of Illinois Press.

McConnell, Stuart (1992) *Glorious Contentment: The Grand Army of the Republic, 1865–1900*. Chapel Hill, NC: University of North Carolina Press.

McCoy, Drew (1989) *The Last of the Fathers: James Madison and the Republican Legacy*. New York: Cambridge University Press.

McCurry, Stephanie (1995) *Masters of Small Worlds: Yeoman Households, Gender Relations, and the Political Culture of the Antebellum South Carolina Low Country*. New York: Oxford University Press.

McDonald, Forrest and McWhiney, Grady (1980) "The South from Self-Sufficiency to Peonage: An Interpretation," *American Historical Review* 85: 1095–118.

McDonald, Roderick (1993) *The Economy and Material Culture of Slaves: Goods and Chattels on the Plantations of Jamaica and Louisiana*. Baton Rouge, La.: Louisiana State University Press.

McDonough, James Lee (1980) *Stones River: Bloody Winter in Tennessee*. Knoxville, Tenn.: University of Tennessee Press.

McFeely, William S. (1968) *Yankee Stepfather: General O. O. Howard and the Freedmen*. New Haven, Conn.: Yale University Press.

McGlynn, Frank and Drescher, Seymour (eds.) (1992) *The Meaning of Freedom: Economics, Politics, and Culture after Slavery*. Pittsburgh, Pa.: University of Pittsburgh Press.

McHenry, Elizabeth (2002) *Forgotten Readers: Recovering the Lost History of African American Literary Societies*. Durham, NC: Duke University Press.

McKenzie, Robert Tracy (1994) *One South or Many? Plantation Belt and Upcountry in Civil-War Era Tennessee*. New York: Cambridge University Press.

McKenzie, Robert Tracy (1995) "Rediscovering the 'Farmless' Farm Population: The Nineteenth-Century Census and the Postbellum Reorganization of Agriculture in the US South, 1860–1900," *Histoire Sociale* 28: 501–20.

McKitrick, Eric L. (1960) *Andrew Johnson and Reconstruction*. Chicago: University of Chicago Press.

McLaurin, Melton (1991) *Celia: A Slave*. Athens, Ga.: University of Georgia Press.

McManus, William (1970) *Black Bondage in the North*. New York: Oxford University Press.

McMillen, Sally G. (1990) *Motherhood in the Old South: Pregnancy, Childbirth and Infant Rearing*. Baton Rouge, La.: Louisiana State University Press.

McMurry, Richard M. (2000) *Atlanta 1864: Last Chance for the Confederacy*. Lincoln, Nebr.: University of Nebraska Press.

McPherson, James M. (1965) *The Struggle for Equality: The Abolitionists during the Civil War and Reconstruction*. Princeton, NJ: Princeton University Press.

McPherson, James M. (1982) *Ordeal by Fire: The Civil War and Reconstruction*. New York: Oxford University Press.

McPherson, James M. (1983) "Southern Exceptionalism: A New Look at an Old Question," *Civil War History* 29 (Sept.): 230–44.

McPherson, James M. (1988) *Battle Cry of Freedom: The Civil War Era*. New York: Oxford University Press.

McPherson, James M. (1991) "Abraham Lincoln and the Second American Revolution," in *Abraham Lincoln and the Second American Revolution*. New York: Oxford University Press.

McPherson, James M. (1992) "American Victory, American Defeat," in Gabor S. Boritt (ed.) *Why the Confederacy Lost*. New York: Oxford University Press.

McPherson, James M. (1996a) "The War of Southern Aggression," in McPherson, *Drawn with the Sword: Reflections on the American Civil War*. New York: Oxford University Press.

McPherson, James M. (1996b) "Who Freed the Slaves?," in McPherson, *Drawn with the Sword: Reflections on the American Civil War*. New York: Oxford University Press.

McPherson, James M. (1997) *For Cause and Comrades: Why Men Fought in the Civil War*. New York: Oxford University Press.

McWhiney, Grady (1983) "General Beauregard's 'Complete Victory' at Shiloh: An Interpretation," *Journal of Southern History* 49: 421–34.

McWhiney, Grady (1988) *Cracker Culture: Celtic Ways in the Old South*. Tuscaloosa, Ala.: University of Alabama Press.

Malone, Ann Patton (1992) *Sweet Chariot: Slave Family and Household Structure in Nineteenth Century Louisiana*. Chapel Hill, NC: University of North Carolina Press.

Malone, Dumas (1948–81) *Jefferson and his Time*, six vols. Boston, Mass.: Little, Brown.

Malvasi, M. G. (1997) *The Unregenerate South: The Agrarian Thought of John Crowe Ransom, Allen Tate, and Donald Davidson*. Baton Rouge, La.: Louisiana State University Press.

Mandle, Jay R. (1978) *The Roots of Black Poverty: The Southern Plantation Economy after the Civil War*. Durham, NC: Duke University Press.

Mandle, Jay R. (1992) *Not Slave, Not Free: The African American Economic Experience since the Civil War*. Durham, NC: Duke University Press.

Manis, A. M. (1987) *Southern Civil Religions in Conflict: Black and White Baptists and Civil Rights, 1947–1957*. Athens, Ga.: University of Georgia Press.

Mann, Susan Archer (1994) *Agrarian Capitalism in Theory and Practice*. Chapel Hill, NC: University of North Carolina Press.

Margo, Robert A. (1995) "The South as an Economic Problem: Fact or Fiction?," in Larry J. Griffin and Don H. Doyle (eds.) *The South as an American Problem*. Athens, Ga.: University of Georgia Press.

Marler, Scott P. (2001) "Merchants in the Transition to a New South: Central Louisiana, 1840–1880," *Louisiana History* 42: 165–92.

Marler, Scott P. (2004) "Fables of the Reconstruction: Reconstruction of the Fables," *Journal of the Historical Society* 4: 113–37.

Marten, James (1998) *The Children's Civil War*. Chapel Hill, NC: University of North Carolina Press.

Martinez, J. M., Richardson, W. D., and McNinch-Su, R. (eds.) (2000) *Confederate Symbols in the Contemporary South*. Gainesville, Fla.: University Press of Florida.

Massey, Mary Elizabeth (1966) *Bonnet Brigades: American Women in the Civil War*. New York: Alfred A. Knopf.

Masur, Louis (2001) *1831: The Year of Eclipse*. New York: Hill and Wang.

Mathews, Donald (1977) *Religion in the Old South*. Chicago, Ill.: University of Chicago Press.

Meinig, D. W. (1998) *The Shaping of America: A Geographical Perspective on 500 Years of History*, four vols. Volume 2: *Continental America, 1800–1867*. New Haven, Conn.: Yale University Press.

Melish, Joanne Pope (1998) *Disowning Slavery: Gradual Emancipation and "Race" in New England, 1780–1860*. Ithaca, NY: Cornell University Press.

Merk, Frederick (1972) *Slavery and the Annexation of Texas*. New York: Knopf.

Miller, John Chester (1977) *The Wolf by the Ears: Thomas Jefferson and Slavery*. New York: Free Press.

Milton, George F. (1930) *The Age of Hate: Andrew Johnson and the Radicals*. New York: Howard-McCann.

Mitchell, Reid (1995) *The Vacant Chair: The Northern Soldier Leaves Home*. New York: Oxford University Press.

Mohr, Clarence L. (2001 [1986]) *On the Threshold of Freedom: Masters and Slaves in Civil War Georgia*. Baton Rouge, La.: Louisiana State University Press.

Moneyhon, Carl H. (1994) *The Impact of the Civil War and Reconstruction on Arkansas: Persistence in the Midst of Ruin*. Baton Rouge, La.: Louisiana State University Press.

Montgomery, David (1967) *Beyond Equality: Labor and the Radical Republicans, 1862–1872*. New York: Alfred A. Knopf.

Montgomery, David (1987) *Fall of the House of Labor: The Workplace, the State, and Labor Activism, 1865–1925*. Cambridge: Cambridge University Press.

Montgomery, R. (2000) "Lost Cause Mythology in New South Reform: Gender, Class, Race, and the Politics of Patriotic Citizenship in Georgia, 1890–1925," in J. L. Coryell et al. (eds.) *Negotiating Boundaries of Southern Womanhood: Dealing with the Powers that Be*. Columbia, Mo.: University of Missouri Press.

Moore, Barrington, Jr (1966) *Social Origins of Dictatorship and Democracy: Lord and Peasant in the Making of the Modern World*. Boston, Mass.: Beacon Press.

Moore, Frank (1866) *Women of the War: Their Heroism and Self-Sacrifice.* Hartford, Conn.: Scranton.

Moore, Glover (1953) *The Missouri Controversy, 1819–1821.* Lexington, Ky.: University Press of Kentucky.

Morgan, C. M. (1985) *Redneck Liberal: Theodore G. Bilbo and the New Deal.* Baton Rouge, La.: Louisiana State University Press.

Morgan, Edmund S. (1975) *American Slavery, American Freedom: The Ordeal of Revolutionary Virginia.* New York: Norton.

Morgan, Lynda J. (1992) *Emancipation in Virginia's Tobacco Belt, 1850–1870.* Athens, Ga.: University of Georgia Press.

Morgan, Phillip D. (1998) *Slave Counterpoint: Black Culture in the Eighteenth-Century Chesapeake and Lowcountry.* Chapel Hill, NC: University of North Carolina Press.

Morrison, Michael A. (1997) *Slavery and the American West: The Eclipse of Manifest Destiny and the Coming of the Civil War.* Chapel Hill, NC: University of North Carolina Press.

Morrow, Diane Batts (2002) *Persons of Color and Religious at the Same Time: The Oblate Sisters of Providence, 1828–1860.* Chapel Hill, NC: University of North Carolina Press.

Morton, Patricia (ed.) (1996) *Discovering the Women in Slavery: Emancipating Perspectives on the American Past.* Athens, Ga.: University of Georgia Press.

Moynihan, Daniel P. (1967) "The Negro Family: The Case for National Action," in Lee Rainwater and William Yancey, *The Moynihan Report and the Politics of Controversy.* Cambridge: MIT Press.

Murphy, Teresa (1992) *Ten Hours' Labor: Religion, Reform, and Gender in Early New England.* Ithaca, NY: Cornell University Press.

Nash, Gary (1990) *Race and Revolution.* Madison, Wis.: Madison House.

Nash, Gary and Soderlund, Jean (1991) *Freedom by Degrees: Emancipation and its Aftermath in Pennsylvania.* New York: Oxford University Press.

National Bureau of Economic Research (NBER) (1960) *Trends in the Nineteenth-Century Economy* [Studies in Income and Wealth, Volume 24]. Princeton, NJ: Princeton University Press.

Nevins, Allan (1950) *The Emergence of Lincoln,* two vols. New York: Charles Scribner's Sons.

Nevins, Allan (1959) *The War for the Union.* Volume 1: *The Improvised War, 1861–1862.* New York: Charles Scribner's Sons.

Nevins, Allan (1971 [1947]) *Ordeal of the Union.* Volume 8: *The War for the Union: The Organized War to Victory, 1864–1865.* New York: Charles Scribner's Sons.

Newman, Richard S. (2002) *The Transformation of American Abolitionism: Fighting Slavery in the Early Republic.* Chapel Hill, NC: University of North Carolina Press.

Nichols, Roy Franklin (1967 [1948]) *The Disruption of the American Democracy.* New York: Free Press.

Noble, David F. (1977) *America by Design: Science, Technology, and the Rise of Corporate Capitalism.* New York: Alfred A. Knopf.

Norton, Mary Beth (1996) *Founding Mothers and Fathers: Gendered Power and the Forming of American Society.* New York: Alfred A. Knopf.

Novak, William J. (1996) *The People's Welfare: Law and Regulation in Nineteenth-Century America.* Chapel Hill, NC: University of North Carolina Press.

Nye, Russel B. (1949) *Fettered Freedom: The Slavery Controversy and Civil Liberties.* Ann Arbor, Mich.: University of Michigan Press.

Oakes, James (1982) *The Ruling Race: A History of American Slaveholders.* New York: Alfred A. Knopf.

Oakes, James (1990) *Slavery and Freedom: An Interpretation of the Old South.* New York: Alfred A. Knopf.

Oates, Stephen (1995) *A Woman of Valor: Clara Barton and the Civil War.* New York: Free Press.

O'Brien, Patrick K. (1988) *The Economic Effects of the American Civil War.* London: Macmillan.

Ochiltree, Ian D. (1998) "'A Just and Self-Respecting System?' Black Independence, Share-cropping, and Paternalistic Relations in the American South and South Africa," *Agricultural History* 72: 352–80.

Olsen, Christopher J. (2000) *Political Culture and Secession in Mississippi: Masculinity, Honor, and the Antiparty Tradition, 1830–1860.* New York: Oxford University Press.

O'Reilly, Francis Augustin (2002) *The Fredericksburg Campaign: Winter War on the Rappahannock.* Baton Rouge, La.: Louisiana State University Press.

Osterweis, R. G. (1973) *The Myth of the Lost Cause, 1865–1900.* Hamden, Conn.: Archon.

Ott, Thomas (1973) *The Haitian Revolution, 1789–1804.* Knoxville, Tenn.: University of Tennessee Press.

Owsley, Frank L. (1949) *Plain Folk of the Old South.* Chicago: Quadrangle.

Painter, Nell (1996) *Sojourner Truth, a Life, a Symbol.* New York: Norton.

Palladino, Grace (1990) *Another Civil War: Labor, Capital and the State in the Anthracite Regions of Pennsylvania, 1840–1868.* Urbana, Ill.: University of Illinois Press.

Palmer, Colin A. (1996) "Rethinking American Slavery," in Alusine Jalloh and Stephen E. Maizlish (eds.) *The African Diaspora.* College Station, Tex.: Texas A & M University Press.

Paludan, Phillip Shaw (1988) *A People's Contest: The Union and Civil War, 1861–1865.* New York: Charles Scribner's Sons.

Paludan, Phillip Shaw (1994) *The Presidency of Abraham Lincoln.* Lawrence, Kan.: University Press of Kansas.

Paquette, Robert L. (1997) "Saint Domingue and the Making of Territorial Louisiana," in David Barry Gaspar and David Patrick Geggus (eds.) *A Turbulent Time: The French Revolution and the Greater Caribbean.* Bloomington, Ind.: Indiana University Press.

Parker, W. N. (1980) "The South in the National Economy, 1865–1970," *Southern Economic Journal* 46: 1019–48.

Patterson, Orlando (1982) *Slavery and Social Death: A Comparative Study.* Cambridge, Mass.: Harvard University Press.

Patterson, Orlando (1991) *Freedom.* Volume 1: *Freedom in the Making of the Modern World.* New York: Basic Books.

Pavich-Lindsay, Melanie (ed.) (2002) *Anna: The Letters of a St. Simons Island Plantation Mistress, 1817–1859.* Athens, Ga.: University of Georgia Press.

Pearson, Edward A. (ed.) (1999) *Designs against Charleston: The Trial Record of the Denmark Vesey Slave Conspiracy of 1822.* Chapel Hill, NC: University of North Carolina Press.

Pease, Jane H. and Pease, William H. (1999) *A Family of Women: The Carolina Petigrus in Peace and War.* Chapel Hill, NC: University of North Carolina Press.

Pease, William H. and Pease, Jane H. (1974) *They Who Would be Free: Blacks' Search for Freedom.* New York: Oxford University Press.

Peiss, Kathy (1986) *Cheap Amusements: Working Women and Leisure in Turn-of-the-Century New York.* Philadelphia, Pa.: Temple University Press.

Perdue, Theda (1998) *Cherokee Women: Gender and Culture Change, 1700–1835.* Lincoln, Nebr.: University of Nebraska Press.

Perkins, Edwin J. (1994) *American Public Finance and Financial Services, 1700–1815.* Columbus, Ohio: Ohio State University Press.

Perkins, Howard C. (ed.) (1942) *Northern Editorials on Secession,* two vols. New York: Appleton-Century for the American Historical Association.

Perman, Michael (1973) *Reunion without Compromise: The South and Reconstruction, 1865–1868.* New York: Cambridge University Press.

Perman, Michael (1984) *The Road to Redemption: Southern Politics, 1869–1879*. Chapel Hill, NC: University of North Carolina Press.

Perman, Michael (1989) "Eric Foner's Reconstruction: A Finished Revolution," *Reviews in American History* 17: 73–8.

Perman, Michael (1991) "Counter Reconstruction: The Role of Violence in Southern Redemption," in Eric Anderson and Alfred A. Moss, Jr (eds.) *The Facts of Reconstruction*. Baton Rouge, La.: Louisiana State University Press.

Perman, Michael (2001) *Struggle for Mastery: Disfranchisement in the South, 1888–1908*. Chapel Hill, NC: University of North Carolina Press.

Perry, Lewis C. (1973) *Radical Abolitionism: Anarchy and the Government of God in Antislavery Thought*. Ithaca, NY: Cornell University Press.

Peskin, Allan (1973) "Was There a Compromise of 1877?" *Journal of American History*, 60: 63–75.

Peterson, Merrill D. (1994) *Lincoln in American Memory*. New York: Oxford.

Pickett, LaSalle Corbell (1908) "My Soldier," *McClure's Magazine*.

Piersen, William D. (1993) *Black Legacy: America's Hidden Heritage*. University of Massachusetts Press.

Pierson, William D. (1996) *From African to African American: From the Colonial Era to the Early Republic, 1526–1790*. New York: Twayne.

Piston, William Garrett and Hatcher, Richard W., III (2000) *Wilson's Creek: The Second Battle of the Civil War and the Men Who Fought It*. Chapel Hill, NC: University of North Carolina Press.

Pocock, J. G. A. (1975) *The Machiavellian Moment: Florentine Political Thought and the Atlantic Republican Tradition*. Princeton, NJ: Princeton University Press.

Polakoff, Keith Ian (1973) *The Politics of Inertia: The Election of 1876 and the End of Reconstruction*. Baton Rouge, La.: Louisiana State University Press.

Pollack, Norman (ed.) (1967) *The Populist Mind*. Indianapolis, Ind.: Bobbs-Merrill.

Porter, Glenn and Livesay, Harold C. (1971) *Merchants and Manufacturers: Studies in the Changing Structure of Nineteenth-Century Marketing*. Baltimore, Md.: Johns Hopkins University Press.

Potter, David M. (1954) *People of Plenty, Economic Abundance and the American Character*. Chicago: University of Chicago Press.

Potter, David M. (1960) "Jefferson Davis and the Political Factors in Confederate Defeat," in David Donald (ed.) *Why the North Won the Civil War*. Baton Rouge, La.: Louisiana State University Press.

Potter, David M. (1968) *The South and the Sectional Conflict*. Baton Rouge, La.: Louisiana State University Press.

Potter, David M. (1972) *The South and the Concurrent Majority*, ed. Don E. Fehrenbacher and C. N. Degler. Baton Rouge, La.: Louisiana State University Press.

Potter, David M. (1976) *The Impending Crisis, 1848–1861*, completed and ed. Don E. Fehrenbacher. New York: Harper and Row.

Potter, David M. (1995 [1942]) *Lincoln and his Party in the Secession Crisis*. New Haven, Conn.: Yale University Press; reissued with new introduction by Daniel W. Crofts. Baton Rouge, La.: Louisiana State University Press.

Powderly, Terence V. (1967 [1890]) *Thirty Years of Labor: 1859–1889*. New York: A. M. Kelley.

Powell, William H. (1892) "Ulysses S. Grant," in *War Papers and Reminiscences 1861–1865 Reard Before the Commandery of the State of Missouri, Military Order of the Loyal Legion of the United States*, vol. 1, St. Louis, Miss.: Becktold & Co.

Pred, Alan R. (1973) *Urban Growth and the Circulation of Information: The United States System of Cities, 1790–1840*. Cambridge, Mass.: Harvard University Press.

Pressly, Thomas J. (1954) *Americans Interpret their Civil War*. Princeton, NJ: Princeton University Press.

Pressly, Thomas J. (1962 [1954]) *Americans Interpret their Civil War*, rev edn. New York: Free Press.

Price, George and Stewart, James Brewer (eds.) (1999) *To Heal the Scourge of Prejudice: The Life and Writings of Hosea Easton*. Amherst, Mass.: University of Massachusetts Press.

Prude, Jonathan (1983) *The Coming of Industrial Order: Town and Factory Life in Massachusetts, 1810–1860*. New York: Cambridge University Press.

Prude, Jonathan and Hahn, Steven (eds.) (1985) *The Countryside in the Age of Capitalist Transformation*. Chapel Hill, NC: University of North Carolina Press.

Rable, George C. (1984) *But There Was No Peace: The Role of Violence in the Politics of Reconstruction*. Athens, Ga.: University of Georgia Press.

Rable, George C. (1989) *Civil Wars: Women and the Crisis of Southern Nationalism*. Urbana, Ill.: University of Illinois Press.

Raboteau, Albert J. (1978) *Slave Religion: "The Invisible Institution" in the Antebellum South*. New York: Oxford University Press.

Rafuse, Ethan S. (2002) *A Single Grand Victory: The First Bull Run Campaign*. Wilmington, Del.: Scholarly Resources.

Raimy, Daina L. (1998) "'She Do a Heap of Work': Female Slave Labor on Glynn County Rice and Cotton Plantations," *Georgia Historical Quarterly* 82: 707–34.

Rakove, Jack N. (1986) *Original Meanings: Politics and Ideas in the Making of the Constitution*. New York: Knopf.

Ramsdell, Charles W. (1972 [1944]) *Behind the Lines in the Southern Confederacy*. Baton Rouge, La.: Louisiana State University Press.

Randall, James Garfield (1940) "The Blundering Generation," *Mississippi Valley Historical Review* 27: 3–28.

Randall, James Garfield (1945) *Lincoln the President: Springfield to Gettysburg*, two vols. New York: Dodd Mead.

Randall, James Garfield (1947) *Lincoln the Liberal Statesman*. New York: Dodd Mead.

Ranney, Austin (1975) *Curing the Mischiefs of Faction: Party Reform in America*. Berkeley, Calif.: University of California Press.

Ransom, Roger L. (1989) *Conflict and Compromise: The Political Economy of Slavery, Emancipation, and the American Civil War*. New York: Cambridge University Press.

Ransom, Roger L. and Sutch, Richard (1977) *One Kind of Freedom: The Economic Consequences of Emancipation*. Cambridge: Cambridge University Press.

Ransom, Roger L. and Sutch, Richard (2001a) *One Kind of Freedom: The Economic Consequences of Emancipation*, 2nd edn. New York: Cambridge University Press.

Ransom, Roger L. and Sutch, Richard (2001b) "*One Kind of Freedom*: Reconsidered (and Turbo Charged)," *Explorations in Economic History* 38: 6–39.

Ray, C. (1998) "Scottish Heritage Southern Style," *Southern Cultures* 4: 28–45.

Reed, J. S. (1983) *Southerners: The Social Psychology of Sectionalism*. Chapel Hill, NC: University of North Carolina Press.

Reed, J. S. (2001) "Lay My Burden of Southern History Down," *Southern Cultures* 7: 100–3.

Reid, Joseph (1973) "Sharecropping as an Understandable Market Response: The Post-Bellum South," *Journal of Economic History* 33: 106–30.

Reidy, Joseph P. (1992) *From Slavery to Agrarian Capitalism in the Cotton Plantation South: Central Georgia, 1800–1880*. Chapel Hill, NC: University of North Carolina Press.

Remini, Robert V. (1984) *Andrew Jackson and the Course of American Democracy, 1833–1845*. 3 vols. New York: Harper and Row.

Remini, Robert V. (1988) *The Legacy of Andrew Jackson: Essays on Democracy, Indian Removal, and Slavery*. Baton Rouge, La.: Louisiana State University Press.

Remini, Robert V. (1991) *Henry Clay*. New York: Norton.

Remini, Robert V. (1997) *Daniel Webster: The Man and His Time*. New York: Norton.

Rhea, Gordon C. (1994) *The Battle of the Wilderness, May 5 and 6, 1864*. Baton Rouge, La.: Louisiana State University Press.

Rhea, Gordon C. (1997) *The Battles for Spotsylvania Court House and the Road to Yellow Tavern, May 7–12, 1864*. Baton Rouge, La.: Louisiana State University Press.

Rhea, Gordon C. (2000) *To the North Anna River: Grant and Lee, May 13–25, 1864*. Baton Rouge, La.: Louisiana State University Press.

Rhea, Gordon C. (2002) *Cold Harbor: Grant and Lee, May 26–June 3, 1864*. Baton Rouge, La.: Louisiana State University Press.

Rhodes, James Ford (1892–1918) *History of the United States from the Compromise of 1850*. 7 vols. New York: Harper.

Richards, Leonard D. (1971) *"Gentlemen of Property and Standing": Anti-abolition Mobs in Jacksonian America*. New York: Oxford University Press.

Richards, Leonard L. (2000) *The Slave Power: The Free North and Southern Domination, 1780–1860*. Baton Rouge, La.: Louisiana State University Press.

Richardson, Heather Cox (1997) *The Greatest Nation on Earth: Republican Economic Policies during the Civil War*. Cambridge, Mass.: Harvard University Press.

Richardson, Heather Cox (2001) *The Death of Reconstruction: Race, Labor, and Politics in the Post-Civil War North*. Cambridge, Mass.: Harvard University Press.

Rilling, Donna J. (2000) *Making Houses, Crafting Capitalism: Builders in Philadelphia, 1790–1850*. Philadelphia, Pa.: University of Pennsylvania Press.

Roark, James L. (1977) *Masters Without Slaves: Southern Planters in the Civil War and Reconstruction*. New York: Norton.

Rodrigue, John C. (2001) *Reconstruction in the Cane Fields: From Slavery to Free Labor in Louisiana's Sugar Parishes, 1862–1880*. Baton Rouge, La.: Louisiana State University Press.

Rodrigue, John C. (2002) "More Souths?," *Reviews in American History* 30: 66–71.

Roediger, David (1991) *The Wages of Whiteness: Race and the Formation of the American Working Class*. London: Verso.

Rohrbough, Malcolm J. (1978) *The Trans-Appalachian Frontier: People, Societies, and Institutions, 1775–1850*. New York: Oxford University Press.

Rose, Anne (1992) *Victorian America and the Civil War*. New York: Cambridge University Press.

Rose, Willie Lee (1964) *Rehearsal for Reconstruction: The Port Royal Experiment*. Indianapolis, Ind.: Bobbs-Merrill.

Rosenberg, Nathan (1972) *Technology and American Economic Growth*. New York: Harper and Row.

Ross, Michael A. (2003) *Justice of Shattered Dreams: Samuel Freeman Miller and the Supreme Court during the Civil War Era*. Baton Rouge, La.: Louisiana State University Press.

Ross, Steven J. (1985) *Workers on the Edge: Work, Leisure, and Politics in Industrializing Cincinnati, 1788–1890*. New York: Columbia University Press.

Rostow, W. W. (1956) "The Take-off into Sustained Growth," *Economic Journal* 66: 25–48.

Rothenberg, Winifred Barr (1992) *From Market-Places to a Market Economy: The Transformation of Rural Massachusetts, 1750–1850*. Chicago: University of Chicago Press.

Rothstein, Morton (1966) "Antebellum Wheat and Cotton Exports: A Contrast in Marketing Organization and Economic Development," *Agricultural History* 40: 91–100.

Roy, William G. (1997) *Socializing Capital: The Rise of the Large Industrial Corporation in America*. Princeton, NJ: Princeton University Press.

Royce, Edward (1993) *The Origins of Southern Sharecropping*. Philadelphia, Pa.: Temple University Press.

Royster, Charles (1991) *The Destructive War: William Tecumseh Sherman, Stonewall Jackson, and the Americans*. New York: Alfred A. Knopf.

Ryan, Mary (1981) *The Cradle of the Middle Class: The Family in Oneida County, New York, 1780–1865*. New York: Cambridge University Press.

Salsbury, Stephen (1962) "The Effect of the Civil War on American Industrial Development," in Ralph Andreano (ed.) *The Economic Impact of the American Civil War*. Cambridge, Mass.: Schenkman.

Salvatore, Nick (1982) *Eugene V. Debs: Citizen and Socialist*. Urbana, Ill.: University of Illinois Press.

Salvatore, Nick (1996) *We All Got History: The Memory Books of Amos Webber*. New York: Times Books.

Samuels, Shirley (ed.) (1992) *The Culture of Sentiment: Race, Gender, and Sentimentality in Nineteenth-Century America*. New York: Oxford University Press.

Sánchez-Eppler, Karen (1993) *Touching Liberty: Abolition, Feminism, and the Politics of the Body*. Berkeley, Calif.: University of California Press.

Sanders, Elizabeth (1999) *Roots of Reform: Farmers, Workers, and the American State, 1877–1917*. Chicago: University of Chicago Press.

Saville, Julie (1994) *The Work of Reconstruction: From Slave to Wage Laborer in South Carolina, 1860–1870*. New York: Cambridge University Press.

Sawislak, Karin (1995) *Smouldering City: Chicagoans and the Great Fire, 1871–1874*. Chicago: University of Chicago Press.

Saxton, Alexander (1990) *The Rise and Fall of the White Republic: Class Politics and Mass Culture in Nineteenth-Century America*. London: Verso.

Scarborough, William K. (ed.) (1972–89) *The Diary of Edmund Ruffin*, three vols. Baton Rouge, La.: Louisiana State University Press.

Scarborough, William K. (2003) *Masters of the Big House: The Elite Slaveholders of the Mid-Nineteenth Century South*. Baton Rouge, La.: Louisiana State University Press.

Schlesinger, Arthur M., Jr (1949) "The Causes of the Civil War: A Note on Historical Sentimentalism," *Partisan Review* 16: 968–81.

Schlomowitz, Ralph (1979) "The Transition from Slave to Freedman: Labor Arrangements in Southern Agriculture," unpublished PhD dissertation, University of Chicago.

Schlotterbeck, John T. (1991) "The Internal Economy of Slavery in Rural Piedmont," in Ira Berlin and Philip D. Morgan (eds.) *The Slaves' Economy: Independent Production by Slaves in the Americas*. London: Frank Cass.

Schmidt, B. C. (1986) *The Judiciary and Responsible Government, 1910–1921*, Vol. 9, Pt. 1 of *The Oliver Wendell Holmes Devise History of the Supreme Court of the United States*. New York: Macmillan.

Schmidt, James D. (1999) *Free to Work: Labor Law, Emancipation, and Reconstruction, 1815–1880* [Studies in the Legal History of the South]. Athens, Ga.: University of Georgia Press.

Schulman, B. J. (1991) *From Cotton Belt to Sunbelt: Federal Policy, Economic Development, and the Transformation of the South, 1938–1980*. New York: Oxford University Press.

Schultz, Jane (1992) "The Inhospitable Hospital: Gender and Professionalism in Civil War Medicine," *Signs* 17: 363–92.

Schultz, Jane (1995) "'Are We Not All Soldiers?': Northern Women in the Civil War Hospital Service," *Prospects* 20: 38–56.

Schwalm, Leslie A. (1997) *A Hard Fight for We: Women's Transition from Slavery to Freedom in South Carolina*. Urbana, Ill.: University of Illinois Press.

Schwartz, Marie Jenkins (2000) *Born in Bondage: Growing up Enslaved in the American South*. Cambridge, Mass.: Harvard University Press.

Schwarz, J. A. (1994) *The New Dealers: Power Politics in the Age of Roosevelt*. New York: Vintage.

Schweiger, Beth Barton (2000) *The Gospel Working Up: Progress and the Pulpit in Nineteenth-Century Virginia*. Oxford: Oxford University Press.

Schweninger, Loren (1990) *Black Property Owners in the South, 1790–1915.* Urbana, Ill.: University of Illinois Press.

Schweninger, Loren and Franklin, John Hope (1999) *Runaway Slaves: Rebels on the Plantation.* New York: Oxford University Press.

Scott, Ann Firor (1970) *The Southern Lady: From Pedestal to Politics, 1830–1930.* Chicago: University of Chicago Press.

Scott, Ann Firor (ed.) (1993) *Unheard Voices: The First Historians of Southern Women.* Charlottesville, Va.: University of Virginia Press.

Scott, Rebecca J. (1994) "Defining the Boundaries of Freedom in the World of Cane: Cuba, Brazil, and Louisiana after Emancipation," *American Historical Review* 99: 70–102.

Scranton, Philip (1983) *Proprietary Capitalism: The Textile Manufacture at Philadelphia, 1800–1885.* New York: Cambridge University Press.

Scranton, Philip (1997) *Endless Novelty: Specialty Production and American Industrialization, 1865–1925.* Princeton, NJ: Princeton University Press.

Sears, Stephen W. (1983) *Landscape Turned Red: The Battle of Antietam.* New Haven, Conn.: Ticknor and Fields.

Sears, Stephen W. (1988) *George B. McClellan: The Young Napoleon.* New York: Ticknor and Fields.

Sears, Stephen W. (1994) "Lincoln and McClellan," in Gabor S. Boritt (ed.) *Lincoln and his Generals.* New York: Oxford University Press.

Sears, Stephen W. (1996) *To the Gates of Richmond: The Peninsula Campaign.* New York: Ticknor and Fields.

Seavoy, Ronald E. (1998) *The American Peasantry: Southern Agricultural Labor and its Legacy, 1850–1995.* Westport, Conn.: Greenwood Press.

Seip, Terry L. (1983) *The South Returns to Congress: Men, Economic Measures, and Intersectional Relationships, 1868–1879.* Baton Rouge, La.: Louisiana State University Press.

Sellers, Charles G., Jr (1965) "Comment on Avery O. Craven, 'Why the Southern States Seceded'," in George H. Knoles (ed.) *The Crisis of the Union, 1860–1861.* Baton Rouge, La.: Louisiana State University Press.

Sellers, Charles G. (1991) *The Market Revolution: Jacksonian America, 1815–1846.* New York: Oxford University Press.

Sewell, Richard H. (1976) *Ballots for Freedom: Antislavery Politics in the United States, 1848–1865.* New York: Oxford University Press.

Sharkey, Robert P. (1959) *Money, Class and Party: An Economic Study of Civil War and Reconstruction.* Baltimore, Md.: Johns Hopkins University Press.

Sheridan, Philip H. (1888) *The Personal Memoirs of P.H. Sheridan, General United States Army,* two vols. New York: Charles H. Webster.

Sigerman, Harriet (2000a) "An Unfinished Battle: 1848–1865," in Nancy Cott (ed.) *No Small Courage: A History of Women in the United States.* New York: Oxford University Press.

Sigerman, Harriet (2000b) "Laborers for Liberty: 1865–1890," in Nancy Cott (ed.) *No Small Courage: A History of Women in the United States.* New York: Oxford University Press.

Silber, Nina (1993) *The Romance of Reunion: Northerners and the South, 1865–1900.* Chapel Hill, NC: University of North Carolina Press.

Silbey, Joel H. (1977) *A Respectable Minority: The Democratic Party in the Civil War Era, 1860–1868.* New York: Norton.

Silbey, Joel H. (1985) *The Partisan Imperative: The Dynamics of American Politics before the Civil War.* New York: Oxford University Press.

Simkins, Francis B. and Woody, Robert H. (1932) *South Carolina During Reconstruction.* Chapel Hill, NC: University of North Carolina Press.

Simon, John Y. (1994) "Grant, Lincoln, and Unconditional Surrender," in Gabor S. Boritt (ed.) *Lincoln and his Generals.* New York: Oxford University Press.

Sims, A. (1997) *The Power of Femininity in the New South: Women's Organizations and Politics in North Carolina, 1880–1930.* Columbia, SC: University of South Carolina Press.

Singal, D. J. (1982) *The War Within: From Victorian to Modernist Thought in the South, 1919–1945.* Chapel Hill, NC: University of North Carolina Press.

Sinha, Manisha (2000) *The Counter-revolution of Slavery: Politics and Ideology in Antebellum South Carolina.* Chapel Hill, NC: University of North Carolina Press.

Sizer, Lyde (2000) *The Political Work of Northern Women Writers and the Civil War, 1850–1872.* Chapel Hill, NC: University of North Carolina Press.

Sklar, Kathryn (1973) *Catherine Beecher: A Study in American Domesticity.* New York: Norton.

Skocpol, Theda (1992) *Protecting Soldiers and Mothers: The Political Origins of Social Policy in the United States.* Cambridge, Mass.: Belknap Press.

Skowronek, Stephen (1992) *Building a New American State: The Expansion of National Administrative Capacities, 1877–1920.* New York: Cambridge University Press.

Slaughter, Philip (1855) *The Virginian History of African Colonization.* Richmond, Va.: MacFarlane.

Sloan, William M. (1891) "Pensions and Socialism," *Century* 42 (June): 179–88.

Smith, Adam (1993 [1776]) *The Wealth of Nations: An Inquiry into the Nature and Causes of the Wealth of Nations.* Oxford: Oxford University Press.

Smith, Margaret Supplee and Wilson, Emily Herring (1999) *North Carolina Women: Making History.* Chapel Hill, NC: University of North Carolina Press.

Smith-Rosenberg, Carroll (1985) *Disorderly Conduct: Visions of Gender in Victorian America.* New York: Oxford University Press.

Soderlund, Jean R. (1985) *Quakers & Slavery: A Divided Spirit.* Princeton, NJ: Princeton University Press.

Solomon, Barbara (1985) *In the Company of Educated Women: A History of Women and Higher Education in America.* New Haven, Conn.: Yale University Press.

Somerville, Diane Miller (1995) "The Rape Myth in the Old South Reconsidered," *Journal of Southern History* 61: 481–518.

Southern Poverty Law Center (2000) *Intelligence Report* 99: 28–9.

Speicher, Anne M. (2000) *The Religious World of Antislavery Women: Spirituality in the Lives of Five Abolitionist Lecturers.* Syracuse, NY: Syracuse University Press.

Sproat, John G. (1968) *"The Best Men": Liberal Reformers in the Gilded Age.* New York: Oxford University Press.

Spruill, Julia Cherry (1938) *Women's Life and Work in the Southern Colonies.* Chapel Hill, NC: University of North Carolina Press.

Stadenraus, Philip (1961) *The African Colonization Movement.* Ithaca, NY: Cornell University Press.

Stampp, Kenneth M. (1950) *And the War Came: The North and the Secession Crisis.* Baton Rouge, La.: Louisiana State University Press.

Stampp, Kenneth M. (1956) *Peculiar Institution: Slavery in the Antebellum South.* New York: Knopf.

Stampp, Kenneth M. (1965) *The Era of Reconstruction, 1865–1877.* New York: Alfred A.Knopf.

Stampp, Kenneth M. (1990) *America in 1857: A Nation on the Brink.* New York: Oxford University Press.

Stanley, Amy Dru (1988) "Conjugal Bonds and Wage Labor: Rights of Contract in the Age of Emancipation," *Journal of American History* 75: 471–500.

Stanley, Amy Dru (1998) *From Bondage to Contract: Wage Labor, Marriage, and the Market in the Age of Slave Emancipation.* New York: Cambridge University Press.

Stansell, Christine (1987) *City of Women: Sex and Class in New York, 1789–1860.* Urbana, Ill.: University of Illinois Press.

Steele, Matthew Forney (1909) *American Campaigns,* two vols. Washington, DC: Byron S. Adams.

Stevenson, Brenda E. (1996) *Life in Black and White: Family and Community in the Slave South*. New York: Oxford University Press.

Stewart, James Brewer (1997) *Holy Warriors: The Abolitionists and American Slavery*. New York: Hill and Wang.

Stewart, James Brewer (1998) "The Emergence of Racial Modernity and the Rise of the White North, 1776–1840," *Journal of the Early Republic* 18: 181–217.

Storey, Margaret (1999) "Southern Ishmaelites, Wartime Unionism and its Consequences in Alabama, 1860–1884," unpublished PhD dissertation, Emory University, Atlanta, Ga.

Stowe, Steven (1987) *Intimacy and Power in the Old South*. Baltimore, Md.: Johns Hopkins University Press.

Stowell, Daniel (1998) *Rebuilding Zion: The Religious Reconstruction of the South, 1863–1877*. New York: Oxford University Press.

Strozier, Charles B. (1988) "Lincoln's Quest for Union: Public and Private Meanings," in Gabor S. Boritt (ed.) *The Historian's Lincoln: Pseudohistory, Psychohistory, and History*. Urbana, Ill.: University of Illinois Press.

Stryker, Lloyd P. (1929) *Andrew Johnson: A Study in Courage*. New York: Macmillan.

Stuckey, Sterling (1987) *Slave Culture: Nationalist Theory and the Foundations of Black America*. New York: Oxford University Press.

Summers, Mark W. (1984) *Railroads, Reconstruction, and the Gospel of Prosperity: Aid under the Radical Republicans, 1865–1877*. Princeton, NJ: Princeton University Press.

Summers, Mark W. (1987) *The Plundering Generation: Corruption and the Crisis of Union, 1849–1860*. New York: Oxford University Press.

Sutherland, Daniel E. (1995) *Season of War: The Ordeal of a Confederate Community, 1861–1865*. New York: Free Press.

Sword, Wiley (1992) *Embrace an Angry Wind: The Confederacy's Last Hurrah: Spring Hill, Franklin, and Nashville*. New York: HarperCollins.

Tadman, Michael (1989) *Speculators and Slaves: Masters, Traders, and Slaves in the Old South*. Madison, Wis.: University of Wisconsin Press.

Tanner, Robert G. (1996) *Stonewall in the Valley: Thomas J. "Stonewall" Jackson's Shenandoah Valley Campaign, Spring 1862*. Mechanicsville, Pa.: Stackpole.

Tatum, Georgia Lee (1934) *Disloyalty in the Confederacy*. Chapel Hill, NC: University of North Carolina Press.

Taylor, Alan (1996) *William Cooper's Town: Power and Persuasion on the Frontier of the Early American Republic*. New York: Random House.

Taylor, Alrutheus A. (1924) *The Negro in South Carolina during the Reconstruction*. Washington, DC: Association for the Study of Negro Life and History.

Taylor, Alrutheus A. (1926) *The Negro in the Reconstruction of Virginia*. Washington, DC: Association for the Study of Negro Life and History.

Taylor, Alrutheus A. (1941) *The Negro in Tennessee, 1865–1880*. Washington, DC: Associated Publishers.

Taylor, George R. (1951) *The Transportation Revolution, 1815–1860*. New York: Rinehart.

Temin, P. (1976) "The Post-Bellum Recovery of the South and the Cost of the Civil War," *Journal of Economic History* 36: 898–907.

Thomas, Emory M. (1979) *The Confederate Nation: 1861–1865*. New York: Harper and Row.

Thomas, Emory M. (1994) *Robert E. Lee: A Biography*. New York: Norton.

Thompson, E. P. (1971) "The Moral Economy of the English Crowd in the Eighteenth Century," *Past & Present* 50: 76–136.

Thompson, E. T. (1965) "Presbyterians North and South: Efforts toward Reunion," *Journal of Presbyterian History* 43: 1–15.

Thornton, J. Mills, III (1978) *Politics and Power in a Slave Society: Alabama, 1800–1860*. Baton Rouge, La.: Louisiana State University Press.

Thornton, J. Mills, III (1980) "Fiscal Policy and the Failure of Radical Reconstruction in the Lower South," in J. Morgan Kousser and James M. McPherson (eds.) *Region, Race, and Reconstruction: Essays in Honor of C. Vann Woodward.* New York: Oxford University Press.

Tindall, George Brown (1952) *South Carolina Negroes, 1877–1900.* Columbia, SC: University of South Carolina Press.

Tindall, George Brown (1965) "Southern Negroes Since Reconstruction: Dissolving the Static Image," in Arthur S. Link and Rembert W. Patrick (eds.) *Writing Southern History.* Baton Rouge, La.: Louisiana State University Press.

Tompkins, Jane (1985) *Sensational Designs: The Cultural Work of American Fiction, 1790–1860.* New York: Oxford University Press.

Trefousse, Hans L. (1969) *The Radical Republicans: Lincoln's Vanguard for Racial Justice.* New York: Alfred A. Knopf.

Trelease, Allen W. (1971) *White Terror: The Ku Klux Klan Conspiracy and Southern Reconstruction.* New York: Harper and Row.

Trollope, Frances (1993) *Domestic Manners of the Americans.* Edited and with an introduction by John Lauritz Larson. St James, NY: Brandywine Press.

Tucker, Barbara M. (1984) *Samuel Slater and the Origins of the American Textile Industry, 1790–1860.* Ithaca, NY: Cornell University Press.

Tucker, Robert W. and Hendrickson, David C. (1990) *Empire of Liberty: The Statecraft of Thomas Jefferson.* New York: Oxford University Press.

Tunnell, Ted (1984) *Crucible of Reconstruction: War, Rebellion and Race in Louisiana, 1862–1877.* Baton Rouge, La.: Louisiana State University Press.

Unger, Irwin (1964) *The Greenback Era: A Social and Political History of American Finance.* Princeton, NJ: Princeton University Press.

US War Department (1881–1901) *The War of the Rebellion: Official Records of the Union and Confederate Armies,* series 1, vol. 19, pt. 2. Washington, DC: Government Printing Office.

Van Doren, Carl (1948) *The Great Rehearsal: The Story of the Making and Ratifying of the Constitution of the United States.* New York: Viking.

Varon, Elizabeth (1998) *We Mean to Be Counted: White Women and Politics in Antebellum Virginia.* Chapel Hill, NC: University of North Carolina Press.

Venet, Wendy (1991) *Neither Ballots nor Bullets: Women Abolitionists and the Civil War.* Charlottesville, Va.: University of Virginia Press.

Vorenberg, Michael (2001) *Final Freedom: The Civil War, the Abolition of Slavery, and the Thirteenth Amendment.* Cambridge: Cambridge University Press.

Wade, Richard C. (1959) *The Urban Frontier: The Rise of Western Cities, 1790–1830.* Cambridge, Mass.: Harvard University Press.

Wallenstein, Peter (1987) *From Slave South to New South: Public Policy in Nineteenth-Century Georgia.* Chapel Hill, NC: University of North Carolina Press.

Walters, Ronald (1976) *The Antislavery Appeal: American Abolitionism after 1830.* Baltimore, Md.: Johns Hopkins University Press.

Walther, Eric H. (1992) *The Fire-Eaters.* Baton Rouge, La.: Louisiana State University Press.

Walton, Gary M. and Shepherd, James F. (eds.) (1981) *Market Institutions and Economic Change in the New South, 1865–1900.* New York: Academic Press.

Wang, Xi (1997) *The Trial of Democracy: Black Suffrage and Northern Republicans, 1860–1910.* Athens, Ga.: University of Georgia Press.

Warren, R. P. (1964) *The Legacy of the Civil War: Meditations on the Centennial.* New York: Vintage.

Watson, Harry L. (1990) *Liberty and Power: The Politics of Jacksonian America.* New York: Noonday Press.

Wattenberg, Ben J. (ed.) (1976) *The Statistical History of the United States.* New York: Basic Books.

Wayne, Michael (1983) *The Reshaping of Plantation Society: The Natchez District, 1860–1880.* Baton Rouge, La.: Louisiana State University Press.

Weaver, R. M. (1968) *The Southern Tradition at Bay: A History of Postbellum Thought,* ed. G. Core and M. E. Bradford. New Rochelle, NY: Arlington House.

Weigley, Russell F. (1973) *The American Way of War: A History of United States Military Strategy and Policy.* New York: Macmillan.

Weigley, Russell F. (2000) *A Great Civil War: A Military and Political History, 1861–1865.* Bloomington, Ind.: Indiana University Press.

Weiner, Marli F. (1998) *Mistresses and Slaves: Plantation Women in South Carolina, 1830–1880.* Urbana, Ill.: University of Illinois Press.

Weisberger, Bernard (1959) "The Dark and Bloody Ground of Reconstruction," *Journal of Southern History* 25: 427–47.

Weisenburger, Steven (1998) *Modern Medea: A Family Story of Slavery and Child Murder from the Old South.* New York: Hill and Wang.

Welter, Barbara (1966) "The Cult of True Womanhood: 1820–1860," *American Quarterly* 18: 151–74.

West, Elliott (2003) "Reconstructing Race," *Western Historical Quarterly* 34 (Spring): 7–26.

Wharton, Vernon Lane (1947) *The Negro in Mississippi, 1865–1900.* Chapel Hill, NC: University of North Carolina Press.

Wheeler, M. S. (1993) *New Women of the New South: The Leaders of the Woman Suffrage Movement in the Southern States.* New York: Oxford University Press.

White, Deborah Gray (1985) *Ar'n't I a Woman? Female Slaves in the Plantation South.* New York: Norton.

Whites, LeeAnn (1995) *The Civil War as a Crisis in Gender: Augusta, Georgia, 1860–1890.* Athens, Ga.: University of Georgia Press.

Whitman, Walt (1882–3) *Specimen Days.* Philadelphia, Pa.: Rees Walsh.

Wiener, Jonathan M. (1975) "Planter-Merchant Conflict in Reconstruction Alabama," *Past and Present* 68 (Aug.): 73–94.

Wiener, Jonathan M. (1976) "Planter Persistence and Social Change: Alabama, 1850–1870," *Journal of Interdisciplinary History* 7 (Aut.): 235–60.

Wiener, Jonathan M. (1978) *Social Origins of the New South: Alabama, 1860–1885.* Baton Rouge, La.: Louisiana State University Press.

Wiener, Jonathan M. (1979) "Class Structure and Economic Development in the American South, 1865–1955," *American Historical Review* 84: 970–1006.

Wilentz, Sean (1984) *Chants Democratic: New York City and the Rise of the American Working Class, 1788–1850.* New York: Oxford University Press.

Wiley, Bell I. (1938) *Southern Negroes, 1861–1865.* New Haven, Conn.: Yale University Press.

Wiley, Bell I. (1944) *The Plain People of the Confederacy.* Baton Rouge, La.: Louisiana State University Press.

Wiley, Bell I. (1975) *Confederate Women.* Westport, Conn.: Greenwood Press.

Williams, Eric Eustace (1994 [1944]) *Capitalism and Slavery.* Chapel Hill, NC: University of North Carolina Press.

Williams, Kenneth P. (1949–59) *Lincoln Finds a General: A Military Study of the Civil War.* New York: Macmillan.

Williams, T. Harry (1941) *Lincoln and the Radicals.* Madison, Wis.: University of Wisconsin Press.

Williams, T. Harry (1952) *Lincoln and his Generals.* New York: Alfred A. Knopf.

Williams, T. Harry (1955) *P. G. T. Beauregard: Napoleon in Gray.* Baton Rouge, La.: Louisiana State University Press.

Williams, T. Harry (1960) "The Military Leadership of North and South," in David Donald (ed.) *Why the North Won the Civil War.* Baton Rouge, La.: Louisiana State University Press.

Williamson, Jeffrey G. (1974a) "Watersheds and Turning Points: Conjectures on the Long-Term Impact of Civil War Financing," *Journal of Economic History* 34: 636–61.

Williamson, Jeffrey G. (1974b) *Late Nineteenth-Century American Development: A General Equilibrium History*. New York: Cambridge University Press.

Williamson, Joel (1965) *After Slavery: The Negro in South Carolina during Reconstruction, 1861–1877*. Chapel Hill, NC: University of North Carolina Press.

Williamson, Joel (1984) *The Crucible of Race: Black-White Relations in the American South since Emancipation*. New York: Oxford University Press.

Wilson, C. R. (1980) *Baptized in Blood: The Religion of the Lost Cause, 1865–1920*. Athens, Ga.: University of Georgia Press.

Wilson, Henry (1872–7) *History of the Rise and Fall of the Slave Power in America*, three vols. Boston, Mass.: J. R. Osgood.

Wilson, Major L. (1974 [1877]) *Space, Time, and Freedom: The Quest for Nationality and the Irrepressible Conflict, 1815–1861*. Westport, Conn.: Greenwood Press.

Winch, Julie (1988) *Philadelphia's Black Elite: Activism, Accommodation, and the Struggle for Autonomy*. Philadelphia, Penn.: Temple University Press.

Winston, Robert W. (1928) *Andrew Johnson, Plebeian and Patriot*, New York: Holt and Sons.

Wolfe, Margaret Ripley (1995) *Daughters of Canaan: A Saga of Southern Women*. Louisville, Ky.: University Press of Kentucky.

Wood, Ann Douglas (1972) "The War Within a War: Women Nurses in the Union Army," *Civil War History* 18: 197–212.

Wood, Betty (1995) *Women's Work, Men's Work: The Informal Slave Economies of Lowcountry Georgia*. Athens, Ga.: University of Georgia Press.

Wood, Forrest G. (1968) *Black Scare: The Racist Response to Emancipation and Reconstruction*. Berkeley, Calif.: University of California Press.

Wood, Gordon S. (1969) *The Creation of the American Republic, 1776–1787*. Chapel Hill, NC: University of North Carolina Press.

Wood, Gordon S. (1992) *Radicalism of the American Revolution*. New York: Alfred A. Knopf.

Wood, Kirsten E. (2004) *Masterful Women: Slaveholding Widows from the American Revolution through the Civil War*. Chapel Hill, NC: University of North Carolina Press.

Wood, Peter (1974) *Black Majority: Negroes in Colonial South Carolina from 1670 through the Stono Rebellion*. New York: Norton.

Woodman, Harold D. (1968) *King Cotton and his Retainers: Financing and Marketing the Cotton Crop of the South, 1800–1925*. Lexington, Ky.: University Press of Kentucky.

Woodman, Harold D. (1987) "Economic Reconstruction and the Rise of the New South, 1865–1900," in John B. Boles and Evelyn Thomas Nolen (eds.) *Interpreting Southern History: Essays in Honor of Sanford W. Higginbotham*. Baton Rouge, La.: Louisiana State University Press.

Woodman, Harold D. (1995) *New South – New Law: The Legal Foundations of Credit and Labor Relations in the Postbellum Agricultural South*. Baton Rouge, La.: Louisiana State University Press.

Woodman, Harold D. (2001a) "*One Kind of Freedom* after 20 Years," *Explorations in Economic History* 38: 48–57.

Woodman, Harold D. (2001b) "The Political Economy of the New South: Retrospects and Prospects," *Journal of Southern History* 67: 789–810.

Woods, James M. (1987) *Rebellion and Realignment: Arkansas's Road to Secession*. Fayetteville, Ark.: University of Arkansas Press.

Woodward, C. Vann (1951a) *Origins of the New South, 1877–1913*. Baton Rouge, La.: Louisiana State University Press.

Woodward, C. Vann (1951b) *Reunion and Reaction: The Compromise of 1877 and the End of Reconstruction*. Boston, Mass.: Little, Brown.

Woodward, C. Vann (1960) *The Burden of Southern History*. New York: Vintage.

Woodward, C. Vann (1965) "An Expert," *New York Times Book Review* Christmas issue, Section 7, December 5.

Woodward, C. Vann (1966) *The Strange Career of Jim Crow*. New York: Oxford University Press.

Woodward, C. Vann (1974) *The Strange Career of Jim Crow*, 3rd edn. New York: Oxford University Press.

Woodward, C. Vann (ed.) (1981) *Mary Chestnut's Civil War*. New Haven, Conn.: Yale University Press.

Woodward, C. Vann (1986) *Thinking Back: The Perils of Writing History*. Baton Rouge, La.: Louisiana State University Press.

Woodward, C. Vann (1989) *The Future of the Past*. New York: Oxford University Press.

Woodworth, Steven E. (1990) *Jefferson Davis and his Generals: The Failure of Confederate Command in the West*. Lawrence, Kan.: University Press of Kansas.

Woodworth, Steven E. (1992) "'The Indeterminate Quantities': Jefferson Davis, Leonidas Polk, and the End of Kentucky Neutrality, September 1861," *Civil War History* 38: 289–97.

Woodworth, Steven E. (1995) *Davis and Lee at War*. Lawrence, Kan.: University Press of Kansas.

Woodworth, Steven E. (1998) *Six Armies in Tennessee: The Chickamauga and Chattanooga Campaigns*. Lincoln, Nebr.: University of Nebraska Press.

Wright, Donald R. (1993) *African Americans in the Early Republic, 1789–1831*. Arlington Heights, Ill.: Harlan Davidson.

Wright, Gavin (1978) *The Political Economy of the Cotton South: Households, Markets, and Wealth in the Nineteenth Century*. New York: Norton.

Wright, Gavin (1982) "The Strange Career of the New Southern Economic History," *Reviews in American History* 10: 164–80.

Wright, Gavin (1986) *Old South, New South: Revolutions in the Southern Economy since the Civil War*. New York: Basic Books.

Wright, Gavin (2001) "Reflections on *One Kind of Freedom* and the Southern Economy," *Explorations in Economic History* 38: 40–7.

Wyatt-Brown, Bertram (1982) *Southern Honor: Ethics and Behavior in the Old South*. New York: Oxford University Press.

Wyatt-Brown, Bertram (1985) *Yankee Saints and Southern Sinners*. Baton Rouge, La.: Louisiana State University Press.

Wyatt-Brown, Bertram (2001) *The Shaping of Southern Culture: Honor, Grace, and War, 1760s–1880s*. Chapel Hill, NC: University of North Carolina Press.

Yancey, William L. (ed.) (1967) *The Moynihan Report and the Politics of Controversy*. Cambridge, Mass.: MIT Press.

Young, Agatha (1959) *Women and the Crisis: Women of the North in the Civil War*. New York: McDowell Obelensky.

Young, Elizabeth (1999) *Disarming the Nation: Women's Writing and the American Civil War*. Chicago: University of Chicago Press.

Zaeske, Susan (2003) *Signatures of Citizenship: Petitioning, Antislavery, and Women's Political Identity*. Chapel Hill, NC: University of North Carolina Press.

Zagarri, Rosemarie (1988) "The Rights of Man and Woman in Post-Revolutionary America," *William and Mary Quarterly* 3rd ser., 55: 203–30.

Zilversmidt, Arthur (1967) *The First Emancipation: Gradual Emancipation in the North*. Chicago: University of Chicago Press.

Zinn, H. (1964) *The Southern Mystique*. New York: Alfred A. Knopf.

Zuczek, Richard (1996) *State of Rebellion: Reconstruction in South Carolina*. Columbia, SC: University of South Carolina Press.

Index